The Contemporary Novel in France

The Contemporary Novel in France

Edited by William Thompson

University Press of Florida

Gainesville ♦ Tallahassee ♦ Tampa ♦ Boca Raton

Pensacola ♦ Orlando ♦ Miami ♦ Jacksonville

Library of Congress Cataloging-in-Publication Data
The contemporary novel in France / edited by William Thompson.
p.   cm.
Includes bibliographical references and index.
ISBN 0-8130-1409-3 (alk. paper) ∞
1. French fiction—20th century—History and criticism. I. Thompson, William, 1961–   .
PQ671.C56   1995
843'.9109—dc20   95-19048

The University Press of Florida is the scholarly publishing agency for the
State University System of Florida, comprised of Florida A & M University,
Florida Atlantic University, Florida International University, Florida State
University, University of Central Florida, University of Florida, University of
North Florida, University of South Florida, and University of West Florida.

University Press of Florida
15 Northwest 15th Street
Gainesville, FL 32611

Contents

Preface

In a controversial essay that appeared in the *Stanford French Review* in 1991, Antoine Compagnon lamented what he called the "diminishing canon" of French literary studies in the United States, contending that the focus of French specialists in America has become increasingly limited and that the number of authors deemed worthy of analysis has consequently diminished.[1] The favorites (Proust and Duras are the two he mentions by name) undergo a seemingly endless barrage of analysis while other, equally talented and intriguing writers receive scant attention—both those whose careers have long reached a conclusion and those more contemporary writers who have received critical or popular acclaim in France, but who remain relatively obscure in the United States. Another phenomenon on which Compagnon touches is the fascination by many American literature specialists with postwar French thought (literary, sociological, and philosophical; structuralism, poststructuralism, deconstruction, feminism, etc.)—again at the expense of novelists, poets, and playwrights, in other words, those writers who have been the traditional focus of literary analysis. Few major institutions of higher education in the United States today do not have in their curriculum at least one course on or encompassing literary theory from France. Familiarity with literary theory has increasingly become a prerequisite for young scholars attempting to obtain an academic position in the area of French literary studies, and the likes of Barthes, Foucault, Derrida, Lacan, and their successors are the subjects of an overwhelming number of scholarly books and articles.

These latter authors have intrigued both French and North American intellectual circles and inspired a generation of critics and imitators.

But those writers pursuing more traditional forms of literary expression continue to produce a considerable number of novels, short stories, plays, and poetry, all competing against one another for popular and critical acclaim (if that is in fact their goal). In a few privileged cases, these works also compete for recognition from those scholars and serious readers whose decisions and reading practices will largely dictate which works will achieve a more than ephemeral fame.

In an effort to help mitigate the absence of detailed study of the contemporary French literary scene, and to provide the reader with an appreciation of the richness of the recent novel production in France (albeit with no pretense of being exhaustive or conclusive in its presentation), this collection focuses on the novel form in contemporary France through analyses of a selection of novelists whose works are representative of the genre since the height of the nouveau roman, arguably the most significant "movement" in the novel in France since World War II. More specifically, each chapter considers the work of one author (with the exception of the first chapter, which investigates the autobiographical fictions of the nouveaux romanciers). In order to assure a thorough and scholarly contribution on every novelist included, thereby strengthening the overall impact of the collection, each chapter has been written by a different scholar specializing in French literature (and in the contemporary novel in particular). The essays consider a variety of writers who, at times, reflect radically divergent personal backgrounds and attitudes toward the novel genre: those whose careers were well established before the nouveau roman (such as Green and Gracq), those whose works are or were initially greatly influenced by the experimentation promoted and practiced by the nouveaux romanciers (such as Sollers and Ricardou), and those whose writings reflect vastly different preoccupations (Cixous and Tournier, for example). There are older and younger writers, women and men, gays and straights, Catholics, Jews, and unbelievers, those with a wide readership and those read by a select few.

Special emphasis is placed on those writers whose careers begin after the nouveau roman (whether influenced by it or not), as it is this group of writers whose works are less known to North American readers, and whose works we must consider if we are to comprehend in an intelligent manner the status and character of the novel in contemporary France. While most recent studies of "contemporary" French literature hesitate to discuss any writers whose careers begin after the nouveau roman—out of a fear of privileging one author whose works may eventually be overshadowed by those of another, currently neglected author—this collection, by its very composition, stresses that to neglect these novelists is to neglect more than three decades in the development of the most prominent literary genre of twentieth-century France. With the exception of Marguerite Duras, the major figures of the nouveau roman, who have been the subject of a great deal of critical evaluation and debate, are discussed only in the first chapter on autobiographical fictions. In order to focus the scope of the collection even further, all the writers included are published in France (and the majority spend most of their time in France). This last criterion does not imply a voluntary exclusion of the rich body of work being produced in Québec, the Caribbean, and in North and West Africa. However, for the sake of cohesion and in order to keep the collection within manageable parameters, the choice was made to restrict the discussion to writers published in, and mostly living in, France.

The choice of these authors also does not imply that they are necessarily the only prominent, talented, or representative authors in the novel scene in France, and certainly questions will be raised concerning the exclusion of several authors. (For various reasons, both practical and unpredictable, some important authors, such as J.-M. G. Le Clézio and Georges Perec, have not been included.) Given the enormous quantity of literary production in France every year, and given the substantial number of novelists active in the period covered by this collection, it is apparent that not every writer can be included. One hopes, however, that the reader will realize the pragmatic difficulties of discussing the contemporary novel and will acknowledge the effort of making appropriate choices concerning the inclusion and exclusion of material.

In addition, the reader will notice that no specific time frame has been delineated to mark the boundaries of the collection, with the exception of the admittedly vague reference point of the "height of the nouveau roman." One might have chosen as logical starting and finishing points the dates of 1958 (the initiation of the Fifth Republic, which coincides with the publication of several of the critical and creative works that would solidify the status of the nouveau roman in France) and of 1992 (the year during which this collection was first conceived and, of course, the year of unification for the European Community). However, when speaking of literature, any such demarcations are obviously and necessarily arbitrary and therefore best avoided. The authors included here, when considered in their entirety, should not be categorized as a homogeneous group representative of each and every trend, development, and style in the novel in France over a period of thirty or forty years. The novel has not "grown" or developed in any one direction, as the essays in this collection certainly demonstrate, and if there is one characteristic of the contemporary novel in France, it is diversity, one that is impossible to delineate in a fixed and convincing manner.

The introduction to the collection traces the prominent trends and movements in the novel as well as the critical and scholarly reception and evaluation of the contemporary novel in France from the end of World War II until the early 1990s. Although we categorize the writers with reluctance, this enables us to consider the manner in which the novel has been treated in the hands of its more critical readers, in order to comprehend some of the creative and theoretical points of view that have dominated the recent literary scene. The chapters after the introduction have been grouped under four headings. Although these may appear arbitrary and restrictive to some, the aim of these headings is to provide some guidance as to the basic similarities of the origins, styles, and preoccupations of the authors within the context of the contemporary novel in general. Part I, "Continuing 'Traditions' and Changing Styles," groups together those novelists whose careers predate or begin with the nouveau roman and who continue to write (most of them even today, albeit often utilizing forms other than the novel). Part II, "Innovations in Language and Form," includes those writers whose works are representative of the constant and continuing interest in experimentation with language and with form in the contemporary novel in France, a trend that has received a considerable amount of both positive and negative commentary in discussions of the novel in recent times; some (Ricardou, Sollers) initially influenced by the innovations of the nouveau roman, some (Roubaud, Echenoz) engaging in the light-hearted wordplay and parody encouraged by the Oulipiens, and still others (here exemplified by Cixous) utilizing language as a vehicle to challenge social, literary, and linguistic commonplaces whose authority can no longer be taken for granted.

The writers covered in Part III, "Writing, History, and Myth," represent the many authors who have been fascinated by, and who have subsequently used, genuine and fictional events and characters from the past in their works, or have created, based on fact and myth, new "mythologies," new worlds in which to place their fictions. Some, like Elie Wiesel, regard the past as very personal and very real, and describe the horrors of World War II, the Holocaust, and their consequences on contemporary society. Others, like Patrick Modiano, describe pasts, in particular the events of World War II, that they have not experienced personally; they use the so-called mode rétro to depict events in a frame of reference of their own invention, yet based on "real" historical events. Tournier and Wittig, like many other writers, see the novel as a vehicle for depictions of worlds based on, or countering, existing histories or mythologies; worlds beyond the scope of Western patriarchal structures, worlds where once "marginal" characters such as homosexuals and women now take precedence, where attitudes toward sexuality are continually confronted, and where long-accepted myths are transformed and parodied.

Part IV is at first glance the least coherent: "New Narratives, New Traditions." The stories told by the authors included in this category have little in common, and the techniques they utilize, some experimental, some pseudo-biographical, some relatively traditional, differ greatly. The emphasis is indeed on the new: new concepts of narrative, in which content and form seem to have been given equal importance (as the technical innovations of the 1950s and 1960s and more traditional modes of narration each have influenced the novelist's style); new stories, as the general return to the art of "story-telling," to the depiction of complex characters dealing with personal situations, facilitated by an ever-increasing choice of subject matter, continues to characterize much of the prose fiction writing in France; new writers, who are similar in that they are perhaps lesser known to readers of French literature, yet who are vastly different in their origins, their choice of style, and their subject matter, as the novel, in all its diversity, continues to expand beyond any previously established guidelines concerning form and content.

It is hoped that this collection will appeal to scholars, students, and casual readers alike, providing all with some indication of what has happened recently in the domain of the novel in France at the hands of various representative authors. Aimed primarily at an English-speaking audience, this work will serve as both a critical appraisal of and as an introduction for many to an entire generation of French novelists.

This collection strives to bridge the large (and potentially growing) gap in the chronicle of French literature studies, created by the preoccupation with French theory and by the reluctance to consider seriously the works of a vast and varied generation of writers, by providing both scholarly analyses of the work of prominent and talented authors and valuable resource information for anyone interested in further study of these authors and works.

A collection of this nature requires the cooperation and assistance of all those involved, and the editor would like to take this opportunity to thank all the contributors for their initial interest in submitting a chapter to the collection, for their constant enthusiasm about the project, and for their assistance in the editing of the manuscript. They have all demonstrated patience and continued unqualified support for the project, and for this they are to be lauded and thanked. I would also like to thank various individuals and academic units at the University of Memphis for their support: first, the Center for the Humanities, which generously granted a one-semester fellowship that allowed for release time to work on the manuscript; second, my colleagues in the Department of Foreign Languages and Literatures, in particular, the chairman, Ralph Albanese, who provided constant guidance, encouragement, and friendship; and third, Marc Shannon and Ellan Pinter, two of my graduate students who provided invaluable assistance in the compilation of bibliographical data. I certainly could not fail to acknowledge here the unfailing support of Kenneth Davis, Jr., and that of my parents, Ivan and Nora Thompson.

Notes

1. Antoine Compagnon, "The Diminishing Canon of French Literature in America," *Stanford French Review* 15, nos. 1–2 (1991), pp. 103–15.

Introduction

The Contemporary Novel in France:
A Generation of Writing and Criticism

William Thompson

For as long as writers, critics, and readers have discussed the past, present, and future of French literature, laments have been voiced about a "crisis" in this literature. In particular, the latter half of the twentieth century—with its discussions about modernity and postmodernity, the role of the intellectual, the nuclear age, technological advances in entertainment—has questioned the status of literature, often condemning the latter to an imminent demise. To a great extent, the recent debates about the purpose of literature in France are hardly surprising if one considers the succession of events that have had such a profound impact on French society in general over the course of the past few decades: World War II, the Algerian war, the events of May 1968, nuclear proliferation, and the cold war, as well as the endless list of scientific discoveries that have altered the shape of modern society.

Perhaps no one genre in any period in France has suffered more from the negative advertising associated with this lament of a crisis than the novel since the end of World War II. The discussion about literature's social purpose (its "engagement"), the challenges to traditional modes of writing on the part of the nouveaux romanciers and the participants of *Tel Quel*, the rise of television and cinema as competing sources of entertainment in a society endowed with an increasing amount of leisure time—all these factors, so varied and all so influential, have caused the status and the fate of the novel in France to be a continual subject of both amicable and hostile debate.

While these arguments about the future of the novel have been perpetuated, and while structuralist and poststructuralist thought have

1

come to dominate the field of literary criticism in France (and have been the primary content of intellectual material exported to the United States), increasingly little attention has been paid to the actual production of the novel in France. If the experimentation in the novel in the 1950s and 1960s on the part of writers such as Robbe-Grillet, Butor, Sarraute, and Sollers has led to volumes of critical praise and bashing, the subsequent literary achievements in France have elicited relatively sparse commentary (both in North America and, significantly, in France itself). Consequently, the concept of a crisis in the contemporary novel in France has become even more acute. This concept has undoubtedly become the most prominent recurring theme in discussions of this genre, as critics and readers, in the aftermath of the nouveau roman and its descendants, have been unable to detect any clear development in the novel, and have, concurrently, been suspicious of the theoretical bases of the nouveau roman. These factors have, moreover, led to a negative, albeit ill-based assessment of the genre as a whole.

We might first document the discussion of a crisis in the novel in France, especially as this so-called crisis has been depicted after the advent of the nouveau roman, in order to comprehend how the novel has appeared to fall on hard times (at least in the opinions of its critics). First, does a crisis in fact exist? In a chapter entitled "De crise en crise" (which leads one to believe that we should be considering a sequence of crises rather than a single phenomenon), Roger Laufer, Bernard Lecherbonnier, and Henri Mitterand in *Thèmes et langages de la culture moderne* discuss the apparently universal agreement about a crisis, specifically as regards the novel: "Les romanciers, les critiques, les historiens de la littérature, les théoriciens les plus abstrus comme les lecteurs les plus naïfs, s'accordent sur un point, sur un seul point: *le roman est en crise* ."[1] But they continue by indicating that a precise definition of the nature of this crisis is far from complete: "Cette constatation faite, les analyses divergent, bien entendu. Mais il apparaît que chacun, à sa façon, dans son langage, admet grosso modo que cette crise du roman ne fait que refléter la crise de civilisation où nous sommes plongés depuis la fin du XIXe siècle" (p. 228). Unlike the writers whose many other references to a crisis in French literature we consider here, these three authors establish a parallel between the situation of the novel and that of society as a whole (although they hardly succeed in pinpointing the source of this crisis affecting mankind in contemporary times by attributing it to a state of mind prevalent for almost a century).

Jacques Brenner seems less than convinced about the existence of a crisis, his attitude reflecting, perhaps, a growing apathy toward the lengthy feud between the partisans of "realistic" or "traditional" novels and those of the nouveau roman and its immediate descendents: "La crise de la littérature est une vieille histoire. Elle peut s'observer de divers points de vue. Elle tient à la mauvaise conscience des écrivains, au comportement suicidaire de quelques-uns d'entre eux (parmi les plus fa-meux), à l'évolution de la société, aux transformations du monde de l'édition."[2] By assuming the stance of an (apparently amused) bystander, Brenner seems to suggest that one would be far better off ignoring warning cries of a crisis (with the writers themselves being the guiltiest parties) and forging ahead instead with the actual writing of the novel itself. The incredible variety of literary production in France and throughout the world, whether of lasting artistic value or not, certainly gives rise to a diverse wealth of possible readings and approaches, for which the critic can hardly remain thankless.

Perhaps the most pessimistic statement about the contemporary novel is that made by Bernard Gros when he questions the very possibility of writing novels in such chaotic times: "De quoi peut-on faire des romans, quand on guette un champignon atomique, quand on regarde passer des présidents, lorsqu'on écoute le Tiers Monde renvoyer, sous forme de cris de haine, les thèmes qui étaient l'honneur de l'Occident?"[3] But faced with this relentless pessimism, we might at the same time refer to the title of another chapter on the novel since the war found in another overview of the twentieth century: André Daspre and Michel Décaudin call their chapter "L'Interminable mutation," envisaging the apparent disorder of the contemporary novel not as a crisis to be lamented, but as the inevitable process of change characteristic of the contemporary world in general.[4]

It is remarkable that, despite general agreement among many critics about the existence of a crisis, little agreement is found about the cause and the actual character of this crisis. For example, some of the most negative comments on the postwar French literary scene can be found in Maurice Blanchot's *Le Livre à venir* (1959). In spite of a promising title, promising in that it might seem to introduce a discussion of the vibrancy of a literature on the verge of continuing greatness, Blanchot moves far beyond talk of mere crisis to suggest the very death of literature: "L'art touche-t-il à sa fin? La poésie périt-elle pour s'être regardée en face, de même que celui qui a vu Dieu meurt? Le critique qui considère notre temps, en le comparant au passé, ne peut qu'exprimer un doute et, au sujet des artistes qui malgré tout produisent encore, une admiration désespérée."[5] Blanchot regrets the demise of the novel form as it was practiced before World War II, when it was the domain of monumental writers such as Gide, Bernanos, François Mauriac, Giraudoux, and Malraux. Blanchot also suggests that no writer after the war could hope to claim the status that these great writers had enjoyed in their time.

On the other hand, for Pierre Vanbergen, if indeed there is a crisis, this situation is actually beneficial to literature, in that it forces both the writer and the reader to refocus their attention and to reconsider a genre that they have long taken for granted: "Il semble bien que le roman ne se soit jamais mieux porté que depuis que l'on disserte de sa 'crise.' "[6] Similarly, Pierre Brunel and his colleagues see a crisis in the novel (one that has existed since the beginning of the century) as a necessary and positive feature: "Régulièrement mis en question depuis la fin du XIXe siècle, le roman semble vivre au XXe de crises continuelles qui, loin de l'affaiblir, le régénèrent et accroissent ses moyens."[7] Without any crisis or questioning of the nature of the novel form, the latter, in the opinion of these writers, could not progress. It is precisely the existence of a crisis or crises that has allowed for positive developments in the novel form.

For Pierre de Boisdeffre, writing in 1962, the crisis of the novel is not necessarily related to the radical transformations the genre has undergone at the hands of various writers (although Boisdeffre was far from an enthusiastic supporter of the nouveaux romanciers). For Boisdeffre, it is in the domain of the more "popular" novel in France that there exists a crisis: "le roman n'est pas seulement en pleine métamorphose, il est aussi en pleine crise. Dans le roman de 'consommation courante,' ce ne sont plus des Français qui, à quelques exceptions près, fournissent les meilleurs crus, mais des étrangers."[8] And in a radio conversation published in 1974, Maurice Nadeau suggests to Roland Barthes that the presence of a crisis concerns not simply the literature being written, but the entire "industry": "depuis que j'exerce mes activités, j'ai toujours entendu parler de crise. Crise de l'édition, crise de la librairie et, bien entendu, crise de la lecture. Ne s'agirait-il pas d'un état endémique?,"[9] suggesting that a crisis in just one domain of this industry would necessarily cause a domino effect. Barthes, for his part, is much more precise in defining this crisis: "il y a crise, quand l'écrivain est obligé ou bien de répéter ce qui s'est déjà fait, ou bien de cesser d'écrire; quand il est pris dans une alternative draconienne: ou bien répéter ou bien se retirer" (p. 20). The crisis in this case is neither the incapacity of the writer to practice his craft nor necessarily a lack of imagination. The crisis is an inability to innovate.

In his superb *Histoire de la littérature de langue française des années 1930 aux années 1980*,[10] Pierre de Boisdeffre entitles one section "Une crise du roman français (1953–1968)." If he, on the one hand, uses the date of the publication of Robbe-Grillet's *Les Gommes* as a starting point for the crisis (implying, perhaps, that the nouveau roman is responsible for this crisis), Boisdeffre also seems to situate the end of the crisis in 1968. While some critics have seen the crisis in the novel as parallel to, or as the direct result of, crises affecting French society as a whole, Boisdeffre chooses a date symbolic of a major crisis in French society (the year of the May student-initiated protests) as the logical concluding moment of the crisis in the novel. Boisdeffre seems to suggest that the events of May 1968 render the arguments about a crisis in the novel irrelevant and insignificant in comparison. Whether the entire debate circulating around the crisis or crises is valid or not, the existence of such debate demonstrates the continuing lively interest in contemporary French letters, and in the novel genre in particular, on the part of critics, scholars, as well as the general public—whose interests, we must admit, differ greatly from those of critics and scholars, but whose tastes are much more difficult to document.

Any discussion of the contemporary novel in France must take into account the two overwhelmingly prominent postwar "attitudes" toward this genre: existentialism and the nouveau roman. Although the former has its origins in a distinctly philosophical tradition, while the latter refers to a loosely connected group of writers who rejected most attempts at categorization and "collectivization," the two have undoubtedly colored more subsequent developments and trends in the novel, both directly and indirectly, than any other factors.

In the case of existentialism, the impact of this school of thought on the contemporary novel lies perhaps less in its philosophical point of view than in the literary aspirations of its dominant figure—Jean-Paul Sartre—and even more so in a subsequent rejection of the political and social agenda that Sartre encouraged for literature.

In *Qu'est-ce que la littérature?*, the primary work in which he elaborates his concept of "littérature engagée," Sartre analyzes the situation of the author in France vis-à-vis the bourgeoisie and the proletariat (and, by extension, the Communist Party). For Sartre, the written word is capable of changing the world: "L'écrivain 'engagé' sait que la parole est action: il sait que dévoiler c'est changer et qu'on ne peut dévoiler qu'en projetant de changer. Il a abandonné le rêve impossible de faire une peinture impartiale de la Société et de la condition humaine."[11] The writer has not only the capability to change the world but the obligation: "qu'il soit essayiste, pamphlétaire, satiriste ou romancier, qu'il parle seulement des passions individuelles ou qu'il s'attaque au régime de la société, l'écrivain, homme libre s'adressant à des hommes libres, n'a qu'un seul sujet: la liberté" (p. 81). Purely artistic notions are secondary to the social message that literature must convey: "Il n'est plus temps de *décrire* ni de *narrer*; nous ne pouvons pas non plus nous borner à *expliquer*. La description, fût-elle psychologique, est pure jouissance contemplative; l'explication est acceptation, elle excuse tout; l'une et l'autre supposent que les jeux sont faits . . . nous avons à révéler au lecteur, en chaque cas concret, sa puissance de faire et de défaire, bref, d'agir" (p. 349).

Yet it is this very rejection of the artistic element, and the rather authoritarian manner in which Sartre would impose his philosophy of literature, that left later generations indifferent to these notions: "what makes Sartre's idea of literature impossible for the Nouveau Roman to accept is not so much the importance he attaches to political reality as the definition of *language* that follows from it. For Sartre and for the reflectionist Marxism underpinning social realism, the language of a novel is necessarily subordinate to the world-view it presents."[12] As the following generation proclaims the death of the intellectual, and becomes more interested in the possibilities of language (largely under the influence of structuralism), Sartre's ideas will become quickly outdated, artistic ideals taking precedence over social issues. And, as Maurice Nadeau (and many other critics) point out, literature, no matter what its goal, is still literature, is still to be read, and therefore must still attract an audience: "s'il est souhaitable qu'un romancier soit 'engagé,' il faut d'abord qu'il soit 'romancier.' "[13] Nadeau considers the failure of Sartrian preoccupations as the consequence not of the political message inherent in his approach but of the abandonment of a care for style and readability. Even Sartre himself will eventually move beyond the idealism of *Qu'est-ce que la littérature?*, eschewing fiction and drama for political causes.

His changing attitude toward literature is most apparent in his declaration "that in a world of starving millions literature itself was useless and wicked if it appealed simply to a cultured minority."[14]

One must also acknowledge that the majority of novelists writing during this period chose to follow paths independent of the more prominent and well-advertised attitudes of the times. In spite of their enduring renown, by no means were existentialism and the nouveau roman the only, or even the dominant, tendencies in the novel in France during the period between the end of World War II and the end of the 1950s. Many fine novelists chose to perpetuate the "traditional" novel à la Balzac, making their priority an elegant style and an intriguing plot. A few of these novelists, among them Roger Nimier, Michel Déon, and Antoine Blondin, collectively referred to as the "Hussards," specifically chose a traditional, or so-called neoclassical, style in direct reaction against Sartrian existentialism: "Revenons au beau langage, aux romans bien faits, à la gratuité, à la désinvolture, à l'évasion. Au roman à thèse et d'ambitions métaphysiques, ils entendent substituer le roman distrayant, spirituel, 'bien écrit.' "[15] Indeed, if any one "style" of novel continues to prosper through the twentieth century, it is the "traditional" novel: "il ne se borne pas à survivre, il prolifère. Il reste même aux yeux d'un vaste public la forme la plus attirante, la plus rassurante aussi, de la littérature."[16]

Authors such as Simenon, Bazin, Troyat, Green, and Giono have followed their own agenda, their own style, enjoying great success (especially in comparison to the relative paucity of sales of the nouveau roman). Many others—Queneau, Bataille, Blanchot, Leiris, Beckett, Vian, Gracq, and Klossowski—have been innovators, but have not adhered to any "school" or movement suggestive of an ideology (Gracq, in fact, demonstrates his complete disdain for the literary scene in *La Littérature à l'estomac*). Still others (Yourcenar, Merle, and Gary) have explored the events of recent and distant history, composing various forms of "historical" novel, and this variety of agendas pursued by writers, hand in hand with the much publicized efforts of the nouveaux romanciers, will assure the novel a broad and undefinable character for years to come.

In *Le Livre à venir*, Maurice Blanchot questioned any attempt at a definition of literature: "l'essence de la littérature, c'est d'échapper à toute détermination essentielle, à toute affirmation qui la stabilise ou même la réalise: elle n'est jamais déjà là, elle est toujours à retrouver ou à réinventer. Il n'est même jamais sûr que le mot littérature ou le mot art réponde à rien de réel, rien de possible ou rien d'important. Cela a été dit: être artiste, c'est ne jamais savoir qu'il y a déjà un art, ni non plus qu'il y a déjà un monde."[17] Indeed, Blanchot considers that nothing is more detrimental to literature than the constant process of categorization and classification that it seems to undergo: "La littérature n'est domaine de la cohérence et région commune qu'aussi longtemps qu'elle n'existe pas, qu'elle n'existe pas pour elle-même et se dissimule. Dès qu'elle apparaît dans le lointain pressentiment de ce qu'elle semble être, elle vole en éclats, elle entre dans la voie de la dispersion où elle refuse de se laisser reconnaître par des signes précis et déterminables" (p. 277). For Blanchot in 1959, the future of literature appeared bleak: "Il arrive qu'on s'entende poser d'étranges questions, celle-ci par exemple: 'Quelles sont les tendances de la littérature actuelle?' ou encore: 'Où va la littérature?' Oui, question étonnante, mais le plus étonnant, c'est que s'il y a une réponse, elle est facile: la littérature va vers elle-même, vers son essence qui est la disparition" (p. 265).

No single event, movement, author, or work has had a greater impact on the study of the French novel since World War II or produced more commentary than the careers of those novelists who came to be known collectively as the "nouveaux romanciers." Many volumes and even more articles and essays have discussed the characteristics, styles, and impact of the nouveau roman (as the bibliography at the end of this collection demonstrates). At this point we limit our analysis to mentioning the major traits of the nouveau roman, considering what the writers of the nouveau roman say about their work (as they were often their own best explicators), and finally discussing the impact of the nouveau roman on the novel in France as a whole.

The common denominator of the nouveaux romanciers (in particular, Alain Robbe-Grillet, Michel Butor, Nathalie Sarraute, and Claude Simon) is their rejection of the accepted trademarks of the so-called traditional novel (well-delineated characters and a logical, consequential narrative, for example). However, as Claude Simon points out, this rejection is virtually the only common feature of those associated with the nouveau roman: "Je crois que ce que l'on peut dire c'est que nous nous trouvons spontanément d'accord pour rejeter un certain nombre de conventions qui régissent le roman traditionnel. Mais à partir de là, chacun de nous œuvre selon son tempérament."[18] Indeed, it is advisable to avoid the restrictive terms "school" or "movement" when discussing the nouveaux romanciers, for they shared far more differences than similarities. Barthes prefers to call the nouveau roman a sociological phenomenon: "j'avoue que j'hésite beaucoup à voir dans le Nouveau Roman autre chose qu'un phénomène sociologique, un mythe littéraire dont les sources et la fonction peuvent être aisément situées."[19] It is only by chance that the term *nouveau roman* (first used by critic Emile Henriot) has come to represent this group of writers. Various other terms were suggested by other critics, some more accurately reflecting the tendencies of the individual novels concerned: roman blanc, anti-roman, anté-roman, pré-roman, roman expérimental, jeune roman, nouveau réalisme, école du regard, école de l'objet, école objectale, école du refus, chosisme, mouvement chosiste, alittérature, école de minuit.[20]

Beyond their common rejection of the traditional novel, the nouveaux romanciers (either in their entirety or individually) may be characterized by the following elements:

Disappearance of the traditional character as center of the novel
Alteration of the logical sequence of actions
Formal experimentation
Questioning of reality and imagination
Self-generative language
Concern with the creative act
Challenging of traditional author/reader relationships
Preoccupation with perception and description
Experimentation with temporal aspects
Questioning of psychology
Experimentation with conversation and subconversation

These features are obviously not the exclusive property of the small group of writers published by Editions de Minuit during the 1950s. Several critics have accurately pointed out that the nouveaux romanciers, in challenging traditional modes of writing, are themselves actually participating in a long-standing tradition of writers (such as Proust, Gide, Woolf, and Joyce) who have questioned and attempted to transform the novel, a "tradition" as strong and detailed as that of the conventional novel. And at the important conference on the nouveau roman at Cerisy in 1970, critic Françoise von Rossum-Guyon claimed that the term *nouveau roman* may apply to a considerably larger number of texts than originally intended: "le Nouveau Roman s'insère dans un champ plus large que celui dans lequel on a dû l'enfermer provisoirement. Le roman nouveau ne désigne pas un groupe, encore moins une école, mais *tout texte qui pose à l'intérieur de lui-même le problème de son fonctionnement*" (emphasis in original).[21]

The first extensive critical examination of the nouveau roman was conducted by Roland Barthes in a series of articles on the novels of Robbe-Grillet. In "Littérature objective," as the title suggests, Barthes focuses on Robbe-Grillet's preoccupation with objects and their depiction (hence the early labels of "école du regard" and "école de l'objet"). Barthes sees in Robbe-Grillet's work a challenge to traditional modes of written representation:

> Le réalisme traditionnel additionne des qualités en fonction d'un jugement implicite: ses objets ont des formes, mais aussi des odeurs, des propriétés tactiles, des souvenirs, des analogies, bref ils fourmillent de significations; ils ont mille modes d'être perçus, et jamais impunément, puisqu'ils entraînent un mouvement humain de dégoût ou d'appétit. En face de ce syncrétisme sensoriel, à la fois anarchique et orienté, Robbe-Grillet impose un ordre unique de saisie: la vue. L'objet n'est plus ici un foyer de correspondances, un foisonnement de sensations et de symboles: il est seulement une résistance optique.[22]

For Barthes, "les objets de Robbe-Grillet . . . sont faits pour être là. Tout l'art de l'auteur, c'est de donner à l'objet un 'être là' et de lui ôter un 'être quelque chose'" (p. 31). In contrast to the traditional novel with its omniscient narrator and psychological preoccupations, Barthes sees a dependency in Robbe-Grillet's work on the immediate reaction to one's visual surroundings. In other words, the narrator can describe only what he sees or experiences directly.

> Le roman devient expérience directe de l'entour de l'homme, sans que cet homme puisse se prévaloir d'une psychologie, d'une métaphysique ou d'une psychanalyse pour aborder le milieu objectif qu'il découvre. Le roman, ici, n'est plus d'ordre

chthonien, infernal, il est terrestre: il enseigne à regarder le monde non plus avec les yeux du confesseur, du médecin ou de Dieu, toutes hypostases significatives du romancier classique, mais avec ceux d'un homme qui marche dans la ville sans d'autre horizon que le spectacle, sans d'autre pouvoir que celui-là même de ses yeux. (pp. 39–40)

In fact, it is this preoccupation with description in the nouveau roman that will interest (and horrify) many critics.

Over the course of the years after Robbe-Grillet's first novel and Barthes's first articles, writers and critics alike delineated, categorized, and dissected the nouveau roman. Opinions about what the nouveaux romanciers were attempting to achieve varied greatly, just as the novels themselves differed. One favorable interpretation considered that the nouveaux romanciers were attempting "l'invention d'un univers neuf" and "la libération des capacités inventives du langage narratif."[23] Robbe-Grillet himself would declare in an interview, "The role of the novelist today isn't to explore social values, for those already exist: it is to discover *new* values."[24] Lucien Goldmann was one of many critics to agree that both the form and the content of the nouveau roman must differ from those of the nineteenth-century novel, just as the culture of the 1950s differs from nineteenth-century culture: "si [Sarraute et Robbe-Grillet] ont adopté une forme différente de celle des romanciers du XIXe siècle, c'est en premier lieu parce qu'ils avaient à décrire et à exprimer une réalité humaine . . . différente de celle qu'avaient à décrire et à exprimer ces derniers."[25] In this vein, some have suggested that the nouveau roman may accurately reflect the preoccupations of a consumer society,[26] the nouveaux romanciers having chosen to explore this avenue of writing in a direct response to the social developments transpiring around them.

Undoubtedly the most prominent and influential theoretical statements to come out of the nouveau roman era are those found in the essays of Alain Robbe-Grillet himself, written during the 1950s and collected in *Pour un nouveau roman*. Although theory and practice did not always coincide in Robbe-Grillet's case, and although many of his comments he would later refute or tone down, these declarations are worth examining as they have influenced an entire generation of writers.

Writing in the latter half of the 1950s, Robbe-Grillet, like many writers and critics, considered the novel in France to be in a state of crisis and lamented in particular the perpetuation of a novel form relatively unchanged for more than a century: "La seule conception romanesque qui ait cours aujourd'hui est, en fait, celle de Balzac."[27] Robbe-Grillet saw the continuing exploitation of traditional modes of narrative expression as the indication of a potential demise of the genre: "Devant l'art romanesque actuel . . . la lassitude est si grande—enregistrée et commentée par l'ensemble de la critique—qu'on imagine mal que cet art puisse survivre bien longtemps sans quelque changement radical" (p. 16). It is clear that Robbe-Grillet had a specific "changement radical" in mind, for he wrote these words after several of his novels had already been published.

Robbe-Grillet encouraged an open-mindedness about new explorations in the novel: "Le nouveau-né balbutiant sera toujours considéré comme un monstre, même par ceux que l'expérience passionne. Il y aura de la curiosité, des mouvements d'intérêt, des réserves quant à l'avenir" (p. 17). In addition, a rejection of outdated techniques and preoccupations with psychological and social significance is necessary, so that author and reader alike may appreciate their surroundings in a new objective, realistic manner: "ce qui nous atteint, ce qui persiste dans notre mémoire, ce qui apparaît comme essentiel et irréductible à de vagues notions mentales, ce sont les gestes eux-mêmes, les objets, les déplacements et les contours, auxquels l'image a restitué d'un seul coup (sans le vouloir) leur *réalité*" (p. 19; emphasis in original).

Robbe-Grillet has little respect for the components of the traditional novel, such as plot, and demonstrates how these features have lost their once consistent (and now anachronistic) status over the course of the twentieth century: "il suffit de lire les grands romans du début de notre siècle pour constater que, si la désagrégation de l'intrigue n'a fait que se préciser au cours des dernières années, elle avait déjà cessé depuis longtemps de constituer l'armature du récit. . . . Il s'agit désormais d'autre chose. Raconter est devenu proprement impossible" (p. 31). His greatest frustration seems to lie with the concept of character: "nous en a-t-on assez parlé, du 'personnage'! Et ça ne semble, hélas, pas près de finir. Cinquante années de maladie, le constat de son décès enregistré à maintes reprises par les plus sérieux essayistes, rien n'a encore réussi à le faire tomber du piédestal où l'avait placé le XIXe siècle" (p. 26). As the central component of conventional narrative, character is consequently most open to alteration in the experimentation of the *nouveaux romanciers*, becoming nameless, faceless, and at times seemingly nonexistent.

Robbe-Grillet also attacks Sartre's goals for literature: "cette façon généreuse, mais utopique, de parler d'un roman, d'un tableau ou d'une statue comme s'ils pouvaient avoir le même poids dans l'action quotidienne qu'une grève, une mutinerie, ou le cri d'une victime dénonçant ses bourreaux, dessert à la fois, en fin de compte, et l'Art et la Révolution" (p. 36). For Robbe-Grillet, the writer's interests must be purely literary and oblivious to outside social influences: "Le seul engagement possible, pour l'écrivain, c'est la littérature" (p. 120). Acknowledging that the nouveau roman, with its particular goals, is at first a difficult enterprise for the uninitiated reader, Robbe-Grillet suggests that this confrontation with the new is consistent with life in a rapidly changing modern world: "Si le lecteur a quelquefois du mal à se retrouver dans le roman moderne, c'est de la même façon qu'il se perd quelquefois dans le monde même où il vit, lorsque tout cède autour de lui des vieilles constructions et des vieilles normes" (p. 116).

Like Robbe-Grillet, Nathalie Sarraute devotes considerable attention to the changing nature of the concept of character in the modern novel, noting in particular the reduction of the traditional character to its most basic framework: "Il était très richement pourvu, comblé de biens de toute sorte, entouré de soins minutieux; rien ne lui manquait, depuis les boucles d'argent de sa culotte jusqu'à la loupe veinée au bout de son nez. Il a, peu à peu, tout perdu: ses ancêtres, sa maison soigneusement bâtie ... son corps, son visage, et, surtout, ce bien précieux entre tous, son caractère qui n'appartenait qu'à lui, et souvent jusqu'à son nom."[28] In fact, the title of Sarraute's collection of essays—*L'Ere du soupçon*—originates in her discussion of the tenuous relationship between the reader and the author caused by the dramatic changes in the depiction of character: "Non seulement ils (le lecteur et l'auteur) se méfient du personnage de roman, mais, à travers lui, ils se méfient l'un de l'autre. Il était le terrain d'entente, la base solide d'où ils pouvaient d'un commun effort s'élancer vers des recherches et des découvertes nouvelles. Il est devenu le lieu de leur méfiance réciproque, le terrain dévasté où ils s'affrontent. ... Nous sommes entrés dans l'ère du soupçon" (pp. 73–74).

In her discussion of the traditional novel, Sarraute acknowledges the lasting attraction of a form capable of adaptation, while she points out that the "modern" novel, by its very originality, is virtually inimitable.

> On ne peut, répète-t-on, refaire ce qu'ils [the Moderns] ont fait. Leurs techniques, aux mains de ceux qui essaient de s'en servir, tournent aussitôt au procédé; le roman traditionnel, au contraire, conserve une jeunesse éternelle: ses formes généreuses et souples continuent, sans avoir besoin de subir de notables changements, à s'adapter à toutes les nouvelles histoires, à tous les nouveaux personnages et les nouveaux conflits qui s'élèvent au sein des sociétés qui se succèdent. (p. 111)

What does the traditional, so-called realist novel offer readers? ". . . un secours dans leur solitude, une description de leur situation, des révélations sur les côtés secrets de la vie des autres, des conseils pleins de sagesse, des solutions justes aux conflits dont ils souffrent, un élargissement de leur expérience, l'impression de vivre d'autres vies" (p. 160). But Sarraute warns against the false security of such novels, stating that only the modern novel can truly open the reader's eyes to what is "real":

> Le lecteur, privé de tous ses jalons habituels et de ses points de repère, soustrait à toute autorité, mis brusquement en présence d'une matière inconnue, désemparé et méfiant, au lieu de s'abandonner les yeux fermés comme il aime tant à le faire, a été obligé de confronter à tout moment ce qu'on lui montrait avec ce qu'il voyait par lui-même. Il n'a pas dû peu s'étonner alors, soit dit en passant, de l'opacité des conventions romanesques qui avaient réussi à masquer pendant si longtemps ce qui aurait dû crever tous les yeux. (p. 114)

Perhaps more so than Robbe-Grillet and Sarraute, with whom he is often associated, Michel Butor in his critical writings promotes the potential experimental nature of the novel: "Alors que le récit véridique a toujours l'appui, la ressource d'une évidence extérieure, le roman doit suffire à susciter ce dont il nous entretient. C'est pourquoi il est le domaine phénoménologique par excellence, le lieu par excellence où étudier de quelle façon la réalité nous apparaît ou peut nous apparaître; c'est pourquoi le roman est le laboratoire du récit."[29] He even considers formal innovation a *necessary* requirement of the novel: "L'invention formelle dans le roman, bien loin de s'opposer au réalisme comme l'imagine trop souvent une critique à courte vue, est la condition *sine qua non* d'un réalisme plus poussé" (p. 11). Realism is, in fact, a problematic term, in that two periods or two centuries will obviously have vastly different concepts of reality.

Four dates stand out in the history of the nouveau roman and the critical debate that followed: 1955—when the first articles by Barthes, Robbe-Grillet, and Sarraute appeared about these new novels; 1958—when the special issue of *Esprit* was published devoted to the nouveaux romanciers (the first collection of critical analyses of the nouveau roman as a group); 1963—when the first book-length critical studies of the nouveau roman and its authors appeared; and 1971—the *décade* of Cerisy, the most extensive analysis to date of the nouveau roman by its critics and its authors. Each of these dates also marks a significant stage in the actual production of the nouveau roman: by 1955 most of the authors were associated with some kind of "movement"; by 1958 the major works of what would come to be known as the nouveau roman had been published; by 1963 the movement had been well documented, while its writers were beginning to pursue other interests; by 1971 the nouveau roman had largely become an integral component of the French literary "tradition" that it had attempted to counter, and had itself been imitated and surpassed.

What, exactly, has been the impact of the nouveau roman (and the critical debate surrounding this phenomenon) on the subsequent development of the novel in France? For his part, Roland Barthes minimizes this impact when he states, "Le nouveau roman a modifié certaines techniques de description, certaines techniques d'énonciation, il a subtilisé les notions de psychologie du personnage, mais on ne peut pas dire qu'il représente une littérature-limite, une littérature d'expérience."[30] In the same collection, Philippe Sollers, once a fervent admirer and potential descendant of the nouveau roman, denies any significant role at all for the latter, seeing in the nouveau roman a pale imitation of other more vigorous creative enterprises: "ce n'est certainement pas ce qu'on a appelé le *nouveau roman*, qui est au fond une faible répétition d'expériences menées ailleurs dans d'autres langues et dans d'autres pays, comme c'est aisément démontrable, qui peut ici apporter un démenti quelconque à ce que je suis en train de décrire comme le recul de la littérature française" (p. 76).

For some, the nouveau roman is an insignificant attempt to deviate from the only true form which the novel can possibly take: "Il n'y a qu'un progrès dans l'art du roman, c'est d'être capable d'en écrire d'authentiques et non de s'épuiser à construire des mécaniques scripturales que l'on appelle romans et qui ne sont, en somme, que des constructions savantes, des séquences linguistiques laborieusement fabriquées, de prétentieux exercices d'écriture dépourvus du moindre souffle de vie, la plupart du temps illisibles."[31] Admittedly, many such commentaries were made on the basis of reading only one novel, or with the work of one particular novelist in mind, but other negative criticism might apply to any one of these works, for example, this comment by Jean-Bertrand Barrère: "La technique, il semble, doit réussir à s'effacer, au lieu de s'interposer entre l'auteur et le lecteur, absorbant son attention au détriment de ce que nous persistons à estimer l'essentiel."[32]

For other critics, however, the nouveau roman sparked a renewal of interest in the possibilities in the novel form above and beyond those practiced by the vast majority of writers, as well as a rejection of those aspects of the genre that had become overused: "Le nouveau roman . . . a rendu l'immense service de nettoyer le genre de la crasse des clichés et des procédés usés qui s'était accumulée au cours des siècles."[33] While some critics saw the nouveaux romanciers as *provoking* a crisis in the novel, Pierre de Boisdeffre could see their arrival as a possible solution to this crisis, although he does not believe that their works have any lasting value: "L'importance du 'Nouveau Roman' tient donc moins à ce qu'il apporte qu'au fait qu'il est apparu en pleine 'crise' du roman: on a accueilli ses représentants avec d'autant plus de curiosité qu'on estimait, à tort ou à raison, le roman conventionnel engagé dans une impasse."[34]

In another work, however, Boisdeffre criticizes not the nouveaux romanciers, but those who would embrace the nouveau roman as the epitome of the novel genre, although they often do not comprehend the texts which they idolize: " 'Le Robbe-Grillet' n'est pas un *produit* que l'on *consomme*, c'est un *vêtement* que l'on *porte*. L'essentiel n'est pas de le lire, c'est de pouvoir en parler."[35] Boisdeffre considers the novel not only in terms of its literary merit, but also in terms of its beneficent effect on the reader: "S'il est un objet de consommation, le roman a aussi un autre rôle—et c'est ici que la 'création' dépasse la 'production.' Dans la mesure où il relève de la 'littérature,' il doit encore, en dehors de toute utilité immédiate, concourir à la *promotion des valeurs*: le plus grand rôle de la fiction consiste à incarner ces valeurs en des héros ou des situations exemplaires."[36] Similarly, J. M. Cocking warns, in a discussion of the nouveau roman, against overestimating a work without first consider- ing the presence or lack of artistic merit in this work: "people who value the arts have now become so involved with the fear of not recognising future greatness that they are leaning over backwards to accept gim- mickry as a worth-while kind of originality."[37]

Despite, or perhaps as a result of, the debate revolving around the nouveau roman, the traditional novel thrives and even increases in popu- larity. While Pierre de Boisdeffre sees this proliferation as a reaction against the nouveau roman ("nous assisterons donc au retour en force de tout un roman de tradition: 'romans d'amour,' reportages, romans de l'aventure individuelle, romans de la révolution"),[38] in fact the tradi- tional novel benefits from the existence of the nouveau roman, as the intense critical debate focused on the latter encourages a closer atten- tion to form and content in the novel as a whole in France, the influence of the nouveau roman gradually infiltrating the works of many novel- ists who would not otherwise consider themselves overtly experimen- tal: "The elements of fiction that are re-evaluated by the nouveau roman affect our reading of those novels that the nouveau roman supposedly subverts. The entire genre is reassessed in a perspective that alters the way in which we see even the most familiar examples of it."[39] If the period of creativity of the nouveau roman itself may be of limited dura- tion, its influence is much more profound: "the New Novel is an ex- haustible form, in the sense that puzzles lose their attraction once they become too easily solved."[40] Although the nouveau roman itself may see its readership decline, and its interest for scholars abate, readers and critics alike appreciate the influence of this phenomenon in the works of other writers.

If there is a direct successor to the nouveau roman, it is perhaps the writings in, and the activities revolving around, the journal *Tel Quel* (whose first issue appeared in 1961). As was the case with the nouveau roman, *Tel Quel* will never attain the broader popularity achieved by Sartrian existentialism; it will remain a relatively exclusive intellectual enterprise, but one deeply involved in the major literary and social debates of the times. Although the cofounder and key figure of *Tel Quel*, Philippe Sollers, writes novels, the best known contributors are theoreticians and philosophers: Roland Barthes, Jacques Derrida, Michel Foucault, Gérard Genette, Julia Kristeva, Tzvetan Todorov, and Jean Ricardou, to name just a few.

The primary initial interest of *Tel Quel*, as revealed in the "Déclaration" that appeared in the first issue, is an investigation into the nature of writing: "Ce qu'il faut dire aujourd'hui, c'est que l'écriture n'est plus concevable sans une claire prévision de ses pouvoirs, un sang-froid à la mesure du chaos où elle s'éveille, une détermination qui mettra la poésie à la plus haute place de l'esprit. Tout le reste *ne sera pas* littérature" (emphasis in original).[41] However, as this statement suggests, the focus on writing is not purely a literary investigation in the traditional sense (and as the nouveaux romanciers explored the genre), a point stressed by Celia Britton: "*Tel Quel* are concerned above all to institute a division within the field of literary practice, because their position is fundamentally *militant*. That is, they are putting forward a programme for a certain kind of revolutionary literature, defined as 'écriture' (writing) in opposition to bourgeois 'littérature' (literature)."[42] However, unlike Sartre, for whom writing was merely a vehicle through which his philosophical thought could be expressed, *Tel Quel* envisages writing as the manifestation of revolutionary principles. Bourgeois language and writing must both be challenged in order for true and complete social change to be realized.

Just as the nouveau roman had no one distinct goal, *Tel Quel* and its contributors embrace a diverse program of issues, literary and social, over the course of the journal's existence, such as:

> The distinction between writing and literature
> The relationship between writing and social change
> A questioning of the notions of author and text
> The impact of Freud and Lacan on writing
> An understanding of the signifying process
> The relationship of Marxism and literature

Danielle Marx-Scouras even sees in *Tel Quel* the ultimate stage in postwar intellectual development: "The rehabilitation of literature in 1960 implied the liquidation of postwar ideologies, and particularly, of engagement. With respect to literature and ideology, *Tel Quel* marks a closing chapter in French intellectual history. Its first phase from 1960–62 constitutes a requiem for the postwar years."[43]

As was the case for the nouveaux romanciers, the contributors to *Tel Quel* reject conventional notions of literature and encourage new approaches to the writing process in order to avoid what Sollers in *Logiques* calls a process of replacement: "On ne lit peut-être plus que par allusion à la Bibliothèque achevée ou à l'organisation audio-visuelle, et l'on pourrait dire sans exagération que la presque totalité des livres encore publiés sont d'ores et déjà des produits de remplacement."[44] The new focus on writing, according to Sollers, transfers the focus from the author to the activities of writing and reading: "Nous voyons donc que la question essentielle n'est plus aujourd'hui celle de l'*écrivain* et de l'*œuvre* (encore moins de 'l'œuvre d'art'), mais celle de l'*écriture* et de la *lecture*" (pp. 237–38; emphasis in original). With this new concept of writing, the very notions of writer and reader find themselves under attack: "par définition, l'écriture doit s'inscrire dans les intervalles entre les individus qui se livrent à son expérience et comme de l'un à l'autre, en retrait de chaque personnalisation qui n'est jamais, au fond, qu'un effet de marché. Le texte appartient à tous, à personne."[45] Sollers goes as far as to suggest that the contemporary writer or reader is incapable of understanding of what writing and reading truly consist: "nous sommes sans cesse en train de lire et d'écrire, dans nos rêves, notre perception, nos actes, nos fantasmes, notre pensée—mais nous l'ignorons dans la mesure où nous *croyons savoir lire et écrire*" (emphasis in original).[46] Writing is no longer necessarily a conscious, intellectual enterprise: "Ecrire, faire apparaître l'écriture, ce n'est pas disposer d'un savoir privilégié: c'est essayer de découvrir ce que tout le monde sait et que personne ne peut dire" (p. 248), and by questioning the writing process itself, by investigating theories of writing, one may improve the practice of writing.

Although the contributors to *Tel Quel* at first praised the efforts of the nouveaux romanciers (only to criticize them later), the two envisaged literature in radically different terms. The nouveaux romanciers' primary interest is still the form and composition of the novel, while the focus of *Tel Quel* is writing ("l'écriture") and text and their philosophical and political implications: "Where in Robbe-Grillet or Butor the creative process is embodied quite robustly in terms of physical environment or 'characters,' with Sollers and others it is reduced to little more than the adventure of a language or *parole* itself."[47] As Jean Ricardou so succinctly expressed it, the focus has shifted from "l'écriture d'une aventure" to "l'aventure d'une écriture."[48] Finally, critics and authors alike have come to refer to the "nouveau nouveau roman," which has surpassed the nouveau roman in its preoccupation with language and with writing. The reader too becomes an active participant in the creative process, abandoning the passive stance encouraged by the conventional novel: "le 'nouveau nouveau roman' faisait du lecteur un producteur, puisqu'il exige une lecture productive qui recrée en quelque sorte le texte, et qu'il peut aussi susciter en lui le désir d'explorer par lui-même quelques-unes des infinies possibilités de l'écriture."[49]

The preoccupations of *Tel Quel* (largely dependent on Sollers's pre-occupations) varied greatly over the twenty-three years of its existence, demonstrating the constantly changing interests of a whole generation of writers and thinkers. Several specific developments can be traced in *Tel Quel*'s history: from 1960 to 1969 the preoccupation was with writing, although the emphasis changed over the course of the decade from fiction to theory (structuralism, semiology, Russian formalism); after the events of May 1968 the journal became sympathetic to Communist China and Maoism; in 1976 begins a move in ideology from left to right, followed in 1977 by an increased focus on the United States. Finally, in 1983, *Tel Quel* was replaced by *L'Infini*, with yet another change in emphasis; the most commonly cited authors in the new journal became Dante, Joyce, and Pound, and the most commonly cited book, the Bible.[50]

As the example of *Tel Quel* demonstrates, the widely perceived notion of the novel as a text written by an author for a reader is far too simplistic for contemporary times, as even the example of the nouveau roman remains rooted in a consideration of traditional concepts of the novel: "La littérature cesse d'être un discours s'efforçant d'aller d'un émetteur à un récepteur qu'il s'agit d'influencer: elle est une structure qu'il s'agit de démonter hors de toute sédimentation mythique, lexicologique, morale ou charnelle."[51] The traditional novel survived the onslaught of theoretical and social concerns imposed on it by some writers and critics. Just as the nouveau roman exerted only a limited influence on writing practices in the 1950s, the programs of *Tel Quel* and other journals and currents of thought affected only a small percentage of writers during the 1960s and 1970s, and many critics have pointed out the limited appeal of those writers preoccupied by theory and concerned with innovation for innovation's sake: "La recherche de l'originalité à tout prix a beau être l'une des prétentions les plus remarquables de ce temps—et probablement la plus décevante de toutes—on se dit parfois que l'historien futur de notre littérature actuelle n'aura pas besoin, sans doute, de multiplier les sous-titres, car les œuvres du moment ont un air de famille."[52] Yet even those critics vehemently opposed to the ideologies of writers and thinkers like the members of *Tel Quel* acknowledge the place that such ideologies inevitably occupy in the world of literature: "On peut briser les cadres, s'évader des anciennes formes, en inventer de nouvelles, mettre le genre en doute, la littérature en question, nier la réalité, aspirer au silence et au néant, tous ces massacres, ces négations, ces renaissances prennent corps dans une 'fable' dont nous avons besoin parce qu'elle s'adresse à l'ensemble du complexe humain, sur tous les plans, de la réalité quotidienne au mythe."[53]

Traditional and more "popular" modes of literary expression will also benefit from the mistrust in which many readers held the experimental writings of the 1950s and 1960s: "Rebuté par des écrivains qui, loin de l'aider à mieux comprendre et à mieux accepter sa tâche, ne cessent, d'une manière qui n'est pas toujours essentielle à leur propos, de la lui compliquer... comment s'étonner que le grand public, à défaut de ces maîtres à penser dont il a gardé la nostalgie, se rabatte sur des maîtres à rêver?"[54] The experimental works will always provoke considerable interest on the part of critics and especially scholars because of their originality and because, quite simply, they are different from the norm: "Les livres 'dont on parle' (qu'on ne lit pas toujours), ceux qui 'font du bruit,' sont des œuvres de provocation, de contestation ou de rupture. Le sens esthétique—ce qu'on appelait hier le *goût*—ne guide plus les créateurs."[55]

Yet while the events of May 1968 will encourage the writers of *Tel Quel* to embark on a more overtly political agenda, abandoning literary topics such as the question of "écriture," these same events will also mark a general refocusing on more human problems in the novel in France, whether this is a direct consequence of May 1968 or not: "les événements de 1968, même s'ils n'ont été qu'une parodie d'histoire, ont eu pour conséquence de poser, ou de reposer, les problèmes urgents qui concernent les hommes, leur vie, leur avenir, leur espérance. Certes, on a continué à écrire des 'nouveaux romans'—mais la nouveauté, la puissance d'impact, soudain, n'était plus de ce côté-là: c'est le roman historique qui a, durant quelques années, occupé le devant de la scène."[56] However, many critics will point out that the interest in history is not accompanied by an interest in contemporary social issues and that, compared to the era of Balzac and Stendhal, our own generation will leave little literary analysis of current social and cultural questions. The diversity of subject matter found in the contemporary novel in France might be best interpreted not as a crisis, or as an indication of indecisiveness or lack of direction by authors who are not, after all, a homogeneous group, but rather as an indication of the infinite number of worthy topics available for discussing humankind's position in the modern world, a richness of possibilities much more promising than the avenues open to those interested in formal experiment: "Depuis Baudelaire, en France, des 'avant-gardes' se sont succédé. Cela finissait par être un autre conformisme; nier, transgresser devenait un rite. C'est plutôt le besoin d'affirmer l'homme et de lui trouver un sens qui se manifeste dans la littérature depuis une quinzaine d'années, à travers une mosaïque de productions diverses."[57]

The variety that characterizes the novel in France from the 1950s on makes any generalizations about this genre difficult, if not impossible. As Albérès points out, one should not seek any sort of "révélation littéraire, sociale, sociologique, structuraliste, psychophénoménologiste, politique" in tracing the tendencies of the contemporary novel in France, a task made all the more difficult, he adds, by the lack of any one dominant figure, like Sartre, Camus, Malraux, or Gide, writers who had such a broad impact in the years preceding the advent of the nouveau roman and later textual innovations.[58]

Yet the lack of a dominant figure, accompanied by the presence of increasingly divergent styles in the novel, does not preclude the possibility that one or many among the current group of writers might gain lasting recognition, a fact vigorously supported by the present collection. Obviously the differences lie not only in the works being produced but also in the tastes of the reading public: "On assiste à une parcellarisation du champ littéraire, à une atomisation du public en sous-ensembles relativement clos bien qu'il ne soit pas exclu qu'à long terme ces écritures, qui font d'un groupe à la fois le sujet d'élection et le destinataire privilégié, puissent atteindre, par des voies détournées, l'universel."[59] Indeed, close critical attention to these different styles should be encouraged rather than withheld if we are to understand what has occurred in the wake of the impact of the nouveau roman.

For most critics, the experiments of the 1950s and 1960s are unrepeatable and now of only limited relevance to the genre's development. Boisdeffre summarizes the legacy of the nouveau roman (especially as practiced by Robbe-Grillet) by claiming, "Le romancier d'aujourd'hui ne peut plus se contenter de mesurer des objets."[60] Yet the impact of these formal innovations, whether considered as a positive or negative influence, has lingered; as recently as 1989, Lecherbonnier could see "le retour à un certain classicisme et le désir de renouveler un genre quelque peu asphyxié par les expériences outrancières des générations précédentes."[61] Indeed, the nouveau roman has become a fixed component of French literary history, finding its place on university reading lists and in the critical analyses of various scholars and, thereby, has been relegated, somewhat, to the past. Concurrently, more than one critic has hailed the apparent return to more "traditional" modes of storytelling, undoubtedly the most significant development in the novel since the height of the nouveau roman, as writers have rejected the more overtly experimental forms of "écriture," preferring instead to attract the reader (and a larger number of readers at that) with rich, intriguing narrations. Calling the nouveaux romanciers and their descendants "les bricoleurs du roman," Jacques Brenner calls the newer generation of storytellers—Le Clézio, Tournier, Modiano, Fernandez, for example— the writers of "la nouvelle fable."[62]

At the same time, the subjects available to the writer have multiplied at an astounding rate, as mass communication and the availability of global transportation have made the world much more accessible. Formerly forbidden topics have become more acceptable since the end of World War II, as social and so-called sexual revolutions have relaxed existing interdictions: "Literary language has been liberated to talk, and talk freely, about once taboo subjects (sex, expecially, but not only)."[63] For example, in this collection alone we encounter authors openly discussing female sexuality (Wittig, Cixous, and Groult), homosexuality (Tournier, Fernandez, and Drevet), and contemporary attitudes toward sex and promiscuity (Sollers and Queffélec).

However, as far as defining the major currents of the novel is concerned, several critics have lamented the lack of a trend that stands as the center of attention, even if not as a dominant tendency. Speaking in 1989, Angelo Rinaldi could even say that such a trend is a necessity when speaking of French literature: "Nous traversons une période de désarroi. Il y a vingt ans encore, on pouvait parler d'avant-garde, de structuralisme et autres 'ismes.' Brutalement tout s'est effondré. Les gens sont devenus perplexes. Par nature, le Français a besoin d'écoles, d'étiquettes."[64]

Even those who have been associated with more experimental investigations of the novel have turned to styles that find a larger audience, abandoning the techniques that moved them to the forefront of the avant-garde in favor of autobiography and conventional story-telling, albeit often with traces of their earlier preoccupations: "Le retour du sujet, qui n'existe que doté de son imaginaire va automatiquement de pair avec le retour du récit. L'écriture semble redevenir le lieu d'une aventure humaine . . . les grands écrivains de l'avant-garde des années soixante-dix deviennent, vingt ans plus tard, des hommes et des femmes qui se rapprochent du lecteur, qui s'ouvrent à lui à travers des récits autobiographiques."[65] Michel Raimond suggests that the predilection for autobiographical or semiautobiographical forms (such as those practiced by the nouveaux romanciers) has left readers more interested in forms of narration with a personal tone, one absent from the experimental literature of the 1950s and 1960s: "Le lecteur de nos jours n'est-il pas plus sensible, dans la fiction, à la voix du romancier qu'aux tableaux qu'il peint? N'est-il pas plus attentif à la qualité d'une présence qu'aux performances de la description ou aux habiletés de la narration? Ne préfère-t-il pas au tableau objectif du monde de son temps . . . la sincérité d'un témoignage personnel?"[66]

Several critics have attempted to trace developments in the novel since the height of the nouveau roman, with varying results, and we might consider some of these trends, in which many of the authors studied in this collection are implicated. Although most of these critics acknowledge the arbitrary manner in which they choose means of categorization, they are largely successful in delineating the prominent themes and undercurrents in the recent novel. Bersani et al., for example, trace four principal movements in the novel in the wake of the May 1968 events through the 1970s: an increase in autobiographical fiction, a return to a preoccupation with history, the evocation of the concerns raised by the May 1968 events, and a reflection on the status of women. At the same time, they detect a continuing division between tradition and experimentation: "Entre roman traditionnel et roman nouveau, la distance n'a fait que s'accroître."[67] Yet they also suggest that the dominant preoccupations of the postwar era have lost their appeal: "Fini le temps de littératures engagées, des illusions lyriques, des avant-gardes extrémistes et des départs pour la Bolivie ou le Bangla-Desh" (p. 839). Kibédi-Varga suggests that many of the more interesting works—some experimental, others combining intriguing stories with innovative narrative techniques—may be placed under the ill-defined heading of "postmodern." In particular, he refers to the "mode ironique" of much contemporary writing, involving the processes of "réécriture" and "renarrativisation"— the rewriting of history or of existing stories, for which he provides the examples of Toussaint, Echenoz, and Tournier, or the process of "déguisement"—the cloaking of the story in unexpected and unusual forms— of which the works of Georges Perec are cited as the most representative example.[68] Certainly the characteristics generally associated with postmodernism dominate the contemporary novel form in both its traditional and experimental manifestations: "randomness, pluralism, heterogeneity, multiplicity, dispersion, and indeterminacy rather than univocity, totality, wholeness, hierarchy, and polarity."[69] Indeed, it appears that many authors see no other choice than to use and abuse their literary heritage: "Plutôt que de créer du 'nouveau,' l'artiste joue dès lors à décomposer et recomposer ce qui existe déjà. Il devient le metteur en scène de son héritage. Ou son conservateur. Ou son démolisseur. Il procède par citations ou plagiats. Il joue aussi bien avec les œuvres du passé qu'avec les déchets ou les signes de la consommation de masse."[70]

Other compilers of literary histories have restricted themselves to classifying the contemporary novel in France according to the major themes that seem to dominate, neglecting the more obvious opposition of tradition versus innovation. Michel Raimond divides the postwar novel into six categories: roman d'aventures, roman historique, connaissances du réel, historiens du temps présent, le témoignage, and les choses de la vie.[71] Another such categorization utilizes seven headings that reflect a more sociohistorical point of view: la deuxième guerre, l'intellectuel et la société, la décolonisation, la crise des valeurs bourgeoises, la condition ouvrière, Mai 1968, and la civilisation de l'objet.[72]

The subject matter of the novelists included in this collection certainly attests to the diversity suggested in the preceding lists. No one style or topic has come to dominate discussion of the genre in the way that the nouveau roman and existentialist thought prevailed in their time. Yet although the individual chapters isolate the novelists discussed here, themes and preoccupations do persist throughout the collection, giving the whole an element of unity. Beyond the interest in formal innovation that several of the novelists demonstrate (Sollers, Ricardou, and Roubaud, for example), the choice of subject matter alone reveals a seemingly endless list of possibilities: the horrors of wars, both real and imaginary (Green, Gracq, and Chedid), World War II and the Holocaust (Wiesel, Tournier, and Modiano), the former French colonies (Tournier, Queffélec, and Duras), the United States (Green, Sollers, and Groult), the status of women (Cixous and Wittig), music (Fernandez, Drevet, and Echenoz), death (Pinget and Chedid), faith (Green and Wiesel), photography (Toussaint and Tournier), film (Modiano and Drevet), the detective novel (Modiano and Echenoz), all in a vast range of settings, again both real and imaginary: Vietnam, America, Israel, Russia, Italy, the Maghreb, and Lebanon, as well as every corner of France.

Yet for all the diversity and seemingly limitless possibilities available to current and future writers, negative and pessimistic evaluations of the contemporary state of affairs continue to emerge. Pierre de Boisdeffre, for example, depicts the literary scene in a perhaps excessively negative light: "Il y a crise—et même éclatement—du 'concept de littérature.' Aggravation du fossé entre tradition et modernité. Contamination, idéologique et politisation de la vie littéraire. Enfin, concentration du succès sur un petit nombre de best-sellers sélectionnés par les médias."[73] Vercier and Lecarme as well point out the difficult task of the contemporary novelist forced to compete for the attention of a discriminating public: "le romancier a beaucoup plus de mal que par le passé à imposer sa part de transposition, de fiction ou de création. A peine a-t-il écrit son livre qu'il doit le présenter et le représenter, dans diverses interviews dont l'émission *Apostrophes* est la plus indispensable."[74]

These two statements reflect an inevitable reality of the contemporary literary scene. Any consideration of the novel in France today must acknowledge the great influence on the world of the novel in France of the publishing houses, the media, and the literary prizes. The success of any author's work, whether his or her appeal be popular or "literary," is unquestionably dependent in part on factors such as the name of the "maison d'édition" that publishes the work, on the reception of this work in the many periodicals that include book reviews, and finally, on the attribution of a literary prize, especially the major awards announced every November: Goncourt, Fémina, Renaudot, Médicis, Interallié, and so on. Even the season during which the novelist's work is released can determine the fate of this work, as both author and reader may find themselves depending on the choices and caprices of a publisher: "Equinoxe d'automne des prix littéraires, solstice d'été des romans de plage, l'édition a ses saisons et ses poussées de fièvre. De même avec une frénésie accrue, les médias allument et éteignent des gloriettes éphémères. . . . Dans un tel contexte, quelles chances le lecteur conserve-t-il de discerner les œuvres véritablement nouvelles, exigeantes et aventureuses?"[75]

In addition, the world of literature has expanded to include genres that barely existed a generation or two ago. Certainly we must mention the "paraliterary" forms that have made a considerable contribution to the realm of the novel since World War II. These works are worthy of our attention for several reasons: they are among the most widely read works by the general public; they are increasingly the focus of attention of critics and scholars, as their inherent artistic value has been recognized; and they are often a considerable influence on other, more "serious" novelists. From the world of the roman policier alone, names such as Simenon, A. D. G., Boileau-Narcejac, and Japrisot have become common components of discussions of the contemporary novel in France. Authors such as René Barjavel, Gérard Klein, and Jacques Sternberg, if less known than their American counterparts, have found success in the world of science fiction. Vercier and Lecarme suggest that these latter two forms of the novel are in fact a more accurate reflection of the interests of modern society than their traditional counterparts: "notre société se reconnaît sans doute davantage dans les miroirs du roman policier et de la science-fiction que dans celui du roman, qu'il soit d'avant-garde ou de tradition."[76] Even the "la bande dessinée," the comic strip, published in hardcover in France and a passion for the French difficult for many North Americans to appreciate, has been the object of considerable critical attention, and Astérix, Tintin, and Lucky Luke are undoubtedly more familiar fictional characters to much of the French public than those found in best-selling novels.

What might we say of the status of the novel in France in order to understand not only its present but also its future? We might consider what several French writers and critics have written on this subject. The opin-

ions are, not surprisingly, diverse, and range from the most gloomy pessimism and predictions of the imminent death of the novel, to eager
anticipation. In 1972 Edouard Gaede asked more than three hundred
writers to reply to twenty-two questions about their craft, one of these
questions asking for their predictions about the future of literature.[77]
Some of the replies, such as that of René Clair, appear quite accurate
and timely in their consideration of the ongoing status of literature in
contemporary society: "Je pense qu'à la fin de notre siècle, la 'littérature,'
au sens que nous donnons aujourd'hui à ce mot, aura perdu une grande
part de son importance. Radio, télévision, cinéma ne sont sans doute
que les précurseurs de moyens d'expression que nous sommes en ce
moment incapables de concevoir" (p. 661).

Other notable replies envisaged the future of literature in a variety
of manners, from the positive ("Il y aura toujours des poètes," Albert
Fabre, p. 664), to the carefree ("Peu m'importe! Travaillons!" Armand
Lunel, p. 671). Some hoped for a narrowing of the gap between tradition and innovation: "Elle doit trouver une synthèse entre les formes
traditionnelles et les tendances nouvelles" (Jean-Alfred Noël, p. 674).
For his part, Michel Tournier, probably the most prominent of those who
responded, saw literature as remaining true to a tradition of unpredictability: "Tout à fait imprévisible et en même temps absolument fidèle
à son passé. L'œuvre sera d'autant plus surprenante et inattendue que
la fonction restera identique à ce qu'elle était les siècles passés. Vouloir
changer la fonction dans l'espoir de renouveler l'œuvre, c'est le faux
calcul de l'impuissance" (p. 682).

Although Gaede's survey dates from 1972, many of the comments
made by the respondents still appear relevant to any discussion of the
novel. For all the debate concerning the traditional versus the experimental novel, a far more compelling question asks what place these
works occupy in a world overwhelmed by technological advances, many
of which are intended to entertain and to assume a role that literature
has fulfilled for centuries. Jacques Brenner points out that if there is a
crisis in the novel in France, its origins lie not in any lack of quality
works, but in a lack of "l'attention que l'on porte aux œuvres de l'esprit."[78]
Michel Butor suggests that writers must reconsider the unique structures and possibilities of the novel, if they wish this genre to remain
competitive with television and film: "Cet objet [le livre] par lequel tant
d'événements ont eu lieu, convient-il de s'y tenir encore, et pourquoi?
Quelles sont ses véritables supériorités, s'il en a, sur les autres moyens

de conserver nos discours? Comment utiliser au mieux ses avantages?"[79] In response to Butor's questions, we might offer the pessimistic evaluation of one prominent novelist, Patrick Modiano: "Faute d'audience, faute de pouvoir s'adapter au rythme du monde moderne . . . il y a simplement le fait que le roman ne peut plus, à mon sens, déterminer ou orienter la sensibilité commune, comme il pouvait encore le faire au début de ce siècle."[80]

On a more positive note, Maurice Nadeau believes that as long as people attempt to explain our existence on this planet, the novel will have its place: "On peut briser les cadres, s'évader des anciennes formes, en inventer de nouvelles, mettre le genre en doute, la littérature en question, nier la réalité, aspirer au silence et au néant, tous ces massacres, ces négations, ces renaissances prennent corps dans une 'fable' dont nous avons besoin parce qu'elle s'adresse à l'ensemble du complexe humain, sur tous les plans, de la réalité quotidienne au mythe."[81] Jean Ricardou, who could not have a more different approach to the novel than Nadeau, also recognizes the unique function of literature in modern society: "Si donc, comme on l'a maintes fois noté, la littérature nous fait mieux voir le monde, nous le révèle, et, d'un mot, en accomplit la critique, c'est dans l'exacte mesure où, loin d'en offrir un substitut, une image, une représentation, elle est capable, en sa textualité, de lui opposer la différence d'un tout autre système d'éléments et de rapports."[82] Yet the novel and literature as a whole will continue to change, on the one hand, because they have always been changing and, on the other hand, because our ever-changing modern world demands it: "La vie littéraire, pour demeurer fidèle à sa qualité et à sa propre histoire, en est encore à chercher de nouvelles formes d'expression, dans une société où les besoins culturels s'infléchissent et se modifient à des rythmes plus rapides qu'autrefois, et dans des directions encore imprévisibles."[83]

Ultimately, the purpose of the novel, if it indeed has one, may be to express the reality of a particular period or society, although such expression shall undoubtedly take an infinite variety of forms, from the most conventional narrative to the most complex and difficult "écriture." It would appear that as far as the present and future of the novel in France are concerned, tradition and experimentation find themselves (and despite themselves) sharing a common goal, in what one might call an eternal, and uneasy, balance, a balance constantly challenged by the multitude of new works appearing every year.

And the reader certainly has a wealth of possible works from which to choose: several hundred new novels are released annually in France, and a significant percentage of these are the products of newly published novelists. One can only hope to read a fraction of what Pierre de Boisdeffre calls "l'innombrable roman,"[84] and ascertaining some coherent trend or common orientation in these works is a formidable, if not impossible task. Even in 1967, Michel Butor wondered why anyone would want to add anything new to this overwhelming quantity of works: "Toute invention littéraire aujourd'hui se produit à l'intérieur d'un milieu déjà saturé de littérature. Tout roman, poème, tout écrit nouveau est une intervention dans ce paysage antérieur. . . . Pourquoi dès lors, à cette énorme masse, dont nous ne connaîtrons qu'une minuscule partie, vouloir ajouter encore des volumes?"[85]

Evidently, in considering authors who are still writing and developing their style, in considering a literature that is still "en train de se faire," one always risks the danger of drawing premature and inaccurate conclusions about these authors and their works, perhaps neglecting works that future generations will appreciate and canonize, while favoring works that may have only an ephemeral impact. Perhaps the most accurate reflection of this hesitation to pass judgment, of this difficulty in assessing the contemporary novel, can be found in a novel by one of the authors discussed in this collection: *Les Fruits d'or* by Nathalie Sarraute.

> Est-ce bon? Est-ce mauvais? Il vous faut des règles impérieuses qu'il serait obligatoire d'appliquer. Vous voulez à toute force qu'il y ait une vérité à laquelle on soit contraint de se soumettre coûte que coûte. . . . L'Art, comme vous dites, une œuvre d'art n'est jamais une valeur sûre. C'est bien connu, c'est évident. On se trompe beaucoup, c'est naturel. Comment savoir? Qui peut dire qu'il sait? Même pour les valeurs les plus éprouvées, les chefs-d'œuvre du passé, on voit tout à coup des revirements, on assiste à de brusques engouements. . . . Les goûts changent. Il y a à certains moments certains besoins. Et après on veut autre chose. Comment voulez-vous empêcher les gens de suivre la mode, ici comme en tout? Qui se trompe? Qu'en restera-t-il? Mais que veut dire restera? Restera pour qui? Jusqu'à quand? Comment prévoir?[86]

To neglect the developments in the novel in France since World War II out of a fear of erroneous statements would be both negligent and unfortunate. Negligent, in that we would be, in a spirit of excessive conservatism, reserving judgment on an aspect of contemporary French culture that is both worthy of attention and necessary for understanding this culture. Unfortunate, in that we would be depriving ourselves and others (scholars, students, and the general public) of the opportunity and the pleasure of performing that act for which these works are intended: reading. And indeed, it is for those who have a sincere interest in the novel in France that the following chapters are intended: for those interested in tracing some of the important developments since the height of the nouveau roman, for those with a specific interest in one or more particular authors, for those interested in French culture (of which the novel is, of course, an integral component), and for those seeking the pure joy of reading rich, intriguing, and thought-provoking works of fiction.

Notes

1. Roger Laufer, Bernard Lecherbonnier, and Henri Mitterand, *Thèmes et langages de la culture moderne. Littérature et langages 5. Les genres et les thèmes* (Paris: Nathan, 1977), p. 228.

2. Jacques Brenner, *Tableau de la vie littéraire en France d'avant-guerre à nos jours* (Paris: Fayard, 1978), p. 109.

3. In Bernard Gros, ed., *La Littérature (du symbolisme au nouveau roman)* (Paris: Denoël/CEPL, 1970), p. 247.

4. André Daspre and Michel Décaudin, eds., *Histoire littéraire de la France. Tome 12, 1939–1970* (Paris: Editions Sociales, 1980).

5. Maurice Blanchot, *Le Livre à venir* (Paris: Gallimard, 1959), p. 147.

6. Pierre Vanbergen, *Aspects de la littérature française contemporaine* (Brussels: Labor, 1973), p. 141.

7. Pierre Brunel et al., *Histoire de la littérature française. Vol. II: XIXe et XXe siècles* (Paris: Bordas, 1986), p. 715.

8. Pierre de Boisdeffre, *Où va le roman?* (Paris: Del Duca, 1962), p. 97.

9. Maurice Nadeau, in *Ecrire . . . pour quoi? pour qui?* ed., Roger Pillaudin (Grenoble: Presses Universitaires de Grenoble, 1974), pp. 19–20.

10. Boisdeffre, *Histoire de la littérature de langue française des années 1930 aux années 1980* (Paris: Perrin, 1985).

11. Jean-Paul Sartre, *Qu'est-ce que la littérature* (Paris: Gallimard, 1948), p. 30.

12. Celia Britton, "The Nouveau Roman and *Tel Quel* Marxism," *Paragraph* 12, no. 1 (March 1989), pp. 68–69.

13. Nadeau, *Ecrire*, p. 96.

14. Quoted in John Ardagh, *The New France* (Harmondsworth: Penguin, 1973), p. 522.

15. Nadeau, *Ecrire*, p. 143.

16. Jacques Bersani et al., *La Littérature en France depuis 1945* (Paris: Bordas, 1970), p. 291.

17. Blanchot, *Livre à venir*, p. 273.

18. Quoted in Nicole Bothorel et al., *Les Nouveaux Romanciers* (Paris: Bordas, 1976), p. 7.

19. Roland Barthes, "La Littérature d'aujourd'hui," *Tel Quel*, no. 7 (autumn 1961), p. 40.

20. See Stephen Heath, *The Nouveau Roman: A Study in the Practice of Writing* (Philadelphia: Temple University Press), pp. 40–41; Bruce Morrissette, "The New Novel in France," *Chicago Review* 15, no. 3 (winter–spring 1962), p. 1.

21. Françoise van Rossum-Guyon, in *Nouveau Roman: Hier, aujourd'hui, vol. I* (Paris: UGE, 1972), p. 415.

22. Barthes, "Littérature objective," *Essais critiques* (Paris: Seuil, 1964), p. 30.

23. Brunel et al., *Histoire*, p. 722.

24. Ardagh, *New France*, p. 546.

25. Lucien Goldmann, *Pour une sociologie du roman* (Paris: Gallimard, 1964), pp. 283–84.

26. Jean-Michel Maulpoix et al., *Histoire de la littérature française: XXe, 1950–1990* (Paris: Hatier, 1991), p. 148.

27. Alain Robbe-Grillet, *Pour un nouveau roman* (Paris: Gallimard, 1963), p. 15.

28. Nathalie Sarraute, *L'Ere du soupçon* (Paris: Gallimard, 1956), pp. 71–72.

29. Michel Butor, *Essais sur le roman* (Paris: Gallimard, 1964), p. 9.

30. In Pillaudin, *Ecrire*, p. 29.

31. Albert Léonard, *La Crise du concept de littérature en France au XXe siècle* (Paris: Corti, 1974), p. 168.

32. Jean-Bertrand Barrère, *Le Cure d'amaigrissement du roman* (Paris: Albin Michel, 1964), p. 118.

33. André Maurois, *Nouvelles directions de la littérature française* (Oxford: Clarendon, 1967), p. 23.

34. Boisdeffre, *Où va le roman?*, pp. 294–95.

35. Boisdeffre, *La Cafetière est sur la table* (Paris: Table Ronde, 1967), p. 9.

36. Boisdeffre, *Où va le roman?*, p. 17.

37. J. M. Cocking, "The 'Nouveau Roman' in France," *Essays in French Literature*, no. 2 (November 1965), p. 3.

38. Boisdeffre, *Histoire de la littérature de langue française*, p. 1122.

39. Ann Jefferson, *The Nouveau Roman and the Poetics of Fiction* (Cambridge: Cambridge University Presses, 1980), p. 6.

40. John Sturrock, *The French New Novel: Claude Simon, Michel Butor, Alain Robbe-Grillet* (London: Oxford University Press, 1969), p. 34.

41. *Tel Quel*, no. 1 (1961), p. 3.

42. Britton, "*Tel Quel* Marxism," p. 73.

43. Danielle Marx-Scouras, "Requiem for the Postwar Years: The Rise of Tel Quel," *French Review* 64, no. 3 (February 1991), p. 411.

44. Philippe Sollers, *Logiques* (Paris: Seuil, 1968), p. 229.

45. Sollers, "Ecriture et révolution," in *Théorie d'ensemble* (Paris: Seuil, 1968), p. 69.

46. Sollers, *Logiques*, p. 247.

47. Sturrock, *New Novel*, p. 37.

48. Jean Ricardou, *Pour une théorie du nouveau roman* (Paris: Seuil, 1971), p. 32.

49. Liliane Temime-Chedeau, in *Nouveau Roman: Hier, aujourd'hui*: I, p. 424.

50. See Jean-Francois Fourny, "From *Tel Quel* to *L'Infini*," *Contemporary French Civilization* 11, no. 2 (spring–summer 1987), pp. 189–99.

51. Gros, *Littérature*, p. 207.

52. Régis Boyer, "Romans actuels, œuvres de recherche et de cri," *Le Français dans le Monde*, no. 48 (April–May 1967), p. 6.

53. Nadeau, *Ecrire*, pp. 185–86.

54. Bersani et al., *Littérature en France depuis 1945*, p. 844.

55. Boisdeffre, *Histoire de la littérature de langue française*, p. 1116.

56. Michel Raimond, *Le Roman* (Paris: Armand Colin, 1988), p. 17.

57. Marie-Claire Bancquart and Pierre Cahné, *Littérature française du XXe siècle* (Paris: PUF, 1992), p. 444.

58. R.-M. Albérès, *Le Roman d'aujourd'hui. 1960–1970* (Paris: Albin Michel, 1970), p. 272.

59. Bruno Vercier and Jacques Lecarme, *La Littérature en France depuis 1968* (Paris: Bordas, 1982), p. 12.

60. Boisdeffre, *Le Roman français depuis 1900* (Paris: PUF, 1985), p. 123.

61. Bernard Lecherbonnier et al., eds., *Littérature. Textes et documents: XXe siècle* (Paris: Nathan, 1989), p. 791.

62. Jacques Brenner, *Histoire de la littérature française de 1940 à nos jours* (Paris: Fayard, 1978).

63. Charles Porter, "Foreword," *Yale French Studies*, Special Issue (1988), pp. 2–3.

64. Eric Conan and Olivier Mongin, "La Comédie des prix littéraires. Entretien avec Angelo Rinaldi," *Esprit*, no. 156 (November 1989), p. 10.

65. Sophie Bertho, "L'Attente postmoderne. A propos de la littérature contemporaine en France," *Revue d'Histoire Littéraire de la France* 91, nos. 4-5 (July–October 1991), p. 737. See also Chapter I of this collection.

66. Raimond, *Le Roman*, p. 73.

67. Bersani et al., *Littérature en France depuis 1945* (1980 edition), p. 865.

68. A. Kibédi-Varga, "Le Récit postmoderne," *Littérature*, no. 77 (February 1990), pp. 3–22.

69. Dina Sherzer, *Representation in Contemporary French Fiction* (Lincoln: University of Nebraska Press), p. 3.

70. Maulpoix et al., *Histoire*, p. 403.

71. See Raimond, *Le Roman*.

72. In René Lasserre, *La France contemporaine* (Tübingen: Max Niemeyer Verlag, 1980).

73. Boisdeffre, *Histoire de la littérature de langue française*, p. 1123.

74. Vercier and Lecarme, *Littérature en France depuis 1968*, p. 105.

75. Maulpoix et al., *Histoire*, p. 404.

76. Vercier and Lecarme, *Littérature en France depuis 1968*, p. 249.

77. Edouard Gaede, *L'Ecrivain et la société* (Nice: Université de Nice, 1972).

78. Jacques Brenner and Jean-Pierre Salgas. *Le Roman français contemporain* (Paris: Ministère des Affaires Etrangères, 1990), p. 5.

79. Butor, *Essais*, p. 131.

80. Patrick Modiano, in Jean-Louis Ezine, *Les Ecrivains sur la sellette* (Paris: Seuil, 1981), pp. 25–26.

81. Nadeau, *Ecrire*, pp. 185–86.

82. Ricardou, *Pour une théorie*, pp. 23–24.

83. Françoise Gerbod and Paul Gerbod, I*ntroduction à la vie littéraire du XXe siècle* (Paris: Bordas, 1986), p. 148.

84. Boisdeffre, *Histoire de la littérature de langue française*, p. 679.

85. Butor, *Répertoire IV* (Paris: Minuit, 1973), p. 7.

86. Sarraute, *Les Fruits d'or* (Paris: Gallimard, 1963), p. 170.

Part I.
Continuing "Traditions" and Changing Styles

1

Autobiographical Fictions

Raylene Ramsay

The experimental new autobiographies that have marked characteristic shifts in the work of the "nouveaux romanciers" since the early 1970s are contributing to a rethinking and a rereading of both autobiographical and fictional writing. *Roland Barthes par Roland Barthes* (1974) signaled the new directions, followed by Marguerite Duras's *L'Amant* (1984), *La Douleur* (1985), *Emily L.* (1987), *L'Amant de la Chine du nord* (1991), and *Yann Andréa Steiner* (1992); *Frontières* by Michel Butor (1985); Claude Ollier's *Déconnections* (1988); Alain Robbe-Grillet's *Le Miroir qui revient* (1984), *Angélique ou l'enchantement* (1988), and *La Mort de Corinthe* (1994); *Enfance* (1983) and *Tu ne t'aimes pas* (1989) by Nathalie Sarraute; and *L'Invitation* (1989) and *L'Acacia* (1989) by Claude Simon.[1]

What are the significant innovations of this experimental new genre that might feed into and modify ways of organizing our contemporary texts or model new relations between the writer and the reader? Like the nouveau roman of the 1960s and the so-called nouveau nouveau roman of the late 1970s and 1980s, the "autofictions," to use Doubrovsky's term, unfold in a world of ontological and epistemological uncertainty. Meaning is placed under erasure as the text is deconstructed and reconstructed circling in invaginating structures, like the Moebius strip that provides only double (and contradictory) answers to questions of origins. The new genre is characterized by a telescoping of personal story and history and a reversible movement between inside and outside, in a "complementary" (contradictory but not mutually exclusive) movement of the writing that redefines story and history and rewrites a self. Such movements take the autofictions beyond the traditional retrospective autobiographical narrative of the development of a personality, a confessional narrative that observes a pact of truth and sincerity. They suggest the reader's own splitting and require her/him to examine the expectations or knowledge of the law that she/he brings to the reading of the text.

The transformed self of the new autobiographical fictions is not the traditional single and centering Cartesian subject present to itself in thought. Nor is it simply the postmodern decentered, overdetermined play of linguistic signifiers, a game of textual mirrors in which the person is endlessly deferred. It is neither wholly phantasmatical, the imaginary speaking of memory, as Robbe-Grillet puts it, nor wholly referential. Rather, in a new logically contradictory and characteristically postmodern structure one might call "complementarity" by analogy with Heisenberg's theory of the "complementary" nature of matter (at once wave and particle, continuity and discontinuity), the autofiction walks an emotional and logical tightrope between these pairs, seeking new forms better adapted to new visions of self, of language, and of world, and venturing into limit zones.

While the writing of the new autobiography is language-based and, as such, has connections with rationality, with historical moment, and with pre-existing texts (that is, with the collective), as textual creation, texture, interweaving of linguistic elements, images and forms, this discourse is "writing" in the most recent Barthesian sense. It is a sensuous and semiotic exploration, a passionate, individuated enterprise whose truth is finally affect identified. In *La Chambre claire,* love alone, for the mature Barthes, can decide whether the photo of an object (the mother) reveals its truth. Sarraute asserts the "truth" of the memory of an idyllic childhood excursion to the park with the mother recounted in *Enfance* because she can "hear" the little bells and the whirling celluloid flowers. To authenticate her narrative, Duras invites her reader to "look" with her at her adolescent self in her gold lamé high-heeled shoes and man's hat on the ferry crossing the Mekong river ("Regardez-moi"). Robbe-Grillet evokes the strong feelings aroused by the present crushing of a muskrat underfoot as evidence of the reality of the memory from his early childhood in which he kills a wounded sparrow. He is able to see himself only in the mirror of his writing. The ludic intertextual play of these texts and their self-conscious metacommentaries on their own functioning also designate their origins as a bodily production of desire, and of desire's concomitant pleasure/pain.

Revisions in the ready-made discourse of the self (autobiography as a retrospective narrative in prose recounting the history of a personality), then, become, in the new genre, an individuated practice of writing (fictions) from the body, bringing together the "bios" and the "graphy," that is, both the local and particular life or sensation and the pre-existing collective text. And, in their preoccupation with a present of the writing and the suspicion of the representational fallacy—the illusion that the text adheres naturally to the world—the new autobiographies, like the earlier new novels, initially appear resistant to history.

The earlier fictional work of these writers was interpreted persuasively as dislocating historical and literary chronology and the causality and connective coherence this sustains. Yet although they have all spoken of their new autobiographies as open, mobile, linguistic creations in the present moment, the inspiration for their multiple perceptions and imaginings also derives from memory of past events. At the level of the metatext, Robbe-Grillet's *Le Miroir qui revient* and Nathalie Sarraute's *Enfance* probe the very questions of the distortions and limitations of the past by the frames of the present (the frames of knowledge) that attempt to recapture it. The adult imposes her/his itinerary and present vision on the recreation of the child she/he once was. The past is also altered by the often aleatory processes of choice and the uncertainties of recollection, and the nature of the strategies (fictional and narrative) by which the past is recovered. There is no necessary causal relation between past and present, life and text; these relationships become reversible. As in the New Histories concerned with the trivia and the minutia of the past or with those groups and persons traditionally without voice, theirs is a new focus on the organic and the microscopic. Time and history are thus transformed but not eliminated as the reader is led to ask, not "Is this really the true story of the writer's history and origins?," but "What does it mean to ask such questions?"

What are the conceptions of self and history that the forms of these novels produce? Time/history has, of course, always been presented as what is unwritten by History (capitalized) in the work of Claude Simon: the wind blowing, the grass growing, and the old lady in black passing, a bundle of firewood on her back. In the 1983 and 1987 autofictions of Nathalie Sarraute (*Enfance* and *Tu ne t'aimes pas*), time/history is constituted as in her earliest work *Tropismes* (1937) and as in all her novels by tiny protoplasmic, contradictory movements of the psyche seeking security and pleasure, immobilizing or fleeing to avoid destruction or pain, dominating or submitting in psychological intrasubjective and intersubjective dramas repeated in competing dialogic narrative voices. In Marguerite Duras, it is once again the submerging seas (the homophonic mer/mère, sea/mother) of the fierceness and annihilating power of the violence of desire, the spontaneous fusion of the nonsocialized child with the natural world (the Lacanian presymbolic), set against the flat gray expanse of socialized ennui (the symbolic). For Robbe-Grillet, time is the precise, meticulously described swell of the wave, breaking and repeating at regular intervals, always already there, eternally, along the same (or almost same) line, yet slipping imperceptibly by the tiny imperfection into monstrous disorder, ready to suck one down to green depths, and back again.

Recursive patterns of sexual violence concealed/revealed in Robbe-Grillet's selection and organization of its disparate debris mark both the strata of Western history and culture (Greco-Roman/Judaic/Christian/Germanic) and the topologies of the phantom cities of Robbe-Grillet's own *imaginaire*. Time, in the new autobiographies as in the earliest novels, is at once the vertigo of libidinal obsession and new statistical scientific orders such as those emerging from the very unpredictability of the turbulent flows, the self-similar fractal shapes and the sensitive dependency on initial conditions that chaos theory models as it incorporates both randomness and order. The past in the autofictions, in another oxymoron, is the past present in the confused multiplicity of the moment, a past that, if no longer unproblematically and simply an origin or immediate apprehension of the real, is at the least a material re-membered from the past, reworked in the present of the time/experience of the writing.

L'Amant and its cinematic rewriting, *L'Amant de la Chine du nord*, are exemplary in this respect. They can be read as a somewhat fragmented account, most often narrated in the present, of Duras's childhood played out against the historical scene of French Indochina in the 1920s and 1930s. The grandiose tragedy of the widowed mother's purchase of a land grant that turns out to be regularly flooded by the sea constitutes both a central event in the emotional family saga that saw the young Marguerite (and indeed also the older writer) taking form and a criticism of a corrupt French colonial administration. The adolescent heroine's defiance of familial, social, and colonial taboos and racial discrimination in her passionate relationship with a wealthy Chinese man is the projection of an individuated subjectivity and psychic life into a colonial history, a social situation, and an ideology that derive from the domain of collective experience and inherited text. At first sight, nothing seems particularly new in this apparently dialectical functioning of private and public spheres, of history and self, Indochina and Duras. But the collective and the individual have in fact become two "complementary" faces (contradictory but not mutually exclusive) of the same phenomenon. There is both splitting and merging of a third-person character (now the adolescent girl or "the little one," and now the narrator-writer) and the first-person narrator (now the young girl, now the elderly narrator, now Duras the writer); of a personal "je" and an only apparently more distant "elle"/"la petite." The metacommentary that breaks the narrative flow and momentarily destroys the referential illusion identifies writer, narrator, and character yet establishes tensions between them. World War II, for example, the central event of the historical period these writers share, is represented in Duras as a lived familial or sexual power struggle. It takes the form of a primitive scene of "masculine" domination and "feminine" submission, introjected and experienced in the material body, that is, physically and emotionally. The war assumes the metaphorical face of the hated but seductive, bigger, stronger brother, "invading," "occupying," "destroying" the body (the territory) of the weaker, beloved, "little" brother for his own pleasure and the affirming of his power:

> Je vois la guerre sous les mêmes couleurs que mon enfance.
> Je confonds le temps de la guerre avec le règne de mon frère
> aîné. . . . Je vois la guerre comme lui était, partout se répandre,
> partout pénétrer, voler, emprisonner, partout être là, à tout
> mélangée, mêlée, présente dans le corps, dans la pensée, dans
> la veille, dans le sommeil, tout le temps, en proie à la passion
> saoulante d'occuper le territoire adorable du corps de l'enfant,
> du corps des moins forts, des peuples vaincus, cela parce que
> le mal est là, aux portes, contre la peau. (p. 78)

For Duras, what can be "known" of the immediacy of history, war, or holocaust comes not so much from classification of the past or from the power that access to or control of ready-made historical discourses brings as from a power-renouncing movement between self and language, between the present of the writing and the past, between self and other (the sliding reference of the same pronoun), in self-loss (in language) and intersubjectivity. In this process, fiction (self-exploration and wish fulfillment through doubles) and confession become coextensive. Writing is a function of life as self is a function of rewriting in the present. Perhaps this explains the many and major discrepancies between the versions of Duras's life. The enamored but scorned suitor M. Jo, largely unsuccessful in spite of his seductive diamond in *Un Barrage contre le Pacifique,* is replaced in *L'Amant* by the wealthy Chinese lover whose seduction is partly an effect of his diamond ring and partly a result of the child's need to assert her own sexual desire and independence from the intense jealousies and passions within her family circle. In *L'Amant de la Chine du nord,* the seducing and seduced fifteen-and-a-half-year-old adolescent turns out to be only fourteen; the mother, in the final instance, is complicitous with her daughter's relationship; the weak lover stands up to the detested dominating older brother; and the protective relationship with the "little" brother is presented as incestuous.

Autofiction, then, is a "complementary" relation (contradictory but not mutually exclusive) between passion and the linguistic play that must double passion to bring it to consciousness, that is, between the wild territories of the unsayable presymbolic and the symbolic linguistic order that constitutes the social self, between memory and the imagination. Such a relation arises in the writing of/with the powerless "feminine" body at the level of disordered personal experience of the senses close to the unconscious or the Kristevan Chora in fusion with the mother. Writing is also necessarily a linguistic cutting up and conscious "remembering" (and thus loss) of these events. Sharon Willis's subtle study of the obsessive theme of desire and lack (loss or lack inherent in the act of representation) and its relation to violence in Duras gives voice to the reader's dual sense of familiarity and loss in a world of deeply private fantasies that appear also to be the anonymous displacements and metaphorizations of collective sexuality.[2] Violence inheres in individuated psyche, in writing, and in the "real."

Madeleine Cottenet-Hage recalls that in the second of the *Aurelia Steiner* films (1979), the character, spoken by Duras and identified only at the end of the film as Aurelia speaking from Vancouver, enacts at once a personal, a historical, and a universal story. This archetypal Durassian story of pain is the story of the loss of Aurelia Steiner's parents in a concentration camp, "the story of the Jews," "the story of humankind," and Duras's own history/story, become legend.[3]

In Duras's pseudo-diary *La Douleur*, the global, objective, or outside events that constitute the Resistance and the Holocaust are refracted through the textual mirrors of the local inner experiences of feminine waiting and emotional pain: the pain of the loss of her unborn child or, later, more problematically for the reader, the pain of childbirth. Knowledge of history here also emerges through the other, from Marguerite's waiting for Robert L. (Robert Antelme, "L/il/elle"), *her* husband, imprisoned in 1944 for his activities in the Resistance and deported from the French prison of Fresne. The intensity of this emotionally and physically experienced waiting holds center stage and not the events of Robert's dramatic rescue, orchestrated by François Morland (alias François Mitterrand) from the barracks for the dying in Dachau. Marguerite's own timeless, careful, nursing vigil over the pain of Robert's slow return to the living is given precedence over any account of heroic sequential external events of war or rescue.

Pain, as the other and chosen face of pleasure in the scenes of the French actress-protagonist's encounter with a fictional Japanese lover in the film-text *Hiroshima mon amour*, returns in the affair with the "autobiographical" Chinese lover. These "feminized," minority lovers themselves weep and suffer. They experience passively both complicity with and victimization by forces of historical injustice, racism, and nuclear holocaust and the pleasure/pain of both a self-affirming desire and a self-loss in the other that they do not resist. The ballet of bodily linguistic experience of pleasure and pain and of abstract collective forces— that is, of the drive for domination that is history and of the master-servant structure of the psyche—in Duras's work, derives, then, from monsters encountered in her history. The humiliations, wild freedoms, and passions of her childhood in Indochina, like her experiences of the war, or of the sufferings and joys of human bonding, reflect both a sociohistorical situation and an individuated psyche characterized by a fascination with, fear of, and movement between, domination and self-loss.

The (elder?) brother as strong hunter of the tiger in the forests of Siam, envied object of the mother's adoration, free and predatory, played a major role in Duras's early traditional novel set in French Indochina, *Un Barrage contre le Pacifique* (1950). The relationship with this brother who, in this first writing of childhood experience, is merged with the beloved "little" brother of *L'Amant,* is one of strong fascination. A later short work, *Agatha* (1981), is an intense drama of the remeeting and subsequent separation of a brother and sister who recall together the power of their early and overwhelming incestuous love. Even in *L'Amant,* where the beloved "little" brother is identified with the lover in his fear of the elder brother, the passionate hatred expressed for the older brother/the war (responsible for the death of the little brother) thus seems ambivalent, troubled by the erotic attraction of, and fear of complicity with, the simultaneously destroyed and revived fascinating, brutal order of "masculine" power. The maternal, incestuous relation with the "little" brother of *L'Amant de la Chine du nord,* like the relation with the homosexual Yann Andréa identified with the powerless by the name Steiner, may be the other face of this attraction to power.

In Duras's "Albert des Capitales," a short fragment in *La Douleur,* the exploration of the pull between inner poles of "masculine" power and control or "feminine" powerlessness and passivity takes the dramatic form of a historical event. During the liberation of France, the female narrator, Thérèse, orchestrates a ritualistic interrogation in which a middle-class collaborator-traitor is humiliated and beaten to extract a confession. Although her leadership in the sadistic "trial" is justified by her desire for solidarity with the proletarian Resistance, at the end of the story Thérèse weeps. The implication is that her actions are an unacceptable exclusive identification with the active and oppressive "masculine."

Duras's autobiographical fiction, *Emily L.,* also contains both historical and self-reference in the evocation of the ruins of the German factory beyond the sunless forest, the history and personal history abstracted in the appearance in the white spaces of the square of a group of self-similar "Koreans" who recall the unself-aware cruelty of the Asian youths of Duras's childhood experience, killing the starving dogs on the Kampot plain for their sport. Emily L.'s inarticulate cries of fear and pain that elide the boundaries between the inner and the outer world, between self and text, like the Durassian text itself, are a paradoxical literary articulation of a space of movement between preverbal experience and conscious historical text, between the individual life in the novel and the novel of life.

Nathalie Sarraute's *Enfance* is played out against historical back-drops that change from the absolutist prerevolutionary tsarist Russia of her earliest childhood at the beginning of the century to the middle-class France of her mother's remarriage and her father and stepmother's later political exile. Natacha's story/history, like Marguerite's, is again generated out of the child's difficult relations with figures of familial authority and affective power within a specific historical frame. This autofiction introduces dialogic and "complementary" voices. An inter-ruptive, judgmental voice gendered "masculine" by the adjectives ("outrecuidant," "grandiloquent," p. 10) used to describe him, a voice that addresses the first voice familiarly as "tu," is characterized by Car-tesian rationality, exactitude, and critical distance, particularly in his analysis of the mother's faults. A first-person voice marked as feminine in gender and moving between the responses of the writer-interlocutor ("je me suis un peu laissée aller," p. 21) and the words of young Natacha ("elle m'a vue venir," p. 24; "je suis morte," p. 29) evoke the welling up and irruption of tropistic psychological movement. This voice suggests the child's passionate desire for the mother and the power of the mother's words, both the fear of rejection by mother and stepmother, and the attempts at separation from the fascination of the mother and self-affir-mation. In the final instance, both voices are controlled by the aging writer, Nathalie Sarraute, consciously orchestrating the choices and or-der of the fragments spoken or remembered by both voices.

Yet the writings of the interchange between masculine and femi-nine voices re-evokes the feelings and tensions in the child Natacha Tcherniak's life, pulled in opposite directions by loyalties to divorced parents. The charming, silken, adored mother demands absolute loy-alty and devotion from her daughter, but several scenes show the mother as lying to the child about an impending tonsillectomy or the mortal danger of touching a telegraph pole, or where babies come from, as im-patient with the nursing duties imposed on her by a sick Natacha, as mean with the servants' dinner servings, and as closer to her new hus-band than to her daughter, who is abandoned at eight to her father and stepfather. The fewer but less critical sketches of the responsible, sternly moral, more cerebral, reserved, but austerely loving and silently complicitous father also appear to be part of the writer's attempt to un-derstand the sentiments of those close to her by the recreation of psy-chological minidramas and by implicit or explicit analysis. But like the child, the adult writer is, at the same time, recreating feelings close to the child's trembling, listening still for the complex emotional movements that might lie beneath the *lieux communs* of parental phrase or her own *énoncés*. She too is searching for love as well as for knowledge. At the level of the *énoncé* Sarraute perhaps identifies more closely with the critical, investigative masculine voice. Yet at the level of the *énonciation*, aware that words are flattening and inadequate and that single, reasoned judgments are simplifying, the uncertain emotional feminine voice paradoxically seems stronger than the self-assertive masculine voice.

Sarraute does not discuss the historical events of her father's exile under the tsar, or the Russian revolution, or the later Stalinist era that she experienced on a visit to terrorized relatives. Forced to live under an assumed name and to go into hiding during the Occupation, narrowly escaping arrest by fleeing from the village of Janvry after being denounced as a Jew, she makes no mention of the war and the Holocaust. In all her texts, however, underlying the orderings of feelings and experience by cliché and dialogic social interactions, as yet dimly perceived and preceding dialogue, lurk "subconversations" that may well be a reemergence of these violent, suppressed historical events. In the polyphony of different voices that constitute the "nous" in *Tu ne t'aimes pas,* it is finally the unself-loving voice, on the side of guilt for the victims and the outstretched hands it has to ignore, that is preferred to the voices of self-satisfaction and self-love.

The commonplaces of the language do seem to attach themselves in some way to common psychological movements, and Sarraute's relationship with her mother is a saga of the movement between the child's early adoring loyalty to that parent's injunctions and a fierce resistance to the hidden control exerted by her words. Cliché confronts cliché: the mother's edict "un enfant qui aime sa mère trouve que personne n'est plus beau qu'elle" (p. 93) is resisted by the child's thoughts on the doll—"Elle est plus belle que Maman" (p. 92)—and negative judgments: "Maman a la peau d'un singe" (p. 96). Perhaps Sarraute's works can all be characterized by the piercing of the silken skin of the mother('s language), the movement between the safety and belonging of her soft order and the impulse to resist appearances, to question her authority and influence.

"Subconversations," then, consist of disordered but precise, contradictory affective movements (tropisms) revolving around the desire to master and control and the instinct to submit, flee, or build defense.

The need of the baker of Janvry to denounce her, claimed Sarraute in a rare interview with Marc Saporta, derived from just such movements, from the baker's fear of disorder, his desire to be "right," to impose the security of the law, and protect himself from the hidden threat. These tropistic movements of aggression, the fear of disorder, and the attempt to impose an absolute and infallible order, at once collective and individually experienced, are at the heart both of the history that she lived and of the hidden source of her own autofictions that explore the simultaneous temptation and rejection of the authoritative masculine voice and of self-satisfaction.

However, Sarraute is as categorical at the beginning of *Enfance* as our other writers. For her, language is not life. It does not translate a plenitude of origins. It is a paper copy, a cardboard cutout of experience, incapable of representing the confused tropistic "real" behind its networks of signs in order to better bring hidden aspects of life to consciousness. For History too is a rule-bound narrative, involving selection and exclusion and just such a ready-made doubling/linguistic suppressing of the real.

The admission of the relative powerlessness of the new language, which creates linguistically mediated worlds but cannot clearly reflect the nonlinguistic world or the unconscious mind and the monsters of our being (drive to domination/desire for submission), is echoed by Robbe-Grillet. For the latter, in *Le Miroir qui revient*, all reality is "indescribable" as, for the later Barthes, the real is the "uncoded." In *Roland Barthes par Roland Barthes*, the autobiographical "I" can be only a multiple experimental linguistic self or "character in a novel." Yet, the figures of the war in Robbe-Grillet's work seem to echo, if more faintly, Marguerite Duras's insistence on any knowledge of history being grounded in the nonordered experience of the body, in the felt reality of power and humiliation. In *Le Miroir qui revient*, this takes the form of a dissolution of clear boundaries between the external historical event and the unconscious impulse in the phantasmatic figure of the Comte de Corinthe: Resistance hero and Nazi collaborator, sexual sadist and victim of the (female) vampire, literary, legendary, and real father, wounded in World War I. The shock of the fall of the Third Reich and the discovery of the Holocaust in the light of a right-wing, anti-Semitic Robbe-Grillet family ideology is overlaid by the narrator's revelation of his own sadistic sexual fantasies. In *Angélique ou l'enchantement*, the historico-cultural myths of the cavalry officer in the forests on the Franco-German frontier and his encounters with the dangerous spy, or of the knight-errant in thrall to only seemingly fair maidens, become inextricably interwoven with phantasmatic scenes of "feminine" bondage and sado-erotic "masculine" power. This suppression of woman's body seems to derive from a barely conscious anxiety (the anguish and fascination of death and disintegration) provoked by the attraction of the seductive and vulnerable "enchanting" feminine other in the self. Such an active sadistic suppression of the fear of the "feminine" is the other face of the "ravishing" by the "masculine" in Duras. Even in these postmodern texts, some dualities persist. While Duras introduces a certain degree of role reversibility, however, Robbe-Grillet fixes the female at the very traditional cultural pole of masochism and domination.

For Claude Simon, the linearity of traditional linguistic organization betrays the complexity of the simultaneous sensory, intellectual, and phantasmatic associations and memories of the writer. Such a linear organization is a misrepresentation of the discontinuity both of experience and of history. Yet, as Joan Brandt points out, Simon too is aware that "*all* words cut up, set in concrete, and annihilate by replacing" what they represent.[4] Simon, says Brandt, calls upon the formal orders of art, the frame, the techniques and images of overlapping and superposition, to seek out "that ideal perspective which would make an all-encompassing vision possible" (p. 380). But, as the writer himself admits, his new text is "aussi dépourvu d'épaisseur et d'existence qu'une feuille de papier" (p. 67). For Brandt, the "effort to enclose the discontinuity of experience fails either because it leads to an annihilation of the real by substituting its own flattened image or [because it] is undermined by the temporality and the expansiveness of what it seeks to enclose" (p. 383).

Perhaps that is why the central event concealed behind Claude Simon's "impossible" ideal perspective is also inevitably absent. Already in the novel *La Route des Flandres* (1960) Claude Simon's cavalry officer/fictional protagonist/father/self circles obstinately seeking orders in the chaos of the 1940 debacle around an absent center: a disintegrating dead horse. Like the "lack" in his own "signifying unity" that Robbe-Grillet pursues in *Le Miroir qui revient*—the hole at the center of the golden ring that gives the ring its form in the sequel *Angélique ou l'enchantement*—this void is not only absence, or degree zero, or disorder, but also the feminine principle of postmodern linguistic regeneration and emergence of new orders. The void is a recurring figure in all these works. In Duras's *L'Amant* (which was to have been called "Absolute Photography"), this degree zero takes the form of the imaginatively powerful photo that "had never been taken" of the adolescent self. In *Emily L.*, it is the missing unfinished poem, the "minimal internal difference," sensed but imperfectly detected, that lies at the heart of the poet's life and death. In *Angélique*, it is the crime that is always, already there, displayed as the absent center of the labyrinth.

The void of self, as Keren Smith defines it in an article that compares the voyeur-criminal protagonists in Robbe-Grillet's *Voyeur* and Dostoyevsky's *Crime and Punishment*,[5] is the lack of any unifying or transcendental principle (God, history, man) that can give meaning to the self and to the world. This void of self distinguishes traditional fiction (in which the void exists only in a binary organization of void or redemptive meaning, of purity or criminality) from the postmodern. In the former, a mediation can be effected and a metaphysical or moral solution is possible. Dostoyevsky's protagonist, Raskolnikov, lost in the void ("If God were dead then everything would be possible") is redeemed from his crime by punishment and perhaps by female (self-) sacrifice. The nondialectical, chaotic, postmodern void of self does not permit mediation. It is, however, a site at which what is repressed by language and the social order—the monsters of will to power and will to self-dissolution, of the narcissistic (sado-masochistic) psyche—can take form, a site at which authenticity might be sought.

The polysemous title of Claude Simon's 1967 novel *Histoire* had already suggested the public history and private story telescoped in the author's fiction. The early novels had moved between chaos and formal orders in the new reversible topological space of the Moebius strip, where inside and outside, cause and effect become indeterminate. In *Les Géorgiques* (1981), a text that is itself constructed, in a now-familiar postmodern strategy, from other texts of Western tradition (from Vergil and from Michelet's *Histoire de la révolution*, for example), the chaotic yet strangely patterned and recursive overlapping circles of military defeats and victories around a hollow sexualized matrix of birth and death constitute a collective male experience of Western history, the personal text of military father and ancestor, and the historical text of Simon's own participation in the French debacle. In the more recent "autobiographical" evocation of an invitation to Soviet Russia, history is the personal assemblage of the fragments of the disparate official and private discourses overheard. Meaning, like the text itself, is produced in the infinitely branching interactions of the syntagmatic and paradigmatic axes of the working of the language that create effects of the mind and of the emotion, and yet the war, like the visit to Russia, is grounded in Simon's own lived past/currently recalled experience, generated by perception, memory, and desire and by the ready-made texts of history including those of great men (the father, the great general). The encounter with Gorbachev described in *L'Invitation* is overlaid by these pretexts. The new textual/physical body in Simon also models fields of complex interaction between biology and history, language and the self.

The new autobiographical fictions lead not to classical self-knowledge, or to modern self-consciousness, but rather to a postmodern sense of reflexivity among linguistic mirrors. Yet they do involve a shift marked by the foregrounding of pronominal shifts, from "je" to "il" or "Corinthe," from "je" to "elle" or "the little white girl" (Duras), from "je" to "tu" or to "nous" (Sarraute). As Lois Oppenheim argues, they slip from the focus on the anonymity of collective forms to forms of individuation.[6] The theoretical "death" of the author as origin and finality is replaced by a concern with what might constitute the specificity of an individual (style). As in the New Historicism, history is indeed story, narrative forms, and strategies, but it is also, as Veeser has shown, the social, political, and personal contexts out of which the story arises.[7]

The experiences of twentieth-century French history (the world wars) serve as a pre-text for the fictions of a returning if altered and constantly splitting self in these new, individuated and ground-breaking texts. Yet in an interesting slippage, the texts emerging at other collective cultural sites, new sciences such as quantum physics (the principle of complementarity) and chaos theory, postmodernisms of various kinds, appear to influence the reconstruction of this self around a subversion of the boundaries of order and chaos, of inner and outer, feminine and masculine, power and powerlessness, autobiography and fiction, and the binary oppositions and categories that these poles subsume. The telescoping of these opposites creates complementary forms (contradictory but not mutually exclusive) of self and writing, history and story, that intimate the revolutionary interest of these new intergeneric, bio (and) graphical autofictions.

Notes

1. This chapter draws on an article entitled "Autobiographical Fictions: Duras, Sarraute, Simon, Robbe-Grillet Rewriting History, Story, Self," published in *International Fiction Review* 18, no. 1 (winter 1991), parts of which are reproduced here with the permission of the editor.

2. Sharon Willis, *Marguerite Duras: Writing on the Body* (Urbana: University of Illinois Press, 1987).

3. Madeleine Cottenet-Hage and Robert Kolker, "The Cinema of Duras in Search of an Ideal Image," *French Review* 63, no. 1 (October 1989), pp. 88–98. The quotation is taken from the catalogue for the film, p. 59.

4. Joan Brandt, "History and Art in Claude Simon's *Histoire*," *Romanic Review* 73, no. 3 (May 1982), pp. 373–84.

5. Keren Smith, "Voyeurism and the Void of Self: The Problem of Human Identity in Robbe-Grillet's *Le Voyeur* and Dostoyevsky's *Crime and Punishment*," *New Zealand Journal of French Studies* 9, no. 2 (1988), pp. 34–41.

6. Lois Oppenheim, "From Anonymity to Individuation in the Nouveau Roman," paper read at a special session entitled "The French Nouveau Roman Thirty Years On" at the Modern Language Association convention, New York, December 29, 1988.

7. Aram Veeser, ed., *The New Historicism* (New York and London: Routledge, 1989).

Bibliography

Creative Works

Barthes, Roland. *Roland Barthes par Roland Barthes*. Paris: Seuil, 1974.

Butor, Michel. *Frontières*. Marseille: Le Temps Parallèle, 1985. Translated by Elinor Miller and Warren Miller as *Frontiers*. Birmingham, AL: Summa, 1989.

Duras, Marguerite. *L'Amant*. Paris: Minuit, 1984. Translated by Barbara Bray as *The Lover*. New York: HarperCollins, 1986.

———. *La Douleur*. Paris: P.O.L., 1985. Translated by Barbara Bray as *The Malady of Death*. New York: Grove, 1988.

———. *Emily L.* Paris: Minuit, 1987. Translated by Barbara Bray. New York: Pantheon, 1989.

———. *L'Amant de la Chine du nord*. Paris: Gallimard, 1991. Translated by Leigh Hafrey as *The North China Lover*. New York: New Press, 1992.

———. *Yann Andréa Steiner*. Paris: P.O.L., 1992.

Ollier, Claude. *Déconnections*. Paris: Minuit, 1988. Translated by Dominic Di Bernardi as *Disconnections*. Normal, IL: Dalkey Archive, 1989.

Robbe-Grillet, Alain. *Le Miroir qui revient.* Paris: Minuit, 1984. Translated by Jo
    Levy as *Ghosts in the Mirror.* New York: Grove, 1989.
———. *Angélique ou l'enchantement.* Paris: Minuit, 1988.
———. *La Mort de Corinthe.* Paris: Minuit, 1994.
Sarraute, Nathalie. *Enfance.* Paris: Gallimard, 1983. Translated by Barbara Wright
    as *Childhood.* New York: Braziller, 1985.
———. *Tu ne t'aimes pas.* Paris: Gallimard, 1989. Translated by Barbara Wright as
    You Don't Love Yourself. New York: Braziller, 1990.
Simon, Claude. *L'Invitation.* Paris: Minuit, 1989. Translated by Jim Cross as *The
    Invitation.* Normal, IL: Dalkey Archive, 1991.
———. *L'Acacia.* Paris: Minuit, 1989. Translated by Richard Howard as *The Aca-
    cia.* New York: Pantheon, 1991.

Selected Critical Works

Armel, Aliette. *Marguerite Duras et l'autobiographie.* Paris: Le Castor Astral, 1990.
Assouline, Pierre. "La Vraie Vie de Marguerite Duras." *Lire* (October 1991): 49–
    59.
Barthes, Roland. *Chambre claire. Note sur la photographie.* Paris: Seuil, 1980.
Beaujour, Michel. *Miroirs d'encre: rhétorique de l'autoportrait.* Paris: Seuil, 1980.
Benmussa, Simone. *Nathalie Sarraute: qui êtes-vous?* Lyon: La Manufacture, 1987.
Calle-Gruber, Mireille. "Quand le nouveau roman prend les risques du roma-
    nesque." In *Autobiographie et biographie. Colloque franco-allemand de Heidelberg,*
    ed. Mireille Calle-Gruber and Arnold Rothe, 185–99. Paris: Nizet, 1989.
Clayton, Alan J. *Nathalie Sarraute ou le tremblement de l'écriture.* Paris: Archives
    des Lettres Modernes, 1989.
De Man, Paul. "Autobiography as De-Facement." *Modern Language Notes* 94, no.
    5 (1979): 919–30.
Doubrovsky, Serge. "Autobiographie/Vérité/Psychanalyse." *L'Esprit Créateur*
    20, no. 3 (fall 1980): 87–97.
Garis, Leslie. "The Life and Loves of Marguerite Duras." *New York Times Maga-
    zine* (October 20, 1991): 44–61.
Hewitt, Leah D. *Autobiographical Tightropes.* Lincoln: University of Nebraska Press,
    1990.
Houppermans, Sjef. "Un Miroir enchanté." *Dalhousie French Studies* 17 (fall–winter
    1989): 37–45.
Lejeune, Philippe. *Moi aussi.* Paris: Seuil, 1986.
———. "Paroles d'enfance." *Revue des Sciences Humaines,* no. 217 (January–March
    1990): 23–38.
Minogue, Valerie. "Fragments of a Childhood: Nathalie Sarraute's *Enfance.*"
    Romance Studies, no. 9 (1986): 71–83.
———. "Le Cheval de Troie. A propos de *Tu ne t'aimes pas.*" *Revue des Sciences
    Humaines,* no. 217 (January–March 1990): 151–61.

O'Callaghan (Ramsay), Raylene. "The Art of the (Im)possible: The Autobiography of the French New Novelists." *Australian Journal of French Studies* 25, no. 1 (1988): 71–91.

———. "Reading Nathalie Sarraute's *Enfance:* Reflections on Critical Validity." *Romanic Review* 80, no. 3 (May 1989): 445–61.

———. "The Uses and Abuses of Enchantment in Robbe-Grillet's *Angélique ou l'enchantement.*" *Dalhousie French Studies* 17 (fall–winter 1989): 109–16.

———. "Voice(s) in Nathalie Sarraute's *Enfance.*" *New Zealand Journal of French Studies,* Special Issue (1989): 83–94.

Ramsay, Raylene. *Alain Robbe-Grillet and Modernity: Science, Sexuality, and Subversion.* Gainesville: University Press of Florida, 1992.

Riffaterre, Michael. *Fictional Truth.* Baltimore: Johns Hopkins University Press, 1990.

Sankey, Margaret. "Time and Autobiography in *L'Amant* by Marguerite Duras." *Australian Journal of French Studies* 25, no. 1 (1988): 58–70.

Saporta, Marc; Sarraute, Nathalie. "Portrait d'une inconnue: conversation biographique." *L'Arc,* no. 95 (1984): 5–23.

Sheringham, Michael. "French Autobiography: Texts, Contexts, Poetics." *Journal of European Studies* 16, no. 1 (March 1986): 59–71.

———. "*Ego redux*? Stategies in New French Autobiography." *Dalhousie French Studies* 17 (fall–winter 1989): 27–35.

Smith, Sidonie. "Self, Subject and Resistance: Marginalities and Twentieth-Century Autobiographical Practice." *Tulsa Studies in Women's Literature* 9, no. 1 (spring 1990): 11–24.

Stoltzfus, Ben. "The Language of Autobiography and Fiction: Gide, Barthes, and Robbe-Grillet." *International Fiction Review* 15, no. 1 (winter 1988): 3–8.

2

Julien Green

Robert Stanley

Julien Green, born in Paris of American parents on September 6, 1900, has had a remarkable literary career. Although one would not be surprised if he decided to rest on his laurels, that has certainly not been the case. Known primarily as a novelist, Julien Green is also the author of a highly respected *Journal*, five published plays, several short stories, an autobiography, a biography of Saint Francis of Assisi, several essays, and a "conte pour enfants." *L'Expatrié*, the portion of his diary published in 1990, lists under the rubric "A paraître" no fewer than six titles. If the contents of *L'Expatrié* are to be believed, Green continues to keep up with current events, to travel extensively, and, most importantly from the point of view of this collection, to practice his profession as a creative writer.

While acknowledging the considerable interest of Green's other works, we must remember that his novels are the bedrock of his literary production. Brian Fitch says of these novels: "On comprend qu'encouragé par l'auteur du *Journal,* on a pu soutenir que c'est dans ses romans qu'il faut chercher Green et à travers eux seulement qu'on peut saisir l'homme dans toute sa complexité humaine."[1] We need to know, too, that although Green has often been called an "écrivain catholique" and (probably) correctly so, he himself dislikes the term. If the term "écrivain catholique" means an author who constantly indulges in moralizing or preachifying in his literary products, then Green is certainly not that. But "écrivain catholique" does not have to imply moralizing and preachifying. It can also indicate an author who, as a Roman Catholic, writes novels that contain spiritual dimensions and express spiritual longings. Green's work is deeply marked by the struggle between the flesh and the spirit. Since Green's own life—he was a homosexual in his younger years—has been profoundly influenced by this struggle, it is not surprising that echoes of this dichotomy should occur frequently in his novels. One can cite in this regard one of his earlier novels, *Adrienne Mesurat* (1927), in which a repressed and intimidated young woman struggles to break out of a psychologically suffocating family situation, and his most recent novel, *Les Etoiles du sud* (1989), in which a young woman, whose first husband dies in a duel, remarries, to lose her second husband in America's Civil War, all the while remembering the love affair she had with the man who killed her first husband. If matters of a sexual/social nature almost always occur in Green's novels, spiritual/religious concerns are not far below the surface.

Since 1960 Green has written five novels, which will be the focus of this chapter: *Chaque homme dans sa nuit* (1960), *L'Autre* (1971), *Le Mauvais Lieu* (1977), *Les Pays lointains* (1987), and *Les Etoiles du sud* (1989). Because the last two novels are closely related and may eventually form part of a trilogy, it is natural that they be considered together. They are also historical novels, quite different from anything Julien Green has previously produced. At the same time, the first three novels, being more traditional Green novels, may conveniently be grouped together.

It has been stated above that Green's entire literary œuvre—novels as well as drama and short stories—may be characterized as the struggle between the desires of the flesh and the aspirations of the spirit, as well as man's misery without God's grace. These two major themes are certainly present in *Chaque homme dans sa nuit*, *L'Autre*, and *Le Mauvais Lieu*. It would be worthwhile to examine how these themes are handled in the three novels in question and to discuss the novels' strengths and weaknesses.

In its own unique way, love (specifically sexual love) dominates the thoughts of many characters in these three works. Some are obsessed and even destroyed by sensuality; others are given new insights into their own lives and natures. One of them, Louise, the young protagonist of *Le Mauvais Lieu*, is even mysteriously and inexplicably "snatched away" from the sordid world in which she moves with almost perfect innocence. In *Chaque homme dans sa nuit*, a young man named Wilfred Ingram tries to live his Roman Catholic faith in addition to—one could say in spite of—his frequent (and frequently anonymous) sexual encounters with various women. In *L'Autre,* Roger seeks sexual gratification with Karin in the summer of 1939, whereas after the war, when he returns to look her up again, he seeks to convert her to Catholicism, while she goes to the church only in fits and starts. In *Le Mauvais Lieu,* Louise, a thirteen-year-old adolescent who moves quietly through life, yet who has an enormous influence on those who come into contact with her, is a paragon of moral innocence and physical beauty and stands in sharp contrast to her tawdry surroundings.

Wilfred Ingram is destined to go through life not only representing his faith in the eyes of his Protestant relatives but also struggling between the moral imperatives of that faith and his own gnawing sexual desires. This is no easy task, yet it does not prevent Wilfred from functioning. Unlike some of Green's characters, Wilfred accepts his sexual nature and his proclivity to frequent sexual encounters. As one critic expresses the situation: "Wilfred Ingram has been able to accept sexuality and to integrate it into his life. Nevertheless, this statement of fact requires considerable qualification: Wilfred does lead a life that includes, indeed is dominated by, sensuality, but at great cost; for the tension between his sensual nature and activity and his religious faith and aspirations inescapably results in anguish and distress."[2]

Even more frustrating to him is the fact that others consider him a model of virtue, while he knows that he is not. In the seventh chapter of the first part of *Chaque homme dans sa nuit,* Wilfred thinks to himself: "La vérité n'était pas en lui. Ce qui était en lui, c'était le diable. Il était plongé dans le péché comme dans une boue suffocante et Angus le croyait pur. Angus valait mieux que lui. Avec son élégance, sa richesse, son cynisme, Angus eût fait aux yeux de bien des catholiques figure de réprouvé, mais le réprouvé valait mieux que lui, Wilfred, le croyant" (p. 447). This is, to be sure, only in Wilfred's imagination, for his cousin Angus is far from morally superior to his "simpler" Catholic cousin. On the contrary, Angus, as the reader later learns, is involved in unsavory sexual encounters with other men and is miserably unhappy. Yet he and others, including Wifred's dying Uncle Horace, persist in thinking that young Wilfred is a model of Christian virtue.

In a remarkable scene that takes place in the bedroom of the dying uncle, the latter asks Wilfred to pray for him and Wilfred experiences the greatest difficulty and embarrassment in doing so. A short portion of the conversation between the two is enlightening:

—Mon oncle, dit Wilfred, vous vous fatiguez à parler.

—Non, je veux dire ce que j'ai à dire. Je me trompais, mais je voulais croire. Toi, tu as la foi.

Je le sais. On me l'a dit. La vraie foi. Dis-moi que tu as la foi.

—Oui.

—Tu crois tout ce que dit l'Eglise.

—Oui je le crois, fit le jeune homme avec une énergie subite. . . . "Ah, fit-il dans un souffle, qu'est-ce que cela veut dire: croire?

—Je ne sais pas.

—Tu ne sais pas!

—Mon oncle, on sait qu'on croit comme on sait qu'on est amoureux. (pp. 461–62)

Later in this scene, Wilfred will attempt to pray for his uncle at the latter's insistence, but the prayer is not satisfactory for, as Wilfred candidly admits to his uncle, he does not really know how to pray. After much frustration, he does say "Tout est bien" (p. 464). But as is the case elsewhere in this novel, he does not understand who or what inspires him to utter these words; there are times when Wilfred, perhaps moved by divine grace, says or does things of which he would normally not be capable. Green writes of this phenomenon: "Ces paroles sortirent de sa bouche comme si elles eussent été prononcées par un autre et avec une netteté qui le tira brusquement de sa torpeur. Il resta quelque temps à genoux, dégrisé, l'âme tranquille, et il lui semble pendant l'espace d'une minute qu'il était absent du monde, mais aucune idée précise ne se formait dans son cerveau, sinon que le bonheur envahissait tout, un bonheur étrange qui effaçait la vie quotidienne, le temps et la terre" (pp. 464–65). There are similar moments elsewhere in the novel. When asked by his uncle to cure him, Wilfred says that, to do so, he would have to be a saint, and a saint he is not. In an odd reply, Uncle Horace says: "Si! . . . En ce moment tu es comme un saint. Nous le sommes tous à une minute ou autre de notre vie" (p. 465). This scene is important for the character delineation of Wilfred, because it shows what later parts of the novel will further corroborate: in spite of his misgivings and feelings of unworthiness, Wilfred is able to be of genuine help to others.

In L'Autre, a man and a woman who had been lovers in Copenhagen in 1939 meet again in the same city ten years later. The man, Roger, has fought in the war and was actually a prisoner of war, though his experiences as a P.O.W. are never alluded to in detail; and the woman, as a result of her fraternization with the occupying German officers in Denmark, is ostracized by everyone after the war. When, in fact, they see each other again in 1949, it is learned that the man has undergone a religious conversion, the precise nature of which he is at a loss to explain, and he desires to "undo" the damage he had done earlier in disparaging her faith and in pursuing a love affair with her. As is often the case, the conversion itself is a matter of some mystery, even to the one who undergoes it. Roger relates to Karin that he was in a small Romanesque church in a province of France. He is intrigued by the sight of two elderly women who appear to be in a sort of religious trance. They are looking at something, but Roger cannot say what:

> Rien ne se lisait sur leurs traits contourés par l'âge, mais l'idée me vint tout à coup qu'elles regardaient quelque chose—ou quelqu'un. Ce fut comme un éclair déchirant la nuit. Pendant quelques minutes, je restai dans un coin de l'église, ne sachant plus bien où j'étais. Une chose me parut certaine: il y avait entre ces murs, sous ces voûtes, une présence qui n'était pas sensible à ma vue. C'est tout. Je sortis. . . . Quand je sortis de cette église, j'étais converti sans bien m'en rendre compte. Le reste suivit tout naturellement. (pp. 860–61)

This is really the only description in the novel of Roger's conversion, but the influence of that conversion pervades the second half of the novel known as the "Récit de Karin (mars–avril 1949)." His conversion was a radical change from his previous sensuality: his primary reason for spending the summer of 1939 in Copenhagen was in order to experience sensual, that is to say sexual, pleasure. He met Karin by chance and pursued her amorously. But his contact with women, in the fateful summer of 1939, was not limited to women he knew; occasionally, he went to prostitutes. After a particularly frustrating evening with Karin, and an equally frustrating conversation the next day with a secondary character named Mlle Ott, Roger considers the implications of seeking solace with a prostitute: "Qu'est-ce qui me retenait dans cette ville? La peur et le désir. J'imaginai le dégoût qui suivrait la nuit passée en compagnie d'une prostituée avec qui je n'échangerais pas une parole. Je voyais d'avance le nombre de doigts qu'elle lèverait demain matin pour indiquer son prix. Tout était médiocre, et même triste, mais j'avais envie de cette fille" (p. 775).

As is so often the case in Green's novels, sexual activity, particularly of an illicit nature, is seen as sad, depressing, even disgusting. It is, however, important for us to consider this aspect of Roger's life before his religious conversion.

One more aspect of Roger's character at this point should be taken into consideration, namely, his hostility to religion, of which numerous examples could be cited. After a very keen disappointment at not being able to dine with a beautiful Danish woman whose charms have an impact upon him, Roger is irritated by references to religion in another conversation with Mlle Ott: "Une conversation avec Mlle Ott me laissait un souvenir de dégoût, surtout ses allusions patelines à la religion. Il y avait en moi quelque chose qui se révoltait à la pensée d'une foi asservissant l'homme, et qu'on m'en parlât dans ce restaurant où j'attendais en vain une prostituée mettait le comble à mon impatience. L'envie me prit de quitter cette ville dès le lendemain matin. . . . Il y avait déjà trop de souffrance pour moi dans ces rues" (p. 786).

When the reader compares the selfish, pleasure-seeking Roger of 1939 to the committed Christian, concerned with the salvation of a soul, whom the reader encounters in the second half of the novel, he/she realizes just what a profound change has come about in the mind and soul of this man. Such a profound change in a single character is somewhat unusual in Green's novels. More common is the character who develops in a continuum (for example, Adrienne Mesurat or Daniel O'Donovan in the short story "Le Voyageur sur la terre"), even though the final outcome may be death. Far less frequent is the *major* character who undergoes a *major* transformation for the better. In the case of Roger, this change is the result primarily of his conversion, which itself could have been brought about at least partially because of his suffering as a P.O.W. in World War II.

Louise, the child-protagonist of *Le Mauvais Lieu*, moves through the novel protected, as it were, from the sordid characters and circumstances surrounding her. Despite two men, one her uncle, who would like to possess her sexually, and her rather scatterbrained and venal aunt, Gertrude, who showers her with a suffocating (and somewhat misplaced) maternal love, Louise manages to avoid catastrophe and, when things become too difficult, disappears without a trace in a way that is as fully mysterious as her protection from worldly contamination.

Louise is part of a tradition of lonely children or young people who frequent the works of Julien Green: from Daniel O'Donovan in "Le Voyageur sur la terre," to the little girl in *Christine,* to Elizabeth in *Les Pays lointains* (though Elizabeth is lonely, but far from alone at the plantation Dimwood), such characters often have to deal with loneliness, frequently in large, somewhat spooky old houses. These children are usually without playmates and must deal with adults who, for whatever reasons, are preoccupied and somewhat outside the bounds of "normal" men and women. Naturally, these lonely children will have problems and sometimes neuroses that have an impact over the course of the work of fiction. In order to understand Louise and to analyze her situation, it is helpful to realize the Greenian tradition in which she stands. One must also understand that Louise is the daughter of Gertrude's late brother and sister-in-law, both killed in a car accident. By terms of the will, Gertrude, a childless widow, was named as Louise's guardian. Although Gertrude has enough money for a very comfortable life-style, she is portrayed as naive, self-indulgent, and very gullible, albeit not evil or cruel.

Throughout the novel, Green pokes gentle and sometimes not so gentle fun at Gertrude. In her own way, she tries to be good to Louise, who, for her part, does little to make things easier for Gertrude or most other adults. The novelist's description of Louise's bedroom, no doubt lovingly decorated by Gertrude, is not without humor:

> Dans la chambre de Louise où les murs et les meubles essaient de parler le langage de l'enfance, avec la maladresse propre aux adultes, une suite de bariolages naïfs racontait l'histoire du Petit Poucet et du Chaperon rouge. Un coucou annonçait les heures, mettant une note de gaieté conventionnelle dans ce décor d'une futilité douceâtre. Là pourtant, Gertrude était aux pieds de sa nièce qui se tenait debout et toute droite, pareille à une idole indifférente aux supplications des humains. (p. 63)

Louise is perhaps the most resolutely taciturn of Green's protagonists. She is also perhaps the most other-wordly, but if one is aware of Green's thirst for purity and sanctity, a trait evident throughout his literary career, the character of Louise is probably not so surprising.

One critic comments on Green's desire for purity and how this desire profoundly affected his literary career: "The angelism of Green's adolescent spiritual aspirations was never to be outgrown. The rest of his life Green was obliged to live with a bitter nostalgia for lost sainthood. But he was on the verge of discovering a vocation that would afford him a means of coming to grips with his most disturbing problems, both the spiritual anxiety of the mystic and the sexual obsessions of the sensualist."[3] Because Louise is a representative of the "angelism" side of Julien Green, she stands for a degree of purity that the author himself was not able to maintain, at least as a young man. Louise is not unaware of her own sensual beauty; as an example, one thinks of the scene in which Gertrude catches Louise standing on a piece of furniture and observing her own naked body in a mirror. But Louise seems to be genuinely unaware of the effect she has on others.

Let us consider briefly three instances in the novel where Louise influences another character, without intending to do so and without, at least in two of the three cases, even realizing that she has this influence. Although these three characters (Brochard, Perrotte, and Marthe Réau) are quite different from one another, they all appear to be similarly influenced by the young girl of almost unearthly beauty.

Brochard is a widower of somewhat uncertain financial security, who has the unfortunate characteristic that he likes to have sex with twelve-year-old girls. This penchant takes him into degrading and even dangerous situations (Green describes a visit made by Brochard to a brothel in an abandoned building in the dead of night). He is warned by Gustave, Gertrude's brother and Louise's uncle, to stay away from Louise. The reader can hence imagine Brochard's surprise when, during the course of a "randonnée nocturne" in search of sexual adventures, he comes across Louise, the very object of his passionate longing and concupiscence: "Ce fut à ce moment qu'une chose se produisit qui lui fit ouvrir la bouche de stupeur. A vingt mètres de l'endroit où il se tenait, Louise traversa la rue. Elle allait vite, sans regarder à droite ni à gauche et ses cheveux couvraient ses épaules dans une sorte d'épanchement doré. Ses jambes nues brillaient avec des reflets de pierre polie" (p. 114). When one has dreamed of seeing someone for whom one has an immense passion, the shock of seeing that person can be great. So great is the shock for Brochard that he attributes it at first to the cognac he had consumed to give himself courage. He loses sight of her and never sees her again.

The second person who "loves" Louise is an elderly woman called simply Perrotte. Perrotte had previously been one of Gustave's employees, but now she is Louise's tutor, whose efforts in the field of education Gustave ridicules. It is evident that Perrotte is very fond of her young charge, but there is no suggestion of impropriety on her part. In an alarming scene, in which Louise first is spoken to and interrogated by her uncle and then faints because of fear, Perrotte tries to make the best of a bad situation. As Louise lies in a faint, Perrotte refers to her as "Mon adorée!" (p. 175). During a final conversation between Louise and Perrotte, before the former's departure for Chanteleu, a private school, Perrotte makes references to the suffering associated with love. These references, in all likelihood, surpass Louise's understanding:

> —Louise, essayez de me comprendre. Je suis une mauvaise femme. Si, je sais ce que je dis, mais c'est parce que je n'ai jamais été aimée.
> Louise lui posa doucement une main sur la tête et lui dit doucement:
> —Moi, je vous aime.
> Perrotte éclata en sanglots.
> — Vous ne pouvez pas savoir ce que cela veut dire: aimer. Vous ne savez pas. On souffre trop. (p. 182)

Perrotte, as the novelist makes clear, is an unhappy and probably thoroughly repressed woman, one of the most pathetic figures in the novel. But when she is in Louise's presence, she experiences happiness, a strange sort of happiness she has rarely known elsewhere.

The third character profoundly influenced by Louise is Marthe Réau, a teacher at the Chanteleu school who has been a lesbian. She is Louise's protector and mentor in Chanteleu. Though she is not sexually tempted by the golden-haired girl, her affection for her can best be described as love. The following conversation between Mlle Réau and the headmistress is enlightening as regards the two women and their attitudes toward Louise. The headmistress lets it be known that she almost did not admit Louise and was persuaded finally by the financial generosity of Louise's Uncle Gustave, whose sexual penchant for young girls is only too well known. Marthe Réau is sensitive to the headmistress's knowledge of Marthe's sexual preferences, as the headmistress states:

> —J'ai eu raison de vous permettre de la prendre chez vous. [Louise's bedroom is across a small living room from Marthe's, and on a different floor from where the other students reside.] Elle est beaucoup trop vulnérable et beaucoup trop jolie pour l'exposer au voisinage de nos petites.
>
> Sa voix restait ferme et claire malgré soixante-dix ans largement dépassés. Il y eut un silence, puis elle demanda:
> — Si elle est vulnérable, ne craignez-vous pas de l'être vous-même? Saurez-vous résister?
> Le visage de Mademoiselle Réau s'empourpra.
> — Vous me permettrez de ne pas répondre à une question aussi surprenante. (p. 231)

Both women seem to realize that Louise must be protected not only from students—"toutes nos écervelées," as they are called (p. 232)—but also from her dangerous Uncle Gustave. After Louise's mysterious disappearance, Mlle Réau is terribly distraught and is unable to function as a teacher. The artistry of Green in *Le Mauvais Lieu* is evident in the way he presents a figure of profound innocence who moves through the world of the most sordid and jaded passions without being sullied by them.

At this juncture, the question can be asked concerning the major protagonists in *Chaque homme dans sa nuit*, *L'Autre*, and *Le Mauvais Lieu*: do they attain salvation or, to use a term of Catholic theology, do they die in a state of grace? The answer in all three cases would appear to be affirmative. Wilfred Ingram dies as result of being shot by a friend of dubious moral character, yet who begs Wilfred to forgive him. Karin, whose death by drowning is not suicide, as those around her believe, seems to have worked out her salvation or at least to be headed in that direction, under the beneficent influence of Roger. Louise, the figure of profound innocence in *Le Mauvais Lieu*, does not die but rather disappears without a trace; she does not *die* so much as *remain* in a state of grace, and this despite the sordid world in which she lives.

Wilfred, in *Chaque homme dans sa nuit,* is a young man whom many others in the novel regard as either actively religious or at least a source of information and encouragement when it comes to religious matters. It is interesting—and possibly no mere coincidence—that so many other characters in the novel speak to Wilfred about religion, God, and moral values: Uncle Horace Ingram, the old black male servant at Uncle Horace's house, James Knight, Max (the deeply troubled young man who later shoots Wilfred fatally), Tommy (a friend from childhood days), Freddie (a coworker who, shortly before his death, is baptized by Wilfred in hospital), Angus Howard (Wilfred's cousin who is, figuratively speaking, paralyzed by guilt and despair and who learns from James Knight about Wilfred's beatific death). All these characters, to various degrees, discuss religious matters with Wilfred or look to him for some kind of spiritual help. As a case in point, let us examine briefly two statements made by James Knight.

When Knight first meets Wilfred, the former, a strict Presbyterian, is hostile to the latter, a Roman Catholic suspected of moral laxity. But when Knight has a nearly fatal illness some time later, he discovers that his main concern is not his faith in God but a desire to stay alive. Afterward, his religious faith—and its concomitant "triumphalism"—are significantly weaker. In a conversation with Wilfred one evening, when Wilfred and Knight's wife, Phoebé, have declared their love for each other (obviously not in Knight's presence), the latter speaks of Judas and Jesus and of how Judas made a dreadful mistake in hanging himself instead of asking Jesus for forgiveness:

> Jésus aimait Judas. Or, si trahir Jésus était une grande faute, elle était malgré tout pardonnable. L'erreur de Judas a été de croire qu'elle ne l'était pas, et de se pendre. Imaginez tout se passant d'une autre manière, Judas courant à Jésus alors que celui-ci butait et trébuchait sous le poids de sa croix. Dans des cris et des larmes, le traître se jette à genoux, demande pardon à sa victime. . . . Quel regard tombe alors sur lui, pensez-vous? Un regard de haine? Je ne le crois pas. Un regard d'amour, Wilfred, un regard d'amour. Il y a eu dans la Passion une minute où seul Judas pouvait consoler Jésus en lui demandant pardon. Le scandale est que cette minute ait

passé sans que Judas se soit trouvé là. C'est ainsi que je vois les choses. (pp. 658–59)

There is no doubt that James Knight, as a (formerly good, now not so staunch) Presbyterian, knows Holy Scripture well. He was highly critical of Wilfred at one time, at least in part because of the latter's Roman Catholicism. But he now has a much more relaxed approach to religion, partly because the faith he had has been firmly shaken. Nevertheless, he is still concerned with religious and moral questions. Knight's statement has two noteworthy consequences: it makes Wilfred feel guilty about his relation to Phoebé, and it also, to a degree, presages an event associated with the death of Wilfred himself. Shortly after Wilfred is shot by Max, the latter kneels on the sidewalk and begs for his victim's forgiveness: "Un mot fut prononcé pourtant, un mot qui effaçait tout, parce que seul parlait le plus grand amour. Si faiblement que Max l'entendait à peine, la bouche murmura: 'Oui . . . '" (p. 702). Knight had posed the question of what things would have been like had Judas asked Jesus for forgiveness. (Anthony Newbury refers to two diary entries made by the novelist in the 1950s concerning Judas as evidence of Green's interest in Christ's betrayer.)[4] In the case of Wilfred, his murderer asks for and receives his forgiveness, and this would seem to be one indication of the blessedness of his death.

In the last chapter of the novel, Green has James Knight describe to Angus the death of Wilfred, as he witnessed it. Though skeptical of the Roman rite of Extreme Unction, Knight goes to speak to the priest who had administered it to Wilfred, and then together the two men go to Wilfred's room: "J'ai vécu de longues années. Je n'ai pas encore vu sur le visage d'un être humain une expression de bonheur comparable à celle qui éclairait les traits de Wilfred. . . . Je ne pouvais détacher les yeux de Wilfred. On aurait dit qu'il souriait de ma surprise et qu'il connaissait des choses secrètes qu'il gardait pour lui. Malgré ses paupières closes, il semblait nous observer de loin, comme d'une région de lumière" (p. 708).

Wilfred is one of Green's protagonists most struck by divine grace, although this would not be evident to the reader in many parts of the novel nor to Wilfred himself. Yet Wilfred, for all his doubts, for all his sins of the flesh, for all his reluctance to talk about religion, even with those who desperately want to discuss it with him, manages to hold on to his faith and to point himself in the right direction. The novelist himself considered *Chaque homme dans sa nuit* to be his first "livre optimiste."[5] This attitude would seem to be corroborated by the scene of Wilfred's death in hospital. Even more than Karin, his counterpart in *L'Autre*, Wilfred convinces the reader that salvation is possible.

But let us briefly consider Karin. In some ways, *L'Autre* is a more enigmatic novel than *Chaque homme dans sa nuit*, even though its plot has fewer convolutions. Karin, like other Greenian protagonists, is attempting to work out her salvation, though she herself might not phrase this so directly. Karin wants the love of Roger, a love she enjoyed briefly in the summer of 1939. But Roger comes back to Denmark in the spring of 1949 not to resume an old love affair, but to try to "undo" the moral damage he had caused earlier and to "direct" Karin toward Christianity and Catholicism. He puts her in touch with a priest whom she sees and with whom she speaks from time to time. Karin's attitude toward the priest as a representative of the church varies from receptive to hostile. The same can be said of her attitude toward God. In her conversations with the priest, she challenges him to prove to her that there exists a personal and loving God; he answers her as gently, as patiently, and as charitably as possible. During their initial conversation, the novelist makes us privy to the thoughts in Karin's mind: "Pour la première fois de ma vie, je goûtai l'étrange plaisir de me mettre en accusation pour me délivrer d'un poids intolérable. De cette manière, je donnais tout à la ville entière qui m'avait si durement chargée. Une sorte d'équilibre se rétablissait par le seul fait de mes aveux" (p. 917). Though Karin does not make a formal confession as a practicing Catholic, nonetheless she reminds the reader of Wilfred in *Chaque homme dans sa nuit*, for whom confession is always a source of spiritual consolation.

Later Karin finds herself again in the same church, again seeking consolation and answers for her many questions. She speaks to a girl who says to her "Madame, la foi n'a pas besoin de voir" (p. 984). Though she is full of questioning and doubt, Karin decides to kneel, as others often do in church. The emotion she feels is remarkable:

> Fallait-il me mettre à genoux comme la vieille femme à deux
> pas de moi? J'y résistai un long moment, puis, le visage en
> feu et le cœur battant, l'orgueilleuse se mit à genoux. Que se

passa-t-il? Je ne pourrais le dire au juste, mais tout à coup je me sentis calme et heureuse. Me frappa surtout cette tranquillité soudaine. Il me semble que toute crainte avait disparu de mon être, comme si un grand vent l'eût balayée. Pour la première fois, je me sentis en sécurité, à l'abri de tout malheur et de toute tristesse, mais cette halte délicieuse dans le temps ne dura pas. (p. 984)

Green has written elsewhere of moments in his own life when he experienced great peace, tranquility, and assurance. Doubtless he has transposed such an episode of peace into this scene involving Karin. One cannot be sure of Karin's "permanent" acceptance of this peace that comes from faith. But we do learn, from the last few pages of the novel, that her death by drowning is not suicide but the result of an accident that occurred when she was trying to escape from two men pursuing her on the quay.

The Biblical quotation chosen by Green to head the fourth part of *L'Autre* is most appropriate: "Ne craignez point ceux qui tuent le corps et qui ne peuvent tuer l'âme" (Matthew 10: 28). Karin dies, but it would seem that her soul is safe. Anthony Newbury writes of this juncture of the novel: "Set against the possible loss of spiritual life, the death of the body is for Green correspondingly less dreadful to contemplate. . . . Karin's aggressors will indeed bear the responsibility for snuffing out her bodily existence, but the essential Karin, her soul, is inviolate. . . . Green has nevertheless finely pointed his Christian message and expressed with equal force his own thought on sexuality and its relationship to the Christian religion."[6] Tormented by sexual desire and plagued by questions of religious faith, Karin has finally arrived at some measure of peace, if not total fulfillment. The fact that her life ends so suddenly and unexpectedly is a tragedy in secular terms, but not so on the level of eternity.

And what of the chaste and innocent Louise, heroine of *Le Mauvais Lieu*? She does not die, or at least we are not told of her death. On the contrary, she disappears from the confines of the boarding school, during the time of a heavy snowstorm, virtually on Christmas Eve. As has been mentioned, Louise has the ability to maintain innocence and purity in the midst of the most sordid goings-on. She values Marthe Réau's friendship and is upset one day by the mistaken belief that Marthe no longer loves her. She leaves a handwritten note, naively stating that she is departing. Green ends the novel with a statement as enigmatic as it is fascinating: "Mais chercher l'enfant par les chemins obscurs de notre monde était bien inutile. L'innocence avait disparu dans ce qui lui ressemblait le plus: dans la neige" (p. 295).

Because Green's two most recent novels—*Les Pays lointains* and its sequel, *Les Etoiles du sud*—are also his longest (891 and 745 pages respectively), they will be considered by concentrating on various episodes of pivotal importance. Green began *Les Pays lointains* in the 1930s but abandoned the project, supposedly because of the similarities to *Gone with the Wind,* only to take it up again many years later. Both have as their heroine Elizabeth Escridge, a young and beautiful Englishwoman who comes to the ante-bellum American South with her mother to seek help from the man whom a paternal aunt had married. The plot of the two novels is relatively complicated, especially since both novels move at a leisurely pace and employ numerous subplots and a multiplicity of major and minor characters. These two novels are also a "first" for Green insofar as they are historical novels. Though the old concerns of sin and moral values are present here, they are, so to speak, somewhat diluted from the high intensity with which they occur in the earlier works.

Green, whose parents came from the South and who knew it from his own sojourns there, has gone to great trouble to create the atmosphere of the South both before and during the Civil War. Much emphasis is given to the endless discussions of politics and propaganda concerning the questions of slavery, the U.S. Constitution, calls for secession, the actions of the U.S. Congress, and so on. Green has steeped himself in the history of this period. One paragraph provides a reasonably good idea of the political conversations that abound throughout the novels:

> A déjeuner, il fut convenu qu'on ne parlerait pas de politique, afin de ne pas troubler les délices de la table, mais cinq minutes ne s'étaient pas écoulées qu'il ne fut plus question que du Compromis et des chances de paix. . . . Les rumeurs qui circulaient à présent laissaient prévoir un accord. Rassurés, les convives s'offraient le plaisir de le mettre en pièces: c'était sur l'honneur du Sud une honteuse éclaboussure et de plus une filouterie politique. Calhoun pouvait se retourner dans sa tombe. (p. 340)

There are times when the discussions become very heated, especially when the younger men of the family, in particular Fred and Billy Hargrove, express their desire for a war between North and South. The war does not break out until the period covered in *Les Etoiles du sud*, but it casts a long shadow over the first novel.

The episode of the ball at Dimwood, given supposedly to celebrate the acceptance of a compromise to save the Union in 1850, is a great social event for those involved and is described by the novelist with gusto. Green is thoroughly imbued not only with Southern history, but also with the social customs and traditions of the Old South. The invitations are carefully considered for those who are likely to accept, because too many refusals would impinge on family pride. The social intricacies of choosing dance partners are a cause both of delight and some consternation among the dancers. The older ladies, not given to dancing, sit on the side and, from time to time, help themselves generously at the buffet. The subject of daughters to be married off is a frequent topic of conversation. As one of the ladies observes, "Evidemment . . . la dépense est forte, mais on a des filles à marier et si même une seule des quatre était casée, l'opération justifierait les frais" (p. 358).

In point of fact, an engagement does result during the evening of the ball. A Lieutenant Boulton, who cuts a very dashing figure, asks for the hand of Susanna Hargrove. Her father virtually forces her to accept, despite her disinclination to marry the young man, whom she scarcely knew previously. Her description to her cousin Elizabeth of the scene with her father reveals her distress: "—Tu ne peux pas savoir. Papa a été horrible. Il est venu me chercher dans ma chambre. Il est entré de force. Il m'a dit que pour toute la famille c'était une chance inattendue, qu'il m'ordonnait de dire oui, que désobéir à son père, c'était désobéir à Dieu et que désobéir à Dieu c'était l'enfer, j'ai eu peur. . . . Je ne l'ai jamais vu comme ça. . . . Il était rouge, j'ai cru qu'il allait me tuer" (p. 363). One is quite aware that many marriages were arranged rather than entered into voluntarily by both partners. The injustice of such a system is made more apparent by Susanna's disinclination toward marriage in general. After her subsequent attempt at suicide, in fact, the engagement is broken off.

Perhaps the most "historical" part of these two novels is the section of *Les Etoiles du sud* entitled "Dixie," in which the events from November 6, 1860 (Election Day, when Lincoln was elected), to the Battle of Bull Run are described. Again, it is obvious that Green knows the history of this era well. Very impressive is his indictment of war that accompanies a description of the suffering of soldiers who had participated in Bull Run. The train carrying Confederate wounded stops in the small town of Gainesville, Virginia:

> Ceux des blessés qui pouvaient tenir debout se serraient aux fenêtres et réclamaient à boire. . . . La foule qui s'attendait à une célébration d'héroïsme se trouvait face à la souffrance et demeura un instant silencieux. Quelqu'un entonna *Dixie*, puis se tut presque aussitôt. Libre aux civils de chanter victoire chez eux! La guerre, ce n'était pas les fanfares, les drapeaux claquant au vent, les hauts faits, l'héroïsme en peinture, non, c'était une jeunesse mutilée qui avait mal, secouée dans les compartiments d'un chemin de fer. (pp. 740–41)

Green expresses here his own pacifism and hatred of war, as he wants the reader to be keenly aware of the suffering that war can inflict upon both military and civilians.

There is much that can be said about Julien Green's distinguished literary career and much that can be said about the five novels included in this study. Green is a very humane and compassionate individual. He is concerned about the struggle between spiritual aspirations and carnal demands, and this struggle may be said to dominate his work. He is also a consummate craftsman of the French language. Green can weave a story combining human interest, suspense, and his perennial concern for moral values. One does not always realize, perhaps, just how much effort and labor go into a work such as *Chaque homme dans sa nuit*, which on the surface may appear at first glance effortless. But the relatively complex plot, with its highly developed characters, is anything but simple, and certainly not easy.

Green's perspective is that of a Christian, specifically, Catholic writer. He *does* believe that salvation is possible, but that by no means implies that life will always be easy or that the good individuals will always triumph, at least *ici-bas*. Wilfred Ingram dies from a gunshot wound, though he is resolutely trying to do the right thing. Karin drowns because she falls from a quay, though she was slowly but surely coming to terms with the God of Christianity; certainly she did want to live, not to perish. Louise disappears during a heavy snowstorm at Christmas, leaving the world, in some respects, as mysteriously as Jesus came into it. In the two Southern novels, Elizabeth experiences love, marriage, and a brief adulterous affair, before enduring the death of two husbands. The last two novels both present a vast panorama of the life and culture of the ante-bellum South. Though the stage is vast, it is never so vast that one loses sight of the major players. If writing novels that deal with believable men and women, and the considerable burdens they must bear, makes a writer worthy of critical attention in the late twentieth century, then Julien Green is such a creative artist. Because of his efforts over the course of more than sixty years, the French novel is all the richer.

Notes

1. Brian T. Fitch, "Préface," *Configuration critique de Julien Green* (Paris: M. J. Minard [*Revue des Lettres Modernes* 130–33], 1966), p. 10.

2. Anthony H. Newbury, *Julien Green: Religion and Sensuality* (Amsterdam: Rodopi, 1986), p. 139.

3. John M. Dunaway, *The Metamorphoses of the Self: The Mystic, the Sensualist, and the Artist in the Works of Julien Green* (Lexington: University Press of Kentucky, 1978), p. 30.

4. Newbury, *Julien Green*, p. 153.

5. Interview with Guy Dupré, *Arts* (April 27 to May 3, 1960). Quoted in Julien Green, *Œuvres complètes, vol. III* (Paris: Gallimard [La Pléiade], 1973), p. 1515.

6. Newbury, *Julien Green*, p. 189.

Bibliography

Works by Julien Green

Mont-Cinère. Paris: Plon, 1926.

Adrienne Mesurat. Paris: Plon, 1927.

Christine, suivi de Léviathan. Paris: Cahiers libres, 1928.

L'Autre sommeil. Paris: Gallimard, 1931.

Epaves. Paris: Plon, 1932.

Le Visionnaire. Paris: Plon, 1934.

Minuit. Paris: Plon, 1936.

Si j'étais vous . . . . Paris: Plon, 1947.

Moïra. Paris: Plon, 1950.

Sud, play. Paris: Plon, 1953.

L'Ennemi, play. Paris: Plon, 1954.

Le Malfaiteur. Paris: Plon, 1955.

L'Ombre, play. Paris: Plon, 1958.

Chaque homme dans sa nuit. Paris: Plon, 1960. Translated by A. Green as *Each Man in His Darkness.* London: Quartet, 1991.

L'Autre. Paris: Plon, 1971. Translated by Bernard Wall as *The Other One.* London: Collins and Harvill, 1973.

Le Mauvais Lieu. Paris: Plon, 1977.

Frère François, biography. Paris: Seuil, 1983.

Les Pays lointains. Paris: Seuil, 1987. Translated by Barbara Beaumont as *The Distant Lands.* New York: Marion Boyars, 1991.

Les Etoiles du sud. Paris: Seuil, 1989.

Selected Critical Works

Brodin, Pierre. *Julien Green.* Paris: Editions Universitaires (Classiques du XXe siècle), 1957.

Burne, Glenn S. *Julien Green.* New York: Twayne, 1972.

Carrel, Janine. *L'Expérience du seuil dans l'œuvre de Julien Green.* Zurich: Juris Druck und Verlag, 1967.

Cooke, Mother M. Gerard. *Hallucination and Death as Motifs of Escape in the Novels of Julien Green.* Washington, D.C.: Catholic University of America Press (Studies in Romance Languages and Literatures), 1960.

Dunaway, John M. *The Metamorphoses of the Self: The Mystic, the Sensualist and the Artist in the Works of Julien Green.* Lexington: University Press of Kentucky (Studies in Romance Languages, no. 19), 1978.

Eigeldinger, Marc. *Julien Green et la tentation de l'irréel.* Paris: Editions des Portes de France, 1947.

Kostis, Nicholas. *The Exorcism of Sex and Death in Julien Green's Novels.* The Hague, Paris: Mouton ("De proprietatibus litterarum," Series practica 71), 1973.

Mor, Antonio. *Julien Green, témoin de l'invisible.* Translated from the Italian by Hélène Pasquier. Paris: Plon, 1973.

Muff, Oswald. *La Dialectique du néant et du désir dans l'œuvre de Julien Green.* Zurich: P. G. Keller, 1967.

Newbury, Anthony H. *Julien Green: Religion and Sensuality.* Amsterdam: Rodopi, 1986.

Petit, Jacques. *Julien Green, "l'homme qui venait d'ailleurs."* Paris: Desclée de Brouwer, 1969.

Piriou, Jean-Pierre. *Sexualité, religion et art chez Julien Green.* Paris: A. G. Nizet, 1976.

Prévost, Jean-Laurent. *Julien Green ou l'âme engagée.* Lyon: Emmanuel Vitte, 1960.

Raclot, Michèle. *Le Sens du mystère dans l'œuvre romanesque de Julien Green.* Paris: Aux amateurs de livres, 1988.

Rose, Marilyn Gaddis. *Julien Green. Gallic-American Novelist.* Berne, Frankfurt am Main: Herbert Lang and Co. (European University Papers), 1971.

Rousseau, Guy-Noël. *Sur le chemin de Julien Green.* Neuchâtel: A la Baconnière, 1965.

Saint Jean, Robert de. *Julien Green par lui-même.* Paris: Seuil ("Ecrivains de toujours"), 1967.

Sémolué, Jean. *Julien Green ou l'obsession du mal.* Paris: Editions du Centurion, 1964.

Stokes, Samuel. *Julien Green and the Thorn of Puritanism.* New York: King's Crown Press, 1955; Westport, CT: Greenwood, 1972.

Tamuly, Annette. *Julien Green à la recherche du réel: approche phénoménologique.* Sherbrooke: Editions Naaman, 1976.

Wildgen, Kathryn. *Julien Green: The Great Themes.* Birmingham, AL: Summa Publications, 1993.

3

Julien Gracq

Michel Viegnes

Few contemporary French authors suffer from a more perplexing disparity between their literary importance in France and their reputation in North America than does Julien Gracq, born Louis Poirier. Despite the excellent translation of Gracq's master-novel *Le Rivage des Syrtes* by Richard Howard,[1] his works are still somewhat esoteric, even among initiates who know everything important written beyond the Atlantic in the language of Rimbaud and Breton.

One explanation could be Gracq's well-known (to his readers, at least) aversion for publicity and trendiness. Often characterized as a "natural child of Surrealism," Gracq is a fiercely individualistic writer, full of scorn for literary movements (except Surrealism) and critical dictates. There is nothing in him of the "écrivain engagé," the Sartrian type who would refuse to distill the magic of a landscape lest (s)he be accused of collaborating with the ruling class by offering esthetic diversion from social problems; nothing either of the "nouveau romancier" type who thinks that the primary duty of the fiction writer is to denounce the fallacy of fiction writing. Gracq, as he repeatedly claims in his critical essays, loves literature, and his favorite authors—Melville, Jünger, Tolkien, among others—have no complexes whatsoever about the "hubris" of literary enchantments.

Louis Poirier was born on July 27, 1910, in a small town of the Loire River valley. His childhood was quiet and introverted. In 1928, he went to Paris to pursue his education and two years later was admitted to the prestigious Ecole Normale Supérieure, where he studied to become a professor of history and geography. During these years in the

74

capital, his cultural and literary horizons expanded: he read a great deal and discovered German Romanticism and Wagner's music, including *Parsifal,* which inspired a lifelong fascination with the story of the Holy Grail. He also read Breton's *Nadja* and saw in Surrealism a reconquest, through poetry, of an entire dimension of the psyche that the Cartesian tradition had repressed: a sort of superromanticism. He met Breton in 1939 and nine years later published what is still considered one of the most penetrating studies on the author of *Les Manifestes du surréalisme* and his movement: *André Breton. Quelques aspects de l'écrivain.* Yet, despite his admiration for Breton, he would never be part of the Surrealist group. In one of the rare interviews he granted, he explained his position: "Mes relations avec le Surréalisme ont été surtout des relations avec Breton, des relations d'admiration et d'amitié mais qui n'ont jamais été d'adhésion totale. . . . Ma non-appartenance au groupe avait été une question réglée, il me semble, dès ma première rencontre avec Breton. Je n'ai jamais signé de manifeste ou de texte collectif, ni participé aux exclusions lancées contre tel ou tel."[2]

In 1938, Poirier published his first novel, *Au château d'Argol,* under the "nom de plume" he would keep for the rest of his literary career—Julien Gracq—the first name being a tribute to Stendhal's *Le Rouge et le noir,* the book that sparked his passion for literature as a child. The novel was published by a very small publisher, José Corti, to whom Gracq would reserve total exclusivity until 1989, when the publication of his complete works began in the Gallimard "Pléiade" collection. The book sold only 150 copies, but was acclaimed by several influential critics. One of the most enthusiastic readers was Breton himself.

Au château d'Argol is a relatively short novel, without dialogue, so much inspired by the Gothic novel that it verges at times on parody. Its substance is difficult to summarize. At first sight it may appear as a love triangle, as we witness the complex relationships between three characters, a woman named Heide and two men, Albert and Herminien. Ambiguous, allegorical events take place in Brittany, in a medieval castle, the forest surrounding it, and the ocean. In addition to vague Hegelian references, the Grail story is the fundamental intertext of this initiatic novel, Heide and Herminien representing spiritual and cosmic forces that Albert has to conquer in his quest. At the very end, he kills Herminien.

It is no small paradox that while writing a novel so aloof from contemporary issues, Gracq was having a very militant political life within the Communist Party, which he had joined in 1936 during the Front Populaire. In 1938, he even intended to travel to the Soviet Union, but was denied a visa. For Gracq, 1939 was a turning point: it is the year he met Breton for the first time, but it also marked the declaration of war and the beginning of the so-called drôle de guerre that became the framework of his novel *Un balcon en forêt*, published in 1958. It was also the year of the infamous Nazi-Soviet pact, which had on Gracq the same effect that the Budapest repression later had on other French Communist intellectuals in 1956. From then on, Gracq lost interest in politics.

During the war, he was taken prisoner, sent to a prison camp in Germany, and then was returned to France because of illness. It was during the last years of the war, while he resumed his professional life as a teacher, that he discovered Ernst Jünger's *Auf der Marmorklippen*, a novel that had a major impact on him.

In 1945, two books appeared: a collection of prose poems, *Liberté grande,* and his second novel, *Un beau ténébreux.* Set (again) in Brittany, at a seashore hotel, *Un beau ténébreux* consists of a summer in the life of a little group of wealthy socialites, whose vacation was fairly dull until the arrival of Allan, a perfect dark romantic stereotype, and his companion, Dolorès. The novel explores the devastating effect Allan has on this nebula of mediocre lives. A typical Poe-esque figure, as his name suggests, his fascination has something to do with the secret reasons why he came to the hotel, reasons that are gradually revealed.

By 1948, when he published his essay on Breton, Gracq's name was well established in the microcosm of Parisian letters. But the performance, in 1949, of his play *Le Roi pêcheur,* another avatar of the Grail legend, attracted much negative reaction, which crystallized in him a latent, intense hatred for the snobbery of the intellectual "tout-Paris." One year later, he expressed his feelings in a bitter pamphlet called *La Littérature à l'estomac.* The next year, in 1951, to further manifest his contempt for the literary establishment of the capital, he refused the Prix Goncourt awarded to him for *Le Rivage des Syrtes.*

This novel has been compared to the one by Jünger mentioned above and to Dino Buzzati's *Il Deserto dei Tartari.* Like these two books, *Le Rivage des Syrtes* is a historico-geographic fiction. Set in an undefined epoch that could be the late nineteenth century, it is an account of the subtle circumstances leading to a war between two empires. The

Seigneurie d'Orsenna, a once mighty mercantile nation, reminiscent of the Repubblica Serenissima of Venice, has been for three centuries in a state of "cold war" with Farghestan, a Turkish-like Muslim empire. The two territories are separated by a narrow sea, beyond a marshy, desolate southern province of Orsenna called the Syrtes. The narrator and protagonist Aldo, son of a rich family of the capital, tired of the elegant but empty life he enjoyed with other sybarites of his age, obtains from the government an assignment as political observer to a military outpost on the Syrtes seashore. During his tenure, he becomes obsessed with the "opposing shore" of the enemy land, and, with the complicity of Vanessa, a seductive double agent, provokes a naval skirmish with Farghestan. It triggers an all-out war, which the novel does not narrate, except to say that it annihilates Orsenna. Summoned back to the capital city, Aldo meets the shadowy master of Orsenna, Danielo, only to discover that he had been the pawn of a suicidal conspiracy at the highest level, intended to deal the fatal blow to the decadent, self-hating civilization.

Though most discerning readers acclaimed it as a great text, some found this novel imbued with "fascist romanticism" because certain passages seem to convey an apology of brutal, vitalistic ideologies. At any rate, after the Prix Goncourt refusal, Gracq withdrew increasingly from the literary circles and began to acquire a reputation as a solitary, misanthropic, secretive writer. In 1958, he published *Un balcon en forêt*, which may reflect his aspirations to escape a world marred by violence and ugliness. The novel is set in the first year of World War II. A French soldier named Grange, along with three other privates, waits for the hypothetical German offensive in a bunker called Les Falizes, in the thick of the Ardennes forest. There, like the Duke in Shakespeare's *As You Like It*, Grange persuades himself that he has found one of these magical refuges away from the so-called real world of vulgarity, absurdity, and death. Two factors consolidate his sylvan mirage: the strange nonevent of the "drôle de guerre," and Mona, a no less strange woman living in a small house in the forest. This house and its inhabitant seem to come out from a German or Celtic folktale. For Grange and his fellow soldiers, it appears that history has forgotten them. It makes it all the harder to wake up one fine morning of May 1940. None of them will survive.

In 1955, Gracq had started another novel, which, like *Le Rivage des Syrtes*, was set in an imaginary time and space. The novel was aborted and became, under the title "La Route," one of the three short stories of *La Presqu'île*, along with the one that gives its title to the collection, and a third entitled "Le Roi Cophetua." This collection, Gracq's own *Trois contes*, appeared in 1970 and is his last published work of fiction. In 1961, he had published a collection of critical essays, *Préférences*, followed, in 1967 and 1974, by *Lettrines I* and *Lettrines II*, and finally by *En lisant, en écrivant* in 1981. In these critical reflections, Gracq reveals much about himself and his own poetics through his comments on Novalis, Balzac, Lautréamont, Poe, and others.

Finally, during the last part of his life Gracq has seemed to lose interest in fiction in favor of poetic meditations with an autobiographical basis. *Les Eaux étroites*, in 1976, is a short text evoking his favorite hiking trail on the banks of the Evre, a small affluent of the Loire. The little river and its landscapes are transfigured by Gracq into an initiatic itinerary. The title of *La Forme d'une ville* (1985) is an allusion to Baudelaire's poem "Le Cygne," where the author of *Les Fleurs du mal*, seeing Haussmann's innovations destroy the old Paris, complained, "Le vieux Paris n'est plus—la forme d'une ville/Change plus vite, hélas! que le cœur d'un mortel." He is one of the few French authors, along with Gide and Giono, who has seen himself being "canonized" (his enemies said "mummified") through a Pléiade edition of his works during his lifetime. His most recent published works are *Autour des sept collines* (1988) and *Carnets du grand chemin* (1992), two miscellanea of travel impressions, autobiographical references, and meditations on art and literature.

As already indicated, Gracq's contribution to the exploration of new narrative forms that characterizes the postwar French novel is not as visible as in the nouveau roman; even though inspired by Surrealism, his concept of the poetic novel has nothing to do with texts such as Aragon's *Blanche ou l'oubli* or Boris Vian's *L'Ecume des jours*. At first sight, each of his four novels seems to fit within a well-established literary model: the Gothic novel for *Au château d'Argol*, the polyphonic, psychological étude for *Un beau ténébreux* (a text replete, moreover, with literary allusions), the Stendhalian adventure novel for *Le Rivage des Syrtes*, and the World War II story for *Un balcon en forêt*. Yet, after a few pages the reader is caught within a kind of poetic trap, not unlike the fly within the invisible spider web, and realizes, however confusedly, that all these models are being subverted from within. In the adventure novel, for instance, the plot, the events, and the facts are essential: they are the true skeleton of the text. Gracq respects the plot structure in a paradoxical fashion, through a poetics of absence that he calls the "intrigue en creux."

Gracq has appropriated Breton's maxim "c'est l'attente qui est magnifique." The whole narrative line of Le Rivage des Syrtes leads to a crucial event that remains beyond the scope of the novel: the outbreak of the war between Orsenna and Farghestan. The novel ends before the actual war begins: the focus is on the many, sometimes microscopic facts and signs that lead to it and gradually make inevitable what was at first a most unlikely outcome. The traditional plot structure is to this novel what a metal printing character is to the hollow clay mold from which it was molded. The event will emerge from the "intrigue en creux" "comme une vague naît du creux qui la précède," to use Gracq's own words in Un beau ténébreux (p. 161). The excipit, or final sentence, of Le Rivage des Syrtes contains another metaphor in the same vein. Says Aldo, walking in the streets of his soon-to-be-destroyed city, after his fateful interview with Orsenna's master: "je savais pourquoi désormais le décor était planté" (p. 839). This theatrical image conjures up the world of trag-edy—for it will surely be "full of sound and fury"—with the sense of inescapable fatality that comes with it. Averting the war, then, is as un-thinkable as stopping "deux corps qui commencent à faire les gestes de l'amour" (p. 838).

The "intrigue en creux," with its expectative poetics, although at its best in Le Rivage des Syrtes, is nonetheless at work in all four novels, as well as in the short story entitled "La Presqu'île." Nearly all of Gracq's narratives follow the same model: a poetic milieu—what Breton would have called a "champ magnétique"—is carefully built up, where every detail points toward a final event that may or may not be presented to the reader, but the coming of which dissolves the fabric of ordinary, re-assuring (i.e., nonpoetic) reality. Thus magnified, this final occurrence—Allan's suicide, the war with Farghestan, the German offensive in the Ardennes forest—functions as a minor apocalypse, a catastrophic rev-elation that sheds light on the enigma of living. So illuminating is it that merely waiting for it, feeling the magnetic premonitions of its advent, following the signs that lead to it, is already an initiatic journey. Para-doxically, as waiting for the final event is more meaningful than the event itself, the latter can remain forever virtual, and never materialize. In "La Presqu'île," the narrator decides not to go and meet Irmgard: she might not live up to the expectations he nurtured during his wait. Perhaps she would not be the real Irmgard: the real one lives within his heart. In a similar fashion, the knight seeking the Grail may find that it is hidden in the quest itself. No less a literary thinker than Maurice Blanchot puts Gracq's fiction in the broad category of "le monde littéraire magique," whose essence, he observes, is descriptive rather than narrative. Says Blanchot: "Il peut s'y passer quelque chose, il ne s'y passe rien: tout est en place pour l'événement, les préludes s'ajoutent aux préludes, les préparatifs sont infinis, mais l'événement lui-même ne peut être présent que dans un avenir sans cesse reporté, comme toujours menaçant, comme irrémédiablement futur."[3] We return below to this essentially initiatic dimension of Gracq's novels.

One characteristic of the poetic novel is precisely that it tends to subsume the habitual duality between narration and description. This is true in Gracq's fiction, and this resolution of the two poles is realized through various means, one of which is the narrative use, or narrativization, of metaphors. *Le Rivage des Syrtes* is the finest example of a mythopoetic network of metaphors that echo one another from the beginning to the end of the novel. Thus, the rather peculiar image of a "nocturnal egg" is used in two key passages. During the Christmas office at the Saint-Damase church, where a strange priest has just prophesied the coming of the Horsemen of the Apocalypse—a veiled allusion to the forthcoming invasion by Farghestan—the protagonist Aldo compares the night enveloping this church and its frightened flock to an "œuf nocturne" (p. 707). The same phrase had occurred in the middle of the novel, when the small contingent of the Syrtes outpost had undertaken, against Captain Marino's will, the renovation of the old fortress. The ancient building, dating back to centuries of bloody warfare, now stands on the desolated shore as an "énorme œuf nocturne" (p. 667). Adding to the obvious intrinsic symbolism of the egg—that from which something is to be born—the echo establishes a logical link between two apparently unrelated events and enhances their common function as invitation to war. This interplay of malleable signifiers is only one example among many that shows how Gracq, through metaphoric devices, turns description into a parallel narrative.

One sees in *Le Rivage des Syrtes* and throughout his works examples of Gracq's heavy use of italics. This device is not limited to the fictional texts, but appears in virtually everything he has written. It might be the most conspicuous "signature" left by Gracq, as the reader can find an average of two or three phrases in italics on every page. Several critics have devoted in-depth studies to this phenomenon and its stylistic, as well as linguistic, significance. The distancing effect of italics operates at various levels and is quite complex.

Most often the italics signal affinities between the literal meaning of a word or locution and their figurative significance. Sometimes the shift from one level to the other is quite obvious: thus during the scene in *Au château d'Argol* when Heide, Herminien, and Albert swim away from the shore to the extreme limit of their strength, risking their lives, it seems that Heide is trying to lead both men to *"l'autre rivage de l'Océan"* (p. 69). The italics only enhance the already potent symbolic charge of the "opposing shore" image, which is central to *Le Rivage des Syrtes* as well: in most mystical and initiatic imagery, the opposing shore of the ocean is the very goal of the quest, the Beyond, the threshold of revelation, just as the crossing of the waters is the epiphanic journey itself. In other cases, the use of italics cannot be explained by the confrontation between a literal and a figurative meaning. Gracq may italicize a word whose meaning is apparently so simple and obvious that the reader might otherwise overlook it, without stopping for a second. The italics invite—or force—the reader to question the apparent straightforwardness of the signified, just as Gracq's poetics, as a whole, reflects an inquiry beyond the deceptive surface of reality.

In *En lisant, en écrivant,* Gracq reflects on a particularity of the French curriculum with which he was quite familiar. One remembers that he was, under his real name, a professor of history and geography (the two disciplines are taught together in French secondary schools). Much could be said about the pros and cons of this curricular junction, but it certainly underlines the two categories in which any human experience takes place: time and space. Poirier's academic training has had a most profound impact on Gracq's approach to the novel: in his novels geography, topography, and the natural and material surroundings, are the prime reality from which everything else derives. Gracq's human characters have the psychology of their natural surroundings, as countries, according to Napoleon, have the politics of their geographies. In a text entitled "La Plante humaine," Gracq theorized this symbiosis between the individual and the geographical milieu. The human "plant" is the recipient, like any other plant, of the telluric forces that continually shape the appearances of nature. Thus, the dark powers of the forest, so richly thematized in many myths, folktales, and medieval romances, largely determine the functioning of the dramatis personae in *Au château d'Argol* and even more so those in *Un balcon en forêt*, in which Mona is clearly a "génie du lieu," a pure emanation of the Ardennes.

In a similar vein, seascapes and desolate shores constitute the living milieu where the characters of *Un beau ténébreux* and *Le Rivage des Syrtes* evolve according to their internal logic. In the former text, long walks on the beach are occasions to discuss Allan's enigmatic personality, and the headquarters of the little society revolving around this dark star are located at the Hôtel des Vagues, a name that obviously connects the building to the sea. In *Le Rivage des Syrtes*, the sea is also a key element, as are the shores and marshes of the Syrtes province. Several studies of this novel have analyzed, inspired by Bachelard, the symbiosis between characters and elements: Aldo is clearly in harmony with the sea, while Marino, despite the connotations of his name, is a man of the land, with all the negative ideas that come with it. There is throughout the novel a dichotomy between the land, emblematic of the sterility, stagnation, and unimaginative passivity of the doomed civilization of Orsenna, and the sea, engrossed with all the virtualities of risk, adventure, and revelation. Aldo spends days contemplating the sea, and finally crosses to the "opposing shore," while Marino visits the inland farms. Interestingly enough, Vanessa, the initiatic mediator between Aldo and his destiny, lives in Maremma, a city described as "la Venise des Syrtes," built on marshes, where land and waters intermingle.

No fictional topography would be complete without the structures superimposed by man on nature. Architecture and buildings play an essential role in Gracq. In *Au château d'Argol*, as the title indicates, the castle is as much a persona as the mystical triangle of Heide, Herminien, and Albert. The symbiosis between the humans and the edifice is reminiscent of "The Fall of the House of Usher" and of the Gothic novels by Horace Walpole and Ann Radcliffe. As important is the so-called *chapelle des abîmes*, where Herminien and Albert find the objects associated with the Grail legend. The Gothic intertext is also at work, more indirectly, in the long descriptions of the Syrtes fortress. A living thing, a sentinel of stone watching over the horizon of Farghestan, the fortress bears within itself the first intimations of Aldo's destiny. Like a sanctuary, it contains a forbidden "inner sanctum," the "chambre des cartes," where Marino has hidden the maps of Farghestan, as if to exorcise their dangerous talismanic power. Aldo, expectedly, finds his way thereto, through dark complicated corridors. Even in *Un balcon en forêt*, the bunker of Les Falizes functions as a nerve center, although the forest is the overpowering presence in the novel. Characterized as a "piège à cons" by an army officer visiting Grange and his friends, the bunker is indeed a trap, albeit a cozy one, a deceptive shelter in which this group of soldiers of the "drôle de guerre" will indulge for a while under the illusion that they can escape the nightmare of history, until Guderian's Panzers break through the supposedly impenetrable forest.

Whether they are natural or man-made, Gracq is obviously fascinated with locations that mark the border between two worlds and, at a higher level, two realities. Both the fortress of the Syrtes and the bunker in the Ardennes are the most advanced outposts of a cultural territory— Orsenna or the Allies—in which a character is waiting for an ultimate encounter with the Other. A particular spatial symbolism is contained in the very titles of some of his texts, through words like "rivage," "balcon," "presqu'île," which indicate a point of contact, an intersection of two domains.

Roads and pathways are also key elements in Gracq's fantasmatic topography. The short story entitled "La Route" is exemplary of this poetic treatment: nothing happens in this brief remnant of an aborted novel, where description reigns supreme. A group of riders is traveling along an ancient paved road, partially destroyed and buried, cutting through fields, forests, deserted villages. This road, evoked through a constellation of metaphors, is magnified to become a sign of the deepest meanings of existence: as a pathway, it indicates the "sens," both as direction and meaning.

Time in the Gracquian world is both future-oriented and circular. The present is determined by the "minor apocalypse" looming over the horizon of a not too distant future, an event that brings destruction but also revelation, in keeping with the original meaning of the Greek. In *Le Rivage des Syrtes* and *Un balcon en forêt*, this event is the outbreak of the hostilities that will turn these funny wars into "serious" ones. In *Un beau ténébreux*, it is Allan's carefully planned suicide. The day he has set for it, materialized by a mark on a calendar discovered in his hotel room, functions as the eye of a psychological hurricane that devastates the lives of nearly all those who approach him during his final months at the

Hôtel des Vagues. Like a black hole, this point in the future when time will stop for him sucks in the present and gives the key to his enigma. The mesmerizing radiance of this man is explained by the control he now has over his life: having decided how and when he will die enables him to be above the common fears and limitations of mankind. Thus he can lose huge sums of money at the casino without apparent emotion. One may wonder whether Gracq, who acknowledged *La Condition humaine* as a great novel, has not been impressed by Malraux's view that death—especially when it is chosen—"transforme la vie en destin."

But if individual time always seems to be determined by the magnetic attraction of a capital virtuality in the future, historical time is definitely cyclical in Gracq's world. Thus, in *Au château d'Argol,* the mystic drama of the Grail story transcends historical time. It unfolds in an eternal present and will time and again upset the lives of those who seek to conquer its mystery. As for *Le Rivage des Syrtes,* Gracq admits, in one of his rare moments of self-analysis, that it is a parable about "l'esprit de l'histoire,"[4] or the forces that drive its long-term cycles. He acknowledges Oswald Spengler as his main inspiration for a cyclical view of the rise and fall of civilizations, which the old Machiavellian archon of Orsenna expounds in these terms: "Un état ne meurt pas, ce n'est qu'une forme qui se défait. Un faisceau qui se dénoue. Et il vient un moment où ce qui a été lié aspire à se délier, et la forme trop précise à rentrer dans l'indistinction. Et quand l'heure est venue, j'appelle cela une chose désirable et bonne. Cela s'appelle mourir de sa *bonne mort*" (p. 835).

Gracq's modes of thought are definitely initiatic. Every element of his fiction fits within the powerful mechanism of a quest for ultimate meanings. As in the myth of Acteon, the vision of the naked truth, being a transgression, will inevitably bring death. But the price to pay for knowledge is accepted. The would-be initiates instinctively know that there is no way back, and they undertake without hesitation what Allan calls "le voyage sans retour de la révélation" (p. 146). As they come closer to the locus of their epiphany, they have a sense that their destiny is being fulfilled. Says Aldo, as he arrives by night (this, of course, is no accident) at the Syrtes: "je me baignais pour la première fois dans ces nuits du Sud inconnues d'Orsenna, comme dans une eau initiatique. Quelque chose m'était promis, quelque chose m'était dévoilé; j'entrais sans éclaircissement aucun dans une intimité presque angoissante . . . comme on s'avance les yeux bandés vers le lieu de la révélation" (p. 565).

As if to prepare them for this esoteric quest, Gracq frees his male protagonists from the usual burdens and attachments of life within society. This is how he ironically describes his typical protagonist in an often cited passage of *Lettrines:*

Lieu de naissance: non précisé
Date de naissance: inconnue
Nationalité: frontalière
Parents: éloignés
Etat civil: célibataire
Enfants à charge: néant
Profession: sans
Activités: en vacances
Situation militaire: marginale
Moyens d'existence: hypothétiques
Domicile: n'habitent jamais chez eux
Résidences secondaires: mer et forêt (p. 35)

The role of female characters is no less essential in Gracq's fiction. Femininity, for Gracq, means mystery. This is most explicit in one of the short stories of *La Presqu'île,* entitled "Le Roi Cophetua," after a famous painting by Dante Gabriel Rossetti. A World War I aviator visits the house of his friend Nueil, who is absent and perhaps dead. There he meets his silent and subservient maid. After serving him dinner, she shows him to his guestroom and quite naturally offers herself to him. The next morning, oppressed by the silence and dereliction of this house and its ghostlike servant, he leaves. The brief encounter causes him to reflect on female nature, which is "une énigme, une question pure" (p. 238).

The nameless maidservant in "Le Roi Cophetua" possesses the three characteristics of the Gracquian woman: she is enigmatic, she fulfills the narratological function of "auxiliary" to the male protagonist, and, most important, she acts as an emissary of another dimension of reality, inaccessible to rational inquiry or straightforward action. She belongs to what anthropologist Gilbert Durand calls the "nocturnal" order, while man is "diurnal."[5] In other terms, being more in tune than the male with the "other side," she is a necessary mediator between the "hero" and the object of his quest.

Although nearly all Gracquian women possess this last, fundamental attribute, they are not as self-effaced as this character. Heide, in *Au château d'Argol,* could also be characterized as a "passive" mediator, but the Mona of *Un balcon en forêt,* and even more so the Vanessa of *Le Rivage des Syrtes* are very "active" in their initiation of the male hero. Sex is an element of this initiatic process: the female "mediator" reveals something of the "other side" to the male protagonist by making him share her intimacy, for she is not only the door into the nocturnal realm of life, she is herself this realm, to a certain degree. Yves Bridel, who devotes a whole chapter to female characters in *Julien Gracq et la dynamique de l'imaginaire,* is right to stress that it is always thanks to a woman that the hero can penetrate into this new world, "dont la femme est reine, mais où elle ne peut régner que par l'homme qu'elle initie."[6] The Celtologist Jean Markale has linked Gracq's whole feminine mythology to the ancient Celts' concept of women as intermediate between men and the unseen.[7] The only exception to this rule would be found in *Un beau ténébreux,* where Allan, contrary to most of Gracq's male protagonists, seems to be complete in himself, not needing a high priestess to show him the way through the underworld with a golden bough.

In conclusion, we must admit that this short study will necessarily fall short of opening all the secret doors of Gracq's labyrinth. It provides only some essential keys. Gracq is indeed a "continuing tradition" in French letters: he represents one of the last believers in the magic powers of language, and of fiction as mythmaking.

Notes

1. Julien Gracq, *The Opposing Shore,* trans. Richard Howard (New York: Columbia University Press, 1987).

2. Hervé Cain, "Conversation avec Julien Gracq," *Givre,* no. 1 (1986), p. 24.

3. Maurice Blanchot, "Grève désolée, obscur malaise," *Givre,* no. 1 (1986), p. 50.

4. Gracq, *En lisant, en écrivant* (Paris: José Corti, 1981), p. 216.

5. Gilbert Durand, *L'Imagination symbolique* (Paris: PUF, 1964), pp. 94–95.

6. Yves Bridel, *Julien Gracq et la dynamique de l'imaginaire* (Lausanne: L'Age d'Homme, 1981), p. 85.

7. Jean Markale, "Julien Gracq ou le Celte janséniste," *Givre,* no. 1 (1986).

Bibliography

Works by Julien Gracq

Œuvres complètes. Vol. I, edited and with an introduction by Bernhild Boie. Paris: Gallimard ("La Pléiade"), 1989. This volume contains all the works published between 1938 and 1954, plus *Préférences*. Those cited in this chapter, with the page numbers corresponding to this edition, are: (1) *Au château d'Argol*, (2) *Un beau ténébreux*, (3) *Liberté grande*, (4) *Le Roi pêcheur*, (5) *André Breton. Quelques aspects de l'écrivain*, (6) *La Littérature à l'estomac*, (7) *Le Rivage des Syrtes*, (8) *Préférences*. For the works published afterward, a second Pléiade volume is still in preparation. The references to these works are taken from the original José Corti editions. *Au château d'Argol* was translated by Louise Varese as *The Castle of Argol* (Venice, CA: Lapis Press, 1991); *Le Rivage des Syrtes* was translated by Richard Howard as *The Opposing Shore* (New York: Columbia University Press, 1987).

Un balcon en forêt. Paris: José Corti, 1958. Translated by Richard Howard as *Balcony in the Forest*. New York: Columbia University Press, 1987.

Lettrines I. Paris: José Corti, 1967.

La Presqu'île. Paris: José Corti, 1970.

Lettrines II. Paris: José Corti, 1974.

Les Eaux étroites. Paris: José Corti, 1976.

En lisant, en écrivant. Paris: José Corti, 1981.

La Forme d'une ville. Paris: José Corti, 1985.

Autour des sept collines. Paris: José Corti, 1992.

Carnets du grand chemin. Paris: José Corti, 1992.

Secondary Critical Works

Amossy, Ruth. *Les Jeux de l'allusion littérature dans 'Un beau ténébreux' de Julien Gracq*. Neuchâtel: La Baconnière, 1980.

―――. *Parcours symbolique chez Julien Gracq: 'Le Rivage des Syrtes'*. Paris: CDU-SEDES, 1982.

Berthier, Philippe. *Julien Gracq critique d'un certain usage de la littérature*. Lyon: Presses Universitaires de Lyon, 1990.

Borgal, Clément. *Julien Gracq: l'écrivain et les sortilèges*. Paris: Presses Universitaires de la France, 1993.

Bridel, Yves. *Julien Gracq et la dynamique de l'imaginaire*. Lausanne: L'Age d'Homme, 1981.

Cahiers de l'Herne, no. 20 (1972). Special issue on Julien Gracq.

Cardonne-Arlyck, Elisabeth. *La Métaphore raconte. Pratique de Julien Gracq*. Paris: Klincksieck, 1984.

Carrière, Jean. *Julien Gracq. Qui êtes-vous?* Lyon: La Manufacture, 1986.

Cesbron, Georges. "Etat des recherches." In *Actes du Colloque International Julien Gracq, May 21–24 1981*. Angers: Presses Universitaires d'Angers, 1981.

Dobbs, Annie-Claude. *Dramaturgie et liturgie dans l'œuvre de Julien Gracq*. Paris: José Corti, 1972.

Francis, Marie. *Forme et signification de l'attente chez Julien Gracq*. Paris: Nizet, 1979.

Givre, no. 1 (1986). Special issue on Julien Gracq.

Grossman, Simone. *Julien Gracq et le surréalisme*. Paris: José Corti, 1980.

Hoy, Peter. *Julien Gracq, essai de bibliographie 1938–1972*. London: Grant and Cutler, 1973.

———. *Julien Gracq, œuvres et critique 1988–1990*. Paris: Lettres Modernes [Revue des Lettres Modernes, no. 1093–1095], 1992.

Leutrat, Jean-Louis. *Julien Gracq*. Paris: Editions Universitaires, 1967.

Marot, Patrick. "Plénitude et effacement de l'écriture gracquienne." *Revue des Lettres Modernes*, no. 1000–1006 (1991): 125–74.

Murat, Michel. *'Le Rivage des Syrtes': Etude de style*. 2 vols. Paris: José Corti, 1982.

———. *Julien Gracq*. Paris: Pierre Belfond, 1991.

Vouilloux, Bernard. *Mimesis: sacrifice et carnaval dans la fiction gracquienne*. Paris: Lettres Modernes, 1991.

———. *De la peinture au texte. L'Image dans l'œuvre de Julien Gracq*. Genève: Droz, 1989.

4

Marguerite Duras

Thomas Broden

Marguerite Duras's works privilege the temporal figures of duration, repetition, and the moment; haunted by the past, the typical Durassian character is neither engaged in the present nor thrown to the future by any compelling project. Dynamic processes such as development, change, and renewal start up but tend to deviate, dissipate, or turn back on themselves, able to pose questions and point to problems but rarely to resolve them. The characters frequently seem unwilling or unable to envisage a narrative time of transformation, exhibiting an "incompréhension des causes, [une] ignorance des raisons."[1] The threatened eclipse of these temporal dimensions fundamental to narrative can make Duras's writing seem to negate time itself,[2] to stray from novelistic development and dramatic resolution and arrive instead at a poetic contemplation, a lyrical *écriture* in between or beyond genres. Her treatment of temporality resonates with an essential inertia in the texts; lacking compelling projects or engaging relationships, characters find themselves alienated from their milieu and cut off from action in the world. Interpreted in all its polysemic ramifications, the French phrase "le temps de l'ennui" sums up these key features of her work, configured differently at various stages of her career. Appearing at once as the characterized condition of modernism and as the peculiar mode of Duras's expression, ennui threatens to suspend the subject's desire for change in both the private and the public spheres.

    The time of ennui designates the kind of time many Durassian subjects have: neither a pleasant nor a harrowing time, but one marked by the passions peculiar to ennui. To be metaphorically "on Durassian time" is to enter the world of ennui evoked in her fiction, to lodge in the emotional niche created by her works. In early texts the ennui ranges from the restless boredom of *L'Après-midi de Monsieur Andesmas*'s eponymous hero to the stagnation of *Les Petits Chevaux de Tarquinia*'s vacationers and *Moderato cantabile*'s Anne Desbaresdes. In later works a graver listlessness, detachment, and spiritual emptiness inhabit the cosmopolitan elite of *Le Vice-consul,* as a clinical melancholy afflicts Alissa of *Détruire dit-elle,* the mother of *L'Amant,* and the trio of *L'Amour.* Older acceptations of ennui—sorrow—and "s'ennuyer de quelqu'un"—to suffer from someone's absence—also find deep resonance with the works, in which losing a beloved can provoke the sadness that permeates *Le Navire Night* and *L'Homme atlantique,* the grief and covetous desire of the hero in *Les Yeux bleus cheveux noirs,* or the depression of Lol V. Stein and the heroine of *Hiroshima mon amour.* The loss and its attendant ennui determine temporal structures in the texts, producing specific narrative "temps de l'ennui." Earlier Duras novels stage a recurrent atmospheric environment of ennui, moreover, defining a meteorological "temps de l'ennui" (le temps = weather). In its different acceptations, "le temps de l'ennui" colors both inner and outer worlds, permeates subjects and settings, and affects even description and lighting in the texts and their relation to the characters' emotional climate. Exploring the potentialities of the phrase leads one to unfolding layers of the Durassian œuvre.

The *Robert* dictionary defines the expression "s'ennuyer de quelqu'un" thus: "(vieilli, régional) souffrir de son absence" and glosses the former sense of the noun "ennui" as: "tristesse profonde, grand chagrin." Carol Murphy has demonstrated the central importance of absence in the novels of Marguerite Duras and initiated its analysis;[3] many of Duras's works turn precisely on a structure comprising the loss of a loved one resulting in an acute sorrow. The absence of the beloved can result in a severe depression, which forms the extreme end of the Durassian spectrum of ennui. Lol V. Stein collapses and goes into depression some time after being abandoned by her fiancé in *Le Ravissement de Lol V. Stein.* The protagonist of *Les Yeux bleus cheveux noirs* gives free reign to utter narcissistic collapse and crying as he mourns the loss of the stranger with blue eyes and black hair. In both of these texts, the loss is positioned near the outset of the story; in *Un Barrage contre le Pacifique,* it is at the end of the work that her son's apparent definitive departure drives the mother to a similar state. The adolescent heroine of *Hiroshima mon amour* hibernates in the cellar and the bedroom in a depressed state after the trauma of her German lover's death; the sequestration occurs toward the end of the first diptych in the film. Whereas she emerges, phoenixlike, from the ashes of the mourning, the man in *Yeux bleus* makes no break with the past, Lol resembles as much a zombie as a renewed spirit, and the fictional mother of *Un Barrage* undergoes no process of rejuvenation.

The prostration associated with the grief cuts the temporal development of the text, while the abandonment can function as a key element determining the narrative structure of the entire work. The T. Beach scene of desertion and substitution functions as the point of origin for Jacques Hold's portrait of passionate Lol; the entire complex explanatory edifice he constructs refers back to this founding moment. His tale of Lol begins when Anne-Marie Stretter enters the scene accompanied by her daughter, or, as he says: "Je vais donc la [Lol V. Stein] chercher, je la prends, là où je crois devoir le faire, au moment où elle me paraît commencer à bouger pour venir à ma rencontre, au moment précis où les dernières venues, deux femmes, franchissent la porte de la salle de bal du Casino municipal de T. Beach" (p. 14). Abandoned by Michael Richardson, Lol experiences an emotional and symbolic accident (she neglects to suffer), which determines the rest of her development and interactions. The voyeurism and the erotic triangle established in that primal textual scene reassert themselves throughout the narrative as the privileged frameworks in which she will seek transcendance, and as the key architectural figure of the book. The scene of abandonment and the resultant symbolic structures are revisited above all in crucial closing scenes that seem to offer Lol a chance to give events the shape of a recovery narrative and that instead produce repetition in fascination and a new crisis. The novel's narrative configuration as well as Lol's libidinal economy—as portrayed by the narrator and character Doctor Jacques Hold[4]—are governed by the mechanisms of absence and grief.

The beginning and ending of *Yeux bleus* are similarly ordered by a double loss recounted in the opening pages. Both the female and the male protagonists lose the object of their desire when the foreigner with blue eyes and black hair departs; the nighttime mourning scene in the café is at once where the protagonists meet and where the form of their subsequent interaction is established. The loss, with its accompanying mourning process, informs and controls the entire narrative. Just as the

setting of the original observed encounter in the Hôtel des Roches remains the setting for the rest of the play, verbally described as an unfur-
nished bedroom and not as a hotel lobby with mahogany tables and
chairs on stage, so too does the moment of that first encounter prevent
time from moving on to any other meaningful activity. The initial encounters remain the lived temporal framework of the text. The interaction between the woman and the man in the room never denies the original time of narcissistic mourning and heightened emotional expression.
The love the two share for the foreigner remains their true bond: "C'était
cet amour, celui pleuré par eux deux ce soir-là, qui était leur véritable
fidélité à l'un l'autre, cela au-delà de leur histoire présente, et de celles à
venir dans leurs vies" (p. 146). *Yeux bleus* plays with introducing the
original scene at the end of the text to bring the work full circle on the
model of *Lol V. Stein*. After the narrator performs a spatial scene of recognition identifying the stage setting with the Hôtel des Roches lobby,
the work flirts with having the characters themselves recognize who
they are with respect to the roles of the initial scene. In this case, however, the text is left asymmetrical by refusing the closure: "Il lui dit qu'un
seul et même jeune étranger était cause de leur désespoir ce soir-là au
bord de la mer . . . elle dit que non, qu'il leur est impossible de savoir ce
qui s'était passé, qu'ils étaient comme dans les crimes les témoins qui
avaient oublié de regarder" (pp. 146–47). The loss of the beloved at the
outset of the text conditions the temporality of the entire narrative, and
the narrative itself is constructed on the basis that a first moment of loss
generates a story. Whereas the man remains circumscribed by the imaginary confines of the liminal gaze and abandonment, the woman endeavors to construct a new symbolic framework, which results at least in the
fictional product offered to the reader.

"Le temps de l'ennui" also thematizes recurrent weather patterns
in the Durassian texts, which force their oppressive atmosphere on the
characters. The incipit of *Les Petits Chevaux de Tarquinia* establishes its
torpid climate: "Sara se leva tard. Il était un peu plus de dix heures. La
chaleur était là, égale à elle-même. Il fallait toujours quelques secondes
chaque matin pour se souvenir qu'on était là pour passer des vacances"
(p. 9). The book's opening can recall that of Marcel Proust's *A la recherche du temps perdu*, in which the narrator announces his early-to-bed routine, then proceeds to tell of waking up and requiring several moments
to get his bearings in space and time. This pristine, elemental waking

moment, a pure present not yet inserted in the narrative of the subject's past, serves as the exemplary point of departure for Poulet's study of Proustian time.[5] The female protagonist of Tarquinia gets up late; her naive present is occupied entirely by the excruciating heat, before she can entertain the thought that the heat is an elected torture for her August vacation. The harsh sun, especially the August Mediterranean sun, beats on the characters of "La Douleur," of *Le Marin de Gibraltar* and *Tarquinia*, and of *Dix heures et demie du soir en été* and *L'Après-midi de Monsieur Andesmas*. The violent heat stifles action, strains relationships, and provokes inertia and boredom. The ennui of focus in the texts of the 1950s represents that luxury typical of affluent society on vacation or in retirement. Unlike the persistent pattern of loss and grieving, the stifling heat, like the ennui it bears, will be left behind by the characters as they move on to another phase.

The nonsituated, third-person narrator of *Tarquinia* decribes the Italian seaside village, an "endroit infernal" as Sara lives it the first morning of the book: "Seul le bourdonnement des frelons autour des fleurs dérangeait l'air épais, sirupeux, du matin. Et le soleil ne brillait pas, étouffé qu'il était par l'épaisse brume qui enserrait le ciel dans un carcan de fer. Il n'y avait rien à faire, ici, les livres fondaient dans les mains. Et les histoires tombaient en pièces sous les coups sombres et silencieux des frelons à l'affût. Oui, la chaleur lacérait le cœur. Et seule lui résistait, entière, vierge, l'envie de la mer" (pp. 22–23). The weight of the air, the "iron grip" of the morning mist immobilize the characters; the heavy heat turns solids to liquids, defied only by the already aqueous sea. "Les histoires tombaient en pièces": the joints and clasps that hold the stories/affairs together dissolve, allowing the fragments to fall away; so with the book Sara is reading, as with her marriage. As she shrugs off the affectionate grasp of Jacques, he asks her:

> —Tu t'ennuies? C'est ça?
> Elle ne répondit pas.
> — C'est ça ou autre chose?
> — C'est ça. Je m'ennuie, dit Sara.
> — Moi aussi, je m'ennuie beaucoup, dit-il. Il ajouta: Et de quoi t'ennuies-tu?
> Elle se redressa et essaya de lui sourire.
> — Je ne sais pas très bien. (*Tarquinia*, p. 68)

In this scene ennui functions at least in part as a screen Sara uses to avoid raising other issues.

The August heat of Florence beats down in similar fashion on the male narrator of *Gibraltar:* "ce jour fut le plus chaud de la canicule. Le goudron des rues était en bouillie. On se déplaçait comme dans le sirop des cauchemars. Les tempes battaient, les poumons brûlaient" (p. 49). All day long the narrator's thoughts are occupied by his female friend of whom he is becoming aware for the first time since they met, and with whom he will soon break. At night her person is associated with the oppressive heat: "Je ne pouvais plus faire la part de la chaleur de la ville et celle de sa chaleur à elle" (p. 48).

In an insightful study, Danielle Bajomée defines the quintessential temporality in Duras as a moment cut off from any duration or process: "Les créatures de Duras ne sont qu'une conscience aiguë de l'instant, de sa précarité et de son intensité."[6] Much like the Proustian present *hors temps* identified by Poulet, Bajomé's Durassian moment figures as a dramatic epiphany at the expense of any vectorial, linear time. For the critic, the defining instant is purely phenomenological and represents a sudden and ultimately atemporal revelation of being; the Durassian text thus seeks to "ranimer l'intemporel, cette qualité de présence qui escamoterait les accidents de la durée en ressuscitant le frémissement, l'instantanéité du jaillissement de l'être, la sauvagerie d'un moment singulier" (p. 111). The preceding discussion leads to developing or amending Bajomée's observation by noting, first, that such a moment often contrasts sharply with a *duration* central to the texts[7] and, second, that many important Durassian texts juxtapose at least two distinctive "moments"—be they instants or durations—where the collocation triggers a dialectical impetus and not stasis. *Gibraltar* thus counterpoises to the above evocation of torrid heat the narrator's nocturnal waking fantasy, making up the first euphoric scenario that comes in response to the dysphoric ennui. At this early point, the scenario highlights cool flowing water—an escape from the heat—and a silent swim with a male acquaintance: an escape from the woman, and from women in general. The fantasy has its roots in descriptions the acquaintance gave of the seaside Italian town Rocca traversed by a river, La Magra:

C'est alors que chaque nuit, un même fleuve m'apparaissait.
Il était grand. Il était glacé, vierge de toute trace de femme. Je

l'appelais doucement la Magra. Ce nom à lui seul me ra-
fraîchissait le cœur. Nous étions seuls, lui, ce chauffeur, et
moi. Il n'y avait personne dans le paysage que nous deux . . .
c'était un long samedi. Le ciel était couvert. De temps en temps
nous nagions côte à côte dans un univers inconnu, d'une verte
et sombre phosphorescence . . . nous ne parlions pas, nous ne
nous disions rien, aucun besoin n'en faisait sentir. (*Gibraltar*,
p. 48)

The passage links the water's icy bracing quality to the virginal exclusion of women. The long, lingering character of the time associated with
ennui subsists even in the contradictory euphoric scenario: the day chosen is a Saturday, whose midday traditionally begins the French weekend, and it is a "long" Saturday. Clouds veil the sun, source of torment,
and diving down to the depths of the river gives access to an aqueous
alternative to the harsh surface.

At the depths of the river, male silence replaces the chattiness of
the female companion. In the voluptuous images of escape, an all-consuming desire inscribes itself in the sprawled, spread-out, slowed-down
time: "Pendant trois nuits, ce samedi se prolongea. Interminable. Inépuisable. Le désir que j'avais d'être près de lui, sur les berges du fleuve
ou dans le fleuve, était tel qu'il éteignait tout autre désir" (*Gibraltar*, p.
48). The alternative and opposite moment possesses a scope and weight
comparable to the first. The topography of Rocca–La Magra parallels
that of the Italian vacation site of *Tarquinia:* fresh and salt water, river
and sea, a small seaside village, mountains dominating the coast (*Gibraltar*, pp. 19–20). In *Tarquinia* as well, the cool water stands as the respite from the heat. The motorboat excursion *cum* swim at La Pointa
Bianca reiterates the same underwater universe, a cool, blue-green wa-
tery alternative to the punishing earth:

Le fond de la mer semblait très proche, il brillait comme un
clair de lune parfois traversé des rayures vertes du jour . . .
c'était l'envers du monde. Une nuit lumineuse et calme vous
portait, foisonnante des algues calmes et glacées du silence.
La course des poissons striait son épaisseur d'insaisissables
percées. De loin en loin, la vie apparemment cessait. Alors
des gouffres nus et vides apparaissaient. Une ombre bleue

s'en élevait, délicieuse, qui était celle d'une pure et indécelable
profondeur, aussi probante sans doute de la vie que le spectacle même de la mort. (*Tarquinia*, pp. 152–54)

The man who desires Sara and with whom she will spend a night forms
part of the euphoric water thematics: "Cet homme avait un corps fluide,
un peu fragile même, et brun, fait pour la mer" (p. 25); he is initially
known as the man with the motorboat. The weather of Duras's ennui
contrasts with and quite nearly reverses the typical meteorology of
Baudelairean and Laforgean spleen. The torrid summer Mediterranean
sun that hurts the eyes, beats on the head, and enervates the body replaces the rain and low-lying gray clouds over the city. Cool alcoholic
drinks provide an artificial paradise, a cultural reflex of the dominant
natural escape from the heat in the Durassian works, menthe à l'eau for
the *Gibraltar* narrator and bitter Campari for Sara, Diana, and the others
in *Tarquinia*.

The time of ennui in these texts stems from the regular repetition
of the same: the quoted opening of *Tarquinia* is repeated word for word
the second morning, the heat returning as relentlessly as the child in *Le
Square*. The endlessly deferred ending of the side plot, in which the
mother refuses to confront her son's death, causes the languid, repeti-
tive, insignificant gestures of the French vacationers to appear all the
more desultory. The relief envisaged in the euphoric fantasy of the
Gibraltar narrator entails stopping the return of the same by opening up
a hole in time ("Pendant trois nuits, ce samedi se prolongea. Interminable. Inépuisable," p. 48). Yet the Durassian texts break the lyric stases
of the moment and the dichotomy by sketching the attempt at a narrative reversal of fortunes, underscoring the dynamism inherent in the
contrastive vision to ennui in the texts. The novels thus entail several
crucial, interrelated moments, not just one; in both *Gibraltar* and *Tarquinia*,
the seemingly atemporal moment is already a carnival escape and a dialectical response to the eleven-month workaday grind regimented by
work and schedules. The heat follows a prior event: the character leaves
work and home and departs on vacation. The subsequent ennui already
mingles with an attendant willingness to entertain alternatives to the
status quo. The new, contrasting vision of relief through water and cool-
ness leads in turn to the attempt at or the temptation of a decisive event
such as a significant decision or encounter, an event that takes shape

through but also against the backdrop of the preceding ennui. Through voyages and quests, fugues and getaways, spatio-temporal movement often translates the dynamic impetus, whether escapist as on the motor-boat of *Tarquinia*, escapist and utopian as on the yacht of *Gibraltar*, or potentially therapeutic and corrective as in the envisioned departure for Tarquinia. The Durassian texts at the same time stage and trope spatio-temporal movement, as they present and quote narrative succession as explanation when Peter Morgan of *Le Vice-consul* and Jacques Hold of *Lol V. Stein* elaborate their matrices generative of women.

Artifice doubles with natural settings to prod the subjects into leaving ennui and initiating an alternative. The *Gibraltar* narrator makes his major decision, experiences some lucidity, and resolves to embrace honesty upon contemplating a fresco, Giotto's *Annunciation* in Florence. Sara too makes her significant decision—to stay with her husband—and hopes to reconstruct an intimacy armed with a new lucidity upon gazing at the frescos at Tarquinia. The characters perceive wisdom in the ciphered aesthetic beauty as so many other Durassian characters find emotional significance in piano playing and chamber music. The texts manifest perhaps not so much an "oubli du devenir, pour laisser scintiller la splendeur originaire de l'être, dans le fantasme du figé," as Bajomée affirms,[8] but rather the uncertain struggle of becoming against the force of the inert, atemporal moment.

Other Durassian novels of the 1950s stage an inactive time, a temporality that is a nontime, a suspension of real time to follow afterward or that is already past. In *L'Après-midi de Monsieur Andesmas* the motif of waiting controls the time of the novel. The text is practically free of temporal ellipsis, analepsis, or other figure, so that the time of reading would quite nearly match the time of action. Throughout the entire book, Andesmas awaits the arrival of a character with whom he has an appointment. *Dix heures et demie du soir en été* illustrates a similar time of waiting, while juxtaposing that waiting to a point in time where the decisive event occurs, ten-thirty one summer night. *Hiroshima* constructs a cyclical time, a time that repeats instead of moving beyond; forgetfulness stalks memory and indirectly deflates the importance one can attribute to the present.

A break in the pattern of Duras's "temps de l'ennui" comes in the 1960s and 1970s, when a much more somber view of ennui emerges in the India cycle. The treatment maintains similarities with the preceding period but reverses the proportions and the "rapport de forces" of the key ingredients. The characters live, rather than vacation in, a climate they find sweltering (Calcutta). As in *La Guerre de Troie n'aura pas lieu*, the works' central, decisive event does not take place: the heroine Anne-Marie Stretter declines the Vice-Consul's offer of love (*Le Vice-consul* and *India Song*) as Lol V. Stein fails to suffer jealousy; in the transitional *Moderato cantabile*, action is arrested as soon as broached, as is the characters' kiss. These texts inaugurate an escalation of ennui. The *Robert's* third definition of ennui—"impression de vide, de lassitude crée par le désœuvrement, par une occupation monotone ou dépourvue d'intérêt"—provides a fair characterization of ennui in the Durassian texts from the 1950s. The formulation compares with the fourth definition proposed in the *Robert*: "mélancolie vague, lassitude morale qui fait qu'on ne prend d'intérêt, de plaisir à rien." A first difference between the two stems from a contrast in intensity: "mélancolie" replaces the milder "impression de vide." More important, however, the relation of cause and effect is reversed from one definition to the next: whereas in the third it is an event ("désœuvrement," "occupation monotone") that determines the sentiment of ennui, in the fourth it is endemic ennui that determines events ("on ne prend plaisir à rien"). In the first case, a specific situation causes an impermanent dejection, while in the second, a lasting melancholy without particular cause expresses itself in an inability to interest oneself in anything: "L'ennui, ici, c'est un sentiment d'abandon colossal, à la mesure de l'Inde elle-même, ce pays donne le ton" (*Le Vice-consul*, p. 116). *Le Vice-consul* describes the life of the white colonial women in India: "Les femmes, pour la plupart, ont la peau blanche de recluses. Elles vivent volets clos à l'abri du soleil-qui-tue, elles ne font presque rien aux Indes, elles sont regardées, heureuses ce soir, sorties de chez elles, en France aux Indes" (*Le Vice-consul*, p. 100). The heroine, Anne-Marie Stretter, incarnates this inactivity and exhaustion; she suggests to her friends "ne faisons rien," upon which they proceed to spend their time drinking champagne (*Le Vice-consul*, p. 136). In the film *India Song* the excessive slowness of the characters' delivery, gestures, and movements expresses in particularly dramatic fashion the listlessness of the characters, the slowness of time, and the lack of action. Similarly, many of Duras's later male characters make love too slowly (the man in the hotel in *Yeux bleus*, for example).

Kristeva situates this Durassian ennui in the field of melancholy and depression, connecting the author to postwar, post-concentration-camp, nuclear-age apocalyptic thinking.[9] Durassian melancholy inscribes silence in the text,[10] reduces the message of discourse to the conclusion that there is nothing to say, and stalls time by reproducing mirror images of characters in the texts. The radical developments undergone by Alissa and Elisa in *Détruire dit-elle* are thus taken out of narrative time and structured instead as repetition and circularity since Elisa becomes (like) Alissa and Alissa (like) Elisa. *Moderato cantabile* similarly makes Anne Desbaresdes tentatively seek to echo an earlier heroine rather than strike out in new directions of her own. The traumas of the second half of the twentieth century provoke a suffering in Duras that determines a new expression of the socio-historical moment as an inner experience of pain and not as a situation chronicled in (external, official) history.[11] *Hiroshima* already points to Duras's strategy of reworking the public/ private interface: the film emphasizes the subjective experience of history as it impinges from the present moment, but also from the past through memory and repetition. The script and the filmic writing also emphasize the woman's struggle to affirm herself as a historical and historiographic subject.[12] The *Aurélia Steiner* series similarly juxtaposes, then interweaves the holocaust past and the present of suffering.

In the texts of this period, the temporal moment is conjoined to waiting, in turn often linked to watching. The works disperse the instant, as *Le Vice-consul* and most strikingly *India Song* spread the embassy reception over a long textual expanse, and throughout a multitude of variously elaborated characters, some central figures such as Anne-Marie Stretter and Charles Rossett, others the "on dit" that prefigure the voices of the film and play. The focal temporal point in *Le Vice-consul* and *India Song* occurs when the vice-consul from Lahore screams out to stay with Anne-Marie Stretter for the evening, the moment Duras implicitly evokes in her summary of *India Song*: "l'histoire est une histoire d'amour immobilisée dans la culminance de la passion" (*India Song*, p. 148). Yet even this absolute, determining instant finds its signification in that other, unending durative time that serves as the backdrop informing and defining the drama of the individuals: the horror of famine and leprosy.

The works construct the temporality of "too late," of "after the fact." "Très vite dans ma vie il a été trop tard," muses the narrator of *L'Amant* (p. 9), recalling a physical loss of youth and freshness in her face even before any events that would have inflicted a sense of loss or sorrow. This lingering time after the critical moment, at "the end of the world,"[13]

takes over *India Song:* after the characters have died, after the civilization that they epitomized has become extinct, and after the personal
dramas of the individuals are no more than whispered legends and viti-
ated, altered fragments of stories and gossip, the text begins. The Anne-
Marie Stretter character establishes this time, as indeed the entire *dramatis
personæ* represent ambulatory sculptures, monuments to their characters. *L'Amour* communicates the apocalyptic moment in a form resembling the science fiction time of "after the great conflict" destructive of
civilization. In the text, S. Thala—the hometown of Lol V. Stein—is burning and the beach is in flames; all the characters of *Lol V. Stein* reappear
in *L'Amour* reduced to hollow shells, amnesiacs, emotionally broken and
suicidal; the hotel is almost deserted, as if condemned. The works dra-
matize the end of things, dwelling on the moments of their agony, death,
and commemoration.

Certain Durassian texts show a comparable treatment of time and
maintain the narrative configurations of inaction, but invert the thematics
of ennui by entertaining utopian visions of peace, leisure, and quiet communication, which Kristeva's tragic portrait of the author and œuvre
fails to address. The tranquility of the two female friends in *Nathalie
Granger* stands as a positive counterpoint to the ennui of the preceding
works. Lingering scenes such as the clearing of the breakfast table and
the silent, rhythmed performance of daytime tasks parallel the drawn-
out time of the moment and highlight a lack of critical action and conflict, but convey a warmth generated by the interaction between the two
women. Opposed not to ennui but to danger and violence, to selling
and commercialism, this quiet, women's time resembles a subdued lack
of pain more than the *jouissance* of the sea. The *farniente* of the hotel-
sanatorium in *Détruire dit-elle* again presents a wry but upbeat version
of killing time and doing nothing. The problems faced by the group lack
the dark edge of the brooding Durassian texts; the general comfort with
the open relationships defuses some of the impetus to repression present
in earlier works. These genial fictional scenes parallel the serene encounters evoked by Xavière Gauthier in her preface to *Les Parleuses,* in which
she speaks of spending the summer with Duras conversing and making
jam.

The ennui of the earlier texts abates when the status quo is reaf-
firmed (*Tarquinia*) or bracketed (*Gibraltar*); the underlying resignation to
(or confidence in) order neutralizes ennui in the same way as it defines

critique as irony, and change as respite, escape, and fantasy. The works of Duras's mid-career radicalize both the ennui and the response to it; they stage the crumbling and death of order in both political and personal spheres, casting the projected alternatives no longer as mere side shows, but as potential new solutions. Whereas in the early *Un Barrage contre le Pacifique* the colonial milieu figures as a place from which to escape, by *Le Vice-consul* and *India Song* it has become an ancien régime and a lost civilization. Similarly, the endings of *La Vie tranquille* and *Tarquinia* repudiate infidelity and celebrate the married couple, while the later *La Musica* and *L'Amante anglaise* portray the withering and suspension of the spouses' relationships, as *Lol V. Stein*, *Le Vice-consul*, and *Détruire dit-elle* sketch alternatives to the couple, monogamy, and heterosexuality, not as temporary, partial, or fantastic diversions, but as new modes of interaction. As the ennui takes on more ominous proportions, the attempts to defeat it likewise intensify. The fictional evolution resonates with historical developments of importance to Duras. The postwar irony of Duras and Sartre resonates with the cold war and French parliamentary democracy that strangled the hopes of Resistance idealists. The darker ennui coincides in turn with the increasingly distant and gerontocratic Fifth Republic, as the heightened importance attributed to marginalized responses to power in the works corresponds to the concomitant rise of gauchisme, the decentralized and often disorganized grass-roots radicalism that, as of the Algerian war of independence, began to replace the French Communist Party as the force of the far left in France and for Duras. In a more personal sphere, Duras seems to have forsworn marriage as an institution after a second attempt unraveled in the late 1950s, granting a new importance to encounters, brief relations, and other avenues of intimacy.[14]

After the late 1970s, Duras's works at once highlight and question the ability of chronological structures to give form to critical events and human experience. The texts accentuate both tensions and crucial connections between the solar calendar of days and weeks upon which depend organized society, on the one hand, and the vital dramas of the characters and their expression in narrative, on the other. *Yeux bleus* blurs the boundaries among days and constructs a strong although hazy impression of significant time elapsed, then retrospectively imposes the allegorical and crisply defined temporal frame of "six days and nights" on the interaction recounted; in the time that it took to create the world the couple has not managed to accomplish anything. Inversely, *Emily L.* and "La Douleur" establish a dramatic time structure based on long scenes, then close by abandoning that duration and jumping to an implicit time of summary, clouding the temporal specification of the end and disrupting the rhythm of the texts. "La Douleur" does so after prominently displaying signs of a personal diary, dating its "entries," before it confounds the calendar by having the days run into one another without distinction, feigning ignorance of dates, and constructing an alternative symbolic calendar of events. The first-person narrator thus claims not to know when she learned her spouse was alive (p. 61), then marks it as the date of the end of the fighting in Europe (p. 62), as she pegs the date of his sister's death to the Armistice (p. 77). The texts argue whether temporal patterns can inform and give meaning to events and human experience or whether the latter necessarily elude and resist chronology. As the first-person narrator/character of *L'Amant* observes, "L'histoire de ma vie n'existe pas . . . il y a de vastes endroits où l'on fait croire qu'il y avait quelqu'un, ce n'est pas vrai: il n'y avait personne" (p. 14). Enunciative structures in the works advance the same thesis by using and abusing frames to split the time of the text in two, the mutually exclusive alternatives cancelling each other out (*Le Camion, Yeux bleus*).

At the same time, the works published in this later period make the most convincing attempts at a narrative time of transformation and development in Duras's œuvre, thus posing the possibility of breaking out of the preceding cycles of ennui. The end of "La Douleur," a text written just after the war but edited only in 1985, unravels and problematizes the temporal and emotional forms that organize its principal scenes, but affirms nonetheless the life after death of the concentration camp survivor: "il savait qu'à chaque heure de chaque jour, je le pensais: 'Il n'est pas mort au camp de concentration'" (p. 81). The figures of cyclical time, of the suspended moment, and of the never-ending ending that pervade *Yeux bleus* must confront the heterosexual woman's effort to learn how to love the gay man, a process strongly marked as transformational and authentic. Whereas the 1982 *La Maladie de la mort* closes by cutting its protagonist out of temporal development—"Ainsi cependant vous avez pu vivre cet amour de la seule façon qui puisse se faire pour vous, en le perdant avant qu'il ne soit advenu" (p. 57)—the 1986 *Yeux bleus* rewrites the same story but directs it toward an ending that opens as much as it closes, leaving the couple in an intense happiness (p. 148).

Duras's œuvre follows the lead of *Le Camion,* where the time in which at least *something* is possible follows the end of the time in which *everything* was thought possible: in the film the deaths of civilization and revolution, of the body and absolute love have opened up a window, a time after time, in which acts that make modest differences can be attempted on an uncharted landscape. For months in 1980 Duras was thought to lie on the verge of death, but she emerged from the crisis having successfully completed a course of alcohol detoxification. The first text to follow, *L'Eté 80,* represents the fruit of a 'life on the installment plan' strategy that initiated the author's return to writing after her crisis and after a decade focused on the performance media of theater and film. The book's Normandy Beach, its account of the Gdansk revolution, and its couple composed of a young boy and a female camp counselor turned storyteller sound notes that recur and are developed in many of the author's late works. The evolution in her œuvre resonates with a stable, close companionship that took the place in her life of earlier relationships and encounters. It coincides as well with the presidency of her friend François Mitterrand, under whose leadership socialism in France left the opposition and entered the arena of political action in which the visionaries of a new era needed to confront and solve everyday problems.

The texts written in the last two decades endeavor to better define this space left after the destruction of *everything. Emily L.* proposes a kind of narrative closure to *Le Marin de Gibraltar* as *La Musica deuxième* does to *La Musica,* the later works sketching at least the material framework for a resolution of the earlier open ended texts. Similarly, whereas the earlier accounts of the author's adolescence in *Un Barrage contre le Pacifique* and *L'Eden cinéma* recount a love put off in protracted fashion before being refused (compare *Moderato cantabile*), the 1984 *L'Amant,* written after the death of her mother and older brother, portrays an intense, intimate relationship between the fifteen-year-old Creole and the Chinese lover and describes it as an experience of growth and change. Ennui per se disappears from center stage in these works, leaving instead more active passions attached to exertion, struggle, and suffering. Displacing the sun and torpor of both Calcutta and the earlier Mediterranean vacation sites, a new setting and climate permeate the texts, that of the Normandy coast, with the varied force and cadence of the sea, from a murmur to a crash, with its often cloudy days of green and gray water. The most recent texts become a medium conveying "l'assaut des vagues contre le mur de la chambre et leur déferlement à travers les paroles" (*Yeux bleus*, p. 152). They enact the author's attempt to redefine, reposition, or even overcome the time of ennui.

Notes

1. Danielle Bajomée, *Duras ou la douleur* (Brussels: De Boeck, 1989), p. 120.

2. See Helga Steinmetz-Schünemenn, *Bedeutung der Zeit in Marguerite Duras* (Amsterdam: Rodopi, 1976).

3. Carol Murphy, *Alienation and Absence in the Novels of Marguerite Duras* (Lexington, KY: French Forum, 1982).

4. See Martha Noel Evans, "Marguerite Duras: The Whore," in *Masks of Tradition. Women and the Politics of Writing in Twentieth-Century France* (Ithaca: Cornell University Press, 1987), pp. 123–56.

5. Georges Poulet, *Etudes sur le temps humain*, vol. 1 (Paris: Plon, 1949), p. 366.

6. Bajomée, *Duras*, p. 110.

7. See Jean-Luc Seylaz's classic study *Les Romans de Marguerite Duras: Essai sur une thématique de la durée* (Paris: Minard, 1963).

8. Bajomée, *Duras*, p. 111.

9. Julia Kristeva, "La Maladie de la douleur: Duras," in *Soleil noir: Dépression et mélancolie* (Paris: Gallimard Blanche, 1987), pp. 227–65.

10. On the importance and function of silence in Duras's texts, see also Michèle Montrelay, "Sur *Le Ravissement de Lol V. Stein*," in *L'Ombre et le nom* (Paris: Minuit, 1977), pp. 9–23; Madeleine Borgomano, "Une écriture féminine? A propos de Marguerite Duras," *Littérature*, no. 53 (1984), pp. 59–68; Liliane Papin, *L'Autre scène: Le théâtre de Marguerite Duras* (Saratoga, CA: Anma Libri, 1988), p. 91; and Susan D. Cohen, *Women and Discourse in the Fiction of Marguerite Duras* (Amherst: University of Massachusetts Press, 1993), pp. 149–54.

11. Kristeva, *Soleil noir*, p. 243.

12. See Deborah Glassman, "The Feminine Subject as History Writer in *Hiroshima mon amour*," *Enclitic* 5, no. 1 (1981), pp. 45–54.

13. Duras, *Les Lieux de Marguerite Duras* (Paris: Minuit, 1977), p. 77.

14. Alain Vircondelet, *Duras: Biographie* (Paris: Bourin, 1991), pp. 226, 258–59.

Bibliography

Works by Marguerite Duras

Les Impudents. Paris: Plon, 1943.
La Vie tranquille. Paris: Gallimard, 1944.
Un Barrage contre le Pacifique. Paris: Gallimard, 1950. Translated by Herma Briffault as *The Sea Wall*. New York: Farrar, Straus and Giroux, 1985.

Le Marin de Gibraltar. Paris: Gallimard, 1952. [Pages refer to 1987 printing.] Translated by Barbara Bray as *The Sailor from Gibraltar.* New York: Riverrun, 1980.

Les Petits Chevaux de Tarquinia. Paris: Gallimard, 1953. Translated by Peter Du Berg as *The Little Horses of Tarquinia.* New York: Riverrun, 1980.

Des Journées entières dans les arbres. Paris: Gallimard, 1954. Translated by Anita Barrows as *Whole Days in the Trees and Other Stories.* New York: Riverrun, 1984.

Le Square. Paris: Gallimard, 1955. Translated in *Four Novels by Marguerite Duras: The Square, Moderato cantabile, Ten-Thirty on a Summer Night, The Afternoon of Monsieur Andesmas,* Introduction by Germaine Brée. New York: Grove Press, 1965.

Moderato cantabile. Paris: Minuit, 1958. Translated in *Four Novels by Marguerite Duras.*

Dix heures et demie du soir en été. Paris: Gallimard, 1960. Translated in *Four Novels by Marguerite Duras.*

Hiroshima mon amour. Script of the film directed by Alain Resnais. Paris: Gallimard, 1961. Translated by Richard Seaver as *Hiroshima mon amour.* New York: Grove Press, 1966.

L'Après-midi de Monsieur Andesmas. Paris: Gallimard, 1962. Translated in *Four Novels by Marguerite Duras.*

Le Ravissement de Lol V. Stein. Paris: Gallimard, 1964. Translated by Richard Seaver as *The Ravishing of Lol V. Stein.* New York: Grove Press, 1966.

Théâtre I, II, III. Paris: Gallimard, 1965, 1968, 1984. Translated as *Three Plays: The Square, Days in the Trees, The Viaducts of Seine-et-Oise.* London: Calder and Boyars, 1967; *Suzanna Andler, La Musica, L'Amante anglaise.* London: Calder, 1975

Le Vice-consul. Paris: Gallimard, 1965. Translated by Eileen Ellenbogen as *The Vice Consul.* London: Hamish Hamilton, 1968.

L'Amante anglaise. Paris: Cahiers du Théâtre National Populaire, 1968. Translated by Barbara Bray as *L'Amante anglaise.* London: Hamish Hamilton, 1968.

Détruire, dit-elle. Paris: Minuit, 1969. Translated by Barbara Bray as *Destroy, She Said.* New York: Grove Press, 1970.

Abahn, Sabana, David. Paris: Gallimard, 1970.

L'Amour. Paris: Gallimard, 1971.

Les Parleuses. Interviews with Xavière Gauthier. Paris: Minuit, 1974. Translated by Katharine A. Jensen as *Woman to Woman.* Lincoln: University of Nebraska Press, 1987.

India Song. Paris: Gallimard, 1973. Translated by Barbara Bray as *India Song.* New York: Grove Press, 1976.

L'Eden cinéma. Paris: Mercure de France, 1977.

Les Lieux de Marguerite Duras. Interviews with Michelle Porte. Paris: Minuit, 1977.

Le Navire Night; Césarée; Les Mains négatives; Aurélia Steiner. Paris: Mercure de France, 1980.

L'Eté 80. Paris: Minuit, 1980.

L'Homme assis dans le couloir. Paris: Minuit, 1980. Translated by Barbara Bray as *Man Sitting in the Corridor.* New York: Blue Moon Books, 1991.

Les Yeux verts. Paris: Cahiers du Cinéma, 1980. Translated by Carol Barko as *Green Eyes.* Boulder: Colorado University Press, 1990.

Agatha. Paris: Minuit, 1981. Translated by Howard Linolli in *Agatha and Savannah Bay: Plays.* Sausolito, CA: Post Apollo, 1992.

Outside. Paris: Albin Michel, 1981. Translated by Arthur Goldhammer as *Outside: Selected Writings.* Boston: Beacon Press, 1986.

La Maladie de la mort. Paris: Minuit, 1982. Translated by Barbara Bray as *The Malady of Death.* New York: Grove Press, 1986.

L'Amant. Paris: Minuit, 1984. Translated by Barbara Bray as *The Lover.* New York: Pantheon, 1985.

La Douleur. Paris: P.O.L., 1985. Translated by Barbara Bray as *The War. A Memoir.* New York: Pantheon, 1986.

Les Yeux bleus cheveux noirs. Paris: Minuit, 1986. Translated by Barbara Bray as *Blue Eyes, Black Hair.* New York: Pantheon, 1987.

Emily L. Paris: Minuit, 1987. Translated by Barbara Bray as *Emily L.* New York: Pantheon, 1989.

La Vie matérielle. Paris: P.O.L., 1987. Translated by Barbara Bray as *Practicalities.* New York: Grove, 1990.

La Pluie d'été. Paris: P.O.L., 1990. Translated by Barbara Bray as *Summer Rain.* New York: Macmillan, 1992.

L'Amant de la Chine du nord. Paris: Gallimard, 1991. Translated by Leigh Hafrey as *The North China Lover.* New York: New Press, 1992.

Yann Andréa Steiner. Paris: P.O.L., 1992.

Ecrire. Paris: Gallimard, 1993.

Le Monde extérieur. Vol. 2 of *Outside.* Edited by Christiane Blot-Labarrère. Paris: P.O.L., 1993.

Selected Critical Works

Alazet, Bernard. *'Le Navire Night' de Marguerite Duras: Ecrire l'effacement.* Lille: Presses Universitaires de Lille, 1992.

Ames, Sanford Scribner, ed. *Remains to Be Seen: Essays on Marguerite Duras.* New York: Peter Lang, 1989.

L'Arc, no. 98 (1985). Special issue on Duras.

Armel, Aliette. *Marguerite Duras et l'autobiographie.* Paris: Le Castor Astral, 1990.

Bajomée, Danielle. *Duras ou la douleur.* Brussels: De Boeck, 1989.

Bajomée, Danielle, and Ralph Heyndels, eds. *Ecrire dit-elle.* Brussels: Editions de l'Université de Bruxelles, 1985.

Blanchot, Maurice. *La Communauté inavouable.* Paris: Minuit, 1983. See especially pp. 51–93.

Blot-Labarrère, Christiane. *Marguerite Duras.* Paris: Seuil, 1992.

Borgomano, Madeleine. *Duras. Une lecture des fantasmes.* Petit Roeulx (Belgium): Cistre Essais, 1985.

Cismaru, Alfred. *Marguerite Duras.* New York: Twayne Publishers, World Authors Series, 1971.

Cahiers du Cerf XX (Brest), no. 7 (1991). Special issue on Duras.

Cohen, Susan D. *Women and Discourse in the Fiction of Marguerite Duras: Love, Legends, Language.* Amherst: University of Massachusetts Press, 1993.

Cranston, Mechthild, ed. *In Language and in Love. Marguerite Duras: The Unspeakable.* Potomac: Scripta Humanistica, 1992.

Duras, Marguerite, et al. *Marguerite Duras.* Paris: Albatros, 1977, 1979. Translated by Edith Cohen and Peter Connor. San Francisco: City Lights, 1987.

L'Esprit Créateur 30, no. 1 (spring 1990). Special issue on Duras.

Glassman, Deborah N. *Marguerite Duras: Fascinating Vision and Narrative Cure.* Rutherford: Fairleigh Dickinson University Press; Toronto: Associated University Presses, 1991.

Guers-Villate, Yvonne. *Continuité/Discontinuité de l'œuvre durassienne.* Brussels: Editions de l'Université de Bruxelles, 1985.

Hill, Leslie. *Marguerite Duras: Apocalyptic Desires.* New York: Routledge, 1993.

Hofmann, Carol Anne. *Forgetting and Marguerite Duras.* Niwot: University Press of Colorado, 1991.

Lebelley, Frédérique. *Duras ou le poids d'une plume.* Paris: Grasset, 1994.

Lamy, Suzanne, and André Roy, eds. *Marguerite Duras à Montréal.* Montréal: Spirale, 1981

Magazine Littéraire, no. 278 (June 1990). Special issue on Duras.

Marini, Marcelle. *Territoires du féminin. Avec Marguerite Duras.* Paris: Minuit, 1977.

Micciollo, Henri. *Moderato cantabile de Marguerite Duras: Lire aujourd'hui.* Paris: Hachette, 1979.

Murphy, Carol J. *Alienation and Absence in the Novels of Marguerite Duras.* Lexington, KY: French Forum, 1982.

Pierrot, Jean. *Marguerite Duras.* Paris: José Corti, 1986.

Ricouart, Janine. *Ecriture féminine et violence: Une étude de Marguerite Duras.* Birmingham, AL: Summa, 1991.

Selous, Trista. *The Other Woman: Feminism and Femininity in the Works of Marguerite Duras.* New Haven: Yale University Press, 1988.

Seylaz, Jean-Luc. *Les Romans de Marguerite Duras. Essai sur une thématique de la durée.* Paris: Minard (Archives des Lettres Modernes, no. 47), 1963.

Steinmetz-Schünemenn, Helga. *Bedeutung der Zeit in Marguerite Duras*. Amsterdam: Rodopi, 1976.

Tison-Braun, Micheline. *Marguerite Duras*. Amsterdam: Rodopi (Collection Littérature Française Contemporaine no. 2), 1985.

Udris, Raynelle. *Welcome Unreason: A Study of 'Madness' in the Novels of Marguerite Duras*. Amsterdam: Rodopi, 1993.

Vircondelet, Alain. *Duras: Biographie*. Paris: Bourin, 1991.

———, ed. *Marguerite Duras: Rencontres de Cerisy*. Paris: Ecriture, 1994.

Willis, Sharon. *Marguerite Duras: Writing on the Body*. Urbana: University of Illinois Press, 1987.

5

Robert Pinget

Robert Henkels

"Tout redire pour tout renouveler." This lapidary phrase which echoes through the novels and plays of Robert Pinget expresses, in epigrammatic form, the goals and techniques that are commonly held by the new novelists. Like his fellow authors at the Editions de Minuit, Robert Pinget has striven, and continues to strive (with notable success), to push off against narrative conventions inherited from the past and to form new ones by reshaping the old. The quest to renew through retelling lies at the cornerstone of the overarching shape of his fiction. Recurrence and alternation drive the presentation of his characters. Waves of reminiscence and change flow through his narratives. Repetition and variation constitute the sinews of his paradoxically down-to-earth and poetic prose.

Pinget's school years in Geneva were marked by an interest in the Classics (particularly the pastoral poetry of Vergil). He wrote a good deal of his own poetry while in school (which does not appear to have survived in print). After obtaining a law degree he moved to Paris, where he tried his hand as an artist (he continues to paint as an avocation and to play the cello). Sketches, drawings and caricatures crowd the pages of his manuscripts and the influence of music makes itself felt in his later work. Pinget's first book, *Entre Fantoine et Agapa* (1951), placed itself clearly outside the mainstream of existentialist writing in vogue at the time. Whimsical, humorous, devoid of any social message, and espousing no political cause more specific than the freedom of the imagination to express itself by playing with language, this short collection of fanciful descriptions of an imaginary province recalled Max Jacob and

Henri Michaux. Yet it was also highly original. Pinget's second book, *Mahu ou le matériau* (1952), a "récit," consisted of a collection of short, surrealistic chapters loosely strung together. It caught the eye of Albert Camus and, as a result, his third book, *Le Renard et la boussole* (1953), was published by Gallimard. Like its predecessors, Pinget's third book—and his first novel—was a quirky parody of the travel journal. The author's deft twisting of established conventions caught the eye of Alain Robbe-Grillet, who was assisting Jerôme Lindon in the selection of manuscripts for the Editions de Minuit. So Pinget's fourth volume, *Graal Flibuste* (1956), appeared under the colors of Minuit, the publishing house with which he has remained ever since.

Being published by Minuit meant more than a convenient mailing address (Pinget's Paris apartment being located minutes away). It meant that Pinget's work would be associated with (although never appropriated by) the group of innovative novelists whose spokesman was Robbe-Grillet. Its members included Samuel Beckett (who was to become a close friend), Claude Simon, and Nathalie Sarraute. Critics soon began referring to the collective work of this highly individualistic group as "le nouveau roman" and to Pinget as a "nouveau romancier," and the label has stuck ever since.

This association is justifiable, up to a point. Like Samuel Beckett, Pinget has written extensively and successfully for the theater. Like Nathalie Sarraute, although in a completely different vein, he has explored the nuances of spoken language. But the association with the nouveau roman has proved to be something of a mixed blessing. It has led to false expectations and inaccurate comparisons. For although Pinget shares the group's interest in innovating through parody (his favorite novel is *Don Quixote*), Pinget's is a unique voice, highly individual and nonderivative. "Voice" is used advisedly here since, unlike Robbe-Grillet, who writes for the eye, or Claude Simon, whose inspired verbal "bricolage" alludes frequently to architecture, Pinget writes essentially by and for the ear. A poet by instinct, he has used the necessity for linear development required by narration as a counterbalance for his verbal flights of fancy.

Whereas humor is usually conspicuously absent from the nouveau roman, or often appears there only in its most gallowslike manifestations, Pinget's writing abounds in malapropisms, wordplay, and "contrepéties." Unlike most of his colleagues, he is frequently and consistently funny. Another fundamental aspect of his work sets him apart.

Alone among Jerôme Lindon's authors, Pinget remains firmly attached to the Christian tradition and belief. His fiction, even at its darkest, never completely rejects the hope of the possibility of transcendence.

Having pointed out the caveats and limitations of grouping Pinget among the writers who shaped the nouveau roman, it is also fair to say that like many of the authors who have published at the Editions de Minuit, Pinget's work can be described as passing through three distinct, if somewhat overlapping, phases. He begins by distancing his writing from such forms and conventions of traditional, "well-made," nineteenth-century fiction as the omniscient author, linear plot construction, reliance on chronological time, and the depiction of comprehensible psychological motivation. At this point in his career, Pinget is preoccupied with what first appears to be a negative pushing-off from the recent literary past, an effort that he accomplishes largely through parody. In this first phase (from *Entre Fantoine et Agapa* through *Clope au dossier*), Pinget turns the conventions of the quest narrative inside out, particularly fictionalized biography and the detective story. He makes the writing of the novel itself the work's subject and object, as narration becomes the subject of the narrative.

In the second phase, (from *L'Inquisitoire* in 1962 to *Quelqu'un* in 1965), elements of parody gradually disappear as Pinget explores analogies between reading and writing and develops a complex and dynamic relationship between the writer and the reader. At this stage, deciphering the text or assigning a single meaning to it becomes as challenging (and ultimately as impossible) a task as Pinget's writer-narrators face when they try to reduce the ambiguities, complexities, and contradictions of their experiences to the page. In the works of this period Pinget strives to develop narrative structures and techniques suitable to express his vision as a series of elliptical cycles of change through recurrence.

Most recently, in his work from *Le Libéra* (1968) to the present, he has reduced linear, cause-and-effect anecdotal elements to a bare minimum. The texts of this period engage the reader even more directly in the joys and tribulations of creation. In works that explore the boundaries that separate prose from poetry, the everyday from the transcendent, and the written word from music, Pinget's language undergoes the continuing process of repetition and variation that recalls the baroque music he loves so deeply.

Since an attempt to describe one author's work in terms of another's is approximative and inaccurate at best, particularly in the case of an author as distinctive as Pinget, this chapter centers presentation of his work on discussions of representative texts from the author's first two periods, *Graal Flibuste* and *L'Inquisitoire*. Since Pinget continues to publish innovative works of the highest caliber, the present discussion concludes the description of the innovative work of this "writer's writer" with a more detailed discussion of one of his later novels, *L'Apocryphe* (1980), emphasizing the ways in which Pinget's treatment of myth is a continuation of the themes and techniques of his earlier writing and an extension of them. Perhaps this discussion will suggest why, as the nouveau roman has given way to the nouveau nouveau roman, and the nouveau nouveau roman to a return to more traditional forms of narration, Pinget's is a voice that has captured and retained the close attention of discriminating and appreciative readers and critics and will continue to do so.

Pinget once concluded a lecture on his conception of the act of creation with the remark "Tout ce que je viens de dire est vrai. Tout ce que je viens de dire est faux. Tout ce que je viens de dire est vrai et faux à la fois." His early fictional works enact that cryptic remark writ large. As Cervantes does in *Don Quixote*, Pinget and his writer-protagonists create the new by rewriting the old. As suggested above, Pinget has explained his attraction to prose narrative by remarking that the linearity of the novel imposes on his free-wheeling poetic associations a certain forward motion. For example, *Graal Flibuste* shapes the flights of fancy of his first two works into a loosely sequential and often interrupted narrative line of sorts.

The reader is presented with a voyage journal in the first person, describing the adventures of an explorer visiting the realm ruled by the deity Graal Flibuste. Short entries enumerate the aspects of the kingdom that strike the observer's fancy. We are informed about the mores of the natives, the topography and geography of the territory, the genealogy of the reigning deity, the favorite sports and pastimes of the inhabitants, the flora and fauna and architectural monuments of town and country. All of this is recounted in a matter-of-fact tone reminiscent of French voyage-narratives from the eighteenth century. Occasionally, though, the narrator's self-satisfied remarks are undercut by his servant, Brindon, who plays Sancho Panza to his master's Don Quixote.

If the tone remains resolutely prosaic, the subject matter is fanciful to the point of being surreal. The list of the pantheon of local deities, for example, includes Gloria, the patron saint of pharmacists and the god of thunder and vengeance, and Patrona, who gave birth to a child covered with vegetation from head to toe after being inseminated by a watercress plant. The vegetation and animals described run to hybrid species that could only have come from a Creator with a keen sense of humor. Pinget provides the reader with glimpses of such delightful creatures as "les joies du matin," "les oublieuses d'amertume," "les lièvres de vase," "les papillons-singes," "les écureuils-bougies," "les pavots-chiens," and "les frotte-mignon." The enumeration of these wonders is interspersed with a fragment from an epic poem, "La Quête d'amour de la sorcière Vaoua," with the genealogy of Graal Flibuste, with a "Dialogue philosophique," and with the pastiche of a mystery story, and other whimsical matters.

Pinget clearly enjoys taking his imagination for an airing and the freedom to create neologisms. He plays with words and sounds, taking full advantage of the tongue-in-cheek parody of the voyage account. There is a danger in whimsical works of this kind that the fanciful material may proliferate to the point where the reader loses patience or the author's vision becomes so idiosyncratic as to become hermetic. Pinget avoids this trap by keeping the journal entries short, by varying the tone and content of the journal, and by striking a balance between arabesques of fancy and the sequential demands of story-telling. The overall impression is one of energy, imagination, and zest reminiscent of Rabelais.

Graal Flibuste and the other early works help to explain why Pinget was somewhat reluctant at first to be grouped by critics as one of the nouveaux romanciers. At first glance this exuberant, amusing text with its emphasis on verbal acrobatics and sound associations seems worlds away from the abstract geometry of Robbe-Grillet's fiction or the grim, spare parables of Samuel Beckett. Nevertheless, as the reader penetrates further into the account of the kingdom of Graal Flibuste, several disquieting questions are posed obliquely, and they are questions raised by several other authors who publish at Minuit. What does it mean to tell a story, for instance, and what are the limits of language? Must every element of the narrative necessarily fit neatly into a decipherable whole?

Many of these questions make themselves felt more clearly in the second edition, or "l'edition intégrale," which ends with a six-page description of the decorative ornamentation of a mysterious triumphal arch framing the horizon. Despite the portal image, which might suggest it, this final fragment provides no sense of closure. The reader is left instead with the sense that the act of telling can never be completed since the quest for complete self-expression is impossible and since language itself is unequal to the task. The narrator warned that such may be the case earlier in the text when he says: "J'ai progressé pour ainsi dire à rebours et me voilà plus démuni qu'un nouveau-né. J'entends bien surseoir, puisque j'ai pris le parti d'écrire, à l'arrêt de mort qu'il me faudra prononcer contre moi, mais tiens à prévenir le lecteur que ce livre, à l'instar de qui le composa, diminue d'importance à mesure qu'il grossit, contrairement à l'usage" (p. 33).

In other words, *Graal Flibuste* is constructed like a "poupée gigogne" or a "roman à tiroirs," which may be expanded indefinitely. And so Pinget's narrator will never be able to express completely the vagaries of his imaginary world. Nor can the reader and the writer ever capture in words the kaleidoscopic reality of our daily lives. The attempt to do so, however, by casting a net of words over the world, remains an unrealizable quest that lies at the very heart of the human spirit. Ultimately, *Graal Flibuste* is really not "about" a voyage to a fantastic kingdom at all. It enacts the compelling, alternately amusing and disturbing act of writing, its joys, its sorrows, and its frustrations. This self-consciousness, the demands Pinget makes upon the reader, and the effective parody of conventions handed down from the "well-made" novel of the nineteenth century justify the inclusion of Pinget's fiction in the "nouveau roman" group.

Pinget continued to rely on parody in his other early works. *Le Fiston,* one of the most successful of these texts, unfolds as a spoof of the "roman réaliste" and the "roman policier," in which the novel first appears to follow the investigation of a young girl's death and gradually turns into another affecting exploration of writing itself. Pinget's novels of the late 1950s seemed to be undergoing the same process of diminution that shaped Samuel Beckett's writing. As his books shrank in length, Pinget's editor eventually bet him that he could not write a novel of more than 250 pages. The author won the wager by producing *L'Inquisitoire* in 1962, considered by most critics to be his magnum opus, that is, arguably the most innovative work of the second phase of his novelistic production.

L'Inquisitoire literally contains "a cast of thousands." The 489 over-sized pages of the original Editions de Minuit edition (since accompa-

nied by the Union Générale des Editeurs edition with an excellent introduction by Jean-Claude Liéber), contain allusions to over a thousand
characters and place names. The scope of the provincial world revealed
in the novel and Pinget's painstaking evocation of place caused one critic,
rather misguidedly, to describe Pinget as "un Balzac moderne." The
novel's pages teem with stories of hushed-up scandals, allegations of
criminal activity, complex social structures, and extensive enumerations
of settings and furnishing worthy of Balzac's "Scènes de la vie de province."

But all this material is presented to the reader not through the convention of the omniscient authorial presence of Balzac, who intervenes
frequently in the narrative, but in the form of an extended dialogue. The
tone of this conversation is clearly "inquisitory" in the investigative sense
of the word. The person asking the questions seems to have judicial standing and to possess a sort of inquisitorial power over his interlocutor.
Perhaps he is a detective or a prosecuting attorney. In any case, it is the
questioner who directs the line of questioning and his quarry, an elderly
man, responds to it. The latter, answering (or avoiding) the questions, is
an old, family servant, long retired from the service of his masters, two
old bachelors, who lived in a local château.

The questioner seems very curious to know what went on in this
household, so his questions keep returning to that subject. But "la vie de
château" is not the only subject of discourse. It lies at the center of the
dialogue as other subjects of inquiry radiate from it, like spokes on a
wheel. The investigator bores in on implied allegations calculated to
tantalize the reader's interest. The château may have been the site of
homosexual orgies. One of the other domestics may have been a child
abuser and murderer. The servant's masters may have been addicted to
drugs. Their business manager may have been running a tax-evasion
ring.

But every time the questioner seems about to close in on these allegations, the old man scuttles away, changing the subject, refusing to
answer, or launching into seemingly endless enumerations of furniture
contained in a room, the distribution of rooms in the house, or the topography of points of interest in the town and the grid of streets connecting them, or a detailed, if garbled, description of a painting:

il y a contre le mur un grand tableau qui représente des
paysans ils jouent à toutes sortes de jeu comme colin-maillard,

> dans le coin gauche on voit une fille les yeux bandés et les
> garçons qui rigolent autour un lui lève la jupe ou plutôt non
> ça c'est le milieu, à gauche il y en a qui jouent au croquet
> parfaitement à gauche le croquet et un des joueurs se tourne
> vers la fille colin-maillard en levant son maillet comme pour
> l'assommer, un autre essaie de passer la cloche on le voit tout
> penché en avant en train de viser et tout à fait à gauche tenez
> ça me revient il y a un joueur en train de pousser sa boule du
> pied pendant que les autres ont le dos tourné. (p. 362)

If the prose of Graal Flibuste rises out of the ordinary, the old servant's replies seem mired in the prosaic. And yet the sheer accumulation of detail, the doubling back of the descriptions, the cascade of "mises au point," coupled with the lack of punctuation and the length of the digressions, has a liberating effect upon the reader's imagination. One feels lost and disoriented in this unbroken flow of words and images.

To make matters even more confusing (and amusing), the old man suffers from severe deafness. This condition often disqualifies him as an accurate witness since he may not have heard or may have misunderstood what was being said. As a result he comes up with several highly amusing spoonerisms, particularly when foreign words or idiomatic expressions fracture his lexicon. "Clergyman" becomes "Kleptomane." "A la bonne franquette" comes out as "à la bonne flanquette." And "épidémies" becomes "épidermies."

Although they may first appear to be minor comic touches, these verbal lapses and spoonerisms point toward the novel's true subject, i.e., language. Subsequent to the publication of L'Inquisitoire, Pinget observed that the identity of the two interlocutors was not really the investigator and the old man at all. Instead, the two voices project a division in the author's persona as he questions his imagination. His creative self responds, and both collaborate to win the wager with Jerôme Lindon by producing the book that will eventually become L'Inquisitoire.

Once again, the narrative becomes its own subject and object as the expressive limits and possibilities of language meet on the page. The old man's story will never be finished because nothing can ever be told completely. All the same, the compulsion to try to tell a story, and by doing so to try to find meaning in events around us, seems to be unavoidable for human beings, endowed with language and reason. In other words, as Pinget concludes in *Le Fiston,* "En dehors de l'écrit, c'est la mort" (p. 173). Furthermore, since language, like knowledge, is imprecise and we never know the definitive truth about persons and events, "il faut tout redire pour tout renouveler." Perhaps that is why in *L'Inquisitoire* Pinget accentuates his use of recurrence and alteration. After *L'Inquisitoire,* the people, places, and events of Pinget's world will continue to reappear from book to book. Unlike Balzac's use of recurrence in *La Comédie humaine,* however, Pinget's characters reappear each time in slightly altered form, and the stories in which they are involved recur in a succession of variants.

Just as *L'Inquisitoire* tells us more about many of the characters that have appeared before by reintroducing them, the broad outlines of Pinget's fiction as a whole come into clearer focus. The chronicle of the imaginary province between Fantoine and Agapa with which he begins expands into a continuing "roman fleuve," which develops through the alternation of recurrence (the reintroduction of old material) and alteration (unpredictable changes and retellings of previous givens). From 1969 on Pinget extends this broad treatment of characters, places, and plot down to the basic level of words and phrases.

The structure of the texts of this period reflects Pinget's interest in the forms of music and acts out the dictum alluded to here in various configurations. Elements of straightforward, ABCD narration are cut to a minimum, leaving a series of fragments that recur and shift meaning like the repeated variations of themes, or leitmotifs, in music. As Pinget observed of this technique in remarks delivered at a retrospective symposium on the nouveau roman at New York University:

> If it is de rigueur in this assembly to speak of technique, I will very briefly say that the structure of my novels is often built on recurrences. These recurrences, or repetitions, are of four kinds.
>
> (1) Complete recurrence, ab initio or repetition of the first part of the book in the second. Bipartite structure, then. Typical examples *Le Fiston, Fable, L'Apocryphe.* What is important here is the repetition of all the themes, but with perceptible or imperceptible modifications, distortions, variations, transformations, which finally destroy, or at least shake, the certainties that the reader may have fastened on in the first part.

Hence the impression that the book is being composed, and decomposed, under his very eyes. The formula I have employed to define this procedure and which applies to all my books is: Nothing is ever said, since it can be said otherwise.

(2) Partial and progressive recurrence, all the way through the book. After a certain number of pages, let us say, recapitulation of themes with variations, and so on with different themes. Typical examples: *Quelqu'un, Le Libera me domine, Passacaille.* "Unipartite" structure, then.

(3) Complete but reversed recurrence, starting from the middle of the book, of the first part in the second, which thus repeats it by going back to the beginning, Bipartite structure, but disguised as "unipartite," as the book is all of a piece. . . . Unique example, *Cette voix.* Variations and hypotheses proliferate, as in (1) and (2). It is only the stimulus that differs. I would, therefore, stress the fact that in order to write, I need a positive stimulus to trigger the creative process.

(4) A fourth kind of recurrence is the pure and simple repetition of certain key phrases, or leitmotifs, throughout the book, which thus increase its resemblance to a musical composition.[1]

The abstract formulation of these devices sounds mechanical or tedious. In actual practice the contrary is true. Because of Pinget's keen sense of nuance and his acute ear for the modulations of spoken language and his treatment of words as sounds, his utilization of recurrence and alternation gives his work a high degree of resonance, both within individual texts and within the overarching structure of the chronicle as a whole. The use of these devices also makes possible a paradoxical and poetic language in which something may indeed be true, or false, or be true and false at the same time.

L'Apocryphe combines apparently contradictory themes that have preoccupied Pinget in recent years: the indignities of old age, the reinvigoration of fresh perspective, the fear of death, the hope of transcendence, the threat of creative impotence, and the possibility of new ways of writing. He reassembles a familiar cast of characters: the old, crotchety, reclusive writer, his friend, the doctor, the maid, and the old man's nephews. The "story" (if one could call it that) recounts the effort to piece together a manuscript composed of fragments from an old almanac, the reclusive writer's journal, and his disparate writings, all of them amended by a series of putative editors after his death. Structurally, the novel keeps coming back to the figure of a shepherd. He first appears as the idealized, classical figure of the pastoral swain in Vergil's *Eclogues.* He next enters the text as a real-life, contemporary shepherd guiding his flock over the fields near Pinget's country house near Amboise. And finally, the figure appears as an avatar of Christ, the Good Shepherd, when the novel ends, just as it begins, with an evocation of the Christmas season. The novel concludes with a strong suggestion of the shepherds in Luke who were the first to receive the glad tidings of the birth of Christ.

Each representation of the figure points to a different way to read the text. The classical shepherd suggests the circular notion of the "éternel retour," and the novel does, in a sense, end where it began, i.e., in the Christmas season. The reader thus experiences a sense of circularity as he/she goes through the text. The French herdsman recurs in the strand of the narrative that has a linear (this-happened-that-happened-next) movement to it, and suggests a straight, or chronological, reading. The Christian shepherd enacts the spiral reading of the text in which the reader continually refers back to reappearing leitmotifs without going all the way back to the beginning. It recalls that, in Christian iconography, everything is, at once, the same and different after the birth of Christ, a chronology that may be represented by an ellipse or a spiral. The shepherd of *L'Apocryphe* blends the three figures just as the text makes possible three ways of reading. Perhaps because of these apparently contradictory strands, as the novel's title suggests, the true significance of the figure and of the novel itself remains secret and ambiguous, unrevealed or revealed in indeferable terms like the Apocrypha of the Bible.

The texts of Pinget's third period, or his third way of writing, contain other many figures and structures of a similar richness of association and resonance. They are, of course, difficult to summarize since not a great deal "happens" in them, or rather sometimes so many contradictory things are alleged to have occurred that the text modulates into the conditional tense, the mode of conjecture of which, as Michèle Praeger points out, Pinget is a past master.[2]

Within the nouveau roman group, as was previously remarked, Pinget's work has been described as developing "l'école de l'oreille" in contrast to Robbe-Grillet and Claude Simon, who work more extensively with visual effects. Pinget has distinguished himself as a dramatist as well. His radio plays have been performed by the BBC and Radio Stuttgart. The Comédie Française added several of his dramatic works to its repertoire, and one summer the theater festival at Avignon was devoted to his work. He has also recently been involved with a theater troupe producing for the stage a text derived from *L'Inquisitoire*.

Literary fashion has changed frequently and profoundly since Pinget began writing. The existentialist vogue of the early 1950s gave way, for a time, to the ambitious and innovative projects of the new novelists. The apparent hermeticism of these works posed profound theoretical questions about the nature of literature and how to approach it. For a time, the attention of critics and intellectuals shifted from fiction itself to literary criticism. There can be little doubt, at least to me, that "la nouvelle critique" and its various means of expression (structuralism, Marxist criticism, socioliterary and feminist criticism, and others), have rejuvenated discussion of how to approach literature. It should not be surprising either that, after an extended period of questioning, traditional narrative closer to the model of Balzac has made a comeback.

Through the vicissitudes of literary fashion, Robert Pinget's writing has remained true to itself. Pinget has worked and reworked themes of universal concern with increasing subtlety, developing forms uniquely his own. The soft-spoken voice of Robert Pinget has continued to make itself heard more and more convincingly while many of his fellow nouveaux romanciers have fallen silent or turned to autobiographical reminiscences. His decision to shape his "œuvre" as an ongoing chronicle has given his later work a unique resonance and poignancy.

For those unacquainted with Pinget's work, it might be pointed out that readers interested in intertextuality will find his novels particularly rewarding. The early works allude frequently and effectively to *Don Quixote*. The later novels and "récits" contain quotations, paraphrases, and allusions to Vergil, Catholic liturgy, Saint Augustine, and Jung. Each text also echoes words and phrases (as well as characters and place names) from Pinget's other novels. Many of the dramatic works reshape situations, themes, and motifs from the novels, and Pinget has found several highly successful dramatic devices to make these transpositions come to life on the stage. To read Pinget's work as a whole is therefore particularly rewarding precisely because of the echo effect, the fugal development from work to work. That is not to say, however, that individual novels remain inaccessible to readers unacquainted with Pinget's chronicle. Nor is it necessary to read his work chronologically, since the relationships between volumes are free-flowing, and each work has great interest and integrity in its own right.

Criticized in the 1950s for their playful rejection of narrative tradition and their nonrealistic depiction of the world, in retrospect Pinget's works may be considered to be close to common everyday experience. After all, in a sense the more we know people in real life, the less we understand them. Pinget's recurring characters inscribe that truth on every page. In our daily lives we are accustomed to experiencing time simultaneously, as linear, circular, and as flowing like a spiral. The dance of the seasons is a circular, recurring one. Yet each springtime, each Christmas day seems, somehow, unique. Events in real life, as in Pinget's fictitious province, have as many "true" versions as there are observers of them. Most of us live, whether we admit it or not, in a world where material existence is suffused to some degree by the spiritual. Pinget's fiction, where poetry and prose commingle, reflects and celebrates these paradoxes. The fact that his vision corresponds to contemporary scientific discoveries in relativity and nuclear physics is probably, in a sense, accidental. It is more likely that his use of recurrence and alternation stems from the author's fondness for the affinities I have mentioned and the writings of Jung.

Jung interprets the efforts of the Alchemists to transform base metal into gold as a metaphor for humanity's desire to bring into harmony the material and spiritual parts of the self (the animus and the anima). For Pinget, that effort takes place at the level of language, and the quest itself is subsumed in the endless attempt to "tout redire pour tout renouveler." From the outset Pinget has refused simply to describe the nature of that quest to the reader. The use of recurrence and alternation lies at the center of his attempt to make the reader participate as directly as possible in that quest since it leaves the reader the broadest possible opportunity to tell and retell the story. It is perhaps for that reason that

John Updike described Pinget as "one of the noblest presences in world literature" and that his work continues to grow, to develop, and to win critical acclaim.

Notes

1. Lois Oppenheim, ed., *Three Decades of the New Novel* (Urbana: University of Illinois Press, 1986), p. 147.

2. Michèle Praeger, *Les Romans de Robert Pinget: Une écriture des possibles* (Lexington, KY: French Forum, 1986).

Bibliography

Works by Robert Pinget

Entre Fantoine et Agapa (nouvelles). Jarnac: La Tour de Feu, 1951. Translated by Barbara Wright as *Between Fantoine and Agapa*. New York: Red Dust, 1982.

Mahu ou le matériau. Paris: Robert Laffont, 1952. Translated by Alan Sheridan-Smith as *Mahu or The Material.* London: Calder, 1966.

Le Renard et la boussole. Paris: Gallimard, 1953.

Graal Flibuste. Paris: Editions de Minuit, 1956 (édition intégrale, 1966).

Baga. Paris: Editions de Minuit, 1958. Translated by John Stevenson. London: Calder, 1967.

Le Fiston. Paris: Editions de Minuit, 1959. Translated by Richard Coe as *Monsieur Levert.* New York: Grove, 1961. Translated by Richard N. Coe as *No Answer.* London: Calder, 1961.

Clope au dossier. Paris: Editions de Minuit, 1961.

L'Inquisitoire. Paris: Editions de Minuit, 1962. Translated by Donald Watson as *The Inquisitory.* London: Calder, 1966; New York: Grove Press, 1966.

Quelqu'un. Paris: Editions de Minuit, 1965. Translated by Barbara Wright as *Someone.* New York: Red Dust, 1984.

Le Libera. Paris: Editions de Minuit, 1968. Translated by Barbara Wright as *The Libera me domine.* London: Calder, 1975; New York: Red Dust, 1978.

Passacaille. Paris: Editions de Minuit, 1969. Translated by Barbara Wright as *Recurrent Melody.* London: Calder, 1975. Published as *Passacaglia.* New York: Red Dust, 1978.

Fable (récit). Paris: Editions de Minuit, 1971. Translated by Barbara Wright. London: Calder, 1980; New York: Red Dust, 1980.

Cette voix. Paris: Editions de Minuit, 1975. Translated by Barbara Wright as *That Voice.* New York: Red Dust, 1982.

L'Apocryphe. Paris: Editions de Minuit, 1980.

Monsieur Songe (récit). Paris: Editions de Minuit, 1982.

Le Harnais (carnets). Paris: Editions de Minuit, 1984.

Charrue (carnets). Paris: Editions de Minuit, 1985.
L'Ennemi. Paris: Editions de Minuit, 1987.
Du nerf (carnets). Paris: Editions de Minuit, 1990.
Théo ou le temps neuf. Paris: Editions de Minuit, 1991.
Micrologues: Vouvou Miam-Miam, Les Oignons, Le Hasard, Le Cafard, Le Temps, Conseils. London: *La Chouette* (French Department, Birnbeck College, University of London), 1991.
(Pinget is also the author of several volumes of plays.)

Selected Critical Works

Baetens, Jean. "Passacaille ou la multiplication par zéro." *Littérature,* no. 46 (May 1982): 93–104.

———. *Aux frontières du récit: "Fable" de Robert Pinget comme nouveau nouveau roman.* Toronto: Editions Paratexte; Louvain: Université Pers Leuven, 1987.

Baqué, Françoise. *Le Nouveau roman.* Montréal: Bordas, 1972.

Baril, Germaine. "Robert Pinget's Polyvalent use of parody in *Abel et Bela, Identité* and *Nuit.*" *Degré Second,* no. 7 (July 1983): 109–22.

Bas de casse, no. 2 (1980). Special issue on Pinget.

Bauman, Su. "*Passacaille,* Passacaille? Etude sur un roman de Pinget." *Kentucky Romance Quarterly* 22, no. 1 (1975): 125–35.

Boyer, Phillippe. "Mezzo voce." In *L'Ecarté(e),* pp. 113–45. Paris: Seghers-Laffont, 1973.

Broomer, Peter. "A New Way of Reading Pinget's *Passacaille.*" *Nottingham French Studies* 12, no. 2 (October 1973): 86–99.

Carrabino, Victor. "Pinget's *Passacaille:* The Endless Sonata of the Dead." *Neophilologus,* no. 69 (January 1985): 59–66.

Cismaru, Alfred. "Robert Pinget: *Passacaille.*" *French Review* 44, no. 1 (October 1970): 183.

Crépu, Michel. "Voix: Entretien avec Robert Pinget." *Esprit* n.s. 7, no. 2 (February 1983): 8–14.

Duvert, Tony. "La Parole et la fiction." *Critique,* no. 252 (May 1968): 443–61.

Etudes Littéraires 19, no. 3 (winter 1986–87). Special issue on Pinget.

Henkels, Robert. "Novel Quarters for an Odd Couple: Apollo and Dionysus in Beckett's *Watt* and Pinget's *The Inquisitory.*" *Studies in Twentieth Century Literature* 2, no. 2 (spring 1978): 141–57.

———. *Robert Pinget: The Novel as Quest.* Tuscaloosa: University of Alabama Press, 1979.

———. "Voix et silences: Les pièces radiophoniques de Robert Pinget." *Présence Francophone,* no. 22 (spring 1981): 173–90.

———. "Oublieuse mémoire." In *From Dante to García-Márquez: Studies in Romance Linguistics,* ed. Gene H. Bell-Villada et al., pp. 363–84. Williamstown, MA: Williams College, 1987.

———. "And Behold, There Were Shepherds: The Shepherd Mandala in Pinget's *L'Apocryphe.*" *New Novel Review 2*, no. 1 (1994): 33–48.

Kaempfer, Jean. "Robert Pinget, la description dans quelques états." *Poétique,* no. 88 (November 1991): 387–98.

Knapp, Bettina. "Un interview avec Robert Pinget." *French Review 42*, no. 1 (October 1968): 548–54.

Liéber, Jean-Claude. "Lecture de *Quelqu'un.*" *Littérature,* no. 10 (May 1973): 65–76.

———. "Structure du récit dans *L'Inquisitoire.*" *Poétique,* no. 14 (1973): 250–60.

———. "L'Ecriture de Pinget." *Nouvelle Revue Française,* no. 428 (September 1988): 75–79.

Lindon, Jerôme. "Littérature dégagée." *New Morality 2–3* (1962): 105–14.

Magny, Olivier de. "Robert Pinget ou le palimpseste." Postscript to *Graal Flibuste.* Paris: Union Générale des Editeurs, 10/18, 1963.

Mercier, Vivian. *The New French Novel from Queneau to Pinget.* New York: Farrar, Strauss and Giroux, 1971.

Praeger, Michele. *Les Romans de Robert Pinget: Une écriture des possibles.* Lexington, KY: French Forum, 1986.

———. "Un ennemi qui vous veut du bien." *Critique 43*, no. 485 (October 1987): 844–62.

Pugh, Anthony. "Pinget's Others." *Paragraph: A Journal of Modern Critical Theory 12*, no. 1 (March 1989): 37–55.

Reid, Martine, Brigitte Szymanek, and Karen McPherson. "Robert Pinget." *Yale French Studies,* Special Issue (1988): 97–114.

Renouard, Madeleine. *Robert Pinget à la lettre.* Paris: Belfond, 1993.

Review of Contemporary Fiction 3, no. 2 (summer 1983). Issue on Jack Kerouac and Pinget.

Revue de Belles Lettres, no. 1 (1982). Special issue on Pinget.

Taminiaux, Pierre. *Robert Pinget.* Paris: Seuil, 1994.

Part II.
Innovations in Language
and Form

6

Philippe Sollers

Katherine C. Kurk

Aimons. Rythmons. Et passons.[1]

The variety and volume of his writings, the fervor and contradiction of his literary and political stances, his penetrating eye, close-textured exposition and militant eroticism, and his image as *homo ludens* par excellence, have all made Philippe Sollers a dominant force in the French literary scene for the last thirty years. This is not to say that he is understood or that his path and its followers have been constant. In fact the questions posed by Léon S. Roudiez—"Who is Philippe Sollers? What is he anyway?"[2]—are ones frequently asked and more rhetorically answered by other contemporary critics, including the writer himself. Stephen Heath, one of Sollers's earliest, most astute, and sympathetic readers, now describes him as exemplifying, to an extreme degree, the post-postmodernist desire for publicity:

> Sollers, founder and energizer of the most influential journal of this half-century, *Tel Quel* . . . has gone from a series of uncompromising texts . . . via phases of adulation of the pope and the United States to a trilogy—a trinity—of novels that combine sex, antifeminism, and the chronicles of multinational Parisian cultural life to the taste of a greatly expanded audience. . . . Sollers's significance is now the degree to which he spectacularizes the current reality of the writer as medium, assumes his work as simply the sum of his appearances: penning a piece on Madonna, posing for a car commercial, popping up with [Bernard] Pivot.[3]

Philip Barnard, a longtime Sollers translator, is more positive but equally cautionary: "Today . . . Sollers takes his place as one of the major French authors of the second half of the Twentieth Century. Thus far the career of this protean and always controversial writer and left-bank personality has been complex and eventful; Sollers's gift for self-transformation makes summaries of his career rapidly obsolete."[4] Even Sollers's name, a provocative pseudonym chosen when, as a minor, he published his first story despite familial disapproval, resists singular definition: "Venant de *sollus* (avec deux L!) et *ars*. 'Tout entier art.' *Sollus* est le même radical que le grec *holos*, qui veut dire: 'entièrement, sans reste.' . . . Absolument dédié à l'art. Brûlure! Sacrifice! Sainteté! Mais, en même temps, sollers veut dire: habile, intelligent, ingénieux, adroit, rusé, le terrain le plus apte à produire . . . Sollers, sollertis . . . Sollertia . . . Voilà un nom bien suspect, n'est-ce pas, immoral en diable!"[5]

Born Philippe Joyaux on November 28, 1936, in Talence, a suburb of Bordeaux, Sollers had a childhood marked by asthma and otitis, "le souffle" and "l'oreille."[6] His early schooling was in Bordeaux; he then spent some time at a Jesuit institution in Versailles, from which he was expelled for too little discipline and too much "forbidden" reading. Sollers was also briefly a student at the Ecole Supérieure des Sciences Economiques et Commerciales. His first prose work, "Le Défi," written in September 1956, and his novella *Une curieuse solitude* (1958), both first-person narratives concerning youthful sexual initiation and its consequence, and both greatly influenced by Marcel Proust and André Breton, were praised by such notables as Louis Aragon and François Mauriac. In 1960, Sollers (along with Marcelin Pleynet) founded the review and monograph series *Tel Quel;* it is generally considered the leading journal of European writing and critical discourse of its time. Sollers's prolific critical writings are not restricted to *Tel Quel* and *L'Infini*, nor is there any limit to his subject matter. He is as equally at home discussing Nietzsche's *Ecce homo* or the statuary of Aristide Maillol as he is writing a piece for *Le Monde* on the La Closerie restaurant or a travelogue on the Ile de Ré.

Le Parc (1961, Prix Médicis), a "poème romanesque" that focuses on reading and the viewing process, was published in the wave of temporal and spatial exploration after the appearance of Alain Robbe-Grillet's *Dans le labyrinthe*. Yet Sollers, initiating a series of reversals for which he is famous, soon discarded his affinity with the *nouveau roman*.[7] This volte-face was duly and ironically observed by Robbe-Grillet:

"Sollers, à l'époque où il n'avait pas songé à me condamner définitivement, m'avait demandé un texte pour sa revue."[8] Sollers has rejected predecessors and colleagues with vehemence and sang-froid. His 1968 break with Jean-Pierre Faye, who created the rival journal *Change,* has been well documented.[9] In the rigorous 1970 preface added to *Une curieuse solitude,* he even denied his own early text as belonging to "la tradition culturelle classique bourgeoise, en plein décomposition" and placed himself "depuis longtemps et définitivement de l'autre côté" (p. 7).

In June 1975, Sollers told David Hayman: "I think my books begin with *Drame.* . . . Then you have *Nombres,* followed by *Lois,* which constitutes a break or rupture, then *H,* and then this work [*Paradis*]."[10] The new novelistic canon coincides with a series of ideological shifts showcased by *Tel Quel* and Sollers's other critical writings: from Marxist ("Printemps rouge") to Maoist (a special double issue of *Tel Quel* 48/49, a passionate defense of Maria-Antonietta Macciocchi's *De la Chine,* the Chinese ideograms of *Nombres*), to a mystical adherence to the Holy Catholic and Apostolic Church of Rome (a conversion implicit in *Délivrance*) coupled with an alliance with such nouveaux philosophes as Bernard-Henri Lévy and an interest in the United States. On the surface this trajectory diverges radically, yet there are shared patterns and discernable progressions within *Drame, Nombres, Lois, H, Paradis,* and *Paradis II* that tie to Sollers's more recent works as well. Each text examines the boundaries of the writing process, the interplay of words, sounds, and ideas on the page. *Drame* (1965), a cross-genre title, is divided into sixty-four prose *chants,* a dialectic of "je" and "il" that may also be read as the sixty-four houses of the *I-Ching,* the "changes" that move to divine moral, social, and political enigmas. Simultaneously *Drame* is chess, board game and game board, subject and process intertwined, a war of chance and reason, "pour un joueur, le temps projeté en espace" (*Drame,* cover note). While *Drame* pulsates between the reading and writing couple, Roland Barthes has demonstrated that its true subject is more specifically a narrator's quest: "A searching hero, a searched-for story, an enemy language, an ally language, these are the cardinal functions that make up the meaning . . . and [the] dramatic tension."[11] In *Drame,* one can also recall the young Sollers "tout formé dans la maladie," spending his time playing chess, reading and discovering "des naissances perpétuelles et sans doute des morts perpétuelles."[12]

On several occasions Sollers has called *Drame* and *Nombres* (1968) ascetic and spiritual investigations, and both texts have explicit mathematical ("espèce d'obsession géométrique"[13]) and philosophical frames. *Drame* is composed of binary tension, a dynamics of pairing. *Nombres* is composed of twenty-five prose sections of four sequences apiece, based on a system of ten: "Et je suis comme eux, parmi eux, parmi vous, dans l'opération, dans le nombre, $1 + 2 + 3 + 4 = 10 - $ ⟨𝟙𝟘⟩)———."[14] Yet *Nombres* is equally grounded in Lucretius's "Seminaque inumero numero summaque profunda" ("The seeds of all things are countless in number and are rushing through limitless space impelled by perpetual motion," p. 9), which allows for the division, reconstitution, multiplication, proliferation, and disappearance of words and ideas, textual points of reference. *Nombres* is death and reformation in movable parts. Its "je" persona is a soldier, a victim, an archeologist deciphering the signs of dead culture, dead formations with their "nombres" literally covered in blood, "le récit rouge" (p. 57). Both Jacques Derrida and Julia Kristeva have argued that *Nombres* is built from the dead surfaces of other Sollersian texts as well as their sources.[15] The Kabbalah, the Torah, Vedic hymns, Pythagoras, Bruno, Marx, Nietzsche, Descartes, Lenin, Artaud, Bataille, Mao, Hegel, Aristotle, Leibnitz, Baudelaire, Rimbaud, Mallarmé, Dante, and Pascal are merely a few of the writers or texts that appear in *Nombres* with no identified reference. *Nombres* stands in opposition to the Old Testament Numbers wherein Moses names and enumerates the people of God: "Une textualité générative infinie, plurale remplace le signifiant."[16]

If *Drame* and *Nombres* test the limits of writing, then *Lois* (1972) is the ultimate text of transgression. Canon becomes cannon, a percussive explosion of sound and sacrilege: "Et sonnez hautbois caphonez clairons" (p. 107). Entirely rewritten after the shock of his father's death, *Lois* is removed by Sollers from the perpetual motion of reading and rewriting as intellectual exercise ("Récit de la pensée dans les mots et réciproquement," *Drame*, p. 98) to a more corporeal textual body, a cacophony of voices. *Lois* is based on Mallarmé's dice, on Joyce's *Finnegan's Wake*, laced with Montesquieu's *L'Esprit des lois* and Plato's *Laws*. The reader/writer/actor becomes a channeler whose speech has had a past life and can also take on new life of its own. *Lois* updates Panurge ("La nature en *dette* impose braguette," p. 43) and creates semantic litanies worthy of Rabelais: "Nous vous congelons, nous vous confondons, votre confiture nous inspire en rond . . . nous vous consacrons maître couille en con" (pp. 50–51). It is a Gargantuan laugh in the face of death, a conscious choice of regeneration. The cube of *Lois* is an upending, a death-to-life process: "nié [1] face [2] à face [3], niant [4] la membrane [5], l'entrée [6]: ce qui s'y trouve existe ailleurs, ce qui n'y est pas n'est nulle part: NÉ—" (p. 5). That which is "nié" (rejected, contested) is "NÉ" (born) with majuscular and raucous force. Sollers's form has evolved from the balletic interface of *Drame* to semipunctuated, open-ended groupings in *Lois*, from syntax to "Sein taxe" (p. 69).

Such freedom is expanded in *H* (1973), which Sollers has called a "lyrico-epic,"[17] a "brouillon" written "dans un état de débordement."[18] Its total lack of conventional guideposts—punctuation, narrative, personae—forces the issue of aural reading in much the same way that a person is obligated to swim when thrown into deep waters: "c'est le lieu idéal pour nager entre blanc et noir" (*H*, p. 31); "la nature est pour moi un lac rempli de poissons et moi poisson poisson poisson sans complexes les dauphins suivent dans la mer leurs canaux d'information c'est leur tradition orale imagine un peu qu'ils lisent comme ça en nageant," (p. 63); "il faut nager dans la matière et la transformation de la langue en matière" (p. 100); "j'apprends à nager" (p. 128); "tout est joie poissonneuse" (p. 153). In *Drame*, Sollers envisions "un livre illimité, c'est-à-dire un livre qui soit un mot (un point)" (p. 130), reminiscent of Mallarmé's "expansion totale de la lettre."[19] *H* is that text; infinite readings illuminate and define the ideogrammatic letter without reducing or fixing it. As title, as text, "H" is suspended, an atomic axis. Critics have remarked on the encyclopedic quality of *H*: "at first glance . . . [its] entries are both unlabeled and out of sequence."[20] The letter *H*, based on the Greek *êta* and the Phoenician *heth*, is a trellis, a gate, both entrance and exit. Passing through this gate one can find Friedrich Hölderlin (who signed his personal correspondence with the single initial "H" and whose epistolary *Hyperion* is grounded in voice), a sexual unleashing similar to Rimbaud's *H* in *Illuminations*, "H" as erotic talisman and symbol of the life cycle recalling the signs of Artaud's Tarahumara Indians, the number *huit*, *H* as *hache* ("quel libérateur brandira l'épée invisible où lame et poignée," p. 24) and *hydrogène* ("voilà la bombe qui retombe toute chaude enfumée," p. 9), the *hameçon* of the text, *l'heure H*, and above all, *l'histoire*. *H* may be interpreted as a reaction to May 1968—the historical event filtered through the sieve of its aftermath, as larger sequences of chronological tombstones that become "temps retrouvé" when they relive in the moments of their enunciation, and as Sollers's autobiographical memories.

Paradis (1981), like *H,* continues in unpunctuated and unmediated form, visually emphasized by being in italicized boldface throughout. Sollers has compared its psalmody to the incessant movement of a Tibetan prayer wheel: "il y a à la fois le rythme, la danse, le roulement des syllabes et l'interprétation des événements . . . le flux des générations, de la destruction."[21] He has recorded *Paradis* on tape, broadcast it on the radio, and has given it numerous personal readings, and Jean-Paul Fargier has captured it on video ("Sollers au Paradis"). Of all Sollers's novels, *Paradis* is arguably the one most accompanied by authorial critique since it appeared as *travail en cours* in succeeding issues of *Tel Quel,* often followed by a commentary or interview, and it was published simultaneously with the most overt Sollersian memoirs to date, *Vision à New York,* a series of interviews with David Hayman. *Paradis* is a Dantesque update, a biblical bath in the "wake" of Joyce. In *H,* the reader must swim in a paginal sea; *Paradis* is a flood of personal religious epiphany, its oral rhythm a series of undulating waves with Sollers a neo-Noah: "*il resta là quarante jours et quarante nuits sans manger ni boire écrivant l'écrit s'écrivant au bruit des paroles n'écrivant rien tout en écrivant sans arrêt n'écrivant que ce qui était écrit en train de s'écrire et parfois s'écrivant lui-même*" (p. 53). Noah's entire fabula—masculinity and femininity, catastrophe, salvation, and procreation, culpability or innocence of the intoxicated, erotic body, progenitor of Babel—eddies and swirls while multiple voices including Christ, Odysseus, and Shakespeare intermingle with the quotidian flotsam and jetsam such as tennis du jour ("*deuxième balle net effet spin shot lifté volée revers long des lignes borg connors vilas mac enroe,*" p. 233) or the papal visit to Mexico ("*jean paul 2 pologne se pose alighieri au mexique,*" p. 221). Sollers's *Paradis* is a zestful, unnerving reading experience, in his own terms: "C'est un livre d'un lyrisme fou."[22]

In 1982, Sollers surprised his reading public by moving from the Editions du Seuil to the publishing house of Gallimard and by disbanding *Tel Quel.* A new journal subscription card (1983) announced: "*Tel Quel* est arrêté. *L'Infini* commence . . . Pourquoi *L'Infini*? Parce que l'invention littéraire peut plus que jamais avancer sans justification, à l'air libre. Parce que la pensée doit aller dans tous les sens où son aventure la conduit." The publishing world is under siege in Sollers's more recent fictions, especially in *Portrait du joueur.* Literary critics are captured with equal brio in *Le Cœur absolu.* "Cacadémiciens" and "unifrèrsitaires" (*Lois*) have always been suspect. Obviously Sollers's own "writing adventure" had taken a new route. *Femmes* (1983) is the beginning of a series of novels in the 1980s dealing with journalists, novelists, diarists, artists in various quasi-autobiographical masks: "identités rapprochées multiples."[23] On the surface more accessible to the reader, these works have topped the French best-seller lists for weeks, not only for their eroticism but also for their portrayals, in *roman-à-clef* fashion, or perhaps more accurately their betrayals, of contemporary literati. They dance on the line between fiction and reality, the "intermédiaire," a zone of actuality that Sollers has known since his earliest writings, now recast and foregrounded: "Le moment approche où l'espace va donner sa permission, l'autorisation, dans un déclic, d'être là sans être là, d'être vraiment le spectre du lieu, l'aventurier immobile de la doublure interdite."[24]

The "je"-narrator of *Femmes,* an American journalist named Will (free? possibly; Shakespeare? assuredly. See pp. 539–50), who lives in Paris, is writing a novel, *Femmes,* which will be translated by his friend "S." who is also writing a novel, *Comédie:* "être là sans être là," indeed. Will's other male companions include three thinkers with names of Germanic resonance: Lutz (Louis Althusser), Fals (Jacques Lacan), and Werth (Roland Barthes), and an Italian, Alfredo Malmora (Alberto Moravia). His female friends are more numerous and diverse. Among them one finds Deborah, his wife (Kristeva), Flora (M.-A. Macciocchi) and Elissa (Hélène Cixous). Sollers has been taken to task for his merciless rendition of the personal tragedies of Althusser, Lacan, and, most particularly, of Barthes. Some critics who found Sollers's earlier works "illisible" reproached him for having become comprehensible in *Femmes.* Much attention has been paid to the "collective" women (the feminist group WOMANN, World Organization for Men Annihilation and for a New Natality, is trying either to convert Will or possibly to destroy him), and to Will's varied amorous encounters. The title is an homage to the "Woman" series by Willem de Kooning, with an additional nod to Picasso's "Les Demoiselles d'Avignon." Yet the narrative thread, woven of Célinian ellipses, is Will's odyssey home ("Toujours Homère et Cie," p. 566) and the interplay of elements that conspire to delay, to propel, to instruct him en route. Will is a twentieth-century "frequent flier" in all possible senses, complete with son Stephen (little Daedalus) and a libidinal black box, "mon carnet de jouissance" (p. 32). Like Odysseus, he must confront birth and death in the maternal image. The "character" most alive (by action, and also by being pregnant with Will's child) in *Femmes*, Cyd, is killed in a terrorist bomb attack; WOMANN kills woman before Will boards his flight to New York.

It is no surprise that *Portrait du joueur* (1985) begins with its narrator, Philippe Diamant, returning to his native Gironde, reminiscing at his father's and grandfather's graves, and finding the site of his natal home razed with a SUMA hypermarket in its place. Suspected of being a shoplifter while he roves the SUMA aisles, Diamant assumes the part of an "archeologist," M. Lévi-Strauss, in search of the layers of an ancient civilization. This excavation into the Sollersian past resurrects *Une curieuse solitude* as well with a hilarious confrontation between Diamant, Asunción (his sister's maid, "petite, ronde, brune, les yeux amusés, tablier noir et tablier blanc," p. 16), and her "mec." Role-playing and dual vision—Diamant's good eye plus a literal and figurative black one thanks to the boyfriend's suspicions, and his mother Lena's two-dimensional regard, "au bord de la mort . . . ses deux yeux . . . l'un marron clair, l'autre sombre" (p. 39) mirroring the Aquitaine's double allegiance to France and England—combine to announce the spectral stage. Four women of Diamant's childhood—"le bouquet de femmes" of Lena, grandmother Odette, sisters Laure and Hélène—balance the four women of his adulthood: wife Norma and mistresses Ingrid, Joan, and Sophie. With one home down, one home to find, strata of time and space, of present and memory spliced, the multifaceted Diamant confronts a variety of births and deaths. *Portrait du joueur* is an earthquake, moving and rearranging the world as Diamant knows it, rending it, displaying it, complete with an epistolary epicenter that vibrates and generates aftershocks: the "Lettres de Sophie." Sophie, whom Diamant met in Hölderlin's Tübingen, enjoys setting the stage, inventing scenarios for which she sends Diamant explicit, salacious instructions. Critics have discussed the similarity to the notes that Joyce sent his wife, Nora, and the obvious resemblance of the title to *Portrait of the Artist as a Young Man*.[25] Notice should also be taken of the fact that S.'s Polish wife in *Femmes* is named Sophie (a different character but an apparent textual incest) and of the etymological "wisdom" of this feminine role. In fact, Will calls his wife, Deborah, a true "Sophia," squaring the circular allusion.[26]

Like *Femmes*, *Portrait* has an ominous collective, OEUF. As if metamorphosed by the text's geologic upheavals, its acronymic definition varies (*L'Œil Unifié Fraternel*, *L'Œuvre à Usage Financier*, etc.) but the menace remains. OEUF/SUMA buries the individual. Sollers proclaims himself "polemic with everything that is collective. . . . Everything that does not define the real as intrinsically individual seems false and manipulated to me."[27] The novel closes with a montage of episodes that underscore the singularity and urgency of Diamant's continuing mission: a sudden car crash that interrupts his reverie of suicide (parallel to Cyd's death in *Femmes*), a *somnium avisum* in an underground casino (recalling Mallarmé's "Un coup de dés" and the writer/believer's necessary risk), the discovery of a book belonging to his maternal great-grandfather, and the necessity to participate in his niece's wedding, a blessing of familial line.

The continuum is unequivocal with the appearance of *Paradis II* (1986). *Paradis* "ends" with its *voyageur* seated in a café, drinking water, smoking, drifting into sleep, "*puis soudain relâché léger renverse négligemment la tête au soleil*" (p. 254). *Paradis II*, without italics, does not begin, it reawakens: "soleil voix lumière écho des lumières soleil cœur lumière rouleau des lumières moi dessous" (p. 7). Northrop Frye has discussed the Heraclitan "sense of awakening into a greater degree of reality" present in Genesis: "Creation [is] a sudden coming into being of a world through articulate speech (another aspect of logos), conscious perception, light and stability."[28] As the sense of light may account for the emphasis on "days" in the creation story so it contributes to the temporal awareness within the Sollersian œuvre, its creative process. *Paradis II* emerges from the turbulent *Paradis* but also from the chronometric *Femmes* and *Portrait*, evident especially in its Laure (character)/laurie (sister)/Laura (Petrarchan) sequence: "laurie seize ans rayonnante cheveux blonds yeux bleus visage moqueur d'Athéna c'est ma sœur ma nièce ma fille ma petite fille on s'amuse comme ça tout l'été" (p. 109). Laura is then the name of S.'s wife in *Le Cœur absolu*. The connexity of *Paradis* is, moreover, a demonstrable proof of the totality of Sollers's works, multiform and polytextual.

Le Cœur absolu (1987) likewise reawakens with the question "Toujours vivant?" (p. 13). Its narrator, Ph. S., is a writer beset with Dostoyevskyan seizures, metronomic reminders of the human condition. More specifically S. finds his life calculated by a néantomètre: "Sa fonction? Mesurer le coefficient d'irradiation de la néantisation permanente sur l'animal humain. Ses augmentations brusques. Ses pointes" (p. 233). His current project is a screenplay of *The Divine Comedy,* but it is his *un*commonplace book, "LE CARNET ROUGE" of erotic encounters, that punctuates the text and qualifies temporal passage: "G.A. (Grande Année). P.A. (Petite Année) . . . G.S. (Grande Semaine). P.S. (Petite Semaine)" (p. 103).²⁹ S. is also a cofounder of the secret society, *Le Cœur absolu.* Based on principles of individual pleasure and liberty, its members include musicians Cecilia and Marco, Sigrid (a philosopher), and an actress, Liv. S. himself plays roles—most notably, that of Casanova—at a masked ball, via readings of his *Mémoires,* in action. Like *Portrait, Le Cœur absolu* has a core of letters, sent from wife Laura during a trip to the United States (New York, Chicago), which simultaneously encase, as a jeweler's box, an allegory from Nicolas Fontaine's 1691 *Dictionnaire chrestien* on the "DIAMANT" (pp. 221–22). *Le Cœur absolu,* mirroring the *Comedy,* is richly peopled, from fille de joie Snow to fille en joie Jailey, from Regnard and Mozart to Mme Roland and Rodin. At its close, S. has had to abandon his movie project; his Japanese backers withdraw their support. Yet he is asked, by *Les Editions Aurore* (encore du soleil) to write an introduction for a new translation of the *Odyssey,* and S. and Laura return home to Paris: "une année comme une autre, non?" (p. 423).

Near the end of *Femmes,* S. confides to Will that he has an illegitimate daughter, Laure, whom he sees "Comme par hasard. . . . Avec sa mère, au café. . . . Ou de loin. . . . Furtivement. . . . Elle me ressemble" (p. 510). In *Les Folies françaises* (1988), the forty-three-year-old narrator, Philippe Sollers, meets a child he has not seen for eighteen years. Madame, his generic past female fling, has raised her daughter in the United States and in Switzerland, with Sollers's blessing: "A l'époque, j'étais anarchiste: ce choix me parut sur toute la ligne un défi et une réfutation de mes convictions" (p. 15). The earlier "défi," like *Une curieuse solitude,* has returned. Her name is France, all-encompassing, past and future, but consumedly the present: "tu es ma fille et tu es ma langue" (p. 56); "Selon toute probabilité, je serai enterré en France, autant commencer par toi. . . . Je m'ensevelis dans ton lit" (p. 29). While France studies France—its literature, music and art—the narrator makes his study of her: "Je te peins . . . la peinture est un roman, troisième monde au-delà de la réalité et de son miroir, plus présente que ne le sera jamais la conscience de la réalité redoublée d'un miroir. C'est notre folie visible et

lisible" (p. 117). Among the follies one finds "folie à deux"—Oedipus/
Lear/Joyce and daughter—and "folie raisonnante": a theory-minded,
clearly nonvisionary American graduate student Saul, hagiographer of
Sollers's life and work. There are also Proustian folies for he "re"called
the parks, the "maisons de plaisance" of seventeenth-century court favorites and "les parcs" encompass *Les Folies françaises,* as does Proust
himself with both beginning epigraph and closing allusion. Yet the image of the park (*Le Parc*) is also writer Sollers's past, here fast-forwarded
into the present. *Les Folies françaises* is a fable of time and infinity.

Moving away from protagonists whose names are openly self-
coded, Sollers's novels nonetheless continue to be fabled and to interro-
gate temporality. *Le Lys d'or* (1989) has as its narrator a sinologist, Simon
Rouvray, a twentieth-century manifestation of the duc de Saint-Simon.
Rouvray meets a rich young woman, Reine de Laume (another Proustian
allusion, but she is also féerique, magic queen of the Touraine, complete
with "trésor[s] enterré[s]," p. 20), in an antique shop where she pur-
chases a golden lily, obviously taken from a church's sculpture of the
Anunciation. The lily then is functionally permuted, symbolically displaced from incarnating device/virginal receiver to regal French em-
blem and coinage, *le lys d'or* to Taoist symbol of light, until it is replaced
and restored in Rouvray's hands for services rendered. Reine commis-
sions Rouvray to write a sexually explicit notebook (*Le Lys d'or*), full of
the "délices" he enjoys with mistresses Leslie, Tania, and Odile. The Tarot,
"Barbe bleue," Svengali and Mephistopheles, psychoanalysis and dreams
provide background. Spectator of both erotic text and the actual scene,
Reine becomes the ultimate audience, open to and opened by Rouvray,
a lily changed from "voyeuse" to "joueuse."

La Fête à Venise (1991) also has a narrator whose name crosses time
and who emblematizes comment upon his age: "Pierre" (not Jean)
Froissart. Yet it is a nom de guerre, chosen because Froissart is a member of a clandestine gang based in Venice with curious activities: perhaps drug-running or trafficking stolen art—"le grand banditisme international" (p. 158)—but certainly a group of neo-Maquis who battle
judgmental tyranny. Froissart transports a painting by Antoine Watteau,
"La Fête à Venise," a companion piece for the enigmatic "Fêtes vé-
nitiennes." In fact, some of the characters of *Fête* can be read as projec-
tions of this famous *peinture-à-clef.* Froissart's lover, Luz (an artist's necessary light, reprising "le soleil" in the Sollersian corpus), is "[une] boule

ronde et blonde" (p. 35); she illuminates the text much like the irides-
cent dancer foregrounded in Watteau's painting. Watteau corresponds
well with Sollers. He is an artist known for *déplacements;* even the chronology of his œuvre is suspect given the constant reworkings of his can-
vases. Moreover, critics have constantly misjudged him.

There is another A. W. in *Fête:* Andy Warhol, who embodies the
realization of art perceived and categorized by its time and who refuses
to be held hostage. Homage is also paid to Claude Monet's Venetian
series. Done late in life, finished by memory after an October to December visit in 1908, when Monet was haunted by the death of his wife,
Alice, and surrounded by the *nymphéas* of Giverny, these paintings do
not portray the typical reflections of boat and buildings in water. For
this they have been falsely judged as representative of "death in Venice."
However, light as life ("la fête") is more clearly Monet's focus just as it is
Sollers's. *La Fête à Venise* contains intrigue, criticism of art and society, a
mocking self-reflection manifestly reminiscent of Stendhal, and defiance.

The provocative stance is maintained in *Sade contre l'Etre Suprême*
(1992). Purportedly a letter written by the Divine Marquis to the Cardinal de Bernis on the evening of December 7, 1793, during the most virulent days of the Terror, it is also an incisive indictment of present time.
Epistolier Sade/Sollers denounces the reign of a new deity, a Supreme
Being (Thanatos) whose disciples are perpetrating a razzia of catastrophic
proportion. In denying the individual and the Other, in homogeniza-
tion via death and stultification via servitude, the new order engages in
"une incessante *décréation*" (p. 46). Its trinity "de la bêtise, de l'ignorance
et du préjugé" (pp. 32–33), its perversions of the church/bride, "la veuve"
(the guillotine) and her "éternel mari" (the Supreme Being) (p. 26), can
be countered only by "atheism," denial of patriotism and of artistic cen-
sure, and a total acceptance of the body as emblematized by the agonis-
tic Mme. du Barry or the irreverent, insouciant Girondins (pp. 29–30,
42), of Eros. In his critical essays, Sollers often writes of the twentieth-
century war between north and south, the ironic "Germanic" victory:
"pésanteur, glaciation, volonté de mort."[30] His Sade is aflame with in-
dignation ("Comme les lettres sont puissantes quand l'esprit est en feu!"
p. 49), and this letter is an apologia for all writers and readers who are
combustive, alive.

What, then, exists and persists in the Sollersian oeuvre? A brazen
vitality runs from "Le Défi" through *Sade contre l'Etre Suprême* as do

certain other characteristics: a sense of place and time, the role of view and perception, of *le voyable* and *le voyeur*, exploration and expansion of the self, humor, and finally, liberation in combative, complicit acts of writing and reading whose *casus belli* is death and whose sword/pen is eros, the lightning rods of the human condition.

Sollers's portrayals of place encompass conventional definitions; he captures the flavors and smells of Bordeaux ("Entrepôts gardant l'odeur des Antilles, gingembre, cannelle, girofle, tiédeur du sucre imprégnant les murs," *Portrait du joueur,* p. 40), of the Touraine, consistently of the Parisian contemporary arena. Simultaneously he is the new troubadour of Venice: "Je suis arrivé pour la première fois à Venise . . . en octobre 1963. Je me revois laissant tomber mon sac, la nuit, devant Saint-Marc. J'y suis toujours."[31] Self-accused of being "too French," too Southern,[32] he nonetheless exalts such an epithet with France as woman/country, the erotic landscape (*Les Folies françaises*). Yet Sollers's texts are also their immediate place, the "seen" as "scene," as in *Paradis*. Just as they often portray parks, they *are* parks, composites that foreground the picturesque and the assemblage. They are maps that reorient the cardinal points, requiring active navigation with *sex*tant in hand. In much of his fictional network Sollers temporally codifies with specific dates, hours, periods of time, verb tenses, or enumerations, all traditional chronologic measures. But the effect is to dislocate, to suspend, to collide; his unpunctuated fictions exist in moments of orality.

There is in Sollers's works a particular specularity, an investigation of the gaze that performs and deforms, and of the view that informs. This is often revealed in scenes of mutual self-gratification: the young narrator with his aunt Edith (*Femmes*), the narrator and Liv watching Sig with Jailey (*Le Cœur absolu*). Likewise Sollers employs an artistic frame, from *Une curieuse solitude,* a study in black and white interspersed with Gauguin vignettes, to the paginal configurations of *Drame* and the ideograms and diagrams of *Nombres,* to the crucial appearances of Tiepolo, Watteau, Fragonard, de Kooning, Picasso, Rodin, Monet, and Manet in the more recent works. For Sollers, art is a way to understand "the nervous system"[33] of an age, and his texts comprise a series of personal galleries whose pieces are regrouped, hung and rehung, a constant bringing into view.

These writings are consistently self-ironic, self-laudatory, and self-exploratory. Yet that self is enigmatically divided, masked, alternately revealed and denied. One can never forget that "Philippe Sollers" is, in fact, a fiction himself that corresponds well with the playful vein undergirding his "Sollertia." Heir to Rabelais and to Joyce's "trifid tongue," Sollers's very name moves and divides—"sol-air"—as do his invented words in *Lois*, his protean phrases in *H* and *Paradis*, his neo-Menippean tongues. Sollers's reference to himself as clown and mimic is long-standing and cultivated: "C'est une chose qui m'a toujours paru extrêmement importante comme portée philosophique, la capacité d'imiter de façon à faire ressortir le grotesque."[34] Sollers brings forth the laughable with metaphoric and literal elegies of the bed (*Le Cœur absolu*) and of the bathroom (*L'Intermédiaire*), by desacralizing and provoking.

Such raillery and impudence are parts of the serious game in which Sollers opposes the somnolence of our time and the placid, non-participatory reader. Anyone who deals with the Sollersian text is of necessity put on and in the spot: "Comment revenir? Comment être là? Comment accepter l'aventure?" (*Drame*, p. 16); "Prisonnier du jeu?" (*Drame*, p. 21); "Avouez qu'au fond vous ne lisez que ce qui vous arrange" (*Lois*, p. 111); "Vous n'avez pas la carte, la grille, le code d'accès!" (*La Fête à Venise*, p. 17). If "Philippe Sollers, writer" is an *act*, in its fullest definition of operation and performance, then he requires no less of his reader whom he intimately invites to consume, to consummate, to perpetuate the text, ultimately to share his "clin d'œil au sarcophage du jardin." (*La Fête à Venise*, p. 239).

Notes

1. Philippe Sollers, *Lois* (Paris: Seuil, 1972), p. 142.

2. Léon Roudiez, "Review of *Carnet de nuit*," *World Literature Today* 64, no. 2 (spring 1990), p. 278.

3. Stephen Heath, "Friday Night Books," in *A New History of French Literature*, ed. Denis Hollier (Cambridge: Harvard University Press, 1989), p. 1058.

4. Barnard and Cheryl Lester, "Philippe Sollers: *Femmes*," *Yale French Studies*, Special Issue (1988), p. 163.

5. *Portrait du joueur* (Paris: Gallimard, 1984), p. 71.

6. *Vision à New York*, pp. 35–36.

7. Sollers discusses Robbe-Grillet's impact on his writing process in "Sept Propositions sur Alain Robbe-Grillet," *Tel Quel*, no. 2 (1960), pp. 49–53.

8. Alain Robbe-Grillet, in *Nouveau Roman: hier, aujourd'hui: 2. Pratiques* (Paris: UGE, 1972), p. 173.

9. See, for example, Sollers's own "'Camarade' et camarade," *Tel Quel,* no. 39 (1969), pp. 100–101; Roland Champagne, "The Problem of the One and the Many: A Case for the *Change* Collectif," *Boundary 2* 4, no. 3 (spring 1976), pp. 917–23; Lawrence Kritzman, "The Changing Political Ideology of *Tel Quel,*" *Contemporary French Civilization* 2, no. 3 (spring 1978), pp. 405–21.

10. In "An Interview with Philippe Sollers," *TriQuarterly,* no. 38 (winter 1977), p. 125.

11. In "Event, Poem, Novel," trans. Bruce Benderson and Ursule Moinaro in *Event* (New York: Red Dust, 1986), p. 99.

12. *Vision à New York,* pp. 35, 39.

13. Ibid., p. 80.

14. *Nombres,* p. 17.

15. See Jacques Derrida, *La Dissémination* (Paris: Seuil, 1972), and Julia Kristeva, *Semeiotike* (Paris: Seuil, 1978).

16. Kristeva, *Semeiotike,* p. 303.

17. David Hayman, "An Interview with Philippe Sollers," *Iowa Review* 5, no. 4 (1974), p. 91.

18. *Vision à New York,* p. 88.

19. Stéphane Mallarmé, *Variations sur un sujet,* in *Œuvres complètes* (Paris: Gallimard, 1945), p. 380.

20. Hayman, "Nodality or Plot Displaced: The Dynamics of Sollers's *H,*" *SubStance,* no. 43 (1984), p. 56.

21. *Vision à New York,* p. 94.

22. Ibid., p. 130.

23. *Carnet de nuit,* p. 126.

24. *Portrait du joueur,* p. 268.

25. See Geert Lernout, *The French Joyce* (Ann Arbor: University of Michigan Press, 1990), pp. 160–61.

26. *Femmes,* p. 54.

27. Catherine Cusset, "A Different Measure of Time: Writing or the Consciousness of Pleasure," *Yale French Studies,* Special Issue (1988), pp. 159–60.

28. Northrup Frye, *The Great Code: The Bible and Literature* (New York: Harcourt Brace Jovanovich, 1982), p. 108.

29. See Sollers in Cusset, "A Different Measure of Time," pp. 155–56.

30. Sollers in "Nietzsche et l'esprit français," *Magazine Littéraire,* no. 298 (April 1992), p. 26.

31. *Carnet de nuit,* p. 131.

32. *Théorie des exceptions,* p. 303.

33. *Le Cœur absolu,* p. 323.

34. *Vision à New York,* p. 50.

Bibliography

Works by Philippe Sollers

"Le Défi." *Ecrire*, no. 3 (1957): 1–35. Translated by Jean Stewart as "The Challenge" in *French Short Stories I*, 215–265. New York: Penguin, 1966.

Une curieuse solitude. Paris: Seuil, 1958. Translated by Richard Howard as *A Strange Solitude.* New York: Grove, 1959.

Le Parc. Paris: Seuil, 1961. Translated by A. M. Sheridan Smith as *The Park.* London: Calder and Boyers, 1968; New York: Red Dust, 1969.

L'Intermédiaire. Paris: Seuil, 1963.

Drame. Paris: Seuil, 1965. Translated by Bruce Benderson and Ursule Molinaro as *Event.* New York: Red Dust, 1986.

L'Ecriture et l'expérience des limites. Paris: Seuil, 1968. Translated by David Hayman and Philip Barnard as *Writing and the Experience of Limits.* New York: Columbia University Press, 1983.

Logiques. Paris: Seuil, 1968.

Nombres. Paris: Seuil, 1968.

Lois. Paris: Seuil, 1972.

H. Paris: Seuil, 1973.

Paradis. Paris: Seuil, 1981.

Vision à New York. Paris: Grasset (Collection Figures), 1981; Denoël (Collection Médiations), 1981.

Femmes. Paris: Gallimard, 1983. Translated by Barbara Bray as *Women.* New York: Columbia University Press, 1990.

Portrait du joueur. Paris: Gallimard, 1984.

Paradis II. Paris: Gallimard, 1986.

Théorie des exceptions. Paris: Gallimard, 1986.

Le Cœur absolu. Paris: Gallimard, 1987.

De Kooning, Vite. 2 vols. Paris: Editions de la Différence, 1988.

Les Folies françaises. Paris: Gallimard, 1988.

Carnet de nuit. Paris: Plon, 1989.

Le Lys d'or. Paris: Gallimard, 1989.

La Fête à Venise. Paris: Gallimard, 1991.

Improvisations. Paris: Gallimard, 1991.

Le Rire de Rome. With Frans de Haes. Paris: Gallimard, 1992.

Sade contre l'Etre Suprême. Paris: Quai Voltaire, 1992.

Le Secret. Paris: Gallimard, 1993.

La Guerre du goût. Paris: Gallimard, 1994.

Selected Critical Works

Barthes, Roland. *Sollers Ecrivain.* Paris: Seuil, 1979. Translated and introduced by Philip Thody as *Writer Sollers.* Minneapolis: University of Minnesota Press, 1987.
Brochier, Jean-Jacques; Savigneau, Josyane. "Philippe Sollers: contre la grande tyrannie." *Magazine Littéraire,* no. 285 (February 1991): 96–103.
Caws, Mary Ann. "Tel Quel: Text and Revolution." *Diacritics* 3, no. 1 (spring 1973): 2–8.
Chardin, Brigitte. *Sollers Moravia.* Paris: Ramsay, 1991.
Clark, Hilary. "Joyce, Sollers and the Infinite Text." *Canadian Review of Comparative Literature* 16, nos. 1–2 (March–June 1989), 74–94.
———. *The Fictional Encyclopedia.* New York: Garland, 1990. See 129–70 on *Paradis.*
Cusset, Catherine. " A Different Measure of Time: Writing or the Consciousness of Pleasure." *Yale French Studies,* Special Issue (1988): 155–62.
De Haes, Frans. "Philippos Adamantos, homo Sollers." *L'Infini,* no. 11 (1985): 98–104.
Derrida, Jacques. *La Dissémination.* Paris: Seuil, 1972. Translated and introduced by Barbara Johnson as *Dissemination.* Chicago: University of Chicago Press, 1981.
Forest, Philippe. "D'un paradis l'autre." *L'Infini,* no. 30 (1992): 36–62.
———. *Philippe Sollers.* Paris: Seuil ("Les Contemporains," vol. 15), 1992.
Hayman, David. "Nodality or Plot Displaced: The Dynamic of Sollers's *H.*" *SubStance,* no. 43 (1984): 54–65.
Heath, Stephen. *The Nouveau Roman. A Study in the Practice of Writing.* London: Flek, 1972; Philadelphia: Temple University Press, 1972.
Hill, Leslie. "Philippe Sollers and *Tel Quel.*" In *Beyond the Nouveau Roman: Essays on the Contemporary French Novel,* edited by Michael Tilby, pp. 100–122. New York: Berg, 1990.
Kafalenos, Emma. "Philippe Sollers' *Nombres:* Structure and Sources." *Contemporary Literature* 19, no. 3 (summer 1978): 320–35.
Kao, Shuhsi. "Paradise Lost? An Interview with Philippe Sollers." *SubStance,* no. 30 (1981): 31–50.
Kristeva, Julia. *Semeiotike: Recherches pour une sémanalyse.* Paris: Seuil, 1969.
Kurk, Katherine C. "Nascent Structures of Consummation: Philippe Sollers' *Une curieuse solitude.*" *Degré Second,* no. 7 (1983): 123–32.
———. "Philippe Sollers' 'Le Défi': *texte de plaisir, texte de jouissance.*" *South Atlantic Review* 47, no. 4 (November 1982): 27–36.
Lernout, Geert. *The French Joyce.* Ann Arbor: University of Michigan Press, 1990.

Lynes, Carlos. "Production et théorie romanesques chez Philippe Sollers: Lecture du *Parc.*" *Kentucky Romance Quarterly* 19, no. 1 (1972): 99–121.

Owens, Craig. "Sects and Language." *Art in America* 69, no. 6 (summer 1981): 11–17.

Padis, Marc-Olivier. "Philippe Sollers: Un écrivain d'exception!" *Esprit,* no. 190 (March–April 1993): 135–52.

Roudiez, Léon S. *French Fiction Revisited.* Elmwood Park, IL: Dalkey Archive, 1991.

Scherzer, Dina. *Representation in Contemporary French Fiction.* Lincoln: University of Nebraska Press, 1986.

Sollers, Philippe; de Haes, Frans. "*Femmes* et *Paradis.*" *L'Infini,* no. 4 (1983): 32–43.

Sollers, Philippe; Kirili, Alain. "Sexual Atheism: A Conversation." *Arts Magazine* 65, no. 2 (October 1990): 78–82.

Tel Quel, no. 57 (1974). Special issue on Sollers.

7

Jean Ricardou

Tobin Jones

Placing Jean Ricardou's novels among those of his contemporaries is not easy. Historically, most critics and Ricardou himself have associated his three published novels—*L'Observatoire de Cannes* (1961), *La Prise de Constantinople* (1965), *Les Lieux-dits* (1969)—with developments in the nouveau roman. However, because of its extreme eccentricity, Ricardou's work sets its own traditions far from the more familiar forms of postmodern fiction. Ricardou's novels, indeed all his fictions, seem to offer a reading experience only marginally like those of even the most daring of new fictional structures (most similar in their treatment of linguistic forms are Maurice Roche and Philippe Sollers). His novels contain what one might perceive as the deliberate confusion of their semantic and aesthetic functions with the elaboration of theoretical concerns. Complicating these difficulties even further are Ricardou's *Le Théâtre des métamorphoses*, a mixed genre appearing in 1982, and his *nouvelles*, short fictions published separately between 1960 and 1987 and then rewritten and collected in his *Révolutions minuscules* (1971 and 1988) and *La Cathédrale de sons* (1988). The mutual assimilation of theory and fiction in these more radically experimental works sheds critical light on the novels. Moreover, because these other fictions are intertextually so intimately bound to the novels, they cannot help but complicate our understanding of Ricardou's novelistic work and its place in the whole of his œuvre.

All of Jean Ricardou's work has persistently and aggressively explored relationships between the creative effects and the theoretical underpinnings of writing. His first publications in 1960 (a short fiction,

145

three brief literary reviews, and three critical studies on the works of
Michel Butor, Alain Robbe-Grillet, and Claude Simon) even then reflected
his interest in both the theoretical concerns and technical experimentation of much postmodern French writing. In the next three decades, Jean
Ricardou emerged as one of the most militant theorists and innovative
formalists among French novelists. In addition to his three novels and
other fiction, his publications now include over sixty critical and theoretical articles, three collections of critical essays, and two volumes of
literary theory. During this time, he has also organized, directed and
participated in dozens of debates and colloquia devoted to theoretical
developments and practical concerns in the contemporary novel.
Ricardou's militancy during these years contributed much to the debates from which French postmodern thought has emerged, but it also
earned him a reputation as a writer and theorist at odds not only with
more conservative critics and scholars but all too often with many of the
nouveaux romanciers and other contemporary writers as well. In a period of controversy among the French nouveaux romanciers, Ricardou
responded in "Les Raisons de l'ensemble" to what Alain Robbe-Grillet
and others had some years earlier denounced as a "terrorisme ricar-
dolien."[1]

Ricardou's fictions reflect this militancy, displaying openly and
often didactically the theoretical principles that inform them. Consequently, critics have usually studied his novels as extensions and illus-
trations of those concerns. Moreover, because of their experimental nature, Ricardou's novels are extremely self-conscious literary exercises.
Reading them can be a laboriously intellectual process of deciphering
complex and convoluted forms that refuse to play in traditional ways to
moral and social interests. The esoterism of Ricardou's novels explains
their limited popularity among even the devotees of the nouveau roman. The fact that this small group of readers has generally shown little
interest in his novels as aesthetic objects or cultural artifacts has, in turn,
exaggerated the preferential focus on their critical and theoretical functions. The understanding that Ricardou's novels deserve study because
of their theoretical implications has consequently become nearly universal. However, such a focus on the theoretical neglects aesthetic considerations as much as it refuses social and cultural questions. And, as
critics' attention to the presence of theoretical and critical questions in
Ricardou's fictions has dominated the representation and assessment of

their value, it has obscured the equally problematical concern of where his works might fit in the development of the contemporary French novel.

The emphasis, if not the exclusivity of focus, that critics have placed on the role of theory in the reading and understanding of Jean Ricardou's novels has, of course, had some productive consequences. It has drawn attention to the interplay between those two aspects of postmodern fiction that are so essential to the generation and dynamic manipulation of its meanings: the shifting, polyvalent, representative and referential functions of language and the metatextual, theoretical understandings of these functions, which, implicitly or explicitly, guide the reader to an acceptable, even satisfying intellectual closure for the reading experience. One outcome of this, as Lynn Higgins has argued in her superb study of Ricardou's novels and *nouvelles* as metafictions, is the understanding of them as parables of theory whose complex forms render allegorically the very abstractions that govern their structure.[2]

Although well-founded and logical, such critical analyses do not assess the aesthetic impact of the novel's form on its reader. This neglect of the aesthetic and affective functions leaves Ricardou's novels open to the most conservative critical judgments decrying their formalist sterility. One needs to ask, then, how a sensitive reader of Ricardou's works might draw pleasure from their reading and how that pleasure relates to the aesthetic effect of more familiar and more conventionally representative novelistic forms. How do Ricardou's novels inform their reading as a process? Are they accessible to all thoughtful readers or readable only by those who, with an acquired taste for form, seek the pleasurable "feeling" of a structure rich enough in thematic and formal interrelationships to elicit and sustain aesthetic interest? In short, though there has been critical study on the metafictional aspects of Ricardou's fiction, there has been little discussion of how their readability marks either cultural or artistic boundaries.

Ricardou's first novel, *L'Observatoire de Cannes*, explores the creative potential of narrative description and descriptive techniques as thematic means to generate and motivate the elements of a "story."[3] However, unlike Alain Robbe-Grillet's *La Jalousie*, published some six years earlier, this work makes no concessions to its reader. Description in *L'Observatoire de Cannes* does not invite the reader's inference of an obsessive narrative point of view and consequently of the existence of a character whose presence, albeit suppressed, serves to give psychological and aesthetic unity to the narration. Instead, the structures of narrative description formalize relationships according to thematic criteria of aesthetically affective kinds. From that formalization are then generated relationships whose patterns anticipate a "story" of truly unconventional composition, thereby making this work perhaps the most inaccessible of all Ricardou's novels.

The "story" of *L'Observatoire de Cannes* is best characterized as a formalist quest. The first of the novel's thirty-one chapters is devoted to the description of four people in the compartment of a train departing Cannes and heading west along the French Riviera: a blond girl, a young couple, and a bald, camera-carrying tourist. The compartment's remaining seats are either reserved but unoccupied or presumably vacant. In the second chapter, the focus of description shifts abruptly to a funicular railway leading to an observatory overlooking Cannes. In subsequent chapters, a beach, a clearing on a wooded hillside, a strip-tease cabaret called the "Observatoire," and other places join with scenes presented "as though" depicted in photographs, drawings, or other visual forms.

Movement among the descriptive loci of the novel is effected through a process of association and substitution of both objects and the words that refer to them. These displacements tease the reader's need to establish cause and thus invite inference of psychological motivation. However, like the strip-tease described in the novel's twenty-eighth and twenty-ninth chapters, description in this novel occurs as a progressive revelation, an unveiling of an object of desire. The "object," whether a thing, a person (the young blond girl or one of her many avatars), a place, or an event, can be "known" only by approaching it through textual displacements that allow more commanding points of view, and "possessed" only by creating it from language. While this quest emerges initially in the sequencing of images that suggest an implicit motivation, it becomes definable as "consequential" only in the abstract terms of changing spatial perspectives and their thematically describable language. "Pursuit" of the object of description thus becomes a motivational thread, ultimately evolving a thematically definable form of narrative consciousness.

In this process, Ricardou subverts all distinction between what is imaginary or "virtual" and what is "real." This phenomenal uniformity allows him to deter his reader's imposition of causal logics that conventionalize the chronologies of narrative fiction. Instead, he intertwines three distinct orders of description whose hierarchical relationships supplant causal orders usually associated with more conventional, social visions of the fictional universe. One order organizes the fictional reality as "perceived" from within the train's compartment, a moving, enclosed space that metaphorically frames the novel's visionary narrative consciousness. A second order of description is reflected in the reality verbally depicted in the photographs, sketches, or other forms of graphic representation. These verbal images become "textual" loci helping the reader to situate the novel's themes. However, the contexts they indicate invite but never fully support a belief that the events and relationships they frame are elements from which a plot can be constituted. The third occurs as a synthesis derived from the dialectical opposition and linguistic confusion of the first two orders.

To encourage the reader in the effort to establish textual relationships among the persons and objects it describes, narration in *L'Observatoire de Cannes* draws on the associative potential of a polyvalent language. As the narrative generates themes of pursuit and domination from a montage of descriptions of persons, places, objects, and their relationships, it motivates inference of an *intentio* that is more artistic than psychological in implication. Thus, when textually similar doubles of the blond girl appear in a strip-tease act in the cabaret "L'Observatoire de Cannes" and in a photo essay, each is stripped bare in a ritualistic description that emphasizes the thematic importance of three modes of spatial movement. The first two represent distance and "covering" as obstacles to be overcome through semantic exploitation of lexical fields associated with subjective and physical "approach" and discovery. The third eliminates distance and the protection afforded by a covering through violence. This third mode corresponds to a form of aesthetic closure derived from the anticipation and realization of textual objectives through the implication of sexual fantasies.

The description of the photo essay depicting the onslaught of a storm-tossed sea on an unsuspecting, bikini-clad blond girl (chapters 19 and 20) provides a good example of how a static scene in a Ricardolian text can metamorphose into a dynamically self-generative textual fantasy. As though observed from the sea, the girl is first described in terms of the scant protection she would have in a storm. Initially framed as speculation, the intentionality behind this description soon surfaces in a violent scene depicting the sea overpowering all physical obstacles between it and the girl. "Waves" and "foam-fissured" rocks become linguistic icons for the overwhelming force of erotic motivation and the eventual consummation of desire. The word *aigrette*, which here connotes the feathering of the wave's crest, foreshadows its later use as a plume adorning a blond stripper's costume in the cabaret. *Culbuté*, which describes the overturning of the stone slabs shielding the girl from the sea, assumes sexual connotations as a function of the elimination of constraints to the sea's approach. Paronymic wordplay motivates additional thematic and emotive associations. *Dalles* and *sandales* join to destroy the established order, since *dalles* leads to *san[s] dal[l]es*. Meanwhile, the two superfluous letters "s" and "l" excluded from the homophonic anagram overflow the limits of immediate structure to link the transformations of word and meaning in this first novel to Ricardou's subsequent fictions where they will generate and organize thematic content. Such wordplay, which already had an important intratextual role in *L'Observatoire de Cannes,* thus will become important intertextually in structuring *La Prise de Constantinople* and eventually will find its theoretical explanation in the allegorical form of *Les Lieux-dits.*

What is perhaps most innovative in such passages is the systematic equivocation between two functional understandings of the word as image. One, the more conventionally associative, stresses possibilities of semantic combination to determine new thematic associations. The other is more creative. In this instance, the word is manipulated as a logoform to generate new linguistic realities and associate them according to self-selecting semantic and phonetic principles, thereby implying a textually derived narrative imagination. These associative functions of language require the reader to understand the narrative imagination as an activity of a consciousness that both reveals and creates itself. Accordingly, language becomes more than an instrument of expression and representation. Responsive to the cues of the language it elaborates, the text has considerable artistic independence in the determination of a narrative consciousness. This view thus implies a kind of creative intent that appears self-generative and which invites the reader to induce the principles that generate and select the fiction's elements and determine its composition.

Like the reader in 1961, today's reader of *L'Observatoire de Cannes* will not find aesthetic satisfaction in a socially coherent rendering of its fictional world. Never offering meaningful human interrelationships, the fiction lacks the interest expected of the conventional novel. Even the playful hypothesis of distinctions between the "real" and the virtual and the natural tendency to interpret events or scenes as reflections of character prove ultimately inconsequential and unrewarding in the reading experience. An elaboration of material content and the discovery of the thematic principles motivating its composition, *L'Observatoire de Cannes* proves ultimately to be a difficult lesson in reading form without going beyond it.

La Prise de Constantinople arguably showcases most successfully the metatextual problematics of self-containing narrative fictions. Ricardou's second novel also generates the verbal matter of its own content, but, as its text assumes form, it becomes very clear that its subject is its own evolution and the conceptualization of its composition. Though Ricardou again represents this process thematically as a quest, the fictional text's search for its identity as a literary form emerges here in a dialectical and dynamically mutual interference of its several confluent plots and the language that mediates them.

Ricardou gave *La Prise de Constantinople* a striking format he later claimed had a generative role in the novel's writing.[4] The title *La Prise de Constantinople* appeared on the front cover while the title *La Prose de Constantinople* was on the back. Read as the "taking" and the "telling" of Constantinople, these reveal the polarization and interdependence of the two acts and suggest the role of the narrative in the process of transforming either one to represent the other. Symmetrically opposed are also two dedications to the Egyptian goddess Isis and two epigraphs stressing convergence as an organizing process. Structured as three parts with eight chapters each, the novel has no pagination, chapter numbers, or chapter titles. Chapters are divided into blocks of narration, with noticeable blank spaces separating them on the page. These characteristics encourage the notion that the novel's composition arises in or from a symmetrical but otherwise unconventional opposition of textual and spatial elements.

The novel's first word, "rien," set off from the following text, generates a complicated series of intertwined adventures in several different contexts.[5] This process arises in an opposition of the word's signified conceptual absence and its material presence as signifier. The material presence of the word that at first denotes nothing prompts a speculative realization of content, which, by turning inward, further promotes both conceptualization and description. In the latter case, the existence of the word and its inked blackness opposes the white (*blanc* meaning both white and blankness) of the page and so becomes doubly suggestive of a void. This visual contrast also elicits a graphic rendering of "nothing," first in verbally analogous visual form as a zero, and then as a circle. The circle, in turn, becomes a sphere that, in a process of reversal, takes the form of a full moon lighting the black, night-darkened fictional landscape, where "nothing" else can yet be "perceived." The fictional universe thus evolves through a process of denial, opposition, postulation, and reversal to generate objects, scenes, and eventually characters whose relationships invoke causation and lead thematically to the hypothesis of "plot."

The proliferation of fragmented content in the novel's first part is in obvious conflict with its two symmetrically apposed epigraphs' emphasis on convergence as an embracing principle of organization. As elements without clear causal interrelationship accumulate, divergence and diversity enter into a dynamic tension with convergence and unity. On the one hand, similarities among elements of the narrative gradually permit a coalescence of three distinct but tentative plots: the play of eight young children, the social games of eight young adults, and the adventures of eight members of a space commando on Venus seeking La Cité interdite (the Forbidden City). Simultaneously, however, as textual repetitions of identifiable scenes or passages occur in different contexts, the distinctiveness of these plots erodes and gives way to contradiction and eventual confusion. Finally, in the novel's third part, a fourth group of three characters—a doctor Baseille, a nurse Isa, and a mental patient Edouard seeking his identity—emerges from the textual interplay of passages describing the three initial groups.

Repetition with a constant of variability is an important device for the generative structuring of this novel. On the one hand, verbatim or near-verbatim repetitions of a given text in the contexts of different plots and levels of reality undermine established relationships by destroying their uniqueness as part of a distinct order in the fictional universe. On the other hand, textual repetitions serve to define structural pattern, since they create intersections among variants of scenes in the multiple plots. Textual repetition in *La Prise de Constantinople* causes constant vacillation between a narrative that presents a fictional universe and a narrative that responds to the linguistic character of that universe's composition. Meanwhile, as the narrative form establishes and destroys relationships among the novel's initial three plots, it necessitates the hypothesis of new orders and the election of principles of causation to mark and control the conceptual and textual generation of content.

In this process of textual determination, it is the theme of the textual quest for self-identity that ultimately subsumes all causal relationships as elements in a hierarchical structure. At the level of plot, the narrative consciousness synthesizes the identity of the mental patient Edouard in a fusion of the child Edouard, the young adult Edmond, and the space explorer Ed. Word. When the adult Edouard's "psychological" identity emerges from the continuum of the assumed and then abandoned identities of these other characters, a comparable synthesis occurs at the level of writing in the narrative form. The threads of the parallel quests for psychological (social and emotional) and formal (textual and fictional) self-definition finally converge in the novel's last sentence: "Certaine lecture consciencieuse suffit maintenant pour que l'irradiation de toute la figure élabore qui *JE SUIS*, et par un phénomène réflexif point trop imprévu, en un éclair, me *LE LIVRE*." With the pun on "livre," the narrative concludes. Having united the parallel quests and created from them the story of its own genesis, a dynamic form of writing as a process of self-generation, self-determination, and self-elucidation reveals itself as *La Prose de Constantinople*.

Ricardou offers the reader of *La Prise de Constantinople* many more indications of how it is composed and might be read than he did in *L'Observatoire de Cannes*. A suggestion that access to the novel's meaning lies at the juncture of opposite interpretive paths invites the reader to look to the novel's physical center, where passages prescribe two opposed methods of critical reading. The first supposes that any writing is part of a vast library whose traditions form an intertextual infrastructure for all literature. The second suggests that understanding a fiction depends on intuitive and deductive responses to its text alone. The implications of the two approaches to reading are perhaps most evident in the ways they affect the use of wordplay to generate and control the elements of the novel.

In *La Prise de Constantinople*, Ricardou exploits puns, homonyms, paronyms, anagrams, and cryptograms to derive conceptual and structural associations among words and their immediate contexts and to create correspondences among the larger elements of the text. Homophonic puns (e.g., the name of the Venusian city "Silab Lee" and the phrase "syllabe-les," meaning "syllabize them") or paronymic confusions (e.g., "prose" in the semantic context of "pose") draw attention to the polyvalent and arbitrary nature of the linguistic sign and highlight extreme forms of linguistic plasticity. Homonyms and paronyms, like those based on the pronunciation of "S" and "L" ("est-ce elle?," "aisselle," "Hessel") relate otherwise independent fictional developments. Such kinds of verbal play do not by themselves integrate the associated elements in a meaningful way by subordinating them to the demands or priorities of a system. To create thematic centers for that kind of constellation, Ricardou exploits the name "Isabelle." Seen first as an acrostic formed from the first initials of the eight persons in each of the three groups of characters described in the novel, "Isabelle" is also an anagram. It links many of the objects, places, or persons associated with the novel's various quests: the forbidden city Silab Lee, the castle Bel Asile, the doctor Baseille, and the Lac des Abeilles. Partial anagrams allow for even more suggestive associations. From Bel and Isa, for instance, are formed Blaise and Basile—names whose historical importance bears on the thematic organization of Ricardou's novel.

The reorganization of letters to form and to interrelate new names has its analogous fictional correlation among elements in a system of mythological (fictional) and cultural (historical) references that allude to the narrative's quest for literary self-definition. Reigning over this system is the figure of Isis, who reunited the scattered parts of Osiris's dismembered body and who thus represents integration. "Basile" interrelates three complementary thematic perspectives. The Byzantine rulers, Bazile le Macédonien and Basile II, belong to a set that evokes the historical "reality" of a documentable past. Basile le Vénusien in the space quest, "La Cité interdite," and Basile l'Epouvantable from the medieval quest, "La Princesse interdite," belong to the realm of the fictional, stand for the figurative nature of the literary text, and thus represent the imagined. Finally, the alchemist Basile Valentin stands for the hermetic symbolism of the literary form as a quest structure. Allusions to structural metaphor in the gnostic and symbolic traditions of the Middle Ages thus intersect thematically with references to ancient Egyptian history and mythology to emphasize the metaphorical role of the novel's fictional events and characters in the physical elaboration and theoretical explanation of its form.

Ricardou made the mutual interdependence of theory, criticism, and the practice of writing already evident in *La Prise de Constantinople* even more overtly the subject of *Les Lieux-dits* (1969). His third novel is a lesson in reading and interpretation that proves the most easily accessible if not the most aesthetically interesting of his fictions. The novel's subtitle, *Petit guide d'un voyage dans le livre*, suggests the nature of the analogy at work in the novel's formal makeup. It also points to the novel's interpretation as an allegory of the dialectical resolution of the conflicting narrative forms, semantic conceptions, and aesthetic intents of guidebook and novel. Progressing through the description of each of eight cities on the novel's itinerary, the reader learns the history of a conflict between two doctrinaire sects. One maintains that the character of a place always lies at the origin of its name. The opposing sect defends the creative functions of language and argues that, because words lay at the origin of our conception of reality, we can know that reality only on the basis of the meanings that words allow in their own interaction. Though introduced only as a parenthetical note to the guidebook's description of the city, this conflict between the readings afforded by representational and poetic orders of language soon becomes the novel's central theme.

Ricardou allegorizes these opposing theoretical stances in the creation of his characters. One of the two principal characters, Olivier Lasius, comes into being as a narrative convention, a fictional visitor to the town of Bannière. His creation permits the introduction of a hypothetical point of view. When Olivier learns that a woman dressed in red is following an identical itinerary and asking the same questions as he about certain allegorical paintings by Albert Crucis, he sets out to meet her. The two characters eventually join to follow a common path of discovery that comes to embody metaphorically the themes of quest and conflict: the former in the context of search, pursuit, and capture; the latter in the antagonisms of textual oppositions, conceptual reversals, and thematic and formal paradoxes.

Only near the novel's conclusion does it become clear how completely the composition of *Les Lieux-dits* reflects its own development. Invited to form an acrostic of the chapter titles, the reader discovers "Belcroix" to be the middle ground where the two modes (paths) of narration intersect (cross) in fundamental contradiction. Returning to Belcroix, Olivier, who has come to represent the forces of the poetic, seeks first to seduce the woman Atta, who embodies the representational, and then imagines her destruction. The final lines of the novel, however, shift the emphasis from the conflict between the two allegorical characters to the interpretation of the plot as a dialectical form of structural metaphor whose meaning cannot be grasped by exclusive adherence to either of the opposed manners of reading.

After the publication of *Les Lieux-dits*, Ricardou's writing turned increasingly to the thematics of the contradiction, confrontation, and mutual transgression of theory and fiction. In this development, his two collections of *nouvelles* (*Révolutions minuscules* and *La Cathédrale de sons*) and his *Le Théâtre des métamorphoses*, which he described on the cover as "une nouvelle éducation textuelle," mark a clearly progressive fusion of literary theory, affective reading, and fiction. All these later texts incorporate elements (themes, events, characters, and textual repetitions) already seen by the reader of Ricardou's novels or earlier versions of his shorter fictions. They also explore in more limited and, hence, in more easily defined contexts, the theoretical concerns familiar to readers of his novels.

The two collections of *nouvelles* gather in rewritten form most of his short experimental texts, of which the earliest dates from before the publication of his first novel in 1961 and the most recent from 1987. In their more recent forms, these short fictions mark even more clearly than his novels the successive stages of Ricardou's experimentation with descriptive modes of narrative fiction and the creative potential of the written text. The fictions in *Révolutions minuscules* reflect Ricardou's development of narrative description as a means to derive new textual material from the ambiguities of language and to generate a literary self-consciousness that makes visible the process of its becoming. These literary concerns appear in semantic fields such as that of water (sea, waves, currents, foam, cataracts) already evident in *L'Observatoire de Cannes* and *La Prise de Constantinople*. However, in the fictions of *Révolutions minuscules*, such as "Jeu," "Sur la pierre" ("Epitaphe" in the revised edition), "Lancement d'un voilier," and "Plage blanche," the imagery vacillates between its self-signifying materiality and its self-effacing immateriality as a transparent, representational sign.[6] This ambiguity of function is well marked, for instance, in "Plage blanche," where the *plage* (beach) becomes first the page and then the arena (derived from *arénuleux* or sand-covered) wherein Ricardou's text ceremonially plays out its own dreamlike creation.

Other *nouvelles*, such as "Dyptique" and "Autobiographie," raise questions of a broader, more inclusive kind. "Dyptique" opposes conflict and domination in the fictional frames of pursuit and conquest to evoke the theme of death as a form of aesthetic closure derived dialectically from the textual opposition of beginning and ending. "Autobiographie," the final fiction of *Révolutions minuscules,* merges textual self-generation with the narrative "I" and the thematic concerns of the literary autobiography to implicate the whole of Ricardou's œuvre. The fiction of this *nouvelle* evolves from the illusion of an autobiographical account of events that might have inspired the writing of the eight preceding fictions. The end of "Autobiographie" reaffirms, however, the authority of the creative power of the word. In the fiction's final two paragraphs, the reader finds the allusive images and themes identified with the apparent autobiographical intent to be reduced, fictionally distilled as it were, to "huit jets minimes, en voie de parfaite extinction" (p. 169) and insignificant curves traced in the sand only to be complicated by future writings.

In many respects, Ricardou's blending of fiction and theory in *Le Théâtre des métamorphoses* achieves just that complication. Transformation or metamorphosis of fiction into theory, as seen in the allegorization of theoretical concerns in his earlier work, gives way in *Le Théâtre* to the exploration of the fictional character of both criticism and theory. Thus, the use of "mixte" to describe the merging of the concerns and forms of a given fiction with the critical and theoretical representations of fiction in general should be interpreted as a meld or synthesis rather than a combination or aggregation of dissimilar elements. Much as the theater serves as both a venue and means for the representation of an illusory reality, this *texte mixte* becomes the ground and means for the mutual transgressions, metamorphoses, and transvestism of the languages of abstraction and fiction.

The composition of *Le Théâtre des métamorphoses* reveals how problematical this potential dialectic can become in a genre where no clear distinctions exist between the roles theory and fiction play in eliciting the reader's aesthetic involvement. The work is composed of four major parts. Two, "Mixte" and "Principes pour quelques transformations," are predominantly theoretical and metatextually self-elucidating. They embrace the two central, primarily fictional works, "Communications" and "Improbables strip-teases." Although an opposition between the theoretical and fictional discourses in *Théâtre des métamorphoses* is marked to some degree by a separation of texts, linguistic and thematic transgressions occur throughout, with the ultimate effect that each discourse assumes increasingly the linguistic aspects, the intentional character, and often the affective functions usually associated with the other. (Ricardou later explored these kinds of transgression as the constituent procedures of "l'art du X" in the final *nouvelle* of *La Cathédrale de sons*.) Such transgressions are marked throughout Ricardou's work by various signs of the cross. Along with the syllables *ptyx* (the petit x, or little x) found in many titles and proper names encountered in *Le Théâtre des métamorphoses*, there is the X of intersections, the crossing in the cathedral, the crusades, and numerous names ("Belcroix," "Crucis," and "Dela-croix"). These suggest to the reader that the mutually integrative powers Ricardou has accorded narrative technique and concept in *Le Théâtre* are no less present in his earlier novels and the short fictions of *Révolutions minuscules*. They also anticipate similar concerns in the *nouvelles* to be published six years later in *La Cathédrale de sons*.

Transgression in *Le Théâtre des métamorphoses* extends further the familiar thematic developments of erotic pursuit and sexual conquest to suggest that textual generation implies textual unification. "Communications" and "Improbables strip-teases" thus reinforce the notion of unity in diversity in *Le Théâtre des métamorphoses* through the commixture of opposites. At the same time, however, they suggest that Ricardou's œuvre is a constantly progressive *reprise* of his writing. Characters and thematic elements from *La Prise de Constantinople* and the strip-tease from *L'Observatoire de Cannes*, reproduced virtually unchanged in the second novel, reappear in *Le Théâtre* with the effect not only of motivating its specific thematic developments but also of highlighting threads of continuity and suggestively offering hypothetical solutions to some of the most puzzling aspects of Ricardou's novels.

One of the most characteristic and overt examples of these threads is Ricardou's persistent emphasis on the number eight in all his fictions.[7] In *L'Observatoire de Cannes*, there are eight graffiti whose images are basic to the obsessive generation of the plot. In *La Prise de Constantinople*, eight again recurs to associate chapters, characters, and the several names drawn anagrammatically from "Isabelle." In *Les Lieux-dits*, the number occurs in descriptions of Albert Crucis's allegorical painting, a postcard depicting a factory, and a package of Pall Mall cigarettes. In *Révolutions minuscules*, eight fictions precede "Autobiographie." Associated with the organizing principles of the fictions in which it is found, the number can also mark relationships among works. For instance, in "Résipiscence," the sixth fiction in *La Cathédrale de sons*, multiples of eight appear to link the seven *nouvelles* of this later collection to the nine in *Révolutions minuscules:* "Cependant, en outre, on l'entrevoit, pour satisfaire aux impératifs techniques induits par le principe de mon exercice, ma sédécipartite livrée avait eu à subir plusieurs amendements çà et là" (pp. 160–61). This ambiguously self-conscious remark strongly suggests that all sixteen *nouvelles* divided between his two collections form a unified whole.

The interpretation of the number eight both as a device for generating and organizing these writings and as a kind of signature, though speculative, has some support of a nontextual kind. In 1972, Ricardou visited several universities in the United States and discussed the generation of *La Prise de Constantinople* from elements visible on the cover of the edition published by the Editions de Minuit. One of these was his own eight-letter last name, which he claimed to be a partial anagrammatic generator of Villehardouin, chronicler of the Fourth Crusade and, hence, one of several apocryphal sources of the novel's thematic and formal composition. Until the publication of *Le Théâtre des métamorphoses*, critics considered this explanation a bit specious. But since this work emphasizes these same associations and the generative function of Ricardou's name, it seems reasonable to assume that the consistent use of the figure and homological counterparts of eight is indeed a kind of signature reflecting the meld of theory, criticism, and fiction that has become the benchmark of his writing.

Only three in number (despite indications that others are ready or nearing readiness for publication), Ricardou's published novels nonetheless raise important questions about aesthetic ways of seeing the relationship between the means and the ends of the literary experience. They test many of our cultural conventions that set parameters for the activity of reading and thereby determine not only how one reads a fiction but how that fiction may be appreciated as an aesthetic experience. As lessons in reading, they also help us to understand Jean Ricardou not *either* as a writer of fiction *or* a theorist of the novel but as both simultaneously. Ricardou's practices in the text's composition—its creation in the dynamic interaction between the writer as *scriptor*, the linguistic patterns of the written, and the writer as reader—are common both to his fictions and to his theory. The reader of Ricardou's novels learns that throughout his œuvre the interaction of fiction and theory always assumes form in and determines the nature of an aesthetic whole. Finally, Ricardou's theory, with its thematically coherent but reductive arguments, has consistently shown that the fictional form is first and foremost a process of textual exploration and that, as such, it always precedes its theoretical conceptualization. Ricardou's novels can therefore be said to demonstrate that, if theory is to do justice to the immediacy, power, and richness of those aesthetic effects that arise in the confrontation of a reader and a novel's complex wholeness of form, it too must show itself as born of the novel.

Notes

1. For Ricardou's defense, see his remarks in a note (pp. 232–33) in "Raisons de l'ensemble," published with *Le Nouveau Roman*, 2d ed. (Paris: Seuil, 1990).

2. Lynn A. Higgins, *Parables of Theory: Jean Ricardou's Metafiction* (Birmingham, AL: Summa, 1984).

3. For Ricardou's earliest perspectives on these concerns, see "Description et infraconscience chez Alain Robbe-Grillet," *Nouvelle Revue Française*, no. 95 (November 1960), pp. 890–900. Two other essays treating the creative potential of textual description can be found in *Problèmes du nouveau roman* (Paris: Seuil, 1967): "La Description créatrice: Une course contre le sens" (pp. 91–111), and "Une Description trahie" (pp. 112–21).

4. "Naissance d'une fiction," in *Nouveau Roman: Hier aujourd'hui: 2. Pratiques* (Paris: UGE, 1972), pp. 379–92.

5. For Ricardou's discussion of generative techniques, see "La Bataille de la phrase," in *Pour une théorie du nouveau roman* (Paris: Seuil, 1971), pp. 118–58; "L'Initiative aux mots," in *Nouveaux Problèmes du roman* (Paris: Seuil, 1978), pp. 68–88; and "Esquisse d'une théorie des générateurs," in *Positions et oppositions sur le roman contemporain* (Paris: Klincksieck, 1971), pp. 143–50.

6. See "Expression et fonctionnement," in *Problèmes du nouveau roman*, pp. 125–44.

7. Hélène Prigogine discusses the earlier uses of the number in "L'Aventure ricardolienne du nombre," in *Nouveau Roman: Hier, aujourd'hui: 2. Pratiques*, pp. 354–77.

Bibliography

Works by Jean Ricardou

"Le Roman et ses degrés." *Nouvelle Revue Française*, no. 90 (June 1960): 1157–61.
L'Observatoire de Cannes, roman. Paris: Minuit, 1961.

"Par-delà le réel et l'irréel." *Médiations,* no. 5 (1962): 17–25.

La Prise de Constantinople, roman. Paris: Minuit, 1965.

Que peut la littérature? Meeting of the "Mutualité 1964," with Simone de Beauvoir, Yves Berger, Jean-Pierre Faye, Jean-Paul Sartre, and Jacques Semprun. Paris: Éditions UGE, 1965: 49–61.

Problèmes du nouveau roman, essais. Paris: Seuil, 1967.

Les Lieux-dits, petit guide d'un voyage dans le livre, roman. Paris: Gallimard, 1969.

"Esquisse d'une théorie des générateurs." In *Positions et oppositions sur le roman contemporain,* 143–50, followed by a discussion, 151–62. Paris: Klincksieck, 1971.

Pour une théorie du nouveau roman, essais. Paris: Seuil, 1971.

Révolutions minuscules, nouvelles. Paris: Gallimard, 1971.

Nouveau Roman: Hier, aujourd'hui. Volumes I and II. Direction, contributing presentation, and editing of the presentations of the colloquium at Cerisy. Paris: Editions UGE, 1972.

Le Nouveau Roman, essai. Paris: Seuil, 1973. This first edition was rewritten and augmented in 1990 by the inclusion of the essay, "Les Raisons de l'ensemble."

"La Révolution textuelle." *Esprit* 42, no. 441 (December 1974): 927–45.

Nouveaux Problèmes du roman, essais. Paris: Seuil, 1978.

"Pour une lecture rétrospective." *Revue des Sciences Humaines,* no. 177 (1980): 57–66.

Le Théâtre des métamorphoses, mixte. Paris: Seuil, 1982.

Problèmes actuels de la lecture. Editor and codirector of the proceedings of the colloquium at Cerisy. Paris: Clancier-Guénaud, 1982.

Révélations minuscules, en guise de préface à la gloire de Jean Paulhan, suivi de Révolutions minuscules. Paris: Impressions Nouvelles, 1988.

La Cathédrale de sons, nouvelles. Paris: Impressions Nouvelles, 1988.

Une Maladie chronique. Problèmes de la représentation écrite du simultané, théorie. Paris: Impressions Nouvelles, 1989.

Selected Critical Works

Brée, Germaine. "Novelists in Search of the Novel: The French Scene." *Modern Fiction Studies* 16, no. 1 (spring 1970): 3–11.

Calle-Gruber, Mireille. "Effets d'un texte non-saturé: *La Prise de Constantinople.*" *Poétique,* no. 35 (1978): 325–35.

Caminade, Pierre. "Analogie et métaphore structurelle de Jean Ricardou." In *Images et métaphore, un problème de poétique contemporaine,* pp. 90–96. Paris: Bordas, 1970.

Fried, Ursula. "Lecture créatrice à base structuraliste de 'Plage blanche' par Jean Ricardou." *Bonnes Feuilles,* no. 6 (1976): 3–17.

Higgins, Lynn A.. "Typographical Eros: Reading Ricardou in the Third Dimension." *Yale French Studies,* no. 57 (1979): 80–94.

162   ◆   Tobin Jones

────. "Literature 'à la lettre': Ricardou and the Poetics of Anagram." *Romanic Review* 73, no. 4 (November 1982): 473–88.

────. *Parables of Theory: Jean Ricardou's Metafiction.* Birmingham, AL: Summa, 1984.

Jones, Tobin H. "In Quest of a Newer New Novel: Ricardou's *La Prise de Constantinople.*" *Contemporary Literature* 14, no. 3 (summer 1973): 296–309.

────. "Jean Ricardou." In *French Novelists since 1960,* edited by Catherine Savage Brosman, pp. 187–96. Detroit: Gale (Dictionary of Literary Biography, vol. 83), 1989.

Prigogine, Hélène. "L'Aventure ricardolienne du nombre." In *Nouveau Roman: Hier, aujourd'hui: 2, Pratiques,* pp. 353–78. Paris: UGE, 1972.

Raillon, Jean-Claude. "Une étude périlleusement excessive du texte cité." *Sud,* no. 8 (1972): 47–58.

Rice, Donald B. "The Ex-centricities of Jean Ricardou's *La Prise/Prose de Constantinople.*" *International Fiction Review* 2, no. 2 (summer 1975): 106–12.

Sirvent, Michel. "Chiffrement, déchiffrement: de Paul Valéry à Jean Ricardou." *French Review* 66, no. 2 (December 1992), 255–66.

Simon, Pierre-Henri. "De Jean Ricardou: *L'Observatoire de Cannes.*" In *Diagnostique des lettres françaises contemporaines,* pp. 321–26. Brussels: Renaissance du Livre, 1966.

8

Jacques Roubaud

Susan Ireland

Jacques Roubaud is a professor of mathematics at the Université de Paris and one of France's leading experimental poets. His first collection of poems, Σ, was published in 1967 and his most recent, *Quelque chose noir*, in 1986. He has also written extensively on poetry, particularly on the medieval verse forms of the troubadours and the contemporary works of the Ouvroir de Littérature Potentielle (Oulipo). In recent years, however, he has turned to prose and has published an autobiographical work, *Le Grand Incendie de Londres* (1989), and three novels: *La Belle Hortense* (1985), *L'Enlèvement d'Hortense* (1987), and *L'Exil d'Hortense* (1990).

Roubaud became a member of the Oulipo in 1966 and shares its interest in experimentation as a means of renewal. Since its creation in 1960, the Oulipo has brought together writers from various fields, in particular mathematics and literature, and its members have included Georges Perec, Raymond Queneau, François Le Lionnais, Jacques Bens, Noël Arnaud, Harry Mathews, Marcel Bénabou, and Italo Calvino. The group was formed to explore the field of potential literature, that is, to engage in "la recherche de formes, de structures nouvelles et qui pourront être utilisées par les écrivains de la façon qui leur plaira."[1] In order to produce these new forms, Oulipo members both analyze already existing examples of formal experimentation (an activity they call "anoulipisme") and create new structures themselves ("synthoulipisme"). As Le Lionnais points out, "L'anoulipisme est voué à la découverte, le synthoulipisme à l'invention. De l'un à l'autre existent maints subtils passages" (p. 18). Because of their interest in both past forms and new mod-

163

els, they see themselves as part of an experimental tradition that goes back to Antiquity. The writers they cite as having influenced their work, and whom they playfully call their "plagiaires par anticipation" (p. 23), include the Grands Rhétoriqueurs, Villon, Rabelais, Sterne, and Roussel. Roubaud fits well into this tradition and contributes to both the analytic and synthetic sides of the Oulipo's work: his research on the troubadours analyzes medieval poetic forms, while his own poems and novels illustrate the contemporary search for new forms.

Roubaud discusses his life and work in *Le Grand Incendie de Londres*. His description of the book as "mon autoportrait . . . une enquête de nature historique sur moi-même" (p. 311) suggests a traditional autobiography, but the text resulting from his "investigation" constitutes an example of his formal experimentation. The text does indeed contain elements of a self-portrait, as Roubaud describes, for example, his love of reading, his family home in Provence, his travels in the United States, his favorite places in London, and his daily life in Paris. However, rather than organizing this autobiographical information into a traditional linear account, Roubaud presents it in numbered sections that do not reflect the chronological order of the events of his life. In addition, he juxtaposes traditional autobiographical passages with metafictional commentary on *Le Grand Incendie*. In order to emphasize the unconventional aspects of the text, he describes it in terms of what it is not: "ni poésie, ni roman, ni autobiographie" (p. 309). He thus encourages the reader to compare *Le Grand Incendie* with these genres and to identify the experimental techniques.

The Oulipo writers emphasize the use of formal constraint in the elaboration of new literary forms in the belief that "systems of formal constraint—far from restricting a writer—actually afford a field of creative liberty." Roubaud further states that "a text written according to a constraint must speak of this constraint,"[2] and in *Le Grand Incendie,* he frequently discusses "le rôle essentiel des contraintes" (p. 202). In particular, he notes that while working on the text, "je vivais dans un système de règles. Les règles de l'écriture poétique, les règles de la démonstration mathématique, les règles de vie" (p. 160). These three systems of constraint permeate *Le Grand Incendie* and determine both its structure and much of its subject matter.

Many of the constraints used by the Oulipo are mathematical in nature and reflect their exploration of the relationship between literature and mathematics. "Writing under Oulipian constraint is the equivalent of the drafting of a mathematical text," asserts Roubaud (Motte, p. 15), and *Le Grand Incendie* describes his long-standing interest in both mathematics and literature. He traces his fascination with numbers to his childhood and names some of the mathematical works that have most influenced his writing, in particular the *Eléments de mathématique* by Nicolas Bourbaki and "les nombres de Queneau" (pp. 203, 366). He describes *Le Grand Incendie* itself as an example of "la prose mathématique" (p. 148) and explains the "raison numérologique" of the system he uses to generate the text (p. 366). The system derives from the number 1178, the number of days Roubaud knew his wife before her death, and he uses this figure along with the "nombres de Queneau" to create the architecture of the book. Because of these mathematical explanations and the presence of a number at the beginning of every section, it soon becomes clear to the reader that "les nombres ne cessent de pénétrer cette prose" (p. 141).

Roubaud combines these mathematical constraints with poetic structures to create the unusual form of *Le Grand Incendie*. He sees the apparently unrelated fields of poetry and mathematics as complementary disciplines characterized by the use of formal constraints: just as mathematical operations follow a series of rules, poetry is governed by constraints such as rhythm and versification. Because of these shared properties, the two fields coexist in Roubaud's work: "La voie de poésie et la voie mathématique convergeaient" (p. 191). As he does in the case of mathematics, he refers to the poetry that has most influenced his writing: the verse forms of the Arte Major, the Japanese haiku, and the poems of troubadours such as Arnaut Daniel. He often describes mathematics in terms traditionally associated with poetry—"La mathématique est le rythme du monde" (p. 191)—and in *Le Grand Incendie*, he combines the notion of "branches" in medieval poetry with the concept of branching in modern mathematics. *Le Grand Incendie* thus illustrates how he brings the two disciplines together to produce a new form.

Le Lionnais observes that the abstract structures of contemporary mathematical fields such as topology offer "mille directions d'explorations" (Oulipo, p. 17), and in *Le Grand Incendie* Roubaud's crossing of Arthurian legend with "la mathématique de l'entrelacement" (p. 202) described in Bourbaki's *Topologie générale* demonstrates the potential of this type of exploration. The subtitle of *Le Grand Incendie* describes the book as a "récit, avec incises et bifurcations." The "incises" and "bifurcations" come after the numbered sections of the main narrative and provide additional information on the events recounted. Roubaud's use of them means that the narrative does not progress "en ligne droite" but "par branches" (p. 24), a structure he calls "fiction arborescente" (p. 279). The metaphors he uses to describe the text all draw attention to this nonlinear spatial configuration: crossroads, forking paths, the nervous system, a family tree, and a Métro map. The recurring vocabulary in his descriptions also emphasizes bifurcation and interweaving—"entrelacer," "imbriquer," "enchâsser" (pp. 222–23), "embranchements multiples" (p. 34), "une chevelure de récits" (p. 100). Because of these bifurcations, both author and reader are in the same position as "un chevalier du roi Arthur," choosing paths through the forest and deciding which way to go at every new fork (p. 34). Roubaud therefore encourages the reader to explore the bifurcations by approaching the text as one would a map: "comme la lecture de la carte routière d'un pays . . . du réseau hydrographique des rivières au cœur du continent géologique, du squelette dans le corps, des nervures dans la feuille verte" (p. 35). This approach leads the reader to move back and forth between the main narrative and the following sections and thus break the linear sequence of the text.

The arborescent structure reflects Roubaud's exploration of the nature of memory. Since Le Grand Incendie recounts Roubaud's investigation of his past, memories occupy a central place in it, and Roubaud frequently describes the text in terms of memory, calling it "avant tout une tentative de mémoire" (p. 15), "un traité de mémoire" (p. 100), "la prose de la mémoire" (p. 101). The configuration of the text therefore corresponds to the branching of Roubaud's memories, which move from one topic to another by association. Consequently, the numbering of the sections corresponds to the order in which the memories occur, not to the chronological order in which the events took place. The structure of the text thus illustrates the topology of memory since memory, like Le Grand Incendie, is characterized by its branches and bifurcations.

Many of the memories concern the death of Roubaud's wife and his decision not to complete a novel (also entitled Le Grand Incendie de Londres) and a larger work of which the novel was to be a part (Le Projet). Since Le Grand Incendie contains an account of Roubaud's decision to abandon the two projects, he describes it as an "entreprise de destruction" (p. 261). The destruction takes place through writing as the memories are symbolically buried by giving them a fixed form on the page: "Le souvenir . . . est désormais immobile . . . il est en même temps devenu inoubliable, puisque je peux y avoir accès à tout instant, si je le veux, comme un savoir que je commande" (p. 261). Roubaud calls this process "la prosification de la mémoire" (p. 261), and his search for an appropriate form in which to express the memories creates a link between the "destruction" of memory and the Oulipian "construction" of new forms.

The two poles of destruction and construction recur in the third type of constraint used to write the novel: "les règles de vie" (p. 160). Early in the text, Roubaud explains that he has imposed on himself the rule of writing for a certain number of hours a day in order to enable him to continue his life after the death of his wife. The order of the daily writing sessions therefore provides the only "cohérence chronologique" in the book, and the numbering of the sections reflects that order. The past of memory is thus intertwined with the present of writing, and the many references to the act of writing make Le Grand Incendie a highly reflexive work. In this sense, it is as much an account of its own "mise en route" (p. 15) as it is a "portrait" of Roubaud.

In one of the reflexive segments, Roubaud notes that the two abandoned works would both have contained enigmas and some of the conventions of the detective story. Detective fiction—like mathematics and poetry—involves the use of constraints because it has a formulaic structure characterized by the posing and solving of an enigma. The influence of the genre can be seen in all Roubaud's prose works, and several sections of Le Grand Incendie describe his predilection for the traditional English-style detective novel. The word énigme recurs frequently in the text, and the numerical nature of the enigma provides the link between the conventions of the detective novel and the mathematical constraints at work in the text. Roubaud emphasizes this relationship through his use of the term chiffre. He describes the enigma as being both "chiffrée" and "déchiffrable," and the common root of the two words points to the relationship between his use of numbers to structure the text and the need for the reader-detective to take account of them when solving the enigma.

The Hortense novels contain the same formal experimentation as Le Grand Incendie and illustrate the playful nature of Roubaud's work. In these works he creates a chaotic, carnivalesque world and invites the reader to join in the fun. Nothing escapes his humor, and he parodies every aspect of novel writing and literary theory from characterization and narrative conventions to intertextuality and metafictional devices. Like the other Oulipo members, he sees himself as part of a tradition, noting that "one only writes by continuing other writings: it is hazardous to limit oneself to one or two 'masters,' even worse if these be masters of theory and not writers." He cites Georges Perec, Raymond Queneau, Italo Calvino, and Umberto Eco as examples of writers who have successfully "transmuted" concepts and methods from literary theory into "an inventive prose by the presence of an ironical dimension,"[3] and he follows their example by using parody and ironic inversion to transform the fictional and theoretical works of others and incorporate them into his own novels.

The story line of the Hortense trilogy is based on a potential plot suggested in Raymond Queneau's *Pierrot mon ami.* In the epilogue, Pierrot observes that certain elements of his adventures could have been used to create a detective story,[4] and Roubaud takes up the challenge of writing this potential novel. At the end of *Pierrot mon ami,* a chapel is built in memory of a Poldevian prince who died at the edge of an amusement park, and Roubaud takes these elements as the starting point for his story. In his novels, the discovery of oil under "la place Quenleiff" has enriched the Poldevian dynasty. Its princes are engaged in a struggle over succession to the throne, a murder takes place in the chapel, and Hortense finds herself exiled in Queneau'stown, the capital of Poldevia. Throughout the novels, Roubaud playfully hints at the source of his plot in a series of allusions to Queneau and *Pierrot mon ami,* thus illustrating in humorous fashion his belief that one "writes by continuing other writings" ("What Have They Done to Us?," p. 20).

Roubaud weaves the story inspired by *Pierrot mon ami* with plots from other works, and the intertextual world he creates recalls Barthes's definition of the text as "a multi-dimensional space in which a variety of writings, none of them original, blend and clash."[5] Roubaud suggests his intention is to produce such a "blend and clash" when he creates the composite figures of Henry James Joyce, Tolstoïevski, and Shakespirandello (*Exil d'Hortense,* p. 70). The title of Jim Wedderburn's novel, *Lady Bovary's Lover*—"un roman-valise qui pourrait être signé D. H. Flowbert" (*L'Enlèvement d'Hortense,* p. 123)—again emphasizes the notion of blending material from two different works and provides a ludic illustration of Barthes's concept of intertextuality and authorship.

Besides *Pierrot mon ami*, the main ingredient of the blend in Roubaud's first two novels, *La Belle Hortense* and *L'Enlèvement d'Hortense*, is Flaubert's *Madame Bovary*. Roubaud draws attention to the Flaubert connection in an allusion to Flaubert's well-known comment "Madame Bovary, c'est moi." He first states the obvious—"*Je Ne Suis Pas* Madame Bovary!"—then explains this remark in an absurd syllogism: "autrement dit, la belle Hortense n'est pas Madame Bovary, moi je ne suis pas la belle Hortense, et il s'ensuit que je ne suis pas Madame Bovary" (*Enlèvement d'Hortense*, p. 82). These comments set the tone of the borrowings from Flaubert, and Roubaud subsequently portrays Hortense as a carnivalized Madame Bovary. Her disappointment with her marriage reflects Emma's, and she uses Emma's words to describe it: "C'était donc ça le mariage?" (p. 100). Like Emma, she has a lover, and she meets him in the sordid *Flaubert Hôtel* (p. 132). Roubaud also uses Wedderburn's adaptation of Flaubert to make fun of the conventions of the realist novel. A Mrs. Bovary from Paris, Texas, sues Wedderburn because a review of his novel in the *Cow-Boy Examiner* reveals she is *not* "le portrait tout craché" of the fictional Lady Bovary (p. 124). She wins her suit because American law states that all fiction is biographical; Wedderburn should have found out about the real Mrs. Bovary and portrayed her faithfully in his novel. Like many readers, the courts apparently do not understand the postmodernist practice of borrowing from other writers and they therefore sanction Wedderburn for not providing a realistic picture of the Real World.

In the third novel, *L'Exil d'Hortense*, Roubaud blends Queneau with Shakespeare and articulates the plot around elements borrowed from *Hamlet* and *Othello*. As in the case of Queneau and Flaubert, references to Shakespeare recur throughout the novel, and the various spellings of his name reflect Roubaud's transformation of his plays: Chakespéar, Es'rhaaekpes, chakaispéar, Chaquespéare. In Roubaud's version of Shakespeare, the enemies of Prince Gormanskoï, Hortense's lover, ensnare him in the plot of *Hatmel* in order to deprive him of Hortense and his throne. Unaware of what is happening, Hortense and the Prince begin to behave out of character and start to relive events from *Hamlet*. The subsequent episodes of the plot are thus explained by the fact that Hortense "est allée se fourrer dans Hamlet!" (p. 83). The Prince's position is described in a parody of one of Shakespeare's most famous lines—"To be or not to be Hatmel, that is the question" (p. 138)—while Hortense's friends set out to save her from the fate of Ophelia, Hamlet's fiancée. The first solution they propose involves having Ophélie (a cat) replace Hortense in the role of Ophelia. The second combines the plots of *Hamlet* and *Othello*. In this scenario, the Prince's friends will lead him to identify with Othello rather than Hamlet, and he will therefore see Hortense as Desdemona, not Ophelia (p. 218). Finally, Hotello (another cat) proposes to take the place of the Prince (p. 229).

Besides proposing a complicated new version of the two plays, Roubaud parodies many specific elements within them. He reworks the ghost scene, sets the gravedigger scene in the cemetery of Queneau's-town, plays with famous quotations—"Etre l'être ou le non-être tout en étant l'étant ou le non-étant, telle est la taraudante question" (p. 69)—and produces comic variants of characters' names: Hotello, Gorm-Ham, Thehatmel, Amleth, Theal'm, Yorickskoï. In addition, an *Ur-Hatmel* and an *Ur-Othello* have supposedly inspired the Poldevian *Hatmel* and *Othello*, which Shakespeare later copied. These early versions suggest a long tradition of rewriting the plays (including Eugène Ionesco's *Macbett*, Tom Stoppard's *Rosencrantz and Guildenstern Are Dead*, for example), and Roubaud comically inscribes himself in it.

As the plot of *L'Exil d'Hortense* unfolds, Roubaud further crosses Shakespeare and Queneau with Nathalie Sarraute and Alain Robbe-Grillet. When Prince Gormanskoï's friends decide to save him by moving him from the plot of *Hamlet* to that of *Othello*, they note, "Il fallait jeter *le soupçon* dans l'âme de Gormanskoï, le rendre dévoré de *la jalousie*" (p. 218). Their plan is described as "la campagne de jalousification et othélisation de Gormanskoï" (p. 222), and he thus finds himself embroiled in a plot derived from four different works. The parody of Sarraute's *L'Ere du soupçon* becomes clear in the narrator's observation "Le soupçon pénètre partout. Dans la géographie du roman, c'est l'aire du soupçon" (p. 222). Indeed, doubts and jealousy affect one character after another, a phenomenon emphasized by underlining key words or printing them in boldface type: "Augre commença à avoir le *soupçon*, et bientôt fut *jaloux*" (p. 221). The title of a play described in the text points to Robbe-Grillet's novel *La Jalousie* as the source of the "jalousification":

La Jalousie
par A. . . . R. . . .-G. . . . , lyophilisée du
Jaloux sans sujet, de *de Beys* (p. 129)

The explicit references to Robbe-Grillet and Sarraute again draw attention to the notion of the text as an intertextual space, and the burlesque plot demonstrates in parodic fashion how an original novel is born of the "blend and clash" of other works.

Within this intertextual space, Roubaud appears intent on illustrating an entire catalogue of intertextual devices ranging from the use of quotations to the parody of different types of novelistic discourse. Each episode contains a mosaic of allusions to other writers and their works, all of which appear in an irreverent new context: a chapter of *L'Exil d'Hortense* is entitled "La Prisonnière de Zenda," two more are called "La Chute," the history of the Poldèves and the Poldadams recalls the biblical story of Adam and Eve, and *The Thirty-Nine Steps* is transformed into a television program featuring popular music, in which the thirty-nine steps represent positions in the weekly ratings. Other authors and characters are evoked in carnivalized versions of their names: Voltairskoï, Hotello, Hatmel, Boillaut, le comte de Monte-Cridzoï, Louis Macaniche, John le Circle, and "une belle Hortense au bois dormant" (p. 236). Many other allusions take the form of unattributed quotations or paraphrases such as "en souvenir des jours anciens (ceux qui la faisaient pleurer avec leurs violons et leur langueur monotone)" (p. 60). Some of the quotations are blended to create new versions, as in the composite quotation from Baudelaire and Rimbaud: "Si 'je' est un autre, n'est-il Pas Autre que toi, Lecteur, mon semblable, mon frère" (*L'Enlèvement de Hortense*, p. 12). With their numerous allusions to other works, the Hortense novels form a giant intertextual puzzle and challenge the reader to solve it by identifying the allusions.

The intertextual play extends beyond the references to individual texts to include parodies of novelistic styles, which Roubaud juxtaposes for comic effect. Hortense's story begins in the traditional "realistic" setting of a Parisian neighborhood, but many of her adventures take place in the imaginary country of Poldevia. Between these two poles, Roubaud parodies every style from fairy tales and classical tragedy to adventure novels, science fiction, and detective stories. Traditional motifs and themes frequently appear in unlikely new contexts: after escaping from the pirates who had kidnapped her, Ophelia the cat is reunited with her mother in an animal version of the stock recognition scene (*L'Exil d'Hortense*, p. 154). Her father, a science fiction version of Puss-in-Boots, moves so quickly between worlds that he causes a "warping du chronoclastic infindibulum spatio-temporel" (p. 200), and "La Fausse Hortense," a life-size doll made from modeling clay, comes to life as the object of the wicked prince's desires in a carnivalesque version of the Pygmalion myth. The constant travestying of literary styles and motifs creates many burlesque scenes. Hortense, for example, is rescued by a Poldevian cat (Alexandre Vladimirovitch, alias Hotello), who scales the north face of a belfry on a rope ladder set up by Batwoman, while down below the villain Stéphane falls into a basket full of cream cakes (*L'Enlèvement d'Hortense,* pp. 260–61). No aspect of the novelistic tradition escapes Roubaud's parody, and staple ingredients of seventeenth- and eighteenth-century literature are parodied along with the realist novel and contemporary popular fiction.

Roubaud includes allusions to literary theory alongside the references to fictional works as he parodies the contemporary practice of incorporating critical commentary into a work of fiction. In his article entitled "The Theory Monster and the Writer," he describes the FLT, the French Literary Theorist, as a monster composed of elements from Saussure, Jakobson, Chomsky, Barthes, Greimas, Kristeva, Freud, Lacan, Marx, and Althusser. This beast, he says, spoke only in slogans, and writers "were requested to adore it" (p. 18). He himself deals with the monster by demystifying it in his irreverent references to well-known critics and their work. Psychoanalysis and Julia Kristeva's "sémanalyse" become "la Beeranalyse" and "Julio Bouddheveau's S'aimeanalyse" (*L'Enlèvement d'Hortense,* pp. 113–14). Lacan appears as Dr. N'Laak, and the language of the Lagadonians recalls Foucault's *Les Mots et les choses* because "ils ont, eux, abandonné *tous* les mots. Ils les ont remplacé par les choses" (*L'Exil d'Hortense,* p. 185). The formula "H = O" or "H = deux O" reduces to a mathematical formula the notion that "L'Homme c'est l'Œuvre" (p. 212), and a writer accused of "evacuating" an identifiable subject and story from his work responds by composing a drinking song with the refrain "Zévakuon le Sujé et l'Histoüare!" (pp. 71, 73). Linguistics comes in for similar treatment in the description of the Marché des Bébés Orange. The mock philological analysis of the name traces it back to the fourteenth century, when a sign at the entrance said "Ses brebis on range! Marche!" Over the years, these words have evolved into the present name of the market, and the municipality is consequently promoting tourism by providing babies dressed in orange "afin de réduire l'arbitraire du signe, qui diminue notre part de marchés dans le commerce international" (*L'Enlèvement d'Hortense*, pp. 177–79). Roubaud's parodic use of theory demonstrates that he is not intimidated by the theory monster, and he tames it by adapting it to fit the spirit of his novels.

The parody of critics and critical theory draws attention to the metafictional aspects of Roubaud's work. Besides illustrating a wide range of intertextual practices, he parodies many common metafictional devices. He observes that one of the slogans of "the theory monster" is "Death to the author!" (p. 18), an allusion to Barthes's essay entitled "La Mort de l'auteur." As if to protest this slogan, the figure of Roubaud-the-Author intrudes constantly into the intertextual space, orchestrating events, commenting on the characters, and talking to the reader. Roubaud uses this omnipresent author figure to parody every guise of the author from the self-conscious narrator of the early comic novels to the God-like impersonality of the modernist and the intrusive voice of the contemporary metafictionist. The intrusive voice of the Author first appears at the beginning of *La Belle Hortense* when Roubaud draws attention to the distinction between author and narrator. He explains that "Moi, Jacques Roubaud, je ne suis ici que celui qui tient la plume" (p. 8), whereas the narrator is "le personnage qui dit je et raconte" (*L'Enlèvement d'Hortense*, pp. 41–42). The Author (also called Roubaud) therefore states that his intention is to remain invisible: "m'effacer derrière les personnages de mon récit" (p. 11). He thus draws attention to his guise as invisible Author by paradoxically intervening in the text in order to point out his absence from it. He soon drops the pose, however, and after a dispute with the Narrator, the intrusive Author dominates the text. By *L'Enlèvement d'Hortense*, he has decided to do without the Narrator altogether and demotes him to the role of Character. Throughout the rest of the novel, he comically flaunts his presence and demonstrates that he is now the one who says "je":

> Qui est-ce?
> Moi.
> Oui, moi, l'Auteur de ce livre. (p. 45)

In contrast, the Author seems conspicuously absent from most of *L'Exil d'Hortense*. Traditional third-person narrative replaces the omnipresent "je" of the Author, and a few brief references to an anonymous "on" suggest he may have resumed his impersonal guise. "On" has asked Jim Wedderburn to help save Hortense so that the novel will not be ruined. Laurie retorts, "'on' ne pourrait pas venir demander soi-même?" (p. 86). Given the two earlier novels, this is also the question in the reader's mind. The Author remains absent, however, until chapter 28, when he resurfaces, announcing, "Il est temps de jeter le masque. L'Auteur est là!" (p. 195). He has remained behind the scenes until this point because the Editor objects to his intervening: "Vous, vous êtes là tout le temps, vous intervenez, vous discutez avec les personnages, avec le Lecteur, vous expliquez ce que vous faites, ce que vous allez faire, c'est l'Auteur par-ci, l'Auteur par-là; comment voulez-vous que le public s'y reconnaisse?" (pp. 196–97). Since the Editor has ordered the Author to remain invisible, he has participated in events incognito— "toujours anonyme, clandestine presque" (p. 196)—and he reveals that the strange figure (alias the Shakespearian actor MacPrepared) in a green Burberry raincoat, who appears at the scene of several key events carrying a "Big Shopper" bag with a leek sticking out of it, is in fact the Author in disguise. Thanks to this travestied version of the impersonal author—present everywhere, yet visible nowhere—the Author has been able to orchestrate events from behind the scenes and has made sure that the novel ends well.

The Author's participation in the world he is in the process of creating parodies the postmodernist *topos* of the author entering the world of the characters. Novels using this motif create the illusion that the author can move between the real world and fictional universe, when in fact the frame of the novel has simply been widened to include a fictional version of the author in it. Roubaud plays with the notion of the Author's ontological status by establishing a series of levels of the Author. When the paper Author discusses his plans for a film entitled *LA VIE DE JACQUES ROUBAUD* (*L'Enlèvement d'Hortense*, pp. 165–67), he suggests the possibility of an infinite number of levels of the Author and blurs the boundaries between them. The Author's dealings with "paper" versions of other real-world figures further emphasize the blurring of the boundaries between the real and fictional worlds. In particular, the Author engages in a series of disputes with the Editor and the Publisher, whose voices are integrated into the novel in the form of letters and parenthetical notes. As in the case of the Author, Roubaud parodies the notion that they can move freely between the two worlds.

The Author's relations with his characters serve the same function. He first meets Hortense in the "T" bus and describes "les relations complexes, étroites mais chastes d'un Auteur et de son Héroïne" (*L'Enlèvement d'Hortense*, p. 39). He subsequently portrays himself participating in events alongside his characters: sending messages to Jim Wedderburn, studying geometry with Carlotta, establishing an alibi when Inspector Blognard suspects him of a crime, and having his photograph taken with several characters. In similar fashion, the characters express their opinions of the Author. Carlotta notes that "l'Auteur ne dit pas toujours la vérité" (*L'Exil d'Hortense*, p. 85), while Hortense plans to complain to the Editor because she does not like her role. In order to draw attention to the nature of his relationship with characters, the Author states: "J'aime avoir des rapports *humains* directs avec mes per-sonnages. Nous ne sommes pas que des êtres de papier, que diable" (*L'Enlèvement d'Hortense*, p. 165). His reference to "êtres de papier" recalls Barthes's description of the fictional author as a "paper" author, and Roubaud plays with the notion by stating comically that neither he nor the characters are purely fictional.

Roubaud uses the figure of the author to parody many other common metafictional devices. His references to the tools of his trade parody the *topos* of the writer-at-work: he uses "un feutre noir 'Pilot Razor Point' à pointe fine" (*La Belle Hortense*, p. 8), writes *L'Enlèvement d'Hortense* on "Buro + extra-strong 80 grammes" (p. 81), and at the end of *La Belle Hortense* is still at his post writing: "Ceci est le dernier chapitre, tel que je suis en ce moment en train de l'écrire, à mon bureau, par une belle matinée de printemps" (p. 262). The descriptions of the writer-at-work are accompanied by references to the contemporary cliché that a novel exists as words on a page, and the Author uses "technical parentheses" to explain narrative conventions and to demonstrate his authority as creator of the text. His explanations range from brief comments on specific techniques such as the creation of suspense to more extended discussions of the structure of the novels in terms of chapter division, ending, and the representation of time. In a typical parenthesis, he points out that he is using an interior monologue, which he describes by using a *reductio ad absurdum*: "Nous avons pénétré, en modèles réduits bien entendu, immatériels et impalpables, vous, mon Lecteur fidèle et moi, par l'oreille gauche d'Hortense, qui a un petit lobe particulièrement succulent pour des incisives amoureux, et nous naviguons dans ses cir-convolutions cérébrales" (*L'Enlèvement d'Hortense*, p. 98–99). The reader is referred to Hugo and Conrad to complete the description of an impending storm in *La Belle Hortense*, and character portraits are announced as such: "nous suivrons ici la procédure traditionnelle en matière de description d'Héroïne" (p. 139).

On a more general level, all three novels contain a discussion of endings. In "le dernier chapitre" of *La Belle Hortense*, the Author states that he would rather not have a last chapter, but realizes the only alternative would be to have no chapters at all. He has therefore studied the endings of 366 novels to help him write his own, and the novel ends with a parody of the archetypal happily-ever-after ending followed by "L'après-dernier chapitre." In similar fashion, *L'Exil d'Hortense* ends with a "Post-fin" that contains the parodic promise of a sequel:

> (Seront-ils rejoints et capturés, échapperont-ils? Vous le saurez en lisant la suite de ces aventures dans *Lady Hortense;* le lecteur n'a pas encore rejoint l'Auteur, vlan!)
> Et c'est la Fin Finale. (p. 259)

Chapter division and structure receive similar treatment. Most chapters have traditional titles that refer to the development of the plot, but *La Belle Hortense* also contains three "entre-deux-chapitres" as well as the "après-dernier chapitre." The Author also draws attention to the use of chapter breaks to create suspense or closure. "Tel est le suspens au sein duquel je vous laisse momentanément" (p. 211), he comments at the end of one chapter of *L'Enlèvement d'Hortense*, and the characters too seem aware of the implications of chapter division. The reason given for Hortense's fading desire for the Prince in the last paragraph of a chapter in *L'Exil d'Hortense* is: "Peut-être (mais nous n'en jurerions pas) avaient-ils senti l'approche de la fin du chapitre premier" (p. 19). The narrator makes similar observations about the overall structure of the novel, which he describes primarily in terms of a rise and fall. His most extended comments appear in boldface in the middle of the text:

> **Nous voici arrivés au milieu du roman, et il est nécessaire de le signaler: depuis le début du récit, nous montions la pente des mystères, nous gravissions la pente escarpée semée d'énigmes; et nous voici au sommet. Bientôt, dans**

**quelques lignes à peine, nous allons commencer à re-
descendre vers la plaine encore lointaine et brumeuse où
coule, souverain et tranquille, le fleuve FIN."** (pp. 138–39)

His description of the structure recalls the geography of "La Carte du
Tendre," and it becomes increasingly burlesque when the narrator goes
on to compare crossing the river to crossing the Channel on the hovercraft
and equates the sight of the White Cliffs of Dover with the promise of
new adventures on another shore. The humor derives from the juxtaposition of seventeenth-century style prose and the figurative journey of
the Carte with the realities of modern travel and contemporary
metafictional techniques.

The "entre-deux-chapitres" address the question of novelistic time.
The Author has designed these breaks between chapters as "espaces
verts," "espaces de repos," to allow the reader to step outside the time
of the narrated in order to reflect on the text. Temporal indications given
in terms of lines of text also remind the reader of the time of the narration: "Le tout avait duré six minutes et soixante et une lignes dactylo-
graphiées, une des évasions les plus spectaculaires et les plus courtes de
l'histoire du roman d'aventures" (*L'Enlèvement d'Hortense*, p. 261), and
in the final chapter of *La Belle Hortense*, the Author points out that, as he
has suggested throughout, "Le temps qui a passé est exactement ce qui
a été nécessaire au romancier pour écrire son roman" (p. 264). The
Author's intrusive comments thus focus the reader's attention on the
writing of the text, and like *Le Grand Incendie*, the novels recount their
own "mise en route" as well as the adventures of Hortense.

As part of the metafictional parody, the Author refers to his relationship with the reader. Direct address of the reader is a common feature of both contemporary metafiction and the comic novels of the seventeenth and eighteenth centuries. Roubaud parodies the "dear reader"
tradition of writers such as Fielding and Sterne by having the Author
refer to "la foule de mes chers, de mes innombrables futurs lecteurs"
(*L'Enlèvement d'Hortense*, p. 10). Like his early models, he adopts various attitudes toward the reader: pointing out the qualities of a good
reader, checking the right questions are being asked, and warning the
reader not to jump to the wrong conclusions: "Attention, ce que vous
pensez est faux: ce n'est pas dans ce chapitre qu'Hortense sera enlevée;
il est trop tôt encore" (p. 128). Rather than addressing the reader di-

rectly, other novelists use the first-person plural "nous" to signal the presence of the reader. Roubaud parodies this technique by having the Author give a literal explanation of the referents of the pronoun:

> Qui ça, *nous*?
> Par *nous* je veux dire très précisément:
> a) *Vous,* mon lecteur . . .
> b) *Moi.* Voilà pourquoi nous ne sommes que deux au coin de la rue des Milleguiettes pour le commencement de cette terrible histoire. (pp. 10, 12)

The "vous" is singular, he notes, because there is room for only one reader on the corner. This fictionalized reader is subsequently portrayed as a character in the novel, ordering drinks alongside the Author at the Gudule-Bar (p. 45) and forgetting to close the door after following him into an apartment building (p. 14). Like the other real-world figures, the reader becomes a "paper" reader, and the Author refers to the complexities of this position by concluding: "je vous laisse dépatouiller des implications topologiques et existentielles de votre situation" (p. 46).

The use of the pronoun "nous" suggests the inclusion of the reader in a narrative contract in which author and reader ("vous" and "moi") are equals as encoder and decoder of the text. However, the Author constantly asserts his power over the Reader. As he points out, the reader knows only what the Author has chosen to reveal, whereas the Author's omniscience gives him absolute control over events: "Je le sais parce que c'est moi l'Auteur et que je sais tout, et vous le savez parce que je vous le dis" (p. 73). In *L'Exil d'Hortense,* Roubaud portrays the Author's power in the image of the Reader scurrying along trying to keep up with the Author. Since the reader has to wait for the Author to write the next word, the Author's main advantage is that "nous sommes en avance sur lui. Et il ne peut pas nous rattraper" (p. 209). Through his direct address of the reader and his comic foregrounding of the pronouns "nous," "vous," and "je," Roubaud provides a playful illustration of the dynamics of power implicit in narrative and presents his relationship with his readers as a game of manipulation.

Roubaud's portrayal of the reader also involves two metaphors often used in contemporary criticism to describe the act of reading: those of the detective and the voyeur. A detective in *L'Enlèvement d'Hortense*

solves a crime by rereading the first thirty-five chapters of the novel. By
having him find the answer in the novel of which he is a character,
Roubaud draws attention to the reader's role as detective, and the analogy is made explicit when the reader is told to "Chercher, comme
Inspecteur Blognard, la Solution" (p. 174). The Author makes similar
explicit references to the analogy between reading and voyeurism. He
reminds the readers to use their eyes—"Auteur et Lecteur, nous sommes
des yeux qui voyons" (p. 278)—and when he describes Hortense's naked body, he discusses the ethical problems involved in making the
reader a voyeur, concluding that "il est à craindre que le lecteur ne puisse
éviter d'être voyeur" (*La Belle Hortense*, p. 139). Roubaud's parody of
reader-author relations thus ranges from a burlesque version of the "dear
reader" tradition to a comic portrayal of contemporary discussions of
reading.

Roubaud combines the metafictional and intertextual play with
the use of formal constraints. The constraints he chooses reflect the three
main influences on his work discussed in *Le Grand Incendie*: detective
novels, mathematics, and medieval poetry. Pierrot notes at the end of
Pierrot mon ami that his adventures could have been "un roman policier
avec un crime, un coupable et un détective," but that these essential
ingredients of the genre do not figure in the novel (p. 210). Roubaud
provides these missing elements and, like many contemporary writers,
uses the model of the detective story to structure his novels. *La Belle
Hortense* relates the mystery of the "Terreur des Quincailliers" and introduces Inspecteur Blognard, "le célèbre déchiffreur d'énigmes"
(*L'Enlèvement d'Hortense*, p. 20). The novel thus has an enigma and a
detective, but it still lacks a murder. The Author comments on this situation in one of many explicit references to the detective model: "Dans ce
roman où nous sommes, qui est un roman policier, puisqu'il y a un
détective, deux même, n'est-il pas paradoxal *qu'il n'y ait aucun meurtre?*"
(*La Belle Hortense*, p. 254). The situation is remedied in *L'Enlèvement
d'Hortense*, which begins with the murder of Sinouls's dog Balbastre,
and Blognard immediately starts the investigation, helped by his soft-
ware program and the Poldevian detective Sheralockiszyku Hola-
mesidjudjy, known for short as She. Hol. During the course of the investigation, the Author points out ways in which detective fiction has been
used in the modern novel: "il n'y avait aucune chance que mon livre fût
cette variation incongrue et avant-gardiste du roman policier: celui où

l'*Auteur* est le coupable. Il y a eu le Détective comme Criminel, comme Victime, le Narrateur comme Coupable, on a essayé toutes les combinaisons, mais on n'a pas encore écrit le roman où le Lecteur est coupable, celui où il est Victime" (p. 150). His metafictional comments invite the reader to examine the use of the genre in *L'Enlèvement d'Hortense* and to compare it to both traditional models and contemporary variants.

The solution to the enigma lies in the fictional generators. Identifying the murderer therefore involves discovering the system of formal constraint underlying the structure of the novel. The constraint derives from the form of the sestina, a poem with six stanzas of six lines, in which all the stanzas have the same six words at the end of their lines but in a different order each time. With its "permutation en spirale,"[6] the sestina reflects Roubaud's interest in both medieval poetry and the mathematical field of combinatorics. Queneau traces the sestina to the poetry of Arnaut Daniel in the thirteenth century and notes that its spiral permutation is "particulièrement potentielle" for potential literature.[7] Roubaud points to the origin of the form by inscribing Arnaut Daniel in his novels under the name of Arnaud Danieldzoï, and in *L'Enlèvement d'Hortense,* he exploits the full potential of the sestina as a productive mechanism. Both the characters and the plot derive from the combinatory structure. Danieldzoï, the first Poldevian prince, established the laws of succession of the Poldevian dynasty based on "une permutation fixée immuablement depuis le XIIIe siècle," that of the permutations of the six stanzas of the sestina, which means that "l'ordre initial était rétabli . . . au bout de six générations" (*La Belle Hortense*, pp. 44–45). The structure of *L'Enlèvement d'Hortense* and *L'Exil d'Hortense* reflects the same rules: their six parts, each containing six chapters, mirror the thirty-six lines of the sestina. Likewise, the six Poldevian princes each bear "une marque de fabrique, située sur la fesse gauche. C'est une spirale escargoïde" (*L'Enlèvement d'Hortense*, p. 94). Because of its shape, which reflects the spiraling structure of the sestina, the snail is the sacred animal of Poldevia, and six dots are inscribed in the snail-like spirals of the princes in such a way that they each have a different tattoo and can be numbered from one to six. A diagram illustrates the six permutations of six (p. 176) and thus demonstrates how the tattoos reflect the structure of the text and determine the place of the princes in it.

The novel contains numerous clues as to the mathematical nature of the enigma, and the Author points out that "un rôle important est joué par les nombres" (p. 111). Multiples of six, in particular, recur throughout the novels. The rules of permutation finally reveal the criminal, and in a parody of an Agatha Christie ending, Blognard brings the characters together to explain how a close rereading of the novel has enabled him to identify the murderer. Each of the six princes appears six times, "*dans un certain ordre*," which Blognard expresses numerically:

6 1 5 2 4 3
3 6 4 1 2 5
5 3 2 6 1 4 (pp. 278–79)

The permutation of the numbers corresponds to the permutating words at the end of the lines of the sestina. The murderer, the false Poldevian detective, gives himself away because he appears seven times, thus breaking the pattern: "Cette apparition surnuméraire, désordonnée, démesurée, orgueilleuse, le trahit" (p. 279). Solving the enigma requires that the detective be familiar with medieval poetry and numerical permutations, and the ending of the novel thus brings together three important focuses of Roubaud's work: detective fiction, mathematics, and poetry. At the same time, it provides a perfect illustration of the Oulipian use of constraint and Roubaud's postulate that "a text written according to a constraint must speak of this constraint."[8]

The funny, topsy-turvy world of the Hortense novels places Roubaud in the tradition of the comic novel. His "plagiaires par anticipation" thus include Rabelais, Scarron, Furetière, Sterne, and Diderot, and his attitude toward them is at once one of respect and transgression. He describes his relationship to the poets of the past in similar terms: "J'essayai de me confronter à la tradition, dans une disposition intérieure à la fois respectueuse, exaltée et ironique, furieuse ('hommage et profanation,' dit Octavio Paz), pour à la fois l'exorciser, me soulager de son fardeau."[9] His playful inversion of novelistic conventions recalls the spirit of the carnival, and like earlier carnivalesque forms such as Menippean satire, his novels "exorcise" the past by providing a comic version of the "serious" canon. He thus sets up a dialogue with the Western tradition of novel writing, and his use of dialogic forms such as parody, pastiche, burlesque, and travesty demonstrates that nothing is sacred. His novels both illustrate his debt to the past and emphasize his continuing search for new forms. As the Author points out, "le roman n'arrêtait pas de bouger dans sa forme comme dans ses formats" (*L'Enlèvement d'Hortense*, p. 80), and the exuberance of the Hortense novels communicates the vitality of the novel as a genre. Roubaud's dialogue with the past therefore situates his work at the intersection of continuity and change, as part of a long tradition, yet innovative and experimental in form.

Notes

1. Oulipo, *La Littérature potentielle* (Paris: Gallimard, 1973), p. 33.
2. Warren F. Motte, trans. and ed., *Oulipo: A Primer of Potential Literature* (Lincoln: University of Nebraska Press, 1986), pp. 18, 12.
3. Jacques Roubaud, "What Have They Done to Us?: The Theory Monster and the Writer," in *Ideas from France: The Legacy of French Theory*, ed. Lisa Appignanesi (London: Free Association Books, 1989), pp. 20, 21.
4. Raymond Queneau, *Pierrot mon ami* (Paris: Gallimard, 1943), p. 210.
5. Roland Barthes, "The Death of the Author," in *Image-Music-Text*, trans. Stephen Heath (New York: Hill and Wang, 1977), p. 166.
6. Roubaud, "La Mathématique dans la méthode de Raymond Queneau," *Critique*, no. 359 (1977), p. 397.
7. Raymond Queneau, *Bâtons, chiffres, et lettres* (Paris: Gallimard, 1965), pp. 329–30.
8. Motte, *Oulipo*, p. 18.
9. Robert Davreu, *Jacques Roubaud* (Paris: Seghers, 1985), p. 20.

Bibliography

Works by Jacques Roubaud

FICTION

Graal fiction. Paris: Gallimard, 1978.
La Belle Hortense. Paris: Ramsay, 1985. Translated by David Kornacker as *Our Beautiful Heroine*. New York: Overlook Press, 1987.
L'Enlèvement d'Hortense. Paris: Ramsay, 1987. Translated by Dominic Di Bernardi as *Hortense Is Abducted*. Normal, IL: Dalkey Archive, 1989.
Le Grand Incendie de Londres. Paris: Seuil, 1989. Translated by Dominic Di Bernardi as *The Great Fire of London*. Normal, IL: Dalkey Archive, 1991.
L'Exil d'Hortense. Paris: Seghers, 1990. Translated by Dominic Di Bernardi as *Hortense in Exile*. Normal, IL: Dalkey Archive, 1992.
La Boucle. Paris: Seuil, 1993.

POETRY

Σ. Paris: Gallimard, 1967.

Le Sentiment des choses. Paris: Gallimard, 1970.

Trente et un au cube. Paris: Gallimard, 1973.

Autobiographie, chapitre dix. Paris: Gallimard, 1977.

Dors, preceded by *Dire la poésie.* Paris: Gallimard, 1980.

Quelque chose noir. Paris: Gallimard, 1986. Translated by Rosemarie Waldrop as *Something Black.* Normal, IL: Dalkey Archive, 1990.

OTHER WORKS

Petit Traité invitant à l'art subtil du go. With Georges Perec and Pierre Lusson. Paris: Bourgois, 1969.

Graal théâtre. With Florence Delay. Paris: Gallimard, 1977.

"La Mathématique dans la méthode de Raymond Queneau." *Critique,* no. 359 (1977): 392–413.

Graal théâtre II. With Florence Delay. Paris: Gallimard, 1980.

Partition rouge. With Florence Delay. Paris: Seuil, 1988.

"What Have They Done to Us?: The Theory Monster and the Writer." In *Ideas from France: The Legacy of French Theory,* edited by Lisa Appignanesi. London: Free Association Books, 1989.

La Bibliothèque oulipienne, vols. 1–3. With Paul Fournel. Paris: Seghers, 1990.

Selected Critical Works

Berranger, Marie-Paule. *Poésie en jeu.* Paris: Bordas, 1989.

Davreu, Robert. *Jacques Roubaud.* Paris: Seghers, 1985.

Garcin, Jérôme. *Le Dictionnaire: Littérature française contemporaine.* Paris: François Bourin, 1988. See entry on/by Roubaud.

Ireland, Susan. "The Comic World of Jacques Roubaud." *Esprit Créateur* 31, no. 4 (winter 1991): 22–31.

Motte, Warren F., trans. and ed. *Oulipo: A Primer of Potential Literature.* Lincoln: University of Nebraska Press, 1986.

Oulipo. *La Littérature potentielle.* Paris: Gallimard, 1973.

9

Hélène Cixous

Martine Motard-Noar

Hélène Cixous is one of the most controversial thinkers and writers in France. Despite her unwillingness to be labeled a "feminist," she is considered a representative of one of the major creative and critical drives in the New French Feminism movement. If she has always shown her hostility to the term *feminism*, it is because it symbolizes, according to her, a desire by different political groups to replace male tyranny with another one: that of women. However, the definition of *feminism* in a broader perspective, "as an awareness of women's oppression-repression that initiates both analyses of the dimension of this oppression-repression, and strategies for liberation,"[1] makes it possible for us to describe and discuss her works, in the absence of any other viable terminology. Since her first novel, *Dedans* (1969), she has developed her avant-garde practice of writing in close to thirty novels or fictions, several plays, as well as critical and theoretical books published along with an impressive number of articles.[2] Her position in France in the late 1960s, when she started to write and publish, tells of the publishing situation in France at the time as well as that of literature. Just like another prominent feminist writer of her generation—Monique Wittig—she was quickly confronted with an institution in the middle of a crisis. Two members (Maurice Nadeau and Roger Grenier) of the jury of the traditional Prix Renaudot resigned, thus demonstrating their inability to pursue a now-stale acknowledgment of a line of writing dating back to the beginning of the century. At the same time, the nouveau roman was achieving full recognition for its major writers. Up to 1968, it even seems to have the monopoly over all experimental writing. This, among other reasons, may explain why Wittig, for instance, published *L'Opoponax* in 1964 at the Editions de Minuit, famous for having published the nouveau roman, and why Cixous published her first pieces at Grasset, a still fairly traditional publisher. There was what we can construe now as a total absence of "feminine-minded" publishers. For obvious historical reasons, the status of publishers in France corresponded to that of a society not yet redefined.

These women writers will actually find themselves in the middle of a revolution: the May 1968 revolution. Their works and theories started to take shape at the time of a political, economic, and, as the French soon realized throughout the 1970s, ethical, sociological, and philosophical transformation of the country. The development of a more modern French society, although it had started with the post–World War II reorganization of the economy, had been in slow motion under de Gaulle. The 1967 Neuwirth Law canceled the 1920 ban on the sale of contraceptives, and only in 1974, a few years after the "revolution," was abortion legalized in France. The formation of feminist groups, soon to become factions— one of them called "Psychanalyse et Politique," to which Cixous belonged—and the impact of the 1971 pro-abortion "Appel de 343 femmes" account for the final development of issues brought by women concerning women.[3]

The freedom movement of May 1968 started by a small student strike at the Sorbonne coincided with Cixous's career as a university professor with several other contemporary writers such as Jacques Derrida, Jacques Lacan, and Julia Kristeva. Indeed they seem to represent a whole generation influenced by philosophy and a new approach to psychoanalysis. Although Cixous's fiction can in no way be reduced to the pure application of certain philosophical considerations and the deconstructionist ideology, it appears to have been greatly influenced by the writing of a generation with whom she is often compared and associated in many critical works. Still today, Cixous directs her seminar of her "Centre de recherches en études féminines" at the Collège de Philosophie, a meaningful change of "locus" from the Paris VIII-Vincennes campus.

Once considered an "avant-garde" writer, Hélène Cixous, maybe even more than her contemporaries, is today still criticized for her "unreadibility" or even accused of being too prolific, although her work now belongs to a literary corpus taught in universities, included on reading lists. Against her will, Cixous's criticism and fiction, especially after the widely published "Le Rire de la Méduse,"[4] are part of our academic discourse. For that reason, her works have been translated into several languages, and especially in the United States. What seems to have interested most American feminists and theoreticians of feminism is Cixous's clear position as a feminist critic and, at the same time, her total fictional recreation of a positive basis for further construction of woman's self: the concept of the other present in her idea of "the other bisexuality" as well as that of the father figure.

Her first movement to try to write out of the boundaries set by centuries of patriarchy has been to counter any sign of mastery, any gesture or word of exclusion. There, her experience as the founder of a research center in the French university system was an exact mirror of what her writing strove to accomplish:

> When we founded Paris VIII, at the time of '68, we founded it with the idea that there would be no more professors, no more masters—something that never did materialize, because if one is not the master, the other is, of course. We never did get out of the Hegelian system. What one can do is displace it as much as possible. One has to fight it; one can diminish the degree of mastery, yet without completely eliminating it. There always must be a tiny bit of phallus, so that it is humanly impossible to have an absolute economy without a minimum of mastery. The problem is that one is always with the regime of the maximum and not that of the minimum.[5]

Cixous's realistic approach to the issue of mastery can also be perceived in her publishing career as an example of her drive for more freedom. With no choice other than to publish her work under the traditional nomenclature of *novel*, she was finally granted the freedom of leaving the definition of her books to the vague description of *fiction* later on, and even to delete altogether any generalizing, and therefore reductive categorization of her writing.

And, indeed, Cixous's texts draw lines across several of the traditionally recognized "genres," between literary criticism and poetry, between theoretical presentation and the appearance of the novel. This aspect of her writing alone may actually account for the difficulty that some readers have experienced when opening any of her books for the first time. No convenient classification of our expectations as readers is present and we must be ready to wander through her text and musical language in a fashion similar to some of her oneiric questioning. For, overall, Cixous's quest is that of the dilapidation of all economic status of the text. Her "new insurgent writing"[6] opens onto a new conceptualization of characters, their existence, their numbers, their possessions, and that of a plot. "Le Rire de la Méduse," a now classic manifesto of feminist literature, published by Cixous in 1976, enounces clearly her reach beyond usual writing lines, when she calls for an open space "au-delà de la remise-en-lit de la lutte à mort, de l'amour-guerre qui prétend figurer l'échange, elle [la femme] se rit d'une dynamique d'Erôs que la haine alimenterait—haine: héritage, encore, un reste un asservissement dupant au phallus. Aimer, regarder-penser-chercher l'autre dans l'autre, dé-spéculariser, déspéculer" (p. 54). As seen here, Cixous's notion of women's access to freedom is directly related to her access to writing, and specifically in a different fashion, beyond the traditional empowerment of the author by his/her character(s) and of the character(s) by the author, beyond classical writing, which, according to her, is constantly based on a "plus-value" goal.

In practice, for Cixous, this makes for an almost (but not quite) complete deconstruction of the text. The problematics of the beginning and the end of the text are particularly striking, as Cixous negates any imposed stability of the narration by denying any possibility of locating a beginning, an "origin" to the text. For the concept of origin has now become an integral part of a masculine mythology in conjunction with the origin of sin and Eve's accusation. Disempowerment circulates in her fiction through the absence of a linear motion or resolution, with no particular accounting of a progression. Luce Irigaray, a feminist theoretician of the same generation, accuses the Other, man, of the same drive to calculate all movement. Her description of man echoes that of Cixous: "Tu ne peux faire un geste sans le peser. L'économiser, le compter. L'endetter. M'endetter. . . . Tu inventes l'économie."[7] Cixous's *Le Livre de Promethea*, published in 1983, even tries to propose several other titles for the book at the end. These possibilities create an explosion of potential meanings and a necessity to reconsider the text backward from the last page to the first one. What if the titles were: "Promethea agent secret," or "Les Souffrances de Promethea," or "Promethea ouvre un restaurant" (p. 248)? The irony of the proposal also circulates between the genres that these titles allude to—from the detective novel to a feminized version of *Werther*, from a religious rewriting of the Bible to a realistic narration, which, by its radical title, introduces an almost spiritual image of the text's search (i.e., opening a restaurant or opening the text/food to the clients/readers for *their* choice of the menu).

Partie shows another example of her valorization of free-circulating writing, of the "open," a concept that alludes to a well-known stigmatization of woman in her sexual characterization and, therefore, a highly controversial basis in feminist theory. The title itself, like many of Cixous's titles, allows for several interpretations in French. "Partie" means "part" (of a whole) as well as "game." In effect, *Partie* plays on the two apparently equal parts of the text meeting halfway in the book but presenting the same book cover and title at both ends. There is no beginning, no end. Where is the part or the whole? Where does it start, where does it end? Cixous here introduces us to the impossible univocity of her works.

In order to complete her deconstruction of patriarchal discourse and literature, Cixous will also break away from the organized and organizing discourse of gender representations insofar as it works by binary oppositions, such as superior/inferior, man/woman, master/slave, father/son, activity/passivity,[8] all in a desire to orchestrate and structure patterns of authority. To such a manifestation of power, she opposes her notion of "the other bisexuality" as recognition and respect of difference. She defines it exactly as a place where "chaque sujet non enfermé dans le faux théâtre de la représentation phallocratique, institue son univers érotique. Bisexualité, c'est-à-dire repérage en soi, individuellement, de la présence, diversement manifeste et insistante selon chaque un ou une des deux sexes, non-exclusion de la différence ni d'un sexe, et à partir de cette 'permission' que l'on se donne, multiplication des effets d'inscription du désir, sur toutes les parties de mon corps et de l'autre corps."[9] This may be interpreted at first as a hidden or at least irresistible way of feminizing her text, since the inscription of her desire relates to a specific gender. In *Angst*, for instance, the narrators' various identities are clearly identified as "êtres aimantes" (p. 12) when the noun "être" is normally in the masculine. In other cases, this feminization of the language on top of the clear gender identification of the narrative voices makes Cixous's texts shift to a narrow interpretation of "the other bisexuality." In *Anankè*, the statement is made that "l'amour est plus forte que l'histoire" (p. 123; emphasis added), possibly intimating that love should be put in the feminine. Furthermore, the narrator's "ami K" is described as "cette homme," or "l'amour d'un homme fait mère" (p. 145). However, the transformation of fictional gender identities assumes no "parti pris," as such examples are limited to a handful in an overall large fictional production. For female/male associations also run freely through her fiction, adding a myriad of symbolic associations to an image, a character, or sometimes simply a name, as in the name of Saint-Georges, with whom the narrator writes *Les Commencements:* "Sang et gorges, geint, sage et singe, et scin, or, gain et tain. . . . Phallus des commencements, plume de la narratrice, Saint-Georges défait et refait avec elle le troisième corps du texte" (cover). The freedom of gender construction here works as an open-ended process, a moving signifier exploring conscious and subconscious "rapports de force" within the fiction. In addition, Cixous establishes a balance of female and male images in the narration, as it expresses the dynamics she has proposed, that is to say the "between, the *entre* . . . the neither-one-nor-the-other."[10]

If she privileges the word or the name, in short, the signifier, she particularly enjoys mythology as a preconscious representation of gender power, and, therefore, as an existing history that challenges her attempt. As a body of symbols, traditional mythology prescribes set roles for female and male figures. In order to recover the female characters from their mythological oppression, in an effort similar to what Coppélia Kahn characterizes as "Excavating . . . Maternal Subtexts in Patriarchal Literature,"[11] Cixous presents several Greek, Egyptian, Mesopotamian, and biblical heroines. From Penthesilea to Aphrodite, from Persephone and Demeter to Neith, mythological women come to reinforce Cixous's position as to women's capacity to give, in the absence of desire for investment. Allusions to so many different women from the past also seem to point to women's eternal fight for freedom, for an access to speech.

An example of this reappropriation of traditional mythology can be found in allusions to Ishtar. Ishtar, often compared to the Greek Isis, is present in *With ou l'art de l'innocence* as a synonym of pleasure and innocence, therefore, as the title indicates, as a figure leading the fiction closer to its goal: that of finding the art of innocence again. For, according to the legend and Cixous's reinforcement of its positiveness, Ishtar managed to bring her husband back to earth after his abduction. This allows for a period of intense love and flourishing. Much like Monique Wittig, Cixous seems to present an approach to mythological figures as the constitution of a feminine dictionary. The positive reincarnation of feminine figures helps in writing beyond "his"tory to have access to the creative power of women. That power is to be seen as a multiplying gift, a limitless world. Empowerment of women in a nonaggressive fashion explains the presence of several other heroines, such as Leda in *Les Commencements*. Leda was said to have given birth to two giant eggs, from which two sets of twins were born. In this way, Leda reinforces, through the poetic formulation of the myth, a presymbolic construction of women as an admission of their multiplying power both in quantity and quality.

Other examples of the use of mythological heroines in Cixous's works come to prove and reinforce not simply the strength of female power over life, despite their fate, but also the slow eradication of male figures—even at the mythological level—from the fiction. In the intense relationship between Demeter and Persephone, Cixous sets her fiction and her goal as a writer: "le sens n'est pas sur l'axe des mesures, mais bientôt sur celui de la démesure."[12] Demeter indeed marks *Illa* with a love that shows no sign of restraint, a love unbound for another woman: her daughter who has been abducted. But her chants are not those of hysteria as documented by psychoanalysts like Freud. They are proposed, on the contrary, as a declaration of male destructive power. The accusation of Western culture turns quickly into a change of perspective on the myth as a whole. The traditional understanding of Demeter's wrath as craziness is absent at the moment her name is declared a synonym of "D'AIMER TERRE" (p. 18). Contradicting, or rather ignoring, traditional male symbolic, Cixous presents Demeter in the same light as the Medusa, as Nancy Gray analyzed it:

> in 'The Laugh of the Medusa,' all women have to do 'for history to change its meaning' (for our sense of possibility to be re-visioned) is to stop listening to the myths about us as if they were true: 'You only have to look at the Medusa straight on to see her. And she's not deadly. She's beautiful and she's laughing.' Women's relation to old texts has ever been a discomfited one insofar as we find ourselves the enemy, the dan-

ger, in them; refusing to die when we look straight on at them is a deceptively simple step with profoundly revolutionary consequences. She who is not defined as in or of the phallocentric symbolic order can withstand the prohibitions of that order; it cannot harm her because she does not partake of its codes. Her laughter is uncontainable.[13]

In the end, Demeter and Persephone constitute the New Couple, one of rebirth, one of female reconstruction. A new genealogy is born. From woman to woman, there is no need any longer for the goddess to "déméter" the earth since there is no possibility of rapture by men. (This pun, typical of Cixous, plays on the association of the name Demeter [Déméter in French] with the verb *démettre*, i.e., to undo, to take apart.) In this way, mothers and daughters as women give birth to each other in the total marginalization of male power.

This new genealogy also owes its existence to deconstructionist writing and is heavily influenced by Jacques Derrida's philosophy of the text as a "mouvement 'productif' et conflictuel qu'aucune dialectique philosophique ne saurait *relever*, résoudre ou apaiser, et qui désorganise 'pratiquement,' 'historiquement,' textuellement l'opposition ou la différence."[14] The refusal of any concept of simplicity in a text stands only as the prologue for Cixous's pleasure in working on the metamorphosis of the text and its words. The resulting complexity of her writing is at the core of the controversy about her texts as "readable." Some critics even rejected Cixous's enterprise as a whole until the 1980s introduced more feminine writing and more feminist criticism. As for Cixous, the deconstruction of words constitutes a necessity to break away from the law; it is actually a condition for the infinite succession of female births. In *Le Livre de Promethea* the narrator defines her goal clearly: "je vais te bercer, j'accepte de te séparer de moi, pour te donner une naissance. A nouveau je vais revenir à l'entrée de la vie. Pour toi, le nouveau premier pas. Pour toi, je me fais mère avec une douleur, avec une rage, puisque c'est ce que tu veux, je me défais" (p. 170). The search for the "phrase-femelle" (p. 169) is thus never an easy one. Each fiction has its own spatial presentation able to allow the feminine voice to be heard, and meaning to be wandering. *Tombe*, for instance, is built on thirty-three verses, close to biblical style, developing an incantative tone. *Angst*, on the contrary, breathes with a very staccato tempo, written with short sentences in an attempt to exorcize "la scène de la Grande Souffrance" (p. 9). *Vivre l'orange* uses dashes throughout the fiction to mark the slow, gentle, and sensible approach of the writer Clarice Lispector, to whom the book is dedicated.

Traditional narrative and representative notions are absent in all Cixous's fiction. However, the typographical presentation of the text endows it with a descriptive structure. This is especially true in *Partie*, published only two years after Derrida's *Glas*, where the overall syntax of the text, or deconstruction thereof, can be most startling. *Partie* follows the same pattern as Derrida: "D'abord, deux colonnes. Tronquées . . . incises, tatouages, incrustations. Une première lecture peut faire comme si deux textes dressés, l'un contre l'autre ou l'un sans l'autre entre eux ne communiquaient pas."[15] No hierarchy is possible in this context, where the reader is unable to define which text one is supposed to read first, as there is precisely no supposition made. Accommodating for the two voices, at least, of the narrator, the text in its reading only appears as the transcription of more or less distant approaches and questioning. By themselves though, the two columns reinforce a breathtaking dance between the Self and the Other. In *Partie* as in *Glas*, the coexistence of two voices is a direct presentation of binary forces, life and death, as well as a struggle against death, and with it, any attempt at simplifying the writer-narrator identification. In fact, the two columns even make it possible for the reader to improvise a third text in order to relate one part of the text to the other.

Such destabilization of the top voice tends to propose the topic of the precarious as the central focus of fictional and verbal deconstruction. Since Cixous obviously values the precarious as a historically feminine value, she has also expressed a feeling of achievement toward her ability to represent it and, consequently, to save it from disappearing. In her first novel, *Dedans*, the narrator had concluded: "Je me réjouis de pouvoir parler . . . et de pouvoir dire merde merde merde à la mort" (p. 208). However, this sense of victory is matched only by a constant concern to keep the infinitely small and fragile alive in and with her writing. Following Montaigne's advice, her goal opposes traditional masculine values and construction of the self, insofar as "Il faut légèrement couler le monde et le glisser, non pas l'enfoncer."[16] Therefore, she pays attention to a "soufflelein" (*With ou l'art de l'innocence*), the smallest "veinules" of a leaf (*Souffles*), or the smallest meaningful ways of deconstructing and reconstructing a name (*Vivre l'orange/To Live the Orange*).[17] In the end, Cixous's magical geography extends to an overall relationship of the world with the text as the ultimately precarious representation of life. It is constantly threatened with extinction. Fictional reduction becomes a central source of anxiety as writing mirrors woman's alienation in close connection with that of the text. Images of dispersion and scattered parts of the body occur in several fictions with Cixous's own name as a representative of the text's anxiety. In *Partie*, she writes her last name out in the body of the text in three parts (p. 7). Leaving "OUS" as the last part, she accentuates the ability, enjoyment as well as fear to split apart as "OUS" can be understood in French as the plural of "OU" ("or" or "where"), thus stressing the possible multiplication and dispersion of the self. The ambiguity of her writing thus reads as a "déchiffrure" (p. 7), a pun that alone can convey the danger of "déchirure" and "griffure," while its writing explains the need for a necessary "déchiffrage" of dangers in order to subvert them.

The climactic point of this notion can be found in *Angst*, the title of which summarizes a degree of anxiety soon to reach a state of phobia. The death principle indeed becomes the subject and the object of the deconstruction of the father figure while it also accounts for a personal reconstruction. Cixous's texts struggle against the reality of her father's death when she was still a child in Algeria. From then on, an obsessive fiction attempts to set an autobiographical account among imaginary and phantasmatic passages. The beginning of the novel *Dedans* transforms the reality of "Mon père est mort" (p. 15) into an object of representation worth writing about: "je compris que la mort était une vie mystérieuse. . . . Dans ma vie il n'y avait pas de place pour la mort; ma vie avait l'immensité de l'imaginable" (pp. 21–22). It is surprising and ironic here—but this may be Cixous's biggest laugh in a way—that she is using as a fictional pattern one that was identified by Freud, whose psychoanalytic theories she has so often criticized. For in deconstructing the father figure with that of death, Cixous has mimicked Freud's "Fort/ Da" theory. This theory came about when Freud observed a small child playing with a bobbin whenever his mother would leave him. He came to the conclusion that this young boy was trying to represent and therefore appease his separation anxiety by imitating his mother's departure and return with the bobbin. He would make the bobbin disappear ("fort") and reappear ("da") in an attempt to solve his fears and gain power over the action. Cixous, very much like the little boy, relishes in this presence/absence dichotomy. However, replacing the father's absence is not specific to a first novel that could be considered as a typical first novel, a cathartic one. Cixous, on the contrary, extends her fears and feelings of panic to the rest of her fiction and places it under the general symbol of the limit. At the end of *Angst*, she even admits: "Dix livres à vouloir en finir avec la mort. A la fin arriver à écrire *Angst* à contre-terreur . . . pour faire à la mort son dernier sort. . . . L'écrire, à la limite, après tout, pour ne se distinguer du passé que par un fil de texte" (p. 281).

In 1990, thirteen years after the publication of *Angst*, in a series of lectures at the University of California–Irvine, Cixous reiterated her belief in death as the first step on the journey of writing. Writing must go by the "School of the Dead," because "they are the doorkeepers who while closing one side 'give' way to the other."[18] This may explain why *Angst* is far from being her last text to explore death.

Death as a working concept and representative of the father in the end creates the formation of another presence/absence dichotomy as its own shadow: that of the mother's or woman's presence and absence. Pleasure slowly emerges in the name of the feminine: "J'ai assez d'amour pour sentir tant je te suis mêlée, entre tes désirs et mes lèvres, couler le Baiser lui-même, celui que je n'ai jamais reçu, le baiser qui dévore et nourrit, la langue maternelle dans ma bouche, la langue qui m'a manqué, je la sens encore, celle dont je n'ai jamais cessé d'éprouver l'absence, comme si mon corps n'avait pu effacer la première jouissance."[19] One of the reasons for this "ouverture" also happens to be her proposal not to dispose of sexual difference in her definition of a feminine practice of writing, and of reading as well. Consequently, opening space for the other, according to Cixous, stands as the prime realization of an inexhaustible and forever present desire that represents neither a lack nor a desire for castration. She admonishes: "Femme, n'aie peur ni d'ailleurs, ni de même, ni d'autre. Mes yeux ma langue mes oreilles mon nez ma peau ma bouche mon corps—pour—(l')autre, non que je la désire pour me boucher un trou, parer à quelque mien défaut, ou talonnée destinalement par la féminine 'jalousie.' "[20]

Cixous's discovery in the late 1970s of Clarice Lispector appeased and at the same time reinforced such a desperate attempt at finding a balance between these different personal "mythemes" Cixous had mod-

eled in her writing.[21] She truly turned it into a visionary philosophy
with her new guardian angel from Brazil. She explained in clearer terms
what the limit has been all along: the masculine. Lispector's work stands
as a springboard to a further questioning of the voyage toward and with
the other. Thanks to Lispector, Cixous has come to define the next step
of the approach:

> *Pour laisser entrer une chose avec son étrangeté*, il faut mettre de
> la lumière d'âme dans chaque regard, et mélanger la lumière
> extérieure et la lumière intérieure. Une invisible aura se forme
> autour des êtres bien regardés. Voir avant la vision, voir pour
> voir et voir, avant le récit des yeux, ce n'est pas une magie.
> C'est la science de l'autre! tout un art; et toutes les manières
> pour laisser entrer dans notre proche tous les êtres avec leurs
> étrangetés différentes, sont des régions qui demandent à être
> approchées chacune avec une patience appropriée.[22]

This passage clearly expresses an enlargement of Cixous's earlier claim
to an aura of love for the other, where opening would in no way symbolize a lack, a precarious condition, or a desire to annihilate and engulf. In the same movement, what prevails here in looking at the other
is nonfear of the other, the inside, and the entering. In a 1989 essay, Cixous
proposes to see the limit, the extreme in Lispector's work, a limit that
Cixous herself has explored in the majority of her fictional texts. To be

> the most other possible involved passing into the masculine,
> *passing by way of a man*. Paradoxical step. So, to approach this
> almost-woman, one sees in the text how (Clarice)-I has not
> shaved for several days, has not played football, and so on.
> 'I' goes into the masculine, and this particular masculinity
> impoverishes her. . . . But like every process of impoverish-
> ment with Clarice Lispector, it is a positive movement, a form
> of asceticism, a way of bridling a part of pleasure, to attain a
> strange joy. Moreover, in his turn this man 'monasterizes'
> himself, deprives himself, bows down. Double impoverish-
> ment.[23]

As usual in Cixous, the philosophy of the sexes, while engendering a more intense pleasure for bisexuality, reaches out into the realm of writing. There is much pleasure in the intense questioning of Lispector's text:

> Who is the 'Man' who writes this text? No. Who is the man who writes this text? No. What sex is the writer who is capable of writing this text? No. What sex, then, am I who can write this text? Or: does the text decide the sex of the author? I mean the sex hidden in the sex, the imaginary sex. Or: who is the author of the author? I mean: who makes the author? This is what happens to the author who sees him(her)self constrained to ask by an extremely demanding subject: Who am I, who are I, at this very moment? A flight of questions beating two she-wings one black one white one he-r one h-ymn one sh-he one (s)he-sitation. . . . Mad is the wo(man) who wants to know who I.[24]

Ultimately, Cixous works on the unreadability of the text, on a love for the not-I, the "Clarisk," when words do not attempt to replace things in a movement of nonexclusive difference, a "blanc-dire," a white speech that would let even ugliness be.[25] This might be the reason why she still dreams of a further limit to writing: by definition, the limit, that is, the last text. The proximity of death brings the writer closer to this edge. The relationship between Cixous as a writer and Cixous as a reader/critic can be placed exactly in the search, not for unreadability, but for the mysterious splendor of life and its writing:

> One day I wrote a book called *Lemonade Everything Was So Infinite*—it was a book of meditation on one of Kafka's last phrases, a phrase he wrote down on a sheet of paper, just before his death. During this time he no longer spoke out loud, because of the burning in his throat. A phrase came from that unuttered zone where mute but distinct, the most essential things are said, minuscule things, infinite things, inexpressible outside in the sharp air, because of their fragility and beauty. This phrase is *Limonade es war alles so grenzenlos.* For me this is *The Poem,* the ecstasy and the regret, the very simple heart of life. It is the end. And the end of the end. And the first refreshment.[26]

Thus Cixous places truth as close to death as possible, at the limit between the one (life) and the other (death) in its most radical representation. Kafka's last sentence is to be put in parallel with most of the underlying concerns found in her fiction. From *Dedans* to *L'Ange au secret* her fictional writing has attempted to inscribe and analyze her father's death when she was still a child. One of its chapters in particular, "Nos Morts-nos assassins," is dedicated entirely to the exploration of the meaning of his death. It is only in this way that Cixous's works can escape from all binary oppositions (life vs. death, father vs. mother, and, in general, the feminine, etc.), which she has so vehemently denounced. Ecstasy is crossing over borders. The action itself and its writing make for fictional vertigo.

Notes

1. Elaine Marks and Isabelle de Courtivron, eds., *New French Feminisms* (Amherst: University of Massachusetts Press, 1980), p. x.

2. For an extensive bibliography of Cixous's works, consult Martine Motard-Noar, *Les Fictions d'Hélène Cixous: Une autre langue de femme* (Lexington, KY: French Forum, 1991), and Morag Shiach, *Hélène Cixous: A Politics of Writing* (New York: Routledge, 1991).

3. See Marks and de Courtivron, *New French Feminisms*, pp. 3–38.

4. Hélène Cixous, "Le Rire de la Méduse," *L'Arc*, no. 61 (1975), pp. 39–54.

5. Cixous, "Appendix," in Verena Andermatt Conley, *Hélène Cixous: Writing the Feminine* (Lincoln: University of Nebraska Press, 1984), pp. 138 39.

6. Cixous, "Rire," p. 43.

7. Luce Irigaray, *Passions élémentaires* (Paris: Minuit, 1982), p. 66.

8. Cixous, *La Jeune née* (Paris: 10/18, 1975), p. 115.

9. Cixous, "Rire," p. 46.

10. Cixous, in an interview in Conley, *Hélène Cixous*, p. 136.

11. Coppélia Kahn, "Excavating 'Those Dim Minoan Regions': Maternal Subtexts in Patriarchal Literature," *Diacritics* 12, no. 2 (summer 1982), pp. 32–41.

12. Cixous, *Portrait du soleil* (Paris: Denoël, 1973), p. 59.

13. Nancy Gray, *Language Unbound: On Experimental Writing by Women* (Urbana: University of Illinois Press, 1992), pp. 164–65.

14. Jacques Derrida, *La Dissémination* (Paris: Seuil, 1972), pp. 12–13.

15. Jacques Derrida, *Glas* (Paris: Galilée, 1974), p. 5.

16. Quoted in Jean-Pierre Richard, *Poésie et profondeur* (Paris: Seuil, 1985).

17. Cixous, *With ou l'art de l'innocence* (Paris: des femmes, 1981), p. 97; *Souffles* (Paris: des femmes, 1975), p. 159; *Vivre l'orange/To Live the Orange* (Paris: des femmes, 1979), p. 113.

18. Cixous, *Three Steps on the Ladder of Writing*, trans. Sarah Cornell and Susan Sellers (New York: Columbia University Press, 1993).

19. Cixous, *Préparatifs de noces au-delà de l'abîme* (Paris: des femmes, 1978), pp. 110–11.

20. Cixous, "Rire," p. 51.

21. See Tilde Sankovitch, "Hélène Cixous: The Pervasive Myth," in *French Women Writers: Myths of Access and Desire* (Syracuse: Syracuse University Press, 1988).

22. Cixous, "L'Approche de Clarice Lispector," *Poétique*, no. 40 (November 1979), p. 412.

23. Cixous, *"Coming to Writing" and Other Essays*, trans. Sarah Cornell et al. (Cambridge: Harvard University Press, 1991), pp. 142–43.

24. Ibid., p. 143.

25. Cixous, *Reading with Clarice Lispector*, trans. Verena Andermatt Conley (Minneapolis: University of Minnesota Press, 1990), p. 118.

26. Cixous, *"Coming to Writing,"* pp. 136–37.

Bibliography

Works by Hélène Cixous

Dedans. Paris: Grasset, 1969. Translated by Carol Barko as *Inside.* New York: Schocken, 1986.

Les Commencements. Paris: Grasset, 1970.

Tombe. Paris: Seuil, 1973.

Portrait du soleil. Paris: Denoël, 1973.

La Jeune Née. With Catherine Clément. Paris: UGE, 1975.

"Le Rire de la Méduse." *L'Arc*, no. 61 (1975): 39–54. Translated by Keith Cohen and Paula Cohen as "The Laugh of the Medusa," in *New French Feminisms*, edited by Elaine Marks and Isabelle de Courtivron, pp. 245–64. New York: Schocken, 1981.

Souffles. Paris: des femmes, 1975.

Partie. Paris: des femmes, 1976.

Angst. Paris: des femmes, 1977. Translated by Jo Levy. London: J. Calder, 1985.

Préparatifs de noces au-delà de l'abîme. Paris: des femmes, 1978.

Anankè. Paris: des femmes, 1979.

Vivre l'orange/To Live the Orange. Bilingual edition with translation by Ann Liddle and Sarah Cornell. Paris: des femmes, 1979.

"L'Approche de Clarice Lispector." *Poétique*, no. 40 (November 1979): 408–19.

Illa. Paris: des femmes, 1980.

With ou l'art de l'innocence. Paris: des femmes, 1981.

Le Livre de Promethea. Paris: Gallimard, 1983. Translated by Betsy Wing as *The*

Book of Promethea. Lincoln: University of Nebraska Press, 1991.

Reading with Clarice Lispector. Translated by Verena Andermatt Conley. Minneapolis: University of Minnesota Press, 1990.

L'Ange au secret. Paris: des femmes, 1991.

"Coming to Writing" and Other Essays. Translated by Sarah Cornell et al. Cambridge: Harvard University Press, 1991.

Déluge. Paris: des femmes, 1992.

Three Steps on the Ladder of Writing. Translated by Sarah Cornell and Susan Sellers. New York: Columbia University Press, 1993.

Selected Critical Works

Conley, Verena Andermatt. *Hélène Cixous: Writing the Feminine.* Lincoln: University of Nebraska Press, 1984.

Davis, Robert Con. "Woman as Oppositional Reader: Cixous on Discourse." *Papers on Language and Literature* 24, no. 3 (summer 1988): 265–82.

Gray, Nancy. *Language Unbound: Experimental Writing by Women.* Urbana: University of Illinois Press, 1992.

Kahn, Coppélia. "Excavating 'Those Dim Minoan Regions': Maternal Subtexts in Patriarchal Literature." *Diacritics* 12, no. 2 (summer 1982): 32–41.

Marks, Elaine, and Isabelle de Courtivron, eds. *New French Feminisms.* Amherst: University of Massachusetts Press, 1980.

Motard-Noar, Martine. *Les Fictions d'Hélène Cixous: Une autre langue de femme.* Lexington: French Forum, 1991.

———. "Où en est l'écriture d'Hélène Cixous?" *French Review* 66, no. 2 (December 1992): 286–94.

Sankovitch, Tilde. "Hélène Cixous: The Pervasive Myth." In *French Women Writers: Myths of Access and Desire.* Syracuse: Syracuse University Press, 1988.

Sartori, Eva Martin, and Dorothy Wynne Zimmerman, eds. *French Women Writers: A Bio-Bibliographical Source Book.* New York: Greenwood, 1991.

Shiach, Morag. *Hélène Cixous: A Politics of Writing.* New York: Routledge, 1991.

Van Rossum-Guyon, Françoise, and Myriam Diaz-Diocaretz. *Hélène Cixous, chemins d'une écriture.* Amsterdam: Rodopi, 1990.

10

Jean Echenoz

William Cloonan

Je travaille pour des gens qui sont
intelligents avant d'être sérieux.

François Le Lionnais cites these words of P. Féval at the head of his "Second Manifeste" in the Ouvroir de Littérature Potentielle's (Oulipo's) *Littérature potentielle*,[1] but Féval's comment is delightfully apposite to the entire literary output of Jean Echenoz, who, in his own selective way, shares many of the Oulipians' concerns. Jean Echenoz maintains a low profile on the crowded Parisian literary scene. Apart from occasional newspaper articles, since 1979 he has published five novels: *Le Méridien de Greenwich* (1979), *Cherokee* (1983), *L'Equipée malaise* (1986), *Lac* (1989), and *Nous trois* (1992). He has also published a short story, "L'Occupation des sols" (1988), and one chapter in a novel composed by seven authors collectively referred to as New Smyrna Beach ("Ayez des amis," in *Semaines de Suzanne*, 1991). In every instance his publisher has been Editions de Minuit.

Echenoz's fictional works all share several common elements. The stories are usually set in Paris and its suburbs. Each contains elements of the *roman policier*. References to American films, particularly B movies, abound, as do allusions to comic book characters and situations. The author's debt to Oulipo in general and Raymond Queneau in particular is also evident. The variety of Echenoz's interests and motifs, as well as the irony that pervades every aspect of his writing, both challenge and manipulate his audience. He clearly expects the reader to play an active role in the deciphering and indeed in the creation of his texts.

Since the heyday of the nouveau roman in the 1950s and 1960s, the roman policier has enjoyed a considerable vogue in France. Novels such as Robbe-Grillet's *Les Gommes,* Butor's *L'Emploi du temps,* and Pinget's *L'Inquisitoire* have awakened critics to the myriad possibilities of this genre. As Jean-Claude Vareille has pointed out, the roman policier is first of all a *recherche,* an effort to uncover truth despite human error, duplicity, and various misleading possibilities. For Vareille, the mystery novel is "un genre double, bifide. Si une de ses faces regarde vers l'arrière et la tradition, l'autre jette ses regards vers le futur." Finally, a good roman policier is "une série de romans possibles" that "égarera son lecteur dans un labyrinthe de fausses pistes et de culs-de-sac."[2] All these attributes can be readily applied to Echenoz's work, but with one significant difference. Whereas the nouveau roman's version of the roman policier was serious to the point of solemnity, with characters involved in quests that had mythic and philosophical implications, Echenoz's novels are above all comic, and his use of the roman policier format parodic. They describe the human capacity for self-befuddlement and self-delusion in a world whose complexities are manufactured largely by the protagonists themselves.

The plot of *Le Méridien de Greenwich* hinges on the efforts of one group to steal the plans for a secret project called "Prestidge," a word whose not quite correct spelling foreshadows other errors to come. The deranged inventor of the project, Byron Caine, was supposed to give "une copie factice" of "Prestidge" to a mysterious group that wanted to entice the real owners to pursue them while Caine completed his work in peace, ensconced on a desert island. Caine, however, to amuse himself, unknown to everyone, gives the thieves a true copy of the plans, which, in any case, he has no intention of completing for anyone. *Cherokee* centers on an attempt to unearth a long-lost inheritance. After a series of mad adventures that essentially lead nowhere, the erstwhile principal adversaries are united on the last page, wondering "Qu'est-ce qu'on fait, maintenant?" (p. 247). In *L'Equipée malaise,* a scheme to take over a plantation in Malaysia ends in abject failure, as do the efforts of inept thugs to kidnap a girl in order to extort weapons. *Lac* is a novel of so many double-crosses and triple-crosses that in the end it remains to the reader to decide what, if anything, resulted from these numerous machinations.

In Echenoz's novels references to filmmaking, American movies, and movie stars abound. There is nothing subtle about these allusions, as if the author wishes to plant them in the reader's mind and then invite him or her to draw whatever conclusions seem appropriate. The first and final chapters of *Le Méridien* are a self-conscious attempt to recreate in words the effect of a panning movie camera: "Point un roman, donc. Un film, c'était" (p. 13). A character in the novel is described as resembling Dorothy Gish, and at various points in the text the story of *The Bengal Lancers*, starring Gary Cooper and Franchot Tone, is told. One character, Gutman, looks like Sidney Greenstreet, while in *L'Equipée malaise*, another resembles Elisha Cook, Jr. The apartment of Georges Chave in *Cherokee* is filled with pictures of movie stars, and the main character in *Lac* passes some of his idle moments watching *Forbidden Planet*.

At least one gangster in *Le Méridien*, Buck, consciously models his behavior on actors, while other, minor players resemble figures one sees "dans les bandes dessinées ou dans les films de guerre américains" (p. 103). Russian bodyguards in *Lac* are avid readers of comic books, and Ripert and Bock, two private detectives in *Cherokee*, recall respectively Laurel and Hardy by their physiques "ce genre de grand maigre et petit gros" (p. 32), or the two policemen in *Tintin* by their behavior. Finally, just as in comic books or B movies, the fictional characters are mostly one-dimensional. Whatever intriguing possibilities their personalities may suggest, their potential is never examined, and they are often disposed of in a summary, often violent way, rather like the bad guys in comics and movies.

In *Nord* Céline had predicted the brilliant future awaiting the *bande dessinée*: "*Comics*, voyons! . . . plus important que la bombe d'atomes! . . . la sensa-super de l'époque! . . . Renaissance ah! . . . Quattrocento enfoncé! pfoui! . . . *comics*,"[3] and certainly film is the art form par excellence of the twentieth century. Comics and films play a role in Echenoz's work that is primarily ironic but also serious: ironic, because as shallow as both forms can be, they have long since replaced painting and the novel as sources of culture. Serious, because they are the shapers of the contemporary personality. Film, and to lesser degree comics, do more than reflect human personalities, fantasies, and actions; they also can provide the molds out of which people fashion their identities and dreams and model their behavior. Rather than lament this phenomenon, Echenoz's novels celebrate it. If the word *realism* has any place in a discussion of this author, it is present to the extent that his work reflects the superficiality that pervades so much of contemporary experience.

The preponderance of intertextuality and irony in Echenoz's fiction suggests a debt to Oulipo and its cofounder, Raymond Queneau. Oulipo has its origins in a colloquium on Queneau that took place at Cerisy-la-Salle in 1960. As a result of these deliberations Queneau and François Le Lionnais formed an association of writers, scientists, and mathematicians dedicated to "the search for new forms and structures that may be used by writers in any way they see fit."[4] The Oulipo's goal was not "to create works of literature, but to uncover preexisting structures and to discover new ones that can aid the individual artist in the production of original literary works."[5] To this end they engaged in elaborate experiments with classical figures of rhetoric (anaphora, heterograms, palindromes, etc.), but always in a spirit of fun: "The Oulipians hold fast to the notion of ludic literature."[6] However, an Oulipian text should have nothing of the haphazard about it; Oulipians are strictly antialeatory, despite how much one of their productions may suggest the contrary. As Jacques Bens explains: "On peut admettre, sans tenter pour l'instant d'approfondir, qu'une œuvre potentielle est une œuvre qui ne se limite pas à ses apparences, qui contient des richesses secrètes, qui se prête volontiers à l'exploration."[7] The same author goes on to insist on the reader's important role in the Oulipian endeavor: "La littérature potentielle serait donc celle qui attend un lecteur, qui l'espère, qui a besoin de lui pour se réaliser pleinement" (p. 24). Warren Motte further clarifies the reader's role: "The Oulipian text is quite explicitly offered as a game, as a system of ludic exchange between author and reader."[8]

Jean Echenoz has never been an official Oulipo member, but his fiction does reflect comparable concerns and techniques. In *L'Equipée malaise* there is a cargo ship with the rather bizarre name of *Boustrophédon*. A boustrophedon is a literary device that consists of writing alternatively from right to left and then from left to right, a motion that imitates the rocking of the boat on the high seas. One might be tempted to suggest that the word divulges something about the novel's structure, which consists of thirty-three chapters that often move the reader back and forth from one setting to another. However, such an odd name obviously calls attention to itself and sends readers not well-versed in rhetorical matters scurrying to dictionaries, an inevitable reaction that would

imply that the *Boustrophédon* is less a symbol than a joke, a *clin d'œil* in
the direction of the Oulipian interest in classical figures of rhetoric.

Oulipians speak of two sorts of parody: heteroparody which "imite
les œuvres des autres" and self-parody "où l'auteur renvoie à ses propres
ouvrages."[9] The frequent allusions to film and comics, coupled with
devices like concealing a movie projector in the head of a Cyclops
(*Méridien*, p. 17), might serve as relatively transparent examples of
heteroparody. Less obvious examples of heteroparody take the form of
a homage to Raymond Queneau. In his novel *Pierrot mon ami* (1942) appears Mounnezergues, a maker of figures for wax museums. In Echenoz's
Lac there is the amateur painter and professional spy named Mouezy-
Eon. In Queneau's *Le Chiendent* (1933) an awful dwarf called Bébé-
Toutout terrorizes children and adults, while Bébé-Amour is a yappy
pet dog in *L'Equipée malaise*.

Other possible forms of heteroparody are even less apparent. They
depend on bilingual puns and involve the reader's willingness to stretch
his or her imagination. For example, is the would-be tough guy named
Toon in *Cherokee*, who looks like Elisha Cook, Jr., really a cartoon figure?
Or is his boss, Van Os, the brains of the operation who turns out to be
not as smart as he claims, a reference to the Wizard of Oz? The character
in *Méridien* who resembles Sidney Greenstreet is called Gutman, a name
that embodies the image of the late American actor. Such associations
depend on the reader's sense of humor and openness to verbal games
that have no greater purpose than enhancing *le plaisir du texte*.

Self-parody, which in Echenoz takes the form of self-allusion, is at
times obvious and at times less so. Briffaut, a police informer who has a
minor role in *Cherokee*, is also referred to in *L'Equipée malaise* (p. 196).
One of the ships in *L'Equipée malaise* is called Suzy Delair, and an important character in the later novel, *Lac*, is Suzy Clair. A one-legged man
has an insignificant part in *L'Equipée malaise*, and another plays a somewhat more important role in *Lac*. In *Méridien* a punk named Albin mur-
ders an arms dealer in what amounts to an *acte gratuit*. In *L'Equipée malaise* the reader learns that the reason Toon and Van Os are having
difficulty procuring weapons is that their dealer has been killed.

The ever-present ludic quality in the Oulipian enterprise can easily lead one to forget that they were deeply interested in the creation of
carefully structured works of art. Indeed, they were so concerned with
creating obstacles in order to find brilliant, aesthetically satisfying ways

of overcoming them that an early self-definition of Oulipians was "rats who must build the labyrinth from which they propose to escape."[10] In this context the most famous Oulipian achievement was Georges Perec's *La Disparition*, a full-length novel that never uses the letter *e*, the most commonly employed vowel in French. Jean Echenoz is never that outrageous, but he has never been a perfect Oulipian. He does, however, set considerable obstacles for himself. His novels tell stories that could be described as unbelievable and silly; his characters often have no depth. Yet, despite these apparent handicaps, he has written some of the finest examples of postmodernist fiction and has been called "le romancier le plus marquant des années 80."[11]

Le Méridien de Greenwich, Echenoz's first novel, not only contains the literary devices and influences discussed above but it raises an issue that will be central in all his subsequent fiction: the possibilities of writing a novel in an age when the novel risks becoming an obsolete art form. The first chapter relates practically nothing about the "Prestidge" formula and the frenzied efforts of various groups to obtain it. Instead it explores different means of describing a scene involving two lovers— the mad inventor Byron Caine and his girlfriend, Rachel—who are awaiting a galleon (we are in the twentieth century!) to take her from an island. The author initially suggests the scene is a *tableau* (p. 7), then that it could be the pretext for a *récit* (p. 8), but finally announces that it is a film (p. 13). In fact, it is a film that is being looked at by people anxious to recover "Prestidge." Yet in another sense it is not; it is a chapter in a book published by Editions de Minuit in 1979.

To tell the story the author must constantly subvert the novel form. This is necessary because the mainstay of literary art, words, seem to be losing in the contemporary world whatever force they once possessed. Théo Selmer is a polyglot who works as an interpreter at the United Nations. A day arrives when he can no longer endure translating politico-babble from one group to the next, so he abandons his job. On one of the last occasions in the novel when he has a dictionary in his hands, a gun is concealed within it. The one person who really does like words is the blind assassin, Russel, but words do not really teach him anything—"ils me donnent simplement des idées" (p. 137)—and not enough ideas to keep him from having his head blown off.

Echenoz attempts to revitalize language and the novel by exposing and parodying some of the conventions of fiction. He breaks the narrative flow through an absurd interjection, as when, during a conversation between two people seated in a café, the table suddenly remarks: "impossible de fuir, pensait la table, ils me plaquent au sol avec leurs coudes" (p. 34), or by using in a deliberately clumsy fashion a rhetorical device, in this instance alliteration: "il me semblait que le contenant contînt un contenu" (p. 62). The result is to jolt the reader out of a passive reading mode and make him conscious of language's ability to manipulate, confuse, and amuse the reader.

Echenoz uses film in a comparable fashion. It is a form with which the contemporary audience is more at ease than the novel, but it too is artificial, a purveyor of illusion that, for a limited period, passes for reality. Images of seeing and especially of the eye predominate in *Le Méridien*, but what the human eye and the eye of the camera see with such apparent clarity provide the basis for the misguided pursuit of "Prestidge." Echenoz employs elements from film and comics in a manner that is deliberately self-conscious and apparent. There is never any effort to hide or integrate cinematographic techniques within a text, as if to say that this is not a movie, or a comic book, nor for that matter is this the type of novel you had to read in school; it is instead an amalgam of all of them and, as such, a prime example of contemporary fiction.

In *Le Méridien* the principal illusionist is Byron Caine. His name is, of course, a trap. Lord Byron wrote a long poem, "Cain," which created a furor in its day. The British poet was, however, capable of finishing this work before continuing on to political activity that led to his death in Greece. To the extent that Byron Caine is the contemporary artist (he is frequently referred to as an inventor), his text—*Prestidge*—is unfinished and unfinishable (Caine never had much confidence in the idea in the first place); it is an illusion without any potentially hidden substance, a work from which no one could profit in any sense. Lord Byron's death might have had some significance, and in any case he left a body of poetry behind him. Caine merely blows up the machine whose purpose was never made clear and in so doing kills himself and most of the people on the island. Caine is a failure as a contemporary artist because his text, the machine, is an arbitrary conglomeration of disparate, rather than carefully controlled, elements.

Le Méridien makes a distinction between the arbitrary and the haphazard, most often associated with human action, and a work of art's need for careful structuring in order to capture the aleatory. The Greenwich meridian, which crosses the island, is "un point de la ligne du changement de date" (p. 10); it is the result of a decision of convenience— "une sorte d'artifice intellectuel" (p. 194)—permitting people to demarcate changes in time. Whatever its origins, the meridian is closer to a work of art than *Prestidge* because it has consistency and and imposes an order on an otherwise amorphous mass of time. However, Caine uses it merely to have two Sundays off each week.

Closer still to a work of art is the puzzle Caine works on completing. Although this puzzle recalls the more famous one in Georges Perec's *La Vie, mode d'emploi,* in *Le Méridien* its main function is to represent the multiple elements that must be assembled in inalterable positions in order to have a finished text. Caine accomplishes this task and thus discovers that the puzzle is a *mise en abyme,* but a limited one: "la mise en abyme s'arrêtait là, la peinture ne s'étant pas aventuré plus loin dans l'emboîtement des représentations" (p. 140). The puzzle has a structure and coherence, but in a simplified form. Unlike a novel that can be open to diverse readings, the puzzle, once mastered, will always be the same, no matter how often it is attempted.

An object much sought after by those anxious for the plans to "Prestidge" is a little cube that vibrates. This object is supposed to be crucial to Caine's invention. Since the machine will never work, the cube is insignificant in itself, but for those who indulge in the comic book plottings, chases and shootouts, it is "la matière dont les rêves sont faits" (p. 245). The cube, like "Prestidge" itself, is the fiction that controls the lives of those who consider themselves too down-to-earth to have time for the illusions that literature provides. At the novel's end, the cube explodes, apparently killing those remaining characters interested in obtaining "Prestidge."

The last chapter of *Le Méridien* is practically a recapitulation of the first. The anachronistic galleon appears to return to the island, rescue Théo Selmer and eventually reunite him with the few other characters who were not blinded by the desire for "Prestidge." The narrative, as in the first chapter, provides the impression of a movie camera panning off into the distance as the film ends. Yet the last chapter might be Selmer's dying hallucination (he was shot on the beach). The novel's final image, that of a ship as a scalpel cutting tranquilly through the ocean, which immediately closes upon itself—"reproduisant à l'accéléré l'évolution d'une blessure, le procès de sa cicatrisation" (p. 256)—provides false solace. This reassurance is entirely verbal, perhaps nothing other than an ironic concession on the author's part to how the contemporary lover of movies, comic books, and cheap fiction would like it to be.

Cherokee won the Prix Médicis in 1983. The title refers to a jazz composition by Ray Noble, and the novel represents an attempt to write a fiction that mirrors the themes and variations of jazz. Noble's piece, which lasts two minutes and fifty-two seconds, has been the subject of many improvisations by subsequent musicians. Depending on whose version one hears, it can have a big band sound, with smooth transitions and an ending that trails off, or it can be played by a few instruments, with staccato passages and an abrupt ending. It has often been used to test the skill of jazz players.

Jazz is a form of music that can appear deceptively simple, but in fact it is difficult to play, requires excellent musicians, capable of varying a theme extensively without ever completely departing from the central motif. *Cherokee* exploits these aspects of the jazz tradition. It focuses on a period in Georges Chave's life when he works as a private detective. It starts with the beginning of a friendship between Georges and a gigantic thief named Crocognan (caveman?), then follows Georges through his amorous adventures and his activities as a private eye. Among other things he rescues a stolen parrot named Spielvogel who mentions in its chattering the name of Jenny Weltman, the love of Georges's life, at least for the duration of the novel. At the end of the book the friendship with Crocognan is confirmed and an old friendship, with his crooked cousin and erstwhile nemesis Fred Shapiro, seems reignited.

One could read the novel as a series of adventures, but the jazz allusions are always there to unite the text. The chant of a crazy religious group intones "Severinsen" (Doc Severinsen, the trumpeter). Just before the last scene Georges plays an impromptu trio with Crocognan and his former girlfriend's lover, and the final shootout has jazz music as background accompaniment. The omnipresence of jazz provides a structuring device that turns the seemingly disparate incidents into a series of variations on the theme of loss.

Cherokee is a contemporary, staccato version of the musical piece. Georges is not sure about the origins of his name Chave (p. 71), but he is the key ("chiave" means "key" in Italian) to the story. He meets a girl, Véronique, then loses her. He gets a job with a detective agency, but then has to hide from the other agents and the police. While this is happening, Fred Shapiro is trying to lay his hands on someone else's inheritance by exploiting a credulous religious group. He assumes the identity of the absconded charlatan high priest whose name, Dascalopoulos, is as meaningless in Greek as the rites he imposes on his followers.

A motif that enhances the staccato jazz effect involves automobiles. They are constantly starting, then breaking down, and their herky-jerky motion embodies the movement of the plot, which consists of largely fruitless pursuits culminating in the needless murder of a bumbling detective.

The death of the detective, Ripert, does have some importance. It is the most violent variation on the theme of loss and initially appears to strain the fabric of a novel that is mostly comic. The rationale of the death is, however, implicit in the text. Ripert, the Stan Laurel part of the Laurel and Hardy duo (Bock is Oliver Hardy) is as accident-prone, as much of a sad sack character as his movie prototype. Echenoz uses Ripert as he does many of his cinematic and comic book figures: he establishes the character, permits the reader to recognize the reference, and then pushes the stereotype, like a musical motif, to its logical and extreme conclusion.

Just before the novel's end, Fred is holding a gun on Georges, who understandably expresses annoyance, not simply at his current position with regard to his cousin, but because Fred almost had him killed in the preceding scene. Fred takes it all rather philosophically: "J'ai mes contradictions . . . ne sois pas grossier comme ça" (p. 237). Shapiro is indeed a man of contradictions. Once his cousin's closest friend, he suffered as a young man from unexplained bouts of ill humor that drove him away from Georges. His relatively petty criminal activities as a dishonest businessman and later as a con artist eventually led him to kill one man and wound another. He may also be responsible for his uncle's murder (p. 195). However, throughout all this he has maintained a certain sense of decorum. When his false high priestess cannot play her part correctly, he fires her the way a good musician would need to get rid of a bad one: "Ecoute, Jacqueline. . . . Tu pourrais peut-être faire un petit effort" (p. 141). Fred is the minor chord that makes sense only in relation to the major that Georges represents. Ever since he borrowed his cousin's copy of *Cherokee*, which he has not returned (p. 25), he has not been able to complete anything, and if his character makes sense in the novel, it is only because the reader has been following Georges's story as well as his own. Therefore it is not surprising that he seeks a reconciliation with his cousin at the end. Fred needs Georges to begin the next piece.

The title of Echenoz's third novel, *L'Equipée malaise*, contains many of the elements that will figure in the text. The ostensible main theme is an effort by a group of adventurers to help some natives take over a Malaysian (*malaise*) plantation. However, the venture turns out to be an amateurish escapade (*équipée*) which proves difficult (*malaisé*) and doomed to failure, since the assembled team (*équipe*) is no match for the soldiers who attack them. Finally, the reader who follows the characters' mostly ineffective efforts may have an experience similar to the discomfort (*malaise*) one of the plotters, Paul, has when he is tossed about during a storm on the ship, *Boustrophédon*, itself a word that suggests a back and forth motion.

The planning of the group that tries to seize the plantation is mirrored and parodied in the plottings of the inept thieves and kidnappers, Toon and Van Os. In both instances the human effort to assert control over experience contrasts with the haphazard nature of life itself, represented in the novel by dice. Dice can be loaded, but eventually the trick will be exposed, and a sea storm provides a truer image of people's capacity to take charge of their lives: "les hommes se mirent à rebondir contre les parois, sans plus de libre arbitre qu'une balle de flipper emballée dans du ciré jaune" (p. 172).

The leader of the band that attacks the island is Jean-François Pons, who is abetted by his old friend, Charles Pontiac. Both men once loved Nicole Fischer, who rejected them for a pilot whose plane, perhaps by chance, crashed, killing him, but not before he had impregnated Nicole, who later produces a daughter, Justine. Jean-François leaves France for Malaysia, where he remains for thirty years and eventually rechristens himself *duc*. However, there is nothing particularly ducal about Jean-François. He is half-drunk for most of the novel and fails in all his endeavors. He is last seen discussing what passes for the wisdom of the East with a Parisian soothsayer, Bouc Bel-Air.

Charles Pontiac (the Indian, the car, neither?) is another matter. He becomes a marginal person, a street dweller, or more properly, subway dweller, who frequents museums and libraries by night and emerges from various subterranean hideouts (a ship's hold, a Métro station) to save the day. More than any other character in the novel, Charles is aware of the aleatory nature of life. He helps and then he disappears, seemingly aware that nothing can be made permanent but that the worst human excesses can sometimes be curtailed.

If there is any force capable of imposing order in the world of *L'Equipée malaise*, it is the novel itself, which presents a coherent picture of the chaos human beings create. This chaos is for Echenoz comic rather than tragic; *L'Equipée malaise* laughs at rather than criticizes the nonsense people make of their lives. Paul receives some money from a family printing establishment, and as such he might represent the written word. His more intelligent friend, Bob, works in television, a more contemporary art form. Television may well be the present and future of art, and Bob may prove more successful with Justine, the girl he and Paul love. Yet if Paul is generally a failure, his printing business just may not be. It could, after all, produce a work of fiction that reflects on its own role in the contemporary world. Something like *L'Equipée malaise*.

The first character one meets in Echenoz's fourth novel, *Lac*, is Vito Piranese, who has only one leg. This missing leg is emblematic of the entire story and points to the significance of the title. *Lac* is structured around a bilingual pun. The French *lac* is also the English *lack*. Vito lacks a leg; Suzy Clair lacks her husband, the double agent, Oswald; the French government lacks information that a Russian official, Veber, may be able to provide, and when the French get the papers they seek, they turn out to lack any real interest (p. 186).

The main character's name lacks all its potentially symbolic value. He is neither César Franck nor Frédéric Chopin. Rather he is Franck Chopin, an expert in implanting flies (*les mouches*) with listening devices so they can act as spies (*les mouchards*). At one point in the novel he even lacks enough flies. Also, Franck's hair is continually falling out and he worries about this lack. Finally, even the lake in *Lac* lacks a degree of truth. It is artificial (p. 181).

While *lack* is the central motif in the novel, it nonetheless remains difficult to determine what exactly all the spying is attempting to uncover, or what precisely the motivations of the various characters might be. The reader never learns the nature of the information the French seek, nor the extent to which double agents like Oswald and the black Colonel Seck, who gives orders to Chopin, might be triple agents. At one point Oswald gives his wife, Suzy Clair, whose murky activities belie her family name, a pair of cufflinks containing compasses "qui donnent vraiment le nord" (p. 27), and later she goes out "vers le fin fond d'une jungle avec son équipement de boussoles et de miroirs" (p. 47). The world of *Lac* is a game of mirrors that provide only the superficial image of a nevertheless dangerous jungle where the reader, like the characters in the text, constantly risks losing his or her bearings (*perdre le nord*).

After the numerous variations on *lac*, the second most important word in *Lac* is *surface*. Veber must report to a "comité de surface," an obligation reiterated throughout the novel, and Suzy has "les plus belles jambes de Paris-surface" (p. 51). Despite the suggestion of hidden depths, the labyrinth that *Lac* presents is no Piranese fantasy; it is the confusion of ordinary life, where at times even the simplest actions of people seem either unfathomable or, like *les grandes surfaces* of contemporary Paris, where everything begins to appear the same.

At the end of *Lac* Chopin feels "myope comme une taupe" (p. 188), and Oswald is literally myopic throughout the story. The novel infers that this is humanity's true state in the closing years of the twentieth century, where people's ceaseless activity effectively masks the absence of genuine ideals or self-knowledge. As is typical with Echenoz, the author finds comedy rather than tragedy in this state of affairs. *Lac* suggests that in a world whose complexity no longer has a clear source, and where individuals are unsure of both what they want and what they are doing, all one can count on is what one sees, even if one does not see much beyond the surface. However imperfectly perceived, surfaces are the only discernible reality. In *Lac* the single statement that makes this point most forcefully, while at the same time capturing the novel's tone, is attributed to Woody Woodpecker: "That's all folks" (p. 91).

James Joyce is supposed to have said that the twentieth century would have more than its share of tragedy, so what he proposed writing were comedies. The importance of comedy in the fiction of Jean Echenoz should not be underestimated. Comedy suffuses every aspect of his literary art and in so doing permits the author to describe without judging, to ironize without moralizing. To enter his fictional universe hardly involves abandoning all hope, but it does require the reader to at least indulge the possibility that human beings are much more inept, shallow, and self-deluded than is commonly supposed. The Echenoz character, no matter how wise in the ways of the world he claims to be, is essentially an innocent, a person who, in the guise of bending reality to his will, is actually playing an elaborate game with himself and others. Chance, rather than careful planning, will determine the winner.

The Echenoz novel is an even more elaborate game, one played by the reader, who must follow an often silly, if not unbelievable story line, sift through the plethora of literary and cinematic allusions, and accept the occasional and jarring authorial intrusions that undercut any pretention to fictional verisimilitude. The reader does this not in quest of some great truth, but rather in pursuit of the pleasure that attends the unfolding of the late twentieth century's version of the human comedy. This effort can be frustrating at times, but it is always exhilarating. The act of reading Jean Echenoz ultimately involves one in experiences that parallel the behavior of the author's characters, but which are in fact much closer to what a person might undergo in reading an ideally realized Oulipian text: "Il hésite, il tâtonne, il ne sait plus très bien, il lui faut, qu'il le veuille ou non, apporter sa pierre et jouer le jeu."[12]

Notes

1. François Le Lionnais, "Second Manifeste," in Oulipo, *Littérature potentielle* (Paris: Gallimard, 1973), p. 23.

2. Jean-Claude Vareille, *L'Homme masqué, le justicier et le détective* (Lyon: Presses Universitaires de Lyon, 1989), pp. 191, 199.

3. Louis-Ferdinand Céline, *Nord* (Paris: Gallimard, 1960), p. 507.

4. Cited in Warren F. Motte, ed. and trans., *Oulipo: A Primer of Potential Literature* (Lincoln: University of Nebraska Press, 1986), pp. 2–3.

5. Jane A. Hale, *The Lyric Encyclopedia of Raymond Queneau* (Ann Arbor: University of Michigan Press, 1989), p. 52.

6. Motte, *Oulipo*, p. 21.

7. Jacques Bens, "Queneau Oulipien," in *Atlas de littérature potentielle* (Paris: Gallimard, 1981), p. 23.

8. Motte, *Oulipo*, p. 20.

9. Bens, "Queneau," p. 30.

10. Motte, *Oulipo*, p. 22.

11. Jean Lepape, "Jean Echenoz: pour raconter cette époque," cited in "Parutions de septembre," *Les Editions de Minuit* (1992), p. 1.

12. Bens, "Queneau," p. 28.

Bibliography

Works by Jean Echenoz

Le Méridien de Greenwich. Paris: Minuit, 1979.

"Ayez des amis." In *Semaines de Suzanne,* by New Smyrna Beach. Paris: Minuit, 1981.

Cherokee. Paris: Minuit, 1983. Translated by M. Polizzotti. London: Faber, 1991.
L'Equipée malaise. Paris: Minuit, 1986.
L'Occupation des sols. Paris: Minuit, 1988.
Lac. Paris: Minuit, 1989.
Nous trois. Paris: Minuit, 1992.

Selected Critical Works

Habib, Claude: "Légèreté d'Echenoz." *Esprit,* no. 192 (June 1993): 163–67.

Hale, Jane A. *The Lyric Encyclopedia of Raymond Queneau.* Ann Arbor: University of Michigan Press, 1989.

"Jean Echenoz." *Yale French Studies,* Special Issue (1988): 357–61. Introduction by Dominique Jullien, translation by Mark Polizzotti.

Lebrun, Jean-Claude. *Echenoz.* Monte Carlo: Editions du Rocher, 1992.

Lebrun, Jean-Claude, and Claude Prévost. *Nouveaux Territoires romanesques.* Paris: Messidor/Editions Sociales, 1990.

Leclerc, Yvan. "Autour de Minuit." *Dalhousie French Studies* 17 (fall–winter 1989): 63–74.

Lepape, Jean. "Jean Echenoz: pour raconter cette époque." Originally published in *Le Monde.* Cited in "Parutions de septembre." *Les Editions de Minuit* (1992): 1.

Martin, Jean. "Critiques littéraires à la dérive . . . Lettre à la revue *Esprit.*" *Esprit,* no. 190 (March–April 1993): 153–87.

Motte, Warren F., editor and translator. *Oulipo: A Primer of Potential Literature.* Lincoln: University of Nebraska Press, 1986.

Oulipo. *Atlas de littérature potentielle.* Paris: Gallimard, 1981.

Vareille, Jean-Claude. *L'Homme masqué, le justicier et le détective.* Lyon: Presses Universitaires de Lyon, 1989.

Part III.
Writing, History, and Myth

11

Elie Wiesel

Jack Kolbert

No analysis of Elie Wiesel's novels—or of anything else he has written—should be undertaken without considering not only the texts but also—but especially—his personal experience. In a word, the life and novels of Wiesel are consubstantial. His texts are mirrors of his joyful childhood, of the agony of his internment within the universe of Hitler's concentration camps, and of his miraculous survival after the end of World War II as a scarred member of the Jewish diaspora of America, France, and Israel.

Because Wiesel has chosen to write all his fiction in French, his novels belong to the French literary tradition. But his existence is divided among several places: he resides in New York City, teaches humanities in Boston, is a regular habitué of Paris, and finds his greatest exhilaration in Jerusalem. If officially he is a citizen of the United States, intellectually, literarily, and linguistically he is French, and spiritually and intellectually he is Jewish.

Three events have dominated the life of Elie Wiesel: his boyhood in his hometown of Sighet, Transylvania, the Holocaust, and the postwar years as a survivor and, later, international personality. These events also figure prominently in his novels. Wiesel labels his wandering existence an "itinerary."[1] The following outline of the contours of this "itinerary" discusses briefly each of his major works of fiction in the order of publication.

Born on September 30, 1928, in Sighet, Hungary (now a part of Romania), Eliezar Wiesel was one of four children. The others, his three sisters, were Hilda, Batya (Beatrice), and Tsipora. His father, Shlomo

Wiesel, was a grocer and shopkeeper who encouraged his only son to study the languages and literatures of Hebrew and Yiddish. His devout mother, Sara (née Feig), steered him in the direction of Jewish religious doctrines contained in the Torah and Talmud as well as mysticism. Before the Holocaust, Sighet's sizable Jewish population of ten thousand—out of a total of twenty-five thousand inhabitants—led a largely un-assimilated religious cultural existence. Because of the Nazi extermination attempt only about fifty Jews remain in that city today. The greatest single influence on young Elie was that of Dodye Feig, his maternal grandfather, who had excited his impressionable grandson with fiery tales from the Hasidic tradition. As a boy, Wiesel spent his days mostly in the cheder (Hebrew school), the synagogue, and at play with his friends. He remembers vividly the observance of the Sabbath and other festive occasions in the Jewish calendar, as well as playing games with other children in which they imagined the arrival of the messiah. He also recalls the frequent visits to Sighet of wandering storytellers and the town madmen, all of whom would relate to him countless stories from the Bible as well as tales about the rabbis of old and the people who figure in the Talmud. These tales still infiltrate his fiction.

The ebullience of this largely happy childhood was suddenly interrupted in 1944, when the German armies seized Hungary with strict orders from their high command to arrest Hungary's Jews, transport them in cattle cars to the concentration camps of eastern Germany and Poland, and exterminate them in crematoria, gas chambers, or through other forms of mass execution. Wiesel's entire family was rounded up, and most of them were executed. His mother and youngest sister disappeared; his grandfather was presumably murdered in the gas chambers of Bergen-Belsen; his father died from starvation and physical punishment in Buchenwald before his helpless son's eyes. Only he and his two older sisters somehow managed to survive. Wiesel later recreated the tragedy of the Holocaust in his first—and possibly his most celebrated—novel, *La Nuit*, published some thirteen years after his liberation from the camps.

The trauma of the death camps cast an ineradicable cloud over all of Wiesel's postliberation existence; that terrible cloud hovers over every piece of literature he has written. Although most of his literary critics categorize him, quite aptly, as the most significant literary figure in the Holocaust tradition, Wiesel has unsuccessfully struggled against being boxed in by this label. Even when he does not directly depict the Holocaust, its presence almost always lurks in the background. If he does not generally place his characters within the setting of the concentration camps (as he did in *La Nuit*), he deals either with the psychological after-effects once they have been released or else with the children of the survivors of the Nazi brutalities.

When the Americans freed the inmates of Buchenwald, Wiesel was placed with many other young survivors from the camps on a train bound for Brussels, where he was to be repatriated. But his train was rerouted to Paris under orders of General Charles de Gaulle, the provisional leader of postwar France. There Wiesel soon learned and mastered the French language; when he embarked on a professional career as a writer, it was French that became his medium of literary expression. The postwar period was a heady time in French history: a time when the French felt uplifted by their liberation from the oppressive occupation of the Nazi armies and Paris was experiencing the excitement of Jean-Paul Sartre's existentialist movement in philosophy and literature. It was also the time when the writings of Camus and Malraux dominated the world scene. These literary events proved of utmost importance and timeliness for Wiesel, the budding author. Here is how he explains what French meant to him: "It is my working language. . . . When I came to France in 1945, I needed something. I needed a country. And the language became my country. I needed something different, something new, something strange—something so new that I would be allowed to believe in its possibilities, and French was totally new to me. Before the war I did not know that a country named France existed."[2] The French language was also a protest against Hungarian, a tongue that represented all that he hated. After all, as the Wiesel family was being deported to almost certain death in the concentration camps, their long-time Hungarian neighbors watched from the sideline passively indifferent, and never once attempted to save their lives. Later Wiesel's lifelong motto was to be "Indifference to evil is evil," a motto engraved on the gold Congressional Medal of Achievement presented to him by President Ronald Reagan. His plea against indifference to evil is also the fundamental theme of his novel, *La Ville de la chance*.

After the war, Wiesel dreamed of going to Palestine, but immigration quotas imposed on Jews by the British in order to appease the resident Arab population made it difficult for most Jews to go there before the state of Israel was established in 1948. Between 1948 and 1951 Wiesel took advanced courses in psychology, philosophy, and French literature at the Université de Paris. He made many friends in the Jewish community of Paris and supported himself with various part-time jobs: as a choir director (he had always shown a great deal of talent for and interest in Judaic music), as a teacher of the Old Testament and the Hebrew language, and as a summer camp counselor. One of his many positions, journalist for the Franco-Jewish periodical *L'Arche,* led him to discover how much he enjoyed writing. The magazine assigned him to travel to the newly created state of Israel, where he eventually became the India correspondent for the Tel Aviv daily *Yediot Ahronot.* While in India he learned English, gaining fluency in that language almost equal to his facility in French.

In 1956 the Tel Aviv newspaper gave Wiesel the opportunity to discover America by sending him to New York City to cover the proceedings of the recently formed United Nations. After a serious accident in Times Square, where, as a pedestrian, he had been struck by a reckless cab, he was forced to spend almost an entire year convalescing in a wheelchair. This convalescence gave him leisure to ponder his destiny: why had fate slated him for survival, while so many others had succumbed to the brutalities of the concentration camps? Feeling guilty that he lived while six million others had died, he reflected on the metaphysical significance of life and death and on the symbolic meaning of his accident. Wiesel wondered whether unconsciously he had sought to join the six million as he stepped into the path of the taxi. This experience forms the basis for another novel, *Le Jour.* Out of this psychological crisis he emerged reborn, as someone who realized that ultimately one must choose life, not death. Elie Wiesel thus transformed himself from a young man who struggled to adapt himself to an otherwise evil and absurd world into someone who would commit himself to the betterment of humanity. Humanism became the fundamental strand that would hold together the entire tapestry of his fiction and nonfiction writings.

As Wiesel's French travel documents were about to expire, he applied for U.S. residency and would become a U.S. citizen in 1963. He soon took his first American job, in 1957, as a staff member of New York's leading Yiddish-language newspaper, the *Jewish Daily Forward.* He also wrote his first full-length novel, *Un di Velt Hot Geshvign!* (And the World

Remained Silent), in Yiddish. Dealing realistically with his personal ordeal in Auschwitz and Buchenwald, and describing graphically how he
lost his mother, youngest sister, and father, the nascent author fused
autobiography with fiction as he created an 800-page saga. Published in
Buenos Aires, the novel sold poorly; excessively long and overly detailed, the Yiddish tale could reach only a limited international audience.

For ten years, Wiesel had imposed on himself an oath of silence
concerning his experiences in the camps of death. He could find neither
the words nor the grammatical constructions required to describe the
indescribable, even to imagine the unimaginable. The verbalization of
what he experienced could only aggravate the wounds that had been
festering in his soul. He confessed later that "[he] needed ten years to
collect words and the silence in them," to write about the nightmare of
Auschwitz.[3] He would write a novel in 1973, *Le Serment de Kolvillág*, on
the theme of a man who vows never to reveal the brutalities that he had
personally witnessed.

Wiesel returned to Paris, where his newspaper had assigned him
to interview the great Catholic novelist François Mauriac. The French
writer was so impressed with Wiesel's passionate account of his experiences that he advised the young Jewish journalist to reduce his 800-page
Yiddish novel drastically and rewrite it in French; in this way, Mauriac
believed, the story could be published in a country where a large public
was clamoring for more data concerning the Holocaust. In France,
Mauriac was in a position to help him find an interested publisher.
Wiesel's first French-language novel, *La Nuit*, was thus published in 1958
by the prestigious Editions de Minuit. Mauriac himself wrote the preface, which no doubt contributed to the book's success.

Barely more than 120 pages, *La Nuit* was instantly acclaimed in
France by the professional critics and by an immense public. It was translated immediately into English as *Night* and later into every major language of the world. Thus was launched Elie Wiesel's literary career.

La Nuit's success provided Wiesel with much-needed self-assur-
ance. It also persuaded him to write henceforth in French, not Yiddish,
to ensure a wide audience in one of the great international languages of
the world. The only novel in which Wiesel provides a direct account of
what occurred in the camps, the first-person narrated *La Nuit* is a rivet-
ing, even terrifying piece of prose. This first work offers a glimpse of the

literary style that was to become the trademark of Wiesel's later novels: it is taut, spare, concise, devoid of all but the most indispensable stylistic imagery, and poetic with its captivating rhythms, sonorous effects, and gloomy, dark atmosphere.

In the wake of this initial success, Wiesel published two fairly brief novels concerning the survivors of the Holocaust. His second novel, *L'Aube* (1960), also blends autobiography with fiction. The story tells of a Holocaust survivor who goes to Israel; once there, instead of acting like a victim, he becomes an active participant in another violent historical event, Israel's successful war of independence against the Palestinians and their Arab allies, who were determined to dash the hopes of Jewish nationhood. Wiesel's third novel, entitled *Le Jour* (1961), recaptures the autobiographical drama of a Holocaust survivor's accident in New York City and documents the traumatic psychological self-examination of a young man who, tortured by the guilt of having survived the genocide, decides that he must opt for life, not desire death.

Much later, in 1987, the English translations of *La Nuit, L'Aube,* and *Le Jour* (*Night, Dawn,* and *The Accident,* respectively) were combined into a single volume entitled *Night Trilogy.* Together these three compact works sum up the first period of Wiesel's career as a novelist. They are unified in offering a strange admixture of real life and fiction and at the same time demonstrating the juxtaposition of light and dark in Wiesel's own life. Night symbolizes the Holocaust, while light signifies the troubled existence of one who lives not only to remember but also to build a new life of hope out of the ashes of tragedy.

Since writing this trio of short novels, Wiesel has published about one book-length work a year. A prodigious and indefatigable writer, he once explained: "I work sixteen hours a day, and I work every day except Jewish holidays and Sabbaths. . . . If I have a problem with fiction, I go to non-fiction. One balances the other. Fiction is more taxing. I really can write anywhere—that's my journalistic discipline."[4]

After some fifteen years of trepidation, the author of *La Nuit* finally gathered the courage to return to his hometown of Sighet. For him it was a visit filled with anguish and pain: the once-thriving Jewish sector of the city was now populated by non-Jews. Only three or four dozen of his fellow Jews remained. The synagogue stood empty of congregants. Only the prayer books remained, and he was saddened to realize that hardly anyone was present to make use of them. As he walked through the streets, he saw a silent onlooker gazing at him through a window pane. These eyes caused him to experience a flashback to the past, when he saw from a similar window a similar pair of indifferent eyes peering out as he and his entire family joined the other arrested Jews of Sighet, who were all herded together by the German guards and forced to march to the waiting cattle cars that transported them to an almost certain death. In 1962 Wiesel translated this experience into a novel called *La Ville de la chance,* which received France's Prix Rivarol the following year.

In 1964 Wiesel published his fifth novel, *Les Portes de la forêt.* One of the author's most complex and philosophical pieces of fiction, this novel tells the story of a young Hungarian Jew who survives and even escapes from a concentration camp to join partisans combatting the Nazis. Eventually, after the war, this survivor, like Wiesel, goes to New York, where he is consumed by tormenting philosophical conflicts raging within his soul: how could God have forsaken the very people who had revered him through the millennia? Where was God when people were being sent to Treblinka? Why did he remain silent, even seemingly indifferent as the SS stormtroopers and their cohorts were slaughtering hundreds of thousands of innocent children? As the survivor accusingly protests the apparent indifference of God, he also chants his undying love for and faith in God. In the end he chooses love for his fellow men rather than sterile recriminations against an impassive God.

At the age of forty, Elie Wiesel married Marion Rose, a brilliant woman of Austrian descent who, like Wiesel, had miraculously survived the Holocaust. From all appearances, their marriage joined two people who complement each other both professionally and personally. Marion Wiesel has become the English translator of almost all his works since 1969. In 1972, the couple's only child was born and named after Wiesel's father, Shlomo Elisa. The author viewed his son's existence as a miracle. Despite the fate Hitler had decreed for all Jews, an occupant of Auschwitz had survived to add one more link to the ongoing chain of the Jewish people: "It is impossible that 3,500 years should end with me, so I took those 3,500 years and put them on the shoulders of this little child."[5] Elisha, as he is called by his parents, accompanies his prominent father to many major ceremonial events at which the latter is honored. His presence was particularly significant as he accompanied his father to Oslo, where in 1986 the writer received the Nobel Peace Prize.

The 1967 Six Day War also fueled the imagination of Elie Wiesel.

His beloved Israel had scored a miraculous military and moral victory over vastly superior Arab forces. Wiesel's novel *Le Mendiant de Jérusalem* appeared the next year. A best-seller in both Europe and America, the novel may well be, along with *La Nuit*, one of the finest as well as the most popular novels written by Wiesel. The saga of Israel's victory announces the jubilation felt by the Jewish people as their armed forces capture and unite the Old City of Jerusalem with their own western portion of the venerable city and as they seize control of the Western Wall, the holiest site in Judaism. The prevailing tone in *Le Mendiant de Jérusalem* makes it Wiesel's most optimistic, even joyful, novel to date.

After a six-year period during which Wiesel composed mainly nonfiction, a cantata based on music by the French composer Darius Milhaud, a collection of Hasidic tales, and a play, his yearning to write yet another novel led him in 1973 to pen *Le Serment de Kolvillág*, a novel based on Wiesel's own former oath of silence. The sole survivor of a bloody East European pogrom that wiped out the entire population of Jews and their town of Kolvillág takes an oath of silence that prevents him from describing the devastation he witnessed. Like Wiesel himself, who was both unwilling and unable to find the words necessary to describe the bloodbath that he had experienced, the central figure in the novel is tortured by the burden of an oath of silence. The oath is finally broken when he stumbles upon a young man determined to commit suicide and to whom he can finally reveal what he had witnessed in Kolvillág many years earlier. With powerful language the witness makes the young man renounce suicide by transferring onto his shoulders the memory of the dead. Henceforth, the young man will be obligated to go on living, if for no other reason than to testify to his descendents that once there had existed a Jewish community called Kolvillág.

After the successful publication of this novel, the pendulum of Wiesel's creative urge swung once again to nonfiction. Between 1973 and 1980 he wrote mainly nonfiction works: a collection of biblical portraits, a collection of essays and legends, a second play, dozens of articles, prefaces, and discourses. He launched the 1980s, however, with the novel *Le Testament d'un poète juif assassiné* (1980). The central theme of this book is the plight of the millions of Russian Jews who were trapped inside the anti-Semitic environment of the Soviet Union, where life was unbearable for those who wished to practice their religion, yet which Soviet laws forbade them to leave. Structured as a confessional diary written by a Soviet Jewish poet, who had been murdered in 1952 during the Stalinist era, the novel revolves around the attempts of the poet's only son to discover the true nature of his father's life through the study of this diary. The son learns to his horror that his poet-father had been forced to endure the most painful torture. There is clearly a close analogy between the suffering endured by Wiesel's own father in the camps and what the poet's son learns from his father's diary. The work is a compelling and timely piece of fiction, for it appeared just when the situation of Soviet Jewry was reaching near-tragic proportions.

In 1983 Wiesel published *Le Cinquième Fils.* The geographical settings of his novels are generally locations already familiar to the author: the shtetls of Eastern Europe, Paris, Israel, concentration camps, New York. In *Le Cinquième Fils* Wiesel depicts scenes mostly in Manhattan. The principal character is a young man who devotes his life to a search of his parents' past. Eventually he learns that his parents had been viciously tortured by the Nazis, that they had had a son who had been murdered in the Holocaust, that his father had unsuccessfully attempted to kill his son's murderer, and that the resulting trauma has made it impossible for them to discuss their tragic past. The protagonist then travels to Germany, where his brother's killer has since abandoned his Nazi past and become the chief executive officer of a prestigious German industrial corporation. There the protagonist hopes to confront the ex-Nazi and to kill him in an act of vengeance. However, once he finds his target in a plush German corporate office, he discovers that he cannot simply inflict violence on another human being, even a guilty person. Like Wiesel himself, who has always transmitted a message of peace and of conciliation, the protagonist opts for a nonviolent course of action.

In 1987, the author of *La Nuit* and *Le Jour* published another novel using a time of day for its title: *Le Crépuscule, au loin.* Here the novelist treats a topic over which he has been endlessly obsessing: madness versus sanity. Can one truly draw a line between the two? Did the rest of the world not consider the German people among the most highly educated, most cultured, and the most technologically advanced in the world? But if the Germans were truly sane, how could they have collectively perpetrated an insane, irrational act like their campaign to eradicate millions of people during the Holocaust? Wiesel suggests that if this is what sanity is all about, he prefers insanity. His novel takes place

largely within a mental institution in upstate New York. There the protagonist, in search of a missing friend who, he suspects, has been committed to the asylum, interviews several inmates, all of whom imagine
that they are biblical personages like Cain, Adam, Abraham, even God
himself. As in many of his other novels, Wiesel, possibly under the influence of the nouveaux romanciers of France, leaps back and forth between the past and the present, which become interconnected.

The year 1986 represented a milestone in the career of Elie Wiesel,
as he was selected as a Nobel laureate, not for literature, but for peace.
The Nobel Committee, apparently viewing his worldwide impact as one
that transcended literary art, recognized him for the incalculably important role he played on behalf of peace and understanding among
peoples. Calling Wiesel a "messenger to Mankind," Egal Aarvik, the
Norwegian chairman of the Nobel Committee, stated that "Elie Wiesel
has emerged as one of the spiritual leaders and guides [of our era]."[6]
Shortly afterward President Jimmy Carter appointed Wiesel the chairman of the United States Holocaust Commission, a body of public-spir-
ited citizens with a mission to create a national monument in Washington honoring the victims of the Holocaust. After a period of serving as a
public official, Wiesel resigned his position in order to devote himself
more fully to his career as a writer, as a teacher of university students (as
the Andrew Mellon Professor of the Humanities at Boston University),
and as a public speaker who addresses international audiences on the
theme of peace and commitment to human justice.

His most recent novel, L'Oublié, was published in Paris in 1989.
The novel portrays another typically Wieselean situation: a young man
seeks to break through the barrier of silence of his aging father, who is
losing his ability to speak or to remember. The young man wishes to
learn precisely what happened to his mother and to discover what truly
happened to his parents during the Holocaust. What kinds of experiences had they suffered during the Nazi era and later during the Israeli
war of independence? The central theme here is the search for roots and
identity; but there is a secondary theme, that of a romantic relationship
with a young woman who has a difficult time comprehending her
sweetheart's obsession with a past era of family history.

After years of reflection and daily notekeeping in his journal, in
1994 Wiesel published the first volume of his memoirs, Tous les fleuves
vont à la mer: Mémoires. In this detailed, lengthy volume he relates the

daily events of his existence, from his earliest recollections of childhood until 1969. A second and possibly third volume will surely follow in coming years.

The many significant themes in Elie Wiesel's novels and nonfiction include: his dream of return to his youthful days in Sighet; the uniqueness in human history of the Holocaust; the unquenchable need to remember the past in order to build a better future; the solidarity and universality of the Jewish people and the need for improved relations between Christians and Jews; the role of language and silence in literature; human rights, international peace, and justice; the rights of minorities; the importance of teachers in transmitting knowledge, human memory, and moral values to the young; his high respect for literature, especially the sacred texts of Judaism, the Torah, the Talmud, the great writers of France; the question of faith in God and, especially, the relations between God and mankind. Above all, Wiesel's cumulative works constitute a monumental plea against indifference to evil.

These novels are populated with a special world of characters: madmen, village idiots, beggars, storytellers, Hasids, young men groping to learn more about the mysterious past of their parents and ancestors, beggars, teachers and rabbinic scholars, persecutors and their victims. Wiesel seems more adept at portraying male characters than females. His women are often quite sketchy and appear to have been created mainly as complementary figures in the lives of his male characters.

Wiesel's style is deliberately stark, devoid of ornamentation or unnecessary sentimentality, acutely austere. In many ways, it continues the rich tradition of classical literature in France, but it is enriched with existentialism as well as with some of the innovations of typography (the interplay of italics with nonitalic type) and the experiments with time that one associates with the nouveau roman. He has repeatedly compared his philosophy of literary creation to the work of a sculptor who exerts himself during his creative process to chip away large chunks of marble or stone. Once the sculptor has finished his work, what remains is an absolute, minimalist statement. Wiesel's literary art as well is a monument of reductionism.

In his literature, Elie Wiesel has blended his passionate dedication to artistic perfection with his equally passionate conviction that art must carry a moral and ethical message that is designed to humanize and uplift the world. By no means is this art for art's sake. He once noted with irony that Nazis "pouvaient donc admirer un tableau de maître, savourer un beau poème, apprécier la finesse d'une réflexion philosophique et, en même temps, abattre des milliers et des milliers d'êtres humains."[7] In the view of the author of *La Nuit*, art bears the awesome responsibility of improving the human condition.

Notes

1. Irving Abrahamson and Elie Wiesel, *Against Silence: The Voice and Vision of Elie Wiesel* (New York: Holocaust Library, 1985), vol. 3, p. 8.
2. Ibid., vol. 2, p. 3.
3. Ibid., vol. 3, p. 230.
4. Ibid., vol. 2, p. 117.
5. Ibid., vol. 3, p. 276.
6. Quoted in Jack Kolbert, "Elie Wiesel," *French Novelists since 1960* (Detroit: Gale, 1989), p. 329.
7. Elie Wiesel, *Signes d'exode* (Paris: Bernard Grasset, 1985), p. 105.

Bibliography

Works by Elie Wiesel

La Nuit. Paris: Minuit, 1958. Translated by Stella Rodway as *Night*. New York: Hill and Wang, 1960.
L'Aube. Paris: Seuil, 1960. Translated by Anne Borchardt as *Dawn*. New York: Hill and Wang, 1961.
Le Jour. Paris: Seuil, 1961. Translated by Anne Borchardt as *The Accident*. New York: Hill and Wang, 1962.
La Ville de la chance. Paris: Seuil, 1962. Translated by Steven Becker as *The Town Beyond the Wall*. New York: Atheneum, 1964.
Les Portes de la forêt. Paris: Seuil, 1964. Translated by Frances Frenaye as *The Gates of the Forest*. New York: Holt, Rinehart and Winston, 1966.
Les Juifs du silence. Paris: Seuil, 1966. Translated by Neal Kozodoy from the Hebrew as *The Jews of Silence*. New York: Holt, Rinehart and Winston, 1966.
Les Chants des morts. Paris: Seuil, 1966. Translated by Steven Donadio as *Legends of Our Times*. New York: Holt, Rinehart and Winston, 1968.
Zalmen ou la folie de Dieu. Paris: Seuil, 1968. Translated by Nathan Edelman as *Zalmen or the Madness of God*. New York: Random House, 1974.
Le Mendiant de Jérusalem. Paris: Seuil, 1968. Translated by Lily Edelman and the author as *A Beggar in Jerusalem*. New York: Random House, 1970.
Entre deux soleils. Paris: Seuil, 1970. Translated by Lily Edelman and the author as *One Generation After*. New York: Random House, 1970.

Célébration Hassidique. Paris: Seuil, 1972. Translated by Marion Wiesel as *Souls on Fire*. New York: Random House, 1971.

Le Serment de Kolvillág. Paris: Seuil, 1973. Translated by Marion Wiesel as *The Oath*. New York: Random House, 1973.

Ani Maamin (bilingual edition). Translated by Marion Wiesel. New York: Random House, 1973.

Célébration biblique. Paris: Seuil, 1975. Translated by Marion Wiesel as *Messengers of God*. New York: Random House, 1976.

Un Juif aujourd'hui. Paris: Seuil, 1977. Translated by Marion Wiesel as *A Jew Today*. New York: Random House, 1978.

Four Hasidic Masters and Their Struggle Against Melancholy. Notre Dame: University of Notre Dame Press, 1978.

Le Procès de Shamgorod (tel qu'il se déroula le 25 février, 1649). Paris: Seuil, 1979. Translated by Marion Wiesel as *The Trial of God (as It Was Held on February 25, 1649, in Shamgorod)*. New York: Random House, 1979.

Le Testament d'un poète juif assassiné. Paris: Seuil, 1980. Translated by Marion Wiesel as *The Testament*. New York: Summit, 1981.

Five Biblical Portraits. Notre Dame: University of Notre Dame Press, 1981.

Contre la mélancolie: Célébration Hassidique II. Paris: Seuil, 1981. Translated by Marion Wiesel as *Somewhere a Master: Further Hasidic Portraits and Legends*. New York: Summit, 1982.

Paroles d'étranger. Paris: Seuil, 1982.

The Golem: The Story of a Legend as Told by Elie Wiesel. New York: Summit, 1983.

Le Cinquième Fils. Paris: Grasset, 1983. Translated by Marion Wiesel as *The Fifth Son*. New York: Summit, 1985.

Against Silence: The Voice and Vision of Elie Wiesel. 3 vols. Edited and coauthored by Irving Abrahamson. New York: Holocaust Library, 1985.

Signes d'exode. Paris: Grasset et Fasquelle, 1985.

Job ou Dieu dans la tempête. Paris: Grasset et Fasquelle, 1987.

Le Crépuscule, au loin. Paris: Grasset, 1987. Translated by Marion Wiesel as *Twilight*. New York: Summit, 1988.

The Six Days of Destruction. Coauthored by Albert Friedlander. New York: Paulist Press, 1985.

L'Oublié. Paris: Seuil, 1989. Translated by Marion Wiesel as *The Forgotten*. New York: Summit, 1992.

From the Kingdom of Memory. New York: Summit Press, 1990.

Célébration talmudique. Paris: Seuil, 1991.

Tous les fleuves vont à la mer: Mémoires. Paris: Seuil, 1994.

Selected Critical Works

Berenbaum, Michael. *The Vision of the Void: Theological Reflections on the Works of Elie Wiesel*. Middletown, CT: Wesleyan University Press, 1979.

Brown, Robert McAfee. *Elie Wiesel: Messenger to All Humanity.* Revised edition. Notre Dame: University of Notre Dame Press, 1989.

Cargas, Harry James. *Conversations with Elie Wiesel.* New York: Paulist Press, 1976.

————. *Responses to Elie Wiesel: Critical Essays by Major Jewish and Christian Scholars.* New York: Persea Books, 1978.

Cohen, Brigitte-Fanny. *Elie Wiesel: Qui êtes-vous?* Paris: La Manufacture, 1987.

Estes, Ted L. *Elie Wiesel.* New York: Frederick Ungar, 1980.

Fine, Ellen S. *Legacy of Night: The Literary Universe of Elie Wiesel.* Albany: State University of New York Press, 1982.

Rittner, Carol R. S. M., ed. *Elie Wiesel: Between Memory and Hope.* New York: New York University Press, 1990.

Rosenfeld, Alvin, and Irving Greenbert, eds. *Confronting the Holocaust: The Impact of Elie Wiesel.* Bloomington: Indiana University Press, 1979.

Roth, John K.. *A Consuming Fire: Encounters with Elie Wiesel.* Atlanta: John Knox Press, 1979.

Saint-Cheron, Philippe de. *Le Mal et l'exil: Rencontre avec Elie Wiesel.* Paris: Nouvelle Cité, 1988. Translated by Jon Rothschild as *Evil and Exile.* Notre Dame: University of Notre Dame Press, 1990.

————. *Elie Wiesel: pèlerin de la mémoire.* Paris: Plon, 1994.

Stern, Ellen Norman. *Elie Wiesel: Witness for Life.* New York: KTAV Publishing, 1982.

12

Andrée Chedid

J. D. Mann

J'ai tenté de joindre ma terre, à la terre;
Les mots, à la trame du silence;
Le large, au chant voilé.

Tenté de dire la rencontre possible,
Dégager le lieu de la nasse des refuges;
Fléchir la parole, jusqu'à la partager.[1]

These lines, taken from Andrée Chedid's poem "Démarche I," define a fundamental dimension of her literary production, for such are the voices that make themselves heard throughout her œuvre: fraternal, eager for communication, seeking communion with others and with the world. This approach is that of a poet, novelist, and playwright, a woman who is the product of cultural, linguistic, and geographic pluralism, and who considers this diversity a source of enrichment and inspiration.

Born in Cairo in 1920 of Lebanese parents, Chedid received her secondary education in France. She then returned to Egypt, where she earned a bachelor's degree in journalism at the American University in Cairo. In 1942, she accompanied her husband to Lebanon, where they remained for three years while he pursued his medical studies. They have lived in Paris since 1946 and are naturalized citizens of France.

Chedid's œuvre, which includes ten novels as well as over two dozen volumes of poetry, six plays, and four collections of short stories, has attracted growing critical attention for more than twenty-five years. Her earliest work, a collection of poetry in English entitled *On the Trails*

231

of My Fancy, was published in Cairo in 1943. Since then, however, she has chosen French, her first language, as the vehicle for her literary production. She has been the recipient of numerous literary prizes including the Louise Labé prize for poetry (1966), the Mallarmé prize for poetry (1975), the Grand Prix des Lettres Françaises de l'Académie Royale de Belgique (1975), the Prix Goncourt for the short story (1979), and the Pierre Régnier prize of the Académie Française (1986).

Unlike those who live in the land of her ancestors, Andrée Chedid has not personally known the anguish and struggle that cultural dualism can cause. Rather, for her, the experience of this double reality has been an asset to be treasured and has resulted in a peaceful and rewarding fusion. Her writing shows an ongoing attempt to bring together and reconcile the two elements of certain fundamental dualities and, at the same time, to respect and even to valorize their dialectical opposition. She recognizes that, almost in spite of herself, she often treats the same themes, always expressed in terms of a duality, which she describes as a "balancement des contraires: obscur-clair, horreurs-beauté, grisaille-souffles, puits-ailes, dedans-dehors, chant-contre-chant. Double pays, en apparence; mais que la vie brasse, ensemble, inépuisablement."[2]

Andrée Chedid's works are characterized by a profound sense of interrogation, an ongoing quest for answers to the fundamental questions of the human condition. These questions, echoing through her poetry, fiction, and theater, give rise to the themes of birth and rebirth, death, love, and war, which spring from mankind's shared experience, transcending cultural and linguistic boundaries. She expresses the desire to find common ground, to bring into focus the shared experience that can serve as a basis for tolerance and understanding. She has stated: "Je crois *la communication* possible; pas sans problèmes, mais possible. M'intéresse par dessus tout: la recherche d'un lieu de convergence au fond de l'homme, d'une source commune, d'une terre partagée."[3] Chedid's confidence in the existence of this common ground, her belief in the possibility of conciliation, her call for fraternity, are central, both thematically and structurally, to her fiction, theater, and poetry.

In Chedid's first two novels, *Le Sommeil délivré* (1952) and *Jonathan* (1955), although the message is one of hope, the principal characters have only limited success in overcoming their isolation. For Samya, protagonist of *Le Sommeil délivré,* the words of the title symbolize both a final renunciation of the desire for communication and a refusal of her stultifying daily routine. Although Chedid treats the question of the repression of women in the Arab world, seen in the context of the Egyptian middle-class society of the time, the novel is not primarily a plea for female emancipation or a sociological study of family life. Through this story of an oppressed woman, Chedid inculpates everything that hinders the blossoming of the individual and human solidarity. In *Le Sommeil délivré,* the network of barriers, of interdictions and of prejudices, imposed both by the milieu and by society in general with its climate of male supremacy, imprisons Samya both physically and emotionally.

After the death of her six-year-old daughter, Samya seeks to escape from her invisible bonds by shooting her husband. Yet, rather than a true affirmation of revolt, her act of desperation is primarily a renunciation of all contact and communication with those around her. This murder makes insurmountable the physical and emotional distance that has always isolated her. She surrounds herself with a wall of silence that creates a solitude much deeper than she has known before. Samya has become as immobile and unreachable as a corpse, having totally rejected the past and completely disassociated herself from the present. Once this threshold has been crossed, even the word has lost its power. Despite their sympathy for Samya, her friends Ammal and Om El Kher understand that the abyss separating her from them has now become so great that even *la fraternité de la parole* would be incapable of bridging it.

Samya is overcome by the obstacles to communication that have marked every stage of her life. The distances remain too great and the communion and understanding arising from communication—*le partage de la parole*—are never realized. However, the last image of the novel, that of Ammal running away, provides a glimmer of hope.[4] The little girl finds the courage to attempt what Samya has never been able to do. Thanks to the determination that Samya has nurtured within her, she will have the chance to blossom "loin de ce qui étouffe et de cette pourriture que devient la peur" (p. 226).

In *Jonathan,* Chedid's second novel, although the characters have only a limited capacity to communicate with one another, they desire to seek out and to find common ground and thus to establish the basis for solidarity and brotherhood. The action, which takes place in a large Middle Eastern city, begins when Jonathan leaves the orphanage in which he was raised to become sacristan in the church of Père Antoun. Certain of his vocation, the sensitive and diligent young man experiences a period of peace and happiness in the parish of Sainte-Agnès. Then, increasingly impatient to help his fellow men, but without any concrete means of doing so, he is torn by opposing aspirations for contemplation and for action. He finally decides to join the revolutionary movement forming among the youth of the country under the direction of Alexandre, a young architect. However, on the very day that the two men are to meet, the fighting begins and Jonathan becomes one of its first victims, killed by the senseless violence of a group of revolutionaries who enter his church in search of weapons.

Although he is not able to break down the wall of silence that surrounds him, the sacristan faces death comforted by Alexandre's presence. Without knowing the identity of the dying man, the architect shares Jonathan's last moments and is led to reflect on the meaning of his own actions. The destinies of the two young idealists briefly converge, bringing together individuals who, though outwardly dissimilar, are united by the desire for fraternity and inspired by a similar view of life. Even though death intervenes, preventing any verbal communication with Alexandre, "la longue marche vers l'autre" has been realized and the sacristan finally experiences the communion he has so long desired.[5]

The theme of *la fraternité de la parole* finds more complete expression in the eight novels Chedid has published since 1960. In *Le Sixième Jour* (1960), the protagonist, Om Hassan, struggles to save the life of her young grandson, who has fallen victim to cholera during an epidemic in Cairo. Refusing to comply with the directives of the public health officials, who attempt to ensure that all those who have contracted the disease are properly treated, she decides to keep her grandson with her. She hides him from the authorities so that he will not be transported to the hospital, from where, she is convinced, he will never return. Om Hassan cares for the boy herself, hoping to cure him by the sheer force of her will and boundless love. She awaits the sixth day of the illness, on which, she has heard, "ou bien on meurt ou bien on ressuscite" (p. 33). Om Hassan conceals the boy first in a laundry room and then on a boat descending the Nile toward the sea. On the river as in the city, she is unable to avoid the company of Okkasionne, who turns the epidemic to his own profit by tracking down those afflicted by cholera and turning them in to the authorities.

On the sixth day of the vigil, the young boy dies. Om Hassan sees his death reflected in the eyes of Okkasionne, the person she had chosen to announce the good news of his survival. The grandmother loses consciousness but, in the last moments of her life, hears the voices of all her fellow passengers assuring her that the child is alive and declaring that he will live to reach the sea. Although Om Hassan, with her immeasurable faith in life and the courage of her maternal love, does not triumph over fate, the last pages of the novel relate triumph rather than failure. Her inexhaustible hope communicates itself to all her companions, and by a *partage de la parole* that even defies death, they proclaim with her and for her the continued existence of the child within their own hearts. Just as Om Hassan covers a spatial distance while looking for a hiding place in order to ensure the recovery of her grandson, the abolition of the emotional distance, which results from her conversation with Okkasionne on the eve of the sixth day, brings about the survival of the boy on a symbolic level: the affirmation of faith in love and in life. On the sixth day all barriers crumble, the distances disappear, and there is no more need for dissimulation. The victory of the grandmother and the young boy is found in the spirit of fraternity that fills the witnesses to their drama, and in the *partage de la parole* that proclaims the miracle of hope.

Likewise, Lana, protagonist of Chedid's fourth novel, *Le Survivant* (1963), relies on the power of absolute and unwavering love to bring about the survival of her husband, Pierre. She engages in a two-year-long quest in the Sahara, searching for him and remaining convinced that he is the lone survivor of an airplane crash in the middle of the desert. Disregarding the advice of almost everyone with whom she comes into contact, Lana undertakes and perseveres in her search without a single piece of evidence to support her belief that the seat found intact, safely ejected from the crash site, and the footprints leading away from the wreckage, are those of her husband.

Lana covers a spatial distance separating two continents and including the seemingly limitless expanse of the desert. This physical movement is mirrored by emotional movement, which unites her with several individuals while in Africa. For example, despite differences of nationality, of language, and of culture, an immediate bond forms between Lana and the native women who surround her with their reassuring presence in the train after a terrifying encounter with a man she had believed might be her husband. In this novel, acts of communication abound. Letters, conversations, and stories are among the messages that cross the linguistic and spatial barriers separating sender and recipient.

After two years of fruitless searching, Lana returns to France without having found her husband. She resumes her life resigned to Pierre's death but at the same time closer to him than ever. The more Lana confronts the reality of her husband's fate, the more she addresses an interior discourse to him, and it is this communication that reveals the identity of the true survivor—the "nous" of the couple, the fusion of two beings—which, despite the ultimate separation imposed by death, survives intact.

In each of Chedid's first four novels, the characters struggle to break the silence surrounding them and to diminish the distances blocking understanding, conciliation, and, especially, communication. The protagonists' desire to communicate and to break down the barriers that isolate them is mirrored in the narrative technique, for their voices gradually free themselves from the control of the mediating voice and presence of the narrator and enter into direct communication with the extradiegetic narratee.

This gradual progression in the characters' discourse, from complete subordination to the narrator's discourse to direct, unmediated communication with the extradiegetic narratee, begins with Samya's long interior monologue in *Le Sommeil délivré*. Although Samya's thoughts are transmitted to the reader without interruption, her monologue is not delivered by an autonomous narrative voice speaking directly to the extradiegetic narratee. Rather, it is circumscribed by a framework created by the words of an omniscient, anonymous, third-person narrator. The narrative structure of *Le Sommeil délivré* reflects the enclosure and subordination characterizing the life of the protagonist. Just as Samya ends up immobile and silent as a character, as the narrator of her own story, her voice is virtually cut off from all direct communication with the extradiegetic narratee. In the same way that she had been under the authority of her father and then subject to the control of her husband, because of the hierarchy of narrative levels her voice is subordinated to that of the omniscient third-person narrator. It comes to us through that mediating presence and is surrounded by a discourse that forms the encircling "parentheses" of introduction and epilogue framing her interior monologue.

In *Jonathan, Le Sixième Jour,* and *Le Survivant,* the gradual emancipation of the characters' discourse from the mediating presence of the narrator is due, in part, to the increasing proportion of dialogue and reported speech in the transmission of the characters' spoken words. The growing autonomy of the protagonists' spoken discourse reflects the greater importance and efficacy of the acts of communication at the level of the story. The more the characters talk to one another, the more their voices make themselves heard without the mediation of the narrator.

However, it is primarily the protagonists' interior discourse that provides the pathway by which their voices gradually accede to the autonomy of the third-person narrator. This shift is the result of the increasingly prevalent use of present-tense narration and the tendency of the narrator to identify largely with the protagonist, sharing his/her ideological perspective so completely that it becomes almost impossible to determine who—the character or the narrator—voices certain reflections, observations, and questions. The proportion of this ambiguous or "shared" discourse grows in each succeeding novel, and it is not until *Le Survivant* that all uncertainty regarding the identity of the speaker is resolved. Lana's free direct discourse opens certain sections of the novel, without any trace of the organizing function of the narrator and without any sign of subordination to his/her discourse. Thanks to a subtle *glissement* from the text of the narrator to that of the character, Lana's voice comes to us in a discourse that is neither stated nor mediated by the third-person narrator. In contrast to the enclosure of Samya's interior monologue, Lana's unspoken words make themselves heard directly by the extradiegetic narratee.

The themes of *la fraternité de la parole* and its narrative corollary, *la parole partagée,* find their fullest expression in the six novels Chedid has published since 1969. In her fifth novel, *L'Autre* (1969), which has as its setting a small town situated in an unspecified Middle Eastern country, the old man Simm strives to save a Western tourist who has been buried in the rubble created by an earthquake. Simm had seen the young man lean out of his hotel room window just before the cataclysm completely destroyed the village and had witnessed the young man's fall when the hotel was demolished. He remains convinced that the visitor is alive, buried under the debris, and he devotes himself entirely to ensuring his survival. However, Simm is unable to overcome the incredulity of the members of the rescue team, for without proof of the existence of the young man they refuse to undertake the difficult and expensive work required to bring him to safety. Although everyone has abandoned the site, the old man remains true to his convictions and continues his solitary vigil among the ruins. Patiently, he calls to the young man and listens for a response. An answer finally comes, echoing from the depths of the earth.

This time, Simm succeeds in convincing others to join him in his quest. The rescue effort takes several days, during which he remains lying on the ground, talking to the young foreigner, encouraging him, struggling with him against despair and death. Simm's voice carries through the tons of debris and supports the life of the young man. He awakens in him the desire to live and manages to transmit to him his own enthusiasm for life. The bond of fraternity linking the two men, symbolized by the words and gestures of greeting they exchange before the earthquake and cemented by their shared ordeal, goes beyond the sphere of their personal story. It takes on a universal dimension as they give up their individual identities and adopt new names when speaking to each other. For the earthquake victim, Simm becomes "Ben" and for him, the young man is called "Jeph," a name given to foreigners. When the survivor emerges from the bowels of the earth, he wishes, above all, to find the man whose voice saved him from death. However, Simm has slipped away and stands watching from a distance, refusing to answer to the name "Ben," which remains unknown to all, except the young foreigner.

L'Autre is not the story of two individuals, but rather of two civilizations in dialogue. The dialogue is expressed through two men separated by space and time—Simm representing the past and the other representing the future—who are brought together in an affirmation of life and of hope. The words of two languages, barely shared, unite these two men who remain only voices for each other. This celebration of *la fraternité de la parole* through which the young man is reborn is made possible by the microphone, a sort of umbilical cord, put in place thanks to Simm's stubborn efforts. It provides a pathway leading down into the depths of the earth, amplifying the words that will help the young man to look deep inside himself in order to rediscover a meaning for existence.

Unlike *L'Autre* and most of Chedid's earlier novels, *La Cité fertile* (1972) is not set in the Middle East, but in Paris. In this universe of concrete and steel, the protagonist, Aléfa, thrives. A true nonconformist, she lives outside the boundaries of the traditional female roles of wife and mother. Although she may once have been both of these, in her old age she is simply Aléfa, "la femme-bouffon" (p. 25). She wanders through the streets, capturing the attention and imagination of audiences of children and passersby with her intriguing spectacle of words, mime, and dance. However, her intent is not merely to entertain. By means of her performances, she hopes to communicate better with those around her and, in so doing, to help them find ways better to understand and to communicate with one another.

Even the most impersonal and prosaic words, excerpts selected seemingly at random from the newspaper and declaimed in front of spectators gathered on the banks of the Seine, become a vehicle of communication between Aléfa and her audience. For her, the shared word is not only communion with others. It also becomes (perhaps above all) a way of awakening a feeling of fraternity, for her performances, based in part on the participation of the audience, incite the spectators to find common ground. In *La Cité fertile, la fraternité de la parole* represents an invitation to seek out, together, possible answers to the essential questions of existence: "D'où avons-nous surgi? Où vont nos pas, et pourquoi?" (p. 23). Aléfa, a figure of abundant love, expresses herself using words "venues de loin, transmises de voix en voix, de signes en signes" (p. 64), and in so doing, attempts to give voice to what is most fundamental in man.

Continuing the gradual progression developed in Chedid's first four novels, in *L'Autre* and *La Cité fertile* the voice of the third-person narrator loses its monopoly on direct communication with the extradiegetic narratee. The narrative structure is characterized by a *partage de la parole* foreshadowing the narrative polyphony of Chedid's later works. The protagonists' interior discourse is juxtaposed with, not subordinated to, that of the third-person narrator, and it has been liberated from his/her mediating presence. However, the characters do not specifically address themselves to the extradiegetic narratee, nor do they assume a clearly narrative function. It is in *Nefertiti et le rêve d'Akhnaton*, *Les Marches de sable*, and *La Maison sans racines* that it is possible to see the fullest development of the notion of *la parole partagée*. In these three novels, a new dimension, already present as the source of an enriching ambiguity in the earlier works, arises not from the confusion of voices in a mixed discourse, but rather as the product of an almost dialogic alternation of words and periods of silence.

Chedid's seventh novel, *Nefertiti et le rêve d'Akhnaton* (1974), has as its setting Egypt in the time of the pharaohs. The protagonists are Nefertiti and her scribe Boubastos, to whom she is dictating her memoirs after the disappearance and presumed death of her husband, the rebel pharaoh Akhnaton. Having renounced the polytheism of his ancestors for the worship of a single god, Aton, represented by the symbol of the sun disc, Akhnaton had left Thebes to establish, with his wife, a new capital, the City of the Horizon. In this city they had created, Akhnaton introduced not only the practice of monotheism but also a political and social reform based on freedom, justice, peace, and tolerance. However, his dream began to crumble almost as soon as it had been realized. Upon Akhnaton's disappearance and presumed death, twelve years after the founding of his city, his half-brother, the young Tutankhamen, assumed the throne. Seven years later, the general Horemheb instituted a violent movement of counterreform and had the City of the Horizon completely destroyed in order to obliterate all traces of the project undertaken by Akhnaton. Nefertiti and the scribe Boubastos take refuge in a palace located just outside the ravaged city, and they alone remain to contemplate the ruins.

Faced with the destruction of the dream that she had helped to construct, Nefertiti must overcome her sense of loss in order to recount her life to the scribe, for according to the wishes of her husband, it is up to her to keep alive the memory of the city they had built and to explain the ideals upon which it was founded. Boubastos, formerly in the service of the pharaoh, represents for Nefertiti a sort of dual link, a bridge both to the past and to the future. However, his role is not limited simply to the transcription of her account. In fact, it is the bond of sympathy between these two very different individuals and, even more so, the special kind of dialogue they cultivate, that make possible the very generation of the narrative. This bond uniting the *voix* (Nefertiti), which is dictating the memoirs to the *voie* (the scribe entrusted with transcribing them), will permit the memoirs to touch readers of centuries to come.

In *Nefertiti*, the narration is carried out by two first-person voices, those of the queen herself and of the scribe, Boubastos, who alternate in telling the same story. The scribe recounts the reign of Nefertiti and Akhnaton from his own point of view, often interjecting passages of commentary as well as episodes from his own life. Assuming somewhat the same function as the omniscient, third-person narrators in Chedid's earlier novels, his own narrative establishes the context for the one dictated to him by Nefertiti. He describes the spatial, temporal, and emotional background of the account that he is transcribing and also takes it upon himself to fill in certain aspects of the past that are not mentioned by the queen. Thus, far from taking on the passive and invisible role implied by the image of a scribe who simply records what is told to him, Boubastos, by interpolating segments of his own discourse, provides the historical and religious setting for the reign of Akhnaton. He contributes concrete details and images in contrast to the personal and affective dimension emphasized by Nefertiti. Rather than being in contradiction, the two voices narrating the story of Akhnaton reinforce each other. By its composition, the novel is more like a long dialogue than two independent monologues. The queen speaks to the scribe as a close friend to whom she is entrusting the transmission of her husband's dream. In turn, Boubastos reads to Nefertiti the personal reflections he has written. In this way, he helps her to overcome the enveloping silence and to find the strength to dictate her own thoughts.

In the segments told by Boubastos one finds observations on Nefertiti's emotional state and physical appearance as she struggles against the overwhelming silence and emptiness she feels in order to bring forth her memoirs. The scribe, as both witness and participant, recounts not only the events of the reign of Nefertiti and Akhnaton but also the day-to-day circumstances surrounding the composition of the chronicle itself. By describing the difficult "birth" of the account, which consists of the queen's memoirs, Boubastos affirms the sincerity of Nefertiti as a narrator and her reality as a historical personage. Thanks to these passages of external focalization, Nefertiti becomes more than a faraway, isolated voice. She acquires a concrete existence as the scribe underlines the fundamental resemblances linking her to her readers, even those of generations in the far distant future.

As the setting for *Les Marches de sable* (1981), Chedid chose Egypt of the fourth century A.D., a land torn by religious strife between Christian and pagan factions. Against this backdrop of violence and fanaticism, she presents three women, Cyre, Marie, and Athanasia, each of whom has chosen to exile herself in the desert in search of peace and some personal truth. The women, who for a time become anchorites and encounter one another in their wanderings, are of different ages and come from very dissimilar backgrounds. Cyre is a thirteen-year-old girl of humble origin, Marie is thirty-five and formerly a courtesan in Alexandria, and Athanasia, who is sixty, had been the wife of a magistrate and the devoted mother of two sons. They decide to travel together and make their way to the dwelling of the hermit Macé. They find him in the company of Thémis, an elderly man who has come to the desert to reflect on his experiences and to search for Athanasia, the object of his long-standing, unexpressed love.

Despite the setting characterized by religious persecution and fanaticism, Chedid puts the emphasis on what brings the three female protagonists together. At the moment their paths cross, each has reached a turning point. Seemingly very different, they help one another chart a new direction through the desert and through life. Just as in Chedid's previous novels, the expression of fraternity is found in communication, *le partage de la parole*. This communication is all the more precious because for years, all three women had been deprived of the communion gained through true communication: Cyre, because of her vow of silence and the cruelty of her companions at the convent; Marie, because she had exiled herself in the desert and, as a result, had lost all chance at human contact; and Athanasia, who, in order to respect her husband's decision to lead a life of asceticism, had essentially remained silent in the presence of the one person with whom communication would have brought her some consolation.

The voices of these women echo and call out to one another in a series of conversations that help them to understand and to analyze themselves. They are raised in order to question, and they fall silent in order to listen and to understand. These voices are the sign of a true communion, thanks to which "le manque à vivre se met à vivre" (p. 149). Upon their departure, the paths of Cyre, Marie, and Athanasia diverge, and each must face her own destiny, enriched, aided, and enlightened by this encounter. Just as in *L'Autre* and in *Nefertiti, la fraternité de la parole* opens the way to the future.

In addition to presenting a first-person account of events derived from his own experience, Thémis also describes the experiences that led Cyre, Marie, and Athanasia to take refuge in the desert, and the transformation each undergoes in the time she spends there. In doing so, he adopts the perspective of a seemingly omniscient narrator and refers to himself in the third person. He includes events that he did not witness, and yet, in the course of the narration, he seldom mentions his sources of information, presenting the action as though it were coming directly from his own recollections.

The "je"/"il" alternation represents a trace of the underlying polyphony upon which the composition of Thémis's text is based. By using "il" to refer to himself, he calls attention to the echoes of other narrating voices, especially those of Marie and Athanasia, which make themselves heard through his own. This subtle sharing of the narrative privilege can be compared to a song with several parts that become intermingled or to the interlacing threads of a tapestry. The voice of Thémis assumes the task of imposing order on these different threads and becomes, in a sense, a narrative pathway or vehicle shared by all the protagonists.

The story recounted in *La Maison sans racines* (1985) takes place in Lebanon in the summer of 1975. Kalya, who lives in Paris, and her twelve-year-old American granddaughter, Sybil, have never met, but they arrange to spend several weeks together in and around Beirut, vacationing in the land of their ancestors. However, they are soon embroiled in the fratricidal violence beginning to destroy the capital. Kalya becomes a powerless witness to the destruction of a symbol of peace and fraternity meant as a plea for an end to the hostilities. She watches as two young women, Myriam and Ammal, one Christian and the other Muslim, identically dressed, walk slowly toward each other on a deserted street. This walk, intended to culminate in an embrace, is a public display of unity and tolerance that they hope others will emulate.

Suddenly, when one of the women falls victim to a sniper's bullet, Kalya joins them in the street and, armed with a revolver, advances slowly toward them, hoping to be able to prevent another attack. Once she has reached the two women, believing that the danger has passed, she sees her own granddaughter running toward her, followed by the elderly domestic Slimane, who is trying to bring the little girl back to safety. These two are also shot down by an unseen assassin seeking to perpetuate the violence, unmoved by the kindness and innocence that his victims represent. Set in the volatile climate of the early days of the civil war, the story is a crystallization of the situation, one imagined sequence of events into which all the tragedy and senselessness of the conflict are distilled. Interspersed with the events of July and August 1975 are Kalya's reminiscences of the peace and happiness of a vacation spent in the same location with her own grandmother Nouza, forty-three years earlier.

In this novel the theme of *la fraternité de la parole* finds only limited expression, primarily through the bonds of communication, of understanding, and of solidarity linking individuals separated by differences of age, nationality, and religion. The manifestation of a more general unity in the gathering, which was to follow the symbolic gesture of Myriam and Ammal, the *fraternité de la parole,* which was to help to put an end to the hostilities by facilitating communication between individuals belonging to opposing camps, and the collective *partage de la parole,* which was to demand, in one voice, the end to the bloodshed and reprisals, are never realized. The crowd that was to call for "la fin immédiate de toute dissension, de toute violence" (p. 58) remains scattered and silent. The power of *la parole partagée,* vehicle of fraternity and antidote for intolerance, does not have time to take effect. The project conceived by Myriam and Ammal ends only in a silence pierced by gunfire. The voices, which "hors des appartenances, des clans, des catéchismes, des féodalités, des idéologies . . . éveilleraient celles du silence, dissiperaient les peurs, changeraient ces paroles tues en une seule parole de concorde, de liberté. . . . Une parole pour tous" (p. 209), never have the chance to make themselves heard.

In *La Maison sans racines,* the alternating voices of an omniscient, third-person narrator and of the protagonist, Kalya, tell independent stories and the action thus unfolds on two juxtaposed temporal levels. The third-person narrator is recounting the events of July and August 1975, while in an autobiographical monologue, Kalya is retracing a series of episodes that took place during her youth, especially during the summer of 1932, spent in Lebanon with her grandmother. In this interior monologue she finds a refuge from the tragedy of the present moment through the act of recalling certain past experiences that seem almost to represent a totally different existence.

However, if the two narrating voices tell similar stories meant to contrast with each other by accentuating the differences in historical setting, they seem to reach a level of synthesis in yet a third line of discourse. This is found in ten rather brief sections interspersed with those recounting the events of 1932 and 1975. These passages depict Kalya's walk toward the two women in the street, seemingly in slow motion because of the fragmented and dispersed nature of the segments. In the account of this walking sequence, time seems almost to stop or, at least, the moments seem to dilate, allowing the reader to glimpse, through the present, scenes of the recent and distant past. This fragmented thread in which one finds certain elements of the other two stories represents a synthesis not only in content but also in discourse. The voices of the two narrators become so intermingled that Kalya's discourse appears to infiltrate that of the anonymous third-person narrator without any transition or any sign of subordination. Because of this shift, the third-person narrator seems to adopt Kalya's psychological perspective. The omniscience characterizing this third-person voice gives way to the uncertainty, hopes, and fears felt by Kalya in the course of her walk. The discourse seems to belong, therefore, on the shifting border between the texts of the two narrators, whose voices no longer make themselves heard in counterpoint, but rather in unison, in order to transmit a plea for brotherhood and tolerance.

The setting of *L'Enfant multiple* (1989) is Paris in 1987. The protagonist, "l'enfant multiple," is a twelve-year-old Lebanese boy orphaned when his parents are killed by street violence in Beirut. His name, Omar-Joseph, is indicative of the duality of his background. Upon the death of his Christian mother and his Muslim father, Omar-Jo lives for a short time with his maternal grandfather. The old man makes the difficult decision to send his grandson to live with cousins in Paris, feeling that "Omar-Jo devait bâtir autrement, ailleurs, que sur le seul passé; et transformer les images dévastatrices en images d'avenir" (p. 136). In France, Omar-Jo makes himself indispensable to Maxime, the proprietor of a carousel located on the Place Saint-Jacques. Not only does he reawaken Maxime's zest for life and restore the atmosphere of gaiety and magic to his merry-go-round, but Omar-Jo also attracts crowds with his dances, costumes, and half-serious, half-comic monologues.

One spectator remarks "je n'ai jamais rien vu de plus tragique et de plus drôle que cet enfant" (p. 130). Tragic, because of the images of war-torn Lebanon that his words evoke and also because he is himself a victim of the violence. The explosion that killed his parents left him physically as well as emotionally scarred. Having lost an arm as a result of the blast, Omar-Jo is a living reminder of the conflict. He refuses Maxime's offer of a prosthesis, for to accept such a device, which would mask his wound, would be to deny the tragedy: "On ne pouvait troquer ce bras, ni trahir son image. Son absence était un rappel de toutes les absences, de toutes les morts, de toutes les meurtrissures" (p. 207).

Omar-Jo serves as a symbol of the nation itself, incarnating both its enriching diversity and its destructive oppositions. Born in 1975, as the hostilities were just beginning, he is also a symbol of hope. Unlike the closing sequences of *La Maison sans racines,* in which the attempt to bring about peaceful coexistence does not come to fruition, Omar-Jo—"l'enfant multiple"—does survive. Through the power of the shared word, *la fraternité de la parole,* he communicates to all those who listen the possibility and the need for change; not a change in institutions, in laws, or in governments, but rather, in man himself. For him, as for Andrée Chedid, the real challenge is to take one step beyond the tragedy, to continue to hope and to love: "vivre en gardant le lien et l'espoir" (p. 207).

Notes

1. Andrée Chedid, "Démarche I," *Contre-Chant* (Paris: Flammarion, 1968), p. 11.

2. Chedid, "Chantier du poème," *Cavernes et soleils* (Paris: Flammarion, 1979), p. 29.

3. "Huit questions posées à l'auteur," *A la rencontre d'Andrée Chedid . . .* (Paris: Flammarion, 1982), p. 2.

4. See Hédi A. Bouraoui, "*Le Sommeil délivré* d'Andrée Chedid, ou l'aveuglement d'une société," *L'Afrique Littéraire et Artistique,* no. 41 (1976), p. 40.

5. Chedid, *Jonathan* (Paris: Seuil, 1955), book jacket.

Bibliography

Works by Andrée Chedid

Le Sommeil délivré. Paris: Stock, 1952; Flammarion, 1976. Translated by Sharon Spencer as *From Sleep Unbound.* Athens: Ohio University Press, 1983.
Jonathan. Paris: Seuil, 1955.
Le Sixième Jour. Paris: R. Julliard, 1960; Flammarion, 1971; Livre de Poche, 1976. Translated by I. Strachey as *The Sixth Day.* London: Serpent's Tail, 1987.
Le Survivant. Paris: R. Julliard, 1963; Flammarion, 1982.
L'Autre. Paris: Flammarion, 1969.
La Cité fertile. Paris: Flammarion, 1972.
Nefertiti et le rêve d'Akhnaton. Paris: Flammarion, 1974.
Les Marches de sable. Paris: Flammarion, 1981.
La Maison sans racines. Paris: Flammarion, 1985. Translated by Ros Schwartz as *The Return to Beirut.* Saint Paul, MN: Consortium Book Sales, 1990.
L'Enfant multiple. Paris: Flammarion, 1989.
(In addition to the novels listed above, Chedid is the author of more than twenty

volumes of poetry, as well as numerous plays and short stories. For information about these works, the reader is referred to the critical works listed below.)

Selected Critical Works

Accad, Evelyne. "Entretien avec Andrée Chedid (5 août 1981)." *Présence Francophone*, no. 24 (1982): 157–74.

Bouraoui, Hédi A. "*Le Sommeil délivré* d'Andrée Chedid, ou l'aveuglement d'une société." *L'Afrique Littéraire et Artistique*, no. 41 (third trimester 1976): 36–41.

Francis, Raymond Iskandar. "A l'étude d'Andrée Chedid, romancière." *Revue de l'Occident Musulman et de la Méditerranée*, nos. 13–14 (first semester 1973): 343–56.

Hermey, Carl W., ed. "Andrée Chedid." In *Contemporary French Women Poets: A Bilingual and Critical Anthology*, pp. 2–43. 2d ed. Van Nuys, CA: Perivale Press, 1978.

Izoard, Jacques. *Andrée Chedid.* Paris: Seghers ("Poètes d'aujourd'hui"), 1977.

Khalaf, Saher. "Andrée Chedid." In *Littérature libanaise de langue française*, pp. 81–84. Sherbrooke: Naaman, 1974.

Kieffer, Rosemarie. "L'Œuvre littéraire d'Andrée Chedid." *Les Pages de la Société des Ecrivains Luxembourgeois de Langue Française*, no. 17 (1971): 97–101.

Knapp, Bettina L. "Andrée Chedid." In *French Novelists Speak Out*, pp. 57–64. Troy, NY: Whitston, 1976.

———. "Interview avec Andrée Chedid." *French Review* 57, no. 4 (March 1984): 517–23.

———. *Andrée Chedid.* Amsterdam: Rodopi, 1984.

———. "Andrée Chedid." In *French Women Writers. A Bio-Bibliographical Source Book,* edited by Eva M. Sartori and Dorothy W. Zimmerman, pp. 47–55. New York: Greenwood, 1991.

Linkhorn, Renée. "Andrée Chedid: Quête poétique d'une fraternité." *French Review* 58, no. 4 (March 1985): 559–65.

———. *The Prose and Poetry of Andrée Chedid.* Birmingham, AL: Summa, 1990.

Rose, Marilyn Gaddis. "When an Author Chooses/Uses French: Hébert and Chedid." *Quebec Studies* 3 (fall 1985): 148–59.

Trèves, Nicole. "Andrée Chedid et le geste exemplaire." *Dalhousie French Studies*, no. 13 (fall–winter 1987): 80–88.

Viatte, Auguste. "Le Corps et son dépassement dans l'œuvre d'Andrée Chedid." *Présence Francophone*, no. 18 (spring 1979): 29–39.

Viegnes, Michel. "Parole et utopie: la réécriture de l'histoire dans *Nefertiti et le rêve d'Akhnaton* d'Andrée Chedid." *Australian Journal of French Studies* 24, no. 2 (May–August 1987): 215–23.

Yacout, Ragâa. "Andrée Chedid ou la quête de l'absolu." *Lettres et Cultures de Langue Française*, no. 4 (1984): 1–15.

13

Michel Tournier

Susan Petit

Michel Tournier's novels appeal to both a popular and a literary audience. In France all five have been best-sellers and are readily available in inexpensive mass-market editions, while European and North American scholars find them intellectual, complex, and rich with meaning. Tournier's commitment to traditional fiction seems established by his having been a member of the Académie Goncourt since 1972, but a belated recognition of his postmodernism is suggested by the fact that in 1990 he was the subject of a weeklong colloquium at the Centre Culturel International de Cerisy-la-Salle (which Roger Shattuck had criticized in 1983 for ignoring Tournier in favor of the nouveaux romanciers). In fact, Tournier's fiction operates simultaneously on at least two levels: it has a realistic surface with psychologically persuasive characters, interesting plots, witty observations, and amusing and vivid descriptions, but it is also full of allusions, symbols, wordplay, thematic complexities, and even internal textual commentary, all of which help to turn the text into a pretext for new readings. The range of Tournier's talent and interest is indicated by the fact that he is not merely a novelist; he has written autobiography (*Le Vent paraclet*), commentary to accompany or introduce photographs (*Rêves; Vues de dos*), literary criticism and prefaces (*Le Vol du vampire*), short personal meditations (*Le Vagabond immobile; Petites proses*), travel commentary, children's literature, art criticism, and a one-act play, as well as short newspaper and magazine pieces on various subjects. Nevertheless, despite the interest, value, and scope of these works, it is in his novels that Tournier has exercised most fully his considerable talent.

As has been frequently pointed out, Tournier planned originally to teach philosophy at the lycée level, but when he failed the qualifying test, the agrégation, he angrily left the educational system, under what he has called the "illusion" that one can "faire œuvre philosophique seul."[1] After holding various positions connected with publishing and broadcasting, he published his first novel, *Vendredi ou les limbes du Pacifique*, in 1967 at the age of forty-two, in order to practice philosophy through writing fiction. His major technical problem has always been the creation of a realistic narrative built around not only themes but also plot structures embodying philosophical ideas. Patterning is particularly important in his fiction because of his conviction, which he has never entirely abandoned, that philosophy must produce coherent structures. Thus his novels begin with a "dessein" and a "dessin,"[2] not merely a plan but an almost visual plot structure embodying the philosophical idea or problem under consideration, and into which he must fit the details of situation, setting, character, motivation, and action.

The main device Tournier uses to link underlying intellectual structure and realistic surface is myth: his fiction is heavily indebted to well-known stories, from the legend of Saint Christopher through *The Divine Comedy* to the Incarnation. These tales have the advantage of focusing, like Tournier's fiction, on plot rather than character, while also being so familiar that readers accept the plot developments as both believable and inevitable. Also, as many of them are related to Christianity, they lend themselves to philosophical readings. Tournier thus has rejected the nouveau roman from the outset, for he wants to treat his readers to an old-fashioned, exciting story, the better to find a large audience for his philosophical concerns.

He did not entirely reach this goal in his first novel. Tournier himself has said that the philosophy in *Vendredi* is too obvious, to the detriment of more novelistic elements. Nevertheless, the book sold well, won the Grand Prix du Roman de l'Académie Française, and came out five years later in a slightly revised and augmented edition, which is still in print. In fact, it is often read in philosophy classes at the lycée level, while younger children may read a briefer version, *Vendredi ou la vie sauvage* (1971), which Tournier claims is the better of the two because it has less analysis. The story was also made into a five-hour television program and has been dramatized on stage.

On the most obvious level, *Vendredi ou les limbes du Pacifique* is a retelling of Daniel Defoe's *Robinson Crusoe,* the action moved forward one hundred years to 1759 and Robinson's sensibility and language largely attuned to the twentieth century. Unlike Defoe's Eurocentric Crusoe, who recreates English civilization on his island and teaches its ways to his slave Friday, Tournier's Robinson eventually learns from Vendredi that life on a desert island can be lived like an unending Club Med vacation, and he refuses to return to civilization when a ship, the *Whitebird,* lands at the island twenty-eight years after his shipwreck. Tournier is far from the first writer to retell the Crusoe story with a new slant, but he reimagines familiar episodes and creates new ones with wit and verve, as well as a strong sense of irony: the novel satirizes Robinson, sympathetically, for his initial insistence on turning a tropical paradise into a copy of England.

Even as Robinson is grappling with problems of physical survival, he is also engaged in philosophical questioning, primarily about ontology. In the years before Vendredi arrives, Robinson tries to figure out how he knows that he exists and that the island exists, without other people to assure him of the reality of his perceptions, and he records much of his stumbling philosophical analysis in his "logbook," which is part journal and part notebook. He finally opts for a combination of realism and idealism: so long as he is not aware of himself, he does not exist—at least not as a consciousness—but the world does exist (p. 97). However, when something makes him aware of himself, he exists but the world stops existing except in his eye, which becomes "le cadavre de la lumière, de la couleur" (p. 99). The first situation reflects philosophical realism or materialism, while the second reflects idealism.

Robinson also creates a new religion, retracing events in the Old Testament and then departing in a new direction. Some of the wittiest passages are those in which Robinson recreates, largely unconsciously, major Old Testament events, including Cain's killing Abel, Noah's building the ark, and God's leading the Hebrews through the desert to the Promised Land. Vendredi, whose ancestry is part African and part Araucanian, ultimately takes on the role of Christ, showing Robinson by example to love the world around himself without trying to label or control it, to play and enjoy his body as a child might, and to see the sun as a manifestation of God. He also symbolically kills Robinson's judgmental nature, which is represented by a ram called Andoar. The individualism of the religion Robinson develops under Vendredi's guidance is shown through the book's emphasis on the Holy Spirit, both explicitly in Robinson's religious meditations and implicitly through the final plot twist. In it, Vendredi deserts Robinson by leaving on the *Whitebird,* but the cabin boy, Jaan, jumps ship and becomes Robinson's new companion, thus corresponding to the Holy Spirit, which Christians believe came after Christ's departure to comfort believers and which is generally represented by a white bird, the dove.

In this novel, Tournier creates not only a new philosophical theory and a new religion but also a new society and a new sexuality. The copy of European society Robinson creates to occupy his mental and physical energies, complete with a farcically bureaucratic and legalistic government, capitalistic overtones, and slavery reinforced by racism, is first undermined by Robinson's boredom and Vendredi's common sense, then literally blown up by Vendredi's negligence. After Robinson's version of civilization has thus been destroyed, the two men replace the oppressive system with private rituals, friendship, and equality. Robinson has also remade his socially shaped heterosexual self in response to his solitary existence, so that by the time Vendredi arrives, his sexual desires are no longer directed at women but at the island itself. He ultimately replaces genital orgasm with a voluptuousness involving his entire body and deriving from a mystical relationship with the sun in which he feels he plays a female role, or rather, in which he feels gender roles no longer matter (pp. 229–30). *Vendredi ou les limbes du Pacifique,* in short, is an ambitious book presenting not only a new philosophical theory but a new vision of how people can live, at least when they are separated from society.

In Tournier's next novel, *Le Roi des aulnes* (1970), set in France and Germany before and during World War II, the protagonist, Abel Tiffauges, must cope with various repressive societies, from the Collège Saint Christophe he remembers attending as a boy, to Nazi Germany. Tiffauges resembles Robinson by being isolated—in his case, because he is a loner rather than because he is alone—as well as by relentlessly analyzing himself and events and by recording his ruminations in a journal. In these "écrits sinistres" (so named by Tiffauges because he is writing with his left, or sinister, hand, but sinister as well in their content), Tiffauges discusses daily events and current politics, reminisces about his unhappy childhood, and analyzes his world. The analyses are often hilarious, for Tiffauges records his bizarre theorizing with myopic seriousness, as when events lead him to conclude that "la petite fille n'existe pas" (p. 204), "*l'âme humaine est en papier*" (p. 66), and a christening is a "mariage . . . entre un adulte et un enfant" (p. 174). Tiffauges's "écrits sinistres" are more successful than Robinson's "logbook" at integrating analysis into the fiction, for Tiffauges's reasoning derives from his conviction, dramatized throughout the book, that everything around him is a sign that will reveal his momentous, though temporarily hidden, destiny.

The central philosophical issue in *Le Roi des aulnes* is ethics, for Tiffauges becomes a Nazi collaborator when he is a prisoner of war in East Prussia, then rejects that collaboration at the last moment. His experience partly represents that of Germany, for Tiffauges's belief that he has a destiny encoded in nearly everything around him parallels the Nazi belief in a German destiny to rule "inferior" peoples. Tiffauges is not a Nazi and does not take Nazi ideology seriously, but he is so wrapped up in himself that he never wonders how his actions affect other people until it is almost too late, and he is so solipsistic that he believes that World War II has broken out to punish society for believing a false charge of rape against him. Tiffauges is childish, but the same could be said about many of the Nazis, and certainly about Goering, at least as he is portrayed at some length in this novel, with his "face poupine" (p. 324), his mania for reading the "laissées" of animals he is hunting (p. 332), his pet lion, with which he shares huge bites from the thigh of a wild boar (p. 322), and his habit of calming down by running his hands through a huge onyx bowl full of gemstones (p. 345). The ethical implication of the childishness of the Nazis in the book is that only immature people could be attracted to Nazism, an idea Tournier expands on in *Le Vent paraclet*, his literary autobiography, by arguing that Nazi propaganda was particularly aimed at the young (pp. 105–6).

Tiffauges is immature sexually as well as emotionally: though he is just barely capable of heterosexual relations, his strongest impulses center on boys, whom he wants to photograph, tape record, and above all, carry on his shoulders, an act he calls *la phorie*. This sexuality, though strange, is largely inoffensive to others until he rises to power near the war's end in an elite German boys' military school, when he not only recruits but kidnaps children from the surrounding countryside in order to surround himself with boys. Tiffauges does not molest the boys, nor does he want to, but he ignores the fact that forcing them into the military school endangers their lives because they will be required to go to war. Only when he discovers and saves the life of Ephraïm, a Jewish boy who tells Tiffauges details of life in Auschwitz paralleling situations in the school, does Tiffauges realize that he has acted like a Nazi. The uniqueness of Tiffauges's sexual desires has added to his isolation, but his sexuality ultimately helps to break that isolation, for his love for Ephraïm forces him to risk and even lose his life trying to carry the boy to safety when the Russian army attacks the school.

Despite the great detail about Germany and World War II, the book's plot is based not only on history but also on myth. Tiffauges calls himself an ogre, a "monstre féerique, émergeant de la nuit des temps" (p. 13), and he is identified with the ogre-figure of Goethe's poem "Der Erlkönig," called in French "Le Roi des aulnes," who is presented in the novel as a German anti-Christ (p. 294). A more important identification, though, is with the giant Saint Christopher (whose name means Christ-carrier), for the hulking Tiffauges relives the saint's life by serving first the devil, then Christ (first helping the Nazis, then saving Ephraïm), and he carries Ephraïm at the novel's end into the swamps of Mazuria as Christopher is supposed to have carried the Christ child across a river (pp. 71–72). The implication is that, in dying while trying to save the boy, Tiffauges is redeeming himself as Saint Christopher did.

Another structuring device is modeled on Johann Sebastian Bach's last fugues. In fact, just as Bach's final fugues in *The Art of the Fugue* are based on the German notes represented by the letters B-A-C-H, the main episodes in this novel can be represented by the letters of Tournier's name.[3] As in a fugue, key themes recur in this novel in various forms, these themes including carrying, ogritude, impalement, and excrement. As the list indicates, many are connected with the less commonly discussed sides of sexuality. The novel's cool intellectual treatment of highly charged erotic themes gives it great power (which may be one reason that it won the Prix Goncourt, has been translated into at least fifteen languages, was dramatized on stage, and is sometimes taught in lycée philosophy classes). However, the book's politics became an issue as some found it pro-Nazi, even though the entire novel adds up to a condemnation of Nazism. These readers may have been misled by the book's refusal to oversimplify issues (for example, to treat all Germans as evil); instead, it shows both the danger and the appeal of Nazism, which Tournier had seen firsthand on vacations in Germany when he was a child.

His less successful *Les Météores* (1975), which focuses on two generations of a French family from 1937 to 1961, deals with mystical union with God as well as various kinds of unions—mostly sexual—between people. Partly because of its subject matter and partly because of its great length, it has offended and confused more readers than have any of Tournier's other works. Although none of its discussions of sex could be called explicit in the usual sense, the flamboyantly gay Alexandre Surin does meditate at some length on sexuality, his friend Thomas argues that homosexuals are superior in virtually every way to heterosexuals, and Alexandre's twin nephews, Jean and Paul, are characterized in part by their practice of mutual, simultaneous fellatio. Tournier has plausibly claimed that what some readers objected to is not that there are homosexuals in the novel—their presence would hardly be unusual in contemporary fiction—but that Alexandre "fait exister les hétérosexuels! Il parle d'eux sans cesse. . . . Horreur!"[4] In other words, the book questions heterosexuality, rather than accepting it as the norm. Also, both because of Alexandre's sexual proclivities and because of his profession—he manages a company that oversees six municipal garbage dumps—Alexandre's thoughts turn frequently to excrement and other waste matter, and the scatological sections, which are among the cleverest in the book, have been offensive to some.

The book's other stumbling block, its great length, has two causes. First, as Tournier has said, he was "débordé" by Alexandre, so that there is a "déséquilibre" in the character's favor.[5] Alexandre is simply too clever, too energetic, and too interesting to remain in the background, and he seems to run away with parts of the book, which may be longer than objectively necessary. Second, the novel's structures are so complex that it would have been nearly impossible to develop them briefly. Tournier's original plan for the book, he has said, was to unite the meteorological wind to the wind of the Holy Spirit, partly through the theology of Joachim de Fiore.[6] Although he says that this plan did not entirely work out, the novel does have a tripartite division reflecting Joachim's theory of Three Ages, corresponding to the Gospels (Jesus), the Old Testament (God the Father), and the Epistles (the Holy Spirit). The characters relating to these sections are, respectively, Alexandre, his brother Edouard Surin, and Edouard's twin sons, Jean and Paul. At the same time, the book can also be read as a version of *The Divine Comedy*, with Alexandre's chapters corresponding to the Inferno, Edouard's to

Purgatory, and the twins' to Paradise. The problem with this plan, besides its complexity, is that it helps make Alexandre's chapters by far the most interesting part, much as readers prefer the Inferno to the rest of *The Divine Comedy* or the Gospels to the rest of the Bible. So when Alexandre dies two-thirds of the way into the novel, the remainder, concerning the twins, is doomed to anticlimax.

These two structures—the Three Ages of Joachim and *The Divine Comedy*—suggest that the central theme of the novel is salvation. That is so, but the characters generally pursue not a religious but a personal salvation through union with others.[7] There are heterosexual couples, married and unmarried; there are homosexual couples, short term and long term, male and female; and there is the central couple, the twins, who see themselves as the ideal pair, the "frères-pareils," at least until Jean begins to feel suffocated in their symmetrical and seemingly unchanging relationship and flees from Paul. The themes of religious salvation and personal fulfillment join first in the priest Thomas, who has learned to turn his sexual desire for Jesus, whom he imagined as his twin, into love for mankind, so that his "didymie est devenue universelle" (p. 160). Later, the themes are more strongly joined in Paul after he has been definitively separated from his twin and has much of his left side, which represents Jean, amputated. At the novel's end, Paul has visions reminiscent of Dante's at the end of the Paradise, and the language Paul uses to describe his visionary union with Jean suggests that this union resembles union with God: separated from his twin, with whom he shares not only a secret language but also, he thinks, a single soul, he has become "doué d'ubiquité" (p. 623).

Vendredi ou les limbes du Pacifique, Le Roi des aulnes, and *Les Météores* form a kind of trilogy, in part because each shows how someone's fate, a "mécanisme obscur et coercitif," can become an eagerly embraced destiny, "l'élan unanime et chaleureux d'un être vers son accomplissement."[8] Thus the fates of Robinson, Tiffauges, Alexandre, and Paul are set by the structures of the novels, so that Tiffauges is "doomed" to act like Saint Christopher, or Paul is "fated" to live out the archetypal twin story with its inevitable separation. This mechanically set, coercive fate, however, is also eagerly chosen or accepted by each man as well, as shown by Robinson's refusal to leave his island and Alexandre's choosing almost certain death at the docks of Casablanca in pursuit of an Arab boy, his death necessitated by the novel's structure but also deriving from his despair at realizing that he will never find a lover who can perfectly satisfy his narcissism. Thus the characters' psychology is believable, even when one sees the patterns that drive the plots.

In each of these three books, too, the divine has been linked, often in surprising ways, to the quotidian, and even to the sexual and the scatological. Nevertheless, the novels are not "romans à thèse." Readers can regard ironically the protagonists' religious theories, seeing Paul's mystical vision merely as "sublimation" (that is the novel's last word), or they can view them as providing keys to a new kind of Christianity focused on the Holy Spirit. Similarly, one can view the characters' unusual sexualities as evidence of mental instability, or one can believe that these men have found new sexual paths leading to great individual fulfillment. Finally, these three novels are written in a richly allusive, clever, ironic, and entertaining style, which offers layers of meaning for successive readings and which is equally suited to expressing complex theories, narrating realistic events, or providing the large amounts of exposition called for by the works' philosophical underpinnings.

Given the underlying similarities of these three texts, many readers were surprised at Tournier's next novel, *Gaspard, Melchior et Balthazar* (1980), which marked a new direction in his style. This work recounts, often in the manner of a parable or tale, the story of the Wise Men, complete with miracles, from the birth of Christ to the ascent to heaven of one of the Magi. Each of the various miracles has a whimsical side— notably the black king Gaspard's discovery that Jesus is "un bébé tout noir aux cheveux crépus" (p. 220) and the ass's account of the Nativity, at which the busy archangel Gabriel "joue les majordomes" (p. 167)— but the humor does not undermine the seriousness of the ideas. This humor is the sort Tournier calls "l'humour blanc," or "le rire de Dieu," which is caused by the sudden appearance of the absolute in ordinary life.[9] This is the same humor that marks all his works, but this novel insists on the reality of God, at least within the work, so that the book cannot be read as ironic about God, although it is ironic about other things.

The tone of *Gaspard, Melchior et Balthazar*, however, is often jovial, and the book, for all its richly colored passages, which are reminiscent of Flaubert's *Salammbô* and "Hérodias," is less than half the length of *Les Météores*. Is this "slimming down," as Tournier has called it,[10] an improvement, or has Tournier in fact "melted and grown thin,"[11] his works losing their savor as they become shorter, clearer, and less aggressive? It is true that his fiction since *Les Météores* is less inhabited with manic energy; the "mythomanes" who dominated those works and gave them their obsessional power do not appear in the later novels or in the short fiction (*Le Coq de bruyère* and *Le Médianoche amoureux*) with the exception of Martin, the eponymous protagonist of the one-act play *Le Fétichiste*. On the other hand, *Gaspard, Melchior et Balthazar*, like the later novel *La Goutte d'or*, resembles the earlier novels in its biting criticism of society, wicked satire, and rich allusions.

The philosophical issue in *Gaspard, Melchior et Balthazar* is theological: finding salvation through imitating Christ. King Gaspard of Méroé, who has hated his blackness since seeing it through the eyes of Biltine, a white slave, accepts his skin color when he sees that the baby Jesus is African, Christ's blackness being a "surprise miraculeuse que la Sainte Famille avait évidemment préparée" for Gaspard (p. 219). He also realizes that he was wrong to pursue Biltine; he wanted divine, not earthly, love. King Balthazar of Nippur, who has been grieving over God's interdiction of graven images, believes that the Incarnation provides man with permission to represent the human figure in art, and so he will now become a patron of "l'art chrétien" (p. 214). The young Prince Melchior of Palmyrène will give up his attempt to inherit his father's throne and will found a religious community because he has learned "la douceur irrésistible des non-violents" (p. 217). Each has found at Bethlehem a solution that involves, to some small extent, acting like God: giving unconditional love, celebrating the human form, and trying to establish God's kingdom on earth.

Besides the stories of the three Magi, which each king narrates separately, the novel includes Herod's story, which he tells at a banquet he gives for the Wise Men; the tale of Barbedor, which is a parable of the birth of Christ, also told at Herod's banquet; and the story of the Nativity, narrated briefly from the ox's viewpoint, then chattily by the ass. Finally, the last third of the text tells the story of a fourth, forgotten Magus—Taor, prince of Mangalore—whose journey recapitulates those of the other Wise Men but also offers a contrast to them. His story begins in a much lighter vein than theirs but takes him through greater suffering, for he is an archetypal hero moving from innocence to experience, from youth to age, and from life through death into a higher kind of life. Though he sets out from India merely to find a recipe for candy (pistachio Turkish delight), Taor discovers that his derisory quest is also a search for ultimate meaning, and the thirty years he is condemned to spend working in the salt mines of Sodom make his life a true imitation of Christ, not least because he has given up his freedom to save a bankrupt family—that is, to redeem others.

Gaspard, Melchior et Balthazar seems at first more different from Tournier's preceding work than is actually the case. Although it could almost be considered a collection of tales rather than a novel, each of Tournier's previous novels was also built around intertwined and interspersed episodes. Here, the various parts are simply more clearly separated. Sexual themes do not figure as prominently in this work as in the previous ones, but they are present, primarily in the relationship between Gaspard and Biltine and in Taor's observation of the customs of the inhabitants of Sodom, whose city is a sort of hell. Finally, as in his earlier novels, Tournier weaves patterns throughout: the Magi's concern with love, art, and power is echoed in Herod's story, while Taor's interest in food begins as a comic variation on the other themes but attains great force through the book's insistence on Jesus' miracles concerning food, his preaching using food metaphors, and the Last Supper. The primary difference between this novel and the earlier ones is that, for all its wit, it does not allow readers to distance themselves ironically from the characters' religious experiences, because the birth of Christ and Taor's miraculous ascent to heaven are presented as facts. The book loses something in complexity because it presents the Incarnation as true, but it gains in warmth and clarity.

La Goutte d'or (1985), which tells the story of a Muslim Berber named Idriss who becomes an immigrant worker in France, greatly resembles *Gaspard, Melchior et Balthazar* in tone, and Idriss himself is like Taor in various ways. Both are naive, innocent, spontaneous, and disinclined to reflection until near the very end, quite unlike the obsessive, analytical, journal-keeping protagonists of Tournier's first three novels. Idriss also resembles Taor in setting out on a journey for what appears to be a trivial reason—to get back a photograph a blond Frenchwoman has taken of him—and he too goes through a kind of descent into Hell before finding a way out. Finally, King Balthazar's concern with representational art in *Gaspard, Melchior et Balthazar* prefigures this novel's exploration of the relationship between pictorial and written representation, a subject that especially concerns Tournier because he is a technically accomplished photographer and a friend of great photographers. Interestingly, the book itself was first conceived as a television screenplay,[12] and it has since been filmed. Indeed, its comparative lack of analytical passages makes it very visually oriented.

The novel often poses its central philosophical issue in terms of the difference between images and signs, but it is actually a question of interpreting cultural icons and defining the function of art. In Algeria, growing up in the oasis of Tabelbala, Idriss learned to interpret the abstract signs used by the Berbers, such as face painting, but he has not learned to decode representational signs—manmade images—because his culture condemns them. Therefore, Idriss constantly mistakes French visual representations for reality, from the bleached-blond hair of the woman who photographs him at the book's start, through travel posters, comic books, and peep-shows. Not only does he misread what he sees, but in both Algeria and France he constantly is faced with images of himself that he does not recognize, from a laughing donkey to Saint-Exupéry's Little Prince. As he says of the way the French talk to him about himself and Africa, "Je n'y comprends rien, et pourtant ce désert, c'est bien là que je suis né" (p. 142).

The novel thus illustrates Sartre's theory that images do not emanate from the observed object but are produced by the observing subject. When the subject is misinformed or unobservant, the result is a *décalage* between image and reality, whether Idriss is misinterpreting French culture, or whether a photographer, film director, or artist is misinterpreting Idriss. The novel also considers the power of artistic images to mislead viewers. The potentially negative effects of any work of art that is too narrowly representational, and which thus seems too real, are explored by two tales inserted into the narrative—"Barberousse ou le portrait du roi" and "La Reine blonde"—each of which contrasts literally representational portraits with more symbolic ones. Idriss is able to understand the need for interpretation only by studying Arabic calligraphy, which, like all writing, uses abstract symbols so that one must create one's own images. After learning calligraphy, Idriss has the mental tools needed to interpret the cheap, ready-made images with which a tawdry, gaudy Paris surrounds him. That is why, for him at least, "la calligraphie est libération" (p. 201).

Thematic patterns help unify the novel despite its episodic structure. Idriss continually encounters photographers and bleached-blond women, while he is directed toward the power of the word partly through the singers Renaud, Oum Kalsoum, and the presumably fictional Zett Zobeida. Another pattern involves the abstract symbol named in the title, a small drop of gold that Idriss finds and that is "l'émanation d'un monde sans image" (p. 31) and the sign that he is "un enfant libre" (p. 103). He loses it to a bleached-blond prostitute almost as soon as he enters France, recovers it in ironic form when he learns that he is living in the "Goutte d'or" district of Paris, and finds it again at the end of the book in a goldsmith's window in the Place Vendôme. Trying to master a pneumatic hammer, Idriss inadvertently makes the display window crack, as if his new power will return to him his innocence, coupled with strength. This ending, however, is ambiguous, for the cracking of the vitrine summons the police, who may be about to arrest Idriss as the novel ends. Like Idriss learning to decode images, the reader must now find or create an interpretation of these events.

It is clear that Tournier's concerns, though evolving, have always been focused on how to live in the world, how to reconcile the body and the soul, how to seek transcendent relationships, and how to resist pressures to give up one's individuality. His protagonists are all lone seekers after truth or happiness. Each undertakes a journey, usually a physical one, and each—Robinson, Tiffauges, Paul, Taor, and Idriss—grows from immaturity to some degree of maturity. The novels employ traditional techniques, but their perspective is always postmodern, as they blur the line between documented fact and surreal fantasy, between whimsy and horror, and between seriousness and irony. And although the later works do not have the exuberant energy of the first three novels, they have a more delicate touch and greater restraint, and Tournier's style becomes more witty and flexible. The fiction of Michel Tournier embodies the paradox of great literature: it is pleasurably accessible on the first reading, and the pleasure only increases and deepens with later readings.

Notes

1. Michel Tournier, *Le Vent paraclet* (Paris: Gallimard-Folio, 1980), p. 163. All citations from Tournier are to Folio editions where they exist.

2. Ibid., p. 187.

3. Susan Petit, *Michel Tournier's Metaphysical Fictions* (Amsterdam: John Benjamins, 1991), p. 35.

4. *Le Vent paraclet*, p. 264.

5. Ibid., p. 258.

6. Ibid., p. 261.

7. See Petit, "Varieties of Sexuality in Michel Tournier's *Les Météores*," *literature and psychology* 37, nos. 1–2 (1991), pp. 43–61.

8. *Le Vent paraclet*, p. 242.

9. Ibid., pp. 198–99.

10. Petit, *Michel Tournier*, p. 192.

11. Alain Buisine, "A Dispossessed Text: The Writings and Photography of Michel Tournier," *SubStance*, no. 58 (1989), p. 26.

12. Petit, *Michel Tournier*, p. 176.

Bibliography

Works by Michel Tournier

Le Roi des aulnes. Paris: Gallimard, 1970; Gallimard-Folio, 1980. Translated by Barbara Bray as *The Ogre*. Garden City, NY: Doubleday, 1972.

Vendredi ou la vie sauvage. Illus. Georges Lemoine. Paris: Flammarion, 1971. Translated by Ralph Manheim as *Friday and Robinson: Life on Speranza Island*. New York: Knopf, 1972.

Vendredi ou les limbes du Pacifique. Revised and expanded edition. Paris: Gallimard, 1972; Gallimard-Folio, 1980. Translated by Norman Denny as *Friday*. Garden City, NY: Doubleday, 1969.

Les Météores. Paris: Gallimard, 1975; Gallimard-Folio, 1981. Translated by Anne Carter as *Gemini*. Garden City, NY: Doubleday, 1981.

Le Vent paraclet. Paris: Gallimard, 1977; Gallimard Folio, 1980. Translated by Arthur Goldhammer as *The Wind Spirit*. Boston: Beacon Press, 1988.

Le Coq de bruyère. Paris: Gallimard, 1978; Gallimard-Folio, 1982. Translated by Barbara Wright as *The Fetishist*. Garden City, NY: Doubleday, 1984.

Pierrot ou les secrets de la nuit. Illus. Danièle Bour. Paris: Enfantimages/Gallimard, 1979.

Rêves. Photographs by Arthur Tress. Brussels: Complexe, 1979.

Gaspard, Melchior et Balthazar. Paris: Gallimard, 1980; Gallimard-Folio, 1982. Translated by Ralph Manheim as *The Four Wise Men*. Garden City, NY: Doubleday, 1982.

Vues de dos. Photographs by Edouard Boubat. Paris: Gallimard, 1981.

Le Vol du vampire: Notes de lecture. Paris: Mercure de France, 1982.

Gilles et Jeanne. Paris: Gallimard, 1983. Translated by Alan Sheridan as *Gilles and Jeanne*. London: Methuen, 1989.

Les Rois mages. Illus. Michel Charrier. Paris: Gallimard, 1983.

Journal de voyage au Canada. Paris: Laffont, 1984.

Sept contes. Illus. Pierre Hézard. Paris: Gallimard (Folio Junior), 1984.
Le Vagabond immobile. Illus. Jean-Max Toubeau. Paris: Gallimard, 1984.
La Goutte d'or. Paris: Gallimard, 1985; Gallimard-Folio, 1987. Translated by Barbara Wright as *The Golden Droplet.* Garden City, NY: Doubleday, 1987.
Petites proses. Paris: Gallimard (Folio), 1986.
Angus. Illus. Pierre Joubert. N.p.: Signe de Piste, 1988.
Le Tabor et le Sinaï: Essais sur l'art contemporain. Paris: Belfond, 1988.
Le Médianoche amoureux: Contes et nouvelles. Paris: Gallimard, 1989. Translated by Barbara Wright as *The Midnight Love Feast.* London: Collins, 1991.
Le Crépuscule des masques. Paris: Hoëbeke, 1992.
Le Miroir des idées. Paris: Mercure de France, 1994.
Le Pied de la lettre: Trois cents mots propres. Paris: Mercure de France, 1994.

Selected Critical Works

Baroche, Christiane, et al., eds. *Michel Tournier.* Special issue of *Sud* (1980).
————, et al., eds. *Michel Tournier. Sud,* no. 61 (1986): 1–194.
Bevan, D. G. *Michel Tournier.* Amsterdam: Rodopi, 1986.
Bouloumié, Arlette. *Michel Tournier: Le roman mythologique.* Paris: Corti, 1988.
————. "Rencontre avec Michel Tournier." *Europe,* nos. 722–723 (June–July 1989): 147–57.
Buisine, Alain. "A Dispossessed Text: The Writings and Photography of Michel Tournier." *SubStance,* no. 58 (1989): 25–34.
Cloonan, William. "The Spiritual Order of Michel Tournier." *Renascence,* no. 36 (1983–84): 77–86.
————. *Michel Tournier.* Boston: Twayne, 1985.
Davis, Colin. *Michel Tournier: Philosophy and Fiction.* Oxford: Clarendon, 1988.
Deleuze, Gilles. "Michel Tournier et le monde sans autrui." Postface to *Vendredi ou les limbes du Pacifique.* Paris: Gallimard (Folio), 1980: 257–83.
Edwards, Rachel. "Myth, Allegory and Michel Tournier." *Journal of European Studies* 19, no. 2 [no. 74] (June 1989): 99–121.
Fauskevåg, Svein Eirik. *Allégorie et tradition: Etude sur la technique allégorique et la structure mythique dans "Le Roi des aulnes" de Michel Tournier.* Oslo: Solum, 1993.
Gascoigne, David. "Michel Tournier." In *Beyond the Nouveau Roman: Essays on the Contemporary French Novel,* edited by Michael Tilby, pp. 64–99. New York: Berg, 1990.
Hueston, Penny. "An Interview with Michel Tournier." *Meanjin,* no. 38 (1979): 400–405.
Hutton, Margaret-Ann. *"Vendredi ou les limbes du Pacifique."* Glasgow Introductory Guides to French Literature, no. 15. Glasgow: University of Glasgow Press, 1992.

Images et signes de Michel Tournier. Actes du Colloque du Centre Culturel International de Cerisy-la-Salle. Paris: Gallimard, 1991.

Korthals Altes, Liesbeth. *Le Salut par la fiction? Sens, valeurs et narrativité dans "Le Roi des aulnes" de Michel Tournier.* Faux Titre: Etudes de Langue et Littérature Françaises, no. 64. Amsterdam: Rodopi, 1992.

———, ed. *Michel Tournier. Revue des Sciences Humaines,* no. 232 (1993–94).

Koster, Serge. *Michel Tournier.* Paris: Veyrier, 1986.

Krell, Jonathan. *Tournier élémentaire.* Purdue Studies in Romance Literatures. West Lafayette, Ind.: Purdue University Press, 1994.

Ladimer, Bethany. "Overcoming Original Difference: Sexuality in the Work of Michel Tournier." *Modern Language Studies* 21, no. 2 (spring 1991): 76–91.

L'Œil de Bœuf rencontre Michel Tournier. L'Œil de Bœuf, no. 3 (February 1994).

Merllié, Françoise. *Michel Tournier.* Paris: Belfond, 1988.

Petit, Susan. *Michel Tournier's Metaphysical Fictions.* Amsterdam: John Benjamins (Purdue University Monographs in Romance Language 37), 1991.

———. *"Sexualité Alimentaire et Elémentaire:* Michel Tournier's Answer to Freud." In *Diet and Discourse: Eating, Drinking and Literature,* edited and with an introduction by Evelyn J. Hinz, 163–77. Winnipeg: Mosaic, 1991.

———. "Varieties of Sexuality in Michel Tournier's *Les Météores." literature and psychology* 37, nos. 1–2 (1991): 43–61.

Purdy, Anthony. *"Les Météores* de Michel Tournier: Une perspective hétérologique." *Littérature* (December 1980): 32–43.

Redfern, W. D. "Approximating Man: Michel Tournier and Play in Language." *Modern Language Review* 80, no. 2 (April 1985): 304–19.

Rosello, Mireille. *L'In-différence chez Michel Tournier.* Paris: Corti, 1990.

Sbiroli, Lynn Salkin. *Michel Tournier: La Séduction du jeu.* Geneva: Slatkine, 1987.

Shattuck, Roger. "Why Not the Best?" *New York Times Review of Books* (April 28, 1983): 8, 10–15. Reprinted as "Locating Michel Tournier." In *The Innocent Eye: On Modern Literature and the Arts,* pp. 205–18. New York: Farrar, 1984.

Worton, Michael. *"La Goutte d'or."* Glasgow Introductory Guides to French Literature, no. 14. Glasgow: University of Glasgow Press, 1992.

York, R. A. "Thematic Construction in *Le Roi des aulnes." Orbis Litterarum,* 36, no. 1 (1981): 76–91.

14

Patrick Modiano

Katheryn Wright

Est-ce ma faute si je reste
prisonnier de mes souvenirs?
(*Les Boulevards de ceinture*, p. 180)

Jean Patrick Modiano was born in Boulogne-Billancourt on July 30, 1945. His Jewish father, whose name and background have been a carefully kept secret, was apparently an entrepreneur of sorts. His mother, Luisa Colpeyn, was a film actress of Flemish origin. They met and married during the Nazi occupation of France, and Patrick was born a few months after the Liberation. Modiano spent his youth in Paris, residing in an apartment overlooking the Seine on the quai Conti. His younger brother, Rudy, died in childhood, and his death affected Patrick very deeply. His father did not seem to be present much during Modiano's childhood; it would seem that he and Patrick's mother separated during the boy's youth.

Modiano had one year of university training, in 1966, but did not continue as planned. Married in the early 1970s, he now resides in Paris with his wife and children and lives off the income from his writings. Modiano is a private person who seems to relish the unfixed and mysterious identity that has been created around him as a literary figure. His novels reflect his life, at times with remarkable parallels. In some respects, his public persona resembles his heroes' circuitous lives, lives on which one can only speculate because of the secrecy surrounding them or the scarcity of available, reliable information about their pasts. Like his narrators, we are forced to take the role of private detective in order to uncover enough information to give him a documented identity. Failing that, one is tempted, again, to follow the lead of his narrators, filling in with imagination where documentation does not exist.

In 1967, at the age of twenty-one, Patrick Modiano had his first novel, *La Place de l'étoile,* accepted for publication by Gallimard. Because the Israeli-Arab war of 1967 was in full swing at the time the novel was accepted, publication was put on hold because of the anti-Semitism (although largely ironic) expressed in the novel. For this work, he won the Prix Roger Nimier and the Prix Fénéon in 1968. To date, he has published sixteen other novels and several uncollected short stories and wrote the script for Louis Malle's film *Lacombe Lucien.* His sixth novel, *Rue des boutiques obscures* earned him the Prix Goncourt in 1978. Modiano's novels are voyages into the past by first-person narrators who sift through memories in search of a personal and collective identity. The space in which they move is characterized by instability, chance encounters, and compromise. It is a fragile, dysfunctional world in which the past is superimposed on the present and where the memory that retains that past is as fragmented as the world it portrays.

Modiano made his first mark on French literature with the creation and use of memory that predates his heroes' birth. This memory is inspired almost exclusively by the atmosphere, people, and events associated with the Nazi occupation of France and is confined largely to Modiano's first three Jewish hero-narrators: Raphaël Schlemilovitch (*La Place de l'étoile*), Swing Troubadour alias La Princesse de Lamballe (*La Ronde de nuit*) and Serge Alexandre (*Les Boulevards de ceinture*). These three novels, often referred to as Modiano's trilogy, are set in a fictionalized recreation of Nazi-occupied France amid gangsters, black marketeers, prostitutes, French "Gestapistes," and collaborators. The heroes become involved in this murky, inverted underworld in a quest for the father and a viable identity. The narratives portray indecisive beings who suffer from the paradoxical situation of being Jewish adolescents and not knowing precisely what a Jew is. As they ultimately discover, the Jew is a kaleidoscope of stereotypes impossible to assume: traitor and martyr, Semite, anti-Semite, and assimilated Jew, persecutor and persecuted. The ironic undercurrents of these first novels not only exemplify the ambiguities of the Jew's relationship to self and other but illustrate a certain degeneracy in the contemporary society that these novels depict.

While the setting of the Occupation is limited to the trilogy novels, anecdotes and allusions to this period are a consistent feature in Modiano's work as a whole. For not only is the Modianesque atmosphere distinctive in its undercurrent of decomposition but the characters that people the heroes' pasts are frequently curious, sometimes eccentric sorts whose own lives are marred by some unlawful or unethical phenomenon, or whose present existence is marked by what they can never be again. Everyone, it would seem, has a secret to keep. There is the invariably mysterious entrepreneur, the middle-aged celebrity on the decline, the crippled or alcoholic jockey, the person who will eventually commit suicide, the former collaborator, the loner, the person without precise national identity ("l'apatride"), or simply the adolescent adrift in a world of indifference and moral ambiguity. They are the marginals of society, the people whom the hero encounters in his adolescence and to whom the narrator returns in his investigation of the past. It is this murkiness, anonymity, decomposition, mystery, and sense of ruin that informs the Modianesque atmosphere and hangs as an ominous cloud over the narrator whose life has been shaped by it.

Existing in a state of limbo, and bathed in an atmosphere of mystery and half-light, the characters of Modiano's novels issue forth as vague figures of chance, products of the vicissitudes of time, place, and haphazard encounters. The continuum of contrasts typifying the Modianesque landscape projects the contours of their lives, their disquietude, and the phantoms of their past. Passages of minute detail combine with or are juxtaposed to those describing the vaguest of memories: poorly lit streets, hallways, and restaurants and the blinding neon of all-night cafés parallel the faded wallpaper of obscure hotel rooms and the sumptuous decor of velveted apartments and villas long past their prime. Within these walls memories are retrieved; on these streets the hero-narrator searches for clues to his identity. His memories of the past depict him and his acquaintances as a transient community of men, women, and adolescents without social reason, who have lost all ties to their former roots, except in documents and memory. Many are, as Patrick states: "hommes de nulle part" who differ from other marginals in that they often lack what everyone else seems to come by naturally: "un acte de naissance . . . une fiche d'état civil" (*Livret de famille*, p. 130).

Anationalism, a dominant thematic force in Modiano's first six works, is inherently linked to the absence of the father. Indeed, the treatment of the father is of fundamental importance to Modiano's work in general, for the father is closely tied to the quest for identity, roots, civil status, and to the hero's malaise. Rather than a model of stability and protection, the father is presented as a shadowy figure of hollowness, transience, and weakness. The retrospective surveys that compose the narratives often depict individuals who retain vivid memories of fleeting encounters with their fathers, children who were relegated to the position of people-as-objects and who were generally condemned to living in the shadows of indifference. As adolescents, they are neglected, discarded in local or foreign boarding schools, or comparably assigned to someone else's care. They are children who are seen confronting a family life devoid of symbols upon which to model their identity. In *Les Boulevards de ceinture,* where the theme of the father figure is most pervasive, the father is representative of a world of dissolved values whose paucity of ideals is but a veil for expressing the author's views on contemporary society. In part because of this lack of role models Modiano's heroes fall prey to unscrupulous entrepreneurs, languishing eccentrics, and, in the trilogy, to assassins and gangsters. As Serge Alexandre says in *Les Boulevards de ceinture:* "J'aurais préféré que ma vie commençât sous un éclairage plus net. Mais que peut un adolescent livré à lui-même dans Paris? Que peut cet infortuné?" (p. 97).

Modiano's œuvre finds its substance, structure, and style in memory. From *La Place de l'étoile* to *Chien de printemps,* whether prenatal or elicited from the narrator's real or partially invented experience, the Modianesque Muse resides in the past. She becomes visible in the present through the relics that remain of the past in objects, people, places, and atmospheres. Yet the voice of memory that gives life to these elements is often broken, evasive, muted, or inaudible. Although many parallels can be drawn between the workings of postnatal and prenatal memory, the analysis that follows focuses on the use of memory in the posttrilogy novels since they best demonstrate the manner in which "real" memory is elicited in Modiano's œuvre generally, and this memory's importance as a creative literary force.

While prenatal memory situates hero-narrators in a Nazi-occupied France, "real" memory focuses largely on their adolescence in the 1960s. It differs from prenatal memory in that a certain nostalgia is involved, ostensibly generated by phenomena in the present. Whereas Raphaël's narrative in *La Place de l'étoile,* for example, is governed by a bewildering time composite encompassing fragments of the entire history of Jewish exile and persecution, culminating but not ending in the Holocaust, postnatal narratives do not rely on such distinctive telescopic transformations. There is practically no explosion of time and space and the mixing or comparing of past and present is usually supported by visible transition, context or figures of speech. Thus in prenatal memory the past *is* the present. By contrast, in postnatal memory narrators generally recognize the difference (or sameness) between the past, distant past, and present, and between external and subjective reality.

The motivations of the posttrilogy narrators revolve not around their identity as Jews but their identity in a postmodern world. What haunts the more mature narrator's creative mind is not simply the mysteries of his own anationalism and estrangement, but the things, people, and places that have disappeared during his lifetime. Perhaps most important, he is affected by the emptiness these disappearances have caused: "J'ai éprouvé une impression de vide qui m'était familière depuis mon enfance, depuis que j'avais compris que les gens et les choses vous quittent ou disparaissent un jour" (*Livret de famille,* p. 158). Whether such disappearance is due to transiency, modified identities, changing habits, hiding from the law, or death is most often left suggested but unclear. Ultimately, the narrator's curiosity in regard to what constitutes "le cours d'une vie" is also founded on a need to clarify the mysteries of the past and uncover the links that may exist between past and present: "Et si le passé et le présent se mêlaient? Pourquoi n'y aurait-il pas, à travers les péripéties en apparence les plus diverses d'une vie, une unité secrète, un parfum dominant?" (*Quartier perdu,* p. 86).

One of the means by which narrators attempt to uncover this "parfum dominant" is through writing. Indeed, the majority of Modiano's narrators are also (often unstated) writers by profession or future writers. Their retrospective stories most often originate in a near-present (or past) event or situation that stimulates a journey into a more distant past. A typical Modianesque narrative structure begins in the near-present of narration at a time after the period that will become central to the novel itself. To illustrate, the memory initiator for Victor's narrative in *Villa triste* is, in all likelihood, a newspaper obituary recounting the death of an old acquaintance, René Meinthe, the owner of the "villa triste" in Haute Savoie. As readers, we do not discover this until chapter 12. The narrator begins his story in a present of memory/imagination describing the winter appearance of an unnamed summer resort town as though he were viewing it in the "narrating instance."[1] This present of imagination follows René Meinthe's ambulations through town, perhaps on the night he committed suicide. Four brief chapters out of thirteen focus on this present. With few exceptions, the rest recount, in linear fashion, what Victor did one summer in this town twelve years earlier.

While *Villa triste* suspends the chronology of the narrative flow only briefly with incursions into the present, the majority of Modiano's novels are constructed around preparatory allusions that refer to the period that will become the temporal focal point. Achieved largely through working backward and forward again in story time, as in detective fiction, this technique imparts information about the past in piecemeal fashion, usually for about the first half of the novel.[2] These comings and goings between the past, distant past, and near-present serve not just to create a narrative structure found in detective novels but to point to the omnipresence of the past, its unsolved mysteries, and often to the haunting nature of the narrator's memories.

The manner in which the Modianesque narrator imparts information to the reader demonstrates the trajectory of his mind as it works through the near-present (or past) and its memory initiators. While moving backward and forward again in time, the narrator collects clues and new leads and reviews certain scenes and impressions of the past and present in order to reconstruct the "crime," or what has been lost to time or to memory. Yet while gaps may be filled in and tied together (or more frequently left open), rarely does the whole picture emerge fully clarified. For unlike the traditional structure of "genuine" detective fiction, Modiano's conclusions contain none of those reassuring answers to the unknown. The narrator simply does not have the capacity to retrieve enough information in order to fully reconstruct the past. Besides, reality, as Michel Butor explains, is naturally incoherent, alinear, elliptical: "Cette ignorance est un des aspects fondamentaux de la réalité humaine et que les événements de notre vie ne parviennent jamais à s'historiser au point que leur narration ne comporte plus de lacunes."[3] Ultimately, the narrator must acquiesce in the fact that not all the answers can be known, that imagination is the only possible substitute for memory and the unknowable.

The most prevalent solicitor of memory is that of association. Many of the things the hero sees and searches for in the present or near-present of the narrating act—photographs, newspaper items, people, addresses, streets, and buildings—stimulate his mind and elicit other spasms of memory and bring other times, people, places, and events forward to the present or to join other pasts. The most reliable leads that the narrator has to work with in his search are old newspaper clippings, telephone books, and *bottins* (social directories). For Guy Roland and his employer, the latter contained "la plus précieuse et la plus émouvante bibliothèque qu'on pût avoir, car sur leurs pages étaient répertoriés bien des êtres, des choses, des mondes disparus, et dont eux seuls portaient témoignage" (*Rue des boutiques obscures*, p. 8). It is through these memory-documents that the young hero of *Livret de famille* is able to reconstruct, albeit mostly through imagination, the life (or "lives") of Harry Dressel, that Louis recreates his father's life as a champion cyclist in *Une Jeunesse*, that the narrator of *Fleurs de ruine* is able to retrace Urbain and Gisèle T.'s possible itinerary on the night they committed suicide. Like photographs, written documents bear witness to people and a past that might have otherwise remained anonymous or been forgotten entirely in time. Moreover, they often reveal relationships between events and people that provide new clues and different perspectives about the phenomenon under investigation.

In Modiano's work, the photograph serves various functions and appears under several guises. Yet, invariably, its most important feature is that it is a gravestone to the past. Moreover, there is not a single novel in which the photograph does not play a role, from a simple mention to entire investigations revolving around the interpretation of certain pictures. For instance, some photographs are used by narrators to reconstruct (or invent) people's lives: Serge Alexandre (*Les Boulevards de ceinture*) creates a life in the company of his father (which predates his birth) from some old photographs found in a drawer. Guy Roland (*Rue des boutiques obscures*) finds clues to his real identity in a photo in which he believes himself to be present. Patrick (*Livret de famille*) claims, through imagination and from a photograph found in a wallet, the childhood of an unknown man who died beside him in a café one evening. Likewise, Victor (*Villa triste*) repairs his fading memory by means of the unique photograph that he possesses of his girlfriend and their summer spent together in Haute Savoie. Claude Portier (*De si braves garçons*) saves photographs of herself as a young woman, thus furnishing proof of her former beauty and glory. Jean (*Dimanches d'août*) discovers the true identity of the couple claiming to be American by inquiring about a snapshot.

For the narrator delving into the past, photographs seem to materialize those whose traces or youth have been lost and, as a consequence, they give him the momentary sense of retaining something of that past. Yet, as Susan Sontag declares: "A photograph is both a pseudo-presence and a token of absence."[4] Its very nature is intimately related to nostalgia, and as such, the photograph can also be a painful reminder of better days, other worlds, and the disappearance of people, places, and things that so haunt the narrator: "All photographs are 'memento mori.' To take a photograph is to participate in another person's (or thing's) mortality, vulnerability, mutability. Precisely by slicing out this moment and freezing it, all photographs testify to time's relentless melt" (p. 15). In *Une Jeunesse*, Bauer, an older man and amateur photographer, perceives his collection of photographs as follows: "C'est triste de penser que tous ces beaux gosses ont vieilli ou bien disparu . . . Et moi, je reste là, comme un vieux ponton pourri qui les a vus passer. Il ne me reste que leurs photos. . . . Mais quand je feuillette cet album et que je les regarde les uns après les autres, j'ai l'impression que ce sont des vagues qui sont venues se briser au fur et à mesure. . ." (p. 181). Photographs help to underscore a particular climate in Modiano's work: a climate of nostalgia, disappearance, ruin, and has-beens. They are concrete reminders of the fragility of human existence, the fragmentation of a person's identity, and perhaps most painfully, of the fact that the suspense or the future that life once held is now gone.

In addition to the tangible photographs scattered throughout Modiano's fiction, there are also those that memory itself has retained. These visual memories can recall not only the setting or scene but the content, atmosphere, and sensations of the moment frozen in time: "Le train est resté en gare une dizaine de minutes. Je revois comme sur une photo, le quai désert, la lumière jaune de la salle d'attente dont la porte est entrouverte. Et un peu plus loin, les deux ombres du porteur et du chauffeur de la camionnette, assises sur le chariot. Ils fument" (*Quartier perdu*, p. 99). In narrative form, memory's snapshots can be practically verbless and are often dominated by light and shadow. They describe furniture, lamp shades, curtains, spots of sun or moonlight on the floor and, as quoted above, doors that are open to the future. Many are, in fact, cinematographic in quality, combining movement with descriptive portraits; others are still-life photographs of building façades, objects, or rooms:

> Nous sommes restés seuls dans le salon, quelques minutes, et je fais un effort de mémoire pour rassembler le plus de détails possible. Les portes-fenêtres qui donnaient sur le boulevard étaient entrouvertes à cause de la chaleur. C'était au 19 du boulevard Raspail. En 1965. Un piano à queue tout au fond de la pièce. Le canapé et les deux fauteuils étaient du même cuir noir. La table basse, en métal argenté. Un nom comme Devez ou Duvelz. La cicatrice sur la joue. Le chemisier dégrafé. Une lumière très vive de projecteur, ou plutôt de torche électrique. Elle n'éclaire qu'une parcelle d'un décor, un instant isolé, laissant le reste dans l'ombre, car nous ne saurions jamais la suite des événements et qui étaient, au juste, ces deux personnes. (*Fleurs de ruine*, pp. 23–24)

This visual memory, typical of the Modianesque still-life photograph, is characterized by verbal economy, the dominance of substantives, and the absence of verbs. It demonstrates the ingenious subtlety by which Modiano has his narrator pass from the narrative past to a narrative present-in-the-past. By neutralizing objects in time with the imperfect of the verb "être," by eliminating verbs altogether—"la table . . . un nom . . . la cicatrice . . . le chemisier . . . une lumière . . . "—then reinstating verbs with "éclairer" in the present tense, we witness the narrator's mind effacing time as memory projects this scene momentarily into the present. Moreover, combined with his act of narrating—"je fais un effort . . . "— the passage illustrates one of the most important means by which he initiates his recollection of the past: through memory's photographs.

These photographs frequently serve as descriptive summaries from which the narrator draws in order to recreate and sense memories. The immediacy and temporal ambiguity of this momentary immersion into the past provides the context necessary to fill in the photograph-memory with other details and the intervening action. By contrast, such photographs can also serve as atmospheric summaries, as is the case with the Devez/Duvelz anecdote quoted above. The very "raison d'être" for this anecdote is to underscore the sensation of decline, deterioration, and moral ambiguity that the Montparnasse district of the 1960s represents in the eyes of the narrator. Embedded in the investigation into Urbain and Gisèle T.'s mysterious suicide in 1933, the anecdote also demonstrates a personal experience that parallels an imagined setting or situation that could have led the couple to take up company, that fateful night, with a group of people whose social behavior was probably very different from their own.

While odors, music, and other sounds unquestionably play an essential role in recalling certain memories, the Modianesque universe is, in fact, largely visual. It is eye and hair color, clothing, shoes, furnishings, rose-colored drinks, iron gates, streets, and places in general that compose the concrete of the narrators' otherwise fleeting and vaporous world. Moreover, the role of place in Modiano's œuvre is paramount to the workings of associative memory and imagination. The seemingly infinite number of streets, buildings, and cities mentioned within the space of Modiano's fiction testifies not only to the characters' transient nature but often to the only palpable thing they find to hold on to: "Au milieu de tant d'incertitudes, mes seuls points de repère, le seul terrain qui ne se dérobait pas, c'était les carrefours et les trottoirs de cette ville" (*Les Boulevards de ceinture*, p. 105).

Like wars (or for Modiano, the Occupation), places serve as points of reference in the narrators' fragile lives, and initiate the retrieval not only of memories but of certain supersensitive impressions of the past: "Je crois qu'on entend encore dans les entrées d'immeubles l'écho des pas de ceux qui avaient l'habitude de les traverser et qui, depuis, ont disparu. Quelque chose continue de vibrer après leur passage, des ondes de plus en plus faibles, mais que l'on capte si l'on est attentif" (*Rue des boutiques obscures*, p. 105). It is this supersensitive capacity of the Modianesque narrator that both allows and causes him to reflect on the past of certain buildings, entryways, rooms, and streets. As silent landmarks to the past they remain, like the photographer Bauer, as old "floating bridges" on the sea of time. It is the narrator's mission and a personal necessity to capture the memory-echoes these places still emit.

Although Modiano's novels all feature places prominently, *Fleurs de ruine* is particularly rich in its use of places for the revival of memory, both real and supersensitive. Not only are the streets, buildings, and arrondissements of Paris the point of departure and guiding thread of the novel, but memory's anecdotes are largely determined by spatial proximity. Indeed, the surface structure of the novel is none other than a guided tour of the monuments to the narrator's adolescence and early adult life in Paris during the 1960s.

The first page of the novel alone mentions six streets and five institutions and yet consists of only seventeen lines. Each (unmarked) chapter or section begins with an evocation of place: "Ce dimanche soir de novembre, j'étais dans la rue de l'Abbé-de-l'Epée" (p. 11); "Il semble, selon l'enquête, qu'Urbain et Gisèle T., après leur dîner, aient échoué dans un bar de Montparnasse" (p. 16); "Le témoignage d'un serveur qui travaillait dans un restaurant-dancing du Perreux figure en première page d'un journal" (p. 25); "A la sortie du Café de la Marine" (p. 28); "Je me souviens du quai de l'Artois" (p. 32); "Je veux m'attarder sur la Rive gauche" (p. 38); "Je revois les joueurs de billard au premier étage du Café de Cluny" (p. 40); "Le Boulevard Saint-Michel est noyé, ce dimanche soir, dans une brume de décembre" (p. 41). There are in fact only two out of twenty-six "chapters" in which an institution, street, arrondissement, or other place in or near Paris does not initiate the anecdote and the memories these places hold. The novel is not just a review of the people whom the narrator knew or knew of at one time; his identity itself appears as a disordered assemblage of contiguous selves whose faint echoes remain in the places he has chosen to revisit.

The novel begins on a Sunday evening in November, ostensibly in the late 1980s. Although recounted in the past tense, we follow the narrator, block by block, through a certain section of the fifth arrondissement. In doing so, we also listen to him as he reflects on the personal and collective past of some of the streets and institutions that appear before him as he walks. Yet, his unstated destination this evening seems to be a specific address: 26, rue des Fossés-Saint-Jacques. Having found it, or a new version of it ("l'ancien immeuble avait sans doute été rasé une vingtaine d'années auparavant," p. 13), the narrator departs from the first narrative (the walking tour) and enters into an account of the alleged suicide of a couple, Gisèle and Urbain T., that occurred at that address on April 24, 1933. A newspaper report of that time, integrated into the text as if it were the narrator's own, hypothesizes on the suicide and indicates the couple's probable itinerary. The (typically Modianesque) narrator then follows that itinerary, leading us next to the district around Montparnasse, apparently to visit two bars in which the couple had been seen. Yet his ostensible investigation digresses into the memories evoked by places that figure in his own life, so that it becomes evident that this project is not aimed solely at discovering what really happened in the purported suicide of the couple.

In reading this novel, one has the initial impression that it is but a series of disconnected anecdotes held together only by the portrayal of place (Paris) and principal time of focus (the 1960s). Yet, upon closer reading, it becomes clear that the many embedded memories that places elicit are in fact connected to other elements in a network of dead-ends that the novel itself ties together in a limited way. Thus, while the suicide investigation is gradually phased out of the narration (and left unresolved), the couple's name appears again later in the company of a certain alias Pacheco with whom the narrator had become fascinated at the cafeteria of the Cité Universitaire. Indeed, we discover that it was from a newspaper article found in this false Pacheco's wallet (in the 1960s) that the narrator discovered the suicide incident itself. Alias Pacheco is linked to the 1930s and 1940s not only because he appears in another newspaper article describing the itinerary of the T.'s on the night of their suicide, but because of the name he illicitly appropriated, which figures on postwar wanted lists. What could be the false Pacheco from the 1960s appears again in the Luxembourg gardens in the spring of the 1990s. Moreover, Pacheco appears in *Voyage de noces* as a mysterious entrepreneur whom we see only in passing. This recurrence of names and characters is evident throughout Modiano's work. Some names change slightly, others are given only by initial, and some are historical figures: Hayakawa (*La Place de l'étoile, La Ronde de nuit, Livret de famille*); Harry Dressel (*Villa triste, Livret de famille*); Stioppa de Djagoriew (*Rue des boutiques obscures, Remise de peine*); Andrée Karvé (*De si braves garçons, Quartier perdu, Remise de peine*); Pagnon (*Les Boulevards de ceinture, De si braves garçons, Fleurs de ruine*).

The overlapping of temporal zones, combined with the many cross-references, anecdotes begun, left off, and resumed pages later, and photographic images that directly project the past onto the present, demonstrate not just a certain fusion in the perception of time but an interconnectedness of events, people, and places outside of time: "J'ai traversé les jardins. Etait-ce la rencontre de ce fantôme [an old philosophy professor]? Les allées du Luxembourg où je n'avais pas marché depuis une éternité? Dans la lumière de fin d'après-midi, il m'a semblé que les années se confondaient et que le temps devenait transparent" (*Fleurs de ruine*, p. 43).

Like double, triple, or numerous photographic exposures taken of the same object or place on various occasions, memory has recorded certain revealing aspects about people, events, and sensations, rather than time itself. It is only their absence (or age) in the present that measures the passage of time, and memory that exposes the invisible connections between the past, distant past, and the present. In the final analysis, the oscillation between time periods in the narrator's evocation of his life testifies not just to memory's hold over his existence but, because of the inherent comparison that occurs, it shows the present, like an image seen in a vapor-covered mirror, as a reflection of the past.

Modiano's novels are about absence, disappearance, and the search to fill a certain emptiness resulting from both. Haunted by the gratuity of life, its lack of direction, and its discontinuity, narrators seek to find an anchor for their "floating bridge" in a world made up only of "du sable mouvant" (*Les Boulevards de ceinture*, p. 168). As "prisoners of memory," their narratives demonstrate a paradoxical attempt both to break free of the past and to explore its depths. This exploration may answer certain questions, but it also underlines the fragmentation of the narrators' lives and identities. Yet the narrative, as a document that records pieces of the past, ultimately lends a limited sense of presence to a world characterized by absence. Writing (for again, they are all potential writers) helps to materialize the ephemeral, painting a verbal picture of time through the people and events that measure it and give it substance. The narrator and Modiano thus act as witnesses, interpreters, and archivists to a past (and present) that only they, as the last sentinels to a disappearing world, can decipher with any accuracy: "Plus personne ne saurait que ces objets avaient été réunis, pour un temps très bref, dans une chambre de l'avenue Malakoff, par la fille d'Harry Dressel. Sauf moi. J'avais dix-sept ans et il ne me restait plus qu'à devenir un écrivain français" (*Livret de famille*, p. 158). The book may end up on a dusty shelf, as photographs end up in old cookie, cigar, and chocolate boxes (*Rue des boutiques obscures*, p. 81), and thus also be forgotten in time. Yet, unlike photographs, the novel acts as an interpreted document, a verbal photo album to which the narrator can refer even after memory fails completely, after photographs lose their former clarity, and after the last sentinels to a generation have disappeared. In the final analysis, writing is an attempt to overcome the anguish felt upon experiencing the emptiness brought about by the disappearance of people and their memories. Modiano's œuvre, like a collective family album, retrieves both personal and historical memory from oblivion and records his name, through fiction, on the registers of "l'état civil."

Notes

1. Gérard Genette, *Narrative Discourse: An Essay in Method* (Ithaca: Cornell University Press, 1980), p. 31.

2. See Jeanne C. Ewert, "Lost in the Hermeneutic Funhouse: Patrick Modiano's Post-Modern Detective," in *The Cunning Craft: Original Essays on Detective Fiction and Contemporary Literary Theory,* ed. Ronald Walker and June Frazer (Macomb: Western Illinois University Press, 1990), pp. 166–77.

3. Michel Butor, *Répertoire II* (Paris: Minuit, 1964), p. 41.

4. Susan Sontag, *On Photography* (New York: Farrar, Straus and Giroux, 1977), p. 16.

Bibliography

Works by Patrick Modiano

La Place de l'étoile. Paris: Gallimard, 1968.

La Ronde de nuit. Paris: Gallimard, 1969. Translated by Patricia Wolf as *Night Rounds*. New York: Knopf, 1971.

Les Boulevards de ceinture. Paris: Gallimard, 1972. Translated by Caroline Hillier as *Ring Roads*. London: Gollancz, 1974.

Villa triste. Paris: Gallimard, 1975. Translated by Caroline Hillier. London: Gollancz, 1977.

Emmanuel Berl, interrogatoire. Paris: Gallimard, 1976.

Livret de famille. Paris: Gallimard, 1977.

Rue des boutiques obscures. Paris: Gallimard, 1978. Translated by Daniel Weissbort as *Missing Person*. London: Cape, 1980.

Memory Lane. Illus. Pierre Le-Tan. Paris: Hachette, 1981.

Une Jeunesse. Paris: Gallimard, 1981.

De si braves garçons. Paris: Gallimard, 1982.

Quartier perdu. Paris: Gallimard, 1984. Translated by Anthea Bell as *A Trace of Malice*. Henley-on-Thames: Ellis, 1988.

Dimanches d'août. Paris: Gallimard, 1986.

Remise de peine. Paris: Seuil, 1988. Translated by Anthea Bell as *Remission*. Henley-on-Thames: Ellis, 1990.

Vestiaire de l'enfance. Paris: Gallimard, 1989.

Voyage de noces. Paris: Gallimard, 1990. Translated by Barbara Wright as *Honeymoon*. Boston: Godine, 1994.

Fleurs de ruine. Paris: Seuil, 1991.

Un Cirque passe. Paris: Gallimard, 1992.
Chien de printemps. Paris: Seuil, 1993.

Selected Critical Works

Bedner, Jules, ed. *Patrick Modiano*. Amsterdam: Rodopi, 1993.

Bersani, Jacques. "Patrick Modiano, Agent Double." *Nouvelle Revue Française*, no. 298 (November 1, 1977): 78–84.

Chasseguet-Smirgel, Janine. "'La Place de l'étoile' de Patrick Modiano: pour une définition psychanalytique de 'l'authenticité.' " In *Pour une psychanalyse de l'art et de la créativité*, pp. 217–55. Paris: Payot, 1971.

Côté, Paul Raymond. "Aux rives du Lethé: mnémosyne et la quête des origines chez Patrick Modiano." *Symposium* 45, no. 1 (spring 1991): 315–28.

Daprini, Pierre B. "Patrick Modiano: Le temps de l'occupation." *Australian Journal of French Studies* 26, no. 2 (May–August 1989): 194–205.

Ewert, Jeanne C. "Lost in the Hermeneutic Funhouse: Patrick Modiano's Post-Modern Detective." In *The Cunning Craft: Original Essays on Detective Fiction and Contemporary Literary Theory*, edited by Ronald Walker and June Frazer, pp. 166–77. Macomb: Western Illinois University Press, 1990.

Ezine, Jean-Louis. "Patrick Modiano." In *Les Ecrivains sur la sellette*, pp. 16–25. Paris: Seuil, 1981.

Golsan, Richard J. "Collaboration, Alienation and the Crisis of Identity in the Film and Fiction of Patrick Modiano." In *Film and Literature: A Comparative Approach to Adaptation*, edited by Wendell Aycock and Michael Schoenecke, pp. 107–21. Lubbock: Texas Tech University Press, 1988.

Magnan, Jean-Marie. "Un Apatride nommé Modiano." *Sud*, no. 19 (third trimester 1976): 120–31.

Morris, Alan. "Patrick Modiano." In *Beyond the Nouveau Roman: Essays on the Contemporary French Novel*, edited by Michael Tilby, pp. 177–200. New York: Berg, 1990.

Nettelbeck, C. W., and P. A. Hueston. "Anthology as Art: Patrick Modiano's 'Livret de famille.' " *Australian Journal of French Studies* 21, no. 2 (May–August 1984): 213–23.

———. *Patrick Modiano, pièces d'identité: Ecrire l'entretemps*. Archives des lettres modernes (no. 220), 1986.

O'Keefe, Charles. "Patrick Modiano's 'La Place de l'Etoile': Why Name a Narrator 'Raphaël Schlemilovitch'?" *Literary Onomastic Studies*, no. 15 (1988): 67–74.

Prince, Gerald. "Re-membering Modiano: or Something Happened." *Sub-Stance*, no. 49 (1986): 35–43.

Scherman, Timothy H. "Translating from Memory: Patrick Modiano in Postmodern Context." *Studies in Twentieth Century Literature* 16, no. 2 (summer 1992): 289–303.

15

Monique Wittig

Laurence M. Porter

Desire defines the self and gives it a direction. Union with another can obliterate awareness of desire by creating the illusion that we have become complete; but by masking our fundamental lack, gratification also seems to efface our identity. "Que dire maintenant qui ne soit l'histoire de tant d'autres," exclaims the narrator of Nerval's *Sylvie,* once he has committed himself to the ultimately, if only temporarily successful courtship of the actress Aurélie, the shape-shifter whose metamorphoses seem capable of molding themselves to the contours of his desire, as it ebbs and flows. Subordination is a union that is socially defined and mandated as constituting a complete definition of the individual; such a role is demanded of women and not of men. So, to this day, any defection by a woman from the nurturant and reproductive role assigned to her, even if such defection is merely momentary and verbal, creates a scandal. In the 1992 U.S. presidential campaign, the wife of Democratic challenger Bill Clinton was called upon to defend herself against the charge of being insufficiently feminine: she had a brilliantly successful law career, but had produced only one child. Momentarily losing control, Hillary Clinton retorted, "What did you expect me to do? I suppose I should have stayed home and baked cookies." She was ultimately redeemed only after her recipe for homemade cookies was published in *Family Circle* magazine and the readers voted their preference for it over the recipe of Barbara Bush's chef. How much more scandalous, then, is a woman's autobiography? A disloyal demonstration on foreign soil, on a terrain not subordinated to the interests of the family, such literature sticks out of the social fabric like a sore thumb. Conversely, the Symbolic (in Lacan's sense of the word) domain of literature appears essential for many women authors in their quest for self-recognition, self-definition, and self-development, because it helps support what finds insufficient support in the Real.[1]

L'Opoponax (1964), Monique Wittig's first major work, corresponds to the genre of autobiography insofar as it treats the period of separation and individuation in early childhood, typically, up until the end of school and entrance into the adult world (which new phase corresponds to the Bildungsroman, whereas the later transition from society into history corresponds to the self-writing genre of memoirs). Autobiography characteristically relates the constitution of a personal identity through evaluating and then choosing among the various influences acting upon the child; some are accepted and others are rejected. In addition, the as-yet socially insignificant self is affirmed as a unique and irreproducible entity through memorialization.

Wittig's work, however, is less Cartesian. The autobiographical convention of lucidity (reinforced, paradoxically, by repeated expressions of dissatisfaction with the limited insight of the past self by the present-time narrator) is superseded in her novel by the depiction of a collective consciousness in childhood, within which individual identity boundaries blur. Parallel to Nathalie Sarraute in *Tropismes* and to Jacques Lacan's reflections on "the mirror stage"[2] (influenced, in turn, by the hypothesis of "imprinting" in the work of ethologists Konrad Lorenz and William Tinbergen), *L'Opoponax* in its earlier chapters uses mainly the collective pronoun "on" (which, depending on context, can be translated either as "one" or as any personal pronoun), and for a long time the tone of neutral *rapportage* does not particularly single out Catherine Legrand, the center of consciousness. The rare word of the title, whose true meaning is never consciously recognized, evokes female desire.[3] (The third "o" replacing the orthographically correct "a" reinforces the gynosymbolism of the term; "o" is strongly identified with the female in Wittig's next work, *Les Guérillères*.) It refers to an aromatic secretion of a tropical tree and thus in the context of Wittig's career evokes "la cyprine," a word featured prominently on the cover of her *Le Corps lesbien* and designating "cream" (the lubricant secretion of the vagina when the woman is sexually aroused). It constitutes the heroine's self-defining pseudonym when she finally confesses her attachment to her classmate Valérie Borge. The ending in "x" also suggests the Gallic substratum in France and Belgium; the repressed in collective history here connotes the repressed in personal history, as the pen with which Catherine Legrand has so much trouble in learning to write suggests desire sublimated and socialized into conformity. Everyone is supposed to form all her letters according to a universal standard; individuality will have to be recuperated only later by selecting from among the resources offered by literature and by diverting them from their original use in the affirmation of heterosexual desire.

At the beginning of the story, a little boy named Payen (a homonym of *païen,* or pagan) disrupts the class by rushing in to ask who wants to see his "quéquette" (baby talk for penis). At first this disruption would seem to represent an inevitable intrusion of phallic hegemony upon a world of females, but very soon little Payen shows his penis again, and then sickens and dies (pp. 7, 19). The penis has been introduced—into a world where males will appear only in the form of little boys or impotent old men—only to be effaced. What remains is its absence, which will be filled with the phallus, the signifier of desire that manifests itself as a lack. Literature typically defers the sexual maturation of its protagonists to an extraordinary degree, so that their social development can be fictionally interwoven with their sexual development. Here Catherine Legrand and her classmates, who may be six or seven, enter into what Lacan would call the postmirror phase. According to his map of childhood development, the premirror phase, lasting from birth to around six months, is characterized by the infant's experience of fragmentation: it cannot control its body, and it can apprehend only parts of it, such as arms and feet, that come into its field of vision. (Modern research, which shows that tiny infants have the ability to imitate many gestures by the other, such as sticking out the tongue, show a conscious or instinctual awareness greater than that which Lacan seemed to suppose when he first drafted this talk on the mirror phase in 1936.) Schizophrenic states and dreams can recall this experience of the fragmented body. But during the mirror phase from between six to eighteen months, a phase Lacan inserts, in effect, between Freud's oral and his anal phase, the still uncoordinated infant can recognize its image in a mirror and respond to it with playful delight (unlike the infant animal, who is not thus fascinated). Anticipating its later bodily control, the infant now apprehends its body in its totality. At the end of the mirror stage the infant enters the domain of the symbolic by mastering language and by elaborating symbolic substitutions in its unconscious. Thus penis = feces (a detached body part) = baby = gift, for example.

For Catherine Legrand, to possess the penis would be to achieve independence of her mother by becoming differentiated from her. She conceives the idea of becoming independent of her mother when she sees that the little exhibitionistic boy, Robert Payen, ignores *his* mother when she yells at him. Such an awareness allows her to become critical of authority; she realizes that it is not monolithic but that it vacillates when she hears her teacher, the Sister, counting in Belgian style: "septante et un, septante-deux" rather than "soixante et onze, soixante-douze." This insight is reinforced not long afterward when a new teacher and her mother present opposing opinions concerning the reality of ghosts. But in Catherine's subconscious, individuation generates the fear of abandonment, which we can see in the motif of being trapped and screaming; fear of a self-annihilating return to the womb appears in the fantasy that sewer drains could suck you in so you would die, and authority reinforces the imperative of a stifling mother-daughter symbiosis when Sister physically abuses a girl who will not say she loves her mother (pp. 7–24).

In an expression of their growing independence, the little girls then begin to appropriate symbolic substitutes for the penis. At first Catherine is the passive object when the others play doctor, make her disrobe, and poke her just above the anus with a sharp stick; but soon she too becomes active, taking up sticks in the woods, sharpening them into spears to use in war games, throwing them, and using them to stir up the water in bomb craters. Soon, even more assertively, she plays with tools (detachable male parts) and climbs trees until this activity is forbidden her. The point of all these episodes is that in the dawning consciousness of the heroine, power becomes detached from biology (the possession of a penis as body part) and recognized as a potentiality that transcends gender. Many of these scenes depicting little girls wielding symbolic penises will be reworked in several chapters of *Les Guérillères*. But when Catherine tries to attract attention by displaying as a penis-surrogate part of her own body (not susceptible of exchange and therefore of creating a social nexus), she is ignored and rejected. She tries to assume the role of the exhibitionistic little boy by putting her bare foot upon the desk, but none of her girl classmates acknowledge her:

On peut dire que ça n'a pas plu que c'est pour ça qu'il y a quelque chose qui se met à tourner à toute vitesse dans cette espèce de chose qui a l'air d'être Catherine Legrand, et quand Catherine Legrand a fini de lacer sa chaussure, c'est tout lourd au-dedans d'elle, c'est immobile à la hauteur des yeux, ça regarde dehors à travers les orbites, c'est pris, ça ne pourra jamais être autre chose que Catherine Legrand. (p. 95)

She has the sense of being imprisoned in her female identity because she has momentarily fallen into the trap of apprehending her identity as biological: the Real (in the Lacanian sense) imposes itself as a barrier, as the ultimate absence, as Death. And now, for the moment, even the symbolic appropriation and display of the phallus are forbidden her. The apparition of a little girl with a hole in her palate follows; bodily incompleteness migrates from one location to another. Finally Catherine peeks at another girl's vulva, and once she has located lack in the Real, she can extrapolate to history, from which her sex is excluded; the textbook illustration of Charlemagne elicits the reflection "Il n'y a pas de petites filles sur l'image" (p. 104). A paroxysm of symbolic reaction follows as Catherine plays with a gun, knives, missiles, and snakes, and finally a tube of toothpaste that she squeezes out entirely on a little boy, outdoing the male emission. But taking in hand symbolic substitutes for the penis will not in and of itself allow her to have or understand the phallus; as if by way of warning, one of her female companions gets her hand impaled on the teeth of a harrow; and the boy Vincent on whom she squirted the toothpaste cannot tell her what a muraena (moray eel as phallus) is (pp. 145, 147).

Catherine will have to discover and choose her own heroines, to find her own detour around the Real (here, the suppression of women in official recorded history) through a personal and intersubjective Symbolic elaborated along the margins of the official version of the past. By imaginatively transforming the men of Old French legends into female warriors, she attempts to have and to be the phallus both at once. The split between the male-dominated world of the school texts and the assertive females in her fantasy prepares her to learn to dissemble, as she splits the submissive false self that pleases the Sisters and thinks of God from the hidden true self that learns to express in writing admiration and affection for her schoolmates. In contrast, the nuns' names and their femininity have been erased; they belong to male patron saints, and they monotonously recite "non sum dignus."

Since Catherine Legrand cannot have the phallus, she must choose the Oedipal alternative of "being the phallus" or object of desire. To do so she must project her own desire outward in hopes of inspiring a mimetic return from the Other. She unconsciously chooses an object in Valérie Borge. She finds the language for mediating her desire in the love poetry that the girls are beginning to learn in school, and finally she invents the opoponax, the fluid image of her personal desire: she cannot manage to draw it, and "On ne peut pas le décrire parce qu'il n'a jamais la même forme" (p. 179). For a long time she watches Valérie Borge without receiving any attention in return; finally she writes her an anonymous love letter beginning "Je suis l'opoponax." Valérie Borge initially publicizes the existence of the opoponax to her classmates, as befits a condition of diffuse desire, but eventually realizes its identity and lies about it so as to create a private bond with Catherine Legrand. The seventh and final chapter describes their joyful wrestling reunion, their adventuring outdoors, and in conclusion the death of one of their teachers, Mademoiselle Caylus, whose burial concludes the novel as the students symbolically castrate her, playfully pretending to divide her property, taking her false teeth and her cane. As the text closes the heroine anticipates her future by reciting the conclusion of Baudelaire's love poem "L'Invitation au voyage" and a line associating love with immortality from Maurice Scève's Délie. "Je" in place of the anonymous "on" appears in the latter quotation for the first time in the novel. However, one must question "that the appearance of the 'je' represents the emergence into a fully-fledged individualism." In Wittig's ambiguous conclusion, "the individual is as much spoken by the culture she has inherited as she speaks."[4] The derivative conclusion constitutes a covert but pointed self-criticism, and the task of differentiation remains.

If L'Opoponax appropriates love poetry in order to find a way to mediate and thus to discover and define personal feelings and then as a result to be able to bond with another, Les Guérillères must appropriate texts from the revolutionary tradition of the third world, emerging as a group of autonomous political powers (these texts, by Ho Chi Minh, Mao Zedong and others, are obligingly cited by the author at the conclusion of her epic) in order to create the basis for a society of women, the tacit assumption being that since men inevitably enslave, coerce, and exploit women, and since they never can tolerate women's independence, then any self-sufficient society of women can be formed only by a forceful revolutionary act and maintained only through military resistance and constant vigilance. Such a society, of course, would die out in one generation. The biological imperative of insemination for reproduction is elided, and "the little girls" appear as if by magic in order to be trained in the ways of their female warrior society. One imagines a collectivist *crèche* like those in Communist China or a kibbutz like those in Israel. Recruitment poses difficulties in such a monosexual society. To benefit fully from the training, one would have to start young; when one is young, one's political and social conscience has not yet emerged to the point of motivating a conscious choice for separatism; and if new child-members are recruited by recruiting their single parents, then those parents who once chose or were forced to be exploited by men rather than live free from men always pose the risk of recidivism: "In fact, for Wittig, the mother is everything that *is* the socially constructed woman; she is the domesticated woman. In [*Lesbian Peoples*] Wittig opposes the amazon to the mother, the betrayer of free women."[5] Later, in *Virgile, non*, Wittig will ruefully confront the problem of dealing with those whom she wishes to rescue, but who do not want to be free ("My very chains and I grew friends / So much a long communion tends / To make us what we are: even I / Regained my freedom with a sigh," as Byron put it in "The Prisoner of Chillon"). Here in *Les Guérillères*, the self-perpetuating monosexual society is a myth like the myth of Plato's *Republic:* not a blueprint for social legislation, but an incitement and series of guideposts toward reform, as well as a forceful reminder that things could be different and that women need not always accept injustice.

The access to the Symbolic that Catherine Legrand achieves at the end of *L'Opoponax* remains mediated through other people's choices and values, through the prescribed curriculum that is the only source of information about the outside world. (Lacan situates this phase at around eighteen months, when the infant acquires speech and moves past the mirror stage; Wittig, even more than most authors, postpones her heroine's maturation because the emergent lesbian must psychosexually and socially be born a second time to exit from the patriarchy.) Nevertheless, Catherine and her classmates notice that there are no little girls in the pictorial history of Charlemagne, and they select a personal pantheon of female heroes from along the margins of what they are told to read. Their orientation becomes feminocentric, but not revolutionary, because no revolutionary texts are revealed to them by their parents and teachers, who wish to maintain the existing order. In *Les Guérillères* the undifferentiated pronoun "on" that dominated *L'Opononax* becomes "elles" in a way that associates sisterhood with the emergent feminist political consciousness. The pronoun is, for Wittig, the mirror of the self in the Symbolic: "Personal pronouns are, if I may say so, the subject matter of each one of my books."[6] When one says "I," she asserts, one appropriates language as a whole, but in French the adjectives and past participles must agree in gender with the subject. Often their change of spelling, effected through the addition of the mark of the feminine, changes the sound as well. Therefore, in both speech and writing gender particularizes women, robbing them of the universal and its attendant authority that has been usurped as the exclusive property of men: "The result of the imposition of gender, acting as a denial at the very moment when one speaks, is to deprive women of the authority of speech, and to force them to make their entrance in a crablike way, particularizing themselves and apologizing profusely. The result is to deny them any claim to the abstract, philosophical, political discourses that give shape to the social body. Gender then must be destroyed."[7] *L'Opononax* does so by deploying as much as possible the gender-neutral "on." But in the more militant *Les Guérillères*, the elimination of the pronouns "il" and "ils" from the first two of three parts of the work creates an icon of a complete conquest of the world by "elles," the sole, universal, and imperial subject of that world.

The long list of sources at the end of *Les Guérillères* (unfortunately omitted from the English translation) evokes an international revolutionary tradition that transcends the socially imposed boundaries of nation, class, and sexuality. The implied author now maneuvers freely within the domain of the Lacanian Symbolic instead of being obliged to limit herself to choosing from among what is offered by the powers that be through the cultural indoctrination of the educational system. Obliged still to work within the framework of the gender-bound structures of the French language (where the female always is present, in sound or spelling, as something added, as a "marked choice" that connotes inferiority), she tries to universalize the female perspective by consistently using the untranslatable "elles" without antecedent (a possible English rendering would be "shes") and by inventing feminine forms of nouns denoting the performers of activities in which women are ordinarily debarred or restricted: "soldates, parleuses, buveuses."

It is in *Les Guérillères* that Wittig's revolutionary askesis emerges clearly, in the wake of "les Evénements" (the French worker-student protests of May 1968) and the Vietnam War, and just before her emergence as the spokesperson for the antipatriarchal Féministes Révolutionnaires. She does not pander to *revanchisme*: to turn the tables on men and dominate them is still to be preoccupied with them. Instead, she depicts a utopian order where men are, at most, optional, and in general, irrelevant. She does not offer to the reader seductive opportunities for "identification" with a self-conscious author, with an introspective protagonist, or with the inspiring images of an Earth Mother or Nature Goddess. For to depict a single, dominant heroine would be to provide a vehicle for our projected fantasies of personal power and glory, offering a vicarious narcissistic gratification whose enthralling image would distract us from the task of political reflection (one recalls the deliberate distancing from the characters sought in the theater of Bertolt Brecht). Neither does she attempt to ingratiate herself with a *captatio benevolentiae*. In short, she eschews the cult of personality that has undermined so many revolutionary movements and limited them to the lifespan of their founder. Lists of women's first names (liberated from the patronymic) in capital letters, and international in scope, stud the text at intervals of six to eight pages. Typographically framed, these memorializing lists constitute new mirrors, constructed to invite the *prise de conscience* of a sisterly identity and to effect a reparenting of the emerging lesbian self. This self, Wittig believes, ought to be realized in action. To her, literature is not autotelic, but is simply a way station on the long march of universal revolution: "SENS / CE QUI EST A ECRIRE VIOLENCE / HORS TEXTE / DANS UNE AUTRE ECRITURE / ... / SANS RELACHE / GESTE RENVERSEMENT" (p. 205).

Les Guérillères liberates its collective female protagonists, mainly anonymous, by reversing the traditional gendered polarization of space, according to which women belong indoors and men outdoors. A room of one's own is replaced by a battlefield of our own; the phallic locomotor unbinding of the women, who swim, ride, and run freely, leads to their apprehending their bodies "dans leur totalité" (pp. 80–81). Thus, instead of being limited to a narcissistic fixation on those parts of their body that are particularly female, having to do with the housebound occupations of pregnancy and child-rearing (reaction against the glorification of the penis can be a trap, and the women eventually recognize as such their cult of the vulva and vagina), the women can fully exercise their muscles and limbs.

After depicting a feminist *prise de conscience* followed by sociopolitical liberation in her first two published works, Wittig has devoted herself to rewriting the canon and to consolidating lesbian feminist knowledge in encyclopedic and polemical gestures of Aufklärung. Such rewriting inevitably entails restoration for a member of a group whose writings have long been repressed. In both classical antiquity and the Christian era, for example, perhaps nine-tenths of Sappho's love lyrics were permanently destroyed (so were as many of Pindar's odes, but not through virulent censorship and public manuscript burnings). Wittig's third book, *Le Corps lesbien* (1973), expands the motif of apprehending the totality of the body in a way that expresses the exhilaration of lesbian sexuality, rewrites the Song of Songs and the Renaissance *blasons du corps féminin*, but far transcends sexuality to embark upon a passionate anatomy and dissection of the female body, stripping away delusional idealization and relentlessly insisting upon a new Democracy of the Body that is no longer satiric, but celebratory. The split subject, typographically depicted by using barred forms of the first-person singular pronouns and possessive adjectives (j/e, m/a, etc.), functions according to Wittig as a sign of excess in the powerful lesbian subject able to engulf the world. Wittig explains:

> To understand my undertaking in this text, one must go back to *The Opoponax,* in which the only appearance of the narrator comes with a *Je,* 'I,' located at the end of the book in a small sentence untranslated in English, a verse of Maurice Scève, in *La Délie:* 'Tant je l'aimais qu'en elle encore je vis.' This sentence is the key to the text and pours its ultimate light upon the whole of it, demystifying the meaning of the opoponax and establishing a lesbian subject as the absolute subject while lesbian love is the absolute love.[8]

Wittig's procedure here is simple but effective. She has universalized lesbianism by substituting what she considers the metagender term *lesbian* (she who has cast off womanhood and its servitudes, since Wittig defines *woman* as an archaic term describing an archaic social condition, "she who belongs to another"),[9] for the gender-neutral terms *the* and *its*. To rephrase, the phantasm of the opoponax establishes "*the* subject as the absolute subject while *its* love is the absolute love." What does this mean? It means that the bar or *Spaltung* dividing the self from itself (j/e) functions like a mirror reflecting back to the subject her own image so as to effect "la découverte amoureuse de soi." A lesbian object choice means that the image reflected will be anatomically correct. Instead of desiring the penis of the other and engulfing it in the ego-defense mechanism of incorporation ("ingesting" that which one lacks), the female subject can now recuperate the phallus through a complete and not a partial apprehension of the body of the other. The phallus, as Lacan explains, is not a fantasy, nor a part-object, nor the organ that it symbolizes: "The phallus is the privileged signifier of that mark in which the role of the logos is joined with the advent of desire" on the surface of the real or figurative mirror that is the place of the Other. "Desire is neither the appetite for satisfaction, nor the demand for love, but the difference that results from the subtraction of the first from the second," the consciousness of a split between subject and object when the subject realizes that her desire always constitutes an excess in relationship to any possibilities for its fulfillment.[10] This excess assumes the form of the frenzied and violent dismemberment of the other that pervades *Le Corps lesbien*. From the perspective of the implied author, who introduces the intertext of the rending and reassembling of Osiris (who ends up with his penis missing), which corresponds to the rending of the beloved's body, of the text (an assemblage of 110 prose poems), and of the pronoun subject itself, the Bacchantic sacrifice of the *sparagmos* is a necessary prelude to a reconstitution of the self in a new frame of reference.

Wittig's later works, then, constitute acts of consolidation. Her *Brouillon pour un dictionnaire des amantes* (coauthored with Sande Zeig) reinvents origins. The veracity of these stories, which credit lesbian leaders and culture heroines with the invention of all civilization, is not important. The stories serve to reverse lesbians' feelings of disempowerment. In the long central article on history, the degenerate culture of the Mothers, voluntarily trapped in cities, replaces the vibrant nomadism of the Amazons. The refrain, which ascribes the same behaviors to seventeen different tribes under as many headings in the text (they all always carry a double-bitted axe in their belt, never nurse their infants, and never eat bread) removes the various legendary societies of autonomous women from the corrupting flow of time and gathers them together in a collective syncretism that recalls the universal pardon of the various pagan gods near the conclusion of Gérard de Nerval's *Aurélia*. Wittig thereby attempts to create the new identity of a synchronic sisterhood that has resisted oppression. She renames most countries (except for Greece, the land of Sappho) and historical epochs, and insists upon the desirability of "the metamorphosis of words—an avoidance of fixed meanings" (p. 166; I cite Wittig and Zeig's own translation of the French original here and below because it constitutes a revision that achieves greater universality than the first version, by eliminating, for example, "of Amazons" several times in apposition to the word "tribe" in that entry). Socially, the ideal of flexibility is the same as in the linguistic domain: "TRIBE. A tribe can be created by mere decision. One person alone will do. She is the first cell of the new tribe. She may found a hermit tribe or it may multiply. . . . Lack of attachment to a particular locality, sense of adventure, taste for journeys, movement, physical exercises and life in the open air are the characteristics of a tribe" (p. 154). Both modes of flexibility—linguistic and social—converge under the heading NAME (p. 113). Each chooses her own. Wittig attempts to found an absence of foundations, to impart to her fictive, didactic audience the fluidity of desire itself.

Nor can fluidity become a doctrine. Although Wittig published two parodic journey fictions in the same year, 1985 (*Virgile, non*, a reworking of Dante's *Divine Comedy*, and *Le Voyage sans fin*, a reworking of *Don Quixote*, both with female characters), one ends in Paradise and the other does not. Both are haunted by the wraiths of those unfaithful sisters who from Wittig's point of view split the feminist movement. Throughout much of *Virgile, non* the character "Wittig" exhorts the women in hell (in relationships with men) to free themselves, but without success. In *Le Voyage sans fin*, Quichotte is opposed by her own conventional mother and sister. The guiding strand of parody in both these works plays out the clash of autonomy and dependence on dead bourgeois white males (on those who provided the bases for parody). Like Sartre before her, Wittig ends up confronting the aporia of reconciling commitment and freedom of choice. One cannot step through the looking-glass of mediated desire; one cannot fuse with it through homosexuality; and one cannot hold it up to others without becoming trapped behind the image that it presents. Like Sartre, after magnificent achievements, Wittig appears to have been led by the didactic imperative into a dead end.

Notes

1. See, notably, Leah Hewitt, *Autobiographical Tightropes: Simone de Beauvoir, Nathalie Sarraute, Marguerite Duras, Monique Wittig, and Maryse Condé* (Lincoln: University of Nebraska Press, 1990), and Martha Noel Evans, *Masks of Tradition: Women and the Politics of Writing in Twentieth-Century France* (Ithaca: Cornell University Press, 1987).

2. Jacques Lacan, "The Mirror Stage as Formative of the Function of the I," in *Ecrits: A Selection*, ed. and trans. Alan Sheridan (New York: Norton, 1977), pp. 1–7.

3. See Lacan, "Le Désir et son interprétation," *Bulletin de Psychologie,* no. 13 (1959–60), pp. 263–72, 329–35.

4. Jean H. Duffy, "Language and Childhood: *L'Opoponax* by Monique Wittig," *Forum for Modern Language Studies* 19, no. 4 (October 1983), p. 299.

5. Marilyn Farwell, "Toward a Definition of the Lesbian Literary Imagination," *Signs* 14, no. 1 (autumn 1988), p. 117.

6. See Monique Wittig, "The Mark of Gender (1985)," in *The Straight Mind and Other Essays* (Boston: Beacon Press, 1992), pp. 76–89.

7. Ibid., p. 81.

8. Ibid., p. 88.

9. See Wittig, *The Straight Mind,* in particular, "One Is Not Born a Woman (1981)," pp. 9–20, and "The Straight Mind (1980)," pp. 21–32.

10. Lacan, "The Signification of the Phallus," in *Ecrits,* pp. 285–88.

Bibliography

Works by Monique Wittig

L'Opoponax. Paris: Minuit, 1964. Translated by Helen Weaver as *The Opoponax.* New York: Simon and Schuster, 1966.

Les Guerillères. Paris: Minuit, 1969. Translated by David LeVay. Boston: Beacon, 1985.

Le Corps lesbien. Paris: Minuit, 1973. Translated by David LeVay as *The Lesbian Body.* Boston: Beacon, 1986.

Brouillon pour un dictionnaire des amantes (with Sande Zeig). Paris: Grasset, 1976. Translated as *Lesbian Peoples: Material for a Dictionary.* New York: Avon, 1979.

Virgile, non. Paris: Minuit, 1985. Translated by David LeVay and Margaret Cros-
land as *Across the Acheron.* Chester Springs, PA: Dufour, 1987.
Le Voyage sans fin. Paris: Vlasta, 1985.

Selected Critical Works

Auerbach, Nina. *Communities of Women: An Idea in Fiction.* Cambridge: Harvard
University Press, 1978.
Crowder, Diane Griffin. "Amazons and Mothers? Monique Wittig, Hélène Cixous
and Theories of Women's Writing." *Contemporary Literature* 24, no. 3 (fall 1983):
117–44.
Duffy, Jean. "Language and Childhood: *L'Opoponax* by Monique Wittig." *Forum
for Modern Language Studies* 19, no. 4 (October 1983): 289–300.
———. "Women and Language in *Les Guérillères* by Monique Wittig." *Stanford
French Review* 7, no. 3 (1983): 399–412.
———. "Monique Wittig." In *French Novelists since 1960,* edited by Catherine
Savage Brosman, pp. 330–44. Detroit: Gale (Dictionary of Literary Biogra-
phy, vol. 83), 1989.
———. "Monique Wittig." In *Beyond the Nouveau Roman: Essays on the Contempo-
rary French Novel,* edited by Michael Tilby, pp. 201–28. New York: Berg, 1990.
Evans, Martha Noel. *Masks of Tradition: Women and the Politics of Writing in Twen-
tieth-Century France.* Ithaca: Cornell University Press, 1987.
Hewitt, Leah. *Autobiographical Tightropes: Simone de Beauvoir, Nathalie Sarraute,
Marguerite Duras, Monique Wittig, and Maryse Condé.* Lincoln: University of
Nebraska Press, 1990.
Ostrovsky, Erika. *A Constant Journey: The Fiction of Monique Wittig.* Carbondale:
Southern Illinois University Press, 1991.
Porter, Laurence M. "Writing Feminism: Myth, Epic and Utopia in Monique
Wittig's *Les Guérillères.*" *L'Esprit Créateur* 29, no. 3 (fall 1989): 92–100.
———. "Feminist Fantasy and Open Structure in Monique Wittig's *Les Guéri-
llères.*" In *The Celebration of the Fantastic: Selected Papers from the Tenth Anniver-
sary International Conference on the Fantastic in the Arts,* edited by Donald E.
Morse, Marshall B. Tymn, and Csilla Bertha, pp. 261–69. Westport, CT: Green-
wood, 1992.
Sartori, Eva Martin, and Dorothy Wynne Zimmerman, eds. *French Women Writ-
ers: A Bio-Bibliographical Source Book.* New York: Greenwood, 1991.
Shaktini, Namascar. "Displacing the Phallic Subject: Wittig's Lesbian Writings."
Signs 8, no. 1 (autumn 1982): 29–44.
Wenzel, Hélène Vivienne. "The Text as Body/Politics: An Appreciation of Mo-
nique Wittig's Writings in Context." *Feminist Studies* 7, no. 2 (summer 1981):
264–87.
Zerilli, Linda. "The Trojan Horse of Universalism: Language as a 'War Machine'
in the Writings of Monique Wittig." *Social Text,* nos. 25–26 (1990): 146–70.

Part IV.
New Narratives, New Traditions

16

Benoîte Groult

Catherine Slawy-Sutton

Is it possible to rewrite a popular version of the Erotic in the female voice? Can a feminist novelist safely "navigate" in this genre, as she describes the many "channels" through which the female body achieves pleasure? Ever since her first writings, Benoîte Groult has been "sailing" from one feminist topic to another. It seems appropriate, therefore, to use these marine metaphors when one undertakes to examine a text that summarizes the evolution of her career—her 1988 best-seller, *Les Vaisseaux du cœur*—for its title reinforces the prolonged metaphor of the sea with a pun, the French word *vaisseau* designating both a ship and a blood vessel.

When the novel appeared, Groult was invited by Bernard Pivot to his popular weekly talk show, *Apostrophes*. He questioned her on the apparent contradiction between being a feminist and writing such an audacious novel. Benoîte Groult's answer was: "Ce n'est pas parce qu'on est féministe qu'on n'a pas de sentiments contradictoires." The publication of *Les Vaisseaux du cœur* seemed timely, for it occurred during a period when other feminists had also been reexamining the issue of eroticism. Indeed, it is interesting to note that, in the same year, Lucienne Frappier-Mazur published a scholarly article in which she underlined another paradox: the fact that, on the one hand, many feminists have been hostile to erotic literature and, on the other hand, many women have recently felt the urge to "write their bodies."

In 1978, in her informative biography of Benoîte Groult followed by an interview with the writer, Fernande Gontier explored not only the important influences of Groult's family and background but also the main themes recurring through her works: family, friendship, nature, feminism, and so on. In 1980, Margaret Collins Weitz also interviewed Groult on the subject of women's writing and feminism. More recently, Nicole Fouletier-Smith has written an introduction to Groult, with a brief survey of her major themes.[1] But, as this last critic suggests, since Gontier's book, Groult's essays and novels have been the subject only of short reviews. Yet talking about Benoîte Groult raises several questions examined in this essay, more precisely from the vantage point of *Les Vaisseaux du cœur:* is there a contradiction between being a feminist and writing an erotic novel? Does any feminist approach mean having to rethink the erotic? How is this particular novel a feminine version of the erotic?

I shall argue here that in the case of Benoîte Groult's writings, the progression from feminist pamphlet to erotic novel is certainly not contradictory, but indeed logical. In order to do so, I shall first briefly review some of Groult's previous writings, which seem to lead directly to the mature novel examined here, *Les Vaisseaux du cœur.* This article will not attempt to deal with the definition of eroticism as opposed to pornography. I am well aware that at the time of its publication, the second term was used by some critics to describe the novel. But I shall rely on Lucienne Frappier-Mazur's argument that "the sole goal of pornography is to be sexually stimulating and, whatever its form, its primary generic identity is as pornography. *Eroticism,* on the other hand, denotes a quality."[2] As I am convinced that the quality of *Les Vaisseaux du cœur* lies beyond the mere collection of what Frappier-Mazur calls "raw" pornographic passages, I have preferred to use the term *erotic* to refer to this particular text by Groult, in which the main character herself views pornographic movies as a series of "ramonages monotones . . . et minables," which make of sexuality "une activité dérisoire" (p. 137).

As a novelist, Benoîte Groult owes her popularity to the fact that she has always written about women's concerns in an accessible way, with a predilection for the lucid examination of the problems of modern couples. Moreover, throughout her writings, she shows a preference for mixing genres and styles in the same work. Her earlier novels (*Journal à quatre mains, Le Féminin pluriel, Il était deux fois, Histoire de Fidèle*), written in conjunction with her sister Flora, certainly exploited this formula. But Fernande Gontier's statement, based on an examination of Groult's novels before 1978, is certainly still valid for more recent writings: "La forme de l'œuvre est totalement dominée par l'esthétique du journal. Au-delà des sujets qui ne sont que des prétextes, il existe un courant de liberté qui donne un lyrisme au développement, dans le thème récurrent des voyages par exemple."[3] Yet although Fernande Gontier hesitates to label Groult's work before *Ainsi soit-elle* as "feminist," one might argue that indeed it was. In *La Part des choses* (1972), for example, she minutely observed the reactions of several characters confined on a ship. As they were on a cruise around the world, the particularities of their personalities were exacerbated, and the journey only condensed and precipitated the destiny of couples. Each stay in a new port created another emotional crisis. In that novel, Groult showed how men and women age at different rates in a society that idolizes youth, and particularly young women; aging often leads women to bitter despair while their husbands settle for affairs with younger rivals. Far and free from familiar surroundings, the couples of *La Part des choses* are faced with unavoidable confrontation or separation. These many observations about the lives of contemporary couples probably led Benoîte Groult to confide to Fernande Gontier that new models of female heroines were still to be invented: "Je voudrais faire un livre sur les gaietés de la cinquantaine, sur quelque chose qui nous débarrasse de cette tristesse de la femme vieillissante."[4] In the largely autobiographical *Les Trois-quarts du temps* (1983), Groult used first- and third-person narratives again to explore the life of Louise and her evolution from youth to maturity through two marriages and three children. *Les Vaisseaux du cœur* is a logical sequel to such fictional writings: first, because here also Groult favors mixing points of view, adjoining chapters that seem borrowed from a personal journal to those in the third person, inserting dialogues between the female narrator and her moralizing alter-ego (whom she calls "la duègne"); and, second, because this novel goes even further than her previous works in describing femininity and in showing the evolution of a female subjectivity.

As a journalist, Benoîte Groult founded *F Magazine* in 1978, in collaboration with Claude Servan-Schreiber (at the time, the magazine was intellectually oriented). In the 1970s, Groult wrote numerous articles calling for an improvement in the condition of women and for justice for them, both in France and in underdeveloped countries. Most of these articles dealt with the issues of the decade: contraception, pornography, the legalization of abortion, the practice of clitorectomy in many parts of the world, the underlying sexism of many behaviors and of the French language. Groult's arguments and examples are repeated from *Ainsi soit-elle,* a corrosive but successful collection published in 1975, to *La Moitié de la terre,* which came out in 1981. *La Moitié de la terre* includes articles written between 1965 and 1980: most deal with the hidden manifestations of male chauvinism and the exploitation of women. Some of the articles show the evolution in the concerns of women throughout two decades: in the 1960s, they reflected the awareness and demands for rights that, to us, may now seem acquired and elementary; the later pieces examine more subtly the numerous traps surrounding women in their private or public lives, sometimes because of their own complicity with the status quo. Other articles might have seemed rather dated just a few years ago, for instance those dealing with abortion; but they could actually find a new public today. Yet other pieces deserve to be reread by a French public that still tolerates sexism in advertising (female nudity prevails in French ads, and in the summer of 1990 a billboard ad for a *magasin de bricolage,* or do-it-yourself store, showed a woman kneeling down in a sexually provocative position, holding a drill).[5]

In her interview with Fernande Gontier, Groult said that with *Ainsi soit-elle,* she was partly questioning men's appropriation of language:

> Je trouve qu'en littérature, il faut 's'éclater,' c'est utile et encore plus dans une littérature de femme. Je trouve qu'il faut qu'on se réapproprie les mots qui étaient sensés faire partie de la littérature masculine et qui ne sont pas beaux dans la bouche d'une femme. . . . Ils voudraient que les femmes parlent toujours par . . . métaphores. Oui, c'est ça, parler des sources de délices, du siège du bonheur, trouver des expressions imagées pour désigner le sexe féminin. Il m'a semblé que c'était une entreprise utile et saine qu'une femme dise vagin ou clitoris. Je trouvais horrible d'être repoussée dans la littérature fleurie et enrubannée qui est celle réservée aux femmes.[6]

The same motif of the necessity to reappropriate language is reiterated in her interview with Margaret Collins Weitz.[7] Moreover, in an article first published in 1978 in *F Magazine* entitled "Nous, les garces, les femelles, les gonzesses . . . ," she addressed more precisely the language commonly used to designate woman, her sexuality, and her genitals.

She underlined again the derogatory connotation associated with such words in people's minds, since they are used both to "define and denigrate": "Par ses tabous, ses anomalies et ses stéréotypes, [la langue] a pour fonction de fixer et de justifier l'idéologie dominante. Un exemple: sur 1,300 synonymes de 'coït,' 80 seulement le définissent du point de vue féminin, la plupart des autres ayant un sens hostile ou agressif."[8]

It is obvious, therefore, that with *Les Vaisseaux du cœur*, Benoîte Groult continues to deal with an issue that has concerned her for many years: this novel is the logical sequel to her work both as a novelist and as a journalist. Perhaps it is the one that she wanted to write about "les gaietés de la cinquantaine" and about "quelque chose qui nous débarrasse de cette tristesse de la femme vieillissante." Moreover, it hardly seems coincidental that *Les Vaisseaux du cœur* was published two years after she served as president to the "Commission de terminologie pour la féminisation des noms de métiers," which had been created by Yvette Roudy, then Ministre des Droits de la Femme.

Les Vaisseaux de cœur describes the life-long relationship between a Parisian intellectual and a Breton sailor. The journey takes them from a small island in Brittany, where their first amorous encounter takes place, to the many ports throughout the world where they meet periodically to fulfill their intense sexual attraction to each other. George, whose nickname is "Sanzès" (Sans "s") is named after George Sand, whom her mother admired. Like the nineteenth-century writer, she is smart and nonconformist. Gauvain is one of the many children of her neighbors in the small Breton village where George and her family spend their summer vacation. He is handsome, serious, and sincere, but uneducated and very traditional. Everything separates them: their social classes and backgrounds, their educations, their ambitions, their ideas, and their respective marriages, everything but their almost brutal desire for each other. With lucidity, George knows that a marriage to Gauvain would not last; she thinks that he is somewhat silly and naive. Gauvain would be ready to change and uproot himself for her, but George refuses such a sacrifice from him. While she does not want him to lose his authenticity, she also knows that her body needs him. She sees this perfect communion of their two bodies as a gift for which they should be thankful, for she intuitively knows that not everyone is able to accept and assume such a gift. As she says, "la seule connerie impardonnable c'est de résister à un de ces moments comme la vie vous en offre si peu" (p. 48). Therefore George chooses to live this passion for what it has to offer, and not with the secret hope of changing Gauvain or making him part of her world. George and Gauvain will learn to be neither afraid nor ashamed of their bodies and desires. George will know how to make their love last, without becoming a slave to her body and passion. Through their periodical meetings across the world and the ocean, George and Gauvain will live their unique passion for more than thirty years, without having to face the tedious aspects of daily life. At first a moving celebration of two bodies that recognize each other, over time their periodical rendezvous amount to a beautiful, moving love story. "C'est une histoire qui commence sur la peau et se prolonge dans le cœur," as one critic's statement reads on the cover. (Incidentally, the cover includes an illustration of one of Camille Claudel's sculptures, "La Valse," which evokes the same passion as the one described in the novel.)

This story, obviously, is highly unlikely. It is closer to a fantasy. But "realism" is not Benoîte Groult's purpose here. With *Les Vaisseaux du cœur*, she addresses, of course, the terminology used in French to discuss female sexuality. She herself faces, in turn, the dilemma of having to be precise, but without producing a pornographic novel, a textbook, or a manual of sexuality. She accepts the challenge of describing sex and pleasure from a female perspective, but in a book written for a larger public. This in itself constitutes a task paralleling the more theoretical or philosophical writings of contemporary feminisms.

In her preface, Groult notes that she has to rejuvenate the vocabulary of passion. Her recourse to humor—in the text as much as in the preface—underlines the paucity of serious language, and the censorship that novelists have faced, in dealing with eroticism:

> Je sais que le ridicule me guette, que mes sentiments rares vont s'engluer dans la banalité et que chaque mot s'apprête à me trahir, désolant ou vulgaire, fade ou grotesque sinon franchement répugnant. Comment nommer selon mon cœur ces excroissances ou ces incroissances par où s'exprime, se résout et ressuscite le désir? Comment émouvoir en disant 'coït'? .... Alors 'hurtibiller' ou 'fomberger le gingin'? 'Danser le branle' ou 'calmer sa braise'? Ce sont hélas mots oubliés et joyeuses inventions d'une jeune et verte langue qui ne s'était pas encore laissé passer le licou. (p. 13)

Lucienne Frappier-Mazur has shown how erotic literature by

women is doubly marginal, "genre marginal traité par un groupe 'mineur.'"[9] Groult also suggests how doubly hard this task is, when the author is a woman:

> Ce n'est pas sans appréhension pourtant que je vais me mêler à la cohorte des écrivains qui ont tenté de piéger sur une feuille blanche ces plaisirs que l'on dit charnels mais qui nous serrent si fort le cœur parfois. . . . Quand on en vient aux organes qui véhiculent ce plaisir, l'écrivain et peut-être plus encore l'écrivaine se heurtent à de nouveaux écueils. 'La verge de Jean-Phil était roide, tendue à craquer . . . le phallus de Mellors se dressait souverain, terrifiant . . . Les couilles du directeur-adjoint . . . Ton scrotum adoré . . . Son pénis, ton pubis, leurs pénibus . . . Mon vagin denté . . . Votre clitoris, Béatrice . . .' Comment échapper au comique?. . . . Le vocabulaire de la jouissance féminine se révèle, même chez les meilleurs auteurs, d'une pauvreté consternante. (pp. 12–14)[10]

For Benoîte Groult, therefore, writing the feminine necessarily means having to rewrite the erotic. Female writers are faced with an entire mythology that they need to rewrite in their own voice. The difficulty that Groult consciously and conscientiously faces is to rewrite the precise manifestations of female desire with neither vulgarity nor ridicule. The challenge is to amaze the reader through images of the sovereignty of a female body, without falling into the trap of the reification of woman. In this book, her answer is twofold. First, as Groult knows that she is confronted with a problem of language, she attempts to give "une nouvelle jeunesse" to terms used for female organs. Secondly, the story is told by two narrators, somewhat loosely on the same pattern as *Manon Lescaut* and *Carmen*.[11] But contrary to those classic tales, in which male narrators (l'Homme de qualité and Des Grieux in *Manon*, and the frame narrator and Don José in *Carmen*) recount the stories of a strange and voiceless Other (Manon and Carmen), here both the frame narrator and the essential character are females speaking of eroticism in their own voice. As Groult offers the readers an adventure that is both romantic and grounded on "ces plaisirs que l'on dit charnels," she therefore attacks the underlying assumptions that language reveals. Throughout her story, she contrasts her writing to those of the "peloton des écrivains [érotiques]" dating as far back as the Marquis de Sade.

Through this definitely contrasting approach, and through this mixing of the romantic and the erotic, Groult thus participates in what Lucienne Frappier-Mazur calls "le brouillage croissant des définitions génériques" in literature.[12] In order to show how *Les Vaisseaux du cœur* offers a different version of the erotic through the evolution of a female subjectivity, one might compare the motifs in this novel to those identified by Frappier-Mazur in traditional erotic settings. As this critic says:

> La scène érotique représente une version fantasmée de domination sexuelle et peut servir d'exutoire (plus ou moins) ludique, ou de métaphore pour d'autres formes de contrôle. L'anthropologie culturelle nous a appris que nous avons de notre corps une perception médiatisée et socialisée, et que notre corps humain est une métaphore universelle pour le corps social. . . . Traditionnellement, [la] hiérarchie tranchée [de la scène érotique] se justifie par des stéréotypes implicites sur la 'nature masculine'—forte, rationnelle et supposée savoir—et explicites sur la 'nature féminine,' avec sa faiblesse mentale, sa sexualité débridée, sa vocation à la souffrance. Après le XVIIIe siècle et jusqu'à une époque récente, ce type de littérature ne donne plus la parole à la femme: au mieux 'parlée' mais muette, au pire éliminée physiquement.[13]

In many instances in *Les Vaisseaux du cœur*, descriptions of the body seem at first to polarize the feminine and the masculine, and simply to reverse gender roles: "Elle ne connaissait pas d'homme de ce gabarit. Et puis ces poignets épais qui la rassuraient chez un marin l'excitaient chez un amant car 'trop fort n'a jamais manqué'" (p. 87). It is precisely in this direction that the critic Claire Gallois reads the whole novel, when she says: "A y regarder mieux, c'est aussi l'apothéose du féminisme. Adroitement, Benoîte Groult y renverse les rôles. C'est Gauvain à qui est dévolu celui de sois beau et tais-toi."[14] Indeed, when Gauvain's body is described, or said ("dit"), it is certainly tempting to "read" his character as a male object that witnesses the sexual accomplishments of the female partner: "Vous n'auriez pas le même modèle, une taille en dessous? lui dit-elle à l'oreille" (p. 89); "Elle saisit le sexe de Gauvain dans sa main, le soupèse: 'Même vide, il pèse encore . . . je ne sais pas, moi . . . deux cent cinquante grammes?'" (p. 105). Furthermore, the fact that the male character dies at the end of the novel might reinforce the notion of role reversal; here, contrary again to what happens in *Manon Lescaut* or *Carmen*, it is the female narrator who survives to tell her story.

However, the text imposes a more subtle reading. Benoîte Groult is more interested in the *equality* of the partners than in a mere reversal of roles. Reading the book as a version of role reversal would imply that such is always the case throughout the characters' long relationship. But, first, in erotic passages like the ones just quoted, Groult insists primarily on the *ludic* dimension of sexuality; second, one finds many examples in this novel in which the female body also keeps its traditional role as an erotic object, but it is, paradoxically, with what Frappier-Mazur calls the "statut d'un sujet."[15] (Ironically, the author Bataille and the main character in Simon's *La Route des Flandres* are both named "Georges": Benoîte Groult must have had them in mind in writing her erotic novel with "George Sanzès" as the narrator.) When such is the case, the novel leads one to understand that instead of reducing a female character to the purely sexual (i.e., to the status of an erotic object), the erotic liaison that George and Gauvain reserve for each other *liberates* her personality, without her ever totally submitting to her erotic desires: "On abrite comme ça sous sa peau de drôles d'individus. Mais ce n'est pas toujours aux mêmes de faire la loi," George comments with humor (p. 114). Here the issue of the agency of an autonomous *female subject* is central. The affair with Gauvain thus permits the temporary expression of one of the numerous aspects of her intimate self, one that she has been able to discover only with Gauvain: "Elle aime le flatter, dire des choses bêtes, s'agenouiller comme Lady Chatterley, qu'il ne connaît pas, devant le Divin Engin. Lui mentir un peu même pour qu'il se montre plus passionné encore, bref se conduire comme la plus élémentaire des femmes-objets et donner libre cours à cette part de vulgarité, de gauloiserie qu'elle ne connaissait pas en elle. C'est aussi pour cela qu'elle aime Gauvain: pour cette inconnue qu'il fait surgir et qui la squattérise" (p. 105).

The common stereotypes of male and female "natures" thus explode out of their definitions. Benoîte Groult paints the portrait of a woman who is both sexually free and faithful, both rational and sensitive, both strong and feminine. George is the one who initiates their meetings around the world, and she is the one who teaches Gauvain to live their love fully for what it has to offer, illegality but without guilt. But all the same, Groult paints the portrait of a man who, if he does not have any education, has nevertheless a real intelligence of feeling; he is fatalistic but also takes initiatives; he is masculine and willing to sacrifice himself.

George is also an intellectual woman who refuses to make an intellectual topic out of sexuality: "Cette rage de comprendre le sexe comme on comprend les mathématiques! Le sexe n'a d'autre sens que lui-même" (p. 106). The question of sexuality is therefore drawn along lines subtler than those defining a science. This "rage" to intellectualize sex is best exemplified in the novel by George's American adventure (her stay in the United States over several years) and her association with two peripheral characters who embody intelligence and academia: her lover Sydney and her friend Ellen Price. Numerous passages in the novel, full of humor and irony, contrast George's character to Ellen's, whose success in academia is due to her publications "à la Kinsey" on the technical aspects of female sexuality: "Le fait d'enseigner à NYU lavant [Ellen] de tout soupçon de pornographie lui a permis, derrière l'alibi des *Women's Studies,* d'envoyer des questionnaires d'une audace et d'une précision bouleversantes à des milliers de femmes de tous âges, et même d'obtenir une bourse de recherche sur ce sujet, ce qui serait impensable en France" (p. 121). The narrator prefers to mock a scientific discourse on sexuality, which, carried to its extreme, seems to her closer to one on pornography than to one on the alchemy of love: "Ce mot d'orgasme, qui choquait encore chez nous en 1965, prend [aux Etats-Unis] une résonance quasi scientifique. . . . Cependant, le travail d'Ellen n'apporte aucune explication aux intumescences du cœur et son livre s'apparente davantage à une recette de cuisine ou à un manuel de bricolage qu'à une réflexion philosophique sur le plaisir" (pp. 121–23).

Over the course of the novel, the character of Ellen ends up as the very incarnation of the impending failure that results from totally disconnecting pleasure from tenderness and love: "Son livre marche très fort en Amérique, mais son ménage, lui, est en chute libre" (p. 128). After all, Ellen's study of "jouissance féminine," and her way of viewing her friends as many subjects in "travaux pratiques," render lovemaking as just that—a series of mechanical "travaux pratiques" (p. 128)—which include such exercises as the practice of adultery and the toning of intimate muscles (p. 154). "Mais je constate non sans regret que le souvenir de Gauvain me reste assez chevillé au corps pour me détourner d'une participation active à ces jeux," George says (p. 128). As she has discovered, "Sans doute faut-il conclure que le désir n'a pas de configuration descriptible et qu'une rose n'est pas une rose, n'est pas une rose. C'est bien réjouissant, n'en déplaise à Ellen" (p. 124).

All the same, the eventual failure of George's relationship with Sydney, who teaches modern literature and is particularly fond of the nouveau roman, seems to translate into failure the literary study of eroticism by the "avant-garde intellectuelle":

> Les premières années aux Etats-Unis, je m'étais sentie flattée de partager les habitudes érotiques de l'avant-garde intellectuelle. Je pensais encore qu'il existait une avant-garde en amour! Avec Ellen Price et Al et tous nos amis thérapeutes et sexopeutes et analystes et sexanalystes, nous dissertions brillamment de l'amour et du plaisir mais cela ne nous aidait pas tellement à le faire. . . . Cette aisance dans le dillettantisme, que j'avais tant enviée, me paraissait aujourd'hui davantage une infirmité qu'une élégance." (p. 209)

In contrast to the pitfalls of Ellen's "scientific" study of sex and Sydney's "literary" interest in eroticism, George and Gauvain's questioning about their deep attraction to each other remains unsolved. They find that the communion of their bodies has nothing to do with the learning of technical maneuvers, and that their interrogation is closer to one on religious faith: "Et si ce que nous avions de plus profond n'était pas la peau justement? Le corps sait ce qu'il veut au moins, il est imperméable aux raisonnements, il est implacable, le corps. . . . J'ai l'impression d'atteindre à une des sagesses de la vie. Cette union que nous vivons, c'est aussi puissant qu'une communion mystique. C'est comme un décret de la nature qu'on accepterait. Et c'est rare de les entendre, les décrets de la nature" (p. 148). Thus George's realization that Gauvain is much more than a mere erotic object leads us to conclude that, for Groult, rewriting the erotic cannot be reduced to a simple reversal of roles. Rather than reinforcing the stereotype of woman's unbridled sexuality, she presents a female who lives her desires serenely and concretely, *and* also refuses to build her life around her sexuality.

It follows that by mixing male and female stereotypes, as we have seen, the narrator first dissociates the physical from a traditional explanation of relationships between the sexes based on binary oppositions. Second, she destroys the myths of the masculine and the "éternel féminin." Thirdly, while her two main protagonists accept the irrational quality and the mystery of their attraction, Groult also manages to demythicize the erotic.

The explicit description of bodies and of sexual acts is central to the novel, for the woman in this text is not passive either in her way of living her sexuality or in her way of saying it. Interestingly enough, though, the writing of the more daring paragraphs in the novel is always anchored in a comparison to that of other erotic texts, in which the silences and the *non-dit* seem to predominate. For instance, the female voice in this text dares evoke the less romantic sides, the physical consequences, of a passionate "honeymoon" on the most intimate organs, all aspects usually left unsaid in other works: "Tandis que j'étale une crème apaisante sur la région sinistrée, je m'étonne que les auteurs érotiques ne semblent jamais tenir compte de cet accident . . . du plaisir. Les vagins de leurs héroïnes sont présentés comme d'inusables conduits capables de supporter indéfiniment l'intrusion de corps étrangers. Quant au mien, c'est comme si il avait été écorché vif" (p. 54). By thus filling in the silences left by other authors, Groult also underlines how these authors have despised the female sex and caused women to see themselves in a negative manner through many a reflection about their sex:

> George avait toujours douté de son 'bizourlou,' comme disaient ses amies québécoises et l'amour ne pouvait durer selon elle que parce que les hommes ne l'avaient jamais bien regardé. Et ceux qui avaient regardé de près, les auteurs érotiques, ne pouvaient qu'alimenter ses pires craintes et *bousiller son propre érotisme.* Même les écrivains les plus estimés, un Calaferte par exemple, rejoignaient sur ce sujet le peloton immonde dont le seul but semblait être que les femelles se résignent à l'abjection hideuse de leur sexe. . . . L'homme a su vendre et faire respecter [son ahurissant trio]. Les femmes ont manqué leur promotion." (pp. 138–39)

Historically, the erotic novel is based on motives suggesting masculine power, superiority, and voyeurism. As Lucienne Frappier-Mazur states, such writing implicitly links sex with death: "Presque toutes ces situations manifestent la volonté de contrôler ou de supprimer le moi, ou surtout l'autre."[16] These motives underlined by Frappier-Mazur are certainly confirmed by Georges Bataille's earlier philosophical study of eroticism. The first sentence of *L'Erotisme* provides one of the core ideas of his long essay: "De l'érotisme, il est possible de dire qu'il est l'approbation de la vie jusque dans la mort."[17] In his many references to Sade, Bataille seems to generalize this notion: "Il y a dans le passage de l'attitude normale au désir une fascination fondamentale de la mort" (p. 25), and "le mouvement de l'amour, porté à l'extrême est un mouvement de mort" (p. 48). All the same, a critic has been able to say that in Claude Simon's fiction, "ultimately, death becomes the prevailing goal of love" and that "the sexual urge and climax signal the potential destruction of barriers in death-like oblivion."[18] Such a notion of male erotica has been questioned in recent texts by women, one of the most enigmatic being, perhaps, Marguerite Duras's *La Maladie de la mort*. It is therefore revealing that in *Les Vaisseaux du cœur*, neither George nor Gauvain are presented as victims. This novel is also a commentary on the many ways in which humans live their sexuality: out of duty, or in a nonchalant manner, through a taste for technical virtuosity, or philosophical mannerism. But nowhere is it suggested that female eroticism is linked with death. The text contrasts all the better the other protagonists with the couple formed by the two main characters. Through their periodical encounters, George and Gauvain not only "recharge their batteries" but seem to return to the very source of life through difference. Indeed, in this text sex is no longer unconsciously linked to death, but, very powerfully, to *life:* "Chaque lettre, chacun de ses rares coups de téléphone, chaque je t'aime, me semblait une victoire sur les forces de vieillesse et de mort. . . . Lui qui ne voulait croire qu'au devoir et à la noblesse du labeur retrouvait pour m'écrire les mots des poètes. Il m'appelait 'son souffle,' 'sa vie,' 'sa vérité'" (p. 221).

Water—source of life, symbol of femininity—sets the stage for the sovereignty of the characters' bodies and well-being. Like a maternal figure ("la mère"), the sea ("la mer") gives life to their renewed desire. And the Breton islet, on which their young bodies recognize each other for the first time, prefigures all their subsequent encounters: "Gauvain a pris la route de côte bien sûr. Dans des cas comme celui-là, on va d'instinct à la mer. Nous savions qu'elle nous tiendrait lieu de discours et qu'elle nous envelopperait de sa maternelle grandeur, de son silence indulgent" (p. 28).

This theme is not new to Benoîte Groult. As Nicole Fouletier-Smith has already observed, "the sea is a friend, though not always friendly. It is in battling the sea together that many of Groult's torn couples discover how strongly their life together has bonded them."[19] But here more than elsewhere in Groult's work, perhaps, the ocean also polarizes their *differences* from the very beginning: "Gauvain ne savait pas nager. . . . Je m'aperçus que nous n'entretenions pas le même rapport avec la mer. Gauvain et moi ne fréquentions pas la même personne et c'est lui qui connaissait la vraie" (p. 29). The characters' approaches to the sea reveal their totally different personalities, educations, and backgrounds. Yet the sea is the means that allows them to meet periodically in spite of their separate lives; eventually, it symbolizes the very respect in which each character holds the precise differences that keep their love alive. As her desire for Gauvain has remained unchanged throughout the years, George, now middle-aged, questions a common delusion: "J'ai longtemps pensé dans ma jeunesse que s'aimer, c'était fusionner. Je ne le pense plus. [Gauvain] n'est pas, ne sera jamais mon semblable. Mais c'est peut-être ce qui fonde notre passion" (p. 243). Thus, by exploring in this novel the erotic dimension that makes passion last, Benoîte Groult suggests that sexual desire does not erase social, moral, or intellectual differences but feeds on a tender respect for the Other, and for his or her dignity. George and Gauvain will discover that "aimer c'est rester deux jusqu'au déchirement" (p. 243).

"In contrast with men's, women's erotica always introduce some love or passion, and grant the female body some integrity," Frappier-Mazur states.[20] Indeed, in *Les Vaisseaux du cœur,* George's desire for Gauvain becomes inextricably associated with love. The novel not only minimizes the power relationships between the sexes ("Dans ces interminables joutes, pas de gagnant, ni de vaincue," p. 230), but it also partly fills the gap left by other texts on eroticism and middle age. For this "prise de parole féminine" does not avoid speaking up on the bodily changes of the two protagonists, who "connaissent plus de premières nuits que de dixièmes" (p. 229). George faces the fleeting of time with lucidity:

> Je ressentais la nécessité de partir aux Seychelles non seulement pour voir Gauvain mais pour être regardée amoureusement. Ma peau se parcheminait loin de son regard humide. Je voyais aussi ma mère, malgré ses incessants com-

bats, céder peu à peu au temps, lui abandonner des territoires, des activités qu'elle aimait et dont elle feignait de se désintéresser pour ne pas avouer sa défaite. Or vient un âge où les terrains que l'on abandonne ne vous seront plus rendus. (p. 204)

As the female narrator is confronted with middle age, her interior dialogues with her "duègne"—her moralizing, self-righteous alter-ego—intensify. At times, they seem to betray the temptations of defeat, spite, self-denigration, crude observation of the Other, as in such passages in which the "duègne" is particularly eloquent: "Et tu as repéré la peau de son cou ? Elle godaille. —Et ta soeur? —Précisément! Regarde tes bras, toi aussi, ils accusent ton âge. —C'est pas mon âge, c'est le leur" (p. 231); "Un homme, plus encore s'il vit dans une communauté d'hommes, ne pense pas à masquer les petites servitudes de l'âge" (p. 232); "On peut de moins en moins se permettre de faire l'amour en plein jour en vieillissant, ou de circuler nu dans une chambre" (p. 232).

But then, one understands that these short introspective pieces serve also to contrast this female's speech with other erotic writings. The narrator's hesitations when she is faced with aging may seem rather matter of fact, but so much more genuine and healthier than the erotic "adventures" that her open-minded, well-read, intellectual self has read in other texts:

Je sais pourtant qu'un auteur érotique digne de ce nom ne peut faire moins que de montrer son héros regardant déféquer son ou sa partenaire, et ne déchargeant—comme ils disent gracieusement—que si elle a gardé son porte-jarretelles noir, ou s'il lui a uriné au visage. Ces pratiques puériles et malhonnêtes réservent, dit-on, des jouissances seigneuriales. Eh bien nous n'aurons connu que des plaisirs roturiers mais ils ont suffi à nous mettre l'âme au bord des lèvres. Ils m'ont en outre réconciliée avec mon sexe et délivrée de ce malfaisant peloton d'écrivains que j'ai si longtemps cru devoir estimer dans le sillage de Sydney et de ses amis. C'est Gauvain, qui ne les a jamais lus, qui m'a rendu indifférente à leur discours de haine et de mépris. (p. 230)

Throughout the text, humor and compassion prevail. One must

add, however, that *Les Vaisseaux du cœur* certainly has a utopian dimension and is weakened by not going "all the way" in the exploration of the stages of life. One can certainly read the death of the male partner as an ironic return to the traditional confessional récit (on the pattern, already mentioned, of *Manon Lescaut* and *Carmen*), in which the "strange" Other (the female temptress) has to die in order that the narrator may tell his story and return to a virtuous life. But by having Gauvain die at the relatively young age of fifty-seven, the novelist avoids having to think through eroticism and old age. Yet through this touching, though unlikely love story, Groult has rewritten the erotic in the feminine. As we have seen, *Les Vaisseaux du cœur* rewrites the erotic by demystifying it, and linking it to the forces of life. This novel gives a version of female erotica inextricably linked with love. By refusing to give a simplistic version that would merely reverse the roles and power relationships normally exalted in traditional erotic texts, Benoîte Groult has thus created a female character who reconciles us with the erotic, because she has been able to reconcile herself with her sex.

Notes

1. Nicole Fouletier-Smith, "Benoîte Groult," in *French Women Writers: A Bio-Bibliographical Source Book* (New York: Greenwood Press, 1991).

2. See Lucienne Frappier-Mazur, "Marginal Canons: Rewriting the Erotic," *Yale French Studies,* no. 75 (1988), pp. 112–28. Also important to eroticism is the issue of agency in sexuality, as Susan Rubin Suleiman shows in "(Re)Writing the Body: The Politics and Poetics of Female Eroticism," in Suleiman, ed., *The Female Body in Western Culture* (Cambridge: Harvard University Press, 1985). For a concise overview of the feminist debate on pornography and eroticism, see Rosemarie Tong, *Feminist Thought: A Comprehensive Introduction* (Boulder and San Francisco: Westview Press, 1989).

3. Fernande Gontier, *Benoîte Groult* (Paris: Klincksieck, 1978), p. 118.

4. Ibid., p. 212.

5. For more examples of sexism in advertising, see Kathryn A. Murphy-Judy, "Représentations de la femme dans la famille et au travail en France," *Women in French Studies* 2 (fall 1994), pp. 135–57.

6. Gontier, *Benoîte Groult*, pp. 192–93.

7. Margaret Collins Weitz, "Les Dilemmes de la femme écrivain: Entretien avec Benoîte Groult," *Contemporary French Civilization* 4, no. 3 (spring 1980), p. 359.

8. Benoîte Groult, *La Moitié de la terre* (Paris: A. Moreau, 1981), p. 149.

9. Lucienne Frappier-Mazur, "Convention et subversion dans le roman

érotique féminin (1799–1901)," *Romantisme,* no. 18 (1988), p. 108.

10. There is an implicit reference to Colette in "ces plaisirs que l'on dit charnels," she having first given this precise title to a long essay on sexuality that she later retitled *Le Pur et l'impur.*

11. This comment is inspired by a rereading of Naomi Segal's chapter on *Manon Lescaut* and *Carmen* in her book *Narcissus and Echo: Women in the French Récit* (Manchester: Manchester University Press, 1988).

12. Frappier-Mazur, "Convention," p. 117.

13. Ibid., p. 110.

14. Claire Gallois, "Célébration du plaisir," *Magazine Littéraire,* nos. 252/253 (April 1988), p. 131.

15. Frappier-Mazur, "Marginal Canons," p. 126.

16. Frappier-Mazur, "Convention," p. 110.

17. Georges Bataille, *L'Erotisme* (Paris: Minuit, 1957), p. 17.

18. Karen L. Gould, *Claude Simon's Mythic Muse* (Columbia, SC: French Literature Publication Co., 1979), pp. 66–67.

19. Fouletier-Smith, "Benoîte Groult," p. 221.

20. Frappier-Mazur, "Marginal Canons," p. 127.

Bibliography

Works by Benoîte and Flora Groult

Journal à quatre mains. Paris: Denoël-Gonthier, 1962; rev. ed., Denoël, 1994.
Le Féminin pluriel. Paris: Denoël-Gonthier, 1965.
Il était deux fois. Paris: Denoël-Gonthier, 1968.
Histoire de Fidèle. Paris: des femmes, 1976.

Works by Benoîte Groult

La Part des choses. Paris: Grasset, 1972.
Ainsi soit-elle. Paris: Grasset, 1975.
La Moitié de la terre. Paris: A. Moreau, 1981.
Les Trois-quarts de temps. Paris: Grasset, 1983.
Preface to *Œuvres* by Olympe de Gouges. Paris: Mercure de France, 1986.
Les Vaisseaux du cœur. Paris: Grasset, 1988. Translated by Dorothy Rudo as *Salt on our Skin.* New York: Grove, 1991.
Pauline Roland, ou un exécrable héroïsme. Paris: Laffont, 1991.
Cette mâle assurance. Paris: Albin Michel, 1993.

Selected Critical Works

Collins Weitz, Margaret. "Les dilemmes de la femme écrivain: entretien avec Benoîte Groult." *Contemporary French Civilization* 4, no. 3 (spring 1980): 353–

60.

Fouletier-Smith, Nicole. "Benoîte Groult." In *French Women Writers: A Bio-Bibliographical Sourcebook,* edited by Eva M. Sartori and Dorothy W. Zimmerman. New York: Greenwood Press, 1991.

Gallois, Claire. "Célébration du plaisir." *Magazine Littéraire,* nos. 252–253 (April 1988): 131.

Gontier, Fernande. *Benoîte Groult.* Paris: Klincksieck, 1978.

(For a more extensive bibliography of reviews of Benoîte Groult's books, see Fouletier-Smith.)

17

Dominique Fernandez

Marie-Thérèse Noiset

The title of a novel written by Dominique Fernandez in 1987, *La Gloire du paria* is also the title of a chapter devoted to a discussion of his novels in *Le Rapt de Ganymède* (1989), a collection of essays retracing the disapproval of homosexuality through the centuries and the emergence of an openly homosexual literature in recent decades. Assessing the bulk of his novels, Fernandez remarks: "La gloire du paria, c'est-à-dire l'auréole qui magnifie le proscrit, est le sujet de tous mes romans depuis 30 ans, et ils auraient pu tous porter ce titre" (p. 293). One could not wish for a more candid appraisal of literary works in which the fantasies and sensitivities of the writer, the vast erudition of the historian, and the sound judgment of the art critic are all tinged with strong homosexual overtones.

Born in Neuilly-sur-Seine in 1929, Dominique Fernandez is the son of literary critic Ramon Fernandez. After passing his *agrégation* in Italian, he taught for several years at the Institut Français in Naples and began a lifelong love affair with Italy. In 1967, he defended his doctoral dissertation on Cesare Pavese at the Université de Haute-Bretagne, where he was teaching at the time. In this work, which was published the same year as *L'Echec de Pavese*, Fernandez systematically uncovers the obsessional themes of the Pavesian hero. He scrutinizes the various treatments of these themes throughout Pavese's novels and short stories, arriving at a unique reconstruction of the writer's psyche. Even Pavese's style, his staccato prose and elliptical constructions, are signs that help Fernandez capture Pavese's obsession with sexuality, his deep anguish caused by human relationships, his association of women with the mythology of confrontation and calamity, and his crying need for solitude.

Fernandez's strong interest in the psychoanalytical implications of the novel had already been apparent in his first collection of essays on literature, *La Littérature italienne et la crise de la conscience moderne,* published in 1958. Identifying Italian novelist Alberto Moravia as a pioneer psychoanalytical writer, Fernandez pointed out that the Italian novelist was delving into the intricate mechanisms of adult behavior at the same time that Freud was studying them. The parallel he established between Moravia and Freud is comparable to the habitual pairing of the writer and the scientist—Corneille and Descartes, for example—each exploring the same terrain with the particular tools of his trade. Later, in his own novels, Fernandez explored psychoanalytical avenues, concurring with Freud in trying to uncover complex psychological motives for human behavior, in particular for the production of specific artwork. However, he strongly opposed certain Freudian concepts.

L'Arbre jusqu'aux racines, a volume of elaborate essays containing the core of Fernandez's critical thought, was published in 1972. It expounds Fernandez's own rigorous method of criticism, which he calls psychobiography. This work rejects creative imagination as a myth and explains works of art by a painstaking exploration of the artist's early past. At a time when structuralism was flourishing, Fernandez dared to act as a reactionary. He poked fun at the then current dissociation of author and text: "La grande affaire aujourd'hui c'est de traiter la littérature comme un tas de cailloux ramassés dans le désert" (p. 89).

Although he found support in Freud's *Introduction à la psychanalyse,* Fernandez rejected a servile imitation of Freudian models. He defined psychobiography as "l'étude de l'interaction entre l'homme et l'œuvre et de leur unité saisie dans ses motivations inconscientes" (p. 39). It elucidates the mystery of the artist's personality by identifying the primeval experiences transposed into the work of art. Literature and the arts are thus identified as forms of therapy for their creator. Fernandez's method is complex. Fantasies giving birth to art and literature are not, he warns, the direct translation of the artist's infantile experience but spring from that past, modified along the way by life's trials. It is our ignorance about an artist's or writer's biography that often keeps us from deciphering his work by means of his earlier situations and traumas.

The theoretical writings of *L'Arbre jusqu'aux racines* are followed by essays on Michelangelo, Mozart, and Proust, in which the method is put into practice. Fernandez points out that more than half a dozen of Michelangelo's Madonnas have a cold, absent stare. This is in striking contrast to the characteristic representations in Italian art of "the Virgin with child" wherein Mary is depicted as a radiant young mother instinctively and lovingly drawn toward her infant son. Fernandez attributes the peculiarity of Michelangelo's virgins to his feeling of abandonment and betrayal by his mother, who died when he was only six years old. On the other hand, the youthfulness of Mary in the Pietà of St. Peter in Rome is seen as a "blocage affectif" (p. 130). The mother, forever young, is disincarnated and idealized to counteract Michelangelo's distress. The substitution of woman's image for that of mother allows the rise of homosexual fantasies. The ephebic shape and languid pose of the Christ of the Pietà contrast sharply with the rigid attitude of his mother. In Michelangelo's world, only men can be objects of desire, since women are forever out of reach. Fernandez concludes: "La mort de sa mère a tué en lui la possibilité d'aimer les femmes. Et rien n'est plus émouvant que de le voir, en toute sincérité, transformer le mythe de l'incarnation du Christ en mythe de fraternité, de proximité virile" (p. 131).

In Mozart's case, Fernandez disagrees with the great musician's biographers concerning the excellent relationship of Leopold Mozart with his son. He refuses to regard the friction between the two men as a product of the father's excessive solicitude. He identifies "la quête du père" as the central motif in Mozart's operas, noting that Leopold's irritating supervision was aggravated by another torturing father symbol: Mozart's irksome patron, the prince archbishop of Salzburg, Hieronymus Colloredo. In *Idomeneo*, Fernandez identifies a symbolic transposition of Mozart's troubled relationships with paternal figures. The opera represents "le drame des relations entre un père failli et un fils glorieux" (p. 209). *Idomeneo* is a classic case of mutilation of the son by the father. Faced with his father's failure, the successful son is unable to savor his victory. At the end of the opera, Idamante has won the woman of his dreams and the throne of his father, but he stands speechless and is incapable of expressing any joy.

"Proust fils de personne," the last essay of *L'Arbre*, convincingly argues that, despite its reputation of exposing everything, *A la recherche du temps perdu* retreats before unacceptable truths. The characters in *A la recherche*, as Fernandez remarks, are curiously devoid of a past that would explain their eccentricities and neuroses. For instance, the episode of

Mlle Vinteuil's lesbian love, in which she spits at the picture of her father, is presented merely as a horrifying spectacle lacking any profound psychological roots. And since the scene involves secondary characters, it does not disturb the reader's good feelings about the innocence of family life (p. 315).

Fernandez contends that Proust's intricate and lengthy explanations do not clarify what he describes, but obfuscate what he does not want revealed (p. 300). As an example, Fernandez cites the episode in *Combray* in which the ample form of the pregnant kitchen maid reminds young Marcel of Giotto's *Charity*. Here, the alarming sexual turmoil that should normally rock the boy's mind is conveniently replaced by an aesthetic emotion. Fernandez comments: "Chaque fois que des personnages entrent en scène ennoblis, magnifiés par une analogie avec des œuvres d'art, on peut sans se tromper reconnaître la vibration intense du désir" (p. 326). Fernandez's systematic but fruitless search for primordial psychological motives in *A la recherche* convinces him of Proust's dissimulation: "La masse de ce qui est dit cache la masse beaucoup plus importante de ce qui est tu, en sorte qu'on a l'illusion de connaître à fond un homme dans des pages où il s'est constamment dérobé" (p. 299).

L'Arbre jusqu'aux racines was followed, in 1975, by a full-fledged psychobiography of Russian filmmaker Sergei Eisenstein. In *Eisenstein*, subtitled *L'Arbre jusqu'aux racines II*, Fernandez attains full mastery of his method. Analyzing the director's films, he discovers deep psychological truths, while at the same time painting a breathtaking picture of Eisenstein's intellectual depth and diversity.

Fernandez believes that the filmmaker's tormented childhood—the absence of his father and the constant threat of his violent, abusive mother—is the source of his failed relationships with women. Eisenstein was a faithful disciple of Freud. Fighting his strong homosexual tendencies, he felt deeply indebted to Freud's sublimation theory: he once declared that it was Leonardo da Vinci, Marx, and Freud who had kept him from becoming another Oscar Wilde (p. 186). In the angry words of Fernandez, Freud's book on da Vinci convinced Eisenstein that man has only two ways open to him: "Ou le mariage ou la sublimation. Ou la famille ou Léonard de Vinci" (p. 288). Here, as in some of his novels, Fernandez strongly condemns Freud's concept of homosexuality as an arrested stage of development, a perversion of nature that needs to be repressed. Freud's subsequent view of artistic creation as a blessed outlet for repressed homosexuality is also vigorously rejected. These popular Freudian principles are dismissed as "pseudo-scientific ideas" issued from the bourgeois context of nineteenth-century Vienna, where only marriage and its socioeconomic ramifications (children, family, financial stability) could be accepted as a viable way of life (p. 287).

Fernandez scrutinizes Eisenstein's films, searching for hidden psychological signs. He points out the erotic charge of *The Battleship Potemkin* (1925), one of Eisenstein's first films (p. 288). But in *Alexander Nevsky*, a popular epic about the thirteenth-century victory of Prince Nevsky and his Russian subjects against Teutonic invaders, he only detects a strict, impersonal reserve on the part of the artist. This coldness is attributed to the fact that *Alexander*, which premiered in 1938, was commissioned by the Communist government.

October, celebrating the tenth anniversary of the 1917 Revolution, unveils another kind of psychological involvement. Here, the initial image of the government officials' empty seats wrapped in dustcovers, alternating with the picture of the boisterous bourgeois mob, suggests the abandonment by the father in a distant past and the disruptive influence of Eisenstein's chronically enraged mother (p. 156). Fernandez interprets the violent class struggles of *October* as a sublimation of family conflicts (p. 143).

It is with *Ivan the Terrible* (1944–46) that the most brilliant case is made for the hero as an incarnation of Eisenstein's repressive struggles. Recalling the official 1941 showing of the opening segment of the movie, which received a Stalin Prize for this opening segment, Fernandez remarks that Eisenstein was in good standing with the authorities after the completion of *Alexander Nevsky*. The purpose of this new film was to instill deeper patriotic feelings in the Russian people. But as it evolved (it was completed only in 1946), *Ivan the Terrible* was censored by the government. It was not shown in its unabridged version in the Soviet Union until 1958, five years after Stalin's death. Fernandez remarks that *Ivan the Terrible* is the only movie in which Eisenstein gives a complete picture of his hero's tortured childhood (p. 250) and of the psychological consequences it entails. Recognizing Eisenstein's symbolic clues throughout the film, he perceives Ivan as something more than a simple madman desperately fighting his insanity. The legendary Russian tyrant becomes an agonizing rendering of Eisenstein's struggle with his homosexual nature: "Son ennemi, son démon, a un nom bien précis, même s'il l'ignore: l'homosexualité" (p. 267).

When he wrote *L'Arbre jusqu'aux racines*, Fernandez had not yet been able to translate his personal conflicts into his novels. He did not believe it possible to write openly about homosexuality. His early novels (*L'Ecorce des pierres* and *L'Aube*), as he himself confesses in *Le Rapt de Ganymède*, were "closet novels" containing brief, intense tales recording foiled attempts at living. He refers to their distinctive manner as "le style du malaise" (p. 298). Ambivalent treatment of women and masochistic tendencies are the norm for the male characters of these works. Although written ten years before *L'Arbre jusqu'aux racines*, they already exhibit the writer's psychoanalytical concerns. They reveal failed parental images that are part of the scenario of many subsequent novels and, most revealingly, of *Porfirio et Constance* (1992), which treats the tortured marriage of Fernandez's own parents.

In 1971, Fernandez published *Les Enfants de Gogol*. This novel, still marked by reluctance, displays the psychoanalytical current engulfing his thought at the time. Its title owes less to the Russian antecedents and intellectual interests of the characters than to their psychological affinity with the Russian novelist; Gogol, like the three male characters in the book, grew up deprived of his father. The heroes of his fiction are also unchangeable, forever molded by earlier experience. The story is told in the past by Etienne, a young Gogol specialist hired to teach Russian literature to Stéphane, the stepson of Titus Athanazy, a well-known pianist. Etienne introduces himself as "pas seulement l'annaliste d'une adolescence mais aussi l'analyste d'un adolescent" (p. 66). The affinity of the young men's names reinforces the similarities in their lives. Etienne's father, a talented but weak man, killed himself when his son was twelve, and this occurrence had a profound effect on the child. Plagued by a taste for failure, Etienne feels strongly that his life was shaped by the act of his father: "Son ratage, il me l'a pour toujours légué, auréolé du prestige qui reste attaché aux martyrs" (pp. 238–39). As for Stéphane, neither his mother's stifling solicitude nor Athanazy's deep love for him can replace his intense need for paternal approval. The narrator keeps a detailed record of the boy's plight and of his desperate attempts to make contact with Serge Estep, his divorced and absent father. Intermittent postcards devoid of content keep Stéphane's hopes alive for a while. When he receives the long-awaited invitation to visit his father in the

United States, his eagerness to leave greatly disturbs his mother and stepfather. But Estep is an irresponsible individual, a vulgar adventurer who cannot be trusted. Stéphane's trip to New York brings nothing but bitter deception and a desire for self-destruction. Indeed, the elusive father does not appear, and Stéphane becomes lost among the hippies of Washington Square.

Like the characters in Gogol's novels, Stéphane and Etienne are incapable of changing; their lives are determined by their past. Their lot is failure, brought upon them by a thwarted father-son relationship. Etienne, wrapping up his case study, speaks as Stéphane's analyst: "Gogol a définitivement triomphé; nous mourrons tels que nous sommes, tels que nous avons toujours été, tels que nos premiers pas dans le monde nous ont destinés à être. Dites-moi sous quelle constellation parentale votre héros est né, et je vous raconterai sans me tromper son histoire. Seule mon ignorance de certains détails fera une part à l'imprévu. La vérité est aussi simple que cela!" (pp. 238–39).

The 1974 publication of *Porporino ou les mystères de Naples*, which received the Prix Médicis, marks the onset of Fernandez's overt contribution to homosexual literature. The author regards this book as a transitional work: "Porporino m'a servi de transition. La blessure sexuelle infligée au castrat, l'infamie de tels stigmates, dont les ovations du théâtre sont l'amère récompense, symbolise la destinée de l'homosexuel en milieu hostile."[1] *Porporino* inaugurates a series of brilliant novels of gigantic proportions; *L'Etoile rose* (1978), *Dans la main de l'ange* (1982), and *L'Amour* (1986) all belong to this group. These tales are true epics encompassing an entire era, its customs, its history, and its arts. They are written mostly in the first person and their narrators, marginalized artists and writers, are politically conscious individuals, aware of the caprices and failings of their time. Each of these novels is divided into sections corresponding to the various periods of the hero's life and allowing the development of psychological patterns. Historical figures often serve as characters, sometimes even as heroes, giving many episodes a realistic flavor. Fernandez's homosexual production culminates with *La Gloire du paria* (1987), a very moving and thought-provoking novel about the devastation caused by AIDS, and *Le Rapt de Ganymède* (1989), an extensive and extremely well-researched volume on the social rejection of homosexuality and its treatment in literature since the nineteenth century.

Porporino is set in Italy at the end of the eighteenth century. The novel is presented as the memoirs of one of the last Neapolitan castrati. The author pretends to have discovered the text in the basement of a castle in Heidelberg. Many of its characters existed in real life: the sinister prince of Sensevero, Perocades (the Freemason-priest who plays havoc with Porporino's ideas of freedom), Farinelli (the *musico* of divine reputation, now a rich, sad old man). Even young Mozart makes an appearance to warmly endorse the irreplaceable role of castrati in the opera when they were starting to vanish.

Vincenzo Del Prato (renamed Porporino after the famous castrato Porpora) would have been a poor peasant like his father had the priest of San Donato not brought his spectacular voice to the attention of Don Raimondo di Sangro, prince of Sensevero, the village lord. He might even have fared worse: his father was always reprimanding him for his laziness, his lack of skills, and the poor quality of his work. In the first notebook of his chronicle, Porporino relates the ancient customs of his native village, with their amusing mixture of religion and superstition: the priest obligingly undoing a few stitches in a dying man's mattress, at the request of the family, in order to let the soul escape, and Perocades forgetting his masonic training and recoiling in fear at the sight of the lawyer suspected of possessing occult powers. But yet another memory haunts the aging singer, whose career was unimpressive but reasonably happy: from his early years, he dreamed of a world in which the sexes would be less differentiated.

Porporino spends five years at the Conservatoire des Pauvres de Jésus-Christ in Naples, perfecting his voice and establishing friendships with other young singers. Feliciano, more skilled and enterprising than him, better-looking also, becomes his friend and idol, while the prince of Sensevero, Porporino's patron, astonishes and frightens the world with his scientific investigations. The prince is a legendary scientist, whose fertile mind constantly produces new inventions—the unsinkable coach, waterproof cloth—but his lifelong quest is to find the secret of eternal life. This dream leads him to horrible experiments to which Feliciano will eventually fall victim.

In his adult years, as a valued member of the prince's private chapel, Porporino witnesses the splendor and eccentricities of a decadent society where the king himself partakes of the most singular pleasures. He also realizes with satisfaction that the prince's opinion on castrati closely resembles his own; Sensevero believes that the singers, through their blurred sexual differentiation, embody a basic yearning of humanity. This shared ideology lends unity to the novel and comes humorously to light during a discussion of Glück's opera, *Orpheus*. Glück had insisted, in Vienna, that the role of Orpheus be sung by a castrato, but at the time in Naples, the authorities were trying to abolish the custom. The prince justifies Glück's view by insisting on the androgyny of Orpheus, who, although he loved Eurydice even after her disappearance, also sang the beauty of Ganymede and Hyacinth, as recorded in Ovid: "Etait-ce si difficile à admettre? Il [Orpheus] participait à la fois du masculin et du féminin, ne dépendant ni de l'un ni de l'autre. Personne mieux que Glück n'avait pénétré l'énigme de cette nature équivoque" (p. 381). The esteem in which Naples held its famous castrati, in seeming opposition to common sense, answered the deep-seated search of human nature for its original androgyny. Jokingly, the author bestows on the prince a prophetic vision of a future akin to Porporino's wishes, in which sexual differences will be minimized:

> J'imagine . . . une époque devenue totalement inhumaine, asservie comme elle sera aux impératifs du rendement. . . . Alors non seulement on vénérera les enfants, mais la divine ambiguïté de cet âge sera le bien le plus précieux que chacun voudra conserver pour soi. . . . Vous pouvez leur ôter l'opéra, vous ne les empêcherez pas d'inventer dix autres moyens. Par exemple, je vois très bien les deux sexes adopter une mode uniforme, pour leurs vêtements, pour leurs ongles ou leurs perruques, pour leur maquillage. Le renforcement de la division du travail créera le besoin contraire de fusion des attributs sexuels. Qui sait si un jour on n'aura pas du mal à distinguer dans la rue les garçons et les filles? (p. 393)

L'Etoile rose, written four years after *Porporino*, offers a fiery denunciation of the repressive treatment of homosexuality by modern French society. This apologia for the sexual pariah covers a period of about twenty-five years, culminating in the aftermath of May 1968. The book is narrated by David, a teacher and writer, to his lover Alain, a student twenty years his junior whom he met during the revolt. *L'Etoile rose*, recalling the ignominious sign the Nazis imposed on the gay population during World War II, symbolizes the still-extant stigma. Proud but worried about the relaxed demeanor of his friend, David warns him: "J'en connais, qui ne seraient pas fâchés de nous contraindre à sortir marqués du triangle rose au milieu de la poitrine" (p. 16). Alain, however, has experienced rejection himself: he has been thrown out of his father's house because of his sexual preferences.

The older man retraces for his young lover the distress he experienced as a gay youth. Among his early fantasies, David remembers his strong attraction for failed heroes, "Les parias qui brillent de la gloire des élus" (p. 30). The circumstances of his family—a weak, often absent father who allowed himself to be engulfed by Nazi ideology, a strong, courageous mother who struggled to raise her son, a great-grandfather destroyed by an addiction to morphine—closely match the semi-autobiographical disclosures of *L'Ecole du Sud* and *Porfirio et Constance*.

"Pédé à Uckville, Moselle" (p. 91) are the words David uses to recreate the anguish caused by the intolerance that surrounded his burgeoning career. He explains sarcastically: "J'écris ce livre en partie à cause des mots, pour remplacer les vieux mots, qui nous stigmatisaient, par de nouveaux qui nous rendront justice. De 'honteuse,' je suis devenu 'pédé.' De 'pédés,' nous avons accédé . . . au rang d''homosexuels.' Plus de quatre siècles ont été nécessaires pour arriver à ce premier résultat. Songe que 'pédéraste' faisait partie de la langue française depuis 1584, alors que 'homosexuel' n'y est pas entré, selon le petit Robert, avant 1907" (p. 95). David's recollections of his Moselle days alternate between visions of M. de Baïon, a pathetic, aging, aristocratic homosexual trying to put Uckville in the pages of the *Eros-guide*, a sort of *Michelin* guide for gays, and Dr. Dupin, a psychotherapist convinced of the absolute authority of Freud's developmental stages.

The young man who became David's first lover confirmed the strength of the stigma attached to homosexuality. Fag—as he proudly and naively called himself because an American gave him that nickname—found great satisfaction in his relationship with David, as long as he could justify it by its economic advantage. But the proposition of a live-in arrangement made him violently indignant: "Deux mecs vivre ensemble? Mais ça va pas, non? Vous voudriez me faire devenir un pédé?" (p. 208). Fortunately for David, as homosexuality was denounced as "un fléau national" in France and penalized by revolting chemical "cures" in England, he met Donald, a free-spirited American who persuaded him that all antihomosexual propaganda, including Freud's findings, was a direct product of the current industrial technocracy.

Despite his luck in being born twenty years later than David, Alain still encounters society's hatred. Having become a militant member of the Communist Party, he gives of himself with the hotheadedness of youth during the May 1968 incidents. He is even wounded during a skirmish, but soon discovers that revolutionary parties are themselves tainted by prejudice. Banished from the party, Alain is ordered to tear up his membership card beneath the contemptuous gaze of his former comrades. In a surprising gesture, he also destroys his own photograph, satisfying the pariah's secret longing for punishment and, at the same time, fulfilling the ancient paternal curse: "Alain a cherché dans sa poche la petite photographie qu'il venait d'y mettre. Comme une hostie, il l'a élevée devant nous, puis, à son tour, déchirée en menus morceaux . . . achevant l'œuvre commencée par son père" (p. 383).

Dans la main de l'ange (Prix Goncourt 1982) is based on the life of movie producer Pier Paolo Pasolini, who was assassinated on a beach in Ostia in 1975. The narrator is Pasolini himself; most of the events related are real, and many of the characters are well-known. Nevertheless, this work is a novel. Fernandez makes this very clear in a 1987 interview: "Le roman, c'est tout simplement m'imaginer sous d'autres identités. Bien entendu, je m'identifie tantôt au double que j'aurais voulu être et tantôt au double que j'aurais craint d'être. *Dans la main de l'ange* . . . a eu une fonction d'exorcisme, comme pour éloigner de moi la tentation masochiste, suicidaire."[2]

Retracing his youth in the 1940s, the narrator presents a scenario that marks him for a future laden with guilt. He communicates his deep loathing for fascism to his younger brother, Guido, while his father, an officer in Mussolini's army, is held prisoner by the English in Nairobi. Later, Pier Paolo will cower and waver while Guido loses his life in the antifascist resistance.

This work offers no critique of Pasolini's books and films. Instead, it follows the famous iconoclast through his clandestine encounters with Rome's *ragazzi* and recounts the fame he enjoys as well as the hatred and persecution he experiences. It also meticulously recalls the vicious newspaper articles and the countless lawsuits that vilified the writer and filmmaker. It is clearly the most flamboyant "gloire du paria" Fernandez has portrayed.

As in the other novels, dialogues with well-known celebrities add liveliness to the narrative, for example, an encounter between Maria Callas and Pasolini. An even more engaging conversation with the spirit of Gramsci, in the "cimetière des acatholiques" in Rome, convinces the revolutionary to promote Communist ideals in his next book. At times, Pasolini/Fernandez muses on the disgustingly "economic" character of Freud's denunciation of homosexuality: "applique . . . cette notion d'*arrêt dans le développement*, arrêt fatal en économie, au domaine qui nous occupe, et tu découvres, non sans ébahissement, d'où Freud, fils d'un négociant en laines, a tiré ses idées" (p. 360). The narrative ends on the beach at Ostia. In Fernandez's fiction, the pariah, ready for the ultimate sacrifice, provokes his executioner, finally appeasing his lifelong guilt. Commenting on his own death, the narrator says: "De mes lèvres entrouvertes entendit-il le chant de louanges monter vers les cieux? Mon vœu le plus secret venait d'être accompli. J'avais . . . expié autant mes fautes que celles de l'humanité" (p. 599).

L'Amour, written in 1986, is a tribute to gay love untouched by the encumbrances that society heaps on its heterosexual counterpart. Fernandez chooses as his model the German painter Johann Friedrich Overbeck, whom he calls Friedrich in the novel. Napoleon is pursuing his conquest of Europe when the famous Nazarene, then an aspiring young painter, decides on a whim to leave his native Lübeck and join his friend Franz Pforr, who is studying music in Vienna. Unconsciously, he is fleeing the entrapments of bourgeois society: his impending marriage to Elisa, his childhood friend, and the inheritance of his father's prosperous wine business.

As in other novels of Fernandez, many of the characters and events portrayed in this fascinating novel are real. Fernandez retraces the saga of the painter, who, with a few other enthusiastic young artists, founds the "Lucas Brotherhood" and strives to renew art through Christian faith. The novelist adheres to the historical image of the Nazarenes, recounting their disappointment with the Academy of Vienna's pseudo-classicist teachings, their admiration for Italian Renaissance painting, their establishment in Rome as "the Christian Brethren," and their creation of a distinctive, well-delineated, colorful form of religious art.

Besides an enlightening cultural journey through the artistic capitals of nineteenth-century Europe and often humorous encounters with well-known artists and writers of the time—A. W. Schlegel, Ingres, Henri Beyle, Canova, among many others—this novel constantly reflects on love. Friedrich is troubled by the socioeconomic foundation of marriage, which keeps people from being certain of their love: "Trop d'intérêts, et trop divers, soutiennent le mariage, pour qu'on soit certain, même si on aime sa femme, de rester avec elle par amour" (p. 41). Arriving in Vienna with the young artists he meets along the way, Friedrich, like his companions, determined by the accidents of his upbringing, is enthralled by Franz's free spirit: "Pour Friedrich, marqué de façon si profonde par son éducation derrière la façade au pignon en cloche de la Mengstrasse, la liberté de son ami était un sujet perpétuel d'émerveillement" (p. 122). Friedrich rapidly falls in love with Franz. Their affection is mutual, but Franz, driven by his spiritual concerns, seems to have no need for physical love, causing Friedrich to suffer a great deal.

The ongoing discussion on art and artists by the two friends soon revolves around their interpretation of love. After seeing *The Magic Flute,* Franz postulates that Mozart, although married with numerous children, regards sexuality as "impure, superflue, importune" (p. 153). For him, at the end of the opera, Tamino and Pamina revel in their spiritual love, while Papageno and Papagena are merely the necessary agents of propagation. But Friedrich contends that when Pamino and Tamina find each other again after their tribulations, "C'est pour se fondre dans une complète union." He concludes that, for the first time in an opera, "quelqu'un nous dit que la sexualité peut être dissociée de la procréation" (p. 155). Out of compassion, Franz gives in to Friedrich's need for love, but he perseveres in his spiritual outlook. He even suggests that Friedrich may need the reassurance of heterosexual love sanctioned by society. When Franz dies of tuberculosis, Friedrich is ready to return to Elisa and the security of a heterosexual relationship, making him the only pariah in Fernandez's mythology who ultimately succumbs to the pressure of social norms.

La Gloire du paria starts with a period of demystification of gay culture and ends with a grandiose and sinister glorification of the pariah. Fernandez calls it "la célébration du retour, victorieux et terrible, de l'antique malédiction."[3] There is a twenty-year difference between the forty-five-year-old writer Bernard Morin and his lawyer friend, Marc Lavergne. The news of Jean Genet's death at the beginning of the story happily underlines, for Marc, the end of the repressive era. But Bernard, who has always felt proud of his marginality, reacts with a strange ambivalence toward the new freedom. Shortly afterward, an American television documentary reveals the horrible effects of the AIDS virus and changes the attitude of the public. Bernard haughtily stands up to the new ordeal, declaring: "La longue marche des gays se brise contre une fatalité biologique non moins intraitable que le fanatisme des moines dominicains ou la férocité des nazis" (p. 159). Revitalized by the new challenge, he decides to write a play about AIDS, but soon falls victim to the illness himself. Ironically, he had been infected with HIV from a tainted blood transfusion after a hunting accident. Friends quickly disappear as Bernard's sickness progresses, and he remarks with sinister relief: "Autour de celui qui est né paria, les gens ont raison de faire le vide" (p. 218). Following Bernard's strange wishes, Marc unconsciously prepares their grand finale. When, at the end, he injects the deadly syringe into both Bernard's arm and his own, it is in a regal, baroque setting that eloquently translates *la gloire du paria:* four ancient Sicilian candelabras lending their soft, elegant light to the immolation taking place in the middle of the majestic bedroom covered with black hangings.

In *Le Rapt de Ganymède,* a series of well-researched yet passionate essays, Fernandez presents homosexuality as a natural inclination and denounces the myths that have contributed to its disapproval through the centuries. Starting with the condemnation of the *Traité des eunuques* of Charles Ancillon in the eighteenth century, he accuses the French legal and medical authorities of zealously spreading the persecution. He stresses the attempts to end the repression, mainly in twentieth-century England and Germany, and laments the Nazis' ending of these promising efforts. He also indicts psychiatry for subordinating its findings to the economic objectives of industrial society. He contends that by merely substituting the concepts of sickness and neurosis for the age-old stigmas of depravity and degradation attached to homosexuality, psychiatry is simply condoning the modern economic scheme. Fernandez devotes the second part of his book to a penetrating critique of the abundant representations of homosexuality found in art, music, and literature through the ages, including a chapter on his own novels, and offers an edifying statement about his contribution to homosexual literature: "Il me semble que, avec ce dernier livre [*La Gloire du paria*], s'est épuisée ma contribution romanesque à la culture homosexuelle. Raconter des histoires d'homosexuels heureux, en harmonie avec leur entourage? Ce me serait impossible. Le sexe n'est pas ce qui m'intéresse le plus dans l'homosexualité: la condition de marginal, d'exclu, voilà le fantasme qui a toujours mis en train mon imagination" (p. 299).

In addition to his abundant production on homosexual culture,

Fernandez has written two novels based on his parents' lives. These books are not biographies, but they closely follow the path of Ramon and Liliane Fernandez's lives. Their fictional hero, Porfirio Vasconcellos, who narrates both novels, comes from an old Sicilian family, while Ramon Fernandez was of Mexican descent. *L'Ecole du sud* retraces the youth of the writer's parents; *Porfirio et Constance* treats their difficult life together between the two world wars. Fernandez has divided his first book into two parts that recount his parents' early years and underline their incompatibility. The story of Porfirio is told first: his mother, the widow of a Sicilian diplomat, is a fashion journalist in Paris. Porfirio is raised by three doting maiden aunts in the pleasant, anarchic idleness of a Sicilian *palazzo*. At twenty, when his mother calls him to Paris, he is ready for a carefree, frivolous life under her vigilant wing. Constance comes from a much humbler background. The daughter of schoolteachers from Auvergne, she had known adversity at an early age and has been raised under the most austere principles. When, as a brilliant scholarship student at Sèvres, she meets Porfirio at the famous "Décades de Pontigny" of M. Desjardins, their union is inevitably marked for failure.

The north/south opposition of the couple, so well delineated in *L'Ecole du sud,* creates the perfect ground for verifying the accuracy of Fernandez's psychobiographical principles. Formed by diametrically opposed experiences, Porfirio and Constance are marked for a disastrous marriage. But there is no doubt that when he wrote this novel, Fernandez was more interested in exorcising his countless memories than in proving the correctness of his theory with a well-known case study. In *L'Arbre jusqu'aux racines,* he had warned that the main raison d'être for psychobiographical research may be to free the psychobiographer himself of his inner conflicts (p. 69); he is obviously doing this in these two novels. He lends his voice to his father to allow him to confess and exonerate himself. This is an apologia for a pariah of a different sort, a man whose lax upbringing left him incapable of confronting the demands of life.

Porfirio's brilliant mind and his mother's extensive business connections start him on a promising career as a freelance journalist. He moves in the most select political circles but is unable to face up to his responsibilities. Married with two children, he lets Constance support the family while he buys expensive cars. Confronted by his wife's Jansenist outlook, he stands in awe of her iron principles but at the same time takes a mistress. On the eve of World War II, Porfirio is leaning

toward communism. But his admiration for Jacques Doriot (a Communist turned Fascist), his own Italian origin, and his desire to compensate
for his failing marriage make him turn to fascism: "Et maintenant, pour
échapper à l'impression d'avoir tout raté dans son existence, ce Janus à
deux fronts, à deux cœurs, épousait la cause politique des vainqueurs"
(p. 381). This last action, the ultimate proof of his weakness, only sanc-
tions his failure.

Fernandez's tales brilliantly prove that the psychobiographical
novel is a first-rate fictional medium. All his heroes are determined by
accidents of their past. Fernandez's heroes are mostly bright, talented
gays tortured by society's rebukes, but proud of their marginality. His
two works based on his parents' lives confirm that rejection confers a
burdensome but exquisite distinction on its chosen victims. Here, the
homosexual current is absent, but the scenario is similar. Porfirio's comments, at the end of his story, closely resemble Pasolini's on the beach at
Ostia: "Cependant, le matin où je lus dans un numéro de la presse clandestine que le Comité national des écrivains m'avait condamné à mort,
je découvris une jouissance inconnue" (p. 485).

The historical setting of his major novels allows Fernandez to cap-
tivate his reader in different ways. Talking about his fictional work, he
has said: "Le roman, c'est à la fois une promenade, un regard sur les
choses, une réflexion, un essai. Ce n'est pas seulement un langage . . . je
me sens . . . si proche de Stendhal et aussi du XVIIIe siècle, du roman
fourre-tout à la Diderot!"[4] And indeed, Fernandez the historian fasci-
nates with his realistic reconstruction of the period, be it the lavish and
decadent eighteenth-century Italy, or the politically confused pre–World
War II Europe. Fernandez the social critic shatters complacency when
he thunders against the hidden socioeconomic agenda of psychoanalytical pronouncements. Fernandez the æsthete enthralls with his original and sensitive views on music, literature, and the plastic arts. Finally,
Fernandez the Italophile gives his reader a formidable appreciation of
Italy and Italian culture.[5]

Notes

This work was supported in part by funds provided by the University of North
Carolina at Charlotte.

1. Dominique Fernandez, Le Rapt de Ganymède (Paris: Grasset, 1989), p. 299.

2. Frédéric Vitoux, "Dominique Fernandez parle de l'homosexualité, du sida
et du roman," Nouvel Observateur, no. 1165 (March 6, 1987), p. 55.

3. *Le Rapt de Ganymède*, p. 299.
4. Vitoux, "Dominique Fernandez," p. 55.
5. In addition to his theoretical and novelistic œuvre, Dominique Fernandez has written several books on music and art. They are best described as leisurely strolls through artistic cities of the past. Most of them lead the reader through the marvels of Italian architecture, but others, such as *La Rose des Tudors*, revel in English chapels of the eighteenth century. Space limitations prevent a full discussion of these books here, but, in brief, they explicate the marvels, large and small, that often remain hidden from the uninitiated eye.

Bibliography

Works by Dominique Fernandez

NOVELS

L'Ecorce des pierres. Paris: Grasset, 1959.
L'Aube. Paris: Grasset, 1962.
Lettre à Dora. Paris: Grasset, 1969.
Les Enfants de Gogol. Paris: Grasset, 1971.
Porporino ou les mystères de Naples. Paris: Grasset, 1974. (References are to the "Livre de Poche" edition of 1983.) Translated by Eileen Finletter as *Porporino or the Secrets of Naples.* New York: Morrow, 1976.
L'Etoile rose. Paris: Grasset, 1978.
Une Fleur de jasmin à l'oreille. Paris: Grasset, 1980.
Signor Giovanni. Paris: Balland, 1981.
Les Enfants de Gogol. Paris: Grasset, 1981.
Dans la main de l'ange. Paris: Grasset, 1982. (References are to the "Livre de Poche" edition of 1982.)
L'Amour. Paris: Grasset, 1986.
La Gloire du paria. Paris: Grasset, 1987.
L'Ecole du sud. Paris: Grasset, 1991.
Porfirio et Constance. Paris: Grasset, 1992.
Le dernier des Médicis. Paris: Grasset, 1994.

ESSAYS ON LITERATURE

Le Roman italien et la crise de la conscience moderne. Paris: Grasset, 1958.
L'Echec de Pavese. Paris: Grasset, 1967.
L'Arbre jusqu'aux racines. Paris: Grasset, 1972.
Eisenstein: L'Arbre jusqu'aux racines II. Paris: Grasset, 1975.
Le Rapt de Ganymède. Paris: Grasset, 1989.

ESSAYS ON ITALY, TRAVEL, MUSIC, AND ART

Mer Méditerranée. Paris: Grasset, 1965.
Les Evénements de Palerme. Paris: Grasset, 1966.

La Rose des Tudors. Paris: Julliard, 1976.

Amsterdam. Paris: Seuil, 1977.

Le Promeneur amoureux: De Venise à Syracuse. Paris: Plon, 1980.

Le Volcan sous la ville: Promenades dans Naples. Paris: Plon, 1983.

Le Banquet des anges: L'Europe baroque de Rome à Prague. Paris: Plon, 1984.

Le Radeau de la Gorgone: Promenades en Sicile. Paris: Grasset, 1988.

L'Or des tropiques: Promenades dans le Portugal et le Brésil baroques. Paris: Grasset, 1993.

Secondary Critical Works

Brenner, Jacques. *Mon histoire de la littérature française contemporaine.* Paris: Grasset, 1987.

Flügge, Manfred. "Entretien avec Dominique Fernandez." *Lendemains* 15, no. 58 (1990): 138–46.

Naudin, Marie. "Dépaysement avec Dominique Fernandez et Michel del Castillo." *Bulletin 1987–1988, Société des Professeurs Français en Amérique* (1988): 165–72.

Tolstoï, Tatiana. "La Couleur, la grâce, l'élégance." *Quinzaine littéraire,* no. 449 (October 16–31, 1985): 19.

Vitoux, Frédéric. "Dominique Fernandez parle de l'homosexualité, du sida et du roman." *Nouvel Observateur,* no. 1165 (March 6, 1987): 55.

18

Yann Queffélec

Paul Raymond Côté

The narrative structure of Yann Queffélec's first novel, *Le Charme noir*, functions on two distinct levels, creating, on the one hand, an extremely readable work and, on the other, a narration that emphasizes the writing process and the problematic nature of the literary text today. While the first structural conceit invites a conventional, thematic, even mythic approach, the second undermines the traditional, realistic mode to which Queffélec's fictional universe ostensibly subscribes, thereby soliciting an avant-gardist examination centered on what Jean Ricardou calls the adventure of writing, as opposed to the writing of an adventure.[1]

An initial consideration of the adventure per se, that is, the events comprising *Le Charme noir*, indicates a tripartite account dealing with: 1) the childhood and adolescence of the narrator, Marc Frocin; 2) his formative years of military service during the Algerian war; and 3) his adulthood, centering on a sadistic relationship with the last in a series of psychologically and financially abused mistresses. Inscribed in a chronologically linear framework and told almost entirely from a first-person perspective, the narration candidly reveals Frocin's ignoble character: his lowlife activities and petty larcenies, his total lack of scruples ("J'ignore absolument la morale. . . . Moi, je triche à vue: c'est indécent," p. 21), his participation in a group rape culminating in the murder of an American woman in Algeria, the euphoric pleasure he derives from physically brutalizing innocent Algerians, his murder of the despicable Lieutenant Védel, and, in general, his willful lies and deceptions concerning his past. An inveterate alcoholic who subsists by living off the meager salaries of the women he manages to charm, Frocin dubs himself a master in "l'art d'assassiner sans voie de fait" (p. 25). While his last mistress does indeed commit suicide, and the deaths mentioned above can be linked either directly or indirectly to Frocin, the death to which the narrator refers is that of the soul, for his corrosive nature inevitably stifles all life in those with whom he claims to be most intimate.

Certain events, although they do not justify the narrator's behavior, explain various deviant patterns of his character. A host of revelatory details concerning Frocin's childhood are determinant: the striking absence of a maternal figure, the malicious pranks the siblings played on one another, the madness and suicide of the narrator's brother, Marcel, and above all an unqualified lack of affection between family members. At best, Frocin's father considers his offspring as intruders to be avoided and hence places his son in boarding school, "comme on flanque un dangereux malfaiteur sous les verrous" (p. 33). All these factors contribute to the narrator's isolation and inability to communicate with others in a meaningful way. His later sexual conquests merely reiterate the superficial, self-gratifying ethos he was left alone to foster as a child. When confronted with the reality of his own shallowness, as is the case when Madame Horn, the mother of one of his mistresses, unmasks his irresponsible egocentrism, Frocin relieves his misery through drink: "J'avais toujours besoin d'alcool quand la honte s'emparait de moi" (p. 95). This incident is the reenactment of an earlier scene in which Frocin's incapacity to come to terms with situations involving commitment and responsibility is similarly adduced by the nurse tending to his dying uncle: "Je n'avais plus qu'une hâte: retourner dehors et trouver un comptoir où sombrer dans l'amnésie d'une bonne cuite" (p. 68).

The text moves from the level of events concerning the individual in the first section to a more global plane in the second part entitled "Carnets d'Algérie," which proves the novel's most masterfully constructed segment. From a series of preposterous and even repulsive episodes reminiscent of Louis-Ferdinand Céline's *Voyage au bout de la nuit*, there emerges a decidedly flagrant denunciation of society. Using the French army and the Algerian struggle to ridicule all warfare and abuses of authority, Queffélec, by means of his forceful descriptions, exposes the atrocities of armed conflict. Even more tragic than the indiscriminate and barbarous destruction caused by the war is the perverted debasement of those involved. As the young soldiers try to cope with the inanity of daily existence, many embrace the message of the organized killing machine and see in it "une soudaine raison d'espérer" (p. 142).

They become dichotomous thinkers, authoritarians laying claim to all rights: "un uniforme, un moral d'acier comme leur pistolet, et le droit d'humilier n'importe qui" (p. 142). Concerning his own involvement, Frocin explains: "Je simulais la bravoure pour oublier le sentiment d'agir au nom de la connerie" (p. 158).

Frocin's disorientation seems a penetrating reflection of the universal malaise of a world in search of worthwhile values: "J'aimerais bien avoir la foi, et que ma mort offre un sens puisque ma vie n'en a pas" (p. 13). Ironically, Frocin's withdrawal is bolstered by his escapism through literature, alcohol, and the powers of the imagination. These are the three opiates—"la poésie, le pastis et la nuit" (p. 13)—that Queffélec's antihero uses to palliate the personalized *mal du siècle* from which he suffers.

From romanticism to postmodernism, the human dilemma has stemmed from the alienation felt by individuals confronted with social institutions from which they deemed themselves excluded. Queffélec's work further explores that experience of marginality. The narrator's feelings of worthlessness, reinforced by nearly compulsive transgressive behavior, result from his inability to affirm his identity, but more importantly from a pervasive sense of deprivation. Even in his early years Frocin experienced a vague sensation of loss: "J'avais l'impression d'avoir perdu quelque chose et de chercher" (p. 14). Not unlike the *paradis perdu* so lamented by nineteenth-century writers, the void Queffélec's character perceives causes him to drift aimlessly through life on a nebulous quest. Interestingly, the incipit of *Le Charme noir* establishes this theme of ill-defined pursuit while immediately situating the text both thematically and literarily: "Marc Frocin. C'est mon nom. J'ai l'étymologie contre moi" (p. 13). The narcissistic nature of the text is thus affirmed by placing the center of attention on the narrator who straightaway playfully engages in a bit of onomastics, linking his fate with that of King Mark in the Tristan and Isolde legend. In addition to the king's partaking in the quest for the holy grail, the reader might recall the presence of the evil dwarf Frocin in Mark's court. And as in the medieval tale, fatality and misfortune reign in the narrator's life. He deplores the fact that he is homeless, friendless, and without a trade. He likewise bemoans the dissipation of his youthful dreams and aspirations, and most significantly his separation from Christel, the only woman for whom he claims to have felt any real love.

While the thematic elements of *Le Charme noir* are artfully introduced in the first few pages of the work, the title of the first segment, "Marc," and the first two words of the opening chapter, "Marc Frocin," point to the text's literary orientation. This view is supported by Marc Frocin's authorial role (he claims to be working on a manuscript). Frocin therefore functions as a double for Queffélec as writer, a reduplication suggesting that the work is about the writing process. In this vein, critic André Belleau postulates that the inclusion of a writer among a novel's characters, whatever his or her role as far as the intrigue is concerned, challenges the status of the narration because through such a character the work speaks about itself and the discourse becomes self-referential.[2]

In *Le Charme noir*, numerous links exist between the narrator and the written word. Describing himself in his youth as a devourer of books whose literary interests never waned, even when he was a soldier ("Je lisais comme un bon diable, étonné que la guerre accordât aux méninges un dérivatif aussi puissant," p. 144), he claims that he could not survive without novels and confesses that he would write out stories in his mind, imagining the words flowing on paper. Moreover, one of Frocin's mistresses insists that his writing style indicates an outstanding literary sensitivity. During his military service in Algeria, Frocin is in charge of mail distribution, a task that becomes unequivocally identified with literary expression. He delights in opening letters addressed to his fellow soldiers to study the style of the women writing to their lovers and wonders whether, after their men return home, these women will ever have the occasion to write again, "de connaître ce jeu d'écrivain qu'est le transfert de la vie dans les mots" (p. 130). While on mail duty, Frocin tampers with the soldiers' emotions by withholding letters and distributing them at a later time, a seemingly banal act but one that, in the narrator's mind, becomes analogous to André Gide's affective distortion of his diary: "Tel Gide arnaquant son journal intime et se prêtant certains jours, par souci d'équilibrage, des émotions qui l'avaient traversé d'autres jours, je modulais à dîscrétion les rapports du bidasse avec les siens" (pp. 132–33). Another game in which Frocin engages is that of changing his handwriting and corresponding with himself ("J'auto-correspondais," p. 138), sending letters from Algeria to his home in France to have them forwarded (in reality, returned) to him. While this schizophrenic behavior causes him to evoke the dual personality of Stevenson's Dr. Jekyll and Mr. Hyde, it more importantly underscores the narcissistic nature both of Frocin and of his journal (he is, in effect, writing to and for himself), thus becoming a *mise en abyme* of the entire text.

At first glance, the structure of *Le Charme noir* appears unquestionably clear: Marc Frocin, in spite of his overtly nihilistic view of human existence, is finally attaining self-realization through the writing of his journal. The plausibility of this interpretation falters, however, as the reading progresses, especially as concerns the third and final segment of the novel, "Le Carpasson," where a narrative shift to an omniscient third person creates a break, rendering Frocin's journal unassimilable with the text in which it is contained. "Le Carpasson," a fusion of the French words for rug ("carpette") and doormat ("paillasson"), is the pejorative nickname Frocin has surreptitiously given his most recent mistress, Sylvia. It indicates her totally submissive nature and Frocin's insensitive manipulation of her. In this section, Sylvia peruses a manuscript which Frocin has intentionally left for her to find in their squalid apartment, and which reveals details negating all hope of reviving an already strained and empty relationship. The narrative then swings between the pages she is reading and a description of her reaction to them, thus creating a metaphorical representation not only of the text itself but of the *narrataire* or, in this case, the reader. Furthermore, it is not certain whether the text Sylvia is reading corresponds to what the reader has been reading up to this point. There is even a transition to the second person as Frocin addresses Sylvia directly in his journal in his attempt to destroy her psychologically. Set off in italics, the final chapter of *Le Charme noir* returns to Frocin in the present after Sylvia's suicide.

These numerous shifts in point of view produce an ambiguity that envelops the narrative so fully that the reader is never quite certain whether what is transpiring reflects the narrator's personal story or is a part of his delusory world. Did the narrator's mother die or rather did she run off to Mexico with a beekeeper? Did Frocin actually plot and execute Védel's murder or was this event merely symptomatic of the narrator's compulsive fantasizing? Frocin, as he himself admits, assumes a variety of personas, "me cachant, moi, dans tous ces rôles" (p. 92). Sylvia wonders whether or not Frocin wrote the manuscript with the express intention of drawing her into yet another fable (p. 203). Her reception of the text is, in reality, a parody of the reader's potential reaction to the book wherein both ask themselves: "Y avait-il un mot de vrai dans ce fatras qui charriait l'ennui?" (p. 203). Later in the text, Frocin addresses this question without really answering it: "Tu voudrais savoir si c'est vrai ou si c'est faux tout ça, si c'est de la triche ou du solide, mais ne compte pas sur moi pour t'éclairer" (p. 237). Ironically, in spite of the narrator's avowed penchant for lying ("le mensonge est mon radeau de survie," p. 243), his love of words synchronously connotes a search for truth: "la vérité cherche à s'incarner dans les mots," (p. 259). *Le Charme noir* slowly becomes a game of hide-and-seek between the reader and the narrator as the fabricated aspect of Frocin's tale reveals itself: "Si parler de moi m'a toujours passionné, c'est que je pouvais me fuir dans les phrases—ou m'y poursuivre—avec le vague espoir que finirait par se présenter quelque ressemblance entre le personnage et l'acteur" (p. 26). The textual labyrinth unfolding before the reader, the narrator's quest, the thematic and paradoxical treatment of the power of words and the difficulty of communicating—all these elements are a commentary on the precarious situation of contemporary literature and the possible failure of language.

It might be pertinent to note that Queffélec's involvement with literature is of long standing. Journalist and literary critic for *Le Nouvel Observateur* before the publication of *Le Charme noir*, Queffélec began writing at the age of twelve and states that now he could not give it up: "Je vis avec les mots."[3] His father, Henri Queffélec, a fervent Catholic who died in 1991, was the author of over seventy works, most of which celebrate his native Brittany and the sea. Similarities exist between Yann Queffélec's first novel and his father's first published work, *Journal d'un salaud, la Culbute* (1946), in that both texts deal with existential concerns, or the "difficulty of existing," as the narrator of *Journal d'un salaud* puts it. Interestingly, as is the case with Henri Queffélec's novels, symbols of Christianity punctuate *Le Charme noir*. The symbolic connotations of the name of Frocin's lost love, Christel, should not be overlooked. And whereas the men of the sea play a quintessential role in his father's novels, Yann Queffélec's Frocin delights in corrupting his devout military companion Pescatore, whose name signifies fisherman. Images based both on Christianity and the ocean are developed to a greater extent in the works that follow, particularly in the author's second novel, *Les Noces barbares*, where the sea and its symbolic associations become pivotal to the narration.

In recognition of the outstanding literary quality of *Les Noces barbares*, Queffélec was awarded the highly coveted Prix Goncourt in 1985, which immediately catapulted him to the forefront of France's contemporary writers. The novel, like the love-hate relationship it depicts, provoked divergent reactions. A "piece of literary chicanery" and an "overwrought and overrated exercise in Gallic Gothic" for some,[4] *Les Noces barbares* is for others "an excellent novel . . . a novel of great power and beauty."[5] Largely abandoning the first-person perspective found in *Le Charme noir* to espouse an apparently traditional, omniscient, third-person point of view, and adopting a representativeness eschewed by many modern authors, Queffélec weaves a compelling tale vaguely reminiscent of Mauriac's family dynamics of vain destruction and, at times, of Hugo's fixation with the sea and the mother image. In an interview, Queffélec states: "Le nouveau roman nous a fait croire qu'il fallait chasser la sensibilité. C'est une erreur. Moi, je veux avant tout émouvoir."[6] Emotions indeed run high in *Les Noces barbares,* where the author succeeds, in a manner all his own, in rendering a heterocosm structured around repression and isolation.

    Les Noces barbares opens with quasi-ceremonial solemnity as thirteen-year-old Nicole Blanchard prepares for a secret rendezvous with the American soldier who has been ingratiating himself over the past two months with her baker parents. The clandestine meeting abruptly turns into a violent initiatory ritual as the adolescent is the victim of a group rape whose description firmly entrenches the symbols of blood, fire, and water into the thematic fiber of the narrative. Ludovic Blanchard, the child born of this graphically depicted crime, and the real protagonist of *Les Noces barbares,* becomes in turn the victim par excellence, rejected by all, especially and mostly pitilessly by his mother who remains for him an obsessively magnified object of both idealization and fear. The inability of Nicole and her parents to overcome what they see as the shame and ridicule of the community leads them to blatantly negate the child's existence. Relegated to a garret, despoiled of any human affection or attention except that shown by Nicole's cousin, Nanette, Ludo slowly mutates into a monster of innocence and ignorance.

    Like *Le Charme noir, Les Noces barbares* is divided into three parts, each treating a distinct segment in the main character's life: 1) Ludo's sequestered existence above his grandparents' bakery until age eight, followed by his experiences in his stepfather's household after Nicole marries the town mechanic; 2) Ludo's internment at the Centre Saint-Paul, an institution for the mentally deficient; and 3) Ludo's escape from the asylum and discovery of the ruins of a wrecked ship that he adopts as home. This synopsis of the novel's events does not take into account the process of telling that constitutes the core of Queffélec's art. In addition to a style that is direct, straightforward, yet at times poetic, several biblical and archetypal symbols serve as literary vehicles to communicate Ludo's personal drama of dispossession.

Structured around the antithetical themes of innocence and guilt, *Les Noces barbares* contextualizes these elements in the semireligious setting of the Centre Saint-Paul. Indeed, its founder lauded the unspoiled nature of those unable to mentally attain the age of reason: "Ils incarnaient l'innocence édenique, l'espoir lilial du rachat, ils étaient les pur-sang d'une béatitude enseignée par le Christ" (p. 170). And when Ludo naively asks what children are, Mademoiselle Rakoff, head of the institution (and former mistress of its late founder), replies: "Les enfants sont des êtres que le bon Dieu met sur la terre . . . pour donner l'exemple. Quel exemple? Eh bien la pureté, la sincérité, la simplicité, et bien sûr l'innocence" (pp. 177–78). She goes on to explain that children are the guardians of purity and that the lamb symbolizes purity, then presents Ludo with a miniature papier-mâché lamb, which is to represent him in the crèche found in the asylum's dining hall. With jeering irony, the narrator describes how each night, when the children are asleep, Rakoff rearranges the nativity set and how each morning the boarders/patients eagerly look to see the proximity of their lambs to the Christ child. Should the patients fall out of Rakoff's good graces, they inevitably find their lambs far from the infant, a sure sign of disfavor.

The repeated use of the word *innocence* to describe the asylum generates an intentional link with the scriptures. For example, in the evening, pictures are shown commemorating "la Genèse et donc l'innocence—la mer immaculée des premiers jours" (p. 192), and on Wednesdays, patients pay homage to Jesus, "père de l'innocence et doux vainqueur du Malin" (pp. 192–93). The artificiality of this haven from the outside world is vividly exposed, at least to the reader, through the daily practice of drugging the patients with sedatives as well as through Rakoff's bizarre sexual fantasies. In the end, the term *innocent* takes on negative overtones, becoming synonymous with rejecting the outside world and assuming the role of an automaton: "fidèle à ses résolutions, Ludo fut un pur innocent d'une mélancolie souriante, un enfant modèle, et s'aligna si bien sur les autres que son mouton dans la crèche talonna les meilleurs" (p. 228). After curfew, however, Ludo abandons his facade of compliance. Wandering through the asylum and around the grounds, he learns of the clandestine nocturnal activities of the staff members. This encounter with the tree of knowledge, so to speak, marks the end of his physical "innocence." Ludo soon meets a young patient named Lise and in the caress of her arms attempts to overcome the oppressive loneliness he feels. His relation with Lise nevertheless fails to bring him the consolation he needs, since his thoughts unremittingly return to his maternal obsession.

Symbolically, it is with the arrival of Christmas, a feast commemorating the coming of the "Dieu des innocents" (p. 265), that Ludo's emotional state reaches a climax. When his mother, who has thoroughly ignored his existence since he was placed at the Centre Saint-Paul almost a year earlier, does not come to visit him for the holiday, he decides to run away. Before escaping, he sets fire to the crèche, jubilating at the thought that all the artificial lambs and everyone, including his mother, will be swallowed by the flames. Although this is not the case, the scene is crucial since it groups a series of images and themes interspersed throughout the text. First and foremost of these is the inversion of the traditionally joyous implications of Christmas. The narration of *Les Noces barbares* places the event in an ominous trajectory wherein a feast instituted to celebrate the birth of a child reawakens in Nicole feelings of guilt and discord. Ludo is the scapegoat of his mother's hysterics: "Il détestait Noël. Il revoyait les sapins jetés sur la route, les cadeaux piégés, les disputes" (p. 272). The burning of the crèche translates Ludo's desire to efface these unpleasant memories.

It should be stressed that fire is a polysemous symbol with both positive and negative associations. This being so, Ludo's gesture might be interpreted as a frustrated expression of his confused emotional bonds with his mother. But fire is also linked to initiation and purification rites as well as to rites of passage. How revealing the Centre Saint-Paul conflagration becomes when one considers that Nicole placed her son there to break with the past in an effort to cleanse herself of the living proof of her guilt. Previously, she had tried to exterminate this embodiment of her culpability in an aborted attempt to burn her child alive: "Nicole au souvenir du viol, voul[ait] la mettre au feu, cette plaie" (p. 46). Purification and the rite of passage are emphasized here since, in like manner, Nicole burned her childhood dolls immediately after her rape. Furthermore, the blaze set by Ludo at the Centre Saint-Paul definitively puts an end to a segment of his existence and marks his entry into manhood. Thus, as with Nicole, fire becomes for Ludo the catalyst in a symbolic rite of passage.

Like fire, water images carry a rich symbolism. In *Les Noces barbares*, they contribute, often in conjunction with fire images, to the actualization of a significant thematic configuration. If Ludo immediately seeks the ocean after setting fire to the Centre Saint-Paul, it is because of his inherent need to return to his origins and join with the absolute maternal force. Ludo both loves and fears the wave of the ocean: "Elle était belle comme sa mère" (p. 312). On contemplating the sea, Ludo visually soaks in "cet immense lait natal" (p. 61). Again the purificatory qualities of the sea are underscored by Queffélec ("l'innocence—la mer immaculée des premiers jours") as are those of fire ("tout feu qui brûlait donnait à Ludo le sentiment d'approcher la vérité," p. 313). Numerous images fuse the two symbols ("l'océan prenait feu," p. 290) thereby creating an interweaving representative of the inextricable coalescence of Ludo's and Nicole's destinies. Nicole's blond hair is colored a fiery red in Ludo's myriad of drawings, linking her to the many fire images contained in the narration. Ludo's green eyes and fixation with the sea couple him, in turn, with the water images that prevail. The repeated melding of these two opposing elements is a metaphorical articulation of Nicole's phobic visions: "Dans ses fantasmes, il arrivait aussi qu'elle et son fils ne soient plus qu'un seul être, et qu'elle fût obligée de se tuer pour l'oublier" (p. 155). In the context of the images developed throughout the narration, the final scene of the novel is a subtle extension of the fire-water fusion: after killing his mother, Ludo embraces her body, "ses longs cheveux à fleur d'eau lui caress[ant] la bouche" (p. 344), as they both sink to the depths of the ocean.

As in *Le Charme noir*, intertextual references are present in *Les Noces barbares*, the most significant perhaps being *Le Petit Prince*, which Ludo reads at the Centre Saint-Paul. Saint-Exupéry's work seems at times to function as a subtext for Queffélec's narrative describing Ludo's plight, a conflict between childhood and the adult world. A microcosm unto itself suggestive of the Little Prince's distant planet, the Centre Saint-Paul is described as "une planète en quarantaine" (p. 193). More importantly, however, *Le Petit Prince* is the text Ludo's cousin Nanette, a surrogate mother, would read to him when he was confined to the bakery garret. Queffélec includes excerpts from it where reference is made to the other world from which the Little Prince comes as well as to the drawing of a lamb: "Où veux-tu emporter mon mouton?" (p. 42). These details and other phrases taken from *Le Petit Prince*, such as "c'est tellement petit chez moi" (p. 43), are conspicuous commentaries on Ludo's predicament: his hidden origins, his emotional vicissitudes, his circumscribed existence.

La Femme sous l'horizon further explores the drama of family conflict and repudiation, this time in a setting with mythical and at times cabalistic resonances. The title of the novel is derived from astrological principles that are explained to the main character, Tita, in a letter left to her by her deceased mother: "Tu es née sous l'horizon, au bord de la nuit, parmi les soleils de la nuit. Les planètes à ta naissance étaient cachées . . . la lune même était sous l'horizon" (p. 91). This celestial configuration, it would seem, creates conditions favoring accidents and calamitous events, especially those involving fire. This sign of unavoidable fatality dominates not only Tita's existence but that of all her family as well.

Tita, whom her grandmother calls "la fille du péché" (p. 60), has no recollection of her mother, Carmilla, but learns that she resembles her to the finest detail. As in *Les Noces barbares*, where the Blanchards try to deny Ludo's very existence, the Tarassévitch family, led by its matriarch, Zinnaïde, attempts to eradicate any memory of Carmilla's passage. In a bizarre atmosphere steeped in Russian folklore and superstition, the reader follows Tita's investigation into the past to find that her mother was a Romanian gypsy who married Tita's putative father, Vladimir, to gain legal entry into France. When Vladimir refused to let her go to Paris to study, as was agreed, she took on a lover to make her husband jealous. In retaliation, the violent and dipsomaniacal Vladimir decides to play a macabre game of Russian roulette by not repairing the brakes of the family vehicle driven at different times by his wife, his brother, and himself. Fate chooses Carmilla as its victim, and she perishes in a fiery crash.

The divulgence of this hitherto undisclosed information completely alters the relationship between Tita and Vladimir, which degenerates at an accelerated pace as Tita openly goads her father about her mother's death and as Vladimir beats his daughter more frequently. Plagued by gruesome dreams and spectral visions, both seek solace in alcohol. Tita finally goes to live with her cousin in Strasbourg, where she soon real-

342 ♦ Paul Raymond Côté

izes she is pregnant. Although she wants to bear the child to carry out her mother's wishes ("choisis de mettre au monde un enfant qui te délivrera du mal," p. 170), the father, none other than her uncle Lev, tricks Tita into an abortion. Symbols of fire and the sea, prevalent in this section of the text, help convey Tita's complete psychological devastation. Even her encounter with Misha, who sincerely loves her and wishes to marry her, cannot emancipate Tita from the spell of the shadowy phantoms of her past. She begins a double life, creating for Misha's benefit an identity and family history based either on a distortion of real events or on outright fantasy. The mental breakdown she is suffering translates itself in terms of elusive behavior that infuriates and exasperates Misha. In the concluding segments of the narrative, Tita returns to the family manor, where she learns from her grandmother the final truth: Carmilla's lover was Vladimir's brother. Therefore Tita's real father is not Vladimir but rather Lev. Upon learning this, Tita causes a fire that consumes the family manor and its inhabitant. As she runs out to save herself, she is killed by Misha.

Contrary to Queffélec's previous novels constructed in three parts, *La Femme sous l'horizon* comprises two sections. This is significant since the number "two" permeates the narrative, carrying with it a symbolism of conflict and antagonism. Aliette Armel points out several interesting components centered on duality: 1) the double life led by Tita, who by day plays the role of docile fiancée, but by night, unknown to Misha, frequents rowdy discothèques, where she dances feverishly, pretending to be her mother, Carmilla; 2) Misha, who ends up becoming Vladimir's double since Vladimir was responsible for Carmilla's death, much like Misha is for Tita's; 3) the twofold locus of the Tarassévitch estate with the Baba Yaga manor, where fire is forbidden, and Lev's rustic hut, where the warmth of fire is enjoyed to the grandmother's great apprehension.[7] Various other inclusions anchor the symbolic associations of the number in the narration: Zinnaïde had two husbands and two children, Vladimir and Lev; Vladimir raises two children, Tita and Zénia; Zinnaïde dislikes her second son, Lev, just as Vladimir disdains his second daughter, Tita. In addition, Tita is described as possessing a dualistic nature, one aspiring to harmony and motherhood, the other sensual and possessed: "Mystère et mensonge étiraient leur frontière entre les deux femmes" (p. 211). Finally, it is worth noting the role of the caretaker of the cemetery where Carmilla is buried in an unmarked grave.

This character, who helps Tita reconstruct the circumstances surrounding her mother's death, is, like Queffélec, a Breton and becomes the author's double in his role of telling and revealing.

In precise, intense, and lyrical language, *Le Maître des chimères*, which several critics have deemed Queffélec's best novel, deals once again, albeit from an inverse perspective, with the parent-child relationship and the difficulty of coming to terms with reality. Clearly, Queffélec revels in the portrayal of pathologies. The antihero of this work, the protean actor Francis Pavin, a sort of *puer eternus* ("Mais quand cesseras-tu d'être un enfant, lui répétait sa femme," p. 17) is indeed the master of illusions that he actualizes through compulsive prevarication, much like his prototype, Marc Frocin.

Pavin, however, is not a writer but an actor: "il possédait le génie des voix comme celui des costumes" (p. 16). For him theatrics are not limited to the stage. Donning the most bizarre attire to assume various personalities and thus free himself from the codes governing daily existence, Pavin roams the streets of Paris disguised at different times as a doddering old man, a septuagenarian madwoman, and a blind beggar. He even manages to extract a small contribution from his unsuspecting wife, who does not recognize her husband, so complete is his metamorphosis. When in need of solitude, Pavin secludes himself in his secret hideout where he stores his disguises, a shabby rented room unknown even to his wife: "un local aux accessoires . . . une oubliette à prodiges avec démons et métamorphoses" (p. 12).

Pavin's antics carry over to his sexual life, since he thinks nothing of cavorting with a string of mistresses while his wife, Marianne, a successful pediatrician, is either at work or at home taking care of their young daughter, Mimi: "Les jours de cafard il recherchait la trace de ses plus anciennes maîtresses, rebroussant jusqu'à vingt-cinq ans d'absence et de pistes effacées. Il proposait passion, bout du monde ou suicide à des femmes abasourdies, mères de famille, certaines encore éprises et prêtes à renouer le fil du grand amour déserté par lui sans motif" (p. 19). In short, both Pavin's professional and personal duplicity mirror the dissonance between truth and reality, which is at the core of the text's narrative structure.

Despite Pavin's superior gift for drama, he is motivated by an implacable need for self-destruction. Consequently, he does everything in his power to bring about his own ruin, depriving himself of the theatrical success within his reach and transforming his life into a dilatory act of suicide. Indeed, the first segment of the novel relates the actor's professional downfall: breaking character on stage and laughing at his leading lady, missing performances, throwing a brick through the restaurant window where the cast is dining. The most damaging blow to his acting career comes when a demon of the past takes hold of him during a performance of Shakespeare's *Twelfth Night* and makes him once more step out of character to castigate the audience and besiege his admirers with insults.

The second part of the novel describes the disintegration of Pavin's relationship with his wife and his irremediable descent into the abyss of the imaginary as his detachment from reality becomes more acute. While drinking himself into oblivion, rehearsing roles he will never play, and racking up onerous debts his wife invariably pays, he continues his histrionics with one of his mistresses, Anna, promising her marriage and children. So engrossed is he in his roleplaying that he scarcely notices Marianne's distance and the fact that there is no longer any communication with her, a situation that reaches its nadir on Marianne's birthday. After preparing a special meal and purchasing a ring for his wife at great expense, Pavin goes to Pigalle, where he spends over three thousand francs on shoes for one prostitute and gives the ring he bought Marianne to another. His incorrigibility is clearly demonstrated when, returning home completely inebriated to find Anna comparing experiences with Marianne, he attempts to cajole his irate wife while at the same time placating his mistress: "je t'aime [Marianne], souffla-t-il en essayant d'avoir un clin d'œil vers Anna" (pp. 231–32).

In spite of Pavin's blatant deceit and buffoonery, he is not a banal character to be hastily dismissed. On the contrary, Queffélec has endowed him with an enigmatic dimension by means of the veil of mystery that enshrouds *Le Maître des chimères*. In this narration where childhood and death are thematized, the two key events precipitating Pavin's demise (his castigation of the audience while playing Malvolio and his carousing with prostitutes on his wife's birthday) are each immediately preceded by the anonymous arrival of objects from a past that Pavin is desperately trying to bury. Cruelly sent by Pavin's vengeful father-in-law, these objects—the picture of his dead son, Thomas (a child he fathered by a lover before his marriage to Marianne), and a knife, or "languiole," that belonged to Pavin's father—can both be linked to Pavin's nightmarish visions of cradles and coffins in the snow, and to his fixation on the Shakespearean character Malvolio.

Slowly the reader is apprised of facts that make it possible to partially unravel Pavin's labyrinthine past of assumed identities and to understand why the knife is an embodiment of the paternal image that obsesses him. While Francis Pavin, born Lasnier, at one time used the alias "Languiole," his present pseudonym, "Pavin," is derived from the waters where his father drowned: "Il a voulu traverser à pied le lac Pavin comme le Christ, et il s'est noyé" (p. 15). Pavin's profound sense of guilt partially stems from his refusal of his father's humble legacy, his unwillingness to become a cutler: "Il avait refusé le sort des couteliers, refusé ses origines, et voilà qu'il imaginait son père et le père de son père, et tous les hommes de sa lignée" (p. 245). The second memory Pavin attempts to blot out, the death of his infant son from exposure to the cold, is the most incriminating. Since the event transpired while Pavin was at home rehearsing the role of Malvolio so loudly that he drowned out his son's cries, the actor tries to exculpate himself by placing the blame on Malvolio: "Moi, j'ai vu mourir Thomas, mais c'est toi Malvolio qui l'as tué" (p. 278). The two events (the refusal of his origins and the death of his infant son) are closely interrelated, since the first is tacitly presented as a crime of hubris while the second becomes divine retribution for Pavin's offense.

Several narratorial inclusions support this argument. At one point Pavin qualifies himself as both a madman and a megalomaniac (p. 97) and aggrandizes his theatrical glory to mythical proportions: "je vais triompher . . . ils viendront tous m'adorer, tous les morts sortiront des cercueils" (p. 90). He furthermore presents himself as a victimized Christ figure: "D'ailleurs pourquoi Saül me persécutes-tu?" (p. 126). Queffélec's use of Shakespeare's *Twelfth Night*, a play based on disguises and assumed identities, as a sort of metatext, aptly informs Pavin's situation, especially in light of Malvolio's exaggerated pretensions at social ascension. In Shakespeare's work, is not Malvolio called a madman? The play also imparts to Malvolio a double role, which is duplicated in the narrative grounding of *Le Maître des chimères*: "Thou shalt be both the plaintiff and the judge / Of thine own cause" (Act V, scene 1). Throughout Queffélec's text, the reader encounters references to the theme of judgment, and these references transform the narrative into a harangue that is at once paradoxically accusatory and recriminatory. They are also transposed into a Christian context with Pavin's quest for salvation, which he ultimately finds while working in Spain at a restaurant tellingly named "El Pescador."

While the novel opens with the grisly childhood recollection of the slaughter of a pig (named Jesus), it closes with Pavin's death as he pushes a child from the path of an oncoming truck only to be fatally injured himself. This occurs while a bullfight is going on. The matador's name, Jesulin de Ubrique, by virtue of the fact that it contains the name Jesus, helps complete the narrative cycle. Again Pavin's double role is emphasized since he considers himself both as sacrificer and sacrificial victim: "Je suis le matador, le taureau" (p. 294). Realizing Icarus's dream, he is now elevated to the glory to which he has always aspired, as his injured body is lifted toward the sun by the peasants: "la foule battant des mains criait mon nom, c'est moi qu'ils applaudissaient . . . ils me portaient en triomphe, les enfants sanglotaient, je ne m'étais jamais approché si près du soleil" (p. 293). Having succeeded in winning the affection of the little girl whose life he saves, Pavin has earned his salvation through his meritorious act: "il était sauvé, pardonné" (p. 292).

In *Le Maître des chimères*, the alternation between first-person and third-person narration conveys not only Pavin's disorientation and instability but also the binary thematic schema underpinning the novel's structure. In reality, the intertwining of the "je"/"il" perspective is complemented by another narrative device: the interspersing of short italicized passages throughout the text, which articulate a stream of consciousness intervention. This is one of the distinctive markers of Queffélec's style. A similar technique was used in *Les Noces barbares* to reveal the inner feelings of the main character, Ludo, while echoing commentary from other sources, the end result being somewhat analogous to the function of the chorus in Greek tragedy. In *Le Maître des chimères*, these diegetic interruptions evoke haunting memories for Pavin while at the same time creating a curious dialogue between past and present, a sort of *chassé-croisé* that readers must fathom for themselves. Furthermore, the work's narcissistic elements could be analyzed from the standpoint of "the adventure of writing," as a metaphoric variation of the writer's quandary. Such an analysis would be appropriate on two levels: the structural (intertextual references, letters and other self-reflecting strategies) and the thematic (the self-centered creation of alternate realities, the contradistinction of truth and fiction).

Unlike Queffélec's previous antiheroes, Pavin, in the novel's epilogue, becomes a positive character who, guided by his love for his daughter, has shunned his mythomaniacal fantasy world and is at last capable of self-acceptance. Interestingly, this is achieved under his assumed identity of a deaf-mute. Conversing by means of messages scribbled on a notepad or carved in the sand, he transcends himself to establish meaningful bonds with those around him. While *Le Maître des chimères* amplifies the telling process through its triple narrative prism, it also suggests the possibility of valid communication through the written word.

Prends garde au loup takes up many of the narrative techniques and thematic elements found in Queffélec's earlier novels and reweaves them into an intense drama of sexual repression and violence. A kaleidoscopic perspective that fuses characters' thoughts with narratorial commentary; italicized sentences and paragraphs interjecting, usually retrospectively, the first-person viewpoint of the main character; the themes of judgment, guilt, and atonement; fire and water symbols; the depiction of an unavowed and all-consuming prurience are all familiar components of Queffélec's fictional universe. From his earliest recollections, Toni, a timid, frustrated, and cruel boy, incapable of self-affirmation and taunted by his personal failings, has been obsessed by Maï, his cousin by marriage who is two years younger than he. Like Ludo with his abandoned ship and Pavin with his secret rented room, Toni has his "repaire" (p. 24) on an "ilôt secret" (p. 12), aptly named "la Secrète," far from the adult world. There his imagination runs wild as he envisions himself the guardian of fire, living in mythological times, and reflects on Maï's mutable qualities. In his imagination, she can change herself into a flame, a bee, or a violin (p. 25). This internalized childhood world represents a sort of idyllic moment that Toni desperately tries to immortalize ("le rêve de rester toujours deux enfants amoureux," p. 200). Toni's tragic drama is his incapacity to accept the inevitability of change with time: "En fait il n'était pas né pour grandir. . . . Il était né pour l'enfance et les rêves. Il était né pour l'amour de Maï et Maï avait grandi, Maï l'avait trahi" (p. 255).

If time and change are, in essence, symbolic expressions of death, the opening scenes of the novel, depicting the burial of Toni's grandmother, inscribe this existential preoccupation in the narration. More importantly, they reinforce Toni's disdain for the adult world (his grandmother, in his view, has betrayed him by dying: "t'avais pas le droit, fallait pas mourir," p. 16). Toni's subliminal fear of the passage of time and of death becomes explicit to the reader through a nightmare in which a black horse turns endlessly around his grandmother's coffin as Toni struggles in a panic at the bottom of the open grave: he is the one being buried (p. 43).

Archetypal embodiments of time are often theriomorphic in nature, as are figurations of the sexual libido, especially in association with "les symboles de la chute et du péché."[8] All abound in *Prends garde au loup.* An indirect reference to the biblical fall appears near the end of the text when Toni, in a drunken stupor, speaks of his fiancée in cryptic terms, describing her as "une crème de petite vipère . . . qui n'était pas la moitié d'un serpent, surtout pour la pomme!" (p. 257). A previous incident, echoing Pavin's hubris, although not grounded in animal imagery, likewise makes allusion to the mythical fall of humanity by describing Toni's very real fall from a crane, when he tries to outdo his friend, Julius, by climbing higher to be "plus près du ciel" (p. 82). For a few moments, however, high in the air, "il se sentait fort et douloureux comme un dieu" (p. 82). These libidinal fantasies run tandem to Toni's insurmountable fears, which cause objects in the night's shadows to take on the terrifying forms of bats and spiders. In addition, these theriomorphic representations are directly related to "le péché" since Toni's mother requires that her son regularly submit to what she calls the "séance de poux noirs" (p. 34), a euphemism for confessing his sins to her. They are similarly related to the character's confused and ill-defined sexual urges.

Interestingly, much later, when Toni is working as a miner for an engineering firm, he finds himself trapped alone in an underground tunnel with a cow, which he calls a "corne de brume" (p. 232), or foghorn. Yet in the context of the images at hand, the animal suggests a kind of psychological Minotaur, a symbol of Toni's unresolved emotional forces with which he must do battle. It is significant that Toni does not fight the animal that has charged at him, only to break a leg, but ends up lying down beside the injured beast. This unexpected encounter with "la vache sacrée du souvenir de maman" (p. 233) momentarily unleashes in Toni's memory the eerie monsters of his childhood fears, which he now seems able to ponder quite calmly.

As a mechanism of self-defense against time's terrible spectacles, the psyche may invert the negative values they initially inspire and euphemize the objects of fear such that they become shelters from the unknown. Toni's nightmare of being buried alive gives way to his actively seeking the reassurance of subterranean passages. He recalls how, as a miner deep in the bowels of the earth, "toute une montagne le rassurait" (p. 247), as though he were safe in his mother's womb. Textual inclusions comparing Toni to Tom Thumb confirm this imaginary miniaturization, a phenomenon whose psychological implications have been well studied. Indeed, this type of miniaturization is basically a reduction of the male genitals to the infant state. The process seems to denote a psychologically feminine perspective, an expression of fear of the male organ and of intercourse. In the case of Queffélec's character, the refuge offered by the underground network of tunnels becomes a substitute for the sexual fulfillment Toni has never known. In the "nuit du souterrain" he releases his sexual frustrations: "il se caressait les yeux fermés, il frottait sur le roc son sexe baigné de sperme et d'eau froide" (p. 225). Unfortunately, Toni's lifelong fear, which kept him from realizing his love for Maï, has by now degenerated into a morbid physical fixation: "*Maï Maï j'aurai ta fente et je la tuerai*" (p. 225).

Prends garde au loup offers a wealth of symbols and images that cannot be adequately explored here. Attention, however, should be drawn to the setting for the action: a series of small islands, connected by marshes and swamps, suggestive of the characters' isolation and primal impulses. A type of psychological landscape, this "pays d'eaux fermées, sans merci" which has existed "depuis l'arche de Noé" (p. 46), takes on cosmic proportions. It is fundamentally the internal landscape that each of us harbors, the land of tragedy.[9] It is also linked to the basic quest for the innocence to be found at the origin of all things: "l'époque où la Genèse et les Sphaignes ne faisaient qu'une même planète heureuse uniquement peuplée d'enfants" (p. 54). To restore this imagined idyllic state, or at least to annihilate those people and places that have sullied his illusions, Tony imagines burning his secret island (pp. 116, 121) as well as his friendship with Julius, whom he knows is covertly seeing Maï ("incendier leur amitié," p. 117). He likewise imagines dowsing Maï (who has become pregnant by Julius) with gasoline, setting her aflame and then doing the same to his mother (p. 234). While these fiery visions, reminiscent of Saint John's *Apocalypse* (one of Toni's preferred texts), never materialize, Toni is responsible for Julius's drowning.

Much in *Prends garde au loup* is only sketchily revealed, for instance, the reason Toni's father has ostracized himself from the household to inhabit a shed at the other end of the garden, thus renouncing his role of husband and father. In a similar manner, Toni's vague and recurring vision of a man wearing white pants carrying the boy on his shoulders, a vision that seems to hold the key to Toni's identity, is never explained: "il verrait l'homme aux pantalons blancs sur une route de campagne ... et il saurait, il saurait, le jour se lèverait en lui" (pp. 229–30). The final chapter projects the reader into the future. Toni is now being judged for Maï's murder, which apparently took place in the year 2029. Queffélec ends his novel with an ironic twist. "Les hommes en blanc" (p. 266), obviously the medical personnel working on Toni's case to determine his mental state, have replaced the "homme aux pantalons blancs" whose mysterious image pervades the narrative.

As author and editor Françoise Verny states, "the New Novel, with its cerebral stress on form and technique and its disavowal of classic plot, has yielded to a revival of full-blooded 19th-century storytelling. ... There are no schools these days, no currents, no dominant gathering places or literary reviews. We're in a period of individual ferment."[10] Queffélec's novels, especially his most recent works, while not completely discarding the narratorial encoding of the author's function, reflect this trend now prevalent in France. His contribution to French literature is by no means negligible. For literary critic Jean-François Josselin, Queffélec is one of the most original and moving voices in literature today.[11]

Notes

1. Jean Ricardou, *Problèmes du nouveau roman* (Paris: Seuil, 1967), p. 111.

2. André Belleau, *Le Romancier fictif* (Québec: Presses de l'Université du Québec, 1980), p. 23.

3. Gisèle Galante, "Prix Goncourt 1985: Yann Queffélec," *Paris-Match*, no. 1905 (November 29, 1985), p. 13.

4. Ann Moseley, "Sins of the Father and Mother," *Times Literary Supplement* (March 4, 1988), p. 244; Peter Kempt, "Overwrought and Overrated," *Sunday Times* (February 21, 1988), p. 65.

5. Scott Bradfield, "Heir to the Flesh," *New Statesman* 115, no. 2973 (March 18, 1988), p. 28.

6. Galante, "Prix Goncourt 1985," p. 13.

7. Aliette Armel, "Les Cicatrices de l'enfance," *Magazine Littéraire*, no. 254 (May 1988), p. 77.

8. Gilbert Durand, *Les structures anthropologiques de l'imaginaire* (Paris: Bordas, 1969), p. 75.

9. Chantal Davedrin-Liaroutzos, "L'Ange noir," *Magazine Littéraire*, no. 300 (June 1992), p. 84.

10. Richard Bernstein, "Revisionists and Storytellers," *New York Times Book Review* (January 5, 1986), p. 3.

11. Jean-François Josselin, "La Vie est un roman: sang, amour et volupté," *Le Point*, no. 814 (April 22, 1988), p. 65.

Bibliography

Works by Yann Queffélec

Bela Bartok. Paris: Mazarine, 1981.
Le Charme noir. Paris: Gallimard, 1983.
Les Noces barbares. Paris: Gallimard, 1985. Translated by Linda Coverdale as *The Wedding.* New York: Macmillan, 1987.
La Femme sous l'horizon. Paris: Julliard, 1988.
Le Maître des chimères. Paris: Julliard, 1990.
Prends garde au loup. Paris: Julliard, 1992.

Selected Critical Works

Armel, Aliette. "Les Cicatrices de l'enfance." Review of *La Femme sous l'horizon*. *Magazine Littéraire*, no. 254 (May 1988): 76–77.
Bernstein, Richard. "Revisionists and Storytellers." *New York Times Book Review* (January 5, 1986): 3, 29.
Bradfield, Scott. "Heir to the Flesh." Review of *The Wedding*. *New Statesman* 115, no. 2973 (March 18, 1988): 28.
Chassay, Jean-François. "De l'autodestruction considérée comme un art." Review of *Le Charme noir* and interview with Queffélec. *Spirale*, no. 43 (May 1984): 3–4.
Côté, Paul Raymond. Review of *Le Maître des chimères*. *French Review* 65, no. 1 (October 1991): 173 74.
Davedrin-Liaroutzos, Chantal. "L'Ange noir." Review of *Prends garde au loup*. *Magazine Littéraire*, no. 300 (June 1992): 84–85.
Galante, Gisèle. "Prix Goncourt 1985: Yann Queffélec." *Paris-Match*, no. 1905 (November 29, 1985): 12–13.
Josselin, Jean-François. "La Vie est un roman: sang, amour et volupté." Review of *La Femme sous l'horizon*. *Le Point*, no. 814 (April 22, 1988): 65.
Kempt, Peter. "Overwrought and Overrated." Review of *The Wedding*. *Sunday Times* (February 21, 1988): 65.
Moseley, Ann. "Sins of the Father and Mother." Review of *The Wedding*. *Times Literary Supplement* (March 4, 1988): 244.
Queffélec, Yann. "Portrait d'un jeune artiste en vieux singe fatigué." *Nouvel Observateur*, no. 1098 (November 22–28, 1985): 14–15.
———. "Tous comptes faits." Interview. *Nouvel Observateur*, no. 1223 (April 15–21, 1988): 62–63.
Royer, Jean. *Ecrivains contemporains. Entretiens. 4: 1981–1986*, pp. 61–71. Montréal: L'Hexagone, 1987.

19

Patrick Drevet

Gervais E. Reed

A typical French writer working in the classical tradition, Patrick Drevet is a self-conscious artist who has read widely in Greek, Latin, and his native language, keeps a narrow focus, analyzes closely, and writes elegant prose. He continues consideration of ideas that have appeared earlier in twentieth-century French fiction: Gidean problems, a Proustian interest in memory and imagination, undercurrents of Sartrean philosophy and Lacanian psychology, and a Beckettian discouragement that life exceeds the power of human language to express it. Drevet has sustained interest in these ideas throughout his career, and he has expressed them in a fluid, imagistic style that grows out of New Wave novels and films. Nonetheless, he speaks with his own voice. One needs time to read Drevet's novels, récits, stories, and essays—to "browse," as Barthes puts it[1]—because the enjoyment of reading his fiction is an old-fashioned pleasure that requires an aristocratic (again, the word comes from Barthes) and leisured reader. When read slowly, Drevet's writing expands, for his works are about more than appears on the surface. In this sense also, they resemble other late twentieth-century fiction. Like the novels of Nathalie Sarraute,[2] Drevet's work invites readers to examine with a new lens a few phenomena that in their minute details reveal fundamental human concerns. His interest lies not in linear narrative with traditional characters and dialogue, but in the psychological drama that occurs when his narrators view the world, meet other people, face themselves, and contend with their aspiration to express these encounters.

Drevet's works derive from a painterly vision shaped by a keen interest in the history of Western art. In virtually all his writings, he refers implicitly or explicitly to a range of visual artists. Poussin's painting "Echo et Narcisse"—or "La Mort de Narcisse"[3]—figures significantly in his first novel, *Pour Geneviève*, and invites a reading influenced by the myth. Like Narcissus, the narrator yearns for discovery but finds only himself and fails to gain the thing that he loves. One need not dwell on the details of the myth to see a similarity to Drevet's novel. He has structured it as a confrontation between two narratives, both written in the first-person singular, one a notebook filled with drafts for a novel by a persona one might designate as the narrator, the other a commentary on the drafts written later by a second persona, the commentator. Drevet has shaped the novel less as narrative than as literary discourse. His personae are characters, he has said in an interview, echoing Rimbaud: "Dès que je dis JE, j'enfante quelqu'un d'autre."[4] Furthermore, his narrators use the first person as a reminder that the novel is a quest and a construct: "Je tiens à ce que, dans l'objet produit par une forme d'expression artistique, cette forme s'avoue . . . qu'elle rappelle sans cesse qu'elle n'est qu'une recherche" (*Ecrire*, p. 29). These comments recall the words and works of his predecessors, the writers of the French New Wave. In his own manner, however, Drevet invites his reader to scrutinize the process by which visual perception leads to knowledge or, if it fails, to discern the reason why.

Initiating the principal metaphor of *Pour Geneviève*, the narrator/commentator tells how as a boy he saw a bunker, a vestige of World War II built on a beach on the Mediterranean coast, that his mother forbade him to enter. He describes the bunker as it reappears in his memory, and he expresses it as epiphany: "Elle eut tous les caractères que l'on reconnaît aux visions: brutale, fulgurante, totale. J'eus l'impression d'un éclair qui avait illuminé, comme un flash dans la nuit, tout ce que devait contenir mon roman. Oui, tout y était: couleurs, lignes, corps, mains, visages, yeux, regards" (p. 7). In his ambition to reproduce this sudden revelation, the commentator thinks visually. He mentally composes a two-dimensional picture in order to convey the reflective character of his vision, "un vaste tableau en à-plat susceptible de me regarder de la même façon que cette vision du blockhaus m'avait regardé" (p. 7). The commentator begins his project by reading drafts of descriptions of the bunker that, as narrator, he has written years before. Then he becomes more ambitious as he feels the need to lend life to flat description. Forbidden to enter the bunker, the boy lacks historical fact, and the absence of history forces him as an adult to create it. He tells how he imagined a battle, then a wounded soldier lying within the bunker. In his imagination, he associates the prostrate soldier with a friend lying on the beach, then the beach with the sea, then the sea with ideas of death and birth. The bunker on the beach—"mon mythique blockhaus"—informs the novel that the commentator inflates as a metaphor for quest: "Etrange pulsion que celle de l'explorateur ou de l'archéologue, la même que celle du scientifique ou du poète. Cette course au trésor qui anime déjà tous les enfants me reste mystérieuse" (p. 19). Thus the search for the history of the bunker takes the form less of a historical record than of a narrative of imagination. The boy never enters the bunker because of his mother's admonition, but he detects her fear that may go back to her wartime experiences and that he adopts in his own psychology as a fear that the bunker might cave in. Afraid of entering its depths, the boy refrains from entering the bunker except in the privacy of his imagination. Just as the commentator as a boy avoids the risk of entering the bunker, as a man he ultimately refrains from delving into himself. He cannot or will not recognize his homosexuality, characterizing truth again and again as elusive—"insaisissable"—as, of course, it is under the cover of his verbosity. He finds safety in words. Language can convey truth, but it can also protect. The commentator looks constantly for knowledge but hides in the vanity of his sometimes overwrought, often erotic prose. Flowing from his pen, language becomes form without substance.

In this first novel and in subsequent works, Drevet's language expresses visual perception that takes the form of specular effects by which he attempts to understand the psychology of "le regard." As in Robbe-Grillet's film *L'Année dernière à Marienbad,* characters in *Pour Geneviève* live in the consciousness of others. In a causal relationship, the narrator/commentator strives to compose a picture that will reflect his experience and, simultaneously, the persons whom he sees reflect on him. The reciprocity of human consciousness emerges from many visual episodes in the novel, of which two in particular stand out. First, the narrator describes a boy on a beach looking into the distance. Like the narrator who looks at the boy, the anonymous male figure gazes at the horizon, seeking an undefined and perhaps indefinable "essence." As is his wont, the commentator takes the draft of his description and invents its meaning: "Je ne me rappelle plus les traits de ce jeune homme, mais, il est vrai, m'avait retenu l'extraordinaire tension de la recherche que semblait indiquer son attitude. . . . Ce qui m'apparaissait particulier dans le comportement de ce jeune, c'était le sentiment de l'irréalité du présent qu'il me semblait ressentir, et son retour à quelque chose d'essentiel" (p. 275). What the commentator sees most of all in the tension of the boy's stare is its similarity to his mother's staring at the bunker. He combines the two visual images in a symbol of the other in which he senses himself as both fearful and alone: "Et je sens bien qu'en moi leurs comportements coïncident. Qu'est-ce qui les prenait? Cette insoluble question était peut-être moins importante en soi que le fait que je me la posais. Je ne pouvais en tout cas lui donner qu'une réponse: ce qui les prenait, c'était eux-mêmes, et soudain j'étais seul. En même temps que leur irrémédiable solitude, c'était la mienne, tout aussi irrémédiable, qui m'était révélée" (p. 276). This episode comes late in the novel, as if to summarize the psychological process by which solitary human beings yearn to fuse memories and to invent meaning from what they have seen.

In another highly visual sequence—which may well be the most remarkable passage in this carefully crafted novel and the one that most vividly demonstrates the *mise en abîme*—the narrator describes Yves, a *lycéen* whom he loves. Yves, sulking for some unknown reason, is riding in a city bus. The narrator watches both Yves and Yves's reflection in the bus window. Its transparency also permits the narrator to see himself and the passing pedestrians and buildings of the city. In a sullen mood, Yves tries to isolate himself by trying not to look at the other passengers, but he cannot ignore them. They are there, including the narrator, conscious of him, lending him existence. His attempt to escape is a recognition of their power to create him, a superiority that the narrator also recognizes:

N'avais-je pas moi aussi en ce bus l'impression d'être le prisonnier d'un miroir infiniment multiplié, d'un monde où il n'y avait pas de dehors? La vitre de l'autre côté de laquelle j'aurais pu essayer, comme Yves, d'échapper, par un effet de la réflexion du soleil me renvoyait mon image, celle d'Yves, ou celle des gens debout tout près de nous. Et ce jeu même de réverbération était moins l'effet du soleil et des vitres que celui de nos yeux. (p. 294)

Drevet has created a series of specular images reminiscent of Sartre's *Huis clos* or the house in Biskra where Gide's immoralist looks into a mirror and sees Moktir steal a pair of scissors. Inescapable space, in which Drevet's narrator/commentator sees others and is seen by them, both repels and attracts. As in any erotic relationship, it repels because he fears that he will not be able to control what he might find inside. He fears his power to create others that implies their power to create him; their superiority deriving from this power makes him vulnerable. But the space attracts him also because his vanity seduces him into seeking existence in the first place, even in the eyes of others, even at the risk of vulnerability.

Crystalline images show various facets of the narrator's experience and inevitably reflect back on him to reveal the vanity of his quest. In the final section of the novel, Drevet grapples with the effect of photography and of writing. His narrator/commentator and Geneviève look at photographs taken while they were walking on a beach at Saint-Jean-des-Monts. There, as on another beach, he has seen a bunker. The photographs taken of him are good—"réussies," an adjective that takes on ironic implications—but they are beautiful, he says, only in the sense that the elements making up a photograph flatter him. In describing the photograph, however, the commentator's vanity surmounts his defenses and reveals the truth of gesture: "il y a une réticence en tout mon être qui ne veut pas se laisser 'prendre,' qui me guinde, me crispe, qui pâlit mon front, cabre mon cou, bloque ma nuque" (p. 308). The photographs illustrate a rigid posture that suggests his fears, but the pictures don't "take," that is, they do not get to the heart of the matter. On the other hand, his verbal description does take. The reader finds in his perambulations the truth from which the commentator recoils. Although he may be wrong about how a photograph takes, he is right in saying that photographs show only two dimensions. Frequent allusions to the visual arts suggest that painting can convey deeper insights than photography. Drevet's narrator/commentator refers to the depiction of eyes in paintings by Modigliani (p. 119) or to Michelangelo's Sistine Chapel ceiling as an expression of the "esprit créateur" (pp. 43, 204, 234). Moreover, reiteration of Poussin's "Echo et Narcisse" invites a reading of the novel as an expression of the idea that self-love is self-annihilation because Narcissus or the narrator/commentator already possesses what he seeks but refuses to acknowledge that possession. Because the commentator shrinks from what he calls authenticity, becauses he avoids truth in the activity of writing, and because, like Narcissus, he is more interested in the reflection than in what it reflects, the encounter fails. In the last analysis, then, the novel poses the problem of how we grasp truth or beauty and then retain it, a question that has preoccupied Drevet throughout his career.

References to visual art and cinema in *Pour Geneviève* become explicit metaphor in Drevet's second novel, *Les Gardiens des pierres*, in which specular images contribute significantly to the expression of religious truths. Drevet uses the story of a film crew that goes to a monastery to record its closing as an expansion of Lacan's theory of the Other. Four exuberant young men excited by the possibilities of cinema technology and the notion of filming a monastic tradition meet five monks, the only inhabitants of what was once the site of a flourishing religious community in southern France. The film crew is strangely affected by the life of work and prayer taking place in the modest stone structure. The cameraman observes at the beginning of the novel that it was meant to be transformed into a photographic image: "l'abbaye est déjà son propre film, tout est déjà en image" (p. 18). A lighting technician recounts his perceptions of the film crew and the monks they meet. The story becomes—like a film—a sequence of images. It is not a coincidence that Drevet's narrator is the crew's lighting technician and that his responsibilities for lighting scenes carries over figuratively to the prose narrative.

Drevet's leisurely style melds admirably with his subject. Like the persistent flow of frames on a movie screen, the sequences in this novel convey the film crew's experience of coming face to face with the abbey, with others, and with the Other. The novel's first sentence establishes a visual image as the windshield frames a view of the hills of Provence and another world: "L'horizon de la route disparut au bas du pare-brise" (p. 9). Drevet's first-person narrator describes the abbey in explicitly photographic terms: "le regard reconnaissait des formes auxquelles leur caractère régulier, répétitif, donnait l'aspect de points de repère, et bien vite, comme sur le papier sensible plongé dans le bain du révélateur, l'abbaye, à travers les branches crochues des buissons et sous les arbres rares, se dessina en blanc sur le blanc, en gris sur le gris" (p. 11). With remarkable precision and intensity, Drevet transforms the visual description of the monastery into a metaphor for the Other. The men gaze from the top of a hill at the abbey built in the valley below, and they undergo something like Lacan's mirror stage during which the "corps morcelé" anticipates totality: "L'abbaye se présentait encore à nous telle qu'elle avait dû s'immobiliser au moment où, le plus légèrement du monde, la dernière pierre, l'ultime lauze avaient été posées, et nous demeurions ainsi, au-dessus d'elle, comme soulevés dans une position interroga-tive, tenus alertés par une sorte de suspense" (p. 12). Toward the end of the novel, Drevet risks pushing his metaphor too far. The buildings, the abbot explains, are driven into the soil like Christ's flesh nailed to the cross. Like Christ, the monastery aspires to transcend its visible physi-cality and attain the invisible, but it is held back by the earth. The earth limits aspiration to a gaze: "mais voyez comme la dure terre la retient, qui la maintient contre elle, comme cela, face au ciel. . . . La vocation de cette architecture n'est pas de dire mais d'écouter; c'est la nôtre. Elle nous ressemble comme une sœur." Then the abbot reflects self-depre-catingly on the audacity of the image that he has just invented: "Me voici bien lyrique, dit-il" (p. 277).

Dom Bertrand's reductionism calls attention to Drevet's frequently bold style while suggesting at the same time two ideas: the concept of the Other as an invented form, and the notion that the means of human expression are limited. The mirror stage, Lacan asserts in *Ecrits*, "manu-factures" a succession of fantasies that extend from fragmented body-image to its totality.[5] What the child observes in the mirror and what Dom Bertrand observes in the abbey are both abstract ideas that shape the observation, or vice versa, and determine the structure of develop-ing identities. The abbot looks at the monastery and draws together all its secular and spiritual components. Similarly, the cinematographers want to make a film. Drevet's novel records their experiences of aspir-ing to capture on film a certain vision. Ultimately, however, it records their failure. The director, Paco, falls short of the image that he wants. He misses "inscribing" on the screen what he sees on the stone walls and in the monks' gestures. None of the takes satisfies Paco, but all of them demonstrate on one level the distance between ascetic life and a secular point of view, and on another level the disparity between hu-man aspiration to creativity and the realization of that hope. The novel does not lack humor as Paco tries to impose his ideas on the monks. For example, one moment he insists that they be natural, then reproaches them for being less willing than children to take direction. In frustration, he uses makeup on a monk in an attempt to get the right detail, driving the abbot to rebuke him (p. 192). The abbot's gentility contrasts tellingly with Paco's outbursts. Such episodes suggest not only the collision of two cultures—one spiritual, the other secular—but also the lag between idea and its execution. More often than not, the medium fails to register the artist's idea: "Paco s'esclaffa, leva les bras en l'air, puis expliqua qu'un cinéaste ne pouvait être sûr de rien tant que la pellicule n'était pas développée, qu'il ne parvenait du reste presque jamais à ce qu'il avait souhaité et . . . philosopha sur les rapports du réel avec l'imaginaire, sur cette ligne indécise de leur rencontre où se situe la création" (p. 221). Paco blames the medium for his failure to bridge the gap between the real and the abstract.

The idea of the limitations of aesthetic means to express creative aspirations raises important questions, including concern about the novel form itself: does truth always surpass the means of its expression? Paco despairs of ever photographing the monastic architecture in the half-light of dawn, and he says to the abbot: "Vous comprenez . . . la pellicule n'est pas sensible de la même façon que notre œil" (p. 286). Similarly, the narrator cautions the reader about the limitations of language in its failure to convey an image. Having seen the sound technician, Hans, imitating the monks that he is observing and recording, the narrator deprecates his impression: "et sans doute n'était-elle que l'effet de mon imagination romanesque" (p. 247). On the other hand, the abbot summarizes the monastic vocation, suggesting the possibility of merging the components of human existence in a unified life: "Voir enfin pour toujours celui que toujours on a voulu" (p. 201). The narrator wants to reply that we see what we want to see, but he wisely refrains from trivializing the abbot's aphorism. Unlike Paco's exuberance and despair, the narrator's restraint suggests reason for hope. Prose fiction, cinema, or any artistic expression may on occasion and perhaps miraculously integrate with thought and feeling in order to create a unified image of the harmony of human existence and even of peace.

What, the novel invites us to ask, are the conditions for artistic creation? If Drevet's novel succeeds as a metaphor integrating form and content, then the source of its success may lie within the imaginative resources of his narrator. The narrator gathers the fragments of his four-day visit to a monastery into an image of community and spiritual unity. Writing self-consciously in the Proustian tradition, he says that he writes in order to understand Hans's experience in the monastery and that he begins his project by regaining the past, "pour *retrouver* cette ambiance qui me paraît l'avoir retenu" (p. 26; emphasis added). Like Paco, the narrator intends to capture an idea; he differs from Paco, however, in the same way that he resembles Proust. He possesses an increasingly coherent idea of time and memory. Paco's failure to produce a film from discrete takes may be attributed less to the inadequacy of his medium than to lack of a coherent vision. He fails because he understands only part of monastic life, its present, secular dimension: "Si j'ai bien compris . . . ils ne cherchent pas même Dieu, ils ne veulent entretenir en eux que cette volonté et cette capacité que l'on a d'aimer" (p. 152). The point is that Paco has not really understood the monks. In a particularly telling episode, Paco observes the monks as they till their field of lavender, and he envies them their skill and even their grace; but he sees nothing more than meets the eye (pp. 118–19). Ironically, his extension of his observation of the monks to cinema places the focus on himself and calls into question his own artistic intentions. He films the monks tending their fields, reading in the library, taking meals in the refectory, but he never thinks of photographing them at prayer in their chapel. He envies the monks the harmony of their lives, but he does not understand the source of their achievement. His enterprise fails because his filming of the monastery is not informed by the idea of a spiritual tradition. Paco's project remains fragmentary because it lacks a unifying idea.

In contrast, the narrator seeks to understand the deep meaning of his experiences in the monastery. He watches the sound technician, Hans, as the latter watches one of the monks, Père Abel. This series of specular experiences brings Hans to what the narrator wants the reader to understand as a vision of the other and of the Other. From his first meeting with Père Abel, Hans retains an image: "Hans n'eut plus dans les yeux que le pâle cliché de ce visage qui le laissait dans une étrange certitude, il n'aurait su dire de quoi" (pp. 54–55). Hans's encounters with the monk occasion only a few brief verbal exchanges. Usually, discourse between Hans and the monk takes the form of visual exchange. In contemplating the monk, Hans takes cognizance of the Other: "Le visage de Hans pâlit. Il se rendait compte du caractère fatal, à la fois inévitable et inquiétant, d'une rencontre qui imposait avec force à sa conscience la sensation de l'Autre dans toute la violence et toute l'opiniâtreté de sa réalité incompressible, de sa présence ineffaçable, du désir qui le mouvait. Il le savait"

(p. 170). If Hans experiences here what in Lacanian theory is called totality, the monk reciprocates: "en ce même instant Père Abel prenait en lui ce qui lui plaisait et qui était bien plus que ce qu'il pouvait avoir conscience de lui offrir, tout comme son visage et son regard qui lui échappaient étaient pour lui-même source d'un indéfinissable plaisir dont le moine n'aurait su avoir conscience. Il finit par se tourner doucement vers lui. Il ne pouvait que s'étonner de cette amitié qu'il renonçait à comprendre" (pp. 170–71). For the narrator, Père Abel possesses what he calls the root of Otherness—"cette altérité radicale" (p. 260)—that anticipates what Hans will become. At the end of the novel, the narrator reports that Hans has died in an automobile accident. Death removes him from the narrator's life as a physical presence and thus makes of him an abiding memory. The narrator points to the mirror image, saying of Hans what he has said of Père Abel: "Il me reste ce regard, c'est vrai, et ce qu'il continue de désigner. Il me renvoie plus à moi-même qu'il ne me permet de le comprendre" (p. 281). The narrator confronts the fact of human mortality and, consequently, transcends mere observation to see in another way as an artist.

Hans sees in Père Abel specular form, and Père Abel like the other monks sees in the monastery a totalizing image. The narrator sees in Hans the other, creating a *mise en abîme* that ultimately reaches the reader. Drevet joins word and visual image. For example, he describes the refectory where many monks have taken their meals and where light bathes the simple tables and stools, illuminating the sameness of their shape. The repetition of visual forms creates a reflecting image of generations of monks: "bain limpide qui isolait et resserrait les individus dans une pellicule de verre, par ailleurs tout étant nu, éloigné, et les longues tables de bois sombre rangées sur le pourtour de la salle la meublant d'autant moins que la seule où étaient mis les couverts exaltait la vacuité des autres, sous lesquelles les tabourets alignaient leurs pieds avec la rigoureuse patience d'une image sans fin réfléchie" (pp. 150–51). The reflective character of the monastery culminates in a remarkable evocation of matins sung by the monks on their last morning in the community as they have been sung for generations. As he listens, the narrator recognizes a meeting of language and the other, then of silence and vision: "L'air immobile et attentif devenu translucide permit de chacun des moines une vision aussi pure qu'à travers des lentilles" (p. 261). Voices lose their personal quality in chant while habits depersonalize individual monks in order to create, in the words of one of the monks, a community of sensitivity: "ce lieu est une sensibilité commune qui nous lie à tous ceux qui y ont vécu" (p. 177). Shared sensitivity links these human beings, eradicates solitude, and unifies them in an experience of the Other. Nonetheless, a profound irony pervades the monastic experience and this novel. Hans discovers what it is not to be alone when he looks at Père Abel, who, because of his vocation, remains a distant figure, "cet autre auprès duquel il découvrait, dans la distance même qui l'en séparait, ce que c'était que de n'être pas seul" (p. 171). Ironically, however, the more distant he is, the more he seems present to Hans. Similarly, as Dom Bertrand explains to Paco, the monastery has to close or disappear before men can come to know it (p. 34), and Hans has to die before the narrator understands him. Ultimately, then, Drevet's novel expresses the notion of idea as the only reality. As an expression of that neoplatonic concept, the novel aspires, like any work of art, to the absolute.[6]

For Drevet, literary works contain the hope of expressing a totalizing vision, and, in fact, his narrators aspire to the expressive possibilities of visual art. His fourth novel, *Le Visiteur de hasard*, takes the form of a journal, again written in the first person, this time by a teacher in a *lycée* who records his fascination with a handsome adolescent boy, a visual experience so compelling and so astonishing that it blinds him to all other considerations. Questions of marriage, family, or profession are subsumed by the one overwhelming vision of physical beauty. The device of the personal journal reveals his quest as a kind of odyssey— the final word of the novel is *voyage*—during which he suffers self-deception but ultimately experiences the unifying vision that permits him to integrate the aesthetic and moral components of his life. The narrator notes in his journal significant visual episodes. For example, he looks at the cover photograph of a male pornographic magazine, and he contrasts what he takes as a spontaneous visual experience with what he has often felt in looking at paintings. Whereas he understands painting as being deliberately constructed by an artist to create a particular illusion, photography, he believes, offers a direct visual sensation. This distinction leads him to propose photography as a model of candor, for he thinks that it reaches truth free from the interference of the intermediary artist. But this thought turns out a muddled notion. The narrator looks at the magazine, describes in detail how a photographer has arranged lighting in order to create certain effects, yet deceives himself into thinking and writing that photography, unlike painting, provides an immediate vision of truth. In another important episode of this intriguing novel, the narrator accompanies his wife, a knowledgeable balletomane, to a dance performance during which, uninformed and untrained, he glimpses beauty spontaneously. Here the teacher's insights attain the immediate experience that he has yearned for and described in the passage on the photograph. But as in that episode, the narrator fails to recognize that what he has seen falls short of truth, for it is theatrical illusion. His comments on choreography and stage lighting are surprisingly simple-minded. Despite his failure to understand the technical means of creating a vision of beauty, however, the narrator does not fail to desire sincerely the kind of aesthetic experience that dancers offer: "Des fractures que chacun de leurs mouvements opérait dans la lumière jaillissait une écume qui poudroyait autour d'eux et, paraissant porter l'écho de leurs palpitations, renseignait sur la consistance nerveuse et tendre de leur chair, allait jusqu'à propager, parfois, des réactions fibrillaires si intimes que j'en éprouvais une impression obscène" (p. 191).

The epithet "obscène" reveals the narrator's progress from naive gazing at a photograph or unsophisticated attendance at the ballet to a mature understanding of aesthetic experience as erotic. Sexually ambiguous, the narrator reiterates his obsession with Jean-Louis as an object of contemplation, a fascination that forces him to wrestle with his vision: "Il me reste à revenir sur ce qui devait indéfiniment m'échapper, à fixer et saisir ce que, dans l'instant, mes sens se sont révélés incapables de percevoir. Il me reste à découvrir ce que j'ai vu, puisque aussi bien je l'ai eue, ma 'vision'" (p. 248). Describing a final encounter with Jean-Louis, the narrative assumes a liturgical cadence that formalizes the sexual experience and heightens its eroticism. Like the Rimbaud of "Aube," the narrator learns that beauty may be embraced but not retained: "Il n'y avait pas de parole possible entre nous et seulement ce regard nu, total, intense, qui évaporait aussitôt les pensées et les sentiments pour nous donner une perception immédiate, crue, envahissante. Il ne cherchait pas à me retenir. Sa façon de voir le rendait étranger à toute idée d'engagement ou de liaison" (p. 260). As in Thomas Mann's *Death in Venice* and Virginia Woolf's *To the Lighthouse*, *Le Visiteur de hasard* depicts aesthetic experience as integrating all of life but also as fleeting, always in process, like life itself, a concept admirably expressed in the liquid movement of Drevet's prose.

Virtually all his novels and récits convey the communicative possibilities of vision. At the end of one short story, "La Mercedes blanche," Drevet appends a self-portrait that includes the epigraph "Ne touche qu'avec les yeux!" As a lively, curious child, he might often have heard this admonition, which limits relations with the outside world to visual experience and, furthermore, endows the world with an illicit quality. The outside world is too valuable or too dangerous to be experienced directly. It is to be experienced visually. It is not to be handled but to be seen; and if it is to be possessed at all, it is not to be held in the hand but beheld by the eye. The exclusion from tangible possession may well increase desire, however, adding to the contemplation of objects a longing for satisfaction. Objects become obsession, Drevet suggests, and exist in visual memory where the power of imagination reshapes them as aesthetic objects that invite further contemplation and something like erotic enjoyment.[7]

In "La Mercedes blanche," which may be read as an allegory of the aesthetic process, the narrator remembers how as a *lycéen* he would see a white vehicle drive up in front of the school each day at noon as classes were ending and the boys were leaving the building. Remembering this visual experience, the narrator recreates it in imagination, envisioning a driver, another student who asks the driver for a light for his cigarette and other students who cover the automobile with graffiti. Thus an initial perception of probably no particular significance persists in the narrator's memory, where it haunts him, as he says, and where imagination reshapes it as a fiction that he relishes: "Un attachement indéfinissable finit par me lier à cette voiture. Elle fut pour moi comme une personne qui me fixait un rendez-vous et je n'aurais voulu le manquer pour rien au monde" (p. 17). The perception remains elusive, however, because the richness of the visual and imaginative experience exceeds the power of words to express it. If fiction ultimately disappoints the narrator of "La Mercedes blanche," Drevet succeeds, nevertheless, in allegorizing the process by which the writer experiences the world. His persona aspires to experience the richness of memory and imagination to which he lends in the first sentence of the story a visual character and a monumental quality: "L'angle sous lequel m'apparaissent les passants sur les escaliers monumentaux des palais, des églises, des jardins, des gares, est sans doute le plus propre à satisfaire à des aspirations mystérieuses en moi" (p. 13). Delving into the recesses of his psyche, the narrator as creative artist arrives at aesthetic satisfaction and some understanding. But his understanding is not analytic; it is imagistic and erotic. The narrator says that he does not examine the Mercedes critically but that the automobile haunts him like a dream, a fascination, or even a reflex. He speculates on the driver's motives for coming daily to the same place: he can imagine the driver as a divorced parent come to catch a glimpse of his child, as a theatrical agent in search of a child actor, or as a man seeking homoerotic pleasure. Like the narrator who imagines the driver's experience and whose imaginary experience is participation in the driver's life, the reader participates in the imaginary experience of the narrator: "Faute d'avoir ses yeux, son âge, son histoire, la nature du plaisir auquel j'imaginais cet homme venu se livrer continuait à m'intriguer" (p. 21). Like the narrator, the reader aspires to a high level of sensitivity yet, again like him, is bound to be disappointed in an aspiration that can never be complete. Nonetheless, the aspiration and the effort stimulate curiosity, surprise, attraction, and nostalgia. Vision enriches the world: "Je voyais en lui ce genre de personnage non à proprement parler intimidant mais dont le silence donne au monde sa plénitude" (p. 22).

Drevet is interested in the processes of human psychology, especially the root of Otherness—"l'altérité radicale"—offered by acute visual perception. An object, an event, a place or a human relationship bears little interest in itself; each can, however, become an obsession of memory and stimulation to imagination. The narrator of *Le Lieu des passants* catches a glimpse of a school friend in the street: "Inaperçu de Jean-François, je le découvrais tel que jamais je ne l'aurais pu en l'abordant, et je peux en dire autant de tout passant" (p. 187). *Une Chambre dans les bois* tells how a child watches an older boy as a perception of adulthood; *L'Amour nomade* describes the psychology of homosexual infatuation. A brisk pace and lively narrative distinguish *Le Rire de Mandrin* from Drevet's other writing. This swashbuckling tale of the eighteenth-century smuggler retains, however, an imagistic style, remarkable evocations of light, and leisurely descriptions of landscape. Mandrin envisions giving back to the world the purity of the mountains through which he leads his men: "Le caractère puissant de ces défilés inapprivoisés ne devait pas manquer de présenter pour ces hommes en rupture de ban une parenté avec leur nature. Leur vie n'était-elle à l'image de ces montagnes obtuses, de ces monceaux de matière brute, de ces épées de lumière parmi les feuilles ou aiguisant leur fil dans les brèches des crêtes?" (p. 190). The title of the novel *Dieux obscurs* results from a misunderstanding of the word "Dioscures," which a twelve-year-old boy hears and admiringly applies to his godfather and the godfather's companion. The homosexual couple is frequently looked on askance by the boy's family, whose bourgeois values and life-style contrast with the experience of beauty offered by the latter-day Pollux and Castor, a vision that grows secretly to mythic proportions in the boy's imagination. His revelation suggests a parallel in human psychology between erotic and aesthetic desire, and it affirms the superiority over bourgeois values of the often hidden life of the human imagination.

In two autobiographical *récits, Le Gour des abeilles* and *La Micheline,* Drevet recreates as visual experience the river Bienne that he knew as a child and a train trip that he took with his mother from Saint-Claude in the Bienne valley to Saint-Bonnet-le-Château. In "Nature morte au trombone," one of the *Huit petites études sur le désir de voir,* the description of a paper clip, then of the gesture of affixing it to a bundle of scattered papers becomes an image of the satisfaction that the literary artist, like the visual artist, finds in bringing order out of disorder. This essay reflects Drevet's admiration of Dutch and Flemish painting; it might also be taken as a definition of his own art. Every act of seeing is an act of love, each amorous act expresses an aspiration to transcend itself, every act of writing attempts to order random experience as we perceive it. Literature and the visual arts, including film, offer experiences of the gaze that, like the mirror in Jan Van Eyck's "The Arnolfi Wedding," implicates the reader or viewer.[8]

In fact, Drevet has written about the paintings of Georges Adilon as visual apprehension of totality. The encounter with a Rembrandt or a Rouault, he writes, makes the viewer's gaze participate with that of the painter as a response to the glow of what lies beyond the canvas. In such a passage, Drevet intends to suggest that the viewer collaborates with the visual artist to create the vision that is represented and that is apprehended between these two visual sources.[9] In *Récit d'un geste,* Drevet has inferred from Adilon's work that, figuratively speaking, the artist gropes his way toward finding the resin that can fix all colors; he moves toward their beginnings—"l'originalité" (p. 133)—that are the source of their nuance and that maintain each of them as an identified, precise entity. For example, he explains how Adilon came more and more to reduce his use of paint to two colors, black and white, and how he saw white as a primordial color: "La blancheur préexiste. Quelle que soit la perfection de l'œuvre qu'elle contribue à révéler, celle-ci n'atteint jamais la perfection de cette blancheur qui est ce qui est, ce qui fut, ce qui sera" (p. 38). In passages reminiscent of *Les Gardiens des pierres*, Drevet accounts for Adilon's career as a continuous effort to lend visibility to the invisible. Adilon, he says, was driven by a desire to create paintings with the mission of suggesting the trace of a presence capable of accompanying viewers in their own quest, of producing a feeling of fraternity in the confrontation with an effect of color or light, in the experience of lyricism, in the rhythm of brushstrokes, in the movement that music and painting often reach more quickly than words or enliven more effectively than poems (p. 8).

Drevet seeks in a remarkably evocative style to capture the immediate effect of visual art and in his quest bears witness to the infinite possibilities of human vision and creativity. Beginning with his first novel and its references to Poussin's "Echo et Narcisse," the narratives create visual effects that reflect on the narrators, the author, and the reader. Because Drevet's novels form a series of mirror-images, they remind us, writer and readers alike, of our own aspirations. In reading literature or contemplating art, we may hope to join a tradition of searching for ideas that, we remember from one of the passages in *Les Gardiens des pierres*, a monk calls "une sensibilité commune," a community of sensitivity.

Notes

1. Roland Barthes, *Le Plaisir du texte* (Paris: Seuil, 1973), p. 24.

2. Gretchen Rous Besser, *Nathalie Sarraute* (Boston: Twayne, 1979), p. 172.

3. See Hubert Damisch, "D'un narcisse à l'autre," *Nouvelle Revue de Psychanalyse*, no. 13 (1976), p. 123.

4. "Ecrire, questions à Patrick Drevet," *Lyon-maristes*, no. 39 (1981), p. 31.

5. Jacques Lacan, *Ecrits: A Selection*, trans. and ed. Alan Sheridan (New York: Norton, 1977), p. 4.

6. George Steiner, *Real Presences* (Chicago: University of Chicago Press, 1989), pp. 216–27.

7. "Ecrire," pp. 28–29.

8. Svetlana Alpers, *The Art of Describing. Dutch Art in the Seventeenth Century* (Chicago: University of Chicago Press, 1983), p. 179.

9. Patrick Drevet, *Récit d'un geste* (Lyon: MEM/Arte-Facts, 1984), p. 45.

Bibliography

Works by Patrick Drevet

Pour Geneviève. Paris: Gallimard, 1978.

Les Gardiens des pierres. Paris: Gallimard, 1980.

Le Lieu des passants. Paris: Gallimard, 1982.

Récit d'un geste. Sur des peintures de Georges Adilon. Lyon: MEM/Arte-Facts, 1984.

Le Gour des abeilles. Paris: Gallimard, 1985.

Le Visiteur de hasard. Paris: Gallimard, 1987.

Untitled essay on the entrance and chapel of the Externat Sainte-Marie. Lyon: La Montée Saint-Barthélemy, 1988.

Une Chambre dans les bois. Paris: Gallimard, 1989. Translated by James Kirkup as *A Room in the Woods.* London: Quartet Books, 1991.

La Micheline. Paris: Hatier (Collection "Haute Enfance"), 1989; Gallimard, 1994. Translated by James Kirkup as *My Micheline.* London: Quartet Books, 1993.

L'Amour nomade. Paris: Gallimard, 1991.

Huit petites études sur le désir de voir. Paris: Gallimard, 1991.

"La Mercedes blanche." *Nouvelles, nouvelles,* no. 23 (summer 1991): 13–26. Translated by Martin Foreman as "The White Mercedes" in *More Like Minds.* London: GMP, 1992.

"Retour à la mère." *Moule à gaufres,* no. 1 (autumn 1991): 50–57.

Le Rire de Mandrin. Paris: Belfond, 1993.

L'Isle-Adam, avec photographies de Régis Molinard. Auvers-sur-Oise: Molinard, 1993.

"Nuit des temps." *Nouvelle Revue Française,* no. 490 (November 1993): 47–57.

Dieux obscurs. Paris: Belfond, 1994.

Interviews and Articles

"Ecrire, questions à Patrick Drevet." *Lyon-maristes,* no. 39 (1981): 24–35.

"Récit d'un geste" [interview]. *Clémentine* (June 1984).

"La Solitude de l'écrivain." *Magazine littéraire,* no. 290 (July–August 1991): 58–59.

"Ce qu'il y a de meilleur en moi." *Paroles d'amour.* Paris: Syros, 1991.

"Ecrire engage sûrement à aimer." *Paroles d'amour.* Paris: Syros, 1991.

"Si je m'en tiens à mon histoire." *Ecritures,* no. 2 (1992): 110–12.

"L'Azur du roman." *Quai Voltaire,* no. 8 (spring 1993), 52–59.

"Rencontre avec Patrick Drevet." *New Novel Review* 1, no. 2 (April 1994): 62–78.

Richard, Jean-Pierre: "Paysages d'une chair." *Nouvelle Revue Française,* no. 490 (November 1993): 65–78.

20

Jean-Philippe Toussaint

Roy C. Caldwell

Le véritable écrivain n'a rien à dire.[1]

Since 1985, Jean-Philippe Toussaint has published four slim novels with the Paris publishing house Minuit: *La Salle de bain* (1985), *Monsieur* (1986), *L'Appareil-photo* (1988), and *La Réticence* (1991). Readers of these texts have had no difficulty in detecting affinities between them; already the first novel seemed the result of a fully formed, carefully controlled talent. Curiously, the appearance of each new text revealed no "maturation," no "development" of narrative technique or thematic concern, but rather a continuation of an unchanging writing practice: minimalist, composed in blocks of nonsequential text, strangely comic, mixing formal and colloquial linguistic patterns, highly wrought. Toussaint's textual production thus gives the illusion of a certain immobility, fitting perhaps, when one considers that immobility forms a central thematic configuration in each text.

Like Toussaint's writing in the different texts, his narratives display a marked consistency. Each novel centers on a young male protagonist, never named, who displays boyish charm, passivity, and a peculiar ineptitude when faced with social conventions. These characters respond to the anxieties of modern life by flight (to Venice in *La Salle de bain*, to the Midi in *Monsieur*, to London in *L'Appareil-photo*, to Sasuelo in *La Réticence*), and by withdrawing into isolated, often closed spaces to follow the paths of their sedentary thoughts: into the bathtub (*La Salle de bain*), onto the rooftop under the stars (*Monsieur*), behind the doors of a gas station toilet and a self-service photo booth (*L'Appareil-photo*), into an anonymous hotel room in an empty seaside resort (*La Réticence*). In all these novels a certain Sartrean intertextuality may be found. Roquentin's nausea appears in various forms: in the oozing flesh of the "poulpes" (*La Salle de bain* and *La Réticence*), in the disagreeable "odeur de cire mêlé de sperme sec" in *Monsieur*'s rented room (p. 44), in the "réalité brute et presque obscène" that emerges from the stolen photos of *L'Appareil-photo* (p. 120), in the drowned, decomposing cat whose image haunts the narrator of *La Réticence*, and in the rain that falls almost continuously throughout all four novels. Against the fluidity and decay of existence the protagonists attempt to impose images of pure order drawn from geometry, modern physics, and games: darts and Pythagorean theorem in *La Salle de bain*, crystallography and quantum physics in *Monsieur*, chess and photography in *L'Appareil-photo*, the codified narrative practice of the detective novel that forms the subtext of *La Réticence*. But the heroes of Toussaint do not flee harsh reality altogether for the "quiétude [d'une] vie abstraite" (*La Salle de bain*, p. 15). They live in the world and are drawn to its charms. In these stories, women represent the promise—and the threat—of joining the body of life: a lover fled, then nearly killed (*La Salle de bain*), a woman seduced, or rather, seducing (*Monsieur*), a young mother always asleep (*L'Appareil-photo*), a baby son and his entirely absent mother (*La Réticence*). If these are love stories, they lack the closure (either rupture or consummation) that one expects. At the end of *La Salle de bain*, the protagonist may abandon the solitude of the bathroom to rejoin his female companion, but *L'Appareil-photo* closes with the protagonist, lost in thought, waiting in a phonebooth for his lover to return his call. These are faint stories, antinarratives. Very little "happens" in Toussaint's novels, and what does happen tends to occur at the margins of the discourse.

Reviewers in the French press have inevitably attempted to situate Toussaint's enterprise by invoking previous writers whom he seems to resemble. These readers have cited Kafka, Camus, Modiano, Valéry's *Monsieur Teste*, Woody Allen (!), Beckett, the nouveaux romanciers, and other writers recently published by Minuit—Patrick Deville, Jean Echenoz, Marie Redonnet, and the late Hervé Guibert. These may all in some way be useful in explaining certain aspects of Toussaint's work. Nonetheless, the project here is to delineate the figures by which Toussaint structures his narratives, and for this Robbe-Grillet's narrative theory and practice offer the best foundation. In *Le Miroir qui revient,*

Robbe-Grillet divides modern novelists into two groups: those who follow Balzac's realism, and those who "voudront explorer . . . les oppositions insolubles, les éclatements, les apories diégétiques, les cassures, les vides, etc., car ils savent que le réel commence juste au moment où le sens vacille."[2] Toussaint clearly belongs to the second group. Like the juxtaposed snapshots from which Robbe-Grillet forms his narratives in the collection *Instantanés*, Toussaint's stories are composed of fragments, frozen moments, aleatory coincidences, holes, sudden shifts. Like Robbe-Grillet too, Toussaint fills his texts with insignificant details from everyday experience and long, precise descriptions of banal actions (the eating of an olive in *L'Appareil-photo*, for example). Toussaint writes what other writers omit, omits what other writers emphasize. One also finds in Toussaint the *mises en abyme* that Robbe-Grillet employs to duplicate the structure of his narratives: the crystallography of *Monsieur*, the movement of the knight in *L'Appareil-photo*, the purloined letter of *La Réticence*. Unlike Robbe-Grillet, however, Toussaint produces a much more ordered narrative system. The fiction is not *plural*; variants do not accumulate to force the explosion of the unitary récit; in Toussaint events are not blatantly contradictory. Furthermore, Toussaint's texts do not contain strange loops and paradoxical spaces—metaleptic shifts between different diegetic levels—as do Robbe-Grillet's. In Toussaint, we are never taken into the laboratory of fiction where the story—with its dead-ends and false starts—is being composed before our very eyes. At the core of Toussaint's narrative system is an essentially classical principle: the narrator reflects on his past experience and recounts it in well-chosen phrases. Even more than Robbe-Grillet's, Toussaint's narratives appear ludic, that is, governed by arbitrary rules, symmetrical, ritualistic.

Toussaint's protagonists appear strangely passive, strangely empty of desires. In the hotel room, the young father of *La Réticence* expresses what seems the emblematic attitude of these characters: "Je ne faisais rien, je n'attendais rien de particulier" (pp. 14–15). The hero of *La Salle de bain* passes long moments watching the clock's second hand and trying to perceive the minute progress of a crack in the wall. *Monsieur* reaches perhaps a perfect state of well-being when he swings in the hammock, "suivant en pensée le rythme des balancements" (pp. 28–29). But almost in spite of their natural inclination toward immobility, Toussaint's protagonists are possessed of an "élan furieux" (*L'Appareil-photo*, p. 113) and are constantly on the move. To achieve the conditions necessary for serene immobility, paradoxically, they must travel. Each of Toussaint's four narratives has at its center figures of "locomotion," of change of place. These figures assume various forms: in the paths followed by the protagonists, in the different images employed to represent these trajectories, and in the paradoxes of mobility and immobility that emerge from each voyage.

The journeys of Toussaint's novels are fugues, flights from the quotidian and oppressive experience back home. The protagonists of *La Salle de bain* and *Monsieur* both flee women who have rendered their lives too muddled, too murky, too tangled; in escaping the difficulties created by women, they seek to reconstruct the conditions necessary for "the quietude of an abstract life." Each disappears abruptly from Paris for a destination where he will be unknown, out-of-place, and thus exempt from assaults on his solitude. The destinations of these trips seem entirely arbitrary. When *Monsieur*'s fiancée asks him what he plans to do in Cannes, the reply is that "il ne savait pas, il verrait bien" (p. 25).

The protagonist of *La Réticence* displays a similar uncertainty about his trip to the abandoned resort. Inquiring about a room, he asks the hotel-keeper "s'il serait possible d'avoir une chambre pour quelques nuits, même davantage peut-être, jusqu'à la fin de la semaine, je ne savais pas très bien" (p. 13). Although we never learn exactly what situation the protagonist in *La Réticence* has left behind in Paris, the presence of the infant son, and the complete absence of reference to the child's mother, would seem to indicate another flight from complicated, unhappy love. This voyage appears just as unmotivated and haphazard as those in *La Salle de bain* and *Monsieur*. Here the hero's solitude cannot be absolute, however, nor his life abstract, for he has certain "creatural" responsibilities: feeding the baby and changing his diapers. The weekend in London of *L'Appareil-photo* represents a different but essentially related kind of flight. This novel's protagonist has adapted a strategy for handling reality markedly different from that of his *confrères*; he seeks not to escape reality, but to break it down by a slow, deliberate campaign. When he meets Pascale Polougaïevski, his plan to seduce her resembles his elaborate, slow-motion manner of eating olives: "Tout mon jeu d'approche, assez obscur en apparence, avait en quelque sorte pour effet de fatiguer la réalité à laquelle je me heurtais" (p. 14). The trip in this text is thus undertaken not in order to escape love, but rather to promote it. The hotel room here becomes, in theory at least, a closed space where the purity of an erotic *solitude à deux* may be created. The complications the would-be lovers flee are those of the noisy, busy, clutching world which hinders their intimacy: Pascale's family responsibilities (her father and her child), her job, Paris.

The journeys in the four novels are reflected by the protagonists' various meditations on movement. All four of Toussaint's heroes tend to figure the paths of bodies as pure, abstract patterns. For each of them, locomotion becomes trajectory. Motion may be the change of a body's position in time, but these characters seek to represent the entire course of a motion in an image from which time has been removed. The young man in *La Salle de bain* wonders how many times he has followed the trajectory from bathroom to kitchen in his apartment. The geometric figure of his fugue to and from Venice is provided by the text's epigraph: "Le carré de l'hypoténuse est égal à la somme des carrés des deux autres côtés" (p. 7). Monsieur finds peace by contemplating "l'inaccessible pureté des trajectoires" of fish in an aquarium (p. 90). At night on his roof, he finds a similar purity as he attempts to track the repeating paths of the satellites passing overhead. Later in the text he succeeds in transforming the night sky into a metro system where he takes imaginary voyages: "partant du Sirius qu'il repérait sans peine, il évolua du regard vers Montparnasse-Bienvenüe, descendit jusqu'à Sèvres-Babylone et, s'attardant un instant sur Bételgeuse, arriva à l'Odéon, où il voulait en venir" (p. 93). In *L'Appareil-photo,* the main character choreographs his movements to correspond to another celestial sphere; in Milan he spends his time reading newspapers on park benches, "passant de banc en banc pour suivre la progression du soleil" (p. 17). Elsewhere, he compares the real path of the automobile to another perfect, and still more abstract movement from the game of chess: "nous empruntions toujours le même itinéraire maintenant, à quelques nuances près, qui consistait en un parcours qui n'était pas le contraire de celui du cavalier dans la variante Breyer de l'espagnole fermée" (p. 41). In *La Réticence* the young father becomes obsessed with the beam from the lighthouse; he traces its trajectory from the harbor back to its source, where he fantasizes several grim dénouements for the halting fictions he composes.

On the move, Toussaint's protagonist thus manages to pull away from the gravity of a life and to become a particle in pure flight. Alone in the photo booth, the hero of *L'Appareil-photo* follows the course of his thoughts and finds there some kind of solace; he passes from "la difficulté de vivre" to the "désespoir d'être" (p. 94). These characters can grasp existence only in its abstract form, only when they have succeeded in creating a closed space of silence in which the course of their own thoughts may be detected. (Descendants of Descartes, they think therefore they are.) In tranquil solitude thought gathers its innumerable strands and rushes "mystérieusement vers un point immobile et fuyant" (32). This paradox of "fleeing immobility" indeed represents one of the central figures in Toussaint's narratives. In *La Salle de bain*, the paradox appears as the protagonist outlines two fashions of watching the rain: first, "de maintenir son regard fixé sur un point quelconque de l'espace et de voir la succession de pluie à l'endroit choisi" (an approach that renders the rain immobile and furnishes "aucune idée de la finalité du mouvement," p. 36); or, second, "suivre des yeux la chute d'une seule goutte à la fois" (which permits one to "se représenter que le mouvement, aussi fulgurante soit-il en apparence, tend essentiellement vers l'immobilité," p. 36). Immobility, this man concludes, frames motion and thus represents the dominant—and superior—state of affairs. The paradox recurs in *L'Appareil-photo,* where the protagonist, like the raindrop considered in its entire flight, finds himself during a Channel-crossing between two places and thus, he concludes, momentarily nowhere: "L'endroit où je me trouvais s'était peu à peu dissipé de ma conscience et je fus un instant nulle part, si ce n'est pas immobile dans mon esprit" (p. 102). Being nowhere, fixed outside space in a motionless trajectory, he achieves the immobility of spirit that represents for Toussaint's characters the only consolation possible. Movement, concludes the man in the bathroom as he watches the single raindrop, bears bodies continually toward death, which is immobility. Likewise, on the deck, between places, where the division between sea and sky disappears, the Channel-crosser remarks: "Parfois, oui, la mort me manquait" (p. 106). Around the fret and agitation of life, free from time altogether, Toussaint's protagonist finds the pure immobile trajectory that prefigures the perfection of death.

L'Appareil-photo takes as its point of departure the curious coincidence of two distinct events: the narrator decides to learn how to drive, and he receives a letter in which an old friend informs him of his marriage.

After admitting that these two matters "n'avaient malheureusement aucun rapport entre eux" (p. 7), the narrator concludes the section, surprisingly, with the remark that he abhors "amis perdus de vue" (p. 7). This incongruous movement between unrelated sequences seems typical of Toussaint's writing. His narratives often proceed by *parataxis;* there seems to be no link between successive segments. Readers of *L'Appareil-photo* are left to establish for themselves the possible connections between learning to drive, marriage, and friends from the past.

In *Le Miroir qui revient*, Robbe-Grillet claims that, while the classic novel "masked and denied" the problems of representing the instant, the modern novel intentionally exposes these problems and stages the paradoxes of instantaneity. Modern narrative becomes, he claims, "l'impossible mise en ordre de fragments dépareillés, dont les bords incertains ne s'adaptent pas les uns aux autres."[3] Toussaint's composition by unmatched segments appears to correspond to Robbe-Grillet's description of writing in the modern novel. His texts are discontinuous, fragmented, constructed like collages. Parts are unmatched, wrenched from their contexts, and thrust together in jagged patterns. In Toussaint, edges do not disappear; the two never become one. The edge-that-refuses-to-disappear privileges spatial form in the text.

A long theoretical discourse on the nature of images and narrative, of the limits and potentialities of space and time in art, immediately intrudes on the questions raised by Toussaint's novels. Lessing formulated the classical position sharply distinguishing the modes of existence of painting and poetry. Plastic forms, he writes in the *Laocoön*, are spatial, because the visible aspect of objects is best represented in a single instant. By contrast, poetry employs language, which exists as a sequence of words in time. But we know very well that postclassical art refuses to respect genres; it revolts and escapes from the designated territories.[4] As certain kinds of painting seek a temporal dimension, certain kinds of literature attempt to create a spatial dimension. For this kind of painting the problem is narrative: how to represent a series of events—and therefore a duration—in fixed images. For this kind of literature, the problem is pictorial: how to constitute a space with a series of words. Narrative painting wants to seize time, while spatial literature tries to eliminate it. As Toussaint's protagonists consistently convert locomotion into trajectory by eliminating the dimension of time, so too these narratives flee temporal structure for spatial form.

Toussaint's narratives, unlike Robbe-Grillet's, are not fundamentally anachronic: it is possible to reconstruct from the mixed episodes a chronologically consistent narrative. Nevertheless, chronological order is radically fragmented everywhere in Toussaint's novels. The clash of narrative and textual orders is sharpest in *La Salle de bain*, where the text closes by returning to its point of departure: the protagonist exiting his bathroom. We recognize that the trip to Venice, subject of "Hypoténuse," the novel's long middle section, has been an extended analepse. Instead of smoothly narrating continuous actions, Toussaint renders the passing of time through a series of fixed images, minutely detailed and often perfectly banal snapshots. The trip to the Midi in *Monsieur* is not recounted in full, but represented through a sequence of images: a dog's eyes in a flashlight, swinging in a hammock, the bodily sensations of cutting wood: "Puis vint le temps où Monsieur dut rentrer à Paris" (p. 29). As Schrödinger's Copenhagen experiment (which obsesses Monsieur) proves that an electron's leap to another level may not be predicted, Toussaint's narrative seems to shift venues by "sauts discontinus" (p. 78).

Photographs in Toussaint's novels thus play a dual function: they are *mises en abyme* of Toussaint's narrative practice, but they are also of central thematic importance, for they symbolize attempts by the protagonists to control existence by suppressing time. In photographs, the flux of existence is momentarily arrested, providing a transitory image of order. And yet, photographs are simultaneously sources of anxiety for the central characters. Instead of the current identification photos necessary to complete his dossier at the driving school, the narrator of *L'Appareil-photo* brings pictures from his childhood. In these images a past self, secure in the bosom of a child's family relations, is frozen and preserved. But the adult resists the very simple operation of finding a photo booth to obtain the photos he needs to complete his dossier. The anxiety a current photoportrait holds for him seems manifest in the image closing the novel: "Je regardais le jour se lever et songeais simplement au présent, à l'instant présent, tâchant de fixer encore sa fugitive grâce— comme on immobiliserait l'extrémité d'une aiguille dans le corps d'un papillon vivant" (p. 127). Another of Toussaint's paradoxes: how does one capture the instant without killing it? Or, differently stated, where is the unchanging core that constitutes one's essential identity? For the problem of the portrait—the problem of identity—has troubled this man for some time. His suppressed desire to fix his identity surges forth when he finds a camera forgotten by tourists. With it, however, immediately kicks in the vague anxiety that has pursued him through the novel; he panics and races through the ship taking random shots to finish the roll of film as soon as possible. Only when he sees the developed photos does he realize that he has succeeded in taking the self-portrait he had once wished: "C'était comme la photo de l'élan furieux que je portais en moi" (p. 113). Unintentionally, he has managed to snatch from within himself and from the instant a photo that represents both immobility and fluidity: "La photo serait floue mais immobile, le mouvement serait arrêté, rien ne bougerait plus, ni ma présence, ni mon absence, il y aurait là toute l'étendue de l'immobilité qui précède la vie de toute celle qui suit, à peine plus lointaine que le ciel que j'avais sous les yeux" (p. 113).

Roland Barthes has written that photography has created a new category of space-time: "locale immédiate et temporelle antérieure; dans la photographie il se produit une conjonction illogique entre l'*ici* et l'*autrefois*."[5] A photograph, continues Barthes, possesses an "irréalité réelle": "son irréalité est celle de l'*ici*, car la photographie n'est jamais vécue comme une illusion, elle n'est nullement une *présence* . . . et sa réalité est celle de l'*avoir-été-là*, car il y a dans toute photographie l'évidence toujours stupéfiante du: *cela s'est passé ainsi*" (p. 36). In photographs, Toussaint's protagonists perceive not their own presence, but yet another trajectory, the trace of their flight through time. The immobility of photographs is thus paradoxical. Photographs may fix images but they cannot truly *preserve*; they testify only to what has disappeared. Instead of capturing life, photographs become for Toussaint's characters the true image of the terrifying immobility surrounding existence.

When a lady visits Monsieur in his room, he notices, under her "robe moulante," "des traces à peine estompées des sous-vêtements vieux jeu" (p. 52). This detail represents another *mise en abyme* of Toussaint's narrative practice: the lines of his narratives must often be detected across and beneath the text that in part hides them. In these novels occurs a continual play of presence and absence: what appears in the text often seems inconsequential, while the important events occur in the white spaces surrounding the writing. The narrative regularly emerges not as figure, but as ground. Thus, in *Monsieur* the protagonist takes the bus and on it has an altercation with a man who resembles him; in the next block of text, Monsieur has a sprained wrist and arrives at the home of his fiancée needing a place to live. Much later, almost in passing, the text tells us that before living with his fiancée, Monsieur had shared a dwelling with his brother. The conclusion remains for us to draw for ourselves: the man resembling Monsieur on the bus had been his brother, and their quarrel precipitates Monsieur's moving out. What were the reasons for their disagreement? We never know. Likewise, the breaking of his engagement, potentially rich in narrative material, eludes the narrative (and Monsieur himself): "Il avait assez mal suivi l'affaire, en fait, se souvenant seulement que le nombre de choses qui lui avaient été reprochées lui avait paru considérable" (p. 30). The anecdotes Monsieur and Anna tell each other at the party are emblematic of this narrative practice: "Non, ils se racontaient des anecdotes, plutôt, à chacun leur tour, qui à mesure qu'ils les accumulaient, devenaient de plus en plus insignifiantes" (pp. 94–95).

Holes of various sorts appear throughout Toussaint's texts. What does Monsieur burn in the ashtray (p. 20)? What event lies behind the bad blood between Monsieur Parrain and Doctor Douvres (p. 20)? What question by his fiancée provokes Monsieur to respond "Non" (p. 24)? Why would the protagonist of La Salle de bain give his age as "27, bientôt 29 ans" (p. 15)? More significant in the latter text are the larger narrative holes, central events in the narrative for which we never obtain any satisfactory explanation. Thus, we never learn how the protagonist came to receive the mysterious invitation to the Austrian embassy, nor do we witness the internal play of emotions and reasonings that ends in his trip to Venice, or in his self-imposed exile to the bathroom. Gaps configure L'Appareil-photo as well; a rather banal narrative sequence becomes unfamiliar because it suppresses certain intermediate narrative stages. Shortly after the narrator meets Pascale Polougaïevski in the office of the driving school, and with only the faintest signs of developing intimacy, they suddenly arrive in London to spend the weekend together. One block of text leaves them in the Paris metro, while the next block opens with their dining in London: a figure of discontinuity. Other narrative holes operate by what might be called misdirection: instead of the "main event," the text narrates peripheral actions. Thus, as the narrator of L'Appareil-photo and Pascale spend the afternoon in bed together, the text describes at some length the images on the television screen in their room. Similarly, when Monsieur takes Anna to a restaurant, we hear not their conversation, but that of the couple at the table next to them. Toussaint systematically narrates not the central action itself, but rather what occurs in the margins; he writes frames, rituals of opening and closing.

This narrative play of presence and absence assumes its most important function in *La Réticence,* a text whose narrative may be best described as built around or on a network of absence. In this text Barthes's hermeneutic code seems to run in reverse: instead of resolving the mysteries that configure the narrative at its outset, *La Réticence* multiplies them.[6] When the text opens, we may well wonder why the narrator has come to stay in this off-season resort. He supplies a far from satisfactory answer: "C'était en quelque sorte pour voir les Biaggi que je m'étais rendu à Sasuelo" (p. 16). Just who are these Biaggis anyway? How does the protagonist know them, and why has he come to see them just now? This *en quelque sorte* serves to undermine most of the hermeneutic value the explanation may have possessed, but subsequently, as the story unfolds and he hesitates to show these mysterious acquaintances the least sign of his presence, our confusion increases. When he lifts his own letter from the Biaggis' mailbox, thereby hiding his presence in Sasuelo, he has effectively cancelled his original motives for the trip. Reticence, indeed: he resists explaining even to himself why he has taken the letters, why he has come to Sasuelo. And there remains the further question, never articulated but hovering over the entire narrative: where is the mother of the child?

In many ways *La Réticence* seems to be a novel in search of a story. From the beginning it appears to grope toward the narrative form of the detective novel: enigmas are present, and the setting in the abandoned town makes for an atmosphere of decay, suspense, and vague menace. Like a detective, the narrator wanders through town in search of clues. All detective work is analeptic: the effort to reconstruct a series of events in the past from traces left in the present. This protagonist's careful scrutiny reveals only very thin signs: a dead cat, the coming and going of a gray Mercedes, a suspicious fisherman. Nevertheless, he weaves these signs into elaborate and unlikely fictions which attempt to reveal the truth of the past. Tzvetan Todorov has remarked that the *roman à énigmes* is constructed around two temporal sequences, "dont l'une est absente mais réelle, l'autre présente mais insignifiante."[7] In *La Réticence* the absence of the past crime finally overwhelms any reality it might possess, and we are left with only an insignificant present. One by one the imagined crimes dissolve. Biaggi does not drive the gray Mercedes, and he has not taken a room in the narrator's hotel; neither Biaggi nor the cat has been murdered. The dénouement toward which the narrator's fictions build turns comic. Like a long joke without a punchline, the door to the narrator's hotel room slowly opens . . . to reveal the hotelkeeper coming to clean the room! As the narrator telephones Biaggi and leaves on the answering machine a recording of "toutes les imperceptibles variations de [son] silence" (p. 133), Toussaint has recorded the folds of absences: Biaggi, the woman, the narrative itself.

Robbe-Grillet's description of the conflicting tendencies configuring the modern novel applies well to Toussaint's texts: "cette lutte à mort de l'ordre et la liberté, ce conflit insoluble du classement rationnel et de la subversion, autrement nommé désordre."[8] This conflict forms the thematic center of Toussaint's texts. His central characters want to rediscover a male, abstract, Cartesian purity that has been contaminated by the complications of existence, the female, the city, people, modern life. Out-of-step, hopelessly inept, bewildered by life, these protagonists continually seek refuge from the disorder of life in elaborate abstract systems, especially in the pure spaces and actions of games. Thus, Monsieur proves incapable of the effort necessary to find new lodging, but plays soccer, chess, billiards, and ping-pong with passion. Likewise, the protagonist of *La Salle de bain* allows his lover (or wife) to handle the couple's finances, while he crushes his friends at the game of Monopoly; he understands only play money. Then, after he has abandoned her and fled to Venice, he spends his time shut up in his hotel room, where he plays darts, cultivating a Zen-like mental state: "Je fixais le centre de la cible avec une détermination absolue, faisais le vide dans ma tête—et lançais" (p. 60). But even the abstraction of games is not enough for him. Instead of watching football, he prefers to listen to it on the radio, because "le football gagne à être imaginé" (p. 13). In games may be found the neat geometric lines, the clear resolution, the limited perfection that teeming life rarely affords. The protagonist of *L'Appareil-photo* articulates what games represent in Toussaint: "je simulais une autre vie, identique à la vie dans ses formes et dans son souffle, sa respiration et son rythme, une vie en tous points comparables à la vie, mais sans blessure imaginable, sans agression et sans douleur possible" (p. 125). In games Toussaint's central characters find escape from the human condition which haunts them; playing, they enter a simulation of life, a simulation where death does not exist.

Thus Monsieur, unable to decide whether he should pay for Anna's dinner, chooses what he considers the "elegant" solution of dividing the check into four equal parts, paying three. He wins the girl, and the text concludes by celebrating his victory over disorder: "La vie, pour Monsieur, un jeu d'enfant" (p. 111). Narrative itself always represents a kind of game: a playing at war without blood, a playing at finance with phony money, a playing at love without the attendant anguish: a simulation of life. Like his protagonist in *La Salle de bain*, who shifts football to a deeper level of abstraction by imagining it from radio accounts, Toussaint creates stories yet another degree more abstract, more removed from life than conventional stories. His characters flee the pain, the wounds, the aggression of existence; likewise, Toussaint writes fictions that systematically flee the traditional sound and fury of story-telling. He configures his texts to produce not true narratives, but rather simulations of narratives. In his novels literature has become as pure, as innocent, as easy—as illusory—as Monsieur's child's play.

Notes

1. Alain Robbe-Grillet, *Le Miroir qui revient* (Paris: Minuit, 1984), p. 219.

2. Ibid., p. 212.

3. Ibid., pp. 29–30.

4. See Joseph Frank, "Spatial Form in Modern Literature," in *The Widening Gyre: Crisis and Mastery in Modern Literature* (Bloomington: Indiana University Press, 1963), pp. 3–62.

5. Roland Barthes, "Rhétorique de l'image," in *L'Obvie et l'obtus: Essais critiques III* (Paris: Seuil, 1982), pp. 35–36.

6. See Roland Barthes, *S/Z* (Paris: Seuil, 1970).

7. Tzvetan Todorov, *Poétique de la prose* (Paris: Seuil, 1978), p. 13.

8. Robbe-Grillet, *Miroir*, p. 113.

Bibliography

Works by Jean-Philippe Toussaint

La Salle de bain. Paris: Minuit, 1985. Translated by Barbara Bray as *The Bathroom*.
 New York: Boyars, 1991. Film adaptation directed by John Lovoff, 1989.
Monsieur. Paris: Minuit, 1986. Translated by John Lambert. New York: Boyars,
 1991.

L'Appareil-photo. Paris: Minuit, 1988.
La Réticence. Paris: Minuit, 1991.

Selected Critical Works

Anex, Georges. "Jean-Philippe Toussaint: *La Salle de bain.*" In *Le Lecteur complice: Cinquante chroniques de littérature française, 1966–1991,* edited by Georges Anex. Geneva: Zoé, 1991.

Barbedette, Gilles. "Le Métromane." In *Le Lecteur complice.*

DiBernardi, Domenico. "Jean-Philippe Toussaint: *L'Appareil-photo.*" *Review of Contemporary Fiction* 5, no. 1 (spring 1990), 298–301.

Leclerc, Yvan. "Abstraction faite." *Critique,* no. 510 (November 1989): 889–902.

———. "Autour de minuit." *Dalhousie French Studies* 17 (fall–winter 1989): 63–74.

General Bibliography

The following bibliography, without claiming to be exhaustive, is intended for the reader wishing to garner further information about the authors included in this collection, about other major authors of this period, or about trends and developments in the recent novel in France in general. The bibliography has been divided into four parts: book-length works, periodical articles, special issues of periodicals, and bibliographical resources. In order to keep this bibliography to a manageable length, only those works have been included (with a few noted exceptions) that discuss the novel in France since the advent of the *nouveau roman*. In other words, each of these texts includes either analyses of individual authors, overviews of contemporary literature including discussion of the novel, or specific commentary on the development of the novel in contemporary France. Exclusively theoretical works have been omitted, except those that include extensive analysis of the contemporary novel in particular.

The following notes are intended to facilitate usage of this bibliography:

1. Readers should note the date of publication of each text. An article on the "contemporary" novel written in 1958 will certainly differ from one written in 1988.

2. For the sake of uniformity and simplicity, the term *editor* (ed.) has been used to refer to individuals who are not the exclusive authors of works, but who have either edited, compiled, directed, or overseen the compilation of the work in question.

3. The descriptions following each book-length study are not meant to convey the theoretical or philosophical intricacies of these works. The annotations are intended simply to allow readers to sort through the many secondary mate-

rials available and to select works containing analysis appropriate to their interests (Article titles are largely self-explanatory; therefore articles are not annotated.)

4. For the most part, these works are readily available in North America; every book-length work included was examined firsthand by the compiler. Several works that appeared appropriate to the collection have not been included because they are unavailable in North America, or because their existence cannot be verified using OCLC.

5. The reader in need of even further information is referred to the section on bibliographical resources, in particular to the information available in the *French XX Bibliography* and in the *MLA International Bibliography* (the latter available in book form and on CD-ROM).

Book-length Studies

Albérès, R.-M. *Métamorphoses du roman*. Paris: Albin Michel, 1966. On formal development in the twentieth-century novel. Chapters on Robbe-Grillet and the nouveau roman as detective novel, interior monologue, reception of the nouveau roman.

―――. *Le Roman d'aujourd'hui. 1960–1970*. Paris: Albin Michel, 1970. Catalogue of the major writers of the 1960s, categorized by principal themes. Short analyses of about a hundred authors, including Troyat, Cardinal, Sarrazin, Le Clézio, Perec, Sagan, and Duras, as well as the nouveaux romanciers.

―――. *Histoire du roman moderne*. 4th ed. Paris: Albin Michel, 1971. Extensive study of the novel in France. The third part in particular deals with the major tendencies of the postwar novel.

―――. *Littérature horizon 2000*. Paris: Albin Michel, 1974. Traces the major characteristics and developments of the novel from 1945 to 1974.

Allemand, Roger-Michel, ed. *Le "Nouveau Roman" en questions. I: "Nouveau Roman" et archétypes*. Paris: Revue des Lettres Modernes ("L'Icosathèque" 13), 1992. Articles on Duras, Butor, Simon, and Sarraute.

Amette, Jacques-Pierre, et al. *Etat des lieux. Vol I. 40 écrivains d'aujourd'hui*. Paris: La Renaissance, 1982. Collection of short, original works of prose by contemporary novelists including Ben Jelloun, Besson, Bruckner, Chawaf, Hyvrard, Roberts, and Vautrin. Each novelist was asked to contribute a text characteristic of his or her style.

Angenot, Marc. *Le Roman populaire. Recherches en paralittérature*. Montreal: Presses de l'Université du Québec, 1975. Although concerned primarily with the popular novel from 1848 to 1918, this study presents an important analysis of the phenomenon of paraliterature. Excellent bibliography.

Apeldoorn, Jo van. *Pratiques de la description.* Amsterdam: Rodopi, 1982. Theoretical treatment of the nature of description, including analyses of Simon, Duras, and Green.

Ardagh, John. *The New France.* Harmondsworth: Penguin, 1973. On France since the end of World War II. Includes considerable discussion of French culture and letters.

Arnaud, Noël, et al., eds. *Entretiens sur la paralittérature.* Paris: Plon, 1970. Proceedings of the Colloque de Cerisy of September 1–10, 1967. Includes discussion of the popular novel, photoroman, roman policier, and science fiction.

Arnaudiès, Annie. *Le Nouveau Roman. Vol. I: Les Matériaux. Vol. II: Les Formes.* Paris: Hatier, 1974. Consists primarily of texts illustrative of the major characteristics of the nouveau roman. Brief analyses.

Astier, Pierre A. G. *La Crise du roman français et le nouveau réalisme. Encyclopédie du nouveau roman.* Paris: Nouvelles Editions Debresse ("Présences Contemporaines"), 1968. In-depth study of the origins and characteristics of the nouveau roman. Good bibliography.

Atack, Margaret, and Phil Powrie, eds. *Contemporary French Fiction by Women: Feminist Perspectives.* Manchester, England: Manchester University Press, 1991. Chapters on Rochefort, Ernaux, Wittig, Cixous, Cardinal, and Chawaf, among others.

Bancquart, Marie-Claire, and Pierre Cahné. *Littérature française du XXe siècle.* Paris: PUF, 1992. Excellent overview of twentieth-century French literature until 1988.

Baqué, Françoise. *Le Nouveau Roman.* Paris: Bordas, 1972. Short, clear introduction to the nouveau roman, covering the treatment in these works of character and story, objects, time and space, and theme and narration.

Barrère, Jean-Bertrand. *Le Cure d'amaigrissement du roman.* Paris: Albin Michel, 1964. On the lack of substance in the nouveau roman (especially concerning characters and objects).

Barthes, Roland. *Essais critiques.* Paris: Seuil, 1964. Includes the important early articles on Robbe-Grillet and the nouveau roman.

Bédé, Jean-Albert, and William B. Edgerton, general eds. *Columbia Dictionary of Modern European Literature.* 2d ed. New York: Columbia University Press, 1980. Short entries on over 1,800 authors, many of them French.

Bénézet, Mathieu. *Le Roman de la langue.* Paris: UGE 10/18, 1977. Philosophically oriented study of the novel from 1960 to 1975.

Bercot, Martine, et al., eds. *Avant-Garde et modernité.* Paris: Champion, 1988. Includes chapters on the birth of the nouveau roman and the death of *Tel Quel.*

Bersani, Jacques, et al. *La Littérature en France depuis 1945.* Paris: Bordas, 1970, and subsequent revised editions. History and anthology of French literature from 1945 to the present. Several sections on the contemporary novel.

Berton, Jean-Claude. *Histoire de la littérature et des idées en France au XXe siècle. Angoisses, révoltes et vertiges.* Paris: Hatier ("Profil Formation"), 1984. Short outline of twentieth-century French literature. Brief section on the nouveau roman and more recent novelists.

Bessière, Jean, ed. *Récit et histoire.* Paris: PUF, 1984. On the role of history in the novel.

———. *Signes du roman, signes de la transition.* Paris: PUF, 1986. Essays on time and the novel as treated in the works of authors including Sarraute and Duras.

———. *Hybrides romanesques, fiction (1960–1985).* Paris: PUF, 1988. Collection of essays on authors whose works challenge traditional methods of generic categorization.

———. *L'Ordre du descriptif.* Paris: PUF, 1988. Collection of essays on the nature of description. Includes analyses of Simon, Gracq, Yourcenar, and Perec.

———. *Roman, réalités, réalismes.* Paris: PUF, 1989. Articles on the relationship of novel to reality, realism in the novel. Chapters on Duras and Le Clézio.

Blanchot, Maurice. *Le Livre à venir.* Paris: Gallimard, 1959. Collection of essays on contemporary literature. Of particular interest is the section entitled "Où va la littérature?"

Bloch-Michel, Jean. *Le Présent de l'indicatif. Essai sur le nouveau roman.* Paris: Gallimard, 1963 (revised and expanded, 1973). On sociological aspects of the nouveau roman.

Boie, Bernhild, and Daniel Ferrer. *Genèses du roman contemporain: incipit et entrée en écriture.* Paris: CNRS, 1993. On how novels begin. Includes chapters on Simon and Pinget.

Boileau-Narcejac. *Le Roman policier.* Paris: PUF ("Que sais-je"), 1976. On various aspects of the detective novel in world literature.

Boisdeffre, Pierre de. *Où va le roman?* Paris: Del Duca, 1962. Extensive analysis of the status of the novel in France from realism to the nouveau roman.

———. *La Cafetière est sur la table. Contre le nouveau roman.* Paris: Table ronde, 1967. Negative assessment of Robbe-Grillet and the nouveau roman.

———. *La Littérature d'aujourd'hui.* 2 vols. Paris: UGE 10/18, 1969. Abridged paperback version of *Histoire vivante de la littérature d'aujourd'hui* (see below).

———. *L'Ile aux livres. Littérature et critique.* Paris: Seghers, 1980. Short articles on a variety of authors, including Japrisot, Laurent, Modiano, Nourissier, and Decoin.

———. *Le Roman français depuis 1900.* Paris: PUF ("Que sais-je"), 1985. Overview of the twentieth-century French novel. Little analysis, primarily a listing of authors and works.

———. *Les Ecrivains français d'aujourd'hui (1940–1985).* Paris: PUF ("Que sais-je"), 1985. Brief, superficial overview of contemporary French literature.

———. *Histoire de la littérature de langue française des années 1930 aux années 1980.* 2 vols. New edition. Paris: Librairie Académique Perrin, 1985. Unparalleled, massive and thorough history of contemporary French literature. Vol. I: "Roman, Théâtre." Vol. II: "Poésie, Idées, Dictionnaire des auteurs, Bibliographie." Earlier edition entitled *Histoire vivante de la littérature d'aujourd'hui.*

Boisdeffre, Pierre de, ed. *Dictionnaire de la littérature contemporaine.* Paris: Editions Universitaires, 1967. Short entries on a large number of authors. Also several excellent introductory essays by Boisdeffre and others.

Bonn, Anne-Marie. *La Rêverie terrienne et l'espace de la modernité dans quelques romans français parus de 1967 à 1972.* Paris: Klincksieck, 1976. On the depiction of the relationship between man and earth in the contemporary novel.

Bonnefoy, Claude. *Panorama critique de la littérature moderne.* Paris: Belfond, 1980. Collection of articles and reviews, many on the contemporary novel, by a renowned literary critic.

Bonnefoy, Claude, Tony Cartano, and Daniel Oster. *Dictionnaire de la littérature française contemporaine.* Paris: Delarge, 1977. Dictionary of authors, followed by brief overviews of various aspects of French literature since 1945.

Bothorel, Nicole, Francine Dugast, and Jean Thoraval. *Les Nouveaux Romanciers.* Paris: Bordas, 1976. Overview of the history and characteristics of the nouveau roman. Intended for university students.

Bourin, André, and Jean Rousselot;. *Dictionnaire de la littérature française contemporaine.* Paris: Larousse, 1966. Very brief entries on writers active from 1918 to the 1960s.

Bourneuf, Roland, and Réal Ouellet. *L'Univers du roman.* Paris: PUF, 1975. Each chapter deals with a different feature of the novel: narration, character, space, time, point of view. Many references to the contemporary French novel.

Boyer, Alain-Michel. *La Paralittérature.* "Que sais-je?" series. Paris: PUF, 1992. On the features and history of paraliterary genres.

Brée, Germaine, and Edouard Morot-Sir. *Littérature française 9. Du surréalisme à l'empire de la critique.* Paris: Arthaud, 1990. Paperback version of *Littérature française, Vol. 16: 1920–1970* by Germaine Brée. Superb introduction to French literature from 1920 to 1984. Includes an excellent "Dictionnaire des auteurs" and "Chronologie." Translated into English as *Twentieth-Century French Literature.* Chicago: University of Chicago Press, 1983.

Brenner, Jacques. *Histoire de la littérature française de 1940 à nos jours.* Paris: Fayard, 1978. Excellent overview of contemporary French literature, comprised primarily of short essays on individual authors such as the nouveaux romanciers, Le Clézio, Tournier, Modiano, Fernandez, and Berger.

——. *Tableau de la vie littéraire en France d'avant-guerre à nos jours.* Paris: Luneau Ascot, 1982. Less a literary history than a superb overview of the institutions at the basis of French literature, such as the publishing industry, bookstores, the role of the state, literary criticism, and the academies.

——. *Mon histoire de la littérature française contemporaine.* Paris: Grasset, 1987. Intended by Brenner as a supplement to his *Histoire de la littérature française de 1940 à nos jours.* Includes short articles on major contemporary writers, including Duras, Tournier, Le Clézio, Fernandez, and Modiano.

Brenner, Jacques, and Jean-Pierre Salgas. *Le Roman français contemporain.* Paris: Ministère des Affaires Etrangères, 1990. Short overviews accompany lists of prominent writers and works in the contemporary novel in France.

Brincourt, André. *Les Ecrivains du XXe siècle: Un Musée imaginaire de la littérature mondiale.* Paris: Editions Retz, 1979. Dictionary of world authors. Short analyses and brief extracts from their works. Includes entries on Gracq, Green, Le Clézio, Lévy, Modiano, Sollers, and Tournier.

Britton, Celia. *The Nouveau Roman: Fiction, Theory and Politics.* New York: St. Martin's Press, 1992. Excellent study of the history and features of the nouveau roman, including its relationship to Sartre, structuralism, *Tel Quel,* and subsequent developments in French literature and thought.

Brosman, Catharine Savage. *French Novelists since 1960.* Detroit: Gale (Dictionary of Literary Biography, vol. 83), 1989. Impressive and invaluable work consisting of overviews of the work of 32 of France's most important contemporary novelists, including Duras, Gracq, Le Clézio, Modiano, Perec, Pinget, Ricardou, Sollers, Tournier, Wiesel, and Wittig.

Bruézière, Maurice. *Histoire descriptive de la littérature contemporaine. Tome I. Les Classiques contemporains.* Paris: Berger-Levrault, 1975. Introduction to the major figures of twentieth-century French literature. Includes short articles on Green, Duras, Robbe-Grillet, Butor, Sarraute, and Sagan.

———. *Histoire descriptive de la littéraire contemporaine. Tome II. Les Grands Genres.* Paris: Berger-Levrault, 1976. Study of the major and minor figures in twentieth-century French literature. Lengthy section on the novel includes short analyses of Simenon, Bazin, Pinget, Ollier, Sollers, and Le Clézio.

Brunel, Pierre, et al. *Histoire de la littérature française. Vol. II: XIXe et XXe siècles.* Paris: Bordas, 1986. Overview of French literature including section on "La littérature après 1939." Detailed chronology.

Butor, Michel. *Répertoires I–V.* Paris: Minuit, 1960–82. See, in particular, the following articles: Vol. I (1960): "Le Roman comme recherche," "La Crise de croissance de la science-fiction." Vol. II (1964): "Le Roman et la poésie," "Recherches sur la technique du roman," "Réponses à *Tel Quel.*" Vol. III (1968): "La Critique et l'invention." Vol. IV (1973): "Propos sur le livre aujourd'hui." Vol. V (1982): "D'où ça vous vient?"

———. *Essais sur le roman.* Paris: Gallimard ("Idées"), 1964. Important essays by one of the most prominent writers of the postwar period.

Cain, Julien, Robert Escarpit, and Henri-Jean Martin. *Le Livre français, hier, aujourd'hui, demain.* Paris: Imprimerie Nationale, 1972. Published in celebration of the International Year of the Book. Study of the past, present, and future of the book in France. Information on publishers, libraries, writers, and readers.

Cali, Andrea. *Pratiques de lecture et d'écriture.* Paris: Nizet, 1980. Includes analyses of Ollier, Robbe-Grillet, and Simon.

Calle-Gruber, Mireille, and Arnold Rothe, eds. *Autobiographie et biographie. Colloque franco-allemand de Heidelberg.* Paris: Nizet, 1989. Conference proceedings including analyses of Ollier, Cardinal, Perec, and the nouveau roman.

Carroll, David. *The Subject in Question.* Chicago: University of Chicago Press, 1982. Using the works of Claude Simon as a basis, study of the at-times tenuous relationship between contemporary theory and fiction.

Chapsal, Madeleine. *Les Ecrivains en personne.* Paris: Julliard, 1960. Interviews with twelve writers, including Sagan, Vailland, and Butor.

———. *Quinze écrivains.* Paris: Julliard, 1963. Interviews with writers including Duras and Simon.

Chotard, Yvon, et al. *Brûler tous les livres?* Paris: La Nef, 1976. On the status of the book in contemporary French society.

Clark, Priscilla Parkhurst. *Literary France: The Making of a Culture.* Berkeley: University of California Press, 1987. Superb history and analysis of French literary culture.

Clerc, Jeanne-Marie. *Le Cinéma, témoin de l'imaginaire dans le roman français contemporain.* Bern: Peter Lang, 1984. On representations of cinema, photography, and television in the novel.

Colloque international sur le roman contemporain. Pau: Université de Pau et des Pays de l'Adour (*Cahiers de l'Université de Pau et des Pays de l'Adour* 11), 1980. Proceedings include debates on "Recherche et plaisir dans la littérature"; "Ordre et désordre dans le récit"; women in contemporary literature; also several papers on Duras. Participants include several prominent novelists.

Colloque sur la situation de la littérature, du livre et des écrivains. Paris: Editions Sociales, 1976. Proceedings of a conference on the role of the book and the author in contemporary society. Organized by the Centre d'Etudes et de Recherches Marxistes.

Combes, Patrick. *La Littérature et le mouvement de mai 1968.* Paris: Seghers, 1984. On the relationship between French literature and the May 1968 events as well as politics in general.

Cook, Malcolm, ed. *French Culture since 1945.* New York: Longman, 1994. Chapters on various aspects of contemporary French culture, including a lengthy section on literature.

Couégnas, Daniel. *Introduction à la paralittérature.* Paris: Seuil ("Poétique"), 1992. Excellent introduction to the various features of paraliterature.

Dällenbach, Lucien. *Le Récit spéculaire.* Paris: Seuil, 1977. On self-reflexive narrative and the concept of *mise en abyme.* Includes analysis of Butor, Ricardou, Robbe-Grillet, Sarraute, Simon, and Sollers.

Darcos, Xavier, Alain Boissinot, and Bernard Tartayre. *Le XXe siècle en littérature.* Paris: Hachette ("Collection Perspectives et Confrontations"), 1989. Anthol-

ogy of excerpts, with brief commentary. Divided into sections on poetry, theater and prose.

Daspre, André, and Michel Décaudin, eds. *Histoire littéraire de la France. Tome 12,
1939–1970.* Paris: Editions Sociales, 1980. Includes several lengthy overviews
of the contemporary novel.

Débats sur le roman d'aujourd'hui. Paris: Presses de la Renaissance (*Roman*, no. 8),
1984. Text of a colloquium recorded for play on Radio-Gilda in 1984. Discussion of themes such as the "roman réengagé," literature and the human sciences, language in the novel. Participants included Châteaureynaud, Nadaud,
Rihoit, and Tristan.

Dembo, L. S., ed. *Interviews with Contemporary Writers: Second Series, 1972–1982.*
Madison: University of Wisconsin Press, 1983. Interviews with authors including Duras, Sarraute, Robbe-Grillet, and Butor.

D'Haen, Theo, and Hans Bertens, eds. *Postmodern Fiction in Europe and the Ameri-
cas.* Amsterdam: Rodopi; Antwerp: Restat, 1988. Collection of articles on the
postmodern literature of several Western countries. Of particular interest is
A. Kibedi Varga's "Narrative and Postmodernity in France."

Donnat, Olivier, and Denis Cogneau, eds. *Pratiques culturelles des Français, 1973–
1989.* Paris: La Découverte, 1990. Overview of the results of a government-
funded survey of French cultural activities. Interesting chapter on "Le Livre."

Dupuy, Josée. *Le Roman policier.* Paris: Larousse, 1974. Brief history with a selection of short passages representative of the primary characteristics of the
detective novel in France.

Elaho, Raymond Osemwegle. *Entretiens avec le nouveau roman.* Sherbrooke:
Naaman, 1985. Interviews with Butor, Pinget, Robbe-Grillet, Sarraute, and
Simon.

Ellison, David R. *Of Words and the World: Referential Anxiety in Contemporary French
Fiction.* Princeton: Princeton University Press, 1993. On the French novel from
1956 until 1984, including analysis of Robbe-Grillet, Duras, Simon, and
Sarraute.

Engler, Winfried. *The French Novel from 1800 to the Present.* Translated from the
German by Alexander Gode. New York: Frederick Ungar, 1968. Includes chapters on the postwar adventure novel, religious novel, novel of society, and
the nouveau roman.

Engswall, Gunnel. *Vocabulaire du roman français, 1962–1968: Dictionnaire des
fréquences.* Stockholm: Almqvist and Wiksell International, 1984. Statistical
analysis of the vocabulary of 25 French novels of the 1960s.

Enjolras, Laurence. *Femmes écrites: Bilan de deux décennies.* Saratoga, CA: Anma
libri, 1990. Essays on women writers including Chawaf, Cixous, Duras,
Hyvrard, Irigaray, and Wittig.

Escarpit, Robert, ed. *Le Littéraire et le social. Eléments pour une sociologie de la littérature*. Paris: Flammarion (ILTAM), 1970. Sociologically oriented studies of literature in modern society.

Evans, Martha Noel. *Masks of Tradition: Women and the Politics of Writing in Twentieth Century France*. Ithaca: Cornell University Press, 1987. Includes chapters on Duras, Cixous, and Wittig.

Ezine, Jean-Louis. *Les Ecrivains sur la sellette*. Paris: Seuil, 1981. Collection of interviews with writers including Modiano, Sagan, Le Clézio, Simenon, Gracq, Green, Tournier, Perec, Sollers, Robbe-Grillet, and Roche.

Faye, Jean Pierre. *Le Récit hunique*. Paris: Seuil, 1967. Collection of essays on literature (including the nouveau roman) by a member of the *Tel Quel* group.

Federman, Raymond, ed. *Surfiction: Fiction Now . . . and Tomorrow*. Chicago: Swallow Press, 1975. Anthology of essays on innovative contemporary fiction. See, in particular, the contributions by Ricardou, Ehrmann, and Culler.

Fitch, Brian T. *Reflections in the Mind's Eye: Reference and its Problematization in Twentieth-Century French Fiction*. Toronto: University of Toronto Press, 1991. On referentiality in the French novel from 1930 to 1967, including analyses of Beckett, Simon, Blanchot, and Bataille.

Fletcher, John. *New Directions in Literature. Critical Approaches to a Contemporary Phenomenon*. London: Calder and Boyars, 1968. Includes analyses of Robbe-Grillet, Simon, Sarraute, and Duras.

Fletcher, John, and John Calder, eds. *The Nouveau Roman Reader*. London: John Calder, 1985. Collection of extracts from representative works of the nouveau roman with introductions and bibliographies for each author.

Frackman Becker, Lucille. *Twentieth-Century French Women Novelists*. Boston: Twayne, 1989. Includes analyses of Sagan, Etcherelli, Duras, Rochefort, Wittig, and Cixous.

Frohock, W. M. *Style and Temper: Studies in French Fiction, 1925–1960*. Cambridge: Harvard University Press, 1967. Includes chapter on nouveau roman.

Fumaroli, Marc. *L'Etat culturel*. Paris: De Fallois, 1991. On the relationship between culture and the state in France.

Gaede, Edouard. *L'Ecrivain et la société*. 2 vols. Nice: Université de Nice, 1972. Answers from over 300 French writers to 22 questions about their work.

Ganne, Gilbert. *Messieurs les best-sellers*. Paris: Librairie Académique Perrin, 1966. Collection of interviews with some of the best-selling authors of the 1950s and 1960s, including Saint-Laurent, Simenon, Troyat, Sagan, and Bazin. Introduction on the notion of the best-seller.

Garcin, Jérôme. *Le Dictionnaire: Littérature française contemporaine*. Paris: François Bourin, 1988. Garcin asked 250 French writers to compose short pieces about themselves for inclusion in a dictionary. Many of the major contemporary writers contributed, including Ben Jelloun, Cixous, Ernaux, Faye, Fernandez, Groult, Le Clézio, Pinget, Roche, Roubaud, Sollers, and Tournier.

Garvin, Harry R., ed. *Makers of the Twentieth-Century Novel.* Lewisburg: Bucknell University Press; London: Associated University Presses, 1977. Includes chapters on Robbe-Grillet and Sarraute.

Gastaut-Charpy, Danielle. *Le Nouveau Roman. Essai de définition et de "situation".* Aix-en-Provence: Pensée Universitaire, 1966. On various aspects of the nouveau roman, including the treatment of character, time, plot, and point of view.

Gattegno, Jean. *La Science-Fiction.* Paris: PUF ("Que sais-je?"), 1971, and subsequent editions. Overview of the history and the major themes of science fiction writing in French and world literature.

Gerbod, Françoise, and Paul Gerbod. *Introduction à la vie littéraire du XXe siècle.* Paris: Bordas, 1986. Background to the study of contemporary French literature.

Girard, Marcel. *Guide illustré de la littérature française moderne (de 1918 à nos jours).* Paris: Seghers, 1971. Short section on the contemporary novel. Essentially a listing of authors and works.

Goldmann, Lucien. *Pour une sociologie du roman.* Paris: Gallimard, 1964. Classic analysis of the relationship between literature and society.

Gouillou, André. *Le Book Business.* Paris: Tema, 1975. An insider's view of the French publishing world.

Gouze, Roger. *Les Bêtes à Goncourt (un demi-siècle de batailles littéraires).* Paris: Hachette, 1973. Detailed history of the Prix Goncourt and of France's other literary prizes.

———. *Le Bazar des lettres.* Paris: Calmann-Lévy, 1977. On the status, and chances of survival, of literature in modern times.

Green, Robert W. *Just Words: Moralism and Metalanguage in Twentieth-Century French Fiction.* University Park: Pennsylvania State University Press, 1993. Includes chapters on Duras and Sarraute.

Grivel, Charles, and J. A. G. Tans, eds. *Recherches sur le roman I.* Groningen: CRIN, 1979. Collection of analyses of Duras's *Dix heures et demie du soir en été* with the aim of demonstrating the various perspectives available for the study of the novel. Includes a bibliography of the French postwar novel from 1949–1965.

Grivel, Charles, and Frans Rutten, eds. *Recherches sur le roman II, 1950–1970.* Groningen: CRIN, 1984. Collection of formalist analyses, including studies of Green, Simon, and Claude Virmonne.

Gros, Bernard, ed. *La Littérature (du symbolisme au nouveau roman).* Paris: Denoël/CEPL, 1970. Dictionary of authors covering the period from 1870 to 1970 with several fine articles on particular aspects of modern literature, including popular literature, "la nouvelle littérature," and "la littérature de l'engagement."

Guiot, Denis. *La Science-Fiction.* Paris: MA Editions, 1987. Analyses of various authors, including Barjavel and Klein.

Guiral, Pierre, and Emile Temine, eds. *La Société française 1914–1970 à travers la littérature*. Paris: Armand Colin, 1972. Anthology of short texts of fiction and nonfiction representative of the major issues in French society.

Guise, René, and Hans-Jörg Neuschäfer, eds. *Richesses du roman populaire: Actes du colloque international de Pont-à-Mousson, octobre 1983*. Nancy: Centre de Recherches sur le Roman Populaire de l'University de Nancy II, 1986. Includes articles on various aspects of popular literature, including Simenon and le roman rose.

Haedens, Kléber. *Paradoxe sur le roman*. Paris: Grasset, 1964. Two-part study of the novel, the first a study of the difficulty of a precise definition of the novel, the second a bitter attack on the nouveau roman.

Halperin, John, ed. *Theory of the Novel: New Essays*. New York: Oxford University Press, 1974. Collection of theoretical essays on various aspects of the novel. Includes a chapter on contemporary European critics and the novel.

Hamon, Hervé, and Patrick Rotman. *Les Intellocrates*. Paris: Ramsay, 1981; Complexe, 1985. Controversial portrayal of French intellectual and publishing circles.

Harger-Grinling, Virginia A. *Alienation in the New Novel of France and Quebec: An Examination of the Works of Nathalie Sarraute, Michel Butor, Robbe-Grillet, Gérard Bessette, Jean Basile, and Réjean Ducharme*. Fredericton, New Brunswick: York Press, 1985. Analyses of the authors mentioned in the title.

Hargreaves, Alec G. *Voices from the North African Community in France: Immigration and Identity in Beur Fiction*. New York, London: Berg, 1991. Excellent introduction to Beur fiction and its authors.

Hatzfeld, Helmut. *Trends and Styles in Twentieth Century French Literature*. Washington, D.C.: Catholic University of America Press, 1966. Includes a chapter on the nouveau roman with commentary on each of its major practitioners.

Heath, Stephen. *The Nouveau Roman: A Study in the Practice of Writing*. Philadelphia: Temple University Press; London: Elek, 1972. On the nouveau roman as exploration of the possibilities of writing. Chapters on Sarraute, Robbe-Grillet, Simon, and Sollers.

Hewitt, Leah D. *Autobiographical Tightropes*. Lincoln: University of Nebraska Press, 1990. On the autobiographical works of de Beauvoir, Sarraute, Duras, Wittig, and Condé.

Hollier, Denis, ed. *A New History of French Literature*. Cambridge: Harvard University Press, 1990. Massive history composed of short pieces on individual years and major events in French literary history. Includes contributions on the nouveau roman, *Tel Quel*, and *Apostrophes*.

Horn, Pierre L., ed. *The Handbook of French Popular Culture*. Westport, CT: Greenwood, 1991. Each chapter consists of an overview and a bibliography of some aspect of French popular culture and literature, including detective fiction, newspapers and magazines, science fiction, and "les bandes dessinées."

Hornung, Alfred, and Ernstpeter Ruhe, eds. *Autobiographie et Avant-Garde.* Tübingen: Gunter Narr, 1992. Includes analyses of Robbe-Grillet, Doubrovsky, and Boudjedra.

Hoveyda, Fereydoun. *Histoire du roman policier.* Paris: Pavillon, 1965. History of the detective novel in world literature from its origins to the 1960s.

Howarth, Jolyon, and George Ross. *Contemporary France: A Review of Interdisciplinary Studies.* 2 vols. London: Frances Pinter, 1987. Includes articles on media and communications from 1981 to 1986, as well as a chapter on the history and status in 1986 of "les bandes dessinées."

Isou, Isidore. *Les Pompiers du nouveau roman.* Paris: Lettrisme, 1971. Possibly the most negative assessment of the nouveau roman ever written.

Jacquemin, Georges. *Littérature fantastique.* Paris: Fernand Nathan, 1974. Overview of fantastic literature of the nineteenth and twentieth centuries.

Janvier, Ludovic. *Une Parole exigeante: Le nouveau roman.* Paris: Minuit, 1964. Study of the major themes of the nouveau roman, including essays on Sarraute, Robbe-Grillet, Simon, and Butor.

Jardine, Alice, and Anne M. Menke, eds. *Shifting Scenes. Interviews on Women, Writing, and Politics in Post-68 France.* New York: Columbia University Press, 1991. Interviews with the major women writers of contemporary France.

Jean, Raymond. *La Littérature et le réel. De Diderot au "Nouveau roman."* Paris: Albin Michel, 1965. Includes short essays on Robbe-Grillet and Pinget, Faye, and Le Clézio, and the responsibilities of the modern novel.

———. *Pratiques de la littérature.* Paris: Seuil, 1978. First part consists of essays on the nouveau roman and on "écritures féminines." Analyses of the importance of the nouveau roman, Sollers, Faye, Roche, Ricardou, Cixous, Wittig, and Duras.

Jefferson, Ann. *The Nouveau Roman and the Poetics of Fiction.* Cambridge: Cambridge University Press, 1980. Examination of plot, character, and language in the works of Robbe-Grillet, Sarraute, and Butor.

Joye, Jean-Claude. *Littérature immédiate.* Bern: Peter Lang, 1990. Studies of Green, Bourin, Modiano, Navarre, and Sagan.

Kanters, R. *L'Air des lettres, ou tableau raisonnable des lettres françaises d'aujourd'hui.* Paris: Grasset, 1973. Collection of previously published articles, including short pieces on Cixous, Sollers, Le Clézio, Decoin, and Modiano.

Kellman, Steven G. *The Self-Begetting Novel.* New York: Columbia University Press, 1980. On novels that are essentially narratives about their own composition. Includes a chapter entitled "*La Modification* and Beyond."

Kelly, Dorothy. *Telling Glances: Voyeurism in the French Novel.* New Brunswick: Rutgers University Press, 1992. Includes analyses of Robbe-Grillet and Duras.

Kibédi-Varga, A., ed. *Littérature et postmodernité.* Groningen: CRIN, 1986. Includes general essays on postmodernism as well as studies of Robbe-Grillet and Perec.

King, Adele. *French Women Novelists: Defining a Female Style.* New York: St. Martin's Press, 1989. Study of the major themes, such as language and difference, present in the works of twentieth-century French women writers. Specific chapters on Duras and Wittig, among others.

Knapp, Bettina. *French Novelists Speak Out.* Troy, NY: Whitson, 1976. Collection of interviews with several of the major postwar writers, including Pinget, Sabatier, Chédid, Mallet-Joris, Ollier, and Faye.

Lagarde, André, and Laurent Michard. *La Littérature française. Vol. 5. La littérature aujourd'hui.* Paris: Bordas et Laffont, 1972. Overview of the major trends in poetry, theater and the novel from 1950 to 1972. Lengthy section on the novel focuses primarily on the opposition of the traditional novel and the nouveau roman.

Lane-Mercier, Gillian. *La Parole romanesque.* Ottawa: Presses de l'Université d'Ottawa; Paris: Klincksieck, 1989. On the use of direct and indirect speech in the novel.

Laufer, Roger, Bernard Lecherbonnier, and Henri Mitterand. *Thèmes et langages de la culture moderne. Littérature et langages 5. Les genres et les thèmes.* Paris: Nathan, 1977. Consists primarily of excerpts exemplifying major trends in the various genres.

Lebrun, Jean-Claude, and Claude Prévost. *Nouveaux territoires romanesques.* Paris: Messidor/Editions Sociales, 1990. On the "new generation" of writers in 1990. Includes analyses of Ernaux, Echenoz, Nadaud, Bon, and Rio, among others.

Lebrun, Michel, and Jean-Paul Schweighaeuser. *Le Guide du polar.* Paris: Syros, 1987. History of the detective novel in France, focusing primarily on the postwar era. Extensive bibliographical information on individual authors.

Lecherbonnier, Bernard, et al., eds. *Littérature. Textes et documents: XXe siècle.* Collection dirigée par Henri Mitterand. Paris: Nathan, 1989. Excellent, detailed anthology of twentieth-century French literature, including considerable analysis and literary history. See in particular chapters 22 ("Le Nouveau Roman"), 27 ("Ecrits de femmes"), 29 ("Le Roman: Retour au vécu"), 30 ("Le Récit: Permanence de l'écriture"), and 31 ("La Littérature des marges").

Leenhardt, Jacques, and Pierre Józsa. *Lire la lecture. Essai de sociologie de la lecture.* Paris: Le Sycomore, 1982. Survey of readers' responses to George Perec's *Les Choses* and a novel by the Hungarian writer Endre Fejes.

Léonard, Albert. *La Crise du concept de littérature en France au XXe siècle.* Paris: Corti, 1974. Excellent analysis of the concept of literature in twentieth-century France. Relatively unsympathetic chapters on the nouveau roman and *Tel Quel.*

Le Sage, Laurent. *The French New Novel. An Introduction and a Sampler.* University Park: Pennsylvania State University Press, 1962. Lengthy introduction tracing the history and features of the nouveau roman. Followed by excerpts (in English) from the major authors.

Levi, Anthony. *Guide to French Literature: 1789 to Present*. Chicago, London: St. James, 1991. Entries on individual authors and major movements. Includes sections on the life, works, and publications of each author.

La Littérature à l'heure du livre de poche. Bordeaux: Sobodi, 1966. Roundtable discussion of the impact of small-format paperbacks on French literature and writers.

La Littérature fantastique: Colloque de Cérisy. Paris: Albin Michel, 1991. Papers on the theme of fantastic literature.

Lobet, Marcel. *Le Feu du ciel*. Bruxelles: Renaissance du livre, 1969. On the literature of rupture and revolt. Commentary on Klossowski, Le Clézio, and Pieyre de Mandiargues.

Lough, John. *Writer and Public in France from the Middle Ages to the Present Day*. Oxford: Clarendon, 1978. Includes chapter on the financial and social status of the writer in twentieth-century France.

Mansuy, Michel, ed. *Positions et oppositions sur le roman contemporain. Actes du Colloque organisé par le Centre de Philologie et de Littératures Romanes de Strasbourg (Avril 1970)*. Paris: Klincksieck, 1971. Conference proceedings. Papers on novel and autobiography, the nouveau roman, trends in the contemporary novel, Gracq, and Le Clézio.

Marceau, Félicien. *Le Roman en liberté*. Paris: Gallimard, 1977. Collection of short pieces on various characteristics of the novel.

Marks, Elaine, and George Stambolian, eds. *Homosexualities and French Literature*. Ithaca: Cornell University Press, 1979. Includes several general essays on the theme of homosexuality in French literature, as well as interviews with Robbe-Grillet and Cixous and an essay by Wittig.

Matthews, J. H., ed. *Un Nouveau Roman?: Recherches et tradition. La critique étrangère*. Paris: Lettres Modernes, 1964; Mindar, 1983. Excellent collection of essays on the nouveau roman.

Maulpoix, Jean-Michel, et al. *Histoire de la littérature française: XXe, 1950–1990*. Paris: Hatier, 1991. Beautifully illustrated and well-presented anthology and study of French literature from 1950 to 1990.

Mauriac, Claude. *L'Alittérature contemporaine*. Paris: Albin Michel, 1958. On the writers of "aliterature," who have rejected the traditional concepts of story-telling. Chapters on Pinget, Robbe-Grillet, Simon, and Sollers.

Maurois, André. *Nouvelles directions de la littérature française*. Oxford: Clarendon (Zaharoff Lecture for 1967), 1967. Text of a speech providing a succinct analysis of the impact of the nouveau roman.

Mercier, Vivian. *The New Novel from Queneau to Pinget*. New York: Farrar, Straus, and Giroux, 1971. Includes chapters on Queneau, Sarraute, Robbe-Grillet, Butor, Simon, C. Mauriac, and Pinget.

Mertens, Pierre. *L'Agent double*. Bruxelles: Complexe, 1989. Analyses of a number of novelists including Duras and Gracq through the theme of the uneasy position of the author as the link between fiction and reality.

Ministère de la Culture. *Pratiques culturelles des Français: Description socio-démographique. Evolution 1973–1981*. Paris: Dalloz, 1982. Statistical analysis of the pastimes of the French, including their reading habits.

Monnier, Jean-Pierre. *L'Age ingrat du roman*. Neuchâtel: La Baconnière, 1967. Collection of essays on the twentieth-century novel. See, in particular, "Les Nouveaux Maîtres."

Moore, Harry T. *Twentieth-Century French Literature*. Carbondale: Southern Illinois University Press, 1966. Includes a chapter on "antiliterature" and another on other French novelists since 1945. Basically a listing of authors and titles.

Moreau, Jean-Luc. *La Nouvelle Fiction*. Paris: Criterion, 1992. Chapters on several newer writers, including Châteaureynaud, Hubert Haddad, and Frédéric Tristan.

Morris, Alan. *Collaboration and Resistance Reviewed: Writers and "La Mode rétro" in Post-Gaullist France*. Oxford: Berg, 1992. On the treatment in the contemporary novel of the German occupation of France during World War II. Analyses of Modiano, Pascal Jardin, Marie Chaix, and Evelyne Le Garrec.

Moura, Jean-Marc. *L'Image du tiers monde dans le roman français contemporain*. Paris: PUF, 1992. On the depiction of the third world by authors such as Le Clézio, Duras, Lartéguy, and Jules Roy.

Mouralis, Bernard. *Les Contre-littératures*. Paris: PUF, 1975. On the uneasy distinction between "literature" and "paraliterature."

Nadeau, Maurice. *Le Roman français depuis la guerre*. Paris: Gallimard ("Idées"), 1970; Passeur, 1992. Overview of the major novelists from the war to the nouveau roman (1992 edition adds *Tel Quel* and Le Clézio, but nothing else).

Narcejac, Thomas. *Une Machine à lire: Le roman policier*. Paris: Denoël/Gonthier, 1975. Lengthy analysis of the detective novel by one of its leading practitioners in France.

Nélod, Gilles. *Panorama du roman historique*. Paris: SGE/Sodi, 1969. On the historical novel in world literature. Consists primarily of short summaries of a large number of authors.

Neveu, Erik. *L'Idéologie dans le roman d'espionnage*. Paris: Presses de la Fondation nationale des sciences politiques, 1985. Analysis of the relationship between the contemporary detective novel, political ideologies, and mass communication.

Nyssen, Hubert. *Les Voies de l'écriture*. Paris: Mercure de France, 1969. Interviews with six writers (Nourissier, Cabanis, Gascar, Fouchet, Berger, Duras) followed by commentary on their works. Emphasis on the notion of "écriture."

O'Flaherty, Kathleen. *The Novel in France 1945–1965. A General Survey*. Cork: Cork

University Press, 1973. Overview of the postwar novel, categorized by theme (war, religion, childhood) and style (documentary, didactic, traditional, experimental).

Olivier-Martin, Yves. *Histoire du roman populaire en France de 1840–1980.* Paris: Albin Michel, 1980. On the popular novel. Deals primarily with literature from 1840 to 1928.

Oppenheim, Lois, ed. *Three Decades of the French New Novel.* Translated by Lois Oppenheim and Evelyne Costa de Beauregard. Urbana: University of Illinois Press, 1986. Proceedings of a 1982 colloquium on the new novel. Participants include Robbe-Grillet, Wittig, Simon, Sarraute, and Pinget.

Oriol-Boyer, Claudette. *Nouveau Roman et discours critique.* Grenoble: Ellug, 1990. On the nouveau roman and its critical reception.

Ory, Pascal. *L'Entre-deux-mai: Histoire culturelle de la France, mai 1968–mai 1981.* Paris: Seuil, 1983. A cultural history of contemporary France.

———. *L'Aventure culturelle française.* Paris: Flammarion, 1989. A description of postwar French culture.

Ory, Pascal, and Jean-François Sirinelli. *Les Intellectuels en France de l'Affaire Dreyfus à nos jours.* Paris: 1986. Intellectual history of France from 1898 to 1968.

Ouellet, Réal, ed. *Les Critiques de notre temps et le nouveau roman.* Paris: Garnier, 1972. Excellent anthology of short critical pieces on the nouveau roman.

Oulipo. *La Littérature potentielle.* Paris: Gallimard ("Idées"), 1973. History and anthology of the works of the Ouvroir de Littérature Potentielle. Fascinating examples of experimental writing. Translated and edited by Warren F. Motte as *Oulipo: A Primer of Potential Literature* (Lincoln: University of Nebraska Press, 1986). See also the *Atlas de littérature potentielle* (Gallimard, 1981).

Pasco, Allan H. *Novel Configurations: A Study of French Fiction.* Birmingham: Summa, 1987. Introduction and conclusion include numerous reference to the nouveau roman and to the "paramorphous" works of Ricardou and Saporta.

Péquignot, Bruno. *La Relation amoureuse: Analyse sociologique du roman sentimental moderne.* Paris: L'Harmattan, 1991. On the romance novel and its reception in France.

Périsset, Maurice. *Panorama du polar français contemporain.* Paris: Instant, 1986. Composed of a dictionary of authors, authors' answers to a questionnaire, and an overview of literary prizes.

Petruso, Thomas F. *Life Made Real: Characterization in the Novel since Proust and Joyce.* Ann Arbor: University of Michigan Press, 1991. On the contemporary novel as character-centered narrative. Includes numerous references to French authors and analyses of Perec and Queneau.

Peyre, Henri. *French Novelists of Today.* New York: Oxford University Press, 1967. Includes an extremely negative assessment of the postwar novel, as well as a "Panorama of Present-Day Novelists" (short entries on each writer).

Picon, Gaëtan. *Panorame de la nouvelle littérature française.* Paris: Gallimard, 1968; Gallimard (Collection Tel), 1988. On French literature from the 1930s to the 1970s, including chapters on the nouveau roman and on écriture textuelle.

———. *Contemporary French Literature: 1945 and After.* Translated by Kelvin W. Scott and Graham D. Martin. New York: Frederick Ungar, 1974. Includes chapter on the nouveau roman and its successors.

Pillaudin, Roger, ed. *Ecrire . . . pour quoi? pour qui?* Grenoble: Presses Universitaires de Grenoble, 1974. Scripts of seven of the "Dialogues de France-Culture" aired in 1973 and 1974. Includes "Où va la littérature?" (Nadeau and Barthes), "L'Avant-garde aujourd'hui" (Sollers and Pleynet), "Le Nouveau Roman existe-t-il?" (Ricardou and Raillard), and "Langage, puissance et totalitarisme" (Faye and Roubaud).

Pingaud, Bernard, ed. *Ecrivains d'aujourd'hui, 1940–1960.* Paris: Grasset, 1960. Short introductions to and extracts from some of the most important writers of twenty years of French literature, including Duras, Gracq, Mallet-Joris, Pinget, and Sagan.

Porter, Melinda Camber. *Through Parisian Eyes: Reflections on Contemporary French Arts and Culture.* New York: Oxford University Press, 1986. Articles, based on interviews, on various French cultural figures, including Robbe-Grillet, Duras, Wittig, and Sagan.

Poulain, Martine, ed. *Pour une sociologie de la lecture. Lectures et lecteurs dans la France contemporaine.* Paris: Editions du Cercle de la Librairie, 1988. Interesting data and analyses of the reading practices of the French.

Prince, Gerald. *Narrative as Theme. Studies in French Fiction.* Lincoln: University of Nebraska Press, 1992. Investigation into narrative based on eight novels, including Simon's *La Route des Flandres* and Modiano's *Rue des boutiques obscures.*

La Profession d'écrivain. Bordeaux: Sobodi (Université de Bordeaux, Institut de Littérature et de Techniques artistiques de masse), 1968. Roundtable discussion on the definition of a "writer" in contemporary society.

Que peut la littérature? Présentation par Yves Buin. Paris: UGE (10/18), 1965. Text of speeches by Sartre, Faye, Ricardou, and others presented at a debate sponsored by the French Communist student union.

Ragon, Michel. *Histoire de la littérature prolétarienne en France: littérature ouvrière, littérature paysanne, littérature d'expression populaire.* Paris: Albin Michel, 1974. History of working-class literature in France.

Rahv, Betty T. *From Sartre to the New Novel.* Port Washington, NY: Kennikat, 1974. The nouveau roman as direct descendant of Sartre's theories of the novel.

Raimond, Michel. *Le Roman depuis la révolution.* Paris: Armand Colin, 1967 (new edition 1981). Includes a short section on the nouveau roman.

———. *Le Roman.* Paris: Armand Colin, 1988. Excellent introduction to the study of various aspects of the novel (genre, content, narrative).

Rambures, Jean-Louis de. *Comment travaillent les écrivains*. Paris: Flammarion, 1978. Interviews with noted writers on their work habits. Among those interviewed: Cixous, Gracq, Le Clézio, Mallet-Joris, Modiano, Pinget, Rochefort, Sollers, and Tournier.

Ricardou, Jean. *Problèmes du nouveau roman*. Paris: Seuil, 1967. Articles written from 1960 to 1966 on the nouveau roman and on literature in general.

———. *Pour une théorie du nouveau roman*. Paris: Seuil ("Essais"), 1971. More essays on the nouveau roman and literature in general. See in particular "La littérature comme critique" and "Nouveau Roman, Tel Quel."

———. *Le Nouveau Roman*. Paris: Seuil ("Ecrivains de toujours"), 1973. Excellent textual analysis of the nouveau roman, focusing primarily on the notion of "récit." Updated and enlarged as *Le Nouveau Roman, suivi de Les Raisons de l'ensemble*. Paris: Seuil, 1990.

———. *Nouveaux problèmes du roman*. Paris: Seuil, 1978. On the complexities and contradictions of the literary text. Analyses of Robbe-Grillet, Simon, and Ricardou himself, among others.

Ricardou, Jean, and Françoise van Rossum-Guyon, eds. *Nouveau Roman: Hier, aujourd'hui*. 2 vols. Paris: UGE, 1972. Proceedings of the monumental Cerisy conference of 1971. Participants included all the major writers and critics of the nouveau roman. Vol. I ("Problèmes généraux") includes important discussions of the impact and character of the nouveau roman. Vol. II ("Pratiques") consists of analyses of the works of Sarraute, Simon, Robbe-Grillet, Ollier, Butor, Pinget, and Ricardou.

Richard, Jean-Pierre. *L'Etat des choses: Etude sur huit écrivains d'aujourd'hui*. Paris: Gallimard ("NRF Essais"), 1990. Analyses of Réda, Quignard, Djian, and Bergounioux, among others.

Rigby, Brian. *Popular Culture in Modern France: A Study of Cultural Discourse*. London, New York: Routledge, 1991. Excellent study of the concepts of culture and popular culture in France from 1936 to the present.

Ristat, Jean. *Qui sont les contemporains?* Paris: Gallimard, 1975. Includes two interviews with Sollers, one with Denis Roche.

Robbe-Grillet, Alain. *Pour un nouveau roman*. Paris: Gallimard ("Idées"), 1963. Important collection of Robbe-Grillet's essays on his conception of the novel.

Robichez, Jacques, ed. *Précis de littérature française du XXe siècle*. Paris: PUF, 1985. Short introductions to major writers of the twentieth century, including pieces on Tournier, Sollers, Le Clézio, Duras, Bazin, Sagan, Fernandez, Modiano, and Green. Extensive bibliography.

Robichon, Jacques. *Le Défi des Goncourt*. Paris: Denoël, 1975. History of the Prix Goncourt to 1975.

Robinson, Christopher. *French Literature in the Twentieth Century*. Totowa, NJ: Barnes and Noble Books, 1980. Study of the major themes in twentieth-century French literature. Includes section on the nouveau roman and the "new mythologies."

Roudiez, Léon. *French Fiction Today: A New Direction*. New Brunswick: Rutgers University Press, 1972. Includes chapters on the nouveaux romanciers, Claude Mauriac, Saporta, Faye, Sollers, and Ricardou.

————. *French Fiction Revisited*. Elmwood Park, IL: Dalkey Archive, 1991. Updated edition of *French Fiction Today*. Includes earlier chapters as well as new chapters on Roche, Perec, and "The Next Generation."

Royer, Jean. *Ecrivains contemporains. Entretiens*. 4 vols. Montreal: L'Hexagone, 1982–87. Interviews with many authors, including several from France. For example: Vol. 1: Boudjedra, Cardinal, Perec. Vol. 2: Ben Jelloun, Butor, Chédid, Duras, Robbe-Grillet. Vol. 3: Queffélec, Roche, Bianciotti.

Sadoul, Jacques. *Histoire de la science-fiction moderne*. Paris: Albin Michel, 1973 (reprinted in two volumes in the "J'ai lu" collection in 1975). History of English and French-language science fiction from its origins to 1975.

Samuel, Albert. *Regard sur la littérature contemporaine*. Lyon: Chronique Sociale de France, 1974. Includes very sketchy overview of the novel from 1945 to 1972, consisting primarily of lists of authors and titles.

Sarraute, Nathalie. *L'Ere du soupçon*. Paris: Gallimard, 1956. Important collection of essays on the novel by one of the most respected writers of the postwar era.

Sartori, Eva M., and Dorothy W. Zimmerman. *French Women Writers: A Bio-Bibliographical Source Book*. New York: Greenwood, 1991. Includes entries on Wittig, Sarraute, Sagan, Rochefort, Mallet-Joris, Groult, Duras, Cixous, and Chedid.

Sartre, Jean-Paul. *Qu'est-ce que la littérature*. Paris: Gallimard, 1948. The seminal work on "littérature engagée."

Schweighaeuser, Jean-Paul. *Le Roman noir français*. Paris: PUF ("Que sais-je"), 1984. History of the "roman noir" in France from its origins in the nineteenth century. References to San-Antonio, A. D. G., and Vautrin.

Scott, Malcolm. *The Struggle for the Soul of the French Novel: French Catholic and Realist Novels, 1850–1970*. Washington, D.C.: Catholic University of America Press, 1990. Includes chapter on Julien Green.

Sherzer, Dina. *Representation in Contemporary French Fiction*. Lincoln: University of Nebraska Press, 1986. Includes analyses of Ricardou, Robbe-Grillet, Sollers, and Wittig, among others.

Simenon, Georges. *Le Roman de l'homme (suivi d'autres textes)*. Lausanne: De l'Aire, 1980. Three essays by Simenon, and an interview with the author on the art of the novel.

————. *L'Age du roman*. Paris: Complexe ("Le regard littéraire"), 1988. Further reflections on the novel by one of France's most prolific writers.

Simon, Claude. *Discours de Stockholm.* Paris: Minuit, 1986. Acceptance speech of France's 1985 Nobel laureate for literature.

Simon, P. H. *Langage et destin. Diagnostic des lettres françaises contemporaines.* Paris: Renaissance du livre, 1966. Collection of book reviews preceded by three introductory essays, one on contemporary French literature.

Smyth, Edmund J., ed. *Postmodernism and Contemporary Fiction.* London: B. T. Batsford, 1991. Includes chapter on the nouveau roman, as well as more general analyses of postmodernism in relation to feminism, characterization, and narrative.

Sollers, Philippe. *Logiques.* Paris: Seuil, 1968. Essays exposing Sollers's concept of literature and writing. See, in particular, "Logique de la fiction" and "Le Roman et l'expérience des limites."

———. *Théorie des exceptions.* Paris: Gallimard, 1986. Collection of essays by the leader of *Tel Quel* on various authors, including Sollers.

Spire, Antoine, and Jean-Pierre Viala. *La Bataille du livre.* Paris: Editions Sociales, 1976. Left-wing analysis of the publishing industry in contemporary France.

Stambolian, George, ed. *Twentieth Century French Fiction: Essays for Germaine Brée.* New Brunswick: Rutgers University Press, 1975. Includes essays on Gracq, Simon, Robbe-Grillet, Butor, and Wittig.

Stoltzfus, Ben F. *Alain Robbe-Grillet and the New French Novel.* Carbondale: Southern Illinois University Press, 1964. First English-language work on the nouveau roman phenomenon.

Sturrock, John. *The French New Novel: Claude Simon, Michel Butor, Alain Robbe-Grillet.* London: Oxford University Press, 1969. Investigation into the nouveau roman based on the works of Robbe-Grillet, Simon, and Butor.

Tadié, Jean-Yves. *Le Récit poétique.* Paris: PUF, 1978. On the melding of novel and poetry into a new genre: le récit poétique. Includes analyses of Gracq, Mandiargues, and Wittig, among others.

———. *Le Roman au XXe siècle.* Paris: Belfond, 1990. Analysis of the major developments in the treatment of character, structure, and the city in the twentieth-century novel.

Taillandier, François, ed. *L'Année des lettres 1988.* Paris: La Découverte/Ministère de la Culture ("Arts 3"), 1988. Overview of various aspects of the publishing world in one year in France.

Théorie d'ensemble. Paris: Seuil, 1968. Important collection of essays by writers associated with *Tel Quel,* including Foucault, Barthes, Derrida, Sollers, and Kristeva.

Thiher, Allen. *Words in Reflection. Modern Language Theory and Postmodern Fiction.* Chicago: University of Chicago Press, 1984. Using analyses of Wittgenstein, Heidegger, Saussure, and Derrida as a background, examines the characteristics of representation, voice, play, and reference in postmodern fiction (including Robbe-Grillet, Pinget, and Sollers).

Tilby, Michael, ed. *Beyond the Nouveau Roman: Essays on the Contemporary French Novel*. New York and Oxford: Berg (Berg French Studies), 1990. Chapters on the work of nine contemporary novelists, including Duras, Sollers, Tournier, Modiano, and Wittig.

Tint, Herbert. *France since 1918*. New York: St. Martin's Press, 1980. Overview of politics and literature in France since World War I.

Tison-Braun, Micheline. *Le Moi décapité: Le problème de la personnalité dans la littérature française contemporaine*. New York: Peter Lang, 1990. On the question of personality in twentieth-century French literature. Includes analyses of Pinget and Sarraute, among others.

Tournier, Michel. *Le Vent paraclet*. Paris: Gallimard ("Folio"), 1977. Essays on a variety of literary topics by one of the most prominent contemporary novelists.

Tourteau, Jean-Jacques. *D'Arsène Lupin à San-Antonio. Le roman policier français de 1900 à 1970*. Tours: Mame, 1970. Thorough study of the twentieth-century French detective novel.

Valette, Bernard. *Esthétique du roman moderne*. Paris: Nathan, 1985. Theoretical analysis of various aspects of the contemporary novel, such as point of view, time, and description.

Van Herp, Jacques. *Panorama de la science-fiction*. Verniers: André Gérard, 1973. On the major developments in the history of science fiction.

Van Rossum Guyon, Françoise. *Critique du roman. Essai sur "La Modification" de Michel Butor*. Paris: Gallimard, 1970. On Butor's work, but also includes an excellent introduction to the study of the novel in general.

Vanbergen, Pierre. *Aspects de la littérature française contemporaine*. Brussels: Labor, 1973. Overview of the major developments in twentieth-century French literature, including several brief but informative chapters on the contemporary novel.

———. *Pourquoi le roman?* Préface de Henri Mitterand. Paris: Nathan; Brussels: Labor, 1974. A humanistic approach to the contemporary novel.

Vandromme, Pol. *Littérature d'aujourd'hui*. Nivelles (Belgique): Editions de la Francité, 1974. Described by the author as his "journal de lecteur, sous forme de dictionnaire." Short entries on Hallier, Le Clézio, C. Mauriac, and Modiano, among others.

Vannier, Gilles. *XXe siècle. Tome 2, 1945–1988*. Paris: Bordas ("Histoire de la littérature française"), 1988. Short but excellent introduction to postwar literature.

Vareille, Jean-Claude. *L'Homme masqué, le justicier et le détective*. Lyon: Presses

Universitaires de Lyon, 1989. Analyses of the popular novel and detective novel in France.

Vercier, Bruno, and Jacques Lecarme. *La Littérature en France depuis 1968*. Paris: Bordas, 1982. Excellent introduction to the contemporary period, including representative extracts from many authors.

Vessillier-Ressi, Michèle. *Le Métier d'auteur*. Paris: Dunod, 1982. Detailed socioeconomic analysis of the writer's situation in contemporary France.

Vieuille, Chantal. *Histoire régionale de la littérature de France. Tome II: De 1789 à nos jours*. Paris: Plon, 1989. Region-by-region treatment of French literature.

Virmaux, Alain, and Odette Virmaux. *Un Genre nouveau: Le ciné-roman*. Paris: Edilig, 1982. On the various forms film has taken when reproduced as written text.

Weinstein, Arnold L. *Vision and Response in Modern Fiction*. Ithaca: Cornell University Press, 1974. On the perception of and reaction to the world as depicted in the nineteenth- and twentieth-century novel. Includes analysis of Simon and Robbe-Grillet.

West, Paul. *The Modern Novel. Vol. I: England and France*. London: Hutchinson, 1963. Includes short section on the nouveau roman.

Yarrow, Ralph, ed. *Nouveau Roman Handbook*. Norwich: East Anglia, 1984. Textbook to aid students in reading the nouveau roman.

Zants, Emily. *The Aesthetics of the New Novel in France*. Boulder: University of Colorado Press, 1968. Short study of the fundamental principles of the nouveau roman employed by Robbe-Grillet, Sarraute, and Butor, and the application of these principles. Primarily concerned with the theoretical works of these three writers.

Zeltner, Gerda. *La Grande Aventure du roman français au XXe siècle*. Translated from the German by Christine Kubler. Paris: Gonthier, 1967. Includes chapters on the nouveau roman and the novel in the 1960s.

Zéraffa, Michel. *Roman et société*. Paris: PUF, 1971. A sociohistorical consideration of the novel in contemporary society.

Periodical Articles

Albérès, R. A. "Cette nouvelle école littéraire." *A la page*, no. 44 (February 1968): 213–21.

Allaire, Suzanne. "Roman et nouveau roman en France." *Le Français dans le Monde*, no. 212 (October 1987): 48–53.

Alter, Jean. "Faulkner, Sartre and the 'nouveau roman.' " *Symposium* 20, no. 2 (summer 1966): 101–12.

Alter, Robert. "The Self-Conscious Moment: Reflections on the Aftermath of Modernism." *Tri-Quarterly*, no. 33 (spring 1975): 209–30.

Ames, Van Meter. "The Nouveau Roman." *Journal of Aesthetics and Art Criticism* 21, no. 1 (spring 1963): 243–50.

Bars, Henry. "Des modes littéraires de la modernité." *Revue Générale Belge,* no. 8 (August 1966): 1–17.

Barthes, Roland. "La littérature, aujourd'hui." *Tel Quel,* no. 7 (autumn 1961): 32–41.

Berkowitz, Janice, and Daniel Gross. "Change and Exchange. French Periodicals since 1968." *Contemporary French Civilization* 6, nos. 1–2 (fall–winter 1981–82): 237–53.

Bertho, Sophie. "L'Attente postmoderne. A propos de la littérature contemporaine en France." *Revue d'histoire littéraire de la France* 91, nos. 4–5 (July–October 1991): 735–43.

Bertrand, Marc. "Roman contemporain et histoire." *French Review* 56, no. 1 (October 1982): 77–86.

Blanchard, Marc. "Littérature et anthropologie: théorie et pratique de la vie quotidienne dans le nouveau roman." *Romanic Review* 83, no. 2 (March 1992): 217–26.

Blanchot, Maurice. "D'un art sans avenir." *Nouvelle Revue Française,* no. 51 (March 1957): 488–98.

Bleton, Paul. "Mystère, secret et tromperie: sur la généalogie du roman d'espionnage français." *Orbis Litterarum* 39, no. 1 (1984): 65–78.

Boisdeffre, Pierre de. "Un nouveau roman français." *Etudes* 301, no. 4 (April 1959): 70–79.

———. "Audience et limites du 'nouveau roman.'" *Revue des Deux Mondes* (October 1967): 503–13.

Borel, Jacques. "Sur la déshumanisation de la littérature." *Nouvelle Revue Française* 15, no. 177 (September 1967): 397–419.

Boyer, Régis. "Romans actuels, œuvres de recherche et de cri." *Le Français dans le Monde,* no. 48 (April–May 1967): 6–13.

Brée, Germaine. "The 'New' Novelists of France." *Meanjin* 22, no. 3 [no. 94] (1963): 269–79.

———. "Novelists in Search of the Novel. The French Scene." *Modern Fiction Studies* 16, no. 1 (spring 1970): 3–11.

Britton, Celia. "The Nouveau Roman and *Tel Quel* Marxism." *Paragraph* 12, no. 1 (March 1989): 65–96.

Brooke-Rose, Christine. "Transgressions: An Essay-say on the Novel Novel Novel." *Contemporary Literature* 19, no. 3 (summer 1978): 378–407.

Brooks, William. "Nouveau Roman? Old Hat. (Chapeau!)." *Quinquereme* 4, no. 2 (July 1981): 234–45.

Carrabino, Victor. "The Nouveau Roman and the Neo-Romantic Hero." *Comparatist,* no. 7 (May 1983): 29–35.

Champagne, Roland A. "Anti-Structuralist Structures: The Avant-Garde Struggle of French Fiction." *Studies in Twentieth Century Literature* 1, no. 1 (fall 1976): 135–55.

Charney, Hanna. "Pourquoi le 'nouveau roman' policier?" *French Review* 46, no. 1 (October 1972): 17–23.

Clark, Priscilla Parkhurst. "Literary Culture in France and the United States." *American Journal of Sociology* 84, no. 5 (March 1979): 1057–77.

Cloonan, William J. "Prizes and Surprises: L'Année Romanesque 1990." *French Review* 64, no. 6 (May 1991): 915–20.

Cloonan, William, and Jean-Philippe Postel. "New Voices: The French Novel in 1991." *French Review* 65, no. 6 (May 1992): 956–62.

———. "The Business of Literature: The Novel in 1992." *French Review* 66, no. 6 (May 1993): 861–68.

———. "The Bookstore and 'La Diffusion littéraire': The Novel in 1993." *French Review* 68, no. 1 (October 1994): 112–20.

Cocking, J. M. "The 'Nouveau Roman' in France." *Essays in French Literature*, no. 2 (November 1965): 1–14.

Colin, Jean-Paul. "Lire le roman policier." *Esprit Créateur* 26, no. 2 (summer 1986): 26–36.

Compagnon, Antoine. "The Diminishing Canon of French Literature in America." *Stanford French Review* 15, nos. 1–2 (1991): 103–15.

Conan, Eric, and Olivier Mongin. "La Comédie des prix littéraires. Entretien avec Angelo Rinaldi." *Esprit,* no. 156 (November 1989): 5–12.

"The Condition of the Novel." *New Left Review,* no. 29 (January–February 1965): 19–40.

Côté, Francois. "Le Néo-Polar français et les policiers." *Esprit,* no. 135 (February 1988): 46–50.

"La Crise de la littérature." *Lettres françaises,* no. 1361 (November 1970): 4–7.

Dard, Michel. "L'Avenir du roman." *Revue des Deux Mondes* (February 1975): 332–34.

Dean, John. "French Science Fiction: The Intergalactic European Connection." *Stanford French Review* 3, no. 3 (winter 1979): 405–14.

Déjeux, Jean. "Romanciers de l'immigration maghrébine en France." *Francofonia* 5, no. 8 (spring 1985): 93–111.

Elbaz, André. "Les Romanciers juifs français d'aujourd'hui." *Liberté* (July–August 1970): 92–105.

Finch, Alison, and David Kelley. "Propos sur la technique du roman. Nathalie Sarraute interviewée par Alison Finch et David Kelley." *French Studies* 39, no. 3 (July 1985): 305–15.

Fletcher, John. "The Difficult Dialogue: Conflicting Attitudes to the Contemporary Novel." *Journal of European Studies* 4, no. 3 (September 1974): 274–86.

Foucault, Michel, et al. "Débat sur le roman." *Tel Quel*, no. 17 (spring 1964): 12–54.

Fourny, Jean-François. "From *Tel Quel* to *L'Infini*." *Contemporary French Civilization* 11, no. 2 (spring–summer 1987): 189–99.

Fowlie, Wallace. "A Stocktaking. French Literature in the 1960's." *Contemporary Literature* 11, no. 2 (spring 1970): 137–54.

"French Writing Today: Seven Editors Respond." *Literary Review* 30, no. 3 (spring 1987): 309–22.

Galey, Matthieu. "Vie et mort du nouveau roman." *Revue de Paris* 70 (September 1963): 124–27.

Gans, Eric. "The Last French Novels." *Romanic Review* 83, no. 4 (November 1992): 501–16.

Glicksberg, Charles I. "Experimental Fiction: Innovation vs. Form." *Centennial Review* 18, no. 2 (spring 1974): 127–50.

Goldman, Lucien. "Les Deux Avant-gardes." *Médiations* (winter 1961–62): 63–83.

Guérin, Jeanyves, et al. "Y a-t-il encore un roman français?" *Esprit*, no. 101 (May 1985): 111–15.

Hargreaves, Alec G. "Beur Fiction: Voices from the Immigrant Community in France." *French Review* 62, no. 4 (March 1989): 661–68.

———. "History, Gender and Ethnicity in Writing by Women Authors of Maghrebian Origin in France." *Esprit Créateur* 23, no. 2 (summer 1993): 23–34.

Hayman, David. "Double-distancing. An Attribute of the 'Post-Modern' Avant-Garde." *Novel* 12, no. 1 (fall 1978): 33–47.

Hellerstein, Nina S. "Reality and Its Absence in the French New Novel: Butor, Sarraute, Ricardou." *USF Language Quarterly* 20, nos. 1–2 (fall–winter 1981): 27–30, 34.

Henkels, Robert M. "Perversion and the Nouveau Roman." *Kentucky Romance Quarterly* 26, no. 1 (1979): 101–11.

Howlett, Jacques. "Thèmes et tendances d'avant-garde dans le roman, aujourd'hui." *Lettres Nouvelles* 11, no. 32 (February 1963): 139–48.

Hutcheon, Linda. "The Outer Limits of the Novel: Italy and France." *Contemporary Literature* 18, no. 2 (spring 1977): 198–216.

Huvos, Kornel. "Le Roman américaniste français, 1960–1977: Essai de bibliographie annotée." *French-American Review* 3, no. 3 (fall 1979): 85–104.

Jones, Tobin H. "Toward a More Primitive Reading: Aesthetic Response to Radical Form in the New French Novel." *Essays in Literature* 3, no. 2 (fall 1976): 268–84.

Kaeppelin, Olivier. "L'Avant-garde va mal: pourquoi?" *Quinzaine littéraire*, no. 339 (1981): 6–7.

Kanters, Robert. "Sept ans de littérature." *Revue de Paris* 72 (September 1965): 150–58.

Kibédi Varga, A. "Le Récit postmoderne." *Littérature,* no. 77 (February 1990): 3–22.

Kingcaid, Renée A. "After the 'Nouveau Roman': Some New Names in French Fiction." *Review of Contemporary Fiction* 8, no. 2 (summer 1988): 300–12.

Kolbert, Jack, and Nancy L. Cairns. "L'Année littéraire 1989." *French Review* 63, no. 6 (May 1990): 927–49. See also the previous articles on "l'année littéraire" featured annually in the *French Review.*

Köpeczi, Béla. "Les Courants idéologiques de notre époque et la littérature francaise contemporaine." *Acta Litteraria Academiae Scientiarum Hungaricae* 19, nos. 1–2 (1977): 135–46.

Lagrolet, Jean. "Nouveau Réalisme?" *NEF* 15, no. 13 (January 1958): 62–70.

Lévi-Valensi, Jacqueline. "Le Romanesque de l'absurde en France après 1960. Essai de définition," *Revue des Lettres Modernes (Absurde et Renouveaux Romanesques 1960–1980)* (1986): 55–106.

Lindsay, Cecile. "Le Degré zéro de la fiction: La science du nouveau roman." *Romanic Review* 74, no. 2 (March 1983): 221–32.

Linze, Jacques-Gérard. "Lectures de vacances et notes sur l'état du roman." *Revue Générale,* no. 819 (September 1974): 29–43.

———. "Les Retombés du nouveau roman." *Bulletin de l'Académie Royale de Langue et de Littérature Françaises* 66, no. 2 (1985): 62–74.

Lop, Edouard, and André Sauvage. "Le Nouveau Roman." *Nouvelle Critique,* no. 124 (March 1961): 117–34; no. 125 (April 1961): 68–87; no. 127 (June 1961): 83–107.

Magyar, Miklós. "Splendeurs et misères du nouveau roman français." *Acta Litteraria Academiae Scientiarum Hungaricae* 23, nos. 1–2 (1981): 39–47.

Martel, Frédéric. "Littérature et sida." *Esprit,* no. 206 [no. 11] (November 1994): 114–25.

Marwick, Arthur. "Six Novels of the Sixties—Three French, Three Italian." *Journal of Contemporary History* 28, no. 4 (October 1993): 563–91.

Marx-Scouras, Danielle. "The Dissident Politics of *Tel Quel.*" *Esprit Créateur* 27, no. 2 (summer 1987): 101–8.

———. "Requiem for the Postwar Years: The Rise of *Tel Quel.*" *French Review* 64, no. 3 (February 1991): 407–16.

Molino, Jean. "Lettre à mon cousin sur le roman français depuis la guerre." *Commentaire* 11, no. 44 (winter 1988–89): 997–1006.

Mongin, Olivier. "Littérateurs ou écrivains." *Esprit,* no. 181 (May 1992): 102–18.

———. "Le Goût du réel en littérature." *Esprit,* no. 192 (June 1993): 115–26.

Montalbetti, Jean. "15 ans de nouveau roman—enquête." *Magazine littéraire,* no. 6 (April 1967): 4–9.

Morrissette, Bruce. "The New Novel in France." *Chicago Review* 15, no. 3 (winter–spring 1962): 1–19.

———. "Theory and Practice in the Works of Robbe-Grillet." *MLN* 77, no. 3 (May 1962): 257–67.

———. "Topology and the French Nouveau Roman." *Boundary 2* 1, no. 1 (fall 1972): 45–57.

———. "Post-modern Generative Fiction: Novel and Film." *Critical Inquiry* 2, no. 2 (winter 1975): 253–62.

Mouillaud, M. "Le Nouveau Roman: Tentative de roman et roman de la tentative." *Revue d'Esthétique* 17, nos. 3–4 (August–December 1964): 228–63.

Nadaud, Alain. "Où en est la littérature?, ou pour un nouvel imaginaire." *Infini*, no. 19 (1987): 3–13.

Nadeau, Maurice. "Nouvelles formules pour le roman." *Critique* (August–September 1957): 707–22.

Nettelbeck, Colin. "Getting the Story Right: Narratives of World War II in Post-1968 France." *Journal of European Studies* 15, no. 2 (June 1985): 77–116.

Nora, Pierre. "L'Esprit d'Apostrophes—Bernard Pivot: Entretien avec Pierre Nora." *Débat*, no. 60 (May–August 1990): 157–87.

Noreiko, Stephen. "Person to Person: Apostrophe of the Reader in Some Novels in Popular French." *French Studies* 37, no. 1 (January 1983): 59–67.

O'Callaghan, Raylene. "The Art of the (Im)possible: The Autobiography of the French New Novelists." *Australian Journal of French Studies* 25, no. 1 (1988): 71–91.

Opitz, Kurt. "The New Reality of the Continental Novel." *Modern Language Journal* 50, no. 2 (February 1966): 84–92.

Ortel, Philippe. "La Mémoire en noir et blanc." *Esprit*, no. 206 [no. 11] (November 1994): 126–34.

Otten, Anna. "Innovation in Modern French Fiction." *Antioch Review* 45, no. 3 (summer 1987): 266–74.

Padis, Marc-Olivier. "Une Littérature de l'enfermement." *Esprit*, no. 206 [no. 11] (November 1994): 165–73.

Paris, Jean. "The New French Generation." *American Society Legion of Honor Magazine*, no. 31 (1960): 45–51.

Paterson, Janet M. "Le Roman 'postmoderne': Mise au point et perspectives." *Canadian Review of Comparative Literature* 13, no. 2 (June 1986): 238–54.

Picon, Gaëtan. "Le Roman et son avenir." *Mercure de France*, no. 1119 (November 1956): 498–503.

Pingaud, Bernard. "Où va *Tel Quel*." *Quinzaine littéraire* (January 1968): 8–9.

Poole, Roger. "Objectivity and Subjectivity in the Nouveau Roman." *Twentieth Century Studies*, no. 6 (December 1971): 53–73.

Prévost, Claude. "Une nouvelle modernité romanesque?" *Pensée*, nos. 255–260 (July–August 1987): 63–68.

Raimond, Michel. "Aspects nouveaux de la crise du roman de F. Mauriac à J.-M. G. Le Clézio." *Cahiers de Malagar*, no. 3 (1989): 109–25.

Ramsay, Raylene. "Autobiographical Fictions: Duras, Sarraute, Simon, Robbe-Grillet: Re-writing History, Story, Self." *International Fiction Review* 18, no. 1 (1991): 25–33.

Reck, Rima Drell. "Old and New in the French New Novel." *Southern Review* 1, no. 4 [new series] (autumn 1965): 791–802.

Ricardou, Jean. "Nouveau Roman, Tel Quel." *Poétique*, no. 4 (1970): 433–54.

Roudiez, Léon. "In Dubious Battle: Literature vs. Ideology." *Semiotext(e)*, no. 1 (February 1974): 87–95.

———. "Twelve Points from *Tel Quel*." *Esprit Créateur* 14, no. 4 (winter 1974): 291–303.

Saint-Jacques, Denis. "Le Pouvoir du nouveau roman." *Esprit Créateur* 14, no. 4 (winter 1974): 304–11.

Saint-Vincent, Bertrand de. "La République du Goncourt." *Spectacle du Monde*, no. 345 (December 1990): 98–100.

Sénart, Philippe. "Jalons pour le nouveau roman." *Table Ronde*, no. 169 (February 1962): 105–11.

Shroder, Maurice Z. "The Nouveau Roman and the Tradition of the Novel." *Romanic Review* 57, no. 3 (October 1966): 200–214.

Simon, Claude. "Problèmes que posent le roman et l'écriture." *Francofonia* 10, no. 18 (spring 1990): 3–10.

Simon, John K. "Perception and Metaphor in the New Novel." *TriQuarterly*, no. 4 (1965): 153–82.

Stoltzfus, Ben. "The Aesthetics of the Nouveau Roman and Innovative Fiction." *International Fiction Review* 10, no. 2 (summer 1983): 108–16.

Suleiman, Susan. "The Question of Readability in Avant-Garde Fiction." *Studies in Twentieth-Century Literature* 6, nos. 1–2 (fall 1981–spring 1982): 17–35.

Thiébaut, Marcel. "Le Nouveau Roman." *Revue de Paris* 65 (October 1958): 140–55.

Thody, Philip. "New Writing in France." *Critical Quarterly* 28, no. 3 (autumn 1986): 97–101.

Todorov, Tzvetan. "Reflections on Literature in Contemporary France." *New Literary History* 10, no. 3 (spring 1979): 511–31.

Van der Hoeden, Jean-Marie. "Nouveau Roman. Quelle modification littéraire?" *Revue Nouvelle* (November 1986): 429–35.

Vidal, Gore. "French Letters: The Theory of the New Novel." *Encounter* 29, no. 6 (December 1967): 13–23.

Watt, Roderick H. "Andersch, Boll, Lenz and Schnurre on the Nouveau Roman." *New German Studies* 9, no. 2 (summer 1981): 123–44.

Weightman, J. G. "The New Wave in French Culture." *Commentary* 30, no. 3 (September 1960): 230–40.

———. "The French Literary Scene." *Commentary* 41, no. 2 (June 1966): 57–62.

Wood, Philip R. "French Thought under Mitterrand: The Social, Economic and Political Context for the Return of the Subject and Ethics, for the Heidegger Scandal, and for the Demise of the Critical Intellectual." *Contemporary French Civilization* 15, no. 2 (summer–fall 1991): 244–67.

Wurms, Pierre. "Les Courants d'idées dans la nouvelle littérature française." *Die Neueren Sprachen* 66, no. 4 (April 1967): 157–70; 66, no. 5 (May 1967): 209–20; 66, no. 6 (June 1967): 268–78.

Special Issues of Periodicals

Cahiers Internationaux de Symbolisme, nos. 9–10 (1965–66): "Formalisme et signification."

Change, nos. 34–35 (1978): "La Narration nouvelle."

Contemporary French Civilization 6, nos. 1–2 (fall–winter 1981–82): "Intellectual Life in France since 1968."

Contemporary Literature 19, no. 3 (summer 1978): "After the Nouveau Roman: Opinions and Polemics."

Dalhousie French Studies 17 (fall–winter 1989): "De Duras et Robbe-Grillet à Cixous et Deguy."

Digraphe, nos. 39–40 (1987): "Existe-t-il aujourd'hui des écrivains trop connus?"

Esprit, nos. 263–264 (July–August 1958): "Le Nouveau Roman."

———, no. 329 (July 1964): "Colloque est-ouest sur le roman contemporain."

Esprit Créateur 7, no. 2 (summer 1967): "New Directions in the French Novel."

———, 14, no. 4 (winter 1974): "New Critical Practices II (Structuralism, Narratology, *Tel Quel, Change*)."

———, 19, no. 2 (summer 1979): "Contemporary Women Writers in France."

———, 26, no. 2 (summer 1986): "The French Detective."

———, 33, no. 1 (spring 1993): "The Occupation in French Literature and Film."

Infini, no. 19 (1987): "Où en est la littérature?"

Magazine littéraire, no. 43 (August 1970): "Le Roman d'espionnage."

———, no. 65 (June 1972): "Dossier Sollers, Tel Quel."

———, no. 194 (April 1983): "Spécial Polar: Vingt ans de littérature policière."

Marche Romane 21, nos. 1–2 (1971): "Un nouveau nouveau roman."

Modern Fiction Studies 16, no. 1 (spring 1970): "Studies of the Modern French Novel."

Nouvelle Revue Française, no. 214 (October 1970): "Vie ou survie de la littérature."
Paragraph 12, no. 1 (March 1989).
Pratiques, no. 27 (July 1980): "L'Ecrivain aujourd'hui."
Review of Contemporary Fiction 9, no. 1 (spring 1989): Special issue on French fiction.
Science Fiction Studies 16, no. 3 (November 1989): "Science Fiction in France."
Twentieth Century Studies, no. 6 (December 1971): "Directions in the Nouveau Roman."
Yale French Studies, no. 24 (1959): "Midnight Novelists and Others."
———. Special Issue (1988): "After the Age of Suspicion: The French Novel Today."

Bibliographical Resources

Alden, Douglas W., and Richard Brooks, eds. *A Critical Bibliography of French Literature. Vol. VI: The Twentieth Century.* Syracuse: Syracuse University Press, 1980. Part 3 of Vol. VI contains all information pertaining to French literature since 1940.

Bassan, Fernande, Donald C. Spinelli, and Howard A. Sullivan. *French Language and Literature: An Annotated Bibliography.* New York: Garland, 1989. Useful bibliography of materials relating to the study of French literature, including a chapter on twentieth-century literature.

Fitzgerald, Louise S., and Elizabeth I. Kearney. *The Continental Novel: A Checklist of Criticism in English 1900–1966.* Metuchen, NJ: Scarecrow, 1968. Bibliography of critical works, arranged alphabetically by author studied. Updated as *The Continental Novel: A Checklist of Critics in English, 1967–1980.* Metuchen, NJ: Scarecrow, 1983.

French XX Bibliography. Selinsgrove, PA: Susquehanna University Press. The most complete annual bibliography of material pertaining to French literature since 1885, including book-length works, periodical articles, and book reviews for all authors writing in French.

Klapp, Otto, and Astrid Klapp-Lehrmann. *Bibliographie des französischen Literaturwissenschaft.* Frankfurt: Vittorio Klostermann. Annual volume divided by centuries and also by authors.

Lasserre, René, ed. *La France contemporaine. Guide bibliographique et thématique.* Tübingen: Max Niemeyer Verlag, 1980. General bibliography on various aspects of contemporary France.

Les Livres disponibles. Paris: Cercle de la Librairie. Annual listing of French books in print.

MLA International Bibliography. New York: Modern Language Association. Excellent annual bibliography of scholarly works (with brief annotations). Materials since 1980 are also accessible on CD-ROM.

Rancœur, René. *Bibliographie de la littérature française: XVIe–XXe siècles* (annual). Paris: Armand Colin. (Since 1981 in *Revue d'histoire littéraire de la France*). From 1953–1981 published separately under various titles by Armand Colin. Since 1986 this bibliography has been published annually as no. 3 of the *Revue d'histoire littéraire de la France*. From 1981 to 1985 each issue of the above periodical contained a short bibliography of new critical works.

Zéraffa, Michel. "Vingt ans de roman." In *The Present State of French Studies,* ed. Charles B. Osburn, pp. 783–97. Metuchen, NJ: Scarecrow, 1971.

Contributors

Thomas F. Broden is assistant professor of French at Purdue University.

Roy C. Caldwell is associate professor of French at St. Lawrence University.

William Cloonan is professor of French at Florida State University.

Paul Raymond Côté is associate professor of French at American University.

Robert Henkels is professor of French at Auburn University.

Susan Ireland is assistant professor of French at Grinnell College.

Tobin Jones is associate professor of French literature and culture and chairman of the Department of Foreign Languages and Literatures at Colorado State University.

Jack Kolbert is professor of French at Susquehanna University.

Katherine C. Kurk is associate professor of comparative literature and modern languages at Northern Kentucky University.

J. D. Mann is assistant professor of French at Southern Illinois University at Edwardsville.

Martine Motard-Noar is associate professor of French at Western Maryland College.

414

Marie-Thérèse Noiset is assistant professor of French at the University of North Carolina at Charlotte.

Susan Petit is professor of English and French at the College of San Mateo.

Laurence M. Porter is professor of French literature and culture, comparative literature, and critical theory at Michigan State University.

Raylene Ramsay is professor of French and chair of the Department of Romance Languages at the University of Auckland, New Zealand.

Gervais Reed is professor of French at Lawrence University.

Catherine Slawy-Sutton is associate professor of French at Davidson College.

Robert Stanley is associate professor of French and German at the University of Tennessee at Chattanooga.

William Thompson is professor of French at the University of Memphis.

Michel Viegnes is associate professor of French at Bryn Mawr College.

Katheryn Wright is professor of French at Rhodes College.

Index